AUTHOR'S POSTSCRIPT

Because truth was my only goal when I served as counsel to the Warren Commission and when I wrote my book, "November 22, 1963: You Are the Jury," (all royalties from my book and all fees from speaking engagements having been donated to charity);

Because a small group of assassination sensationalists have deliberately covered up the truth about the tragic murders of President John F. Kennedy and Dallas Police Officer J. D. Tippit and have misled a major portion of the American public in general and the intellectual leadership on college campuses in particular;

Because libraries play such a key role in the dissemination of knowledge and because my wife and I believe that if academic scholars have available in their college libraries the salient facts about important historical events, the truth will ultimately prevail;

My wife, Connie, and I are donating to the libraries of leading colleges, universities, and law schools in each of the fifty states, the District of Columbia, and Puerto Rico, a copy of this book.

The reader should know that in October, 1975, after completing my service as Executive Director of the Rockefeller Commission investigating the CIA, I filed with the CIA Freedom of Information requests for all of its files concerning the assassination of President Kennedy. Also, on November 22, 1975, I called for Congress to reopen the investigation of the assassination of President Kennedy, although I stated at the time that a thorough objective investigation would reach the same conclusion reached by the Warren Commission: That Lee Harvey Oswald was the sole gunman who killed President Kennedy and Officer Tippit. The House Select Committee on Assassinations correctly concluded, unanimously, that it was Oswald who shot President Kennedy and Officer Tippit. However, in a complete "flip-flop" in the last three weeks of the investigation, a majority of the Committee incorrectly concluded on the basis of an incomplete investigation by the staff that there was a second gunman firing at President Kennedy, who missed hitting anyone and even missed hitting the Presidential limousine. Because of my unique background and expertise, I sought to testify in an open public hearing before the Committee. Initially, I received written assurances that I would have this opportunity. However, the Committee majority, on the basis of a recommendation by its staff, ultimately denied my request.

Time does not permit me to answer in detail the many questions I still receive concerning the assassination of President Kennedy. However, if the reader desires further information, my more recent writings on the assassination of President Kennedy include articles in the July 15, 1979, NEW YORK SUNDAY TIMES MAGAZINE and the February 6, 1976, April 27, 1979, and September 28, 1979, issues of NATIONAL REVIEW (with a closing "Memo to our Readers" by William F. Buckley, Jr., in the March 21, 1980, issue).

May, 1980

David W. Belin

November 22, 1963:

YOU ARE THE JURY

November 22, 1963

YOU ARE THE JURY

DAVID W. BELIN, ESQ.

QUADRANGLE/THE NEW YORK TIMES BOOK CO.

Library of Congress Catalog Card Number: 73-82479
International Standard Book Number: 0-8129-0374-9

Interior design by: Emily Harste
Second Printing

To Connie, whose warmth, love and keen critical judgment combined to help make this book possible.

CONTENTS

ACKNOWLEDGMENTS

My primary acknowledgment is not to any single person but rather to our American system of government and justice. There are few places in this world where the investigation of the assassination of a fallen leader would be conducted by an independent commission, just as there are few countries in this world where the combination of a free press and separate judicial and legislative branches of government could lead to the exposé of Watergate.

As for individuals, in addition to my wife, who acted as both a sounding board and an editor, there are many others: Harrison E. Salisbury, who was the catalyst in my undertaking to write this book; Herbert Nagourney, able President, and Zinaida Alexi, talented Senior Editor, of Quadrangle/The New York Times Book Company, who realized that truth can be stranger and more interesting than fiction and who in this century of sensationalism had the confidence that a book about the truth of the assassination had merit for publishing and would be read by many people; Irving Horowitz of *The New York Times,* a truly fine copy editor, nearly all of whose suggestions I adopted; Joseph Ball, one of the outstanding lawyers on the West Coast, with whom I worked so closely on the Warren Commission; Howard Willens, a brilliant Washington attorney who while serving with the Department of Justice in 1964 as liaison with the Warren Commission was the first person to contact me to see if I would like to submit my name for consideration as one of the lawyers to be selected from across the country to be appointed as counsel with the Commission; Theodore St. Antoine, the superb Dean of the University of Michigan Law School, who encouraged me to write a book about my work with the Warren Commission; my father, Louis Belin (now deceased), and mother, Esther Belin, who inculcated in their two children a standard of absolute integrity; my brother, Daniel, a Los Angeles attorney of tremendous ability, who made many valuable suggestions; Catherine Sheridan, as fine a secretary as any lawyer could have, whose patience and capacity for work enabled me to meet all deadlines; and last, but surely not least, Jon, Jim, Joy, Tom and Laurie Belin, who helped with such enthusiasm in photocopying and assembling the manuscript and copies.

INTRODUCTION

Harrison E. Salisbury

Ten years have passed since that bright Dallas morning when a sniper took the life of John Fitzgerald Kennedy, ten years which have not eased the anguish of the hour, the tragedy, the mystery. Although President Kennedy's death lies a decade behind us the nation has not ceased to mourn the malevolent circumstances which robbed us of a leader so young, so bold, so promising.

No death in our time has so concentrated a nation's emotions as that of John Kennedy. The fact that his was first in a macabre procession which claimed the lives of his brother, Robert, and a pleiad of Americans—Martin Luther King, Malcolm X, George Lincoln Rockwell, Joseph Yablonski and his family, a remarkable succession of Black Panther figures, including Fred Hampton and George Jackson—and came within a hair's breadth of taking the life of another Presidential candidate, George Wallace, has only intensified the nation's concern.

To many it has seemed that some mad spirit of the Dark Ages has been unleashed within our technological society, striking at random but seeking its victims, in large measure, among men who have sought to put themselves at the service of their fellow citizens through political leadership. To many it has seemed there must be a dark conspiracy running from death to death, linking them all in a sorcerer's web of evil.

Our logical minds have rejected again and again the tawdry evidence which exposes these crimes as the haphazard acts of random psychotics, the by-products of our computerized electronic society, fallout of a civilization programmed to produce metal-and-plastic rather than flesh-and-blood.

In our agony we instinctively clutch for the supernatural. It has seemed too banal to believe that John F. Kennedy could have died less regally than Caesar. Lee Harvey Oswald was a man too trivial to have brought down Camelot. And as the succession of murders thudded across our bulldozed landscape, our minds grasped feverishly at the possibility that there was more in these accidental crimes than met the eye—that behind them all lay some master mind, some sinister power, some ring, some conspiracy of a grandeur to match the stature of the victims.

Particularly in the early months and years after November 22, 1963, there were projected into public consciousness theories to suit the taste of all for whom the dismal facts were unpalatable.

But, let us be realistic: In the ten years since John Kennedy's death not one important clue or fact has been added to that mountainous store so painstakingly and, on the whole, carefully inquired into by the Warren Commission. *Not one fact.* Let us be precise. Theories have been propounded without number. Claim after claim has been advanced—conflicts of evidence, telltale clues overlooked or misinterpreted, and misfeasance and malfeasance by the Warren Commission.

But in all this pawing over the evidence—not one new fact has been turned up. Not one new witness has been ferreted out and brought forward trumpeting: "Yes, I saw the killer!" Not one more bullet than those found immediately after the assassination has been discovered. Not one more weapon which might have been fired at the President. Not one name of a possible co-conspirator of Oswald's. No investigator has produced a link between Oswald and Jack Ruby. Between Ruby and anyone else. Between Oswald and right-wing groups. Between Oswald and left-wing groups. Between Oswald and foreign powers. Or domestic enemies and rivals of the President.

Nothing. Nothing but theory, speculation, sensationalism, juggling and transposition of facts, reordering of what we already knew in order to raise questions (but not to provide answers).

Ten years have passed. It is time to look back to that sunny day in Dallas and, in patience, in quiet, with care and with logic to sum up what we really know. This David W. Belin has done with patience and with eloquence. He has done what no one yet has done (except, of course, for the original Warren report). He has taken all of the evidence and sifted it through. He has concentrated, in particular, on those theses and theories which have been spun by that group which he calls the "assassination sensationalists." He has gone over every one of their contentions, returning to the original testimony, the original evidence, to show how it has been tortured and twisted in order to support cardboard structures. In particular, he has reestablished what has often been overlooked—the primacy of the Tippit killing as demonstrating Oswald's obvious guilt. The evidence here is simply overpowering.

This has been no easy task even for one like Belin, who handled very important segments of the Warren testimony, the processing of evidence and questioning of witnesses. He has had a decade to think and study. He is by no means uncritical of the Commission, of some of its procedures, of some of its methods. But his careful reexamination does not invalidate a single Warren finding. He believes the Commission and Chief Justice Warren, in particular, should not have yielded to the desires of the Kennedy family and should have insisted upon the X rays and medical photographs of the slain President's body. Not because this data would have changed their conclusion but because it would have buttressed the findings and blocked off avenues for turgid sensationalism.

I believe Belin is right. I do not come to that judgment out of hand or simply on the basis of his work. I, too, have labored over the Kennedy facts—first, directing a remarkable team of *New York Times* reporters who, in the first few days after the President's death, themselves uncovered much important information about Oswald and his background independently and before any official investigators; second, in directing, two years later, a careful restudy of the assassination that was designed to accomplish many of the tasks of this book, that is, to examine every major challenge to the Warren thesis (as well as any which *The Times* team was able to generate on its own). That study, unfortunately, was never carried to completion, having been interrupted by my own assignment to Hanoi from December 1966 to January 1967. It is fair to say, however, that our preliminary findings fully support those of this volume.

I do not believe that the Belin study, meticulous, precise and all-embracing as it is, will bring to an end the questions about John Kennedy's death. More than 100 years after the assassination of Abraham Lincoln a new theory of how he met death is periodically advanced. I have found in every part of the world—deep in Soviet Siberia, in the high Himalayas and even in the People's Republic of China—a continuing unwillingness to believe that John Kennedy met his death from a random bullet fired by an insignificant psychopath. In Russia, in China, in France and in England, the theory of the single aberrant assassin is not believed. "There must be more to it." That is the popular belief.

This volume will not crush the mystique of the Kennedy assassination. But for anyone who wishes to know how the crime of this century actually occurred and why it could have occurred in no other way than that which the Warren Commission described, this work tells the story better than it has been told at any time before.

November 22, 1963:

YOU ARE THE JURY

PART I
Overview

1

"AND MY HUSBAND
NEVER MADE ANY SOUND"

The two murders took place within approximately three-quarters of an hour. Our investigation lasted approximately three-quarters of a year.

The ultimate question I had to decide was who killed two men in Dallas, Texas, on Nov. 22, 1963. One was cut down by rifle fire at 12:30 PM. His name was John Fitzgerald Kennedy, thirty-fifth President of the United States. The other was cut down by pistol fire around 1:15 PM. His name was J. D. Tippit, patrolman of the Dallas Police Department.

It was up to me to make the initial determination because I was one of two independent lawyers serving with the Warren Commission assigned to what we called "Area II"—the determination of who killed President Kennedy and who killed Patrolman Tippit. My partner was the outstanding California trial attorney Joseph A. Ball. Together we acted as both the investigator of the facts and the judge of the evidence. By the time we had completed our work we had more firsthand knowledge about the witnesses and the evidence concerning these two murders than any other people in the world.

Unfortunately, though we were supposed to be a totally objective, nonpolitical "blue-ribbon" investigating commission with complete access to all information, our work was hampered by political considerations and errors in judgment made by some of the Commissioners, including Earl Warren, Chief Justice of the United States. These mistakes ranged from overzealous "top-secret" designation of investigative material to our exclusion from direct access to vital portions of the record—most notably the photographs and X rays taken during the autopsy of President Kennedy. More about this later.

We were also hampered by many inaccurate reports from all investigating agencies, including the Federal Bureau of Investigation, the Secret Service, the Dallas Police Department and the Dallas Sheriff's Office.

To all of this were added the myriad problems that stem from natural inconsistencies that inevitably arise within the testimony of different witnesses to an incident. These were compounded because of the nature of the crime, the excitement inherent in the observations of witnesses, the relatively large number of persons who witnessed the assassination and the depth of our investigation.

Most important, we were hampered by the absence of the traditional fair and impartial American jury that would objectively listen to all the vital evidence and reach a true verdict. Instead, we were faced with an emotionally charged jury of world opinion that was typified by my own impressions in Des Moines, Iowa, when I first learned about the assassination and the subsequent murder of the alleged assassin by a figure of some notoriety, Jack Ruby.

In those days immediately following the tragedy, I felt it was highly probable that there was a conspiracy, that Lee Harvey Oswald might not be the real assassin, despite the claims of the FBI, and that Ruby had killed Oswald to silence his victim. Some thought it was a left-wing conspiracy, others thought it was a right-wing conspiracy, and there were innuendos of a conspiracy originating in the Soviet Union, China, Cuba, the Middle East. There was even wild speculation by a few that Lyndon Johnson might in some way be involved.

The susceptibility of human nature to the mystique of conspiracy afforded a fertile field for assassination sensationalists. Through misrepresentation, omission and innuendo they were successful in deceiving a large body of world public opinion for one reason: Few people objectively examined the overall evidence in depth the way a jury would, had there been an actual trial.

The assassination of President Kennedy has been called the crime of the century. For this crime, and for the murder of Officer Tippit, there should be a jury that will render a true verdict based on an objective and dispassionate examination of the key evidence.

I would like you to serve on that jury, to determine for yourself and for the court of world opinion who killed President Kennedy and who killed Officer Tippit. I also want you to see the inside of a so-called "blue-ribbon" commission, particularly since the trend of government is toward more use of such commissions.

In addition, there is a rarely observed side of the FBI that should be disclosed at this time when the possibility of a Federal police force grows more imminent. You will also discover the seemingly insignificant acts of many individuals who singly and collectively changed the course of history.

Finally, you will see how independent citizens in their search for the truth can successfully fight bureaucracy and how important is citizen participation in all levels of government—even "nonpolitical" commissions headed by the Chief Justice of the United States.

At the outset, you should know as a juror that your task is not easy. You will not be spoon-fed one person's conclusions about what someone else said—pure hearsay. Rather, you will hear the heart of the testimony from the key witnesses themselves. It will take time and it may occasionally seem tedious, but the search for the truth is seldom easy. Moreover, as in so many cases, the evidence in this one is full of blind alleys and contradictions.

For instance, James Jarman Jr. stated under oath that Oswald "never hardly worked in a shirt. He worked in a T-shirt." Jarman ought to know. He was an employee of the Texas School Book Depository Company who had daily contact with Lee Harvey Oswald, who also worked there.

But what about the testimony from Troy Eugene West, also an employee of the Texas School Book Depository Company, who also saw Lee Harvey Oswald every day:

I don't believe I ever seen him [Oswald] working in just a T-shirt. He worked in a shirt all right, but I never did see him work in a T-shirt.

Here is another example of the many contradictions in the evidence: Did President Kennedy say anything after he was first hit? It could be important in determining one of the ultimate questions: Did the first bullet that hit the President puncture his windpipe and exit from his throat? If President Kennedy said something after he was first struck, this might constitute strong evidence that the first bullet did not exit from the President's throat.

First, the testimony of the driver of the presidential limousine, Secret Service agent William Greer:

Representative Ford. Did you hear the President say anything after the first shot?
Mr. Greer. No, sir; I never heard him say anything; never at any time did I hear him say anything.

But sitting next to Mr. Greer in the front seat of the presidential limousine was another Secret Service agent, Roy Kellerman. Here is his testimony:

Mr. Specter. . . . Now, describe what occurred as you proceeded down Elm Street after turning off of Houston.
Mr. Kellerman. As we turned off Houston onto Elm and made the short little dip to the left going down grade, as I said, we were away from buildings, and were—there was a sign on the side of the road which I don't recall what it was or what it said, but we no more than passed that and you are out in the open, and there is a report like a firecracker, pop. And I turned my head to the right because whatever this noise was I was sure that it came from the right and perhaps into the rear, and as I turned my head to the right to view whatever it was or see whatever it was, I heard a voice from the back seat and I firmly believe it was the President's, "My God, I am hit," and I turned around and he has got his hands up like this.
Mr. Specter. Indicating right hand up toward his neck?
Mr. Kellerman. That is right, sir. In fact, both hands were up in that direction . . .
Mr. Specter. With relationship to that first noise that you have described, when did you hear the voice?
Mr. Kellerman. His voice?
Mr. Specter. We will start with his voice.
Mr. Kellerman. OK. From the noise of which I was in the process of turning to determine where it was or what it was, it carried on right then. Why I am so positive, gentlemen, that it was his voice—there is only one man in that back seat that was from Boston, and the accents carried very clearly.
Mr. Specter. Well, had you become familiar with the President's voice prior to that day?
Mr. Kellerman. Yes; very much so.
Mr. Specter. And what was the basis for your becoming familiar with his voice prior to that day?
Mr. Kellerman. I have been with him for 3 years.
Mr. Specter. And had you talked with him on a very frequent basis during the course of that association?

Mr. Kellerman. He was a very free man to talk to; yes. He knew most all the men, most everybody who worked in the White House as well as everywhere, and he would call you.

Mr. Specter. And from your experience would you say that you could recognize the voice?

Mr. Kellerman. Very much, sir; I would.

Mr. Specter. Now, I think you may have answered this, but I want to pinpoint just when you heard that statement which you have attributed to President Kennedy in relationship to the sound which you described as a firecracker.

Mr. Kellerman. This noise which I attribute as a firecracker, when this occurred and I am in the process of determining where it comes because I am sure it came off my right rear somewhere; the voice broke in right then.

Mr. Specter. At about the same time?

Mr. Kellerman. That is correct, sir. That is right.

Mr. Specter. Now, did President Kennedy say anything besides, "My God, I am hit."

Mr. Kellerman. That is the last words he said, sir.

Whom do you believe? Secret Service agent Greer or Secret Service agent Kellerman?

Let me give you some assistance. Edward J. Epstein, a purported expert on the assassination of President Kennedy and the investigation by the Warren Commission, wrote a best-selling book, *Inquest.* In this book, Kellerman's testimony forms an essential part of Epstein's thesis. Mr. Epstein writes:

Furthermore, if accurate, the testimony of Secret Service Agent Roy Kellerman makes it extremely doubtful that the throat wound was caused by the first bullet to strike the President. Kellerman, who was in the front seat of the President's limousine, testified that he distinctly heard the President say, "My God, I am hit," *after* the first shot. Since the projectile that caused the throat wound also punctured the windpipe, it is medically highly improbable that the President could speak *after* he received the throat wound. This fact would be consistent with the FBI's version of the autopsy, which implies that the throat wound was caused by a fragment from a later bullet, but inconsistent with the Commission's version of the autopsy, which holds that the first bullet to hit the President exited from his throat.

There is only one thing wrong with Mr. Epstein's judgment: Like the other assassination sensationalists, he is not giving you the whole story.

In addition to Secret Service agents Greer and Kellerman, three other witnesses were riding in the presidential limousine: John Connally, then Governor of Texas; Nellie Connally, wife of the Governor; and Jacqueline Kennedy.

I am sure you jurors want to hear what all the key witnesses said themselves rather than selected hearsay evidence, as presented through the conclusions of third parties. As you put the pieces of the puzzle together, you will get an overall flavor of the people who testified and the underlying nature of their testimony, just as you would in a courtroom. It may at times test your powers of concentration, but the facts will come to you directly from the witnesses themselves. We can start with the rest of the testimony on the question whether President Kennedy said anything after he was first struck.

First, Governor Connally:

Mr. Specter. Did President Kennedy make any statement during the time of the shooting or immediately prior thereto?

Governor Connally. He never uttered a sound at all that I heard.

Mr. Specter. Did Mrs. Kennedy state anything at that time?

Governor Connally. Yes; I have to—I would say it was after the third shot when she said, "They have killed my husband."

Mr. Specter. Did she say anything more?

Governor Connally. Yes; she said, I heard her say one time, "I have got his brains in my hand."

Mr. Specter. Did that constitute everything that she said at that time?

Governor Connally. That is all I heard her say.

Mrs. Connally was also specific on the same question.

Mr. Specter. Mrs. Connally, tell us what happened at the time of the assassination.

Mrs. Connally. We had just finished the motorcade through the downtown Dallas area, and it had been a wonderful motorcade. The people had been very responsive to the President and Mrs. Kennedy, and we were very pleased, I was very pleased.

As we got off Main Street—is that the main thoroughfare?

Mr. Specter. That is the street on which you were proceeding through the town, yes.

Mrs. Connally. In fact the receptions had been so good every place that I had showed much restraint by not mentioning something about it before.

I could resist no longer. When we got past this area I did turn to the President and said, "Mr. President, you can't say Dallas doesn't love you."

Then I don't know how soon, it seems to me it was very soon, that I heard a noise, and not being an expert rifleman, I was not aware that it was a rifle. It was just a frightening noise, and it came from the right.

I turned over my right shoulder and looked back, and saw the President as he had both hands at his neck.

Mr. Specter. And you are indicating with your own hands, two hands crossing over gripping your own neck?

Mrs. Connally. Yes; and it seemed to me there was—*he made no utterance, no cry.* . . . [emphasis added]

And finally, we have the testimony of Mrs. Kennedy, questioned by our General Counsel, J. Lee Rankin:

Mr. Rankin. As you got into the main street of Dallas were there very large crowds on the streets?

Mrs. Kennedy. Yes.

Mr. Rankin. And you waved to them and proceeded down the street with the motorcade?

Mrs. Kennedy. Yes. And in the motorcade, you know, I usually would be waving mostly to the left side and he was waving mostly to the right, which is one reason you are not looking at each other very much. And it was terribly hot. Just blinding all of us.

Mr. Rankin. Now, do you remember as you turned off of the main street onto Houston Street?

Mrs. Kennedy. I don't know the name of the street.

Mr. Rankin. That is that one block before you get to the Depository Building.

Mrs. Kennedy. Well, I remember whenever it was, Mrs. Connally said, "We will soon be there." We could see a tunnel in front of us. Everything was really slow then. And I remember thinking it would be so cool under that tunnel.

Mr. Rankin. And then do you remember as you turned off of Houston onto Elm right by the Depository Building?

Mrs. Kennedy. Well, I don't know the names of the streets, but I suppose right by the Depository is what you are talking about?

Mr. Rankin. Yes; that is the street that sort of curves as you go down under the underpass.

Mrs. Kennedy. Yes; well, that is when she said to President Kennedy, "You certainly can't say that the people of Dallas haven't given you a nice welcome."

Mr. Rankin. What did he say?

Mrs. Kennedy. I think he said—I don't know if I remember it or I have read it, "No, you certainly can't," or something. And you know then the car was very slow and there weren't very many people around.

And then—do you want me to tell you what happened?

Mr. Rankin. Yes; if you would, please.

Mrs. Kennedy. You know, there is always noise in a motorcade and there are always motorcycles beside us, a lot of them backfiring. So I was looking to the left. I guess there was a noise, but it didn't seem like any different noise really because there is so much noise, motorcycles and things. But then suddenly Governor Connally was yelling, "Oh, no, no, no."

Mr. Rankin. Did he turn toward you?

Mrs. Kennedy. No; I was looking this way, to the left, and I heard these terrible noises. You know. *And my husband never made any sound* . . . [emphasis added]

Now, members of the jury, instead of asking whether you believe Secret Service agent Kellerman or Secret Service agent Greer, I will restate the question: Whom do you believe? Secret Service agent Roy Kellerman on the one hand, or Mrs. Kennedy, Governor Connally, Mrs. Connally and Secret Service agent Greer on the other?

And I will leave one additional question. Why, in discussing this vital point, did Mr. Epstein leave out the testimony of Mr. Greer, Governor Connally, Mrs. Connally and Mrs. Kennedy?

Verbatim testimony in this book has been included as it was recorded by the official court reporters transcribing the testimony and as it was published by the United States Government Printing Office in the 26 volumes of testimony and exhibits that were published by the President's Commission on the Assassination of President Kennedy together with the Report. No attempt has been made to correct spelling, punctuation, or other grammatical errors, or words misunderstood by the court reporters such as "lighter" instead of "latter", etc.

2

"TRUTH IS OUR ONLY GOAL"

The Assassination of John Fitzgerald Kennedy on November 22, 1963, was a cruel and shocking act of violence directed against a man, a family, a nation, and against all mankind. A young and vigorous leader whose years of public and private life stretched before him was the victim of the fourth Presidential assassination in the history of a country dedicated to the concepts of reasoned argument and peaceful political change. This Commission was created on November 29, 1963, in recognition of the right of people everywhere to full and truthful knowledge concerning these events. This report endeavors to fulfill that right and to appraise this tragedy by the light of reason and the standard of fairness. It has been prepared with a deep awareness of the Commission's responsibility to present to the American people an objective report of the facts relating to the assassination.

This was the opening paragraph of Chapter I of the Warren Commission Report. It was a declaration of the frame of reference within which we conducted our investigation and wrote this report.

Our frame of reference was established in our first meeting with our chairman, Chief Justice Warren. Regardless of what we found, regardless of how the chips might fall, the Chief Justice said, our only concern was for the truth. We took him at his word. "Truth is our only goal," he said.

The key word was "only." To be sure, in a trial, when examining or cross-examining a witness, I was always concerned with the truth—"the whole truth, and nothing but the truth, so help you God." But my concern was never merely for the sake of the truth itself. There were always other considerations, principally: How does this affect my client? What further steps must be taken in light of the facts to win the lawsuit?

But here there was no lawsuit to win, no special client to serve. We were 14 lawyers selected from across the country. Our only goal was to find the truth, the whole truth, and nothing but the truth—for the sake of finding the truth.

For us lawyers, in contrast to the commissioners, there were no outside influences that might affect our work. We had no government position to protect, no political ax to grind. We were not concerned with judicial precedent. We had no special client paying our fee. If we had any client, it was 190 million Americans who wanted to know the whole truth about the murder of their President. Beyond our shores, people throughout the world also wanted the facts.

Earl Warren spoke with great warmth and sincerity in that first meeting in

9

January. He told us why the Commission had been established. After Lee Harvey Oswald was killed by Jack Ruby, the normal judicial procedures of a trial of the alleged assassin were no longer available. In Texas, there were proposals for an investigation by a Dallas County grand jury. Both the House of Representatives and the United States Senate considered Congressional hearings to try and determine the facts relating to the assassination. Alternative means were discussed, including the possibility of initiating a court of inquiry before a state magistrate in Texas. Killing the President of the United States was not a Federal crime. Therefore, the Texas authorities claimed primary jurisdiction.

Meanwhile, the caldrons of speculation were boiling, particularly after Ruby killed Oswald, the alleged assassin.

The State Department was concerned that the speculation, charges, countercharges and rumors could have adverse effects on American foreign policy, even involving the issues of peace and war. Recommendations were made to President Johnson to appoint an independent nonpartisan fact-finding body with the broadest national mandate. Chief Justice Warren was approached by President Johnson to head this body; Earl Warren told us that he had discussed it with the other members of the Supreme Court. Everyone felt that the Chief Justice should turn down the appointment because it was not proper for a member of the Court to engage in any "extra-curricular activities." Earl Warren told the President, "No."

Then President Johnson called Earl Warren to the White House for a private meeting. The President went over the reports from the State Department. He told the Chief Justice of the rumors and speculation sweeping across the United States and the world. The State Department felt it was essential that there be an independent fact-finding commission that would have the broadest national mandate and that would also have great international standing. The position of Chief Justice of the United States is the apex of the Federal judiciary system; therefore, it symbolizes to most Americans the majesty of reasoned application of justice under the laws of our land. Most Americans considered it fitting that the highest judicial official of their country should head the inquiry into the slaying of a fallen President.

Moreover, Chief Justice Warren and the Court he led had acquired great stature abroad because their dramatic decisions in the field of civil rights had shown a passionate concern for fairness and justice for the individual. President Johnson convinced Chief Justice Warren that an extensive investigation under his leadership would be the most fair and impartial way of finding the truth and would also be accepted and trusted by Americans and by the other peoples of the world.

The President stated that without such a fair and impartial investigation, the increasing speculation could affect the ultimate issues of war or peace. Earl Warren put it simply: When President Johnson said that the assassination of President Kennedy could have an effect on whether there would be war or peace, "I could not turn him down."

The six other Commissioners were chosen by President Johnson with the overall goal of having the "broadest national mandate." From the U. S. Senate he chose Richard B. Russell, Democrat of Georgia, and chairman of the Armed Services Committee, a former Governor and county attorney in his native state; and John Sherman Cooper, Republican of Kentucky, former county and circuit judge in Kentucky and former United States Ambassador to India. Unfortunately, Senator Russell was seldom present at the interrogations of key witnesses brought to Washington to testify. Furthermore, he almost never visited with the lawyers who were conducting the actual investigation.

Two members were drawn from the United States House of Representatives: Hale Boggs, Democrat of Louisiana and majority whip; and Gerald R. Ford, Republican of Michigan, chairman of the House Republican Conference. Congressman Ford was by far the more effective of the two.

From private life, President Johnson selected two lawyers who had served in the administrations of both Democratic and Republican Presidents: Allen W. Dulles, former Director of Central Intelligence; and John J. McCloy, former president of the International Bank for Reconstruction and Development, former United States High Commissioner for Germany, and (during World War II) an Assistant Secretary of War.

Although these individuals might form a body having the "broadest national mandate," there were two major problems: All these men were politically oriented and were either serving in government or had recently held government positions; thus they were not totally devoid of government influence. Moreover, all were busy men with many outside responsibilities; accordingly, none could devote full time to the work of the commission. As a matter of fact, Senator Russell was almost always absent, and, even when the most important witnesses were brought to Washington to testify before the seven commissioners, several of them were almost always absent. Often, only one or two were present, and when we took the testimony of witnesses outside Washington, none of them were present.

To be sure, transcripts were promptly prepared of the testimony of all witnesses. Each commissioner would have a set of the transcripts, if he had the time to read and study them. Even here, however, the procedure left much to be desired. Every experienced trial lawyer knows that the testimony of a witness is not just his actual words. His demeanor, the way in which he answers questions—all the observations of a witness that can be made by a judge and jury in the course of his testimony—are of prime importance. These impressions are lost in the naked transcript. No commissioner not present, no reader, no historian, no scholar, will ever be fully able to recapture them. Thus, it was crucial that the Commission retain a staff that met three basic criteria: (1) competence; (2) experience; (3) independence from all outside political influences and governmental connections.

Fortunately, the Commissioners were aware of this need. As we wrote on page xi of the Foreword to the Report of our Warren Commission:

The Commission took steps immediately to obtain the necessary staff to fulfill its assignment. J. Lee Rankin, former Solicitor General of the United States, was sworn in as general counsel for the Commission on December 16, 1963. Additional members of the legal staff were selected during the next few weeks. The Commission has been aided by 14 assistant counsel with high professional qualifications, selected by it from widely separated parts of the United States. *This staff undertook the work of the Commission with a wealth of legal and investigative experience and a total dedication to the determination of the truth.* [emphasis added]

The staff directed the investigation of the assassination of President Kennedy and wrote the report. And I know from firsthand experience that the work of the staff was performed with "a total dedication to the determination of the truth." Truth was our only goal.

Before getting to the eyewitness evidence directly related to the two murders, you jurors should have a look inside the Warren Commission to see how far we went in the pursuit of the truth. To give you a typical example, let us explore the subject of the paraffin test performed by the Dallas Police Department on the alleged assassin, Lee Harvey Oswald.

3

"IT ONLY MEANS THAT
HE FIRED A GUN"

Members of the jury, the paraffin test is a relatively simple procedure in which liquid wax is applied to a suspect's skin to determine whether he has recently fired a weapon. Before examining our analyses of this test, I want to present three witnesses.

First, Dallas District Attorney Henry Wade: "The paraffin test showed that he [Oswald] had recently fired a gun. It was on both hands."

Mr. Wade's testimony is supported by Dallas Police Chief Jesse E. Curry, who was asked about the results of the paraffin test on Oswald. Chief Curry stated: "I understand that it was positive. . . . It only means that he fired a gun."

However, the third witness, an outspoken critic of the Warren Commission, Mark Lane, takes a diametrically opposite position: "The test, however, showed no gunpowder on either hands or cheek and no nitrates on Oswald's face." Mr. Lane further states that there is ". . . but one possible interpretation—that the paraffin test results were consistent with innocence . . ."

Now, members of the jury, let us go inside the Warren Commission.

Ours was the first commission of its kind that ever investigated such sacrosanct agencies as the FBI. Also, our inquiry required access to the State Department's secret files. The state and local law enforcement authorities in Texas were also on the spot. We would be going over their investigation and would detect any mistakes they had made.

I recall our first meeting with J. Lee Rankin, our general counsel. For more than twenty years Lee Rankin had practiced law in Lincoln, Nebraska, where he attained a reputation as a fine lawyer and a man of high integrity. In January, 1953, he was appointed by President Eisenhower as Assistant Attorney General in charge of the Office of Legal Counsel in the Department of Justice; in August, 1956, he was appointed as Solicitor General of the United States. With his broad background of both private practice and government service, Lee Rankin was well aware of the problems we would encounter in our investigation of government agencies. Accordingly, as general counsel of the Warren Commission, he laid down important procedural rules in our first meeting on Jan. 20, 1964.

After we had assembled in the commission conference room, Rankin warned us that we would be looked upon with great suspicion. Moreover, he said, since this had already been labeled a "blue ribbon" commission with a legal staff composed of "outstanding lawyers selected from across the country," we would be expected to meet the highest standards. We were going to have to be sure of our facts, for we could be certain that government personnel would be more open with us if we showed we knew the facts.

As I left our meeting I thought of the ramifications of what I had been told. If there were problems of executive privilege and lack of full cooperation or full disclosure in a nonpolitical investigation of the assassination of the President of the United States, how could we ever depend on getting the whole truth from our Government in matters of great national importance?

At all times I followed the Rankin rule: I took nothing for granted, including the reports of the FBI, the Secret Service and the Dallas Police Department. In fact, you will find in a later chapter that one FBI report, if correct, would have made it physically impossible for Lee Harvey Oswald to be the assassin of President Kennedy.

Although we did not rely blindly on the findings of the FBI, we necessarily had to take advantage of the investigative work that had already been undertaken. Our first job was to familiarize ourselves with the thousands of pages of data that were being compiled by the FBI, together with all the investigative work of the Secret Service and the Dallas Police Department. Joe Ball and I took almost a month to digest the material that had been obtained from the date of the assassination and that applied to our area.

The procedure that was adopted was to have all investigative material funneled to the commission office, where it would be scanned and copied, with a copy to each lawyer in the areas in which the material was relevant.

This requires a word of explanation. For organizational purposes, our work was divided into six basic areas: Area I centered on the activities of the President, including the background planning of the trip to Texas, the planning of the motorcade through Dallas, the testimony of the persons in the motorcade, the treatment of the President in Parkland Memorial Hospital, and the autopsy.

Area II, in which Joe Ball and I worked, focused on the determination of who was (or were) the assassin(s) of President Kennedy and Officer Tippit.

Area III assumed the correctness of the preliminary reports of the FBI and Secret Service that Lee Harvey Oswald was involved in the assassination of the President. It concentrated on Oswald's life in an effort to determine possible motive and also to determine whether there might have been any domestic conspiracy involved in the assassination, apart from questions involving Jack Ruby. The only areas of Oswald's life that were not covered in Area III were his trips abroad, primarily his sojourn in the Soviet Union and his trip—less than two months before the assassination—to Mexico. These travels were covered in Area IV, which primarily involved whether there were any foreign conspiratorial aspects in the assassination.

Area V concentrated on Jack Ruby. It sought to uncover any relationship between Ruby and the assassination, other than the fact that Ruby had killed Oswald.

The problems pertaining to the protection of the President were the subject of Area VI. This included an evaluation of the standards of Presidential protection that were in effect on Nov. 22, an analysis of how the various governmental agencies met these established standards and recommendations for changes.

The basic plan of organization was to assign two lawyers to each of these six areas.[1] However, we did not work in separate compartments. Nearly every day, we would be in and out of each other's offices, learning facts, questioning theories, arguing and questioning any preliminary conclusions or findings made as we went along. Generally, we went to lunch together in groups. The cross-examination would continue over lunch and during the dinner hours for many of us who were coming back to work in the evening.

We started with no "foregone conclusions"; in fact, I subconsciously wanted to find evidence to prove that Lee Harvey Oswald was *not* the assassin.

After a month of reading, theorizing, cross-examining each other and writing, Joe Ball and I prepared a 248-page first report, primarily for our own use in making further investigation. We set forth our framework in the beginning:

At no time have we assumed that Lee Harvey Oswald was the assassin of President Kennedy. Rather, our entire study has been based on an independent examination of all of the evidence in an effort to determine who was the assassin of President Kennedy.

The initial "assume nothing" standard established by Lee Rankin constituted an important part of the basic framework of our investigation. How important can be illustrated by one example—there were many others—the paraffin test. In our first report, Joe Ball and I commented on the paraffin test. This portion of our report was based on material we had received from the FBI and the Dallas Police Department, which included diagrams of the palm and the back of Lee Harvey Oswald's hands. The FBI material stated that the report of the paraffin test showed the test results on Oswald were "consistent with a person who had handled and/or fired a firearm."

This is the discussion of the paraffin test in our first report:

The report of the paraffin test, together with the drawings thereof, appears in Document #5 at pages 146-149. The paraffin test on the cheek is negative. The

---

[1] One of the best-kept secrets inside the Commission was that Francis W. K. Adams, one of the two lawyers assigned to Area I, performed virtually no work. He should have been asked to resign when it first became apparent that he was not going to undertake his responsibilities, but because of some mistaken fear that this might in some way embarrass the Commission, Mr. Adams was kept on in name only and the entire burden in Area I fell upon Arlen Specter. Fortunately for the Commission, Arlen Specter was able to carry the entire weight of Area I on his own shoulders. Nevertheless, it is indicative of the nature of investigations by governmental commissions that the need for a second lawyer in Area I was outweighed by a political decision. The ramifications of the fact that this decision was made by the Chief Justice of the United States are indeed chilling.

paraffin test on the left hand is positive on the palm of the hand, particularly the area below the middle finger and the fourth finger and on the side of the thumb. Also, on the center of the back of the left hand, there are nitrate positive marks showing. On the right hand on the palm side, there are positive nitrate marks on all fingers and the thumb—the marks on the fingers being around one-third to one-fourth from the end. Also, on the palm and the left portion thereof, not too far from the wrist, there is a positive nitrate showing. On the back of the hand, near the juncture of the thumb and the index finger, there are also nitrate positive marks. The three paraffin casts which were made from the right cheek, right hand and left hand were delivered by Captain George Doughty of the Dallas Police Department to laboratory technician, Al Anderson, and the Dallas City County Criminal Investigation Laboratory and Parkland Hospital; and Anderson assisted Dr. M. F. Mason in processing the nitrate tests and Anderson made the drawings as to where the nitrates were found. The report of Dr. Mason said that in the paraffin tests of the right and left hands, he found "punctate traces of nitrate, which would be consistent with the person who had handled and/or fired a firearm." (Document #5, page 147.)

The complete significance of the paraffin test must be determined. Messrs. Redlich and Eisenberg[2] are working in this area and their findings will be carefully studied by counsel in Area II, particularly since our entire efforts are based on an independent determination of who was the assassin, rather than from the viewpoint of a prosecutor. If anyone firing a rifle within a few hours prior to the submission of a paraffin test on the right cheek with a high degree of certainty would have nitrates on his right cheek which could not be readily removed, this is a factor weighing against the conclusion that Lee Harvey Oswald was the assassin.

The police officer who performed the paraffin test on Oswald was Sergeant W. E. Barnes of the Crime Scene Search Section of the Dallas Police Department. I took his testimony in Dallas on Apr. 7, 1964. Sergeant Barnes told how he brushed layers of warm liquid paraffin on Oswald's hands. As he brushed the wax on, he would periodically interlace layers of gauze that acted as a reinforcing material in the way that steel rods reinforce concrete. The theory of the test is that the warm sticky paraffin opens the skin's pores and picks up any dirt and foreign material present at the surface. When the paraffin cools and hardens, it forms a cast. Then the cast is removed and processed with chemicals that turn blue in the presence of nitrates.

Gunpowder residues contain nitrates. The theory behind the test is that if a cast reacts positively—i.e., if blue dots appear on the paraffin casts—it provides evidence that the suspect recently fired a weapon.

In accordance with the procedures established by Rankin, we made an exhaustive investigation of the significance of the paraffin test before I took the deposition of Sergeant Barnes.

Although the Dallas Police Department used the paraffin test in an effort to determine if Oswald fired a weapon, we found that the *paraffin test is wholly unreliable in determining whether a person has recently fired a*

---

[2]Norman Redlich and Melvin Eisenberg were two of the other assistant counsel.

weapon. The chemicals used in the paraffin test will react positively not only with nitrates from gunpowder residues but also nitrates from any other sources and most oxidizing agents. Thus, contact with tobacco, urine, cosmetics, kitchen matches, fertilizers and many other things may result in a positive reaction to the paraffin test. Also, the mere *handling* of a weapon may leave nitrates on the skin, just as the firing of the weapon may also leave nitrates.

Therefore, a *positive* reaction to the paraffin test is worthless in determining whether a suspect has recently fired a weapon.

The only question that remained was whether a *negative* reaction on the paraffin test would be evidence that a person had *not* fired a weapon. We found that it made a great difference if the weapon was a revolver on the one hand or a rifle or an automatic pistol on the other. A revolver has what is known as an "open cylinder." There is a little space between the cylinder and the weapon, to enable the cylinder to revolve. When a revolver is fired, nitrate-bearing gases escape through this space—and in escaping may leave residues on the hand.

In a rifle and an automatic pistol, however, there is no such gap. Rather, a rifle (and an automatic pistol as well) has what is known as a "sealed chamber." By the time the chamber of a bolt-action rifle would be open for the next bullet to be inserted, the gases already would have gone down the barrel and there would be no pressure that would cause them to be expelled upon the hands (or, for that matter, upon the cheek) of the person who fired the weapon.

None of these facts appeared in the investigation file of the Dallas Police Department, which had performed the paraffin test. *Moreover, there was nothing concerning the paraffin test furnished independently by the FBI that would have shown its unreliability.* Rather, it was only after we had interviewed personnel in the FBI laboratory that we found that the FBI itself, prior to the assassination, had demonstrated the unreliability of the paraffin test.

In an FBI experiment conducted prior to the assassination, paraffin tests were performed on 17 men, each of whom had fired five shots with a .38 caliber revolver. Both the firing hand and the hand that was not involved in the firing were treated with paraffin casts. Then the casts were processed with a chemical, diphenylamine. Under the theory of the paraffin test, all 17 men should have had blue dots on the paraffin casts of the firing hand and no blue dots on the paraffin casts of the other hand.

However, in the experiment:

1. Eight of the seventeen showed negative or essentially negative results on both hands.

2. Three showed positive results on the idle hand, but negative results on the firing hand.

3. Four showed positive on both hands.

4. Only two showed positive results on the firing hand and negative results on the idle hand.

In another experiment conducted by the FBI, nine of 29 people fired weapons; the remaining 20 had paraffin casts made as they went about their normal duties. Some of the weapons fired were automatic pistols and some were revolvers. Theoretically, since an automatic pistol has a sealed chamber, one would say that the paraffin test should be negative. These were the results of this experiment:

1. Of the 20 people who had not come in contact with a gun, every one showed positive tests on either or on both hands.

2. Of the remaining nine, each of whom had fired a weapon, five had fired automatic weapons. Each of these had positive reactions on one or both hands.

3. Of the four persons who fired a revolver, both hands were positive.

This was conclusive evidence that the paraffin test was totally unreliable in proving either that a person had or had not fired a weapon.

We directed that experiments be made with the rifle found on Nov. 22 on the sixth floor of the Texas School Book Depository Building, and we also used the same type of ammunition as the cartridge cases found in that building. There were negative reactions on both hands and on the cheek of the FBI agent who fired the assassination weapon.

Thus, we had the other side of the coin: A negative reaction from the paraffin test did not prove that a person had not fired a rifle.

With this information, we were interested in why any law enforcement agency would give a paraffin test. The question was raised by Representative Ford: "Why are paraffin tests conducted and how extensive are they?"

FBI expert Cortlandt Cunningham, in testimony before the Commission, replied:

Many local law enforcement agencies do conduct these tests, and at their request, the FBI will process them. They take the cast and we will process them. However, in reporting we give them qualified results since we frequently will get some reaction. Numerous reactions or a few reactions will be found on the casts. However, in no way does this indicate that a person has recently fired a weapon. Then we list a few of the oxidizing agents, the common ones, such as urine and tobacco and cosmetics and a few others that one may come in contact with. Even Clorox would give you a positive reaction.

Representative Ford. Is this a test that has been conducted by law enforcement agencies for some time? Is it a new test?

Mr. Cunningham. No, sir; the first tests that I reported on here were conducted in 1935. There may be some law enforcement agencies which use the test for psychological reasons.

Mr. Dulles. Explain that.

Mr. Cunningham. Yes, sir; what they do is they ask, say, "We are going to run a paraffin test on you, you might as well confess now . . . "

Cunningham then testified that the FBI, when conducting its own investi-

gations, does not use the paraffin test because "it is definitely not reliable as
to determining whether or not a person has fired a weapon . . ."

Now that you jurors have the facts, you might be interested in how the
paraffin test was handled in one internationally distributed film about the
assassination. This film, "Rush to Judgment," was described by its copro-
ducers, Emile de Antonio and Mark Lane, as a "brief for the defense" of
Lee Harvey Oswald.

Every experienced trial lawyer knows that when he presents a brief, he
generally starts with his strongest point. The starting point in the moving-
picture "brief for the defense" is the paraffin test.

After an opening attack on the Warren Commission as "insensibly and
progressively" having "emphasized the evidence which seemed to support
Oswald's sole guilt and insensibly and progressively attenuating the
evidence which pointed away from it," the film turns to the paraffin test and
the producers' strawmen, the Dallas Police Department and the Dallas
District Attorney, Henry Wade.

The movie first shows a film clip from a news conference after the
assassination with the Dallas Police Chief, Jesse E. Curry. A reporter asks,
"Chief, we understand you have the results of the paraffin tests which were
made to determine whether Oswald had fired a weapon. Can you tell us
if . . .?"

Chief Curry replies before the question is completed: "I understand that it
was positive."

Asked what that means, Chief Curry replies: "It only means that he fired a
gun."

Then there is another film clip—Dallas District Attorney Henry Wade.
"The paraffin test showed that he had recently fired a gun; it was on both
hands."

From the film clip taken of Wade shortly after the assassination, the
camera then turns to coproducer Mark Lane, who reads:

Gordon Shanklin, the FBI agent in charge of Dallas, added, quote: A paraffin test used
to determine whether a person has fired a weapon recently was administered to
Oswald shortly after he was apprehended on Friday, one hour after the assassination,
which showed that particles of gunpowder from a weapon, probably a rifle, remained
on Oswald's cheek and hands, close quotes.

Lane then concludes:

The test, however, showed no gunpowder on either hands or cheek and no nitrates on
Oswald's face. Confronted with but one possible interpretation that the paraffin test
results were consistent with innocence, the Commission concluded that the test,
formerly presented as a cornerstone in the case against Oswald, was, quote:
completely unreliable.

Note carefully the language of Lane. He does not say that there are no
nitrates on Oswald's hands. Rather, he asserts that the test "showed no
gunpowder" on either hands or cheek.

You jurors now know that Chief Curry, District Attorney Wade and Mark

Lane, all are wrong. What the paraffin test showed was nitrates on Oswald's hands—which could have come from gunpowder but which also could have come from many other substances, such as tobacco, urine or household cleansers. Although the Dallas Police Department used the paraffin test as part of its case against Oswald, we threw out the test because we found on the basis of our independent investigation that the test's showing of nitrates on Oswald's hands did not prove those nitrates were gunpowder. By the same token, it could not be said that the nitrates were not gunpowder. Therefore Lane is wrong when he asserts that the tests showed "no gunpowder." You also know that because a rifle has a "sealed chamber" one would not necessarily find nitrates on the face of the person who had just fired a rifle.

The misrepresentation by Lane in the film is not innocent, for the film was produced after the Warren Commission Report was published. Pages 560-562 of the Warren Commission Report summarize the FBI experiments with the test and show why we concluded the paraffin test was unreliable.

But Lane's film compounds this confusion with a smear; he asserts that the tests were rejected because there was just "one possible interpretation," that the tests "were consistent with innocence." You now know that this statement by Lane is fallacious. The Commission rejected the results of the paraffin test for one reason only: The test had been shown to be an unreliable indicator of whether a person had fired a weapon. You also know that Lane selected this as the opening proposition in his brief. This typifies the attacks on the Warren Commission by assassination sensationalists.

An epilogue in this area turned up in our investigation and was confirmed by Joseph D. Nicol, whom the Commission retained as an independent expert witness. Mr. Nicol, superintendent of the Bureau of Criminal Identification and Investigation for the State of Illinois, said there were cases where people have been convicted of murder in which the paraffin test was part of the evidence.

Why the FBI processes paraffin tests for other law enforcement agencies remains an unanswered question.

PART II
The Murder
of J.D. Tippit

4

"HE JUST LOOKED
FUNNY TO ME"

Members of the jury, the next witness will be brief. He is the internationally renowned professor Hugh Trevor-Roper. Although he has no firsthand knowledge of the events pertaining to either of the two murders in the case before you, Professor Roper has become a self-styled expert based on hearsay evidence that has been presented to him.

"Professor Roper, what do you have to say about the evidence relied upon by the Warren Commission in reaching its findings?"

Professor Roper (writing on page 12 of his introduction to the most widely publicized and distributed book in post-assassination literature, *Rush to Judgment,* by Mark Lane):

The plain fact is that there is no evidence at all to explain how or why the Dallas Police instantly pounced on Oswald, and until some adequate explanation is given, no one can be blamed for entertaining the most likely hypothesis, viz: that the Dallas Police had undisclosed reasons for arresting Oswald even before they had avowable evidence pointing towards him. Once that hypothesis is admitted, almost all the evidence accepted by the Commission can be reinterpreted in a different way.

This goes to the essence of the thesis of almost all of the assassination sensationalists. Implicit in their attacks on the Warren Commission is the idea that Oswald was in some way "framed." Since they adopt this thesis, they have to show that Oswald was innocent not only of the assassination of President Kennedy but also of the murder of Dallas Police Officer J. D. Tippit and that the reason for arresting Oswald had nothing to do with either.

Yet, throughout the mass of post-assassination literature there is almost no mention of the most important witness who can tell why Oswald was arrested, Johnny Calvin Brewer.

The question of Oswald's arrest is one of the most crucial elements in our investigation. Since Brewer is the most important witness in this area, instead of telling you what Brewer said, I want you jurors to hear it in Brewer's own words.

Johnny Calvin Brewer was the manager of Hardy's Shoestore. His store was approximately eight blocks from the scene of the Tippit shooting. I took his testimony in Dallas on Apr. 2, 1964.

Brewer's store was on the north side of West Jefferson Street, a few doors east of the Texas Theatre.

On the afternoon of Nov. 22, 1963, Brewer was in his store listening to a radio report on the shooting of President Kennedy. He heard that a police officer had been shot in the Oak Cliff section of Dallas, the section in which his store was situated.

Mr. Belin. All right, would you describe what happened after you heard on the radio that an officer had been shot?

Mr. Brewer. Well, there was heard a siren coming down East Jefferson headed toward West Jefferson. . . . I looked up and saw the man enter the lobby [which Brewer described as a recessed area, with windows on each side, extending about 15 feet between the sidewalk and the front door of his store].

Mr. Belin. All right, you saw a man going into what you referred to as this lobby area?

Mr. Brewer. Yes; and he stood there with his back to the street.

Mr. Belin. When did he go in now? What did you hear at the time that he stepped into this lobby area?

Mr. Brewer. I heard the police cars coming up Jefferson, and he stepped in, and the police made a U-turn and went back down East Jefferson.

Mr. Belin. Where did they make the U-turn?

Mr. Brewer. At Zangs [Blvd., just east of Brewer's store].

Mr. Belin. Do you remember the sirens going away?

Mr. Brewer. Yes; the sirens were going away. I presume back to where the officer had been shot, because it was back down that way. And when they turned and left, Oswald looked over his shoulder and turned around and walked up West Jefferson towards the theatre.

Mr. Belin. Let me hold you a minute. You used the word Oswald. Did you know who the man was at the time you saw him?

Mr. Brewer. No.

Mr. Belin. So at the time, you didn't know what his name was?

Mr. Brewer. No.

Mr. Belin. Will you describe the man you saw?

Mr. Brewer. He was a little man, about 5'9", and weighed about 150 pounds is all.

Mr. Belin. How tall are you, by the way?

Mr. Brewer. Six three.

Mr. Belin. So you say he was about 5'9"?

Mr. Brewer. About 5'9".

Mr. Belin. And about 150?

Mr. Brewer. And had brown hair. He had a brown sports shirt on. His shirt tail was out.

Mr. Belin. Any jacket?

Mr. Brewer. No.

Mr. Belin. What color of trousers, do you remember?

Mr. Brewer. I don't remember.

Mr. Belin. Light or dark?

Mr. Brewer. I don't remember that either.

Mr. Belin. Any other clothing that you noticed?

Mr. Brewer. He had a T-shirt underneath his shirt.

Mr. Belin. Was his shirt buttoned up all the way?

Mr. Brewer. A couple of buttons were unbuttoned at the time.

Mr. Belin. Light complexioned or dark?

Mr. Brewer. Light complexioned.

Brewer then testified that the police car sirens became fainter indicating the police were going the other way.

Mr. Belin. Then what did you see this man do?

Mr. Brewer. He turned and walked out of the lobby and went up West Jefferson toward the theatre, and I walked out the front and watched him, and he went into the theatre.

Mr. Belin. What theatre is that?

Mr. Brewer. Texas Theatre.

Mr. Belin. Why did you happen to watch this particular man?

Mr. Brewer. He just looked funny to me. Well, in the first place, I had seen him some place before. I think he had been in my store before. And when you wait on somebody, you recognize them, and he just seemed funny. His hair was sort of messed up and looked like he had been running, and he looked scared, and he looked funny.

Mr. Belin. Did you notice any of his actions when he was standing in your lobby there?

Mr. Brewer. No; he just stood there and stared.

Mr. Belin. He stared?

Mr. Brewer. Yes.

Mr. Belin. Was he looking at the merchandise?

Mr. Brewer. Not anything in particular. He was just standing there staring.

Mr. Belin. Well, would you state then what happened? You said that you saw him walk into the Texas Theatre?

Mr. Brewer. He walked into the Texas Theatre and I walked up to the theatre, to the box office and asked Mrs. Postal if she sold a ticket to a man who was wearing a brown shirt, and she said no, she hadn't. She was listening to the radio herself. And I said that a man walked in there, and I was going to go inside and ask the usher if he had seen him. So I walked in and Butch Burroughs—

Mr. Belin. Who was Burroughs?

Mr. Brewer. He was behind the counter. He operated the concession and takes tickets. He was behind the concession stand and I asked him if he had seen a man in a brown shirt of that description, matching that description, and he said he had been working behind the counter and hadn't seen anybody.

And I asked him if he would come with me and show me where the exits were and we would check the exits. And he asked me why.

I told him that I thought the guy looked suspicious.

Brewer and the usher checked the exits to determine whether the man might have left after entering the theatre.

Mr. Belin. What did you and Butch do?

Mr. Brewer. We walked down to the front of the theatre to the stage. First we checked the front exit, and it hadn't been opened. We went to the back and it hadn't been opened.

Mr. Belin. How could you tell that it hadn't been opened?

Mr. Brewer. Well, you open it from the inside, and you raise a bar, and a rod sticks into a hole at the bottom and then you open it. When you close it, it doesn't fall back in. You have to raise the rod again to close it from the inside.

Mr. Belin. In other words, you have to close it from the inside?

Mr. Brewer. You can close it from the outside, but it won't lock.

Mr. Belin. It was locked when you got there?

Mr. Brewer. Yes.

Mr. Belin. So you knew that no one had left?

Mr. Brewer. Yes.

Mr. Belin. Then what did you do?

Mr. Brewer. We went back up front and went in the balcony and looked around but we couldn't see anything.

Mr. Belin. Now you first looked on the bottom floor and you did not see him?

Mr. Brewer. Yes.

Mr. Belin. How many patrons were in the theatre at that time?

Mr. Brewer. I couldn't really tell. There weren't many, but it was dark and we couldn't see how many people were in there. There were 15 or 20, I would say, at the most, upstairs and downstairs.

Mr. Belin. Together, 15 or 20?

Mr. Brewer. Yes.

Mr. Belin. Then you went upstairs. Did you see him upstairs?

Mr. Brewer. No, I couldn't see anything upstairs.

Mr. Belin. Did you hear any noises there?

Mr. Brewer. When we first went down to the exit by the stage, we heard a seat pop up, but couldn't see anybody. And we never did see him.

But we went back and upstairs and checked, and we came down and went back to the box office and told Julia that we hadn't seen him.

Mr. Belin. Julia Postal is the cashier?

Mr. Brewer. Yes; and she called the police, and we went—Butch went to the front exit, and I went down by the stage to the back exit and stood there until the police came.

Mr. Belin. Then what happened?

Mr. Brewer. Well, just before they came, they turned the house lights on, and I looked out from the curtains and saw the man.

Mr. Belin. Where was he when you saw him?

Mr. Brewer. He was in the center section about six or seven rows, from the back, toward the back.

Mr. Belin. Toward the back? Are you sure? Mr. Brewer, do you know exactly which row he was in from the back?

Mr. Brewer. No; I don't know which row.

Mr. Belin. Then what did you see?

Mr. Brewer. He stood up and walked to the aisle to his right and then he turned around and walked back and sat down and at this time there was no place I could see.

Mr. Belin. Did he sit down in the same seat he had been in to begin with?

Mr. Brewer. I don't remember if it was the same seat or not.

Mr. Belin. Then what happened?

Mr. Brewer. I heard a noise outside, and I opened the door, and the alley, I guess it was filled with police cars, and policemen were on the fire exits and stacked around the alley, and they grabbed me, a couple of them, and held and searched me and asked me what I was doing there, and I told them that there was a guy in the theatre that I was suspicious of, and he asked me if he was still there.

And I said, yes, I just seen him. And he asked me if I would point him out.

And I and two or three other officers walked out on the stage and I pointed him out, and there were officers coming in from the front of the show, I guess, coming toward that way, and officers going from the back.

Mr. Belin. Then what did you see?

Mr. Brewer. Well, I saw this policeman approach Oswald, and Oswald stood up and I heard some hollering, I don't know exactly what he said, and this man hit Patrolman McDonald.

Mr. Belin. You say this man hit Patrolman McDonald?

Mr. Brewer. Yes.

Mr. Belin. Did you say this man was the same man?

Mr. Brewer. The same man that had stood in my lobby that I followed to the show.

Mr. Belin. Who hit who first?

Mr. Brewer. Oswald hit McDonald first, and he knocked him to the seat.

Mr. Belin. Who knocked who?

Mr. Brewer. He knocked McDonald down. McDonald fell against one of the seats. And then real quick he was back up.

Mr. Belin. When you say he was—

Mr. Brewer. McDonald was back up. He just knocked him down for a second and he was back up. And I jumped off the stage and was walking toward that, and I saw this gun come up and—in Oswald's hand, a gun up in the air.

Mr. Belin. Did you see from where the gun came?

Mr. Brewer. No.

Mr. Belin. You saw the gun up in the air?

Mr. Brewer. And somebody hollered, "He's got a gun."

And there were a couple of officers fighting him and taking the gun away from him, and they took the gun from him, and he was fighting, still fighting, and I heard some of the police holler, I don't know who it was, "Kill the President, will you." And I saw fists flying and they were hitting him.

Mr. Belin. Was he fighting back at that time?

Mr. Brewer. Yes; he was fighting back.

Mr. Belin. Then what happened?

Mr. Brewer. Well, just in a short time they put the handcuffs on him and they took him out.

Mr. Belin. Did you see police officers hit him after they got the handcuffs on him?

Mr. Brewer. No; I didn't see them.

Mr. Belin. Did you see any police officer hit Oswald after Oswald stopped fighting?

Mr. Brewer. No.

Mr. Belin. Did you hear Oswald say anything?

Mr. Brewer. As they were taking him out, he stopped and turned around and hollered, "I am not resisting arrest," about twice. "I am not resisting arrest." And they took him on outside.

5

"I PROTEST THIS POLICE BRUTALITY"

Mr. Walker. I got back in my car and started cruising the area again. I went up and down the alleys and streets. And there was one incident that really didn't have anything to do with it. I guess I was cruising up the alley with the newspaperman in the car, and I saw a man in long white sleeves, white shirt, walking across the parking lot there of the church, and I couldn't see below his legs, and there was a picket fence there, and when he got about 30 feet from me, I stopped the car, and he was walking toward me, and I had my gun in my lap at the time, and I said, "What is your name?" And he just looked at me. And at that time I didn't know whether he had a rifle or what he had, and he just looked at me, and he bent over, and I stuck my gun in the window and he raised up and had a small dog and he said, "What did you say?" And of course that newspaperman said, "My God, I thought he was going to shoot us."

I said, "I thought he was reaching down for a rifle."

Of course, he reached down and picked up a little dog.

The witness was Dallas Police Officer C. T. Walker, who sped to the scene of the murder of Officer J. D. Tippit after first having gone to the scene of the assassination. On the Dallas police radio, Officer Walker heard about a suspect in the Tippit killing seen running in front of the nearby library. With other police officers, Walker ordered out every person in the downstairs portion of the library building.

And everyone came out, and I saw the person that had run in there, and he said that he had ran there to tell the other people about the shooting. And let's see, that he worked there, he told me he worked there and everything. I soon determined he wasn't the one.

Walker continued cruising the area:

. . . when I heard the call come over the radio that the suspect was supposed to be at the theatre on Jefferson.

Mr. Belin. Was this the Texas Theatre?

Mr. Walker. Texas Theatre; yes.

Mr. Belin. Then what did you do?

Mr. Walker. I went in the alley up to the back door. When I arrived there, there was several officers there. There was a plainclothesman up on the ladder back there. I don't know what he was doing up there, but he was up on the ladder that goes up that door that is in the back. And there were several officers around the back of the theatre, and myself, and McDonald, and Officer Hutson went in the back door. And this man told us, or this boy told us, that there was someone, said the person that he had seen was inside the theatre, and that he had changed seats several times, and he thought he was out there in the middle now.

Mr. Belin. Did he say that he had seen him? Did he tell you what he had seen him do, or not?

Mr. Walker. He said he seen him duck into the store where he worked, kind of looked back, and looked like he was running, and just run into the theatre.

Mr. Belin. Did he say why he seemed to duck in the store at all?

Mr. Walker. No; he didn't. He said he looked like he was scared.

Mr. Belin. Then do you remember this man's name that you talked to?

Mr. Walker. No; it was just for a second, and I went on past him.

Mr. Belin. All right, this was at the back of the theatre?

Mr. Walker. Yes.

Mr. Belin. Did anyone have a gun drawn when this man came?

Mr. Walker. I had my gun out. I had my gun out when I walked in the back of the theatre.

Mr. Belin. Did you have your gun as you continued walking through the back of the theatre?

Mr. Walker. I walked—McDonald and I walked across the stage, and he walked across the farthest away. It would be the south aisle. And I jumped off there where the north aisle runs east and west, and we started up. Hutson went down the steps in front of both of us, and he was slightly in front of me.

Mr. Belin. You are speaking about Officer T. A. Hutson and Officer M. N. McDonald and yourself?

Mr. Walker. Yes, sir.

Mr. Belin. The three of you came in from the back?

Mr. Walker. Yes; and there were probably a couple more, but I just don't remember.

Officer Walker went up the left center aisle of the theatre while Officer McDonald walked up the right center aisle . . .

And he started down that way, and I was walking toward him slightly behind him in the same row of seats that Oswald was sitting.

Mr. Belin. So you approached Oswald from Oswald's left, and McDonald approached Oswald from Oswald's right?

Mr. Walker. That's right.

Mr. Belin. Was Oswald sitting closer to McDonald, or you?

Mr. Walker. Closer to McDonald. He was sitting in the third seat from McDonald's aisle.

Mr. Belin. All right, then, what happened?

Mr. Walker. McDonald approached him, and he said, I don't know exactly, I assumed he said, "Stand up!" And Oswald stood up.

Mr. Belin. Did you hear Oswald say anything?

Mr. Walker. No.

Mr. Belin. Was Oswald facing you as he stood up?

Mr. Walker. No; he faced McDonald.

Mr. Belin. All right.

Mr. Walker. He put his hand up, not exactly as you would raise your hands to be searched, but more or less showing off his muscles, what I call it, kind of hunching his shoulders at the same time, and McDonald put his hand down to Oswald's pocket, it looked like to me, and McDonald's head was tilted slightly to the right, looking down in the right hand.

Mr. Belin. Looking in whose?

Mr. Walker. McDonald's right hand as he was searching, and he felt of his pocket, and Oswald then hit him, it appeared, with his left hand first, and then with his right hand. They was scuffling there, and Officer Hutson and I ran toward the back of Oswald and Hutson threw his arm around his neck, and I grabbed his left arm, and we threw him back over the seat.

At this time I didn't see any gun that was involved. I don't know whether we pulled Oswald away from McDonald for a split second or what, but he was thrown back against the seat, and then the next thing I saw, Oswald's hand was down on the gun in his belt there, and McDonald had came forward again and was holding his, Oswald's, hand.

Mr. Belin. When you saw Oswald's hand by his belt, which hand did you see by his belt?

Mr. Walker. I saw his right hand. I had his left hand, you see.

Mr. Belin. When you saw Oswald's hand by his belt, which hand did you see then?

Mr. Walker. He had a hold of the handle of it.

Mr. Belin. Handle of what?

Mr. Walker. The revolver.

Mr. Belin. Was there a revolver there?

Mr. Walker. Yes; there was.

Mr. Belin. All right.

Mr. Walker. And it stayed there for a second or two. He didn't get it out. McDonald had come forward and was holding his hand.

Ray Hawkins was behind me to my left at that time, and whether or not he came at the same time we did or not, but he was there, and there was a detective.

Oswald had ahold of my shirt and he practically pulled off my nameplate by gripping it with his hand, and I was bent over, and I was in an awkward position, and I could see several hands on the gun.

The gun finally got out of his belt, and it was about waist high and pointed out at about a 45° angle.

I turned around and I was holding Oswald trying to get his arm up behind him in a hammerlock, and I heard it click. I turned around and the gun was still pointing at approximately a 45° angle. Be pointed slightly toward the screen, what I call.

Now Hawkins was in the general direction of the gun.

Mr. Belin. When you heard a click, what kind of click was it?

Mr. Walker. A real light click, real light.

Mr. Belin. Was it a click of the seat?

Mr. Walker. Well, I assume it was a click of a revolver on the shell, and that is when the gun was doing the most moving around. It was moving around in the general area, and they were still fighting. And someone said, "Let go of the gun," and Oswald said, "I can't."

And a detective, I don't recall who it was, there were so many people around by that time, the area was bursting with policemen, and it appeared to me that he reached over and pulled the gun away from everybody, pulled it away from everyone, best I can recall.

Mr. Belin. Okay, what happened then?

Mr. Walker. Ray Hawkins was on my left. He said, "Bring his arm around," and said, "I have the handcuffs."

He said, "Bring his arm around so I can get the cuffs on him."

I finally got his left arm around and I snapped the cuffs on it, and Hawkins went over the seat there and picked up, someone pulled his right arm around there, and Hawkins snapped the handcuffs on him, and turned him around and faced him, Oswald, north.

And Detective Bentley got on his left arm and I took his right arm, and we went out the aisle that I, which would be the left aisle, that I had came in, with Oswald, and walked him out the front.

He was hollering, "I protest this police brutality."

Joe Ball took the testimony of Patrolman McDonald. He testified that he heard about the shooting of Officer J. D. Tippit on the Dallas police radio and went in his squad car to the vicinity of the shooting, and "started cruising the alleys in my squad car."

Mr. Ball. And did you get a call over your radio to go to a certain place?

Mr. McDonald. Well, there was a report from the dispatcher that a suspect was seen running into the public library at Marsalis and Jefferson.

Mr. Ball. You went down there?

Mr. McDonald. Yes, sir. I went directly to Denver Street, which is an alley at that point. It is still designated as Denver Street. I parked the squad car, took my shotgun, and went to the west basement entrance to the public library, and ordered the people in the basement, in the library outside. They came out with their hands up.

The boy immediately said that he had just run into the library to tell the people that the President had been shot. He was a much younger person than what was broadcast on description on the radio.

Mr. Ball. You had heard a broadcast?

Mr. McDonald. Yes.

Mr. Ball. Of a description, of someone to look for?

Mr. McDonald. Yes, sir.

Mr. Ball. What did you hear?

Mr. McDonald. White male, approximately 27 years old, 5 foot 10, weight about 145 pounds, wearing light clothing.

Mr. Ball. When did you hear that? About what time?

Mr. McDonald. It came out on the radio as I was coming to Oak Cliff. There was another general description given on the way to the Texas School Book Depository at Elm and Houston Streets. But it was a vague description.

Mr. Ball. The first description that you heard of a man to look for was on the way downtown to the Texas School Book Depository?

Mr. McDonald. Yes, sir.

Mr. Ball. What was that description?

Mr. McDonald. White male, approximately 27, 29 years old, and he had a white shirt on, weighed about 160 pounds.

Mr. Ball. And that was about 12:40 you got that?

Mr. McDonald. Yes, sir.

Mr. Ball. Now, this later description you got was what point in your travel to Oak Cliff?

Mr. McDonald. That was approximately 1:20 or 1:17.

Mr. Ball. That was after you had heard that Tippit—that the officer had been shot?

Mr. McDonald. Yes, sir.

Mr. Ball. And what was that description?

Mr. McDonald. Well, it was 5 foot 10, white male, 27 years old, wearing a white shirt.

Mr. Ball. Now, as you were cruising the alleys, you had gone into the library basement, and gone to cruising the alleys, did you hear something else over the radio that drew your attention to another part—

Mr. McDonald. Just to report to the public library.

Mr. Ball. After that. Did you receive a report?

Mr. McDonald. After I was satisfied that this teenager that had run into the library didn't fit the description, I went back to my squad car, put my shotgun back in the rack. Just as I got into the squad car, it was reported that a suspect was seen running into the Texas Theatre, 231 West Jefferson.

So I reported to that location Code 3. This is approximately seven blocks from the library, seven blocks west.

Mr. Ball. You went down to the Texas Theatre?

Mr. McDonald. Yes, sir.

Mr. Ball. And that is what address?

Mr. McDonald. 231 West Jefferson.

Mr. Ball. What did you do?

Mr. McDonald. Well, when I got to the front of the theatre there was several police cars already at the scene, and I surmised that officers were already inside the theatre.

So I decided to go to the rear, in the alley, and seal off the rear. I parked my squad car. I noticed there were three or four other officers standing outside with shotguns guarding the rear exits. There were three other officers at the rear door. I joined them. We walked into the rear exit door over the alley.

Mr. Ball. What were their names?

Mr. McDonald. Officer Hawkins, T. A. Hutson, and C. T. Walker. And as we got inside the door, we were met by a man that was in civilian clothes, a suit, and he told us that the man that acted suspiciously as he ran into the theatre was sitting downstairs in the orchestra seats, and not in the balcony. He was sitting at the rear of the theatre alone.

Officer Walker and I went to the exit curtains that is to the left of the movie screen. I looked into the audience. I saw the person that the shoe salesman had pointed out to us.

Mr. Ball. Were the lights on or off?

Mr. McDonald. The lights were up, and the movie was playing at this time.

Mr. Ball. And could you see to the rear of the theatre?

Mr. McDonald. Yes, sir.

Mr. Ball. You could see the man. Did the civilian point out to you the man in one of the rear seats?

Mr. McDonald. He didn't point out personally. He was pointing out the suspect to another officer with him on the right of the stage, just right of the movie screen.

Mr. Ball. What did you do then?

Mr. McDonald. Well, after seeing him, I noticed the other people in the theatre—there was approximately 10 or 15 other people seated throughout the theatre. There were two men sitting in the center, about 10 rows from the front.

I walked up the left center aisle into the row behind these two men, and Officer C. T. Walker was behind me. When I got to these two men, I told them to get on their feet. They got up. I searched them for a weapon.

I looked over my shoulder at the suspect that had been pointed out to me. He remained seated without moving, just looking at me.

Mr. Ball. Why did you frisk these two men in the center of the theatre?

Mr. McDonald. I wanted to make sure that I didn't pass anything or miss anybody. I wanted to make sure I didn't overlook anybody or anything.

Mr. Ball. And you still kept your eye on the suspect?

Mr. McDonald. Yes, sir. He was to my back. I was looking over my shoulder at him.

Mr. Ball. Was he sitting nearest the right or the left aisle as you came in?

Mr. McDonald. The right center aisle. He was in the second seat.

Mr. Ball. What did you do then?

Mr. McDonald. After I was satisfied that these two men were not armed or had a weapon on them, I walked out of this row, up to the right center aisle toward the suspect. And as I walked up there, just at a normal gait, I didn't look directly at him, but I kept my eye on him and any other persons. And to my left was another man and I believe a woman was with him. But he was further back than the suspect.

And just as I got to the row where the suspect was sitting, I stopped abruptly, and turned in and told him to get on his feet. He rose immediately, bringing up both hands. He got this hand about shoulder high, his left hand shoulder high, and he got his right hand about breast high. He said, "Well, it is all over now."

As he said this, I put my left hand on his waist and then his hand went to the waist. And this hand struck me between the eyes on the bridge of the nose.

Mr. Ball. Did he cock his fist?

Mr. McDonald. Yes, sir; knocking my cap off.

Mr. Ball. Which fist did he hit you with?

Mr. McDonald. His left fist.

Mr. Ball. What happened then?

Mr. McDonald. Well, whenever he knocked my hat off, any normal reaction was for me to go at him with this hand.

Mr. Ball. Right hand?

Mr. McDonald. Yes. I went at him with this hand, and I believe I struck him on the face, but I don't know where. And with my hand, that was on his hand over the pistol.

Mr. Ball. Did you feel the pistol?

Mr. McDonald. Yes, sir.

Mr. Ball. Which hand was—was his right hand or his left hand on the pistol?

Mr. McDonald. His right hand was on the pistol.

Mr. Ball. And which of your hands?

Mr. McDonald. My left hand, at this point.

Mr. Ball. And had he withdrawn the pistol—

Mr. McDonald. He was drawing it as I put my hand.

Mr. Ball. From his waist?

Mr. McDonald. Yes, sir.

Mr. Ball. What happened then?

Mr. McDonald. Well, whenever I hit him, we both fell into the seats. While we were struggling around there, with this hand on the gun—

Mr. Ball. Your left hand?

Mr. McDonald. Yes, sir. Somehow I managed to get this hand in the action also.

Mr. Ball. Your right hand?

Mr. McDonald. Yes, sir. Now, as we fell into the seats, I called out, "I have got him," and Officer T. A. Hutson, he came to the row behind us and grabbed Oswald around the neck. And then Officer C. T. Walker came into the row that we were in and grabbed his left arm. And Officer Ray Hawkins came to the row in front of us and grabbed him from the front.

By the time all three of these officers had got there, I had gotten my right hand on the butt of the pistol and jerked it free.

Mr. Ball. Had you felt any movement of the hammer?

Mr. McDonald. Yes, sir. When this hand—we went down into the seats.

Mr. Ball. When your left hand went into the seats, what happened?

Mr. McDonald. It felt like something had grazed across my hand. I felt movement there. And that was the only movement I felt. And I heard a snap. I didn't know what it was at the time.

Mr. Ball. Was the pistol out of his waist at that time?

Mr. McDonald. Yes, sir.

Mr. Ball. Do you know any way it was pointed?

Mr. McDonald. Well, I believe the muzzle was toward me, because the sensation came across this way. To make a movement like that, it would have to be the cylinder or the hammer.

Mr. Ball. Across your left palm?

Mr. McDonald. Yes, sir. And my hand was directly over the pistol in this manner. More or less the butt. But not on the butt.

Mr. Ball. What happened when you jerked the pistol free?

Mr. McDonald. When I jerked it free, I was down in the seats with him, with my head, some reason or other, I don't know why, and when I brought the pistol out, it grazed me across the cheek here, and I put it all the way out to the aisle, holding it by the butt. I gave the pistol to Detective Bob Carroll at that point.

Mr. Ball. Grazed your left cheek?

Mr. McDonald. Yes, sir.

Mr. Ball. Scratched—noticeable scratch?

Mr. McDonald. Yes, sir; about a 4-inch scratch just above the eye to just above the lip.

Mr. Ball. Then what happened after that?

Mr. McDonald. Well, the officers that had come to my aid started handcuffing him and taking him out of the theatre.

Mr. Ball. What did he say—anything?

Mr. McDonald. Well, he was cursing a little bit and hollering police brutality, for one thing.

Mr. Ball. What words did he use?

Mr. McDonald. I couldn't recall the exact words. It was just mixed-up words, people hollering and screaming when they get arrested.

Mr. Ball. What did he say about police brutality?

Mr. McDonald. One thing, "Don't hit me any more." I remember that.

Mr. Ball. Did somebody hit him?

Mr. McDonald. Yes, sir; I guess they did.

Mr. Ball. Who hit him, do you know?

Mr. McDonald. No, sir; I don't, other than myself.

Mr. Ball. You know you hit him?

Mr. McDonald. Yes, sir.

Mr. Ball. Now, did you go with them outside?

Mr. McDonald No, sir.

Mr. Ball. What did you do?

Mr. McDonald. I was looking for my hat and flashlight.

Mr. Ball. Did you go downtown with them?

Mr. McDonald. No, sir.

Mr. Ball. Later you went downtown?

Mr. McDonald. Yes, sir.

Mr. Ball. And did you put a mark on the revolver?

Mr. McDonald. Yes, sir; I did.

Mr. Ball. And did you look at the ammunition in the revolver, the six rounds in the cylinder?

Mr. McDonald. Yes, sir.

Mr. Ball. Did you notice anything unusual about any one of them?

Mr. McDonald. I noticed on the primer of one of the shells it had an indentation on it, but not one that had been fired or anything—not that strong of an indentation.

Mr. Ball. We have here Exhibit 143 for identification. Do you know whether or not this is the revolver that you took from the man that you arrested?

Mr. McDonald. Yes, sir; this is it. I found the mark here.

Mr. Ball. You found your mark?

Mr. McDonald. Yes, sir.

Senator Cooper. What mark is it?

Mr. McDonald. I marked the initial "M."

Mr. Ball. Where?

Mr. McDonald. Right here, on this steel plate.

Mr. Ball. Of the butt?

Mr. McDonald. Yes, sir.

Members of the jury, remember the number of the exhibit on the revolver—Exhibit 143. We are going to come back to that later.

After Joe Ball completed his interrogation of the witness, Senator Cooper asked some additional questions.

Senator Cooper. Who was it that pointed out to you the suspect when you entered the theatre?

Mr. McDonald. I learned his name later.

Senator Cooper. Did some person there point out to you, though, this man sitting in the row whom you later arrested?

Mr. McDonald. Yes, sir. He was a shoestore salesman. His name was Brewer. He was the one that met us at the rear exit door and said that he saw this person run into the Texas Theatre.

Senator Cooper. Did you hear him say that?

Mr. McDonald. Yes, sir.

Senator Cooper. And have you seen him since?

Mr. McDonald. No, sir.

Senator Cooper. But somebody has identified him to you?

Mr. McDonald. Yes, sir. . . .

Senator Cooper. Then when you told the man you arrested to stand up did he immediately pull his pistol out?

Mr. McDonald. No, sir; he stood up and started raising his hands, "Well, it is all over now." But in my opinion, it was an act of giving up or surrendering. It was just natural that my hand went to his waist for a weapon, which was my intent anyway, whether he raised his hands or not. I didn't command him to raise his hands or anything. It was just a reaction of his.

Dallas Police Officer Thomas A. Hutson heard about the shooting of Officer Tippit and went on his motorcycle to the scene. From there, he got in a squad car with two other Dallas police officers and cruised the area.

. . . and as we approached the 100 block of East Jefferson, the radio dispatcher said that a suspect had just entered the Texas Theatre.

The officers drove to the Texas Theatre. I asked Officer Hutson to describe what happened next.

Mr. Hutson. We pulled up to this location and I was the first out of the car to hit the ground. As I walked up to the fire exit doors, Officer Hawkins and Baggett were getting out of the car, and the door to the theatre opened, and this unknown white male was exiting.

I drew my pistol and put it on him and told him to put up his hands and not to make a move, and he was real nervous and scared and said: "I am not the one. I just came back to open the door. I work up the street at the shoestore, and Julia sent me back to open the door so you could get in."

I walked up and searched him briefly and I could see by the description and his clothes that he wasn't the person we were looking for.

Then I entered the theatre from this door, and Officer Hawkins with me, and Officer Baggett stayed behind to cover the fire exit door.

We walked down the bottom floor of the theatre, and I was joined there by Officer Walker by me, and as we walked up the north aisle from the center section, I observed Officer McDonald walking up the south aisle from the center section, and we observed two suspects sitting near the front in the center section.

Mr. Belin. You were on the right center or the left center?

Mr. Hutson. I was on the left center.

Officer Hutson watched Officers McDonald and Walker search two men in the front of the theatre.

Mr. Belin. Then what happened after you saw these two people towards the front of the center section? Were they searched?

Mr. Hutson. Yes, sir.

Mr. Belin. Then what?

Mr. Hutson. Then I proceeded up the aisle toward the back of the theatre, and McDonald was walking toward the back of the theatre in the right center section aisle.

As he approached this person sitting in the same row of seats, he approached this person. I approached from the row behind.

Mr. Belin. You approached from the second row from the back?

Mr. Hutson. Yes, sir.

Mr. Belin. All right, then what did you see happen?

Mr. Hutson. I saw this person stand up, and McDonald and him became engaged in a struggle.

Mr. Belin. Did you see who hit whom first? . . .

Mr. Hutson. No, I didn't. The lights were down. The lights were on in the theatre, but it was dark. Visibility was poor.

Mr. Belin. Then what did you see happen?

Mr. Hutson. I saw McDonald down in the seat beside this person, and this person was in a half standing crouching position pushing down on the left side of McDonald's face, and McDonald was trying to push him off.

Mr. Belin. This person was right-handed?

You have used a motion here that he was pushing on the left side of McDonald's face?

Mr. Hutson. Right. And McDonald was trying to hold him off with his hand . . . I reached over from the back of the seat with my right arm and put it around this person's throat and pulled him back up on the back of the seat that he was originally sitting in.

At this time Officer C. T. Walker came up in the same row of seats that the struggle was taking place in and grabbed this person's left hand and held it. McDonald was at this time simultaneously trying to hold this person's right hand. Somehow this person moved his right hand to his waist, and I saw a revolver come out, and McDonald was holding on to it with his right hand, and this gun was waving up toward the back of the seat like this . . .

Mr. Belin. All right, what happened then?

Mr. Hutson. The gun was taken from the suspect's hand by Officer McDonald and somebody else. I couldn't say exactly. They were all in on the struggle, and Officer Hawkins, in other words, he simultaneously, we decided to handcuff him.

We had restrained him after the pistol was taken, but he was still resisting arrest, and we stood him up and I let go of his neck at this time and took hold of his right arm and attempted to bring it back behind him, and Officer Hawkins and Walker and myself attempted to handcuff him.

At this time Sgt. Jerry Hill came up and assisted as we were handcuffing.

Then Captain Westbrook came in and gave the order to get him out of here as fast as you can and don't let anybody see him, and he was rushed out of the theatre.

I was in the row of seats behind. I saw Officer Walker and Sgt. Jerry Hill had ahold of him, and that is the last I ever saw him.

Mr. Belin. Did you ever see him down at the police station thereafter?

Mr. Hutson. No, sir; I never did see him again.

Mr. Belin. How do you know this was Oswald?

Mr. Hutson. After we finished up in the theatre, I went downtown and went into the office where they were writing up the report, and to tell them the part I took in the arrest of him, to get the information, and at this time they had his name, Lee Harvey Oswald, but all we knew is, he was probably the suspect that shot the officer.

Mr. Belin. In the theatre did you know that he had any connection with the assassination?

Mr. Hutson. No, sir.

Mr. Belin. When did the police stop hitting him?

Mr. Hutson. I never did ever see them hit him.

Mr. Belin. You never saw any police hit him?

Mr. Hutson. No, sir; I didn't.

Mr. Belin. Is there anything else that you can think of about this incident that you haven't related here?

Mr. Hutson. I can't think of anything else right now.

No police officer or patron in the theatre heard anyone say, as Brewer had testified, "Kill the President, will you." Oswald was apprehended in connection with the Tippit murder (although there was a similarity between the police radio's physical descriptions of the assassin of President Kennedy and the murderer of Officer Tippit). Perhaps someone said, "Kill a police officer, will you" and Brewer took this to be "Kill the President, will you" when he learned that Oswald was accused of the assassination of President Kennedy. But regardless of the uncorroborated testimony of what Brewer thought he *heard* a policeman say, there was no doubt about what Brewer *did*—follow a suspicious person into the Texas Theatre and have the cashier call the police. The man that Brewer followed was Lee Harvey Oswald.

Thus you have the answer to the question why Oswald was arrested. Officers of the Dallas Police did not head for the Texas Theatre until after Johnny Calvin Brewer had trailed Lee Harvey Oswald into the theatre and asked the cashier to call the police. In the meantime, a number of police officers had converged on a branch library in the area because of a tip over the police radio that a suspicious-looking person had been seen running into the library.

The police broadcast directing the officers to the theatre as an outgrowth of the acts of Johnny Calvin Brewer was obviously a major factor in the arrest of Oswald. When the police officers found that the suspect was carrying a concealed weapon—which in itself is a crime in Dallas, as in most American cities—and when the police officer found that Oswald pulled out his revolver as he was approached by Officer McDonald, there could be little doubt that he should be arrested and questioned with regard to the Tippit murder, which had taken place in the immediate vicinity.

None of the police officers involved in Oswald's arrest was seriously injured.

Unfortunately, on that same afternoon, Nov. 22, another Dallas police officer who was listening to police broadcasts after the assassination lost his life because he stopped to question a man walking in a residential area, whose description fitted that in the first reports of the assassin of President Kennedy.

J. D. Tippit had been with the Dallas Police Department for more than 11 years. He was assigned to daylight duty in District 78, the Oak Cliff section of Dallas, and drove a police car with the Number 10 prominently displayed on each side. Tippit was alone, for normally only one man was assigned to a patrol car in residential areas in Dallas during daylight shifts.

About 12:44 PM on Nov. 22, 14 minutes after the assassination, the police radio dispatcher ordered all downtown patrol cars to report to the corner of Elm and Houston Streets, Code 3, which was the police code call for an emergency. One minute later, the dispatcher ordered car 10—the one driven by Officer Tippit—to "move into central Oak Cliff area." Tippit followed these orders, reporting at 12:54 PM that he was in the central Oak Cliff area at

Lancaster and Eighth. The police dispatcher then ordered Tippit to be ". . . at large for any emergency that comes in."

Meanwhile, there was a witness who saw the assassin with his rifle in the southeast corner of the sixth floor of the Texas School Book Depository Building. You jurors will soon hear the testimony of this key witness, Howard L. Brennan. Within a few minutes of the assassination, Brennan contacted a police officer and described the man he saw with the rifle in the window. At 12:45 PM and again at 12:48 and 12:55 the suspect in the assassination was described over police radio channel 1 as a "white male, approximately 30, slender build, height 5 foot 10″, weight 165 pounds." This description was given on police radio channel 2 at 12:45 PM.

At approximately 1:15 PM, Officer J. D. Tippit, who had undoubtedly heard the descriptions broadcast over the police radio, was slowly cruising east on 10th Street. He passed the intersection of 10th and Patton, about eight blocks from the point at which he had reported at 12:54 PM. About 100 feet past the intersection, Tippit stopped a man walking east along the south side of Patton Street and whose general description was similar to the one broadcast over the police radio: A white male, slender build, relatively young (around 24 years old) whose height was 5 feet 9″ and whose weight was 150 pounds. What happened after Tippit stopped the man you will soon hear directly from the witnesses who were at the scene on that sunny afternoon of Nov. 22, 1963.

Before turning to the heart of the testimony of these next witnesses, with the facts now available, you jurors might be interested in learning how the assassination sensationalists have treated the question of why Oswald was arrested. We can use a typical exhibit the film coproduced by deAntonio and Lane, the one that used the paraffin test as the opening salvo in the brief for the defense. A key portion of the film concerns itself with the question, "Why was Oswald arrested?"

After asking the question, the film turns to the Dallas District Attorney, Henry Wade. You see a film clip of Mr. Wade speaking after the assassination:

As he was walking toward the theatre a block or so from his house, he ran into a—police officer. Tippit motioned to him to er—said something to him, three witnesses saw him go up and say something to the police officer. As the police officer got out of the car he shot him three times. A civilian there broadcast on the police radio and later picked up the gun and followed him into the Texas Theatre.

As usual, the Dallas District Attorney was in error. Brewer was not at the scene of the murder.

Then the camera turns to the coproducer, Mark Lane, who states:

If Oswald was followed from the murder scene to the place of his arrest, the theatre, that would constitute evidence of his involvement, but the District Attorney was entirely in error. The Commission concedes that no one followed anyone *from the scene of the Tippit slaying* to the theatre. [Emphasis added.]

So far as it goes, Mr. Lane's statement is accurate. Henry Wade was in error, for no one *followed* Oswald *from the scene of the Tippit murder* to the Texas Theatre.

But as you jurors have just been told, an alert citizen, Johnny Calvin Brewer, noticed the suspicious actions of a man when police sirens were coming toward his store. Brewer then followed the man *from his shoe store to the Texas Theatre* and asked the cashier to notify the police.

Johnny Calvin Brewer is never mentioned in the Lane-deAntonio commercial film, in Mark Lane's book or in most of the other books seeking to sensationalize the assassination.

With the facts you now have, you might ask the next obvious question: With the truth so clear, why did Lane and deAntonio pose the question, "Why was Oswald arrested?"

The answer is simple. The conclusions of the Warren Commission are so firmly supported by the record that the only road left open to Lane and deAntonio is outright distortion. You have already seen this approach in connection with the paraffin test, where they falsely stated that the only reason the Warren Commission threw out the paraffin test is because there is "but one possible interpretation—that the paraffin test results were consistent with innocence." And now you see it in the ultimate fraudulent charge: that there was no evidence to explain how or why Oswald was arrested.

Having taken the position that Oswald was somehow "framed" as the assassin of President Kennedy, the assassination sensationalists are forced to assert that Oswald was also innocent of the murder of Dallas Police Officer J. D. Tippit and that the reason for arresting Oswald had nothing to do with either killing.

Of course, you now know the truth—the arrest of Oswald arose from his suspicious actions following the murder of Officer Tippit and the observations of these actions by Johnny Calvin Brewer.

Members of the jury, we can go back to Professor Trevor-Roper's assertion in the introduction to Lane's book:

The plain fact is that there is no evidence at all to explain how or why the Dallas police instantly pounced on Oswald, and until some adequate explanation is given, no one can be blamed for entertaining the most likely hypothesis, viz.: that the Dallas police had undisclosed reasons for arresting Oswald even before they had avowable evidence pointing towards him. Once that hypothesis is admitted, almost all the evidence accepted by the Commission can be reinterpreted in a different way.

The fact is that there is ample evidence to show why Oswald was arrested. The basic hypothesis of most of the assassination sensationalists, as illustrated by the film, is succinctly stated by Professor Trevor-Roper: "That the Dallas police had undisclosed reasons for arresting Oswald even before they had avowable evidence pointing towards him." Having destroyed the basic hypothesis of most of the Warren Commission critics, we have destroyed the entire foundation upon which they have built their misrepresentation.

With the arrest of Oswald as a frame of reference, let us now go to the testimony of the witnesses at the scene of the murder of J. D. Tippit.

6

"I SEEN HIM THROW THE SHELLS"

I could hardly believe what the man was telling me. He had seen the murder of Dallas Police Officer J. D. Tippit. He went to the police car after the gunman ran away and notified police headquarters on the police radio that a Dallas police officer had been shot. He turned over to Dallas police officers two empty cartridge shells that he had seen the gunman throw away in the bushes. Yet the Dallas Police Department never took the man to police headquarters to identify the prime suspect in a police lineup.

Moreover, the witness's name was absent from any written reports of interviews with witnesses conducted by either the Dallas Police Department or the FBI.

Joe Ball and I came across the witness, Domingo Benavides, in the course of our on-the-scene investigation in Dallas and our interrogations of other witnesses. I took his testimony in Dallas on Apr. 2, 1964. Here is how the interrogation began.

Mr. Belin. You want to raise your hand and stand up and be sworn.

Do you solemnly swear to tell the truth, the whole truth, and nothing but the truth, so help you God?

Mr. Benavides. I do.

Mr. Belin. Will you state your name for our reporter, please?

Mr. Benavides. Domingo Benavides.

Mr. Belin. How old are you, sir?

Mr. Benavides. I am 27, April the 9th. I am now 26.

Mr. Belin. Single or married?

Mr. Benavides. Married.

Mr. Belin. Family?

Mr. Benavides. Two children and one expected sometime this month.

Mr. Belin. Where are you from originally?

Mr. Benavides. From Dallas.

Mr. Belin. You were born in Dallas?

Mr. Benavides. Yes, sir.

Mr. Belin. Go to school in Dallas?

Mr. Benavides. Yes, sir.

Mr. Belin. How far did you go through school?

Mr. Benavides. Tenth grade.

Mr. Belin. Then what did you do when you got out of school?

Mr. Benavides. I just went to work.

At the time of the assassination, he was working as a mechanic at Dootch Motors in Dallas.

Mr. Belin. Taking you back to Nov. 22, 1963, anything unusual happen that day?

Mr. Benavides. On the 22d?

Mr. Belin. 22d of November 1963?

Mr. Benavides. This would be embarrassing. Was that the day of the assassination of the President?

Mr. Belin. Yes.

Mr. Benavides. I was thinking it was the 24th. Well, nothing except it seemed like a pretty nice day.

Mr. Belin. Do you remember what day of the week it was?

Mr. Benavides. I don't remember.

Mr. Belin. Do you remember the day that the President was assassinated?

Mr. Benavides. No.

Mr. Belin. Do you remember that he was assassinated in Dallas?

Mr. Benavides. Oh, yes; I remember this.

Mr. Belin. That day you had lunch, were you at work that day?

Mr. Benavides. Yes, sir.

Mr. Belin. You had lunch?

Mr. Benavides. I had lunch. And then this man had stalled this car in the middle of the street and asked me if I would fix it. Something was wrong with the carburetor, or pump that had broken in it, and I went around to the parts house to get the parts for it.

Benavides testified that he was driving a 1958 Chevrolet pickup truck and was heading west on 10th Street and had almost reached the corner of Denver and 10th when he saw a police car stopped along the curb.

Mr. Belin. Where was the police car?

Mr. Benavides. It was sitting about 4 or 5 feet from the curb and down about 2 houses from the corner of Patton Street.

Mr. Belin. All right. Was it between Patton and Denver?

Mr. Benavides. Yes, sir.

Mr. Belin. On what side of East 10th, north or south?

Mr. Benavides. On the south side.

Mr. Belin. What direction was it headed?

Mr. Benavides. It was headed east.

Mr. Belin. What did you see then?

Mr. Benavides. I then pulled on up and I seen this officer standing by the door. The door was open to the car, and I was pretty close to him, and I seen Oswald, or the man that shot him, standing on the other side of the car.

Mr. Belin. All right. Did you see the officer as he was getting out of the car?

Mr. Benavides. No; I seen as he was, well, he had his hand on the door and kind of in a hurry to get out, it seemed like.

Mr. Belin. Had he already gotten out of the car?

Mr. Benavides. He had already gotten around.

Mr. Belin. Where did you see the other man?

Mr. Benavides. The other man was standing to the right side of the car, riders side of the car, and was standing right in front of the windshield on the right front fender. And then I heard the shot. Actually I wasn't looking for anything like that, so I heard the shot, and I just turned into the curb. Looked around to miss a car, I think.

And then I pulled up to the curb, hitting the curb, and I ducked down, and then I heard two more shots.

Mr. Belin. How many shots did you hear all told?

Mr. Benavides. I heard three shots.

Mr. Belin. Where were you when your vehicle stopped?

Mr. Benavides. About 15 foot, just directly across the street and maybe a car length away from the police car.

Mr. Belin. Would you have been a car length to the east or a car length to the west of the police car?

Mr. Benavides. East of the front side of it.

Mr. Belin. So your vehicle wouldn't have quite gotten up to where the police car was?

Mr. Benavides. No; it didn't.

Mr. Belin. How fast were you going when you watched the policeman getting out of his car?

Mr. Benavides. Oh, I imagine not maybe 25 miles an hour. I never did pay much attention to it.

Mr. Belin. You say you stopped the car right away? Your vehicle, I mean?

Mr. Benavides. Yes, sir. I just didn't exactly stop because—I just pulled it into the curb.

Mr. Belin. Then you say you heard a shot and you then ducked?

Mr. Benavides. Yes. No; I heard the shot before I pulled in.

Mr. Belin. Oh, I see. You heard the shot and pulled in and then what?

Mr. Benavides. Then I ducked down.

Mr. Belin. Then what happened?

Mr. Benavides. Then I heard the other two shots and I looked up and the policeman was in, he seemed like he kind of stumbled and fell.

Mr. Belin. Did you see the policeman as he fell?

Mr. Benavides. Yes, sir.

Mr. Belin. What else did you see?

Mr. Benavides. Then I seen the man turn and walk back to the sidewalk and go on the sidewalk and he walked maybe 5 foot and then kind of stalled. He didn't exactly stop. And he threw one shell and must have took five or six more steps and threw the other shell up, and then he kind of stepped up to a pretty good trot going around the corner.

Mr. Belin. You saw the man going around the corner headed in what direction on what street?

Mr. Benavides. On Patton Street. He was going south.

Mr. Belin. Was he on the east or the west side of Patton as he was going?

Mr. Benavides. On the east side.

Mr. Belin. How far did you see him go down Patton?

Mr. Benavides. Just as far as the house would let the view go. In other words, as soon as he went past the house, I couldn't see him any more.

Mr. Belin. Now, the first time that you saw him, what was his position?

Mr. Benavides. He was standing like I say, on the center in front of the windshield, right directly on the right front fender of the car.

Mr. Belin. He was not moving when you saw him?

Mr. Benavides. No; he wasn't moving then.

Mr. Belin. All right, after you saw him turn around the corner, what did you do?

Mr. Benavides. After that, I set there for just a few minutes to kind of, I thought he went in back of the house or something. At the time, I thought maybe he might have lived in there and I didn't want to get out and rush right up. He might start shooting again.

That is when I got out of the truck and walked over to the policeman, and he was lying there and he had, looked like a big clot of blood coming out of his head, and his eyes were sunk back in his head, and just kind of made me feel real funny. I guess I was really scared.

Mr. Belin. Did the policeman say anything?

Mr. Benavides. The policeman, I believe was dead when he hit the ground, because he didn't put his hand out or nothing.

Mr. Belin. Where was the policeman as he fell, as you saw him?

Mr. Benavides. I saw him as he was falling. The door was about half way open, and he was right in front of the door, and just about in front of the fender. I would say he was between the door and the front headlight, about middleway when he started to fall.

Mr. Belin. Did you notice where the gun of the policeman was?

Mr. Benavides. The gun was in his hand and he was partially lying on his gun in his right hand. He was partially lying on his gun and on his hand, too.

Mr. Belin. Then what did you do?

Mr. Benavides. Then I don't know if I opened the car door back further than what it was or not, but anyway, I went in and pulled the radio and I mashed the button and told them that an officer had been shot, and I didn't get an answer, so I said it again, and this guy asked me whereabouts all of a sudden, and I said, on 10th Street. I couldn't remember where it was at the time.

So I looked up and I seen this number and I said 410 East 10th Street.

Mr. Belin. You saw a number on the house then?

Mr. Benavides. Yes.

Mr. Belin. All right.

Mr. Benavides. Then he started to—then I don't know what he said; but I put the radio back. I mean, the microphone back up, and this other guy was standing there, so I got up out of the car, and I don't know, I wasn't sure if he heard me, and the other guy sat down in the car.

Mr. Belin. There was another passerby that stopped?

Mr. Benavides. Yes, sir.

Mr. Belin. Who was he, do you know?

Mr. Benavides. I couldn't tell you. I don't know who he was.

Mr. Belin. Was he driving a car or walking?

Mr. Benavides. I don't know. He was just standing there whenever I looked up. He was standing at the door of the car, and I don't know what he said to the officer or the phone, but the officer told him to keep the line clear, or something, and stay off the phone, or something like that. That he already knew about it.

So then I turned and walked off. I never did assist him after that at all.

Mr. Belin. Then what did you do?

Mr. Benavides. At the time I walked out, I guess I was scared, so I started across the street—alley between the two houses to my mother's house, and I got in the yard and I said I'd better go back, or just caught myself until I got over there, I guess, so I went back around there.

Mr. Belin. When you went back, what did you do?

First of all, was there anything up to that time that you saw there or that you did that you haven't related here that you can think of right now?

Mr. Benavides. Well, I started—I seen him throw the shells and I started to stop and pick them up, and I thought I'd better not, so when I came back, after I had gotten back, I picked up the shells.

Mr. Belin. All right. Now, you said you saw the man with the gun throw the shells?

Mr. Benavides. Yes, sir.

Mr. Belin. Well, did you see the man empty his gun?

Mr. Benavides. That is what he was doing. He took one out and threw it.

Mr. Belin. Do you remember in which hand he was holding his gun?

Mr. Benavides. No; I sure don't.

Mr. Belin. Do you remember if he was trying to put anything in the gun also?

Mr. Benavides. Yes. As he turned the corner he was putting another shell in his gun.

Mr. Belin. You saw him?

Mr. Benavides. I mean, he was acting like. I didn't see him actually put a shell in his gun, but he acted like he was trying to reload it.

Maybe he was trying to take out another shell, but he could have been reloading it or something.

Mr. Belin. Let me ask you now, I would like to have you relate again the action of the man with the gun as you saw him now.

Mr. Benavides. As I saw him, I really—I mean really got a good view of the man after the bullets were fired, he had just turned. He was just turning away.

In other words, he was pointing toward the officer, and he had just turned away to his left, and then he started. There was a big tree, and it seemed like he started back going to the curb of the street and into the sidewalk, and then he turned and went down the sidewalk to, well, until he got in front of the corner house, and then he turned to the left there and went on down Patton Street.

Mr. Belin. When he got in front of the corner, when you say he turned to his left, did he cut across the yard of the house, or did he go clear to the corner and turn off?

Mr. Benavides. There is a big bush and he catty-cornered across the yard.

Mr. Belin. He kitty-cornered across the yard?

Mr. Benavides. Yes. In other words, he didn't go all the way on the sidewalk. He just cut across the yard.

Mr. Belin. Where was he when you saw him throwing shells? Had he already started across the yard?

Mr. Benavides. No, sir. He had just got back to the sidewalk when he threw the first one and when he threw the second one, he had already cut back into the yard. He just sort of cut across.

Mr. Belin. Now you saw him throw two shells?

Mr. Benavides. Yes, sir.

Mr. Belin. You saw where he threw the shells?

Mr. Benavides. Yes, sir.

Mr. Belin. Did you later go back in that area and try and find the shells?

Mr. Benavides. Yes. Well, right after that I went back and I knew exactly where they was at, and I went over and picked up one in my hand, not thinking and I dropped it, that maybe they want fingerprints off it, so I took out an empty pack of cigarettes I had and picked them up with a little stick and put them in this cigarette package; a chrome looking shell.

Mr. Belin. A chrome looking shell?

Mr. Benavides. Yes, sir.

Mr. Belin. About how long did it take you to locate the shells once you started looking for them?

Mr. Benavides. Just a minute. I mean not very long at all. Just walked directly to them.

Mr. Belin. You saw where he had thrown them?

Mr. Benavides. One of them went down inside of a bush, and the other one was by the bush.

Members of the jury, remember these cartridge case shells. They are of crucial evidentiary importance in this case.

Thus you have Mr. Benavides's story of the murder of Officer Tippit. The next series of questions I asked pertained to his description of the gunman.

Mr. Belin. Anything else you can think of about the man after you saw him? What was he wearing? What did he look like?

Mr. Benavides. Well, he was kind of, well, just about your size.

Mr. Belin. About my size? I am standing up.

Mr. Benavides. You are about 5'10"?

Mr. Belin. I am between 5'10" and 5'11". Closer to 5'11", I believe.

Mr. Benavides. I would say he was about your size, and he had a light-beige jacket, and was lightweight.

Mr. Belin. Did it have buttons or a zipper, or do you remember?

Mr. Benavides. It seemed like it was a zipper-type jacket.

Mr. Belin. What color was the trousers?

Mr. Benavides. They were dark.

Mr. Belin. Do you remember what kind of shirt he had on?

Mr. Benavides. It was dark in color, but I don't remember exactly what color.

Mr. Belin. Was he average weight, slender, or heavy?

Mr. Benavides. I would say he was average weight.

Mr. Belin. What color hair did he have?

Mr. Benavides. Oh, dark. I mean not dark.

Mr. Belin. Black hair?

Mr. Benavides. No. Not black or brown, just kind of a—

Mr. Belin. My color hair?

Mr. Benavides. Yes.

Mr. Belin. You say he is my size, my weight, and my color hair?

Mr. Benavides. He kind of looks like—well, his hair was a little bit curlier.

Mr. Belin. Anything else about him that looked like me?

Mr. Benavides. No, that is all.

I then turned to the two cartridge case shells that Benavides said he had found in the bushes.

Mr. Belin. When you put these two shells that you found in this cigarette package, what did you do with them?

Mr. Benavides. I gave them to an officer.

Mr. Belin. That came out to the scene shortly after?

Mr. Benavides. Yes, sir.

Mr. Belin. Do you remember the name of the officer?

Mr. Benavides. No, sir; I didn't even ask him. I just told him that this was the shells that he had fired, and I handed them to him. Seemed like he was a young guy, maybe 24.

Mr. Belin. How old would you say the man that you saw with the gun was?

Mr. Benavides. I figured he was around 25.

Mr. Belin. When the officers came out there, did you tell them what you had seen?

Mr. Benavides. No, sir.

Mr. Belin. What did you do?

Mr. Benavides. I left right after. I give the shells to the officer. I turned around and went back and we returned to work.

Mr. Belin. Then what happened? Did the officers ever get in touch with you?

Mr. Benavides. Later on that evening, about 4 o'clock, there was two officers came by and asked for me. Mr. Callaway asked me—I had told them that I had seen the officer, and the reporters were there and I was trying to hide from the reporters because they will just bother you all the time.

Then I found out that they thought this was the guy that killed the President. At the time I didn't know the President was dead or he had been shot. So I was just trying to hide from the reporters and everything, and these two officers came around and asked me if I'd seen him, and I told them yes, and told them what I had seen, and they asked me if I could identify him, and I said I don't think I could.

At this time I was sure, I wasn't sure that I could or not. I wasn't going to say I could identify and go down and couldn't have.

Mr. Belin. Did he ever take you to the police station and ask you if you could identify him?

Mr. Benavides. No; they didn't.

So even though Benavides had seen the murder and even though he turned over to Dallas police officers two empty cartridge cases that were crucial items of evidence and even though Benavides used a police radio to report the murder to Dallas police headquarters, the Dallas Police Department never took this witness to police headquarters to see if he could identify the suspect.

7

"ANYTHING ELSE
YOU CAN THINK OF?"

Most experienced trial lawyers, when they present a case, "prepare" their key witnesses. I do not mean by this that they try to get a witness to change his testimony or perjure himself. Rather, they review the major facts with the witness in great detail. If there are inconsistencies, the attorney will often point these out to the prospective witness and give him an opportunity to resolve them. In preparing a witness for direct examination, the attorney may ask a witness leading questions to help him—the kinds of questions that are used in cross-examination.

As you jurors can see from the examples of the testimony of the witnesses who have already appeared, the questions that Joe Ball and I asked were not leading ones in which we sought to have the witness arrive at any preconceived conclusion. Moreover, in interviewing these witnesses prior to their formal testimony, our pattern was merely to ask general questions and have the witness relate his story in his own words. If there were inconsistencies within the story of a single witness or if there were inconsistencies in the stories of different witnesses, we let these appear for the world to see. Thus, I concluded my interrogation of Domingo Benavides with the following exchange:

Mr. Belin. You and I never met before today, did we, except that one day when we were around to see Ted Callaway and he introduced you at Dootch Motors and we chatted for 3 or 4 minutes there?

Mr. Benavides. Yes; you and two other men.

Mr. Belin. Today when we met, you came up here and what is the fact as to whether I asked you before the court reporter was able to get here to just relate to me what happened, or did I start questioning you or try to tell you things as I saw them?

Mr. Benavides. No; you just asked me what happened and I described to you what happened.

Mr. Belin. Is there anything you said before the court reporter got here that is different in any way from what you said after the court reporter started taking your testimony?

Mr. Benavides. Maybe now only in the change of time, or I imagine I added a little bit since she was here.

Mr. Belin. Is there anything that would be at variance with what you told me before the court reporter got here?

Mr. Benavides. Well, I don't understand.

Mr. Belin. What I mean is, is there anything that you said before the court reporter got here that you haven't included after the court reporter got here?

Mr. Benavides. No.

Mr. Belin. Anything you have said in front of the court reporter that has been different insofar as being a fact which is opposite or different in anyway from what you told me before?

Mr. Benavides. Different in wording but—

Mr. Belin. But are the facts different?

Mr. Benavides. No; I don't believe the facts are different.

There is one other aspect relating to the manner of our interrogation of witnesses while we served with the Warren Commission.

Every experienced trial lawyer knows that when trying to prove a case you are careful not to ask too many questions. One question can open up "Pandora's box."

I remember a law professor recalling the attorney who asked too many questions in defending a man charged with assault. The defendant supposedly bit the ear off a citizen in the community, and the defendant's attorney was cross-examining the only independent witness for the prosecution. After a series of skillful maneuvers, the defense attorney got the witness to admit that he had never actually seen the defendant bite the other man's ear. Then the attorney asked one question too many:

"Well, if you did not see the man bite the ear, how do you know that the defendant was the one who actually bit the man's ear?"

The response was simple: "Because I saw him spit it out."

We never worried about such problems in our investigation. My standard procedure in interrogating witnesses was to give them every opportunity to add whatever facts they wanted. Domingo Benavides was a typical example. In the concluding portion of the testimony of Benavides, I asked him about the gunman's clothing. Between the scene of the murder and the Texas Theatre a jacket had been found, which we identified as Commission Exhibit 162. I asked Benavides to state whether that jacket bore any similarity to the jacket he saw the gunman wear. He replied, "I would say this looks just like it."[1]

I then asked: "Anything else you can think of?"

Mr. Benavides. Not offhand, except later on, I don't know if I seen it on television but I believe I seen it on television where they was arresting him, the policeman from the theatre. But it didn't seem like he had a jacket on there.

Mr. Belin. When he was being arrested you say he didn't have a jacket on? Now at the time you saw him, did he have a jacket on?

Mr. Benavides. He had a jacket on and it looked like that jacket there.

And then once again I asked, "Anything else?"

Benavides responded: "No, I guess that is all I can think of right now."

Then there was a pause of a minute or two and Benavides added:

[1]Marina Oswald later identified the jacket as Oswald's.

I think there was another car that was in front of me, a red Ford, I believe. I didn't know the man, but I guess he was about 25 or 30, and he pulled over. I didn't never see him get out of his car, but when he heard the scare, I guess he was about six cars from them, and he pulled over, and I don't know if he came back there or not.

Then for a third time, I asked: "Anything else?"

Mr. Benavides. That would be all. I think if anybody had seen anything really close up, that he must have fired just as they got past him, and they must have seen him standing there, because he was right directly in front of me. And whenever you see a squad car parked like that, you think something is wrong. At least that is what comes to my mind.

Mr. Belin. Anything else?

Mr. Benavides. That is all I can think of right now that I can remember.

Mr. Belin. Pardon?

Mr. Benavides. That is all I can think of right now that I can remember.

As Domingo Benavides left the room, I pondered his testimony. On the one hand, he did not want to go to police headquarters to see a lineup because "I wasn't going to say I could identify and couldn't have." Although he might be criticized for this, he did go to the patrol car immediately after the murder and informed police headquarters over the police radio that an officer had been shot. He also returned to the scene to pick up the cartridge cases and turned them over to the police.

Benavides also turned down a request from another citizen, Ted Callaway, at the scene of the Tippit murder. Benavides told about this in the concluding portion of his testimony. I noted that earlier in his testimony he had "used the name Oswald. How did you know this man was Oswald?"

Mr. Benavides. From the pictures I had seen. It looked like a guy, resembled the guy. That was the reason I figured it was Oswald.

Mr. Belin. Were they newspaper pictures or television pictures, or both, or neither?

Mr. Benavides. Well, television pictures and newspaper pictures. The thing lasted about a month, I believe, it seemed like.

Mr. Belin. Pardon.

Mr. Benavides. I showed—I believe they showed pictures of him every day for a long time there.

Mr. Belin. Did you talk to anyone at all there that witnessed what was going on?

Mr. Benavides. No; sure didn't. There was people that asked me what happened, came up in the crowd there and asked me what happened, and I said just the policeman got shot.

Mr. Belin. You talked to Ted Callaway, did you?

Mr. Benavides. No; afterward. You know, I told your—I told him, he asked me when we went, when Ted Callaway got around there, he opened the car door and picked up the phone and called in and told them there was an officer that had been killed. But the officer on the other side of the radio told him to hang up the phone to keep the lines clear, or something of that sort.

Then he jumped out and ran around and he asked me did I see what happened, and I said yes. And he said let's chase him, and I said no.

Mr. Belin. Why did you say "No"?

Mr. Benavides. Well, he was reaching down and getting the gun out of the policeman's hand, and I didn't think he should bother to go like that. So he then turned around and went to the cab that was sitting on the corner.

The man in the taxicab just around the corner from the Tippit shooting was W. C. Scoggins. He is one of the main witnesses in our investigation of these two murders and he will be the next witness.

To help you understand better the testimony of Benavides, Scoggins and the other witnesses who identified the gunman, here is a map showing the scene of the Tippit murder and the location of the witnesses at the time the shots were fired.

Commission Exhibit No. 1305
Location of eyewitnesses to the movements of Lee Harvey Oswald in the vicinity of the Tippit killing.

DENVER ST.

BENAVIDES

X TIPPIT

312 414

410

404

400

BARBARA DAVIS
VIRGINIA DAVIS

FENCE

GUINYARD
CALLAWAY

505

501

500

506

PATTON AVE.

SCOGGINS

MARKHAM

10th ST.

JEFFERSON BLVD.

JACKET

405

401

CRAWFORD ST.

TO TEXAS
THEATRE

OSWALD ROUTE

Known Movements

Assumed Movements

N

SCALE IN FEET

COMMISSION EXHIBIT No. 1305

8

"POOR DAMN COP"

I pulled up and parked at the corner of Patton and 10th and went back down to the club. At first, whenever I passed by, one of the guys hollered at me and asked me did I know the President had been shot, and I made the remark that I had not heard that one. I found a place to park and I came back, and he came back there in a couple of minutes and told me the facts about it. I thought it was some kind of a joke.

So I had to go plumb up to the corner of 10th before I could find a parking place, and I parked right there on the corner and went back and got me a coke and watched the deal, watched the television.

The witness, William C. Scoggins, was a 49-year-old taxicab driver working for the Dallas Transit Company in the Oak Cliff section of Dallas. He was born in Hill County, Texas, and started working after he finished the eighth grade. He had worked at a number of odd jobs and had lived in New York three years and then went to join a Civilian Conservation Corps camp in Connecticut. From there he returned to Texas and had a number of jobs—ranging from farm work to the contracting business. At the time of the assassination, he had been driving a cab for about 21 months.

He picked up a man at the Dallas airport, Love Field, "at approximately 12:35," took him to an address in the Oak Cliff section of Dallas and then went to "the Gentlemen's Club" which I believe is 125 Patton.

I got me a coke and watched television for a few minutes, I would say 10, 12, 15 minutes, there, and went out to eat my lunch.

Mr. Dulles. What were you seeing on television?

Mr. Scoggins. The deal about the President getting assassinated; and when I got back to my cab and got my lunch, and, well, I noticed a police car cruising east there on 10th Street.

Mr. Belin. Where was your cab parked with relationship to the intersection of Patton and 10th?

Mr. Scoggins. Well, it was headed north on Patton, facing 10th Street, on the right-hand side of the street, right close to where the stop sign had been.

Mr. Belin. Now, the right-hand side of the street would be the east or the west?

Mr. Scoggins. It would be the east side. I was headed north.

Scoggins said he had eaten "one or two bites of my sandwich and drank a couple of swallows out of my Coke . . . when I first seen the police car cruising east." He thought it was about 1:20 PM.

54

Mr. Belin. About how fast was it cruising?

Mr. Scoggins. Not more than 10 or 12 miles a hour, I would say.

Mr. Belin. It was going east on what street?

Mr. Scoggins. On Tenth.

Mr. Belin. All right. Did you see the police car go across right in front of yours?

Mr. Scoggins. Yes; he went right down the street. He come from the west, going east on East Tenth.

Mr. Belin. Then what did you see?

Mr. Scoggins. I noticed he stopped down there, and I wasn't paying too much attention to the man, you see, just used to see him every day, but then I kind of looked down the street, saw this, someone, that looked to me like he was going west, now, I couldn't exactly say whether he was going west or was in the process of turning around, but he was facing west when I saw him.

Scoggins testified that the man was wearing a "light-colored jacket" and had stopped along the sidewalk at about the point of the front wheel or bumper area of the police car.

Mr. Belin. All right. Then what did you see the man do?

Mr. Scoggins. I saw him turn facing the street, and then I didn't see him any more after that because he went behind some shrubbery.

Mr. Belin. Did you see the police officer do anything?

Mr. Scoggins. I saw him get out of the police car.

Mr. Belin. Did you see what side he went out of?

Mr. Scoggins. He got out of the driver's side, left-hand side.

Mr. Belin. Then what did you see happen?

Mr. Scoggins. Then he took about a step, I would say, or approximately one or two steps, and then I wasn't really—you know—I went back to my eating, and about that time I heard the shots.

Mr. Belin. How many shots did you hear?

Mr. Scoggins. Three or four, in the neighborhood. They was fast.

Mr. Belin. They were fast shots?

Mr. Scoggins. Yes; they were fast.

Mr. Belin. Then what did you do or say or hear?

Mr. Scoggins. Then I saw the man falling, grab his stomach and fall.

Mr. Belin. Which man did you see fall?

Mr. Scoggins. The policeman. I was excited when I heard them shots, and I started to get out—since we went back over there the other day and reenacted that scene, I must have seen him fall as I was getting out of my cab, because I got out of the cab, and in the process of getting out of the cab I seen this guy coming around, so I got out of sight. I started to cross the street, but I seen I didn't have enough time to cross the street before he got down there, so I got back behind the cab, and as he cut across that yard I heard him running into some bushes, and I looked up and seen him going south on Patton and then when I jumped back in my cab I called my dispatcher.

Mr. Belin. Why did you jump out of your cab first when you heard the shots?

Mr. Scoggins. Because anytime that there is anything going on that is one thing the cab driver wants to do is to get away from that cab, because the man is going to try—if he had ever seen the cab, he looked back over his left shoulder, and I don't think he even seen the cab—he would have probably jumped in the cab and had me take him somewhere or maybe shot me, too, you know, and I didn't want to be around the cab at anytime while he was in the neighborhood, you know, when there was anything like that going on, or anything, robbery, or anything.

Mr. Belin. I believe you said you saw the officer fall. Did you see where he fell?

Mr. Scoggins. Yes; he fell right by the side of the front, about, a little bit forward of the door, right about the door.

Scoggins called his dispatcher and told him about the shooting of the policeman. He identified a picture taken at the scene after the shooting which showed the officer's blood on the street, Commission Exhibit 527.

Mr. Belin. When you saw the officer fall, when was the next place that you saw the man, or did you see him at the same time you saw the officer fall, the other man?

Mr. Scoggins. No. I saw him coming kind of toward me around that cutoff through there, and he never did look at me. He looked back over his left shoulder like that, as he went by. It seemed like I could see his face, his features and everything plain, you see.

Mr. Belin. Was he walking or running or trotting?

Mr. Scoggins. Kind of loping, trotting.

Mr. Belin. Kind of loping or trotting?

Mr. Scoggins. Not in too big a hurry. It didn't seem like at first.

Mr. Belin. At first not too big a hurry?

Mr. Scoggins. Yes.

Mr. Belin. Did he change that at all?

Mr. Scoggins. Never did change his pace as long as I saw him. I don't know where he went after he passed the cab and got down a little piece, because then I was busy trying to get my dispatcher, and I never did look and never did get to see him.

Mr. Belin. Did he have anything in his hand?

Mr. Scoggins. He had a pistol in his left hand.

Mr. Belin. Did the pistol appear to be—did he appear to be doing anything with the pistol or not?

Mr. Scoggins. Yes. He had it, holding it, in his left hand in a manner that the barrel was up like this, and the stock was down here, curved back in here.

Mr. Belin. Did it look like the gun had been flipped open at all or not?

Mr. Scoggins. I wouldn't say.

Mr. Belin. You don't know?

Mr. Scoggins. No; I don't.

Mr. Dulles. You said he had it in his left hand?

Mr. Scoggins. Yes, sir.

Mr. Belin. Did you see where his right hand was?

Mr. Scoggins. He was kind of running, kind of like this, in this manner.

Mr. Belin. Did you hear the man say anything?

Mr. Scoggins. I heard him mutter something like, "poor damn cop," or "poor dumb cop." He said that over twice, and the last, I don't know whether the middle word was "damn" or "dumb," but anyway, he muttered that twice.

Mr. Belin. Did you hear him say any other word or phrase?

Mr. Scoggins. No.

I then showed Scoggins pictures taken when we first interviewed him in Dallas and asked him to reconstruct the events of Nov. 22 showing the location of his cab, the police car and the immediate area. He marked on several of these pictures the location of the gunman when he first saw him and when the gunman came back running toward the cab. I asked Scoggins if—when Scoggins saw the gunman—"were you standing or were you crouched?"

Mr. Scoggins. I was kind of crouched down behind the cab.

Mr. Belin. All right. How did you see him if you were crouched?

Mr. Scoggins. Well, whenever he run through those bushes I looked up again, you see.

Mr. Belin. You looked through your cab window?

Mr. Scoggins. I heard him—whenever I heard him hit those bushes—

Mr. Belin. Did you stand or just look through your cab window?

Mr. Scoggins. I just looked and saw he was going down there.

Mr. Belin. About how close was this man to you when you saw him, the closest when you saw him coming through the bushes, approximately.

Mr. Scoggins. Oh, I would say from here to that chair down there.

Mr. Belin. Pardon?

Mr. Scoggins. About that chair down there.

Mr. Belin. 12 feet?

Mr. Scoggins. Yes.

After calling his dispatcher, Scoggins drove his cab around the corner to where the police car was standing. An ambulance was there picking up the body of J. D. Tippit and he saw a man get on the police radio to report the crime:

. . . and they told him he was going to report it, so they told him to get off the air, that it had already been reported, and he picks up the officer's pistol that was laying on the ground, apparently fell out of his holster when he fell, and says, "Come on, let's go see if we can find him."

Mr. Belin. What did you see him do? This man came up and picked up the policeman's gun. He picked it up and said, "Let's go see if we can find him."

Mr. Scoggins. I thought the man was a kind of police, Secret Service or something. I didn't know, and I take him and we drove around over the neighborhood looking, and I still didn't know what kind—I still thought he was connected with the police department in some way.

Mr. Belin. What route did you take as you drove over the neighborhood?

Mr. Scoggins. I couldn't tell you.

Mr. Belin. You can't tell us the route you took over the neighborhood?

Mr. Scoggins. I was doing the driving and he was doing the directing.

Mr. Belin. He directed you where to go?

Mr. Scoggins. Actually, I couldn't say where he was going.

The man who did the directing was not a police officer—he was Ted Callaway, who will be the next witness to appear before you jurors.

Mr. Belin. After you went around to look for the man, did you find him at all?

Mr. Scoggins. No. We drove around and asked several people, but we did not see anybody that looked like him.

Mr. Belin. Then what did you do?

Mr. Scoggins. Well, by that time there was more policemen there than you can shake a stick at. They were all over that place, and we stopped the cab.

Mr. Belin. At about what time, do you know offhand?

Mr. Scoggins. About 1:30, I guess, approximately 1:30; between 1:20 and 1:35, I would say. We cruised around several blocks looking for him, and we—one of these police cars came by and this fellow who was with me stopped it, and we got back in the car and went back up to the scene, and he give them the pistol, and that time is when I found out he wasn't an officer.

Mr. Belin. Then what happened, or what did you do?

Mr. Scoggins. Well, they was questioning a lot of people and questioning everybody, and they was talking, and so I went back and got on my radio and contacted my supervisor, and they wanted me to come into the office and make a statement, and so I did, the cab company. One of the supervisors got a statement of it, and he asked me did the police, did I give them a statement, and I told him no because, and he said, "Well, why didn't you?" I said, "They didn't ask me. They talked with everybody else."

So the next day they took me down and put me through a lineup, showed me a lineup of four people, and I identified the one that I had seen the day before.

Mr. Belin. Now, let me ask you this question. First of all, do you remember, or can you describe the man you saw on Nov. 22 with the gun?

Mr. Scoggins. He was a medium-height fellow with, kind of a slender look, and approximately, I said 25, 26 years old, somewhere along there.

Mr. Belin. Do you remember the color of his hair?

Mr. Scoggins. Yes. It was light; let's see, was it light or not—medium brown, I would say.

Mr. Belin. Pardon?

Mr. Scoggins. Medium brown, I would say—now, wait a minute. Now, medium brown or dark.

Mr. Belin. Medium brown or dark hair?

Mr. Scoggins. Yes.

Mr. Belin. Was he a Negro or a white man?

Mr. Scoggins. White, light complected, not real brown.

Mr. Belin. Was he fat, average build or thin?

Mr. Scoggins. No, he was slender; not real slender, but you know—

Mr. Belin. Was he wearing glasses or not?

Mr. Scoggins. No.

Mr. Belin. Anything else you remember about him, the color of his shoes?

Mr. Scoggins. No, I can't say that.

Mr. Belin. Do you remember any jewelry he might have had on?

Mr. Scoggins. No.

Mr. Belin. You say you went down to the police station when, Mr. Scoggins, approximately?

Mr. Scoggins. You mean the time of day it was?

Mr. Belin. Was it the same day of the shooting or the next day?

Mr. Scoggins. No, it was the next day.

Mr. Belin. Morning, afternoon, or evening, if you remember?

Mr. Scoggins. Well, the best I can remember, they called me down from the cab stand, the police came down to the office and picked me up. Well, the other guy—I was close to the downtown area, and it didn't take me long to get there, and I waited quite a while before the other man, he was quite out a ways, and it was before dinner.

Mr. Belin. It was before dinner?

Mr. Scoggins. Yes, whenever they called me in.

Mr. Belin. Would it have been on the afternoon of Nov. 23, to the best of your recollection?

Mr. Scoggins. When they took me down there it was along about dinner time.

Representative Ford was following the testimony closely. He caught a point of possible confusion in the witness's use of the word "dinner."

Representative Ford. What do you mean by dinner time? In various parts of the country dinner and supper get confused a little bit. Was it the noon meal or the evening meal?

Mr. Scoggins. Yes.

Representative Ford. Yes what? It was the noon meal?

Mr. Scoggins. Yes.

Mr. Belin. They took you down about the time of the noon meal, is that correct; they took you to the police station?

Mr. Scoggins. I would think that would be about the time.

Mr. Belin. Sometime after you got there after the noon meal you saw the lineup, is that correct?

Mr. Scoggins. Yes.

Mr. Belin. How many people were in the lineup, if you can remember?

Mr. Scoggins. Four.

Mr. Belin. Did you identify anyone in the lineup?

Mr. Scoggins. I identified the one we are talking about, Oswald. I identified him.

Mr. Belin. You didn't know his name as Oswald at that time, did you, or did you not?

Mr. Scoggins. Yes, the next day I did. But, of course I didn't know what his name was the day that I picked him out.

Mr. Belin. You saw a man in the lineup?

Mr. Scoggins. Yes.

Mr. Belin. Did anyone tell you any particular man was Oswald in the lineup?

Mr. Scoggins. No.

Mr. Belin. Well, describe what happened in the police station with regard to the lineup, what they did to you, what they said to you, and what you said to them, and so on.

Mr. Scoggins. Well, they had the four men up there in the lineup, and before they brought them in they told us what they wanted us to do, to look them over and be sure we was, in our estimation, we was right on the man, and which one it was, the one that we saw, the one that I saw.

Mr. Belin. Did they tell you one of the men was the man you saw or not, or did they tell you "See if you can"—just what did they say? Did they say "Here is a lineup, see if you can identify anyone," or did they say, "One of the men in the lineup"—

Mr. Scoggins. Yes, I believe those are the words they used. I am not—

Mr. Belin. Did all of these men look different to you? Were most of them fat, or were most of them thin, or some fat, some thin, some tall, some short?

Mr. Scoggins. There were two of them—the one that I identified as the one I saw over at Oak Cliff, and there was one I saw similar to him, and the other two was a little bit shorter.

Mr. Dulles. Had you been looking at television or seeing television prior to your appearance here at the lineup?

Mr. Scoggins. No.

Representative Ford. Had you been working this Saturday morning with your cab?

Mr. Scoggins. Yes, sir.

Representative Ford. And were working when they asked you to come down to the cab stand to go over to the police station?

Mr. Scoggins. Yes, sir.

Mr. Belin. Had you seen any pictures of Lee Harvey Oswald in the newspapers prior to the time you went to the police station lineup?

Mr. Scoggins. I think I saw one in the morning paper.

Scoggins said the man that he identified in the lineup was No. 3.

Mr. Belin. Did you have the man turn around, or could you—

Mr. Scoggins. Yes, they turned him around.

Mr. Belin. Did they turn just one man around or all of them?

Mr. Scoggins. No; they had them all.

Mr. Belin. Do you remember if the number 3 man in the lineup was wearing the same clothes that the man you saw at the Tippit shooting wore?

Mr. Scoggins. He had on a different shirt, and he didn't have a jacket on. He had on kind of a polo shirt.

Mr. Belin. Before you went to view the lineup, did any of the police officers show you a picture of this man?

Mr. Scoggins. No.

The man in the police lineup that Scoggins identified as the gunman was Lee Harvey Oswald.

9

"HEY MAN, WHAT THE HELL IS GOING ON?"

As I observed Joe Ball interrogate Ted Callaway, I was impressed with the fact that here was a citizen who did not merely stand by when a murder occurred. In the face of an unwilling Domingo Benavides and a not-so-willing William Scoggins, Callaway went after the gunman.

Joe Ball began with some background questions. The witness was 40 years old, had been born and raised in Dallas, graduated high school and attended Southern Methodist University for two years. He had been in the Marine Corps, receiving an honorable discharge in 1954 and had been selling automobiles since 1956.

At the time of the assassination, Callaway was the used car manager for the Harris Bros. Auto Sales Company at 501 East Jefferson—on the northeast corner of 10th and Jefferson—one block south of the scene of the Tippit murder.

Callaway said that at about 1:15 PM on the afternoon of Nov. 22, he was standing on the front porch of his office.

Mr. Ball. What did you hear at that time?

Mr. Callaway. I heard what sounded to me like five pistol shots.

Mr. Ball. Five pistol shots?

Mr. Callaway. Five shots, yes, sir.

Mr. Ball. From the sound, could you tell the source of the sound?

Mr. Callaway. Yes, sir, I could tell it was back of the lot over toward 10th Street.

Mr. Ball. And what did you do?

Mr. Callaway. I ran out to the sidewalk on Patton.

Mr. Ball. And what did you see?

Mr. Callaway. Well, I could see—I was still—before I got to the sidewalk, I could see this taxicab parked down on Patton. I saw the cabdriver beside his cab, and saw a man cutting from one side of the street to the other. That would be the east side of Patton and over to the west side of Patton. And he was running. And he had a gun in his hand, his right hand.

Mr. Ball. And how was he holding the gun?

Mr. Callaway. We used to say in the Marine Corps in a raised pistol position.

Mr. Ball. That would be with the muzzle pointed upward, and with the arm bent at the elbow, is that right?

Mr. Callaway. Yes, sir; just like this.

Joe Ball had Callaway identify the location on pictures we had taken in Dallas when we interviewed Callaway at the site of the shooting.

Mr. Ball. Was he running or walking?

Mr. Callaway. He was running.

Mr. Ball. And where were you when you noticed he had the gun? Or where was he when you noticed he had the gun?

Mr. Callaway. When I first saw the gun, he had already crossed from here to here and was coming up this sidewalk.

Mr. Ball. Coming up the sidewalk on which side of Patton?

Mr. Callaway. West side of Patton.

Mr. Ball. And did he continue to come?

Mr. Callaway. Yes.

Mr. Ball. And did you say anything to him?

Mr. Callaway. Yes.

Mr. Ball. What did you say?

Mr. Callaway. I hollered "Hey, man, what the hell is going on?" When he was right along here.

Joe Ball then had Callaway mark on a picture where the gunman was when Callaway yelled, "What the hell is going on?"

Mr. Ball. What did he do when you hollered at him?

Mr. Callaway. He slowed his pace, almost halted for a minute. And he said something to me, which I could not understand. And then kind of shrugged his shoulders, and kept on going.

Callaway said that when he last saw the gunman, he was going west on Jefferson Street. Callaway then ran to the corner of 10th and Patton after telling a man near him, B. D. Searcy, to keep an eye on the gunman.

Mr. Ball. When you got there what did you see?

Mr. Callaway. I saw a squad car, and by that time there was four or five people that had gathered, a couple of cars had stopped. Then I saw—I went on up to the squad car and saw the police officer lying in the street. I saw he had been shot in the head. So the first thing I did, I ran over to the squad car. I didn't know whether anybody reported it or not. So I got on the police radio and called them, and told them a man had been shot, told them the location, I thought the officer was dead. They said we know about it, stay off the air, so I went back.

By this time an ambulance was coming. The officer was laying on his left side, his pistol was underneath him. I kind of rolled him over and took his gun out from under him. The people wonder whether he ever got his pistol out of his holster. He did.

Mr. Ball. The pistol was out of the holster?

Mr. Callaway. Yes, sir; out of the holster, and it was unsnapped. It was on his right side. He was laying with the gun under him.

Mr. Ball. What did you do?

Mr. Callaway. I picked the gun up and laid it on the hood of the squad car, and then someone put it in the front seat of the squad car. Then after I helped load Officer Tippit in the ambulance, I got the gun out of the car and told this cabdriver, I said, "You saw the guy, didn't you?" He said, yes.

I said, "If he is going up Jefferson, he can't be very far. Let's see if we can find him." So I went with Scoggins in the taxicab, went up to 10th, Crawford, from Crawford up to Jefferson, and down Jefferson to Beckley. And we turned on Beckley. If we had kept going up Jefferson, we probably—there is a good chance we would have seen him, because he was headed right towards the Texas Theatre. But then we circled around several blocks, and ended up coming back to where it happened.

Callaway testified that later that evening "around 6:30 or 7 o'clock" he went to the police station with Sam Guinyard, who worked for Callaway.

Mr. Ball. Now, before you went down there, had you seen any newspaper accounts of this incident?

Mr. Callaway. No, sir; I had been out there on the lot. I hadn't seen a newspaper, hadn't even heard a radio, really.

Mr. Ball. Had you seen any television?

Mr. Callaway. No, sir.

Mr. Ball. Had you seen a picture of a man?

Mr. Callaway. No.

Mr. Ball. The officer show you any pictures?

Mr. Callaway. No, sir.

Mr. Ball. You went into a police lineup, in a room where they had a lineup of men?

Mr. Callaway. Yes.

Mr. Ball. How many?

Mr. Callaway. Four.

Mr. Ball. And were they all the same size, or different sizes?

Mr. Callaway. They were about the same build, but the man that I identified was the shortest one of the bunch.

Mr. Ball. Were they anywhere near the same age?

Mr. Callaway. They were about the same age, yes, sir. They looked—you know.

Mr. Ball. And you say you identified a man. How did you do that?

Mr. Callaway. Well—

Mr. Ball. Tell us what happened.

Mr. Callaway. We first went into the room. There was Jim Leavelle, the detective, Sam Guinyard, and then this busdriver and myself. We waited down there for probably 20 or 30 minutes. And Jim told us, "When I show you these guys, be sure, take your time, see if you can make a positive identification."

Mr. Ball. Had you known him before?

Mr. Callaway. No. And he said, "We want to be sure, we want to try to wrap him up real tight on killing this officer. We think he is the same one that shot the President. But if we can wrap him up tight on killing this officer, we have got him." So they brought four men in.

I stepped to the back of the room, so I could kind of see him from the same distance which I had seen him before. And when he came out, I knew him.

Mr. Ball. You mean he looked like the same man?

Mr. Callaway. Yes.

Callaway said that when Joe Ball and I reconstructed the event with him in Dallas, we measured the distance from the gunman to Callaway at the time he saw the gunman. The closest point was about 56 feet.

Mr. Ball. Did he have the same clothes on in the lineup—did the man have the same clothes?

Mr. Callaway. He had the same trousers and shirt, but he didn't have his jacket on. He had ditched his jacket.

Mr. Ball. What kind—when you talked to the police officers before you saw this man, did you give them a description of the clothing he had on?

Mr. Callaway. Yes, sir.

Mr. Ball. What did you tell them you saw?

Mr. Callaway. I told them he had some dark trousers and a light tannish gray windbreaker jacket, and I told him that he was fair complexion, dark hair.

Mr. Ball. Tell them the size?

Mr. Callaway. Yes; I told them—I think I told them about 5'10".

Mr. Dulles. Did you see his front face at any time, or did you only have a side view of him?

Mr. Callaway. He looked right at me, sir. When I called to him, he looked right at me.

Mr. Dulles. You saw front face?

Mr. Callaway. Yes.

Mr. Ball. I have a jacket here—Commission's Exhibit No. 162. Does this look anything like the jacket that the man had on that you saw across the street with a gun?

Mr. Callaway. Yes; it sure does. Yes, that is the same type jacket. Actually, I thought it had a little more tan to it.

Mr. Ball. Same type?

Mr. Callaway. Yes.

And what about Mr. Searcy, whom Callaway asked to follow the gunman?

Mr. Ball. Did you ever ask Searcy if he followed him?

Mr. Callaway. He didn't follow him. He said something about "Follow him, hell. That man will kill you. He has a gun." So instead of following him, he went back over and got behind the office building.

10
"THAT WAS HIM RIGHT THERE"

Working with Ted Callaway on the afternoon of Nov. 22, 1963, was Sam Guinyard, 28, who was born in Ennis, Texas, and had lived in Dallas since 1957. His testimony was clear and concise:

Mr. Ball. Now, on the day of Nov. 22, 1963, that's the day the President was killed, what were you doing?

Mr. Guinyard. Working there.

Mr. Ball. And you heard about it, that he had been shot? Didn't you?

Mr. Guinyard. Yes; at the time I did.

Mr. Ball. What were you doing and where were you then when you heard that?

Mr. Guinyard. In Oak Cliff at 501 East Jefferson.

Mr. Ball. What were you doing?

Mr. Guinyard. Polishing and waxing a station wagon.

Mr. Ball. And did something else happen that day that you remember?

Mr. Guinyard. Yes, sir.

Mr. Ball. What?

Mr. Guinyard. Well, this was when Oswald shot the policeman.

Mr. Ball. Tell me what you heard—I just want to know what you were doing and what you heard?

Mr. Guinyard. Well, he was about—I guess—

Mr. Ball. Now, wait a minute, were you polishing cars when you heard something?

Mr. Guinyard. When I heard a shot.

Mr. Ball. You heard a noise?

Mr. Guinyard. Yes.

Mr. Ball. And it sounded like shots?

Mr. Guinyard. Yes.

Mr. Ball. How many?

Mr. Guinyard. I heard three.

Mr. Ball. Where did the sound come from?

Mr. Guinyard. Right behind me, north of me—behind me.

Mr. Ball. What street is north of you?

Mr. Guinyard. Tenth.

Mr. Ball. You were on what street—your car lot faces what street?

Mr. Guinyard. It faces Jefferson and 10th.

Mr. Ball. And 10th Street is north?

Mr. Guinyard. Yes; and I was in the back—I was about half way right in the back.

Mr. Ball. The cross street is Patton Street?

Mr. Guinyard. Yes.

Mr. Ball. What did you do when you heard the shots?

Mr. Guinyard. I raised up trying to see where they were coming from, where the sound was coming from.

Mr. Ball. Then what did you do?

Mr. Guinyard. I was looking—trying to see and after I heard the third shot, then Oswald came through on Patton running—came right through the yard in front of the big white house—there's a big two-story white house—there's two of them there and he come through the one right on the corner of Patton.

Mr. Ball. Could you see down to the corner of 10th and Patton to the house?

Mr. Guinyard. I seen him when he come between the two houses, come around in front of the last house to get on Patton Street to come out to Jefferson.

Mr. Ball. Where were you when you saw this?

Mr. Guinyard. I was there at the back, right at the alley back there about as far from Patton Street as—about twice as far from here as to that window.

Mr. Ball. Then you were about 10 feet from Patton Street?

Mr. Guinyard. Yes, sir.

Mr. Ball. So that you could look up Patton Street?

Mr. Guinyard. Yes.

Mr. Ball. North on Patton?

Mr. Guinyard. Yes.

Mr. Ball. And you saw a man, did you?

Mr. Guinyard. Yes.

Mr. Ball. What did you see him doing?

Mr. Guinyard. He came through there running and knocking empty shells out of his pistol and he had it up just like this with his hand.

Mr. Ball. With which hand?

Mr. Guinyard. With his right hand; just kicking them out.

Mr. Ball. He had it up?

Mr. Guinyard. Yes; he had it up just like this.

Mr. Ball. How was he kicking them out?

Mr. Guinyard. He was rolling them with his hand—with his thumb.

Mr. Ball. Rolling them with his thumb?

Mr. Guinyard. Checking them—he had the pistol up just like this [indicating].

Mr. Ball. Did he use his left hand any?

Mr. Guinyard. No; I never did see him use his left hand.

Mr. Ball. He didn't?

Mr. Guinyard. No, sir.

Guinyard said that he saw the gunman cut through a yard at the corner of 10th and Patton and then cut across Patton Street as he approached the corner of Patton and Jefferson.

Mr. Ball. Did you see Mr. Callaway there?

Mr. Guinyard. We was together; yes, sir.

Mr. Ball. You were together?

Mr. Guinyard. Yes, sir; he was at the front and I was at the back.

Mr. Ball. You and Callaway were standing at the alleyway?

Mr. Guinyard. Yes.

Guinyard's testimony differed from Callaway's in that Guinyard said that the gunman came as close to him as 10 feet.

Mr. Ball. How close was he to you when you saw him?

Mr. Guinyard. I guess he was about 10 feet from me—maybe.

Mr. Ball. About 10 feet?

Mr. Guinyard. Yes, sir.

Guinyard testified that he then went with Callaway to the police car, saw the dead policeman and helped put him in the ambulance. He was there when Domingo Benavides came back.

Mr. Ball. And then what did you do after that?

Mr. Guinyard. Well, we stood there a while and talked and I called him Donnie, he picked up all them empty hulls that come out of the gun.

Mr. Ball. Who did—Benavides?

Mr. Guinyard. Yes.

Mr. Ball. Did you pick them up—any of them?

Mr. Guinyard. He picked them up—I didn't pick them up—I was there with him.

Mr. Ball. You were there?

Mr. Guinyard. I was there with him.

Joe Ball then turned to Guinyard's identification of the gunman.

Mr. Ball. Later that day, did you go down to the police department?

Mr. Guinyard. Yes, sir; I went down that night.

Mr. Ball. That same night?

Mr. Guinyard. Yes.

Mr. Ball. Whom did you go down with?

Mr. Guinyard. Me and Ted.

Mr. Ball. You and who?

Mr. Guinyard. Ted—Ted Callaway.

Mr. Ball. And where did you go when you went to the police station?

Mr. Guinyard. I went to the identifying office.

Mr. Ball. You went into a place where there were police officers?

Mr. Guinyard. Yes, sir.

Mr. Ball. And how did you identify him—tell me what happened to you, what you saw?

Mr. Guinyard. Well, I just saw him.

Mr. Ball. Well, were you in a big room?

Mr. Guinyard. Yes—in a big room.

Mr. Ball. With police officers?

Mr. Guinyard. Yes, sir.

Mr. Ball. And what did you see?

Mr. Guinyard. I don't understand you.

Mr. Ball. Did you see some men up ahead of you?

Mr. Guinyard. Yes—four men.

Mr. Ball. Four men?

Mr. Guinyard. Yes—four men—handcuffed together.

Mr. Ball. Were they of different sizes?

Mr. Guinyard. Well, they was pretty close together—there wasn't much difference in size.

Mr. Ball. In height—they were about the same?

Mr. Guinyard. About the same.

Mr. Ball. Were they all about the same color?

Mr. Guinyard. No, sir; they wasn't all about the same color.

Mr. Ball. Did you say anything to any police officer there after you saw them?

Mr. Guinyard. I talked to one—with the detective—after he came out there.

Mr. Ball. What did you tell him—I mean in this room—as you saw these four men up there?

Mr. Guinyard. He just asked me reckon I could identify them and I said I sure could.

Mr. Ball. What did you tell him?

Mr. Guinyard. I just told him I sure could.

Mr. Ball. What did you say to him about it?

Mr. Guinyard. Well, I didn't say anything—I was just waiting on them to bring them in.

Mr. Ball. After they brought them in and after you looked at them, what did you tell the police officers?

Mr. Guinyard. I told them that was him right there—I pointed him out right there. That was him right there.

Mr. Ball. Do you remember where he was standing in the lineup—what number he was?

Mr. Guinyard. I don't know what his number was, but I can tell you where he was standing at.

Mr. Ball. Where was he standing?

Mr. Guinyard. He was standing—the second man from the east side, and that lineup was this way [indicating] and he was the second man from that there end.

Mr. Ball. And did you tell any police officer that you thought that was the man?

Mr. Guinyard. Yes, sir.

Mr. Ball. Whom did you tell; what police officer was it?

Mr. Guinyard. I don't know his name.

Mr. Ball. You don't know his name?

Mr. Guinyard. No, sir; I don't know his name but I know him now if I would see him.

Mr. Ball. Before you went in there, did the police officers show you any pictures?

Mr. Guinyard. No, sir.

Mr. Ball. Did the police officer say anything to you before you went in there?

Mr. Guinyard. No, sir.

Mr. Ball. Did he say that he thought they had the man that killed the police officer?

Mr. Guinyard. No, sir; he didn't tell me that.

Mr. Ball. Did you hear Ted Callaway say anything before you said you thought that was the man?

Mr. Guinyard. No, sir.

The man that both Ted Callaway and Sam Guinyard identified in the police lineup was Lee Harvey Oswald.

11

"SHE SAID HE WAS SHORT, A LITTLE ON THE HEAVY SIDE"

It was 9:10 AM on Mar. 26, 1964. The testimony of the most controversial witness to the murder of Officer Tippit was about to begin. Chief Justice Warren seemed almost like a scholarly minister as he looked and smiled toward the witness, Helen Markham.

As might be expected, she appeared nervous but I knew Joe Ball would handle the questioning informally to help put the witness at ease.

The Chairman.[1] The purpose of the session of the Commission is for the purpose of taking testimony on the assassination of President Kennedy, and it is our information that you have some evidence concerning it and we want to ask you some questions concerning it. You are willing to testify, are you?

Mrs. Markham. Do all I can.

The Chairman. All right. Will you stand up and be sworn, please? Do you solemnly swear the testimony you give before this Commission will be the truth, the whole truth and nothing but the truth, so help you God?

Mrs. Markham. I do.

The Chairman. You may be seated. Mr. Ball will ask you the questions.

Mr. Ball. Mrs. Markham, what is your address?

Mrs. Markham. 328 East Ninth.

Mr. Ball. In Dallas, Tex.?

Mrs. Markham. Dallas, Tex.

Mr. Ball. Where were you born, Mrs. Markham?

Mrs. Markham. Where was I born? Dallas.

Mr. Ball. The Commission would like to know something of your past life and experience, where you were born and your education so I will just ask you a few questions like that.

Take it easy, this is just—

Mrs. Markham. I am very shook up.

Mr. Ball. This is a very informal little conference here.

Mrs. Markham. Well, do you want me to tell you about my life?

Mr. Ball. Yes. Just tell us briefly where you were born and where you went to school and things of that kind.

Helen Markham was born in Dallas. Her father was a farmer and her mother died when she was 6. She had an eighth-grade education and married

[1]"The chairman" is Chief Justice Earl Warren, Chairman of the President's Commission on the Assassination of President Kennedy.

after she dropped out of school. Joe did not ask her how old she was. Mrs. Markham had five children and was divorced at the time she testified. She was a waitress who was working at the Eat Well Restaurant in Dallas on Nov. 22, 1963. Her working hours were 2:30 PM to 10:30 PM. She left her home "a little after one PM" to catch a bus at the corner of Patton and Jefferson, one block south of Patton and East 10th Street, where Officer Tippit was killed. Walking south on the west side of 10th Street toward Jefferson, Mrs. Markham stopped at the northwest corner of 10th and Patton "on account the traffic was coming."

Mr. Ball. Did you see any man walking at that time?

Mrs. Markham. Yes; I seen this man on the opposite side, across the street from me. He was almost across Patton Street.

Mr. Ball. Almost across Patton?

Mrs. Markham. Yes, sir.

Mr. Ball. Walking in what direction?

Mrs. Markham. I guess this would be south.

Mr. Ball. Along 10th, east? Was it along 10th?

Mrs. Markham. Yes, sir.

Mr. Ball. Walking away from you, wasn't he?

Mrs. Markham. He was walking up 10th, away from me.

Mr. Ball. To your left?

Mrs. Markham. Well, he was on the opposite side of the street to me like that.

Mr. Ball. Had he reached the curb yet?

Mrs. Markham. Almost ready to get up on the curb.

Mr. Ball. What did you notice then?

Mrs. Markham. Well, I noticed a police car coming.

Mr. Ball. Where was the police car when you first saw it?

Mrs. Markham. He was driving real slow, almost up to this man, well, say this man, and he kept, this man kept walking, you know, and the police car going real slow now, real slow, and they just kept coming into the curb, and finally they got way up there a little ways up, well, it stopped.

Mr. Ball. The police car stopped?

Mrs. Markham. Yes, sir.

Mr. Ball. What about the man? Was he still walking?

Mrs. Markham. The man stopped.

Mr. Ball. Then what did you see the man do?

Mrs. Markham. I saw the man come over to the car very slow, leaned and put his arms just like this, he leaned over in this window and looked in this window.

Mr. Ball. He put his arms on the window ledge?

Mrs. Markham. The window was down.

Mr. Ball. It was?

Mrs. Markham. Yes, sir.

Mr. Ball. Put his arms on the window ledge?

Mrs. Markham. On the ledge of the window.

Mr. Ball. And the policeman was sitting where?

Mrs. Markham. On the driver's side.

Mr. Ball. He was sitting behind the wheel?

Mrs. Markham. Yes, sir.

Mr. Ball. Was he alone in the car?

Mrs. Markham. Yes.

Mr. Ball. Then what happened?

Mrs. Markham. Well, I didn't think nothing about it; you know, the police are nice and friendly, and I thought friendly conversation. Well, I looked, and there were cars coming, so I had to wait. Well, in a few minutes this man made—

Mr. Ball. What did you see the policeman do?

Mrs. Markham. See the policeman? Well, this man, like I told you, put his arms up, leaned over, he—just a minute, and he drew back and he stepped back about two steps. Mr. Tippit—

Mr. Ball. The policeman?

Mrs. Markham. The policeman calmly opened the car door, very slowly, wasn't angry or nothing, he calmly crawled out of this car, and I still just thought a friendly conversation, maybe disturbance in the house, I did not know; well, just as the policeman got in—

Mr. Ball. Which way did he walk?

Mrs. Markham. Towards the front of the car. And just as he had gotten even with the wheel on the driver's side—

Mr. Ball. You mean the left front wheel?

Mrs. Markham. Yes; this man shot the policeman.

Mr. Ball. You heard the shots, did you?

Mrs. Markham. Yes, sir.

Mr. Ball. How many shots did you hear?

Mrs. Markham. Three.

Mr. Ball. What did you see the policeman do?

Mrs. Markham. He fell to the ground, and his cap went a little ways out on the street.

Mr. Ball. What did the man do?

Mrs. Markham. The man, he just walked calmly, fooling with his gun.

Mr. Ball. Toward what direction did he walk?

Mrs. Markham. Come back towards me, turned around, and went back.

Mr. Ball. Toward Patton?

Mrs. Markham. Yes, sir; towards Patton. He didn't run. It just didn't scare him to death. He didn't run. When he saw me he looked at me, stared at me. I put my hands over my face like this, closed my eyes. I gradually opened my fingers like this, and I opened my eyes, and when I did he started off in kind of a little trot.

Mr. Ball. Which way?

Mrs. Markham. Towards Jefferson, right across that way.

Mr. Dulles. Did he have the pistol in his hand at this time?

Mrs. Markham. He had the gun when I saw him.

Mr. Ball. Did you yell at him?

Mrs. Markham. When I pulled my fingers down where I could see, I got my hand down, he began to trot off, and then I ran to the policeman.

Mr. Ball. Before you put your hands over your eyes, before you put your hand over your eyes, did you see the man walk towards the corner?

Mrs. Markham. Yes.

Mr. Ball. What did he do?

Mrs. Markham. Well, he stared at me.

Mr. Ball. What did you do?

Mrs. Markham. I didn't do anything. I couldn't.

Mr. Ball. Didn't you say something?

Mrs. Markham. No, I couldn't.

Mr. Ball. Or yell or scream?

Mrs. Markham. I could not. I could not say nothing.

Mr. Ball. You looked at him?

Mrs. Markham. Yes, sir. He looked wild. I mean, well, he did to me.

Mr. Ball. And you say you saw him fooling with his gun?

Mrs. Markham. He had it in his hands.

Mr. Ball. Did you see what he was doing with it?

Mrs. Markham. He was just fooling with it. I didn't know what he was doing. I was afraid he was fixing to kill me.

Mrs. Markham said that she ran to the policeman after the gunman ran off. Joe Ball asked the witness:

In what hand did he have his gun, do you know, when he fired the shots?

Mrs. Markham. Sir, I believe it was his right. I am not positive because I was scared.

Mr. Ball. When he came down the street towards you, in what hand did he have his gun?

Mrs. Markham. He had it in both of them.

Mr. Ball. He had it in both of them?

Mrs. Markham. Yes, sir.

Mr. Ball. When he went towards Jefferson you say he went at sort of a trot?

Mrs. Markham. Yes, sir.

Mr. Ball. Did he cross Patton?

Mrs. Markham. Yes, sir.

Later that afternoon, Mrs. Markham was taken to the Dallas Police Department and Joe Ball asked the witness what had happened there. Joe was about to be shocked because he was to use a word in a context that the witness did not understand. The word was "recognize" and the witness thought this meant personally knowing someone.

This is the way it happened:

Mr. Ball. Later that day they had a showup you went to?

Mrs. Markham. A lineup?

Mr. Ball. A lineup.

Mrs. Markham. Yes.

Mr. Ball. How many men were in the lineup?

Mrs. Markham. I believe there were, now I am not positive, I believe there were three besides this man.

Mr. Ball. That would be four people altogether?

Mrs. Markham. I believe that is correct.

Mr. Ball. Were they of anywhere near similar build or size or coloring?

Mrs. Markham. Yes, they were all about the same height.

Mr. Ball. Who were you in the lineup room with?

Mrs. Markham. Who was I [with] in the room where they had this man?

Mr. Ball. Yes.

Mrs. Markham. Policemen.

Mr. Ball. More than one?

Mrs. Markham. The room was full.

Mr. Ball. It was. In this lineup room, the room was full of policemen. Weren't there just one or two men with you?

Mrs. Markham. One or two with me, but I don't know who they were.

Mr. Ball. But there were other officers?

Mrs. Markham. There were all policemen sitting in the back of me, and aside of me.

Mr. Ball. In this room?

Mrs. Markham. Yes, sir. They were doing something.

Mr. Ball. Before you went into this room were you shown a picture of anyone?

Mrs. Markham. I was not.

Mr. Ball. Did you see any television?

Mrs. Markham. I did not.

Mr. Ball. Did a police officer say anything to you before you went in there, to tell you—

Mrs. Markham. No, sir.

Mr. Ball. That he thought "We had the right man," or something of that sort? Anything like that?

Mrs. Markham. No, sir.

Mr. Ball. No statement like that?

Mrs. Markham. No, sir.

Mr. Ball. Did anybody tell you that the man you were looking for would be in a certain position in the lineup, or anything like that?

Mrs. Markham. No, sir.

Mr. Ball. Now when you went into the room you looked these people over, these four men?

Mrs. Markham. Yes, sir.

Mr. Ball. Did you recognize anyone in the lineup?

Mrs. Markham. No, sir.

Mr. Ball. You did not? Did you see anybody—I have asked you that question before—did you recognize anybody from their face?

Mrs. Markham. From their face, no.

Mr. Ball. Did you identify anybody in these four people?

Mrs. Markham. I didn't know nobody.

Mr. Ball. I know you didn't know anybody, but did anybody in that lineup look like anybody you had seen before?

Mrs. Markham. No. I had never seen none of them, none of these men.

Mr. Ball. No one of the four?

Mrs. Markham. No one of them.

Mr. Ball. No one of all four?

Mrs. Markham. No, sir.

Mr. Ball. Was there a number two man in there?

Mrs. Markham. Number two is the one I picked.

Mr. Ball. Well, I thought you just told me that you hadn't—

Mrs. Markham. I thought you wanted me to describe their clothing.

Mr. Ball. No. I wanted to know if that day when you were in there if you saw anyone in there—

Mrs. Markham. Number two.

Mr. Ball. What did you say when you saw number two?

Mrs. Markham. Well, let me tell you. I said the second man, and they kept asking me which one, which one. I said, number two. When I said number two, I just got weak.

Mr. Ball. What about number two, what did you mean when you said number two?

Mrs. Markham. Number two was the man I saw shoot the policeman.

Mr. Ball. You recognized him from his appearance?

Mrs. Markham. I asked—I looked at him. When I saw this man I wasn't sure, but I had cold chills just run all over me.

Mr. Ball. When you saw him?

Mrs. Markham. When I saw the man. But I wasn't sure, so, you see, I told them I wanted to be sure, and looked at his face is what I was looking at, mostly is what I looked at, on account of his eyes, the way he looked at me. So I asked them if they would turn him sideways. They did, and then they turned him back around, and I said the second, and they said, which one, and I said number two. So when I said that, well, I just kind of fell over. Everybody in there, you know, was beginning to talk, and I don't know, just—

Mr. Ball. Did you recognize him from his clothing?

Mrs. Markham. He had on a light short jacket, dark trousers. I looked at his clothing, but I looked at his face, too.

Mr. Ball. Did he have the same clothing on that the man had that you saw shoot the officer?

Mrs. Markham. He had these dark trousers on.

Mr. Ball. Did he have a jacket or a shirt? The man that you saw shoot Officer Tippit and run away, did you notice if he had a jacket on?

Mrs. Markham. He had a jacket on when he done it.

Mr. Ball. What kind of a jacket, what general color of jacket?

Mrs. Markham. It was a short jacket open in the front, kind of a grayish tan.

Mr. Ball. Did you tell the police that?

Mrs. Markham. Yes, I did.

Mr. Ball. Did any man in the lineup have a jacket on?

Mrs. Markham. I can't remember that.

Mr. Ball. Did this number two man that you mentioned to the police have any jacket on when he was in the lineup?

Mrs. Markham. No, sir.

Mr. Ball. What did he have on?

Mrs. Markham. He had on a light shirt and dark trousers.

Mr. Ball. Did you recognize the man from his clothing or from his face?

Mrs. Markham. Mostly from his face.

Mr. Ball. Were you sure it was the same man you had seen before?

Mrs. Markham. I am sure.

Joe Ball then took the witness through some pictures of the scene of the Tippit murder. She marked with an "X" on one of the pictures, Exhibit 521, where she was standing—catercornered from where the Tippit car stopped.

Then Joe Ball went to the essence of the controversy that surrounded the witness—a claim by Mark Lane that he had talked with Mrs. Markham and that she had described the gunman as "short, a little on the heavy side and his hair was somewhat bushy."

Mr. Ball. Mrs. Markham, do you know a man named Mark Lane?

Mrs. Markham. No; I do not.

Mr. Ball. Did you ever hear of the name?

Mrs. Markham. Did not.

Mr. Ball. Did you ever talk to a New York lawyer who says he was from New York?

Mrs. Markham. No, sir.

Mr. Ball. Did you ever talk to a lawyer who was investigating the case in behalf of the deceased man, Lee Oswald?

Mrs. Markham. No, sir.

Mr. Ball. Did you ever talk to a man who said he was representing the mother of Lee Oswald?

Mrs. Markham. No, sir.

Mr. Ball. You don't remember ever talking to a man named Mark Lane?

Mrs. Markham. No, sir.

Mr. Ball. In an appearance before this Commission, a man named Mark Lane has testified this way. Let me read it to you. That was on Wednesday, Mar. 4, 1964, Vol. II of a public hearing before this Commission, page 51. This is what he said:

"I spoke with the deponent"—he is talking about an affidavit that you made to the Dallas Police Department—"I spoke with the deponent, the eyewitness, Helen Louise Markham, and Mrs. Markham told me—Miss or Mrs., I didn't ask her if she was married—told me she was 100 feet away from the police car, not the 50 feet which appears in the affidavit."

Do you recall ever stating that to Mr. Lane or anyone else?

Mrs. Markham. No, sir; no, sir.

Mr. Ball. He testified: "She gave me a more detailed description of the man who she said shot Officer Tippit. She said he was short, a little on the heavy side, and his hair was somewhat bushy." Did you say that to Mark Lane?

Mrs. Markham. No, sir; I don't even know the man.

Mr. Ball. Or anybody else?

Mrs. Markham. No, sir.

Mr. Ball. Did you ever tell anyone that the man who shot Tippit was short, a little on the heavy side, and his hair was somewhat bushy?

Mrs. Markham. No, sir.

Mr. Ball. Was the man, is it your memory now that the man who shot Tippit was short, a little on the heavy side?

Mrs. Markham. No, sir. He wasn't too heavy.

Mr. Ball. Is it your memory that his hair was bushy?

Mrs. Markham. It wasn't so bushy. It was, say, windblown or something. What I mean, he didn't have a lot of hair.

Mr. Ball. He didn't have a lot of hair?

Mrs. Markham. No, sir; that I could see. I don't even know that man; I never talked to nobody.

Representative Ford. You didn't talk to him by telephone or any other means?

Mrs. Markham. No, sir.

Representative Ford. Did you ever get an anonymous phone call from a person who asked you these questions?

Mrs. Markham. No.

Mr. Ball. Now, he also says, and he testified as follows:

"Helen Markham said to me she was taken to the police station on that same day, that she was very upset. She, of course, had never seen anyone killed in front of her eyes before, and in the police station she identified Oswald as the person who had shot Officer Tippit in the lineup, including three other persons. She said no one pointed Oswald out to her, and she said she was just shown four people, and she picked Oswald. She said when he asked her how she could identify him, she said she was able to identify him because of his clothing, a gray jacket and dark trousers."

Did you ever make that statement to him?

Mrs. Markham. I did not, sir.

Mr. Ball. Or to anyone else?

Mrs. Markham. Not to anybody.

Mr. Ball. When you identified Oswald—it was the number 2 man—were you told the number 2 man whom you identified in the lineup?

Mrs. Markham. No, I was not.

Mr. Ball. Were you ever told his name?

Mrs. Markham. No.

Mr. Ball. Ever told his name later?

Mrs. Markham. Nobody, nobody told me nothing.

Mr. Ball. Well, the man that you identified as the number 2 man in the lineup in the police station, you identified him as the man you had seen shoot Officer Tippit?

Mrs. Markham. Yes, I did.

Mr. Ball. Did you identify him because of his clothing that he had on at that time in the lineup?

Mrs. Markham. Just like I told you. I mostly looked at his face, his eyes, and his clothing, too.

Mrs. Markham said that apart from police officers and FBI agents she had talked with two persons—one of whom said he was from Paris and represented a French newspaper and spoke with an accent, and the other who said he was a reporter for *Life* Magazine.

After the gunman left the scene, Mrs. Markham went to the policeman. She recalled someone coming up in a pickup truck but when asked to describe him, she said, "I don't recall. I was screaming and crying and trying to get help, begging for somebody to help me."

Mr. Ball. When did you start screaming?

Mrs. Markham. I started screaming by the time I left where I was standing and screamed plumb across the street.

Mr. Ball. Do you remember what you said?

Mrs. Markham. "The man has killed a policeman." I remember, "Somebody help. He has killed him, he has killed him," I was saying that, I was pulling my hair almost. It is a wonder he did not turn and kill me, really it was.

Mr. Ball. Did you see Mr. Scoggins?

Mrs. Markham. I don't remember—

Mr. Ball. The taxicab driver.

Mrs. Markham. Yes, I saw the taxicab driver.

Mr. Ball. Where was the taxicab?

Mrs. Markham. Parked on Patton.

Mr. Ball. On Patton?

Mrs. Markham. Yes, sir.

Mr. Ball. Did you see the man later, did you see him before the shooting?

Mrs. Markham. Yes, he was sitting in his cab.

Mr. Ball. He was. Then you saw him afterward, didn't you?

Mrs. Markham. Yes, sir.

Mr. Ball. Those are all the questions I have of this witness.

Joe Ball and I were puzzled. Mark Lane had sworn under oath that he talked with Mrs. Markham. Mrs. Markham had sworn under oath that she had never met Mark Lane. "Surely," I said, "Mark Lane would not perjure himself. Helen Markham must be mistaken."

Norman Redlich joined our conversation. He had an idea: Why not show Mrs. Markham a picture of Mark Lane to refresh her recollection? Redlich went to his files and took out two newspaper photographs of Lane, which were marked Exhibits 535 and 536. We recalled Mrs. Markham.

Mr. Ball. I have two Commission Exhibits, 535 and 536. I will show them to you, Mrs. Markham, and I will ask you if you have ever seen the man who is pictured there, whose picture is shown on these two exhibits.

Mrs. Markham. No.

Mr. Ball. Never have seen him before. Do you think he might have been one of the men you talked to before?

Mrs. Markham. No, no.

Mr. Ball. They are pictures of the same man.

Mrs. Markham. No.

Mr. Dulles. We are inquiring whether you had ever seen him after the assassination.

Mrs. Markham. Yes, I know. No; not this man. This man I have never seen—I have never seen this man in my life.

Mr. Ball. I have no further questions.

The witness was then excused and Joe Ball introduced the two newspaper photographs into evidence and Norman Redlich identified these Exhibits 535 and 536 as photographs of Mark Lane.

Mr. Dulles. Can you identify these pictures as pictures of Mr. Lane?

Mr. Redlich. Yes; I can identify these as pictures of Mr. Lane. I would also like for the record to indicate where they came from. Commission Exhibit No. 535 is taken from—Commission Exhibit 536 came from the San Francisco Chronicle, and dated Feb. 8, 1964, and purports to be a photograph of Mark Lane.

Commission No. 535 is a photograph from a newspaper clipping which was in the Commission files, and it is an Associated Press photograph, and appeared, it is taken from the New York Herald Tribune of Mar. 5, 1964, and purports to be a photograph of Mark Lane. I have met Mr. Lane once or twice prior to his appearance before this Commission, and I was present during his testimony before this Commission.

Mr. Dulles. You identify these as pictures of Mr. Lane?

Mr. Redlich. These are photographs of Mark Lane.

Mr. Dulles. And these Exhibits 535 and 536 were the exhibits which were presented to Mrs. Markham?

Mr. Belin. I think the record should show how they were presented. They were clipped out so there was not any writing or anything to indicate whom they were pictures of on their face.

Mr. Dulles. That is on the record.

Mrs. Markham, there is a short question that Congressman Ford wanted to put to you.

Representative Ford. What kind of eyesight do you have, Mrs. Markham?

Mrs. Markham. I have always had good eyesight.

Representative Ford. Do you wear glasses?

Mrs. Markham. No; I don't.

Representative Ford. Have your eyes tested recently?

Mrs. Markham. No; I haven't. I have no cause to.

Representative Ford. You have never worn glasses in your lifetime?

Mrs. Markham. No.

Mr. Dulles. Are you farsighted, nearsighted, or neither, just good-sighted?

Mrs. Markham. Just good-sighted. I did a lot of writing and a cashier and everything. I see pretty good.

Representative Ford. If you go to a movie can you see the picture easily and well?

Mrs. Markham. Oh, yes; yes, sir; real well.

Representative Ford. You can see things at a distance quite well?

Mrs. Markham. Yes, sir. I have never had glasses.

Representative Ford. Thank you very much.

Even though Helen Markham was only one of six eyewitnesses who identified Lee Harvey Oswald as the killer of Officer Tippit, we wanted to resolve the discrepancy between Mark Lane's report of what he said was a conversation with Mrs. Markham and her denial that she had ever met Mark Lane or had ever told anyone that the gunman was short, a little on the heavy side with somewhat bushy hair. Helen Markham was admittedly a "flighty" witness but we wanted to find if she had given this description of the gunman, as alleged by Mark Lane when he testified some three weeks earlier, on Mar. 4.

Here is Mr. Lane's testimony under oath:

Now, it has, of course, been alleged that after Oswald shot the President and took a bus and a taxi, and went home and got a jacket, he then shot and killed Officer Tippit. The affidavit in the District Attorney's office indicates that a person saw a stopped police car, walked up to the police car, leaned on it with his arms on the window, or what would be a window sill or window ledge of the automobile, and then stepped back a step or two, the officer came out, and this person shot Officer Tippit to death.

The affidavit is peculiarly sparse in reference to the description of the assailant, the man who killed Tippit, by an eyewitness who said she was just fifty feet away.

Her description of this person is found in two different portions of the affidavit—he was young, white, male and that is the entire description present in the affidavit at the time.

I spoke with the deponent, the eyewitness, Helen Louise Markham, and Mrs. Markham told me—Miss or Mrs., I didn't ask her if she was married—told me that she was a hundred feet away from the police car, not the fifty feet which appears in the affidavit. She gave me a more detailed description of the man who she said shot Officer Tippit. *She said he was short, a little on the heavy side, and his hair was somewhat bushy.* I think it is fair to state that an accurate description of Oswald would be average height, quite slender with thin and receding hair.

After Mrs. Markham's testimony had been taken, we called back Mark

Lane, who appeared on July 2. In correspondence and statements made as the self-appointed attorney for Oswald, Lane said he had a tape recording of his interview with Helen Markham. The following exchange took place:

Mr. Rankin. Now, Mr. Lane, regarding this tape recording of Helen Markham, and your interview with her, will you tell the Commission when you made this?

Mr. Lane. I had a conversation with Mrs. Markham on the 2nd day of March this year.

Mr. Rankin. Where was that?

Mr. Lane. I have given the Commission the results of that investigation to the best of my ability. I think that, again, Mr. Rankin, your question delves into the functioning of an attorney on behalf of a client, and, therefore, is not proper, and therefore, I decline to answer.

Mr. Rankin. Will you tell the Commission when you made the tape recording that you refer to?

Mr. Lane. I just answered that question, Mr. Rankin. . . .

Mr. Rankin. Mr. Lane, could you tell us whether there was anyone else present at this interview with Helen Markham that you recorded?

Mr. Lane. I don't believe that I said I recorded it. I believe I said it was recorded.

Mr. Rankin. Was it recorded by anyone else?

Lane refused at that time to state how he had recorded it. Later, he agreed to turn over the tape under a promise of immunity from prosecution.[2] It turned out that there had never been a personal interview between Lane and Mrs. Markham. Rather, the recording had been made of a *telephone* conversation. After we received the tape, a transcription was made. We published the transcription in Volume XX, commencing at page 571.

The following appears in this transcript:

Mr. Lane. But, well, just, could you just give me one moment and tell me. I read that you told some of the reporters that he was short, stocky, and had bushy hair.

Mrs. Markham. No, no. I did not say this.

Mr. Lane. You did not say that?

Mrs. Markham. No, sir.

Mr. Lane. Well, would you say that he was stocky?

Mrs. Markham. Uh, he was short.

Mr. Lane. He was short.

Mrs. Markham. Yes.

Mr. Lane. And was he a little bit on the heavy side? [One could hardly ask a question that was more leading and suggestive.]

Mrs. Markham. Uh, not too heavy.

Mr. Lane. Not too heavy, but slightly heavy? [Even more leading.]

Mrs. Markham. Oh, well, he was, no he wasn't, didn't look too heavy, uh–uh.

Mr. Lane. He wasn't too heavy, and would you say that he had rather bushy hair, kind of hair?

Mrs. Markham. Yeh, just a little bit bushy, uh huh.

---

[2]Lane did not say why he wanted immunity, but Lane may have been concerned about federal criminal statutes that prohibit "interception and disclosure of wire or oral communications" (wiretapping) subject to certain exceptions, without the consent of both parties to a communication. (18 USCA 2511)

Mr. Lane. It was a little bit bushy.

Mrs. Markham. Yes.

Then Lane questioned her about the police lineup. Mrs. Markham stated that she identified Oswald in the police lineup. Lane asked whether the police had told her who it might be. Mrs. Markham replied, "They didn't tell me one thing."

Lane then returned to the events of the Tippit shooting and once again went back to Mrs. Markham's description of the gunman:

Mr. Lane. Did you say that he was short and a little bit on the heavy side and had slightly bushy hair?

Mrs. Markham. Uh, no, I did not. They didn't ask me that.

Then Lane asked her again about how she had described Oswald when she made the affidavit.

Mr. Lane. And when you were there, did they ever ask you anything else about Oswald? About whether he was tall or short?

Mrs. Markham. Uh, yes, sir. They asked me that.

Mr. Lane. And you said he was short, eh?

Mrs. Markham. Yes, sir, he is short. He was short.

Mr. Lane. He was short. And they asked if he was thin or heavy, and you said he was a little on the heavy side?

Mrs. Markham. And he was, uh, uh, well not too heavy. Uh, say around 160, maybe 150.

Mr. Lane. Well, did you say he wasn't too heavy, but he was a little heavy?

Mrs. Markham. Uh-huh.

Mr. Lane. You did say that?

Mrs. Markham. I did identify him in the lineup.

Mr. Lane. Yes, and did you say that the man who shot, did you tell the officers that the man who shot Tippit had bushy hair?

Mrs. Markham. Uh, no, I did not.

Mr. Lane. But, but he did have bushy hair you said, just a little bushy?

Mrs. Markham. Well, you wouldn't say it hadn't been combed you know or anything.

Mr. Lane. Yes.

Mrs. Markham. Of course, he probably had been through a lot, and was kind of tore up a little . . .

Lane returned to the shooting of Officer Tippit and what Mrs. Markham saw and then he asked her about her identification of the gunman in the police station. She said that she wanted to be sure, so she had had the police turn the man in the lineup "and they turned him, and it was him."

For a third time Lane tried to have Mrs. Markham state that the person that shot Tippit was short, stocky and had bushy hair.

Mr. Lane. Have you told any reporters about anything?

Mrs. Markham. Well, one. They worried me to death.

Mr. Lane. I'm sure they are after you because you're a very important witness.

Mrs. Markham. Uh-huh.

Mr. Lane. Did any of the reporters, did you tell any reporter that the person that shot Oswald, shot Tippit was short, stocky, and had bushy hair?

Mrs. Markham. I did not.

Mr. Lane. You don't remember telling it because one of the reporters reported that in the newspaper.

Mrs. Markham. Yes, I read that.

Mr. Lane. You read that. What paper was that, do you recall?

Mrs. Markham. Uh, I believe it was in the *Herald.*

Mr. Lane. The *Herald?*

Mrs. Markham. I believe, it might have been the *News.*

Mr. Lane. It was one of the Dallas papers, uh?

Mrs. Markham. Yes, sir.

Mr. Lane. And, do you know what day that was?

Mrs. Markham. No, sir.

Mr. Lane. That was shortly after, though, wasn't it?

Mrs. Markham. Yes, sir. They gave my address, name and everything.

Mr. Lane. Yes, and they had you quoted as saying that he was short, stocky, and had bushy hair.

Mrs. Markham. Well, they are just not right.

Mr. Lane. But that's what they said, though.

Mrs. Markham. I know it. They can put anything in papers.

Try as he could, Mark Lane, legally trained, sought in vain to lead a relatively uneducated person into saying that the man she saw kill Officer Tippit was short, stocky, with bushy hair.

Moreover, under oath Lane had said that Mrs. Markham described Lee Harvey Oswald as being "short, a little on the heavy side, and his hair was somewhat bushy." As you jurors can see, this is fabrication of the substance of his conversation with Mrs. Markham.

As you jurors can also see, when Joe Ball and I interviewed witnesses and questioned them, there was a different approach. We were not trying to get the witnesses to say anything other than what they in their own words thought to be facts. Certainly there were some inconsistencies in Mrs. Markham's testimony, just as there were inconsistencies in the testimony of many other individuals.[3] However, the most important aspect of Mrs. Markham's testimony was that she unequivocally identified Lee Harvey Oswald in the police lineup as having been the person she saw shoot Officer Tippit.

We investigated the composition of that police lineup just as we investigated the composition of all of the other police lineups held by the Dallas Police Department in connection with the shooting of Officer Tippit and we found that this was a fairly conducted one, with people of approximately the same build and with an age range within normal limits.

---

[3]Indeed, most experienced trial lawyers become suspicious of fabrication if no inconsistencies or contradictions are present where there are more than 1 or 2 witnesses to a sudden event.

But even if Mrs. Markham had described the gunman as short, bushy-haired and stocky, the fact remains that not only did she identify the gunman in a police lineup, but so did cab driver W. W. Scoggins who saw Oswald pass with his gun within 12 feet. So did Ted Callaway, so did Sam Guinyard and so did the next two witnesses whose testimony you are about to hear: Barbara Jeanette Davis and Virginia Davis, who were inside the two-story house at the southeast corner of 10th and Patton Streets in Dallas when they heard the shots that killed J. D. Tippit.

12

"HE WAS CUTTING
ACROSS OUR YARD"

Members of the jury, you remember that you heard Domingo Benavides testify that he found two cartridge cases that the gunman tossed in the bushes as he cut across the yard of the house at the intersection of 10th and Patton. Two more cartridge cases were found in the front yard of the house by Barbara Jeanette Davis and her sister-in-law, Virginia Davis, who rented apartments in the two-story frame residential building.

Barbara Davis lived in the front downstairs apartment at the southeast corner of the intersection of 10th and Patton with her husband and two small children. In the same building in another apartment lived her husband's brother and his wife, Virginia Davis.

Barbara Davis was born in Athens, Texas, and had finished "half way through the tenth mid-term" of school when she left to marry. On the afternoon of Nov. 22, Virginia Davis was in her sister-in-law's apartment.

After a few preliminary questions, Joe Ball asked Mrs. Barbara Davis:

On that day did something unusual happen that you observed, on Nov. 22d?
Mrs. Davis. Those gunshots.
Mr. Ball. Gunshots? Where were you when you heard gunshots?
Mrs. Davis. In bed.
Mr. Dulles. Did you say gunshot or gunshots?
Mrs. Davis. Shots.
Mr. Dulles. Plural? How many did you hear?
Mrs. Davis. Just two, they were pretty close together.
Mr. Ball. You were lying on the bed. What did you do?
Mrs. Davis. I got up, put my shoes on to see what it was.
Mr. Ball. Did you ever go outdoors?
Mrs. Davis. At first, I didn't.
Mr. Ball. When you went to the door, did you open the door?
Mrs. Davis. I opened the door and held the screen opened.
Mr. Ball. What did you see?
Mrs. Davis. Mrs. Markham standing across the street over there, and she was standing over there and the man was coming across the yard.
Mr. Ball. A man was coming across what yard?
Mrs. Davis. My yard.
Mr. Ball. And what did you see the man doing?
Mrs. Davis. Well, first off she went to screaming before I had paid too much attention to him, and pointing at him, and he was, what I thought, was emptying the gun.

Mr. Ball. He had a gun in his hand?

Mrs. Davis. Yes.

Mr. Ball. And he was emptying it?

Mrs. Davis. It was open and he had his hands cocked like he was emptying it.

Mr. Dulles. Which hand did he have it?

Mrs. Davis. Right hand.

Mr. Ball. To his left palm?

Mrs. Davis. Yes.

Mr. Ball. Did you see him throw anything away?

Mrs. Davis. No.

Mr. Ball. You didn't?

Mrs. Davis. Yes.

Mr. Ball. What did you do next?

Mrs. Davis. He looked at her first and looked at me and then smiled and went around the corner.

Mr. Ball. Was he running or walking?

Mrs. Davis. He was walking at his normal pace.

Mr. Ball. And he went around the corner?

Mrs. Davis. Yes. He was on the sidewalk right beside the house.

Mr. Ball. Did he go, did he cut across your lawn at all?

Mrs. Davis. Yes.

Mr. Ball. Where?

Mrs. Davis. He cut across the middle of the yard.

Mrs. Davis said she was standing on the porch when she saw the gunman walking across the lawn. She marked the route on a diagram.

Joe Ball then asked her:

After the man left, what did you do, after he went out of sight what did you do?

Mrs. Davis. I went back in and phoned the police.

Mr. Ball. Then what did you tell the police?

Mrs. Davis. I just told them that a policeman had been shot.

Mr. Ball. Then what did you do?

Mrs. Davis. I came back outside and walked down to where the policeman's car was out.

Mr. Ball. Did you see the policeman?

Mrs. Davis. Yes.

Mr. Ball. Where was he?

Mrs. Davis. He was laying on the left-hand side of the car on the ground, by the left-hand fender.

Mr. Ball. Was he alive or what?

Mrs. Davis. I don't know.

Mr. Ball. Did he talk?

Mrs. Davis. No.

Mr. Ball. You didn't know whether he was alive or dead?

Mrs. Davis. No, sir; I didn't get that close.

Mr. Ball. How long did you stay there?

Mrs. Davis. Not 5 minutes, I would imagine, because the police cars started coming, so I went back to my yard.

Mr. Ball. Did you see a man coming and get the policeman's gun?

Mrs. Davis. No, I didn't.

Mr. Ball. Did you later look in the bushes and find something?

Mrs. Davis. Yes; in the grass beside the house.

Mr. Ball. The grass beside the house. What did you find?

Mrs. Davis. We found one shell.

Mr. Ball. One shell?

Mrs. Davis. Yes.

Mr. Ball. And your sister-in-law, did your sister-in-law find something else?

Mrs. Davis. She found one later in the afternoon.

Barbara Davis put a mark on one of the pictures, Commission Exhibit 534, showing where she found the shell. It was "under the window here," referring to a window of the house in the picture.

Mr. Ball. Did you see your sister-in-law find the other shell?

Mrs. Davis. Yes.

Mr. Ball. Where was that found?

Mrs. Davis. There is a little cement walk right here by her door, it was right there, not too far from there.

Barbara Davis then marked on the picture the place where her sister-in-law had found the other shell.

Mr. Ball. You only found two shells, did you, you one and your sister-in-law one?

Mrs. Davis. Yes.

Mr. Ball. What time of day did you find the one shell?

Mrs. Davis. I don't know. This was probably an hour and a half, maybe 2 hours, after the officer was shot.

Mr. Ball. What time of day did your sister-in-law find her shell, find the shell that she found?

Mrs. Davis. Somewhere around 4:30, 5, somewhere in there.

Mr. Ball. Did you later go down to the police station?

Mrs. Davis. Yes, sir.

Mr. Ball. Were you shown a group of people in the police station and asked if you could identify the man?

Mrs. Davis. Yes.

Mr. Ball. Were you alone in that room when you were shown these people?

Mrs. Davis. No, sir.

Mr. Ball. Who was with you?

Mrs. Davis. My husband, my sister-in-law was with me, and some other men.

Mr. Ball. That is your husband Troy, your sister-in-law Virginia Davis, and yourself, and other men?

Mrs. Davis. Yes.

Mr. Ball. Did you know those men?

Mrs. Davis. No, sir.

Mr. Ball. Were police officers there?

Mrs. Davis. They were all in suits, some sat at the back of the room.

Mr. Ball. When those—how many men were shown to you in this lineup?

Mrs. Davis. Four.

Mr. Ball. Were they of the same size or of different sizes?

Mrs. Davis. Most of them was about the same size.

Mr. Ball. All white men, were they?

Mrs. Davis. Yes.

Mr. Ball. Did you recognize anyone in that room?

Mrs. Davis. Yes, sir. I recognized number 2.

Mr. Ball. Number 2 you recognized? Did you tell any policeman there anything after you recognized them?

Mrs. Davis. I told the man who had brought us down there.

Mr. Ball. What did you tell him?

Mrs. Davis. That I thought number 2 was the man that I saw.

Mr. Ball. That you saw?

Mrs. Davis. Yes.

Mr. Ball. By number 2, was the man you saw the man you saw doing what?

Mrs. Davis. Unloading the gun.

Mr. Ball. And going across your yard?

Mrs. Davis. Yes, sir.

Mr. Ball. That was about what time of day that you were at the lineup?

Mrs. Davis. It was after 8, I am sure.

Mr. Ball. After when?

Mrs. Davis. After 8 o'clock.

Mr. Ball. On what day?

Mrs. Davis. On Friday, the same day.

Joe Ball then turned to the question of how the witness identified the gunman.

Mr. Ball. Was he dressed the same in the lineup as he was when you saw him running across the lawn?

Mrs. Davis. All except he didn't have a black coat on when I saw him in the lineup.

Mr. Ball. Did he have a coat on when you saw him?

Mrs. Davis. Yes, sir.

Mr. Ball. What color coat?

Mrs. Davis. A dark coat.

Mr. Ball. Now, did you recognize him from his face or from his clothes when you saw him in the lineup?

Mrs. Davis. Well, I looked at his clothes and then his face from the side because I had seen him from a side view of him. I didn't see him fullface.

Mr. Ball. Now answer the question. Did you recognize him from seeing his face or from his clothes?

Mrs. Davis. From his face because that was all I was looking at.

Finally, Joe Ball wanted to ascertain whether the identification might have been influenced by news coverage.

Mr. Ball. Mrs. Davis, before you went down to look at the man at the police station at 8 o'clock that night, had you seen television pictures of the man on television that he had been arrested?

Mrs. Davis. As far as I can remember I don't remember seeing it because I was out in the yard all the time that was going on, and I don't believe the TV was on.

Mr. Ball. Before you saw the man in the lineup were you shown a picture of any man by a police officer?

Mrs. Davis. No, sir.

Mr. Ball. Did you read a newspaper and see any pictures in a newspaper, picture of a man in the newspaper, before you went down there?

Mrs. Davis. I don't really know. I couldn't be quite sure. I can't remember whether I did or not.

Mr. Ball. Do you take an evening or a morning paper?

Mrs. Davis. We take an afternoon paper, we took an afternoon paper then.

Mr. Ball. Do you recall whether or not you did see a picture in the paper of the man?

Mrs. Davis. I don't remember. I don't even remember whether I read it or not. There was so much excitement.

Mr. Ball. When the man ran over the lawn, can you give me an estimate of how far away he was from you?

Mrs. Davis. I can't.

Mr. Ball. Make a judgment about it as to this room. Is it as far away from you to me?

Mrs. Davis. It was about as far as here to the corner of the room out there, or just a little bit more, the far corner.

Representative Ford. Just a little less, did you say?

Mrs. Davis. About like that.

Mr. Belin. About seven or eight steps?

Mr. Ball. About 20, 25 feet, is that right?

Mrs. Davis. I believe so.

Although the testimony of the witness was unequivocal, Joe Ball added one last series of questions:

Mr. Ball. Let's go back to that afternoon, and you give your best memory of what the man looked like. Don't think of what anybody has told you or what has happened in between. Try to remember the vision you had of that man—the color of his hair, the size of his build and so forth.

Mrs. Davis. You mean weight and like that?

Mr. Ball. He was white, wasn't he?

Mrs. Davis. Yes, sir.

Mr. Ball. Light complexioned, or dark?

Mrs. Davis. He was more light complected than he would have been dark.

Mr. Ball. Color of his hair?

Mrs. Davis. It was either dark brown or black. It was just dark hair.

Mr. Ball. And the color of his clothes?

Mrs. Davis. Well, I said he had on—he looked to me that he had on dark trousers, and it looked like a light colored shirt, with a dark coat over it.

Mr. Ball. About what age would you say the man was?

Mrs. Davis. I am not very good on that. I don't know. I would say he was about 23, 24.

Mr. Ball. And what about his weight and height?

Mrs. Davis. I—

Mr. Ball. You have to be general, I know that.

Mr. Dulles. Just your best recollection. If you haven't any, just tell us.

Mrs. Davis. I just don't know.

Mr. Ball. Was he fat or slender?

Mrs. Davis. He was slender built, and not very heavy.

Mr. Ball. Was he a tall man, or a real short man, or average?

Mrs. Davis. Oh, he wasn't especially tall. I would say he was about medium height or a little taller. I mean he wasn't extra tall.

Mr. Ball. Now, did you have some difficulty in identifying this No. 2 man in the showup when you saw him?

Mrs. Davis. Well, they made us look at him a long time before they let us say anything.

Mr. Ball. What about you? I am not talking about what you told them. What was your reaction when you saw this man?

Mrs. Davis. Well, I was pretty sure it was the same man I saw. When they made him turn sideways, I was positive that was the one I seen.

Virginia Davis was only 16 years old and my overall impression was that she was not nearly so convincing a witness as her sister-in-law. Virginia had also been raised in Athens, Texas, and had completed the ninth grade.

On the afternoon of Nov. 22, Virginia was in her sister-in-law's apartment lying on the couch while her sister-in-law, whom she called Jeanette, and Jeanette's two children were on the bed.

Mr. Belin. Now as you were lying down, what did you see or hear?

Mrs. Davis. We heard a shot.

Mr. Belin. How many shots did you hear?

Mrs. Davis. We heard the first one and then we thought maybe someone had a blowout like a tire or something and we didn't get up to see. Then we heard the second shot and that is when we ran to the front door.

Mr. Belin. Well, now, does that mean that you heard two shots?

Mrs. Davis. Yes, sir.

Mr. Belin. Are you sure there were not more than two, or are you sure that you heard two?

Mrs. Davis. We just heard two.

Mr. Belin. Then what did you do?

Mrs. Davis. Well, Mrs. Markham was trying to say—

Mr. Belin. Mrs. Markham?

Mrs. Davis. Yes, sir.

Mr. Belin. Do you know what her first name is?

Mrs. Davis. No, sir. I just know her by Mrs. Markham.

Mr. Belin. Had you ever known her before?

Mrs. Davis. No, sir.

Mr. Belin. How did you know it was Mrs. Markham?

Mrs. Davis. Well, it said in the paper that it was Mrs. Markham, and my sister-in-law said it was Mrs. Markham. My sister-in-law knows Mrs. Markham.

Mr. Belin. Now you heard the shots. You heard, you say, the second shot and then what did you do?

Mrs. Davis. We was already up. We ran to the door.

Mr. Belin. By we, who do you mean?

Mrs. Davis. Jeanette and I.

Mr. Belin. You went to which door?

Mrs. Davis. The front door.

Mr. Belin. That would be the front of the house facing East 10th Street?

Mrs. Davis. Yes, sir.

Mr. Belin. What did you do when you got to the door?

Mrs. Davis. Mrs. Markham was standing at the tree.

I had the witness mark on a picture the location where she thought she saw Mrs. Markham.

Mr. Belin. I'm going to call that Virginia Davis Deposition, Exhibit 1. What was Mrs. Markham saying, or did you hear her say anything?

Mrs. Davis. We heard her say "He shot him. He is dead. Call the police."

Mr. Belin. Was she saying this in a soft or loud voice?

Mrs. Davis. She was screaming it.

Mr. Belin. Did you see anything else as you heard her screaming?

Mrs. Davis. Well, we saw Oswald. We didn't know it was Oswald at the time. We saw that boy cut across the lawn emptying the shells out of the gun.

Mr. Belin. All right. Now, you saw a boy. Do you know how old he was?

Mrs. Davis. He didn't look like he was over 20.

Mr. Belin. Do you remember what color hair he had?

Mrs. Davis. Let's see, the best I recall, he had sort of light brown.

Mr. Belin. Light brown hair?

Mrs. Davis. Yes.

Mr. Belin. Was he tall or short or average height?

Mrs. Davis. He was about average height.

Mr. Belin. Fat, thin, or average weight?

Mrs. Davis. Slim.

Mr. Belin. Do you remember what he had on?

Mrs. Davis. He had on a light-brown-tan jacket.

Mr. Belin. Do you remember what color his trousers were?

Mrs. Davis. I think they were black. Brown jacket and trousers.

Mr. Belin. The trousers were black?

Mrs. Davis. Yes.

Mr. Belin. Do you remember what kind of shirt he had on?

Mrs. Davis. No, sir; I don't recall that.

Mr. Belin. Was the jacket open or closed up?

Mrs. Davis. It was open.

Mr. Belin. But you don't remember what kind of shirt he had on?

Mrs. Davis. No, sir.

Mr. Belin. Did he look at you?

Mrs. Davis. No, sir; not that I remember. I don't think so.

Mr. Belin. And where was he when you first saw him?

Mrs. Davis. He was cutting across our yard.

Mr. Belin. In what direction was he walking?

Mrs. Davis. He was walking—

Mr. Belin. Away from Patton or towards Patton?

Mrs. Davis. Towards Patton.

Mr. Belin. When you first saw him, had he gotten up to your yard yet or not?

Mrs. Davis. Yes; he was cutting over across our yard.

Mr. Belin. He was cutting across your walk that leads up to the front door?

Mrs. Davis. Yes, sir.

Mr. Belin. About how far from the main sidewalk on East 10th was he?

Mrs. Davis. He was about 3 feet.

Mr. Belin. About 3 feet or so?

Mrs. Davis. Yes; when I first saw him.

Mr. Belin. Then he was cutting across your sidewalk about 3 feet away from the main sidewalk?

Mrs. Davis. Yes, sir.

Mr. Belin. Then did you see him—how long did you see him? Where did you see him go?

Mrs. Davis. We saw him go around the corner of our house.

Mr. Belin. How far did you see him go?

Mrs. Davis. Well, when he disappeared around that corner, that is the last we saw of him.

As the gunman was coming across their front yard, Jeanette Davis and Virginia Davis "watched him unload the shells out of his gun."

Mr. Belin. What hand was he holding the gun in?

Mrs. Davis. In the right.

Mr. Belin. He was holding the gun in his right hand, if you remember?

Mrs. Davis. Yes, sir.

Mr. Belin. What was he doing with his left hand?

Mrs. Davis. He was emptying the shells in his left hand.

Mr. Belin. Was the gun broken open, so to speak? In other words, I don't know if you have ever seen a capgun. When you want to load the capgun, you have to kind of break it apart on a hinge.

Was the gun broken apart like that, or was the barrel straight?

Mrs. Davis. It was like the real gun, little one.

Mr. Belin. What do you mean it was just like?

Mrs. Davis. It was, just as best as I can remember, it was a little pistol, and he was emptying the shells. Where the shell was coming out, he was emptying the shells into his left hand.

Mr. Belin. Did you see what he did with the shells when he emptied them into his left hand?

Mrs. Davis. After we, well, he was dropping them on the ground because we found two.

Mr. Belin. You said that you found two? Did you see him drop them on the ground or not?

Mrs. Davis. No; we didn't see him.

Mr. Belin. You just saw him emptying shells in his hand?

Mrs. Davis. Yes.

Mr. Belin. You didn't actually see what he did with them when he got them in his hand, did you?

Mrs. Davis. No, sir.

Mr. Belin. Then what did you see the man do?

Mrs. Davis. Well, he just cut across. He disappeared from behind the corner of the house.

Mr. Belin. Going toward what street?

Mrs. Davis. Well, going toward Jefferson Street.

Mr. Belin. He was headed on Patton in the direction toward Jefferson?

Mrs. Davis. Yes, sir.

Mr. Belin. Did you see him actually get to Patton Street?

Mrs. Davis. Yes; he was already around the corner.

Mr. Belin. You saw him go around the corner of your home?

Mrs. Davis. Yes.

Later that afternoon, she testified that she went down to the police station with her sister-in-law to see a police lineup.

Mr. Belin. What did you do when you got to the police station?

Mrs. Davis. We stayed there until this detective, some man walked up to us and led us to this dark room.

Mr. Belin. Before they led you to the dark room, did he show you any pictures of anyone?

Mrs. Davis. No.

Mr. Belin. Had you seen any pictures on television of anyone that might be the man you saw walking with the gun?

Mrs. Davis. No.

Mr. Belin. Had you watched television at all?

Mrs. Davis. No; we didn't watch television.

Mr. Belin. Had you seen any newspapers that afternoon?

Mrs. Davis. No, sir; we didn't get the newspapers until that following morning.

Mr. Belin. All right, you went with the detective to a dark room?

Mrs. Davis. Yes.

Mr. Belin. What did you do when you got to the dark room?

Mrs. Davis. He told us to sit down.

Mr. Belin. All right.

Mrs. Davis. And then these five boys, or men walked up on this platform, and he was No. 2.

Mr. Belin. You say he was No. 2. Who was No. 2?

Mrs. Davis. The boy that shot Tippit.

Mr. Belin. You mean the man—did you see him shoot Tippit? Or you mean the man you saw with the gun?

Mrs. Davis. The man I saw carrying the gun.

Mr. Belin. Was he white or a Negro man?

Mrs. Davis. He was white.

Mr. Belin. Were all the men in the lineup white men or some Negroes?

Mrs. Davis. All of them were white.

Mr. Belin. Could you describe any other people in the lineup as to whether they might be fat or thin or short or tall?

Mrs. Davis. Well, one of them was sort, well, he was tall and slim. And then the other one there, he was sort of chubby and he was short. Then this other one, he was about the same height as the other one, the last one I told you about, short and chubby. And the other one was about—medium tall.

Mr. Belin. Now you identified someone in that lineup?

Mrs. Davis. Yes, sir.

Mr. Belin. Did you hear your sister-in-law identify him first, or not?

Mrs. Davis. No, sir; I identified him first.

Mr. Belin. Where was your sister when you identified him?

Mrs. Davis. She was sitting right next to me.

Mr. Belin. How did you identify him? Did you yell that this is the man I saw?

Mrs. Davis. No; I just leaned over and told the detective it was No. 2.

Mr. Belin. Where was the detective? Was he to your right or to your left?

Mrs. Davis. Let's see, to my right.

Mr. Belin. Where was your sister, to your right or to your left?

Mrs. Davis. Right.

Mr. Belin. As she was to your right, so you leaned over to the detective and told the detective it was No. 2?

Mrs. Davis. Yes, sir.

The witness said that she had seen Jeanette Davis find a cartridge case about five feet from the front of the house.

Mr. Belin. What did Jeanette do with it?

Mrs. Davis. She gave it to some detective.

Mr. Belin. Did you see her find any other shells?

Mrs. Davis. I found one after Jeanette, after all the police had gone.

Mr. Belin. When did you find yours?

Mrs. Davis. It was about 10 minutes after all the police had gone.

Mr. Belin. Was that before or after you went down to the police station?

Mrs. Davis. It was before.

Mr. Belin. About when before?

Mrs. Davis. Well, I would say it was about 2:30, or 4.

Mr. Belin. Mrs. Davis, when did you say you found this other shell?

Mrs. Davis. It was about 4.

Mr. Belin. Did you see or know of anyone else finding any other shell?

Mrs. Davis. No, sir; not that I remember.

Mr. Belin. Do you remember what you did with your shell when you found it?

Mrs. Davis. Well, before I picked it up, this boy told me that was walking along with us helping us find, see if we could find anything for evidence, he told me the police would get me if I picked it up by my fingers, and take fingerprints, and I got scared and ran to the house and got a Kleenex tissue and brought back outside and wrapped the shell in.

Mr. Belin. What did you do with it when you wrapped the shell up?

Mrs. Davis. Jeanette took it and put it in her apartment up on the mantleboard.

Mr. Belin. Then what?

Mrs. Davis. Then about 5:30 the same day the police called and wanted us to come down and identify him in the lineup.

Mr. Belin. Then what did you do with the shell?

Mrs. Davis. I gave it to the police.

Mr. Belin. Did you give it to him at your house or down at the police station?

Mrs. Davis. They come and picked us up.

Mr. Belin. You gave it to the officer that came to pick you up?

Mrs. Davis. Yes, sir.

Virginia Davis was totally confused in one area of her testimony: Whether her sister-in-law called the police before or after they saw the gunman cut across the front yard.

It would be reasonable to expect that the call to the police was made after they saw the gunman cut across the front yard. This is what Barbara Jeanette Davis had testified. However, at first Virginia Davis said they called the police "before" they saw the gunman. Then, when she came to the question again, she said that it was after they saw the gunman. Later still, she said it was before they saw the gunman. Then once again, as she reconstructed the evidence, she said it was afterward. Finally, in the concluding portion of her testimony:

Mr. Belin. Now, Mrs. Davis, you and I never talked about this matter until the court reporter started taking your testimony, have we?

Mrs. Davis. No, sir.

Mr. Belin. I never met you before, is that correct?

Mrs. Davis. No, sir.

Mr. Belin. Have you ever talked with any person in connection with the President's Commission before we started taking your testimony here?

Mrs. Davis. No, sir.

Mr. Belin. I want to be certain that we get this time sequence correct as to when you saw the man with the gun and when the police were called, so I am just going to ask you to sit for about 30 seconds and just think as to just what did happen, and then just tell the court reporter in your own words just what did happen there.

(Three minutes of silence.)

Mr. Belin. Now, Mrs. Davis, you may not be able to remember just what exactly the time sequence was. You have been sitting here about 3 minutes, and if you don't remember what the time sequence was, why I would like to have you so state. But if you do remember—or do you want more time to think about it?

Mrs. Davis. Well, the best I can remember, it was before that we saw the boy cut across the yard that we called the police, the best that I can remember.

Mr. Belin. In other words, it is your testimony, as I understand it now, that you heard the shot, and then what did you do?

Mrs. Davis. We heard the second shot and we ran to the front door.

Mr. Belin. What did you see?

Mrs. Davis. We saw this boy cut across the yard, and we had seen this woman was coming home from work, she had on a uniform, that was Mrs. Markham—we didn't know it was at the time, but she saw all that happen.

Mr. Belin. What did you do when you got to the door?

Mrs. Davis. We saw the boy cut across our yard.

Mr. Belin. At the time you got to the door, did you also see Mrs. Markham?

Mrs. Davis. Yes, sir.

Mr. Belin. Did you see both at approximately the same time?

I will ask you whom did you see first, Mrs. Markham, or the boy cutting across the yard?

Mrs. Davis. The boy.

Mr. Belin. You saw the boy first?

Mrs. Davis. That is who we saw first.

Mr. Belin. Then you saw Mrs. Markham second?

Mrs. Davis. Yes, sir.

Mr. Belin. Did the boy say anything?

Mrs. Davis. No, sir.

Mr. Belin. Did Mrs. Markham say anything?

Mrs. Davis. Well, when she got across the other street, 10th, she hollered, "He's dead, he's dead, he shot him."

Mr. Belin. Then what did she say?

Mrs. Davis. She was screaming. I don't know.

Mr. Belin. Then what did you do?

Mrs. Davis. Well, we called the police. Notified them.

Mr. Belin. So you called the police after you saw the boy?

Mrs. Davis. After we saw the boy.

Mr. Belin. And Mrs. Markham?

Mrs. Davis. Yes.

Mr. Belin. You are nodding your head yes. Is that your testimony, to the best of your recollection?

Mrs. Davis. That is my testimony.

Mr. Belin. I want to ask you again, did you call the police before or after you saw the boy?

Mrs. Davis. It was after.

Mr. Belin. It was after?

Mrs. Davis. Yes, sir; after, the best that I can remember.

Mr. Belin. The best you can remember, you called the police before or after you saw the boy?

Mrs. Davis. Yes, sir.

Mr. Belin. Before or after?

Mrs. Davis. After.

Mr. Belin. After you saw the boy, you went back in the house and called the police?

Mrs. Davis. Yes, sir.

Mr. Belin. Is there anything else that you can think of that we haven't talked about that might be helpful in this investigation?

Mrs. Davis. No.

Regardless of Virginia Davis's confusion as to whether the police were called before or after they saw the gunman, both she and her sister-in-law, Barbara Jeanette Davis, were unequivocal in their identification of the gunman as the No. 2 man in the lineup.

Members of the jury, the No. 2 man in the lineup these witnesses saw was Lee Harvey Oswald.

13

"I SAW A PISTOL
POINTING AT ME"

I handed the witness the four cartridge cases that were found at the scene of the Tippit murder.

Mr. Belin. Would you rise and raise your right hand. Do you solemnly swear that the testimony you are about to give will be the truth, the whole truth, and nothing but the truth, so help you God?

Mr. Barnes. I do.

Mr. Belin. Would you please sit down. You can smoke if you want to.

Mr. Barnes. It causes lung cancer.

Mr. Belin. Would you please state your name for the record.

Mr. Barnes. W. E. Barnes.

Barnes was a 42-year-old police sergeant who worked in the Crime Scene Search Section of the Identification Bureau of the Dallas Police Department. On the afternoon of Nov. 22, he went to the scene of the Tippit murder.

Mr. Belin. What did you do when you got to the scene?

Mr. Barnes. The first thing that I did was to check the right side of Tippit's car for fingerprints.

Mr. Belin. Did you find any fingerprints on the right side of the car?

Mr. Barnes. There were several smear prints. None of value.

Mr. Belin. Where were these smear prints located?

Mr. Barnes. Just below the top part of the door, and also on the right front fender.

Mr. Belin. Why did you happen to check that particular portion of the vehicle for fingerprints?

Mr. Barnes. I was told that the suspect which shot Tippit had come up to the right side of the car, and there was a possibility that he might have placed his hands on there.

Barnes said that he had been doing this work in the Crime Scene Search Section since Aug. 1, 1956.

Mr. Belin. Anything else that you did out at the crime scene?

Mr. Barnes. I photographed the scene; yes. There was a couple of hulls that was turned over to me.

Mr. Belin. Do you mean empty shell casings?

Mr. Barnes. Empty .38 caliber hulls was turned over to me at the scene by Patrolman—I believe I would be safe in saying Poe, but I am not sure about that.

Mr. Belin. How do you spell that?

Mr. Barnes. P-o-e, I believe is the way he spells it.

Mr. Belin. You think he was the one that turned over some shells?

Mr. Barnes. I believe it is. I am not too sure right now, but I believe that is what is on the report. I would have to check it to be sure.

Mr. Belin. Would these be on your report?

Mr. Barnes. It would be on our report, at the crime scene search section.

Mr. Belin. Is there anything else that was turned over to you at the scene besides these hulls that you think Patrolman Poe turned over?

Mr. Barnes. Not that I can remember at this time.

Mr. Belin. While you were out there, were any additional hulls found other than these two?

Mr. Barnes. Yes. Captain Doughty picked up another hull, .38 caliber.

Mr. Belin. Did you see Captain Doughty pick it up?

Mr. Barnes. I did not.

After going over in detail some of the pictures that Sergeant Barnes took, I then turned to the four cartridge cases. No identifiable fingerprints were found on the cartridge cases.

Mr. Belin. Sergeant, I will ask you to examine Commission Exhibits Nos. Q-74, Q-75, Q-76, and Q-77, and ask you to state whether or not there appears to be any identification marks on any of these exhibits that appear to show that they were examined or identified by you?

Mr. Barnes. I placed "B," the best that I could, inside of the hull of Exhibit 74—I believe it was Q-74 and Q-75, as you have them identified.

Mr. Belin. Now all four of these exhibits appear to be cartridge case hulls, is that correct?

Mr. Barnes. .38 caliber.

Mr. Belin. .38 caliber pistol?

Mr. Barnes. Yes.

Mr. Belin. They are kind of silver or chrome or grey in color? You can identify it that way?

Mr. Barnes. Yes.

Mr. Belin. How many of these hulls, to the best of your recollection, did you identify out there?

Mr. Barnes. I believe that the patrolman gave me two, and Captain Doughty received the third.

Mr. Belin. The two that the patrolman gave you were the ones that you put this identification mark on the inside of?

Mr. Barnes. Yes.

Mr. Belin. What instrument did you use to place this mark?

Mr. Barnes. I used a diamond point pen.

Mr. Belin. You put it on Q-74 and Q-75?

Mr. Barnes. It looks like there are others that put their markings in there too.

Mr. Belin. Did you have anything to do with identifying either the slugs that were eventually removed from Officer Tippit's body, or the pistol?

Mr. Barnes. No.

Mr. Belin. You never put any identifying marks on those. Is there anything else that you did out at the crime scene?

Mr. Barnes. We made a crime sketch of the scene.

Mr. Belin. You made a crime sketch of the scene?

Mr. Barnes. Yes.

Mr. Belin. Anything else?

Mr. Barnes. No; not that I can recall at this time.

Mr. Belin. What did you do with those cartridge case hulls, Q-74 and Q-75?

Mr. Barnes. We placed them in our evidence room, and turned them over to the FBI. I believe Special Agent Drain of the FBI was the agent that took them.

Mr. Belin. Anything else that you can think of that might be relevant with regard to your work at the Tippit scene?

Mr. Barnes. None. Not at this time.

The cartridge cases were one side of the coin. The other side was the revolver, Exhibit 143, taken from Oswald in the Texas Theatre. The Dallas police officer who had taken the revolver from Oswald during the struggle in the Texas Theatre was Bob K. Carroll. Joe Ball took his testimony on Apr. 3. When Carroll first came to the theatre, he said he went to the balcony. He did not find anyone there that fit the description of the gunman that he had heard on the police radio, and he then went to the main floor of the theatre.

Mr. Ball. What did you see when you came into the entrance to the aisle?

Mr. Carroll. I saw standing up at the time—Oswald was standing up there at that time. Several of us were converging at the same time upon him.

Mr. Ball. Where was McDonald?

Mr. Carroll. He was on Oswald's, let me see, the first time I think I saw Nick was, I believe he was on Oswald's right side.

Mr. Ball. Were they struggling?

Mr. Carroll. Everyone was struggling with him—yes, sir.

Mr. Ball. I mean, were Oswald and McDonald struggling together?

Mr. Carroll. Yes, sir; and then when I got up close enough, I saw a pistol pointing at me so I reached and grabbed the pistol and jerked the pistol away and stuck it in my belt, and then I grabbed Oswald.

Mr. Ball. Who had hold of that pistol at that time?

Mr. Carroll. I don't know, sir. I just saw the pistol pointing at me and I grabbed it and jerked it away from whoever had it and that's all, and by that time then the handcuffs were put on Oswald.

When Joe Ball examined Officer Carroll on Apr. 3, he did not have the revolver, Exhibit 143, in Dallas. That came a few days later. I completed taking the testimony of Officer Carroll on Apr. 9.

I handed the revolver to Officer Carroll and asked him to "state what that is."

Mr. Carroll. Yes, sir. It is a .38 caliber revolver with a blue steel 2″ barrel with wooden handle.

Mr. Belin. Have you ever seen this before?

Mr. Carroll. Yes; I have.

Mr. Belin. Where did you first see it?

Mr. Carroll. I first saw it in the Texas Theatre on Nov. 22, 1963.

Mr. Belin. Would you just tell us about this weapon, when you first saw it?

Mr. Carroll. The first time I saw the weapon, it was pointed in my direction and I reached and grabbed it and stuck it into my belt.

Mr. Belin. What did you happen to be doing at the time?

Mr. Carroll. At the time, I was assisting in the arrest of Lee Harvey Oswald.

Mr. Belin. Do you know whose hand was on the gun when you saw it pointed in your direction?

Mr. Carroll. No; I do not.

Mr. Belin. You just jumped and grabbed it?

Mr. Carroll. I jumped and grabbed the gun; yes, sir.

Mr. Belin. Then what did you do with it?

Mr. Carroll. Stuck it in my belt.

Mr. Belin. And then?

Mr. Carroll. After leaving the theatre and getting into the car, I released the pistol to Sgt. Jerry Hill.

Mr. Belin. Sgt. G. L. Hill?

Mr. Carroll. Yes, sir.

Mr. Belin. Who drove the car down to the station?

Mr. Carroll. I drove the car.

Mr. Belin. Did you give it to him before you started up the car, or after you started up the car, if you remember?

Mr. Carroll. After.

Mr. Belin. How far had you driven when you gave it to him?

Mr. Carroll. I don't recall exactly how far I had driven.

Mr. Belin. Did you put any identification mark at all on this weapon?

Mr. Carroll. Yes, sir; I did. The initials B. C., right above the screw on the inside of the butt of the pistol.

Mr. Belin. That is about an inch or so from the bottom of the pistol?

Mr. Carroll. Approximately an inch from the bottom of the butt of the pistol.

Mr. Belin. As you hold the pistol pointing, that metal strip is pointing up also, is that correct?

Mr. Carroll. That's correct.

Mr. Belin. Where did you put the initials?

Mr. Carroll. Where was I, or where did I put the initials on the pistol?

Mr. Belin. Where were you?

Mr. Carroll. I was in the personnel office of the city of Dallas police department.

Mr. Belin. With Sergeant Hill?

Mr. Carroll. Yes, and others who were present.

Mr. Belin. Did you see Sergeant Hill take it out of his pocket or wherever he had it, or not?

Mr. Carroll. Yes, sir.

Mr. Belin. What day did you put your initials on it?

Mr. Carroll. Nov. 22, 1963.

Sergeant Hill was at the Texas Theatre when Lee Harvey Oswald was apprehended. He got into the front seat of Officer Carroll's car; two other officers got into the back seat with Lee Harvey Oswald.

Mr. Belin. All right; now, let's pick up what happened from the time you started, with the time you opened the doors of the car to put the suspect in the car.

Mr. Hill. Officer Bentley—the suspect was put in the right rear door of the squad car and was instructed to move over to the middle. C. T. Walker got into the rear seat and would have been sitting on the right rear.

Paul Bentley went around the car and got in the left rear door and sat on that side.

Mr. Belin. That would have been from the left to the right, Bentley, Oswald, and Walker? Or Bentley, the suspect, and Walker?

Mr. Hill. K. E. Lyons got in the right front. I entered the door from the driver's side and got in the middle of the front seat.

Mr. Belin. And being that he had the keys to the car, Bob Carroll drove the vehicle.

Mr. Hill. As he started to get in the car, he handed me a pistol, which he identified as the one that had been taken from the suspect in the theatre.

Mr. Belin. When did he identify this to you?

Mr. Hill. I asked him was this his. He said, "No, it is the suspect's."

Mr. Belin. When did he do that?

Mr. Hill. As soon as he handed it to me.

Mr. Belin. When was that?

Mr. Hill. Right as I sat down in the car, he apparently had it in his belt, and as he started to sit down, he handed it to me. I was already in the car and seated.

Mr. Belin. Now I am going to hand you what has been marked Commission Exhibit 143. Would you state if you know what this is?

Mr. Hill. This is a .38 caliber revolver, Smith & Wesson, with a 2″ barrel that would contain six shells. It is an older gun that has been blue steeled, and has a worn wooden handle.

Mr. Belin. Have you ever seen this gun before?

Mr. Hill. I am trying to see my mark on it to make sure, sir. I don't recall specifically where I marked it, but I did mark it, if this is the one. I don't remember where I did mark it, now.

Here it is, Hill right here, right in this crack.

Mr. Belin. Officer, you have just pointed out a place which I will identify as a metal portion running along the butt of the gun. Can you describe it any more fully?

Mr. Hill. It would be to the inside of the pistol grip holding the gun in the air. It would begin under the trigger guard to where the last name H-i-l-l is scratched in the metal.

Mr. Belin. Who put that name in there?

Mr. Hill. I did.

Mr. Belin. When did you do that?

Mr. Hill. This was done at approximately 4 PM, the afternoon of Friday, Nov. 22, 1963, in the personnel office of the police department.

Mr. Belin. Did you keep that gun in your possession until you scratched your name on it?

Mr. Hill. Yes, sir; I did.

Mr. Belin. Was this gun the gun that Officer Carroll handed to you?

Mr. Hill. And identified to me as the suspect's weapon.

Mr. Belin. This is what has now been marked as Commission Exhibit 143, is that correct?

Mr. Hill. Yes, sir; that is what it says.

Mr. Belin. It also says the number on this sack in kind of a red ink or something "C15" on it, too, is that right?

Mr. Hill. It has C15, and on the other side it has 176-G, whatever that is.

Mr. Belin. And then we have marked Commission Exhibit 143?

Mr. Hill. Right.

Mr. Belin. Now, you said as the driver of the car, Bob Carroll, got in the car, he handed this gun to you?

Mr. Hill. Right, sir.

Mr. Belin. All right, then, would you tell us what happened? What was said and what was done?

Mr. Hill. Then I broke the gun open to see how many shells it contained and how many live rounds it had in it.

Mr. Belin. How many did you find?

Mr. Hill. There were six in the chambers of the gun. One of them had an indention in the primer that appeared to be caused by the hammer. There were five others. All of the shells at this time had indentions.

All of the shells appeared to have at one time or another scotch tape on them because in an area that would have been the width of a half inch strip of scotch tape, there was kind of a bit of lint and residue on the jacket of the shell.

Mr. Belin. Did you ever mark those?

Mr. Hill. I can say that I marked all six of them.

I handed Sergeant Hill each of the six bullets and he had scratched the letters "H I L L" on each of them.

Thus, we have the chain of evidence: The .38 caliber pistol, Exhibit 143, that was taken from Oswald at the Texas Theatre and the four cartridge cases that were found at the scene of the Tippit murder and turned over to the FBI by Sergeant Barnes of the Dallas Police Department.

In addition, there were four bullet slugs that were found in the body of Officer Tippit.

The crucial question then became: Were the bullet slugs found in Officer Tippit's body and the cartridge cases found at the scene of the Tippit murder fired by the revolver, Exhibit 143?

14

"SALES APPEAL, I WOULD SAY, IS THE MAIN REASON"

The key phrase: "To the exclusion of all other weapons."

The witness was Robert A. Frazier, Special Agent of the Federal Bureau of Investigation assigned to the FBI laboratory in Washington. For 23 years he had specialized in firearms identification. He was interrogated by Melvin Eisenberg, summa cum laude graduate of Harvard Law School who is now a professor of law at the University of California.

Eisenberg first questioned Frazier about his overall background and experience. The witness had joined the FBI in 1941 after attending the University of Idaho.

Generally in the field of firearms identification, where I have been assigned for 23 years, I received specialized training given in the FBI Laboratory to train me for the position of firearms identification specialist. In that field, we make examinations of bullets and cartridge cases, firearms of various types, for the purpose of identifying weapons as to their caliber, what they are, their manufacturer, their physical characteristics, and determining the type of ammunition which they shoot.

We examine ammunition of various types to identify it as to its caliber, its specific designation, and the type or types of weapons in which it can be fired, and we make comparisons of bullets to determine whether or not they were fired from a particular weapon and make comparisons of cartridge cases for the purpose of determining whether or not they were fired in a particular weapon, or for determining whether or not they had been loaded into or ex-tracted from a particular weapon.

That training course lasted for approximately 1 year. However, of course, the experience in firearms is actually part of the training and continues for the entire time in which you are engaged in examining firearms.

Briefly, that is the summary of the firearms training I have had.

Mr. Eisenberg. Could you estimate the number of examinations you have made of firearms to identify the firearms?

Mr. Frazier. Thousands, I would say—firearms comparisons—I have made in the neighborhood of 50,000 to 60,000.

Mr. McCloy. Have you written any articles on this subject?

Mr. Frazier. Yes. I have prepared an article for the "FBI Law Enforcement Bulletin" on firearms identification, which is published as a reprint and provided to any organization or person interested in the general field of firearms identification.

Mr. McCloy. Have you read most of the literature on the subject?

Mr. Frazier. Yes, I have.

Mr. McCloy. Is there any classical book on this subject?

Mr. Frazier. There are a number of fairly good texts. The basic one, originally published in 1936, is by Maj. Julian S. Hatcher, who later, as a general, rewrote his book "Firearms Investigation, Identification, and Evidence."

There are many other books published on the subject.

Members of the jury, you will soon learn about some rifle bullet cartridge cases and a rifle found in the Texas School Book Depository Building at the scene of the Kennedy assassination. You will also learn about a nearly whole rifle bullet slug found at Parkland Memorial Hospital and two portions of a rifle bullet found in the Presidential limousine that were of sufficient size to be ballistically identifiable.

When Melvin Eisenberg questioned the expert witness, Robert Frazier, he naturally asked him questions applicable both to rifle bullets and cartridge cases and to revolver cartridge cases and bullets.

Mr. Eisenberg. Can you explain how you are able to come to a conclusion that a cartridge case was fired in a particular weapon to the exclusion of all other weapons?

Mr. Frazier. Yes, sir; during the manufacture of a weapon, there are certain things done to the mechanism of it, which are by machine or by filing, by grinding, which form the parts of the weapon into their final shape. These machining and grinding and filing operations will mark the metal with very fine scratches or turning marks and grinding marks in such a way that there will be developed on the surface of the metal a characteristic pattern. This pattern, because it is made by these accidental machine-type operations, will be characteristic of that particular weapon, and will not be reproduced on separate weapons. It may be a combination of marks that—the face of the bolt may be milled, then it may be in part filed to smooth off the corners, and then, as a final operation, it may be polished, or otherwise adjusted during the hand fitting operation, so that it does have its particular pattern of microscopic marks.

The marks produced during manufacture are the marks seen on the bolt face; filing marks, machining marks of the various types, even forging marks or casting marks if the bolt happens to be forged or cast. And then variations which occur in these marks during the life of the weapon are very important in identification, because many of the machining marks can be flattened out, can be changed, by merely a grain of sand between the face of the cartridge case and the bolt at the time a shot is fired, which will itself scratch and dent the bolt face. So the bolt face will pick up a characteristic pattern of marks which are peculiar to it.

Eisenberg asked the witness to explain the basis of the statement "that no two bolt faces would be the same."

Mr. Frazier. Because the marks which are placed on any bolt face are accidental in nature. That is, they are not placed there intentionally in the first place. They are residual to some machining operation, such as a milling machine, in which each cutter of the milling tool cuts away a portion of the metal; then the next tooth comes along and cuts away a little more, and so on, until the final surface bears the combination of the various teeth of the milling cutter. In following that operation, then, the surface is additionally scratched—until you have numerous—we call them microscopic characteristics, a characteristic being a mark which is peculiar to a certain place on the bolt face, and of a certain shape, it is of a certain size, it has a certain contour, it may be just a little dimple in the metal, or a spot of rust at one time on the face of the bolt, or have occurred from some accidental means such as dropping the bolt, or repeated use having flattened or smoothed off the surface of the metal.

Mr. Eisenberg. Why doesn't a series of the same machines, or repeated use of the same machines, cause the same results, apart from future accidental markings?

Mr. Frazier. In some instances a certain type of cutter will duplicate a certain pattern of marks. In general you will find for a milling cutter a circular mark. And you may find the same pattern of circles. But that milling cutter does not actually cut the steel; it tears it out, it chips it out, and the surface of the metal then is rough—even though the circle is there, the circle is not a smooth circle, but it is a result of tearing out the metal, and you will have a very rough surface. When magnified sufficiently, you can detect the difference even between two similarly milled surfaces because of the minor variations in the cutting operation.

Mr. Eisenberg. Have you had occasion to examine such similarly-milled surfaces?

Mr. Frazier. Oh, yes; many times.

Mr. Eisenberg. Would you go into detail on that?

Mr. Frazier. Well, part of my work in the laboratory is dealing with toolmarks of all types, from drills, mills, files, cutting instruments, and so on. And when you are dealing with filing marks or milling marks and so on, it is sometimes possible to identify a particular mill as having made a certain mark on the basis of the grinding marks on that particular mill. But such as a case like this, where the cutting marks have now been altered through use of the weapon and corrosion, or in wear or in filing, some of the original marks are removed, and other marks are in their place, until eventually you reach a condition where that bolt face will be entirely different from any other bolt face. It is a matter actually—when you get down to the basis of it, it is a matter of a mathematical impossibility in the realm of human experience for any two things to ever be exactly alike.

Mr. Eisenberg. That is because the original markings will not be exactly alike, and then you have added accidental markings on top of the original ones?

Mr. Frazier. That is right; yes, sir.

Mr. Eisenberg. Returning for a moment to the original markings, as I understand it, you have worked with the tools themselves and the impressions the tools themselves leave, as opposed to a tooled surface, such as this.

Mr. Frazier. I have worked with both. In other words, in comparing toolmarks, you examine not only the tool, but the marks they produce.

Mr. Eisenberg. And in working with these tools, as I understand your testimony, you have found that the markings which a tool leaves, which the same tool leaves, will be distinctive.

Mr. Frazier. That is true, yes. When it is a scrape or an impression from its surface, or something of that nature, it can be very readily identified. But if it is a drill or something of that nature, where you have a tearing operation, then it is not readily identified, but it occasionally can be identified.

Mr. Eisenberg. Well, how many such examinations do you think you have made?

Mr. Frazier. Thousands of them.

Eisenberg turned to whether there would be any substantial differences between consecutively manufactured bolt faces.

Mr. Eisenberg. Well, will the tool leave different marks on the end of the bolt face from one bolt to the very next bolt face?

Mr. Frazier. Oh, yes; that very often happens. The tool is worn out or the small cuttings get underneath the edge, between the tool, and nick the edge of the tool, so that the tool will gradually change over a period of time. The cutting edge—the amount of change depends upon the amount of wear, the heat involved, and the hardness of the metal—the relative hardness of the metal.

Mr. Eisenberg. Will that particular change be noticed invariably in two consecutive bolt faces?

Mr. Frazier. No, sir.

Mr. Eisenberg. So what is the genesis of the difference in the two consecutive bolt faces as they come from the manufacturer?

Mr. Frazier. The change, as I said, depends on the bolt you are using. It does not always take place, because some bolts are made of a very soft metal, and they will not necessarily change a machining tool to that extent.

Mr. Eisenberg. But the markings, you said, would be different on two consecutive bolt faces?

Mr. Frazier. Oh, yes.

Mr. Eisenberg. And if the tool is not changed, what is the origin of the difference between the markings?

Mr. Frazier. There are other accidental markings placed there during the machining operation.

Mr. Eisenberg. Could you describe that?

Mr. Frazier. For instance, as the blade of a milling machine travels around a surface, it takes off actually a dust—it is not actually a piece of metal—it scrapes a little steel off in the form of a dust—or a very fine powder or chip—that tooth leaves a certain pattern of marks—that edge. That milling cutter may have a dozen of these edges on its surface, and each one takes a little more. Gradually you wear the metal down, you tear it out actually until you are at the proper depth. Those little pieces of metal, as they are traveling around, can also scratch the face of the bolt—unless they are washed away. So that you may have accidental marks from that source, just in the machining operation.

Now, there are two types of marks produced in a cutting operation. One, from the nicks along the cutting edge of the tool, which are produced by a circular operating tool—which produce very fine scratches in a circular pattern. Each time the tool goes around, it erases those marks that were there before. And when the tool is finally lifted out, you have a series of marks which go around the surface which has been machined, and you will find that that pattern of marks, as this tool goes around, will change. In one area, it will be one set of marks—and as you visually examine the surface of the metal, these very fine marks will extend for a short distance, then disappear, and a new mark of a new type will begin and extend for a short distance. The entire surface, then, will have a—be composed of a series of circles, but the individual marks seen in the microscope will not be circular, will not form complete circles around the face of the bolt.

Mr. Eisenberg. Have you had occasion to examine two consecutive bolt faces from a factory?

Mr. Frazier. Oh, yes.

Mr. Eisenberg. And what did you find on that examination?

Mr. Frazier. There would be no similarity in the individual microscopic characteristics between the two bolt faces.

Mr. Eisenberg. There actually was none?

Mr. Frazier. No, there was none.

From cartridge cases, the questioning turned to ballistic identification of a bullet. Frazier used as an example the rifle found in the Texas School Book Depository Building.

Mr. Eisenberg. Can you describe the types of markings which are generated onto a bullet, as opposed to those which are generated onto a cartridge case?

Mr. Frazier. A bullet when it is fired picks up the marks of the barrel of the weapon. These marks consist of rifling marks of the lands and the grooves, the spiral grooves in the barrel, and, in addition, the abrasion marks or rubbing marks which the bullet picks up due to the friction between the barrel and the surface of the copper jacket on the bullet, or if it is a lead bullet, with the lead.

Mr. Eisenberg. How are you able to conclude that a given bullet was fired in a given weapon to the exclusion of all other weapons, Mr. Frazier?

Mr. Frazier. That is based again upon the microscopic marks left on the fired bullets and those marks in turn are based upon the barrel from which the bullets are fired.

The marks in the barrel originate during manufacture. They originate through use of the gun, through accidental marks resulting from cleaning, excessive cleaning, of the weapon, or faulty cleaning.

They result from corrosion in the barrel due to the hot gases and possibly corrosive primer mixtures in the cartridges used, and primarily again they result from wear, that is an eroding of the barrel through friction due to the firing of cartridges, bullets through it.

In this particular barrel the manufacturer's marks are caused by the drill which drills out the barrel, leaving certain marks from the drilling tool. Then portions of these marks are erased by a rifling tool which cuts the four spiral grooves in the barrel and, in turn, leaves marks themselves, and in connection with those marks of course, the drilling marks, being circular in shape, there is a tearing away of the surface of the metal, so that a microscopically rough surface is left.

Then removing part of those marks with a separate tool causes that barrel to assume an individual characteristic, a character all of its own.

In other words, at that time you could identify a bullet fired from that barrel as having been fired from the barrel to the exclusion of all other barrels, because there is no system whatever to the drilling of the barrel. The only system is in the rifling or in the cutting of the grooves, and in this case of rifle barrels, even the cutters wear down as the barrels are made, eventually of course having to be discarded or re-sharpened.

Mr. Eisenberg. Have you examined consecutively manufactured barrels to determine whether their microscopic characteristics are identical?

Mr. Frazier. Yes, sir; I have three different sets of, you might say, paired barrels, which have been manufactured on the same machine, one after the other, under controlled conditions to make them as nearly alike as possible, and in each case fired bullets from those barrels could not be identified with each other; in fact, they looked nothing at all alike as far as individual microscopic characteristics are concerned. Their rifling impressions of course would be identical, but the individual marks there would be entirely different.

Although we found all of the FBI laboratory personnel with whom we had contact to be both competent and objective in their work and analysis, we did not limit ourselves in our ballistic examination to one FBI expert. Moreover, before undertaking any questioning in this area, Melvin Eisenberg extensively studied the field of ballistic identification to be sure that no witness would ever deceive the Commission. Finally, we went outside the FBI and retained independent experts to determine whether bullet slugs or cartridge cases were scientifically identifiable with particular weapons involved in our investigation.

In one instance, there was major disagreement between the independent experts we retained and the FBI. This concerned the bullets fired into Officer Tippit.

The FBI ballistics expert who concentrated on the bullets that killed Officer Tippit and the cartridge cases found at the Tippit killing was Cortlandt Cunningham. You jurors may remember him as the person who showed why the paraffin test was unreliable. Cunningham's educational background included a bachelor's degree from Northwestern University and a law degree from the University of Miami.

Eisenberg handed Cunningham the revolver taken from Oswald at the Texas Theatre, our Exhibit 143, and asked him to describe it. We summarized Cunningham's description on page 558 of our Report.

The revolver taken from Oswald at the time of his arrest was a .38 Special S. & W. Victory Model revolver. It bore the Serial No. V510210, and is the only such revolver with that serial number, since S. & W. does not repeat serial numbers. The revolver was originally made in the United States, but was shipped to England, as shown by the English inspection or proof marks on the chambers. The revolver was originally designed to fire a .38 S. & W. cartridge, whose bullet is approximately 12 or 13 grains lighter than the .38 Special, and approximately .12 inch shorter, but has a somewhat larger diameter. In the United States, the .38 Special is considered to be a better bullet than the .38 S. & W., and the revolver was rechambered for a .38 Special prior to being sold in the United States. The weapon was not rebarreled.

Mr. Eisenberg. Would the failure to rebarrel affect the accuracy of the weapon?

Mr. Cunningham. It should slightly, if you are firing .38 Special bullets, because they are slightly undersized in a .38 S. & W. barrel. On the average, .38 S. & W. barrels are approximately 4/1000ths larger than the normal .38 Special barrel. In this particular weapon, that holds true.

Mr. Eisenberg. Would it affect accuracy at close range?

Mr. Cunningham. None whatsoever. And there, again, the shortening of the barrel would affect the accuracy more than the use of .38 Special, due to the fact that your sight radius has been cut down.

Mr. Eisenberg. That is to say, when you shorten the barrel, the length between the front and the back sights is shorter, therefore giving more room for error?

Mr. Cunningham. Yes, sir. In other words, the movement of the front sight will cause more of a discrepancy at the target at longer ranges, due to the shorter sight radius.

Mr. Eisenberg. Is there any functional reason for cutting the barrel down to its present short size?

Mr. Cunningham. Sales appeal, I would say, is the main reason. Also, concealment.

Mr. Eisenberg. In your experience is a short barrel, cut-down barrel weapon like this usually purchased for legitimate purposes by other than police officers?

Mr. Cunningham. Possibly a collector. Among target shooters, it is not a popular weapon, due to the short sight radius. Revolvers with 6-inch barrels are very accurate weapons. A target shooter would not use a weapon of the short barrel type. Therefore, it is not a very popular weapon for sportsmen.

Mr. Eisenberg. Does the cutting off of the barrel increase the possibility of concealment?

Mr. Cunningham. It does, because it makes it handier. I carried, when I was in the field 5 years—I carried my personally owned firearm, which had a 2-inch barrel, due to the fact that for concealment you could not see it when I wore a suit, and it was more discreet in the type of work I was doing. . . .

Mr. Eisenberg. How much sign of use does it show?

Mr. Cunningham. It has definitely been used, there is no doubt. However, the cylinder is quite tight, and I would say that this weapon is in good operating condition.

On page 558 of our Report, we described the weapon as

a conventional revolver, with a rotating cylinder holding one to six cartridges. It is loaded by swinging out the cylinder and inserting cartridges into the cylinder's chambers. If all six chambers are loaded, the weapon can be fired six consecutive times without reloading. To extract empty cartridge cases, the cylinder is swung out and an ejector rod attached to the cylinder is pushed, simultaneously ejecting all the cartridge cases (and cartridges) in the cylinder. If both live cartridges and expended cartridge cases are in the cylinder, before pushing the ejection rod one can tip the cylinder and dump the live cartridges into his hand. The cartridge cases will not fall out, because they are lighter than the cartridges, and when fired they will have expanded so as to tightly fit the chamber walls.

Mr. Eisenberg. Mr. Cunningham, how fast could one get off shots from this weapon, shooting rapid fire, and without sighting?

Mr. Cunningham. In a combat stance, that is crouched, with a gun at belt level, and your wrist locked, you would have no trouble at all getting off five shots in from 3 to 4 seconds.

Mr. Eisenberg. With what degree of accuracy at close range?

Mr. Cunningham. Excellent. All FBI agents, for instance, practice at 7 yards, which is 21 feet, and we are hitting in the "kill zone" without any problem.

Mr. Eisenberg. How much training would one have to have with this weapon to get four hits in four or five shots at close range into a human body?

Mr. Cunningham. None whatsoever—if you can pull the trigger and point directly at a person, at 8 feet you would not likely miss—with one exception. If you did not lock your wrist, there is a possibility you could shoot too low, or you could pull to the side. Anyone with a little bit of knowledge and with—and really grabbing hold of the weapon, would have little difficulty at all at that distance.

Mr. Eisenberg. When you say "lock your wrist," do you mean just pointing the wrist so that it is in a straight line with your lower forearm?

Mr. Cunningham. Yes. In other words, to tighten it, and not be in a relaxed position. By merely tightening the wrist, you would have no trouble at all hitting a person, approximately the same distance as Mr. Eisenberg and myself.

The four cartridge cases that had been found at the scene of the Tippit murder were introduced together as Commission Exhibit 594. Eisenberg then asked the witness the crucial series of questions:

Mr. Eisenberg. Did you examine the cartridge cases in Exhibit 594 in an attempt to determine whether they had been fired in Exhibit 143, the revolver, to the exclusion of all other revolvers?

Mr. Cunningham. I did.

Mr. Eisenberg. Can you tell us your conclusion?

Mr. Cunningham. As a result of my examination, it is my opinion that those four cartridge cases, Commission Exhibit 594, were fired in the revolver, Commission Exhibit 143, to the exclusion of all other weapons.

Mr. Eisenberg. When did you perform this examination, Mr. Cunningham?

Mr. Cunningham. On Nov. 30, 1963.

Mr. Eisenberg. And how did you make the examination?

Mr. Cunningham. I first marked these cartridge cases upon receiving them. There were four. I would like to state, first of all that Special Agents Frazier and Killion also independently examined these four cartridge cases, and made the same comparisons that I am going to state. I am telling you what I found—although they independently arrived at the same conclusion.

The cartridge cases were first marked and examined for the presence of any individual characteristic marks on these cartridge cases whereby it would be possible to identify them as having been fired in a weapon. I then test-fired Commission Exhibit 143, using similar ammunition, and microscopically compared the four cartridge cases—one at a time—that is Commission Exhibit 594—with the tests obtained from the revolver, Commission Exhibit 143.

Cunningham introduced enlarged photographs as he explained his testimony and pointed out similarities between the four cartridge cases found at the scene of the Tippit murder and test cartridge cases fired from Exhibit 143.

The testimony then went from the cartridge cases to the four bullets:

Mr. Eisenberg. Mr. Cunningham. I hand you four bullets in plastic cases marked C-251, C-252, Q-13, and C-253, which have also certain other markings on them, and I ask you if you are familiar with these bullets.

Mr. Cunningham. I am.

Mr. Eisenberg. Are your marks on these bullets?

Mr. Cunningham. Yes, they are.

Mr. Eisenberg. For the record, I would like to state these four bullets were recovered from the body of Officer Tippit.

When did you receive these bullets, Mr. Cunningham?

Mr. Cunningham. The Q-13 bullet was delivered to the Laboratory the first time on the morning of Nov. 23, and it was delivered to the Laboratory by Special Agent Vincent Drain of the Dallas office of the FBI.

Mr. Eisenberg. And the remaining bullets?

Mr. Cunningham. By the way, it was returned to Dallas, and then it was returned to the Laboratory, delivered again by Special Agent Vincent Drain, of the Dallas office, also, Special Agent Warren De Brueys. They delivered our Q-13 a second time on Nov. 27th.

Representative Ford. When you say "our," what do you mean by "our"?

Mr. Cunningham. In other words, to facilitate reporting in the Laboratory, we usually give these items a Q or a K number. A Q number is a questioned item, like a bullet from a body, and a known is a gun, the K is a known, like a weapon.

That is for reporting purposes. But since this case began, we have so much evidence, and we have received so much evidence, it was considered practical to reassign a C number by us—like Mr. Eisenberg said, they are C-253, C-252, and C-251. They also have a Q number. Q-13 is C-13. That is the reason why I said "our" Q-13.

Mr. Eisenberg. When did you examine Q-13, Mr. Cunningham?

Mr. Cunningham. Nov. 23d, the first time. That was when I made my examination. It was returned on the other date. But it was examined on 11-23.

Mr. Eisenberg. Now, Q-13 has in it a brass colored object, as well as a bullet—that is, the box containing Q-13, your Q-13.

Mr. Cunningham. Yes. That was identified as the button—the button—from the coat of Officer Tippit. The bullet struck that button and when the bullet was removed from the body, the button was also removed.

The numbering of exhibits became somewhat confusing. The four bullets were marked Exhibits 602, 603, 604 and 605.

Mr. Eisenberg. Now, were you able to determine whether those bullets have been fired in this weapon?

Mr. Cunningham. No; I was not.

Mr. Eisenberg. Can you explain why?

Mr. Cunningham. Yes, sir.

First of all, Commission Exhibit No. 602 was too mutilated. There were not sufficient microscopic marks remaining on the surface of this bullet, due to the mutilation, to determine whether or not it had been fired from this weapon.

However, Commission Exhibits 603, 604 and 605 do bear microscopic marks for comparison purposes, but it was not possible from an examination and comparison of these bullets to determine whether or not they had been fired—these bullets themselves—had been fired from one weapon, or whether or not they had been fired from Oswald's revolver.

Further, it was not possible, using .38 Special ammunition, to determine whether or not consecutive test bullets obtained from this revolver had been fired in this weapon.

Mr. Eisenberg. Do you have an opinion as to why it was impossible to make either type of determination?

Mr. Cunningham. Yes, sir; this weapon, using .38 Special bullets, was not producing marks consistent with each other. Each time it was fired, the bullet would seem to pass down the barrel in a different way, which could be due to the slightly undersized bullets in the oversized .38 S. & W. barrel. It would cause an erratic passage down the barrel, and thereby, cause inconsistent individual characteristic marks to be impressed or scratched into the surface of the bullets.

Representative Ford. When you say this weapon, will you identify what you mean by "this weapon"?

Mr. Cunningham. This particular revolver, Commission Exhibit 143.

Mr. Eisenberg. So this brings us back to your earlier testimony, that the gun had been rechambered for a .38 Special, which is slightly smaller in one respect than the .38 S. & W., but it had not been rebarreled for the .38 Special?

Mr. Cunningham. That is correct.

The original .38 Smith and Wesson barrel is still on the weapon.

Mr. Eisenberg. So that the .38 Special, when fired in that gun, might wobble slightly as it passes through the barrel?

Mr. Cunningham. I don't know if wobble is the correct word. But as the bullet is passing down this shortened .38 barrel, we are probably getting an erratic passage, so the marks won't reproduce.

Mr. Eisenberg. Is it possible to say that the bullets were not fired from this weapon, No. 143?

Mr. Cunningham. No, it is not; since the rifling characteristics of Commission Exhibit 143—this revolver—are the same as those present on the four bullets.

Although four cartridge cases were found and four bullets were found, there was evidence indicating that perhaps more than four shots had been fired because three of the bullets were of Western Winchester manufacture and the fourth was of Remington-Peters manufacture, whereas two of the four recovered cartridge cases were of Western Winchester manufacture and two were of Remington-Peters manufacture. Cunningham testified:

Inasmuch as there are three Western bullets, you would be missing one Western cartridge case, and one Remington bullet. You are missing one of each. He could have missed one of the shots. I do not know how many times he actually fired the weapon. But he could have missed once. It is very possible that he could have. And depending on the angle, it would be very difficult to find that bullet unless it struck some close intervening object. Also I have no first-hand information, again, but I believe that some neighbor turned in these cartridge cases to the Dallas Police Department.

Mr. Eisenberg. I believe that is correct.

Mr. Cunningham. You have received a letter from the Dallas office of the FBI just recently, I believe, setting forth that information.

Representative Boggs. That would account for one. There would still be another one, would there not?

Mr. Cunningham. There would be just one cartridge case missing.

Mr. Eisenberg. Is there any other logical theory which could explain the results?

Mr. Cunningham. Of course, he could have had an empty cartridge case remaining in the weapon at the time he fired it. Then he would only have fired four shots, and then a bullet is still unaccounted for. That would explain it also.

In addition to interrogating the ballistics experts of the FBI, the Commission retained an independent ballistic expert, Joseph D. Nicol. At the time of his testimony, Mr. Nicol was Superintendent of the Bureau of Criminal Identification and Investigation for the State of Illinois.

Mr. Eisenberg. Could you briefly describe your qualifications in the field of firearms investigation?

Mr. Nicol. I began studying this field in 1941 in the Chicago Police Crime Laboratory under Charles Wilson, remained there as a firearms technician for approximately 9 years, and then moved to Pittsburgh, where I directed and set up the Pittsburgh and Allegheny County Crime Laboratory, also working in the field of ballistics.

Then I went to Miami, Fla., and set up the Dade County Crime Laboratory and worked there for 5 years. I went to Michigan State and taught for 4 and now I am back in Illinois, in Springfield, as Superintendent of the Bureau.

Mr. Eisenberg. Could you tell us approximately how many bullets and cartridge cases you have examined to identify them or attempt to identify them to suspect weapons?

Mr. Nicol. This would number in the thousands. I do not have an exact figure, but our caseload in Chicago is approximately 4,000 guns annually, of which we would make approximately between 10 and a dozen comparisons, so the comparisons that would be conducted by myself or those under my direct supervision would be approximately 50,000 a year. Now this is just a rough figure. . . .

Mr. Eisenberg. Mr. Nicol, finally I hand you a group of four bullets marked Commission Exhibits 602, 603, 604 and 605, which I state for the record were recovered from the body of Officer Tippit, and a group of two bullets marked Commission Exhibit 606, which I state for the record were fired by the FBI through the revolver, Commission Exhibit 143.

I ask you whether you are familiar with this group of exhibits.

Mr. Nicol. These two are fired lead projectiles that were designated by the FBI as K-3, companions to the tests in 595.

Mr. Eisenberg. When you say companions, you mean they were given to you—

Mr. Nicol. They were given to me simultaneously in an envelope, at that time wrapped in cotton.

Mr. Eisenberg. And the other exhibits?

Mr. Nicol. This was the projectile designated by the FBI, I believe, as Q-13. This is a .38 Special projectile designated Q-502. That would correspond to Commission Exhibit 603.

Mr. Eisenberg. And the item you just identified?

Mr. Nicol. Q-13 would correspond with 602.

This is Q-501, corresponding to Exhibit 604.

This is Q-500, corresponding to Exhibit 605.

Mr. Eisenberg. Are you familiar with all of those?

Mr. Nicol. Yes; I have seen and examined all of these.

Mr. Eisenberg. Did you examine Exhibits 602 through 605 to determine whether they have been fired from the same weapon as fired 606?

Mr. Nicol. Yes; I did.

Mr. Eisenberg. What was your conclusion?

Mr. Nicol. Due to mutilation, I was not able to determine whether 605, 604, and 602 were fired in the same weapon. There were similarity of class characteristics— that is to say, there is nothing evident that would exclude the weapon. However, due to mutilation and apparent variance between the size of the barrel and the size of the projectile, the reproduction of individual characteristics was not good, and therefore I was unable to arrive at a conclusion beyond that of saying that the few lines that were found would indicate a modest possibility. But I would not by any means say that I could be positive.

However, on specimen 602—I'm sorry—603, which I have designated as Q-502, I found sufficient individual characteristics to lead me to the conclusion that that projectile was fired in the same weapon that fired the projectiles in 606.

Mr. Eisenberg. That is to the exclusion of all other weapons?

Mr. Nicol. Yes, sir.

Although Nicol differed from Cunningham in saying one of the bullets, Exhibit 603, was ballistically identifiable with Oswald's revolver to the exclusion of all other weapons in the world, there was no disagreement between the two witnesses on the cartridge cases.

Mr. Eisenberg. Now, for the record, these cartridge cases were earlier identified as having been fired by the FBI in Commission Exhibit No. 143, the revolver believed to have been used to kill Officer Tippit.

Also for the record, I obtained these cartridge cases, both Exhibit 595, which are test cases, and Exhibit 594, which are cases from the murder scene, from the FBI, and transmitted them directly to Mr. Nicol for his examination.

Mr. Nicol, did you examine the cartridge cases in Exhibit 594 to determine whether they had been fired from the weapon in which the cartridge cases in Exhibit 595 had been fired?

Mr. Nicol. Yes, sir; I did.

Mr. Eisenberg. And can you give us your conclusions?

Mr. Nicol. It is my opinion, based upon the similarity of class and individual characteristics, that the four cartridge cases in 594 were fired in the same weapon as produced the cartridge cases in 595.

Melvin Eisenberg momentarily forgot the crucial phrase, "to the exclusion of all other weapons," and after Nicol testified that the bullet, Exhibit 603, was ballistically identifiable to the exclusion of all other weapons, Eisenberg then asked, "By the way, on the cartridge cases, that was also to the exclusion of all other weapons?"

Mr. Nichol: "Correct."

Thus we have the scientific evidence that unequivocally showed that Lee Harvey Oswald killed Officer J. D. Tippit.

Even had there been no eyewitnesses to the Tippit shooting, the apprehension of Oswald less than 45 minutes after the murder with the murder weapon in his possession was certainly strong evidence that Oswald was the killer. And when you add to this evidence the actions of Oswald in the theatre in taking out his gun and resisting arrest and the actions of Oswald before he went into the theatre that aroused the suspicion of Johnny Calvin Brewer, the case against Oswald becomes exceedingly strong. And when you add to all of this the positive identification by the six eyewitnesses who were taken to the Dallas Police Department: W. W. Scoggins, who saw Oswald pass within 12 feet of his cab; Ted Callaway and Sam Guinyard, who saw Oswald running from the scene with gun in hand; Helen Markham, who saw the murder from across the street; and Barbara Jeanette Davis and Virginia Davis, who saw Oswald cut across the front yard of their house—there could be no reasonable doubt that the murderer of Dallas Police Officer J. D. Tippit was Lee Harvey Oswald.

Joe Ball put it succinctly: "In all of my courtroom experience, I have never seen a more 'open and shut case.'"

However, this is for you members of the jury to decide. You may want to take some time in your deliberations to review the evidence before we begin our examination of the other murder that took place in Dallas on November 22: The assassination of John F. Kennedy.

PART III

THE MURDER OF JOHN F. KENNEDY

15

"OH, MY GOD, THEY HAVE SHOT MY HUSBAND"

How do you handle the interrogation of a widow·of a President whose husband was killed as he was sitting next to her in the back seat of an automobile? Chief Justice Warren was extremely sensitive to the situation. The only people present were a court reporter, Jacqueline Kennedy, Robert F. Kennedy, Lee Rankin and the Chief Justice, in his capacity as Chairman of the President's Commission on the Assassination of President Kennedy. The testimony was taken at the Kennedys' Georgetown residence.

Here is what happened:

The Chairman. The Commission will be in order. Mrs. Kennedy, the Commission would just like to have you say in your own words, in your own way, what happened at the time of the assassination of the President. Mr. Rankin will ask you a few questions, just from the time you left the airport until the time you started for the hospital. And we want it to be brief. We want it to be in your own words and want you to say anything that you feel is appropriate to that occasion.

Would you be sworn, please, Mrs. Kennedy?

Do you solemnly swear that the testimony you give before the Commission will be the truth, the whole truth, and nothing but the truth, so help you God?

Mrs. Kennedy. I do.

The Chairman. Would you be seated.

Mr. Rankin. State your name for the record.

Mrs. Kennedy. Jacqueline Kennedy.

Mr. Rankin. And you are the widow of the former President Kennedy?

Mrs. Kennedy. That is right.

Mr. Rankin. You live here in Washington?

Mrs. Kennedy. Yes.

Mr. Rankin. Can you go back to the time that you came to Love Field on Nov. 22 and describe what happened there after you landed in the plane?

Mrs. Kennedy. We got off the plane. The then Vice President and Mrs. Johnson were there. They gave us flowers. And then the car was waiting, but there was a big crowd there, all yelling, with banners and everything. And we went to shake hands with them. It was a very hot day. And you went all along a long line. I tried to stay close to my husband and lots of times you get pushed away, you know, people leaning over and pulling your hand. They were very friendly.

And, finally, I don't know how we got back to the car. I think Congressman Thomas somehow was helping me. There was lots of confusion.

Mr. Rankin. Then you did get into the car. And you sat on the left side of the car, did you, and your husband on your right?

Mrs. Kennedy. Yes.

Mr. Rankin. And was Mrs. Connally—

Mrs. Kennedy. In front of me.

Mr. Rankin. And Governor Connally to your right in the jump seat?

Mrs. Kennedy. Yes.

Mr. Rankin. And Mrs. Connally was in the jump seat?

Mrs. Kennedy. Yes.

Mr. Rankin. And then did you start off on the parade route?

Mrs. Kennedy. Yes.

Mr. Rankin. And were there many people along the route that you waved to?

Mrs. Kennedy. Yes. It was rather scattered going in.

Once there was a crowd of people with a sign saying something like "President Kennedy, please get out and shake our hands, our neighbors said you wouldn't."

Mr. Rankin. Did you?

Mrs. Kennedy. And he stopped and got out. That was, you know, like a little suburb and there were not many crowds. But then the crowds got bigger as you went in.

Mr. Rankin. As you got into the main street of Dallas were there very large crowds on all the streets?

Mrs. Kennedy. Yes.

Mr. Rankin. And you waved to them and proceeded down the street with the motorcade?

Mrs. Kennedy. Yes. And in the motorcade, you know, I usually would be waving mostly to the left side and he was waving mostly to the right, which is one reason you are not looking at each other very much. And it was terribly hot. Just blinding all of us.

Mr. Rankin. Now, do you remember as you turned off of the main street onto Houston Street?

Mrs. Kennedy. I don't know the name of the street.

Mr. Rankin. That is that one block before you get to the Depository Building.

Mrs. Kennedy. Well, I remember whenever it was, Mrs. Connally said, "We will soon be there." We could see a tunnel in front of us. Everything was really slow then. And I remember thinking it would be so cool under that tunnel.

Mr. Rankin. And then do you remember as you turned off of Houston onto Elm right by the Depository Building?

Mrs. Kennedy. Well, I don't know the names of the streets, but I suppose right by the Depository is what you are talking about?

Mr. Rankin. Yes; that is the street that sort of curves as you go down under the underpass.

Mrs. Kennedy. Yes; well, that is when she said to President Kennedy, "You certainly can't say that the people of Dallas haven't given you a nice welcome."

Mr. Rankin. What did he say?

Mrs. Kennedy. I think he said—I don't know if I remember it or I have read it, "No, you certainly can't," or something. And you know then the car was very slow and there weren't very many people around.

And then—do you want me to tell you what happened?

Mr. Rankin. Yes; if you would, please.

Mrs. Kennedy. You know, there is always noise in a motorcade and there are always motorcycles beside us, a lot of them backfiring. So I was looking to the left. I guess there was a noise, but it didn't seem like any different noise really because there is so much noise, motorcycles and things. But then suddenly Governor Connally was yelling, "Oh, no, no, no."

Mr. Rankin. Did he turn toward you?

Mrs. Kennedy. No; I was looking this way, to the left, and I heard these terrible noises. You know. And my husband never made any sound. So I turned to the right. And all I remember is seeing my husband, he had this sort of quizzical look on his face, and his hand was up, it must have been his left hand. And just as I turned and looked at him, I could see a piece of his skull and I remember it was flesh colored. I remember thinking he just looked as if he had a slight headache. And I just remember seeing that. No blood or anything.

And then he sort of did this [indicating], put his hand to his forehead and fell in my lap.

And then I just remember falling on him and saying, "Oh, no, no, no," I mean, "Oh, my God, they have shot my husband." And "I love you, Jack," I remember I was shouting. And just being down in the car with his head in my lap. And it just seemed an eternity.

You know, then, there were pictures later on of me climbing out the back. But I don't remember that at all.

Mr. Rankin. Do you remember Mr. Hill coming to try to help on the car?

Mrs. Kennedy. I don't remember anything. I was just down like that.

And finally I remember a voice behind me, or something, and then I remember the people in the front seat, or somebody, finally knew something was wrong, and a voice yelling, which must have been Mr. Hill, "Get to the hospital," or maybe it was Mr. Kellerman, in the front seat. But someone yelling. I was just down and holding him. [Reference to wounds deleted.]

Mr. Rankin. Do you have any recollection of whether there were one or more shots?

Mrs. Kennedy. Well, there must have been two because the one that made me turn around was Governor Connally yelling. And it used to confuse me because first I remembered there were three and I used to think my husband didn't make any sound when he was shot. And Governor Connally screamed. And then I read the other day that it was the same shot that hit them both. But I used to think if I only had been looking to the right I would have seen the first shot hit him, then I could have pulled him down, and then the second shot would not have hit him. But I heard Governor Connally yelling and that made me turn around, and as I turned to the right my husband was doing this [indicating with hand at neck]. He was receiving a bullet. And those are the only two I remember.

And I read there was a third shot. But I don't know.

Just those two.

Mr. Rankin. Do you have any recollection generally of the speed that you were going, not any precise amount.

Mrs. Kennedy. We were really slowing turning the corner. And there were very few people.

Mr. Rankin. And did you stop at any time after the shots, or proceed about the same way?

Mrs. Kennedy. I don't know, because—I don't think we stopped. But there was such confusion. And I was down in the car and everyone was yelling to get to the hospital and you could hear them on the radio, and then suddenly I remember a sensation of enormous speed, which must have been when we took off.

Mr. Rankin. And then from there you proceeded as rapidly as possible to the hospital, is that right?

Mrs. Kennedy. Yes.

Mr. Rankin. Do you recall anyone saying anything else during the time of the shooting?

Mrs. Kennedy. No; there weren't any words. There was just Governor Connally's. And then I suppose Mrs. Connally was sort of crying and covering her husband. But I don't remember any words.

And there was a big windshield between—you know—I think. Isn't there?

Mr. Rankin. Between the seats.

Mrs. Kennedy. So you know, those poor men in the front, you couldn't hear them.

Mr. Rankin. Can you think of anything more?

The Chairman. No; I think not. I think that is the story and that is what we came for.

We thank you very much, Mrs. Kennedy.

Mr. Rankin. I would just like to ask if you recall Special Agent Kellerman saying anything to you as you came down the street after you turned that corner you referred to.

Mrs. Kennedy. You mean before the shots?

Mr. Rankin. Yes.

Mrs. Kennedy. Well, I don't, because—you know, it is very hard for them to talk. But I do not remember, just as I don't recall climbing out on the back of the car.

Mr. Rankin. Yes. You have told us what you remember about the entire period as far as you can recall, have you?

Mrs. Kennedy. Yes.

The Chairman. Thank you very much, Mrs. Kennedy.

For Mrs. Kennedy, it was a tragic ending to a trip that had begun with high hopes. Such care was taken in planning the trip to combine the maximum political exposure with a reasonable degree of safety. Kenneth O'Donnell, Special Assistant to the President, acted as overall coordinator for the trip.

President Kennedy's attitude on Presidential protection was summarized by O'Donnell in the course of his testimony as he was questioned by Arlen Specter.

Mr. Specter. What was the President's attitude, in a general way, about Presidential protection—that is, President Kennedy's attitude about Presidential protection, Mr. O'Donnell?

Mr. O'Donnell. Well, his general attitude was that the Secret Service—that there was no protection available to a President of a democracy such as the United States from a demented person who was willing to risk his own life; that if someone wanted to kill a President of the United States, who in a sense wears two hats—he is the leader of a political party as well as our Chief Executive—and by the nature of our system must mingle with crowds, must ride through our cities, and must expose himself to the American people—that the Secret Service would not be, other than the protection that they provide by the screening processes prior to the actual carrying out of a political trip—would not be able to guarantee 100 percent protection, considering one has to mingle with crowds of 50,000 to 100,000 people, and mingle with them at handshaking distance.

Mr. Specter. Had you ever discussed the dangers inherent in a motorcade, for example, with the President?

Mr. O'Donnell. Not specifically in a motorcade. I don't think the President's view was—very frankly, we had discussed this general subject. We used to go on trips, and sit around in the evening and this would come up.

Mr. Specter. What was the President's view expressed during those conversations?

Mr. O'Donnell. His view was that a demented person who was willing to sacrifice his own life could take the President's life. And that if it were to happen, I think his general view was it would happen in a crowded situation. I don't think it entered his mind that it might happen in the fashion as of a motorcade.

Mr. Specter. What was his reaction to that risk?

Mr. O'Donnell. I think he felt that was a risk which one assuming the office of the Presidency of the United States inherited. It didn't disturb him at all.

Mr. Specter. When was the last conversation that you had with him on that general topic?

Mr. O'Donnell. The last conversation I had with him on that general topic was the morning of the assassination.

Mr. Specter. Where did the conversation occur?

Mr. O'Donnell. The conversation took place in his room, with Mrs. Kennedy and myself, perhaps a half hour before he left the Hotel Texas to depart for Carswell Air Force Base.

Mr. Specter. That was in Fort Worth?

Mr. O'Donnell. That was in Fort Worth.

Mr. Specter. And tell us, as nearly as you can recollect, exactly what he said at that time, please.

Mr. O'Donnell. Well, as near as I can recollect he was commenting to his wife on the function of the Secret Service, and his interpretation of their role once the trip had commenced, in that their main function was to protect him from crowds, and to see that an unruly or sometimes an overexcited crowd did not generate into a riot, at which the President of the United States could be injured. But he said that if anybody really wanted to shoot the President of the United States, it was not a very difficult job—all one had to do was get a high building some day with a telescopic rifle, and there was nothing anybody could do to defend against such an attempt on the President's life.

Mr. Specter. What was Mrs. Kennedy's reaction to that philosophy?

Mr. O'Donnell. I think—I think she had not quite thought of this at all. She certainly had not thought of it in this way. But I think the general tenor of the conversation was that she agreed that this was—in this democracy, this is inherent.

Mr. Specter. What had her reaction been to the trip to Texas up to that point?

Mr. O'Donnell. She had enjoyed it. She had not been a girl who had loved campaigning. And I thought at the moment, at that very minute, that for the first time—the President and I were discussing a forthcoming trip to the west coast, and he had asked her if she would come, and she said she would be delighted to come, and she would like to go from now on.

The President was delighted. We were all delighted.

Mr. Specter. Had she been on any political trip before this trip to Texas?

Mr. O'Donnell. No; she had not been on a political trip with us for quite awhile.

Mr. Specter. When was the trip immediately prior to the one to Texas that she was last on, if you recall?

Mr. O'Donnell. I don't recall. I don't recall.

Mr. Specter. Was it during the 1960 campaign?

Mr. O'Donnell. She was pregnant, as I recollect, during the 1960 campaign. She had been pregnant just prior to this. So that—and most of the other trips had been really the sort of thing that was difficult for Mrs. Kennedy to go on. But she had never evidenced to me quite as much interest in going on a—continuing to go on these trips, as she was after this.

Mr. Specter. Had she ever been to Texas prior to Nov. 21, 1963?

Mr. O'Donnell. Not to my recollection.

Mr. Specter. After the assassination, had she ever made any comment to you about that conversation which you had in the Hotel Texas in Fort Worth on the morning of Nov. 22?

Mr. O'Donnell. I have never dared bring that conversation up to Mrs. Kennedy.

We summarized the testimony of Kenneth O'Donnell and the other participants involved in the planning and the preparation for the Dallas trip in Chapter II of our Report.

PLANNING THE TEXAS TRIP

President Kennedy's visit to Texas in November 1963 had been under consideration for almost a year before it occurred. He had made only a few brief visits to the State since the 1960 Presidential campaign and in 1962 he began to consider a formal visit. During 1963, the reasons for making the trip became more persuasive. As a political leader, the President wished to resolve the factional controversy within the Democratic Party in Texas before the election of 1964. The party itself saw an opportunity to raise funds by having the President speak at a political dinner eventually planned for Austin. As Chief of State, the President always welcomed the opportunity to learn, firsthand, about the problems which concerned the American people. Moreover, he looked forward to the public appearances which he personally enjoyed.

The basic decision on the November trip to Texas was made at a meeting of President Kennedy, Vice President Johnson, and Governor Connally on June 5, 1963, at the Cortez Hotel in El Paso, Tex. The President had spoken earlier that day at the Air Force Academy in Colorado Springs, Colo., and had stopped in El Paso to discuss the proposed visit and other matters with the Vice President and the Governor. The three agreed that the President would come to Texas in late November 1963. The original plan called for the President to spend only 1 day in the State, making whirlwind visits to Dallas, Fort Worth, San Antonio, and Houston. In September, the White House decided to permit further visits by the President and extended the trip to run from the afternoon of Nov. 21 through the evening of Friday, Nov. 22. When Governor Connally called at the White House on Oct. 4 to discuss the details of the visit, it was agreed that the planning of events in Texas would be left largely to the Governor. At the White House, Kenneth O'Donnell, special assistant to the President, acted as coordinator for the trip.

Everyone agreed that, if there was sufficient time, a motorcade through downtown Dallas would be the best way for the people to see their President. When the trip was planned for only 1 day, Governor Connally had opposed the motorcade because there was not enough time. The Governor stated, however, that "once we got San Antonio moved from Friday to Thursday afternoon, where that was his initial stop in Texas, then we had the time, and I withdrew my objections to a motorcade." According to O'Donnell, "we had a motorcade wherever we went," particularly in large cities where the purpose was to let the President be seen by as many people as possible. In his experience, "it would be automatic" for the Secret Service to arrange a route which would, within the time allotted, bring the President "through an area which exposes him to the greatest number of people."

ADVANCE PREPARATIONS FOR THE DALLAS TRIP

Advance preparations for President Kennedy's visit to Dallas were primarily the responsibility of two Secret Service agents: Special Agent Winston G. Lawson, a member of the White House detail who acted as the advance agent, and Forrest V. Sorrels, special agent in charge of the Dallas office. Both agents were advised of the trip on Nov. 4. Lawson received a tentative schedule of the Texas trip on Nov. 8 from Roy H. Kellerman, assistant special agent in charge of the White House detail, who was the Secret Service official responsible for the entire Texas journey. As advance agent working closely with Sorrels, Lawson had responsibility for arranging the timetable for the President's visit to Dallas and coordinating local activities with the White House staff, the organizations directly concerned with the visit, and local law enforcement officials. Lawson's most important responsibilities were to take preventive action against anyone in Dallas considered a threat to the President, to select the luncheon site and motorcade route, and to plan security measures for the luncheon and the motorcade.

An important purpose of the President's visit to Dallas was to speak at a luncheon given by business and civic leaders. The White House staff informed the Secret Service that the President would arrive and depart from Dallas' Love Field; that a motorcade through the downtown area of Dallas to the luncheon site should be arranged; and that following the luncheon the President would return to the airport by the most direct route. Accordingly, it was important to determine the luncheon site as quickly as possible, so that security could be established at the site and the motorcade route selected.

On Nov. 4, Gerald A. Behn, agent in charge of the White House detail, asked Sorrels to examine three potential sites for the luncheon. One building, Market Hall, was unavailable for Nov. 22. The second, the Women's Building at the State Fair Grounds, was a one-story building with few entrances and easy to make secure, but it lacked necessary food-handling facilities and had certain unattractive features, including a low ceiling with exposed conduits and beams. The third possibility, the Trade Mart, a handsome new building with all the necessary facilities, presented security problems. It had numerous entrances, several tiers of balconies surrounding the central court where the luncheon would be held, and several catwalks crossing the court at each level. On Nov. 4, Sorrels told Behn he believed security difficulties at the Trade Mart could be overcome by special precautions. Lawson also evaluated the security hazards at the Trade Mart on Nov. 13. Kenneth O'Donnell made the final decision to hold the luncheon at the Trade Mart; Behn so notified Lawson on Nov. 14.

Once the Trade Mart had been selected, Sorrels and Lawson worked out detailed arrangements for security at the building. In addition to the preventive measures already mentioned, they provided for controlling access to the building, closing off and policing areas around it, securing the roof and insuring the presence of numerous police officers inside and around the building. Ultimately more than 200 law enforcement officers, mainly Dallas police but including 8 Secret Service agents, were deployed in and around the Trade Mart.

The Motorcade Route

On Nov. 8, when Lawson was briefed on the itinerary for the trip to Dallas, he was told that 45 minutes had been allotted for a motorcade procession from Love Field to the luncheon site. Lawson was not specifically instructed to select the parade route, but he understood that this was one of his functions. Even before the Trade Mart had been definitely selected, Lawson and Sorrels began to consider the best motorcade route from Love Field to the Trade Mart. On Nov. 14, Lawson and Sorrels attended a meeting at Love Field and on their return to Dallas drove over the route which Sorrels believed best suited for the proposed motorcade. This route, eventually selected for the motorcade from the airport to the Trade Mart, measured 10 miles and could be driven easily within the allotted 45 minutes. From Love Field the route passed through a portion of suburban Dallas, through the downtown area along Main Street and then to the Trade Mart via Stemmons Freeway. For the President's return to Love Field following the luncheon, the agents selected the most direct route, which was approximately 4 miles.

After the selection of the Trade Mart as the luncheon site, Lawson and Sorrels met with Dallas Chief of Police Jesse E. Curry, Assistant Chief Charles Batchelor, Deputy Chief N. T. Fisher, and several other command officers to discuss details of the motorcade and possible routes. The route was further reviewed by Lawson and Sorrels with Assistant Chief Batchelor and members of the local host committee on Nov. 15. The police officials agreed that the route recommended by Sorrels was the proper one and did not express a belief that any other route might be better. On Nov. 18, Sorrels and Lawson drove over the selected route with Batchelor and other police officers, verifying that it could be traversed within 45 minutes. Representatives of the local host committee and the White House staff were advised by the Secret Service of the actual route on the afternoon of Nov. 18.

The route impressed the agents as a natural and desirable one. Sorrels, who had participated in Presidential protection assignments in Dallas since a visit by President Franklin D. Roosevelt in 1936, testified that the traditional parade route in Dallas was along Main Street, since the tall buildings along the street gave more people an opportunity to participate. The route chosen from the airport to Main Street was the normal one, except where Harwood Street was selected as the means of access to Main Street in preference to a short stretch of the Central Expressway, which presented a minor safety hazard and could not accommodate spectators as conveniently as Harwood Street. According to Lawson, the chosen route seemed to be the best.

It afforded us wide streets most of the way, because of the buses that were in the motorcade. It afforded us a chance to have alternative routes if something happened on the motorcade route. It was the type of suburban area a good part of the way where the crowds would be able to be controlled for a great distance, and we figured that the largest crowds would be downtown, which they were, and that the wide streets that we would use downtown would be of sufficient width to keep the public out of our way.

Elm Street, parallel to Main Street and one block north, was not used for the main portion of the downtown part of the motorcade because Main Street offered better vantage points for spectators.

To reach the Trade Mart from Main Street the agents decided to use the Stemmons Freeway (Route No. 77), the most direct route. The only practical way for westbound traffic on Main Street to reach the northbound lanes of the Stemmons Freeway is via Elm Street, which Route No. 77 traffic is instructed to follow in this part of the city. Elm Street was to be reached from Main by turning right at Houston, going one block north and then turning left onto Elm. On this last portion of the journey, only 5 minutes from the Trade Mart, the President's motorcade would pass the Texas School Book Depository Building on the northwest corner of Houston and Elm Streets. The building overlooks Dealey Plaza, an attractively landscaped triangle of 3 acres.

The motorcade was led by Dallas police motorcycles followed by a pilot car about a quarter-mile ahead of the motorcade, to alert police along the route that the motorcade was approaching. Then came four to six motorcycle policemen whose main purpose was to keep the crowd back, followed by a lead car driven by the Chief of Police and occupied by two Secret Service agents and the Dallas County Sheriff.

Four to five car lengths behind the lead car was the Presidential limousine, which was driven by Secret Service Agent William R. Greer, with Secret Service Agent Kellerman sitting in the right front seat. In the rear seat was President Kennedy on the right-hand side of the car with Mrs. Kennedy on his left. Between the front and rear seat was a "jump" seat with Governor John Connally of Texas on the right jump seat and Mrs. Connally on the left. Four motorcycles, two on each side, flanked the rear of the Presidential car. Their main purpose was to keep back the crowd.

Closely behind the Presidential automobile was the "Presidential follow-up car," which carried eight Secret Service agents—two in the front seat, two in the rear and two on each of the right and left running boards.

The agents in this car, under established procedure, had instructions to watch the route for signs of trouble, scanning not only the crowds but the windows and roofs of buildings, overpasses, and crossings. They were instructed to watch particularly for thrown objects, sudden actions in the crowd, and any movements toward the Presidential car. The agents on the front of the running boards had directions to move immediately to positions just to the rear of the President and Mrs. Kennedy when the President's car slowed to a walking pace or stopped, or when the press of the crowd made it impossible for the escort motorcycles to stay in position on the car's rear flanks. The two agents on the rear of the running boards were to advance toward the front of the President's car whenever it stopped or slowed down sufficiently for them to do so.

The Vice-Presidential car followed the President's follow-up car by two to three car lengths and immediately behind that was the Vice-Presidential follow-up car. The remainder of the motorcade consisted of five cars for other dignitaries, three cars for press photographers, an official party bus for White House staff members and others and two press buses. A Dallas police car and several motorcycles at the rear kept the motorcade together and prevented unauthorized vehicles from joining the motorcade.

From the Dallas airport to downtown Dallas, the motorcade drove at speeds up to 25 to 30 miles per hour. On two occasions, at the President's direction, the automobile stopped, once to permit President Kennedy to respond to a sign asking him to shake hands and on the other occasion permitting him to speak to a nun and a group of small children.

In the downtown area, the motorcade slowed to 10 to 12 miles per hour. Large crowds of spectators gave the President an enthusiastic reception. The President's motorcade proceeded west through downtown Dallas on Main Street to the intersection of Main and Houston Streets, which marked the beginning of Dealey Plaza.

The motorcade turned to the right on Houston Street and went one block to the north to the intersection of Houston and Elm where the motorcade made a sharp "reflex angle" turn changing from a northerly direction back to a southwesterly direction as you can see on the following map. The Presidential limousine was still traveling relatively slowly, at an average speed of about 11.2 miles per hour.[1]

. Mrs. Connally, elated by the reception, turned to President Kennedy and said, "Mr. President, you can't say Dallas doesn't love you." The President replied, "That is very obvious."

According to the timeclock sign on the top of the Texas School Book Depository Building at the northwest corner of Houston and Elm, it was 12:30 PM.

[1]The speed was determined with the aid of moving picture of the assassination taken by amateur photographer Abraham Zapruder. You will hear more about this.

Commission Exhibit No. 876
DEALEY PLAZA—DALLAS, TEXAS
1. Texas School Book Depository
2. Dal-Tex Building
3. Dallas County Records Building
4. Dallas County Criminal Courts Building
5. Old Court House
6. Neeley Bryan House
7. Dallas County Government Center (Under Construction)
8. United States Post Office Building
9. Pergolas (Grassy Knoll Area)
10. Peristyles and Reflecting Pools
11. Railroad Overpass (Triple Underpass)

16

"AND THIS MAN THAT I SAW PREVIOUSLY WAS AIMING FOR HIS LAST SHOT"

Chief Justice Warren leaned forward and asked the witness, "Would you please rise and be sworn?

"Do you solemnly swear that the testimony you give before this Commission will be the truth, the whole truth, and nothing but the truth, so help you God?"

Mr. Brennan: "I do."

The Chairman (Chief Justice Warren): "You may be seated, Mr. Brennan. Mr. Belin will conduct the interrogation."

I started with some background questions. As with all the witnesses I examined, I used an informal conversational interrogation to put the witness at ease. Howard Leslie Brennan was 45 years old, married with two children and one grandson. He was a steamfitter who on the day of the assassination was fabricating pipe at a location behind the TSBD (Texas School Book Depository) Building in Dallas. At noon he went to eat lunch at a cafeteria at Main and Record Streets in Dallas—one block east and one block south of the front of the TSBD Building, a seven-story building at the northwest corner of the intersection of Houston and Elm Streets in downtown Dallas.

I finished lunch and I glanced at a clock—I don't know exactly where the clock is located—and noticed it was 12:18. So I thought I still had a few minutes, that I might see the parade and the President.

Brennan then walked to the corner of Houston and Elm, where he crossed the street "and I walked over to this retainer wall of this little park pool and jumped up on the top ledge."

The retaining wall was at the southwest corner of the intersection. As Brennan sat on the top, he faced the front of the TSBD Building on the northwest corner.

Mr. Belin. Mr. Brennan, could you please tell the Commission what happened from the time you sat on that retaining wall, what you saw?

Mr. Brennan. Well, I was more or less observing the crowd and the people in different building windows, including the fire escape across from the Texas Book Store, on the east side of the Texas Book Store, and also the Texas Book Store Building windows. I observed quite a few people in different windows. In particular, I saw this one man on the sixth floor which left the window to my knowledge a couple of times.

Mr. Belin. All right. Now, you say the window on the sixth floor. What building are you referring to there?

Mr. Brennan. That is the Texas Book Store.

I then asked Brennan to mark on a photograph marked as a Commission exhibit the window in which he saw the man. He circled the easternmost window on the south side of the sixth floor of the TSBD Building.

Mr. Belin. Did you see any other people in any other windows that you can recollect?

Mr. Brennan. Not on that floor. There was no other person on that floor that ever came to the window that I noticed.

There were people on the next floor down, which is the fifth floor, colored guys. In particular, I only remember two that I identified.

I then asked Brennan to mark on a Commission exhibit the window where he said he saw some black men on the fifth floor. The window that Brennan marked is on the east portion of the south side of the fifth floor of the building. *See the picture on page 128 of Brennan seated on the retaining wall as he was on Nov. 22.*

Then Brennan continued with his story. He watched the motorcade turn right (north) from Main onto Houston and head north and then turn the corner at Houston and Elm in front of him and go (southwest) down the incline toward the railroad underpass. "And after the President had passed my position, I really couldn't say how many feet or how far, a short distance I would say, I heard this crack that I positively thought was a backfire."

Mr. Belin. You thought it was backfire?

Mr. Brennan. Of a motorcycle.

Mr. Belin. All right. Then what did you observe, or hear?

Mr. Brennan. Well, then something, just right after this explosion, made me think that it was a firecracker being thrown from the Texas Book Store. And I glanced up. And this man that I saw previous was aiming for his last shot.

Mr. Belin. This man you saw previous? Which man are you talking about now?

Mr. Brennan. The man in the sixth story window.

Mr. Belin. Would you describe just exactly what you saw when you saw him this last time?

Mr. Brennan. Well, as it appeared to me, he was standing up. I find out later—it appeared to me he was standing up and resting against the left window sill, with gun shouldered to his right shoulder, holding the gun with his left hand and taking positive aim and fired his last shot. As I calculate a couple of seconds. He drew the gun back from the window as though he was drawing it back to his side and maybe paused for another second as though to assure hisself that he hit his mark and then he disappeared. And, at the same moment, I was diving off of that firewall and to the right for bullet protection of this stone wall that is a little higher on the Houston side.

Mr. Belin. Well, let me ask you. What kind of a gun did you see in that window?

Mr. Brennan. I am not an expert on guns. It was as I could observe, some type of a high powered rifle.

Mr. Belin. I believe you said you thought the man was standing. What do you believe was the position of the people on the fifth floor that you saw—standing or sitting?

Commission Exhibit No. 477.
The position of Howard L. Brennan on Nov. 22, 1963, as he sat on a retaining wall facing the Texas School Book Depository (TSBD) Building. The photograph was taken on Mar. 20, 1964, in a reconstruction of Brennan's activities and was marked by Brennan during his testimony to show the window (A) in which he saw a man with a rifle firing at the motorcade and window (B) on the fifth floor in which he saw people watching the motorcade.

Mr. Brennan. I thought they were standing with their elbows on the window sill leaning out.

Mr. Belin. At the time you saw this man on the sixth floor, how much of the man could you see?

Mr. Brennan. Well, I could see—at one time he came to the window and he sat sideways on the window sill. That was previous to President Kennedy getting there. And I could see practically his whole body, from his hips up. But at the time that he was firing the gun, a possibility from his belt up.

Mr. Belin. How much of the gun do you believe that you saw?

Mr. Brennan. I calculate 70 to 85 percent of the gun.

Mr. Belin. Do you know what direction the gun was pointing?

Mr. Brennan. Yes.

Mr. Belin. And what direction was the gun pointing when you saw it?

Mr. Brennan. At somewhat 30 degrees downward and west by south.

Mr. Belin. Do you know down what street it was pointing?

Mr. Brennan. Yes. Down Elm Street toward the railroad underpasses.

I asked Brennan how many shots he heard. At the time of his testimony, it was the consensus of most people that three shots had been fired.

Brennan replied that he heard "positively two" shots. He said that he did not "recall a second shot"—a middle shot between the time he heard the first noise and the time he heard the last noise.

"I don't know what made me think that there was firecrackers throwed out of the Book Store unless I did hear the second shot, because I positively thought the first shot was a backfire, and subconsciously I must have heard a second shot, but I do not recall it. I could not swear to it."

Unfortunately, you readers cannot watch the demeanor of Mr. Brennan as he testifies. But his use of the phrase, "I could not swear to it," is indicative of his seriousness and his efforts to be accurate to the best of his ability. Where he was not sure of his observations, he admitted it.

Mr. Belin. Could you describe the man you saw in the window on the sixth floor?

Mr. Brennan. To my best description, a man in his early thirties, fair complexion, slender but neat, neat slender, possibly 5-foot 10.

Mr. Belin. About what weight?

Mr. Brennan. Oh, at—I calculated, I think, from 160 to 170 pounds.

Mr. Belin. A white man?

Mr. Brennan. Yes.

Mr. Belin. Do you remember what kind of clothes he was wearing?

Mr. Brennan. Light colored clothes, more of a khaki color.

Mr. Belin. Do you remember the color of his hair?

Mr. Brennan. No.

Mr. Belin. Now, I believe you said that after the last shot you jumped off this masonry structure on which you were sitting. Why did you jump off?

Mr. Brennan. Well, it occurred to me that there might be more than one person, that it was a plot which could mean several people, and I knew beyond reasonable doubt that there were going to be bullets flying from every direction.

Mr. Belin. Then what did you do after that? Or what did you see?

Mr. Brennan. I observed to my thinking that they were directing their search towards the west side of the building and down Houston Street.

Mr. Belin. When you say 'they,' who do you mean?

Mr. Brennan. Law enforcement officers.

Mr. Belin. By the west side of the building, you mean towards the underpass or railroad tracks?

Mr. Brennan. Yes.

Mr. Belin. After you saw that, what did you do?

Mr. Brennan. I knew I had to get to someone quick to tell them where the man was. So I ran or I walked—there is a possibility I ran, because I have a habit of, when something has to be done in a hurry, I run. And there was one officer standing at the corner of the Texas Book Store on the street. It didn't seem to me he was going in any direction. He was standing still.

Mr. Belin. What did you do or what did you say to him?

Mr. Brennan. I asked him to get me someone in charge, a Secret Service man or an FBI. That it appeared to me that they were searching in the wrong direction for the man that did the shooting.

And he was definitely in the building on the sixth floor.

I did not say on the sixth floor. Correction there.

I believe I identified the window as one window from the top.

Mr. Belin. All right.

Mr. Brennan. Because, at that time, I did not know how many story building it was.

I asked Brennan what happened after he spoke to the police officer in front of the TSBD Building.

Mr. Brennan. He said, "Just a minute." And he had to give some orders or something on the east side of the building on Houston Street. And then he had taken me to, I believe, Mr. Sorrels, an automobile sitting in front of the Texas Book Store.[1]

Mr. Belin. And then what happened there?

Mr. Brennan. I related my information and there was a few minutes of discussion, and Mr. Sorrels had taken me then across the street to the sheriff's building.

Mr. Belin. Did you describe the man that you saw in the window?

Mr. Brennan. Yes; I believe I did.

Mr. Belin. Mr. Brennan, later that afternoon, or the next day, did you have occasion to go down to the Dallas Police Station to try to identify any person?

Mr. Brennan. That evening, the Secret Service picked me up, Mr. Patterson, I believe, at 6 o'clock, at my home, and taken me to the Dallas Police Station.

Mr. Belin. All right. Could you tell us what happened there, please?

Mr. Brennan. If I might add a part, that I left out a couple of minutes ago—

Mr. Belin. Go right ahead, sir.

Mr. Brennan. As Mr. Sorrels and some more men were discussing this, I mentioned these two colored boys.

Mr. Belin. Yes.

Mr. Brennan. Came out of the book store, running down the steps.

[1]Brennan was mistaken in his identification of the Secret Service agent that he talked to, for according to the testimony of Secret Service agent Sorrels he continued with the motorcade to Parkland Memorial Hospital in Dallas and did not return to the front of the TSBD Building until approximately 12:50 to 12:55. Shortly thereafter he talked to Brennan, who said that he saw ". . . a man at the window on the right-hand side, the second floor from the top. And he said, 'I could see the man taking deliberate aim and saw him fire the third shot,' and said that then he just pulled the rifle back in and moved back from the window, just as unconcerned as could be."

Mr. Belin. You mean the two—

Mr. Brennan. That I had previously saw on the fifth floor.

Mr. Belin. All right.

Mr. Brennan. And I immediately identified these two boys to the officers and Mr. Sorrels as being on the fifth floor.

Mr. Belin. Do you have anything else you wish to add now?

Mr. Brennan. No; that concludes that.

I then asked Brennan one of my "catch-all" questions:

Mr. Belin. Is there anything else now up to the time you got down to the Dallas Police Station?

Mr. Brennan. Well, nothing except that up until that time, through my entire life, I could never remember what a colored person looked like if he got out of my sight. And I always thought that if I had to identify a colored person I could not. But by coincidence that one time I did recognize those two boys.

This portion of Brennan's testimony is extremely important. He said that he could identify two men that he saw in the fifth floor window of the TSBD Building. If he could so identify two such men, particularly when he said that he thought he would never be able to identify a black person, this lends credibility and believability to what you will soon hear from Brennan: The man he saw "at least a couple of times" in the sixth floor window right above these black men on the fifth floor was Lee Harvey Oswald.

I asked Brennan if he remembered the name of the police officer he talked to in front of the TSBD Building. He said that he did not believe he ever heard it. I asked about the names of the Secret Service men he talked to. "I believe one of them was Sorrels." He did not remember the other man's name.

On Friday evening, Nov. 22, Brennan testified, a Secret Service agent picked him up at his home and took him to the Dallas Police Station, where Brennan met Captain Fritz of the Dallas Police Department. They told Brennan ". . . they were going to conduct a lineup and wanted me to view it, which I did."

Now we can picture the crucial confrontation. Here is a witness who says that he could positively identify two Negro men that he saw standing in fifth floor windows of the TSBD Building. On that same day, he is now going to view a police lineup, which includes Lee Harvey Oswald. Brennan had testified that he not only saw the rifleman fire the last shot, but he also saw him come to the window at least a couple of times prior to the motorcade. I watched the witness closely as I continued my interrogation:

Mr. Belin. Do you remember how many people were in the lineup?

Mr. Brennan. No; I don't. A possibility seven more or less one.

Mr. Belin. All right. Did you see anyone in the lineup you recognized?

Mr. Brennan. Yes.

Mr. Belin. And what did you say?

Mr. Brennan. I told Mr. Sorrels and Captain Fritz at that time that Oswald—or the man in the lineup that I identified looking more like a closest resemblance to the man in the window than anyone in the lineup.

Mr. Belin. Were the other people in the lineup, do you remember—were they all white, or were there some Negroes in there, or what?

Mr. Brennan. I do not remember.

Mr. Belin. As I understand your testimony, then, you said that you told him that this particular person looked the most like the man you saw on the sixth floor of the building there.

Mr. Brennan. Yes, sir.

Mr. Belin. In the meantime, had you seen any pictures of Lee Harvey Oswald on television or in the newspapers?

Mr. Brennan. Yes, on television.

Mr. Belin. About when was that, do you believe?

Mr. Brennan. I believe I reach home quarter to three or something of that, 15 minutes either way, and I saw his picture twice on television before I went down to the police station for the lineup.

Mr. Belin. Now, is there anything else you told the officers at the time of the lineup?

Mr. Brennan. Well, I told them I could not make a positive identification.

Mr. Belin. When you told them that, did you ever later tell any officer or investigating person anything different?

Mr. Brennan. Yes.

Mr. Belin. When did that happen?

Mr. Brennan. I believe some days later—I don't recall exactly—and I believe the Secret Service man identified hisself as being Williams, I believe, from Houston. I won't swear to that—whether his name was Williams or not.

Mr. Belin. All right.

Mr. Brennan. And he could have been an FBI. As far as I remember, it could have been FBI instead of Secret Service.

But I believe it was a Secret Service man from Houston.

And I—

Mr. Belin. What did he say to you and what did you say to him?

Mr. Brennan. Well, he asked me—he said, "You said you couldn't make a positive identification."

He said, "Did you do that for security reasons personally, or couldn't you?"

And I told him I could with all honesty, but I did it more or less for security reasons—my family and myself.

Mr. Belin. What do you mean by security reasons for your family and yourself?

Mr. Brennan. I believed at that time, and I still believe it was a Communist activity, and I felt like there hadn't been more than one eyewitness, and if it got to be a known fact that I was an eyewitness, my family or I, either one, might not be safe.

Mr. Belin. If you would not have identified that man positively, might he not have been released by the police?

Mr. Brennan. No. That had a great contributing factor—greater contributing factor than my personal reasons was that I already knew they had the man for murder, and I knew he would not be released.

Mr. Belin. The murder of whom?

Mr. Brennan. Of Officer Tippit.

Mr. Belin. Well, what happened in between to change your mind that you later decided to come forth and tell them you could identify him?

Mr. Brennan. After Oswald was killed, I was relieved quite a bit that as far as pressure on myself of somebody not wanting me to identify anybody, there was no longer that immediate danger.

Mr. Belin. What is the fact as to whether or not your having seen Oswald on television would have affected your identification of him one way or the other?

Mr. Brennan. That is something I do not know.

Mr. Belin. Mr. Brennan, could you tell us now whether you can or cannot positively identify the man you saw on the sixth floor window as the same man that you saw in the police station?

Mr. Brennan. I could at that time—I could, with all sincerity, identify him as being the same man.

Mr. Belin. Was the man that you saw in the window firing the rifle the same man that you had seen earlier in the window, you said at least a couple of times, first stepping up and then going back?

Mr. Brennan. Yes, sir.

Mr. Belin. About how far were you away from that window at the time you saw him, Mr. Brennan?

Mr. Brennan. Well, at that time, I calculated 110 foot at an angle. But closer surveillance I believe it will run close to 122 to 126 feet at an angle.

I then tried to impeach the testimony of Brennan by using FBI reports we had in our files concerning FBI interviews with Brennan.

Mr. Belin. Mr. Brennan, on one of your interviews with the FBI, they record a statement that you estimated your distance between the point you were seated and the window from which the shots were fired as approximately 90 yards.

At that time did you make that statement to the FBI—and this would be on 22 November—to the best of your recollection?

Mr. Brennan. There was a mistake in the FBI recording there. He had asked me the question of how far the shot was fired from too, and also he had asked me the question of how far I was from the shot that was fired. I calculated the distance at the angle his gun was resting that he must have been firing 80 to 90 yards.

Now, I—

Mr. Belin. You mean 80 or 90 yards from where?

Mr. Brennan. From Kennedy's position.

Mr. Belin. But could you see Kennedy's position?

Mr. Brennan. No; I could not. But I could see before and after.

Mr. Belin. In that same interview, you stated that you attended a lineup at the Dallas Police Department at which you picked Lee Harvey Oswald as the person most closely resembling the man you observed with the rifle in the window of the Texas School Book Depository, but you stated you could not positively identify Oswald as the person you saw fire the rifle.

Now, is this an accurate recording of the statement you made to the FBI on or about Nov. 22?

Mr. Brennan. Yes; I believe—

Mr. Belin. In other words, that part of the FBI statement is correct, as to what you told them?

Mr. Brennan. Yes.

I then asked Mr. Brennan:

What was the fact? Could you or could you not actually identify this person as the man you saw firing the rifle?

Mr. Brennan. I believed I could with all fairness and sincerity. As you asked me the question before, had I saw those pictures of Oswald prior, which naturally I don't know whether it confused me or made me feel as though I was taking unfair advantage or what. But with all fairness, I could have positively identified the man.

Mr. Belin. Now, on Dec. 17 there appears to be another interview that you had with an agent of the FBI in which you at that time, according to this report, stated that you could now say that you were sure that Lee Harvey Oswald was the person you saw in the window at the time of the assassination, but that when you first saw him in a lineup you felt positive identification was not necessary, because it was your understanding that Oswald had already been charged with the slaying of Officer Tippit, and you also said that another factor was that you had observed his picture on television prior to the time of identification, and that tended to cloud any identification you made of Oswald at the police department.

Now, does this Dec. 17 interview accurately record what you told the FBI with regard to that matter of identification?

Mr. Brennan. I believe it does.

Mr. Belin. Now, later we have an interview on Jan. 7 with the FBI in which at that time the interview records that while you were at home and before you returned to view the lineup, which included the possible assassin of President Kennedy, you observed Lee Harvey Oswald's picture on television, and that you said that this, of course, did not help you retain the original impression of the man in the window with the rifle, but that upon seeing Lee Harvey Oswald in the police lineup, you felt that Oswald most resembled the man whom you had seen in the window.

Now, is that what you told the man on Jan. 7—that Oswald most resembled the man that you had seen in the window?

Mr. Brennan. Yes.

Mr. Belin. Does that mean you could not give him a positive identification at that time, but could merely say he most resembled the man in the window?

Mr. Brennan. Well, I felt that I could. But for personal reasons I didn't feel like that at that moment it was compulsory and I did not want to give a positive identification at that time.

Mr. Belin. Now, this last interview was on Jan. 7. You still felt these personal reasons as recently as Jan. 7, then?

Mr. Brennan. No. I felt better about it. This is the first guy that—

Mr. Belin. No. I am referring now to the last interview you had on Jan. 7, in which it says that you felt that Oswald most resembled the man you had seen in the window.

Is that what you told them?

Mr. Brennan. Yes.

You mean told this man?

Mr. Belin. On Jan. 7; yes, sir.

Mr. Brennan. No; I don't believe I told this man in those words. I told him what I had said at the lineup. But he might have misinterpreted that I was saying that again.

Mr. Belin. In other words—well, I don't want to say in other words.

When you said on Jan. 7 that upon seeing Lee Harvey Oswald in the lineup you felt that Oswald most resembled the man whom you had seen in the window?

Mr. Brennan. Yes.

Mr. Belin. Now, I am referring to a statement to the FBI on Jan. 7 of this year.

Mr. Brennan. All right.

Mr. Belin. By that, did you have reference to your own personal recollection, or what you said at the time of the Dallas Police Department lineup?

Mr. Brennan. I believe I was referring to what I said at the Dallas Police Department.

Mr. Belin. On Jan. 7 of this year, what is the fact as to whether or not you could give—whether or not you felt on Nov. 22 that the man you saw in the window was the man you saw in the police lineup—not what you told him, but what was the fact?

Mr. Brennan. On Jan. 7, at that time I did believe that I could give positive identification as well as I did later.

Mr. Belin. You mean in the December interview?

Mr. Brennan. Yes.

Mr. Belin. Did you feel that your recollection of the Negroes at that time was as good as the one with the man with the rifle?

Mr. Brennan. Yes—at that time, it was. Now—the boys rode up with me on the plane—of course I recognize them now. But as far as a few days later, I wouldn't positively say that I could identify them. I did identify them that day.

Brennan was then asked several questions by members of the Commission. He thought only three to five minutes elapsed between the time that he jumped behind the retaining wall and the time "I talked to Mr. Sorrels—I believe it was Mr. Sorrels—and the Secret Service men there—I don't believe I talked to them more than three to five minutes."

You will find this next statement hard to believe, but it is true. Even though Brennan is perhaps the most important eyewitness to the assassination, the Dallas Police Department has no record of the composition of the lineup Brennan saw because he went with Secret Service agents instead of police officers. Most likely, it was the same group of men seen by the two Davis sisters-in-law. If it was the same lineup, Brennan was inaccurate as to the number of people in the lineup, for there were only four.

I asked Brennan if he remembered the color of any shirt that the man with the rifle was wearing. He replied, "No, other than light, and a khaki color—maybe in khaki. I mean other than light color—not a real white shirt, in other words. If it was a white shirt, it was on the dingy side."

I then asked Brennan whether or not he remembered the man's trousers.

Mr. Brennan. I remembered them at that time as being similar to the same color of the shirt or a little lighter. And that was another thing that I called their attention to at the lineup.

Mr. Belin. What do you mean by that?

Mr. Brennan. That he was not dressed in the same clothes that I saw the man in the window.

Mr. Belin. You mean with reference to the trousers or the shirt?

Mr. Brennan. Well, not particularly either. In other words, he just didn't have the same clothes on.

Brennan testified that on Nov. 22 he was wearing "grey khaki work-clothes, with a dark grey hard helmet." I handed him Commission Exhibit 479, an enlarged negative from an 8 mm. motion picture film of the Presidential motorcade taken from the other side of Elm Street by an amateur photographer, Abraham Zapruder. Viewing the enlarged negative with a magnifying glass, Brennan was able to find himself sitting on the retaining wall as he watched the motorcade go by. His hard helmet was clearly visible. And it was Mr. Brennan who picked himself out in the picture.

At this point, I asked Brennan a series of questions that illustrated our method of investigation:

Mr. Belin. Well, on Friday you and I met for the first time in Dallas—that would be on Mar. 20th.

Mr. Brennan. Right.

Mr. Belin. And we sat down and I asked you just to tell me what happened, is that correct?

Mr. Brennan. That is right.

Mr. Belin. Did I ask you a general question and say, "What happened?" Or did I just ask you repeated questions?

Mr. Brennan. No.

Well, you more or less told me to tell it in my own way exactly what happened.

Mr. Belin. And you just started to tell it, is that correct?

Mr. Brennan. Yes. I believe that sums it up.

Mr. Belin. And then we then went outside where you pointed out the place where you were sitting?

Mr. Brennan. Yes.

I then asked him:

When we visited on Friday in Dallas, what is the fact as to whether or not I told you what to say or you yourself just told me what you wanted to tell me?

Mr. Brennan. I told you—you did not instruct me what to say at all. I told you in the best words I could to explain exactly my movements and what happened.

Representative Ford. And here today you have testified freely on your own?

Mr. Brennan. Right, I have.

Then, in the concluding part of Brennan's testimony, I asked:

For the record, would you repeat what I would say would be a full statement of the reasons which caused you to state in your December interview to the FBI that you had always been convinced that the man you saw in the lineup was the man you saw firing the rifle, whereas on Nov. 22 you declined to give positive identification. Could you give all of the reasons, please?

Mr. Brennan. Well, as I previously have said, I had saw the man in the window and I had saw him on television. He looked much younger on television than he did from my picture of him in the window—not much younger, but a few years younger—say five years younger.

And then I felt that my family could be in danger, and I, myself, might be in danger. And since they already had the man for murder, that he wasn't going to be set free to escape and get out of the country immediately, and I could very easily sooner than the FBI or the Secret Service wanted me, my testimony in, I could very easily get in touch with them, if they didn't get in touch with me, and to see that the man didn't get loose.

There is no doubt that Brennan gave the Dallas police a description of the man he saw in the window. This description was broadcast several times over the Dallas police radio. We have transcripts of the radio broadcasts.

The first broadcast describing the assassin was at 12:44 PM, only 14 minutes after the assassination. The description is within an inch of Oswald's height and within ten pounds of Oswald's weight. The description is for a white man—not a Negro. The description is within a few years of Oswald's age.

But the fact remains that when Brennan was confronted with Oswald barely six hours after the assassination, he did not make a positive identification. In an age in which people in New York offer no help as a woman is being murdered, in which people in Chicago sitting in a subway car offer no help as another person is being robbed, perhaps it is to be expected that a person, fearing some sort of Communist conspiracy, would not come forth and immediately identify the man who killed the President of the United States.

Before Joe Ball and I decided how much weight should be given Brennan's testimony, we had to take a look at one additional test: Could Brennan, when he testified in Washington, identify the Negro men that he said he had identified as he saw them leave the building while he was talking to a police officer shortly after the assassination? And would these men confirm Brennan's testimony?

Brennan testified in Washington in the morning. I knew that three black men had watched the motorcade from the fifth floor of the TSBD Building. I did not know if any of the three had left the building while Brennan was talking to a police officer, since all three were outside the Commission hearing room in Washington when Brennan first testified. Over the noon hour Joe Ball and I discussed Brennan's testimony. We elected to have all three black men come into the Commission hearing room and let Brennan try to pick out the ones he said he had seen.

If none of these men left the building, it would make our job of evaluating Brennan's testimony much easier. We would disregard his sworn identification of Lee Harvey Oswald and merely state that Brennan's testimony was evidence that the shots were fired from the southeast corner window of the sixth floor of the TSBD Building and also evidence that the man Brennan saw could have been Lee Harvey Oswald because Brennan's identification of the man was relatively close to the identification of Lee Harvey Oswald. On the other hand, if Brennan could correctly pick out at least one of these men, then it could be argued that he was also capable of identifying a man in a window one floor above.

Before adjourning for lunch at 12:40, Joe Ball called the first of the three TSBD employees who were watching the motorcade from the fifth floor of the TSBD Building: Bonnie Ray Williams.

Williams testified in the absence of the two other employees and, of course, in the absence of Brennan. He said that he did not run out with either of the other employees with whom he had watched the motorcade from the fifth floor. Rather, he said, he came out with another employee and some police officers sometime later. Williams also testified that he did not remember seeing Brennan as he (Williams) came out of the building. (Williams' testimony will be reviewed in detail in Chapter 18.)

We reconvened at approximately two o'clock and we brought Williams back. We did not want Williams to leave the hearing room and perhaps tell Brennan about the questions we had asked. So we brought Brennan back into the hearing room as well as the two other employees who were watching the motorcade from the fifth floor: James Jarman Jr. and Harold Norman. Brennan was still under oath.

Mr. Belin. I believe that you testified that you thought you recognized two of the people that you saw looking out of the fifth floor of the School Book Depository Building . . . outside of the building sometime after the assassination, is that correct?

The two people that you saw, are they any of these three people here?

Mr. Brennan. Yes. I believe it is the one on the end and this one here, I am not sure.

The employee that Brennan immediately identified was Harold Norman. But he seemed to hesitate about the other, although he said that he thought that it was James Jarman Jr. I deliberately tried to trip up Brennan:

Mr. Belin. Could it have been neither one of these persons that you saw?

Mr. Brennan. I think it was one of them. I think it was this boy on the end.

Mr. Belin. You thought it was Mr. Norman. And what about Mr. Jarman?

Mr. Brennan. I believe it was him too. Am I right or wrong?

Mr. Ball. I don't know.

And at that time, neither Joe Ball nor I did know whether Brennan was right or wrong. The answer depended on the testimony of Harold Norman and James Jarman Jr.

17
"I BELIEVE IT CAME FROM UP ABOVE US"

I want to give you the following hypothetical facts: Assume a warehouse with floors strong enough to support cartons of books. Assume you are squatting by an open fifth floor window in this warehouse and there is a great deal of noise from the streets below. Assume that immediately above you a person is operating a clip-fed bolt action rifle. Would you believe that you could hear the empty cartridge cases hitting the floor above? Would you believe that you could hear the sound of a bolt going back and forth?

I think that most of you would say, "No." And that is what I said when I first read a Secret Service report that quoted a TSBD employee, Harold Norman, as saying that at the time of the assassination he could hear the sound of cartridge cases hitting the floor above him and that he could also hear the action of the bolt on the rifle above him as he watched the parade from the southeast corner window on the *fifth* floor of the TSBD Building.

We scheduled the testimony of Harold Norman on Mar. 24, 1964. Before he testified, we wanted to interview him on the fifth floor of the TSBD Building and check whether these sounds could be heard. Because we did not want to interfere with the trial of Jack Ruby, all of us in Washington refrained from coming to Dallas until the trial of Ruby had ended in March of 1964. On Mar. 19, Joe Ball and I flew to Dallas and on Mar. 20 we interviewed Harold Norman, Bonnie Ray Williams and James Jarman Jr. on the fifth floor of the TSBD Building. We had with us the equipment necessary to make the test. A Secret Service agent with the bolt action rifle stood with Joe Ball in the southeast corner window on the sixth floor of the TSBD Building. I stayed with Harold Norman on the fifth floor directly below.

Before giving the signal to conduct the experiment, I waited until a train passed on the nearby railroad overpass so there would be plenty of street noise. In addition, at that time, several large trucks were moving down Elm Street. I then yelled to have the test begin.

I smiled, for I really did not expect to hear anything. Then, with remarkable clarity, I could hear the thump as a cartridge case hit the floor. There were two more *thumps* as the two other cartridge cases hit the floor above me.

The Secret Service agent then worked the bolt of the rifle back and forth, and this too could be heard with clarity.

I looked up. The floor acted somewhat as a sounding board. It also had slight cracks through which daylight could be seen. The position of Harold Norman as he was looking out the window was only 12 or 14 feet away from the window where Brennan said he had seen a man with a rifle.

When we reassembled after the re-enactment, I said to my colleague, "Joe, if I had not heard it myself, I would never have believed it."

Four days later, Harold Norman came to Washington, where he testified on Tuesday afternoon, Mar. 24. He was 25 years old, a high school graduate who in November, 1963, was employed as an order filler at the TSBD.

On Nov. 22, Harold Norman ate lunch on the first floor with James Jarman Jr. in a room known as the "Domino Room." (The employees often played dominoes during the noon hour and break periods.)

Harold Norman testified that around 12:00 or 12:10 PM he and James Jarman Jr. (whom he referred to as "Junior") walked outside on the front steps of the TSBD Building where they saw several employees, including Superintendent Roy Truly, a Mr. Campbell, Danny Arce, and Billy Love-lady. Then, he said, he and Junior Jarman went back inside the building and took the west freight elevator to the fifth floor to get a better view of the motorcade. Bonnie Ray Williams joined them on the fifth floor.

Norman identified himself in a picture of the upper stories of the front of the TSBD Building taken by newspaper photographer, Thomas C. Dillard, immediately after the assassination. Norman said he was in the window immediately under the window where Brennan stated the gunman fired the rifle. In the window immediately to Harold Norman's right was Bonnie Ray Williams. James Jarman Jr. was in the next pair of windows immediately to the west.

Although in Dillard's picture it appears that Harold Norman is standing up, he stated that he was in a squatting or "hunched over" position at the time the motorcade went by. (The bottoms of the large warehouse windows come relatively close to the floor.)[1]

Mr. Ball. Now you saw the President go by, did you?

Mr. Norman. Yes.

Mr. Ball. What happened then?

Mr. Norman. About the time that he got past the window where I was, well, it seems as though he was, I mean you know, brushing his hair. Maybe he was looking to the public.

Mr. McCloy. Saluting?

Mr. Norman. Yes.

Mr. Ball. With which arm?

Mr. Norman. I believe it was his right arm, and I can't remember what the exact time was but I know I heard a shot, and then after I heard the shot, well, it seems as

---

[1]This is why Brennan was confused when he testified that he thought the fifth floor employees as well as the gunman in the southeast corner of the sixth floor were all in a standing position. Actually, none of the fifth floor employees was standing, and we are sure that the gunman was not standing, for otherwise he could not have been firing through the lower portion of the window, which was open.

though the President, you know, slumped or something, and then another shot and I believe Jarman or someone told me, he said, "I believe someone is shooting at the President," and I think I made a statement "It is someone shooting at the President, and I believe it came from up above us."

Well, I couldn't see at all during the time but I know I heard a third shot fired, and I could also hear something sounded like the shell hulls hitting the floor and the ejecting of the rifle, it sounded as though it was to me.

Mr. Ball. How many shots did you hear?

Mr. Norman. Three.

Mr. Ball. Do you remember whether or not you said anything to the men then as to whether or not you heard anything from above you?

Mr. Norman. Only I think I remember saying that I thought I could hear the shell hulls and the ejection of the rifle. I didn't tell I think I hear anybody moving, you know.

Mr. Ball. Did anybody say anything as to where they thought the shots came from?

Mr. Norman. Well, I don't recall of either one of them saying they thought where it came from.

Mr. Ball. But you did?

Mr. Norman. Yes.

Mr. Ball. And you said you thought it came from where?

Mr. Norman. Above where we were, above us.

Mr. Ball. Did you see any dust or dirt falling?

Mr. Norman. I didn't see any falling but I saw some in Bonnie Ray Williams' hair.

Mr. Ball. Did anybody say anything about it?

Mr. Norman. I believe Jarman told him that it was in his hair first. Then I, you know, told him it was and I believe Jarman told him not to brush it out of his hair but I think he did anyway.

Mr. Ball. After that happened, what did you do?

Mr. Norman. Well, we ran to the farthest window facing the expressway.

Harold Norman stated that the window was on the west side of the building at the southwest corner of the fifth floor.

Mr. Ball. Why did you run down to that window?

Mr. Norman. Well, it seems as though everyone else was running towards the railroad tracks, and we ran over there. Curious to see why everybody was running that way for. I thought maybe—

Mr. Ball. Did anybody say anything about going up to the sixth floor?

Mr. Norman. I don't remember anyone saying about going up to the sixth floor.

Joe Ball then questioned Harold Norman about a statement that Secret Service agent Carter had taken on Dec. 4, 1963.

Mr. Ball. The document that I have here shows the date 4th of Dec., 1963. Do you remember having made a statement to Mr. Carter, Special agent of the Secret Service, on that day?

Mr. Norman. I can't remember the exact date but I believe I remember Mr. Carter.

Mr. Ball. I want to call your attention to one part of the statement and I will ask you if you told him that:

"Just after the President passed by, I heard a shot and several seconds later I heard two more shots. I knew that the shots had come from directly above me, and I could hear the expended cartridges fall to the floor. I could also hear the bolt action of the rifle. I also saw some dust fall from the ceiling of the fifth floor and I felt sure that whoever had fired the shots was directly above me."

Did you make that statement to the Secret Service man?

Mr. Norman. I don't remember making a statement that I knew the shots came from directly above us. I didn't make that statement. And I don't remember saying I heard several seconds later. I merely told him that I heard three shots because I didn't have any idea what time it was.

Mr. Ball. I see. Did you tell them that you heard the bolt action of the rifle?

Mr. Norman. Yes.

Mr. Ball. And that you heard the expended cartridges fall to the floor?

Mr. Norman. Yes; I heard them making a sound.

Mr. McCloy. You used the expression you heard the ejection. This refers to the bolt action?

Mr. Norman. Yes.

Mr. Ball. Do you remember Friday that we conducted an experiment to see whether or not you could hear?

Mr. Norman. Yes, sir.

Mr. Ball. From the sixth floor?

Mr. Norman. Yes.

Mr. Ball. And where did you put yourself in order to conduct the experiment?

Mr. Norman. In the same window. I may not have been in the same position but I was in the same window.

Mr. Ball. What did you hear on the fifth floor?

Mr. Norman. Well, I heard the same sound, the sound similar. I heard three something that he dropped on the floor and then I could hear the rifle or whatever he had up there.

Mr. Ball. You could hear the rifle, the sound of an ejection?

Mr. Norman. Yes, sir.

Mr. Ball. Did you hear the sound of the bolt going back and forth?

Mr. Norman. Yes, sir; I sure did.

Mr. Ball. You could hear it clearly, could you?

Mr. Norman. Yes, sir.

Mr. Ball. Now there has been a new floor put in on the sixth floor, hasn't there?

Mr. Norman. Yes, sir.

Mr. Ball. The day that you were there on Nov. 22, what was the condition of the ceiling and the floor of the sixth floor?

Mr. Norman. I would say that you could see daylight through there because during the times they put the plywood down you can see the plywood, some portion of the plywood, so I would say you could see a little daylight during that time.

Mr. Ball. When you were there Friday afternoon, did you look up at the ceiling from where you were sitting at the southeast window on the fifth floor?

Mr. Norman. Yes, sir.

Mr. Ball. What could you see on the ceiling?

Mr. Norman. There was one place I could see the plywood and then another place you could still see a little daylight, I mean peering through the crack.

Mr. Ball. What about the joint where the upper floor or the floor of the sixth and ceiling of the fifth floor comes against the wall. Could you see daylight through there?

Mr. Norman. Against the wall?

Mr. Ball. Yes.

Mr. Norman. Yes; in one place you could see a small amount of daylight.

Mr. Ball. Now the day of the experiment last Friday when you heard the cartridges eject, the bolt action and the cartridges ejecting—

Mr. Norman. Yes.

Mr. Ball. Was there any noise outside?

Mr. Norman. Yes; there was.

Mr. Ball. What was it?

Mr. Norman. There was a train and there were trucks and cars.

Mr. Ball. Was there more noise or less noise on the day you conducted the experiment last Friday, Mar. 20, than on Nov. 22, at 12:30?

Mr. Norman. It was more noisy last Friday than it was Nov. 22.

Mr. Ball. Was there any train going by on Nov. 22?

Mr. Norman. No, sir.

Mr. Ball. Were there any trucks going by on Nov. 22?

Mr. Norman. No, sir.

Finally, Harold Norman testified that 10 or 15 minutes after the first shot he came down from the fifth floor to the first floor and went out the front door, where he remembered seeing Mr. Brennan wearing a steel helmet talking to a policeman on the front steps of the TSBD Building.

The Chairman. Did you see Brennan down there when you came downstairs? Did you come out the front door?

Mr. Norman. Yes, sir; I came out the front door and I remember seeing Mr. Brennan.

Mr. Belin. About how long after the shooting was that?

Mr. Norman. It wasn't very long because—I can't remember the time but it wasn't too long a period of time, and I remember seeing him because he had on a steel helmet, a little steel helmet.

Representative Ford. Was he standing with another man and they called you over?

Mr. Norman. I don't know if he was exactly standing with another man, but it was several people standing around there, and I remember him talking and I believe I remember him saying that he saw us when we first went up to the fifth floor window, he saw us then. I believe I heard him say that, but otherwise I don't know if he was standing by. There was quite a few people standing around there.

The Chairman. Then did you go out of the building, away from the building or come back?

Mr. Norman. No, sir; we had to go back inside.

The Chairman. You had to go back?

Mr. Norman. Yes, sir.

Mr. Ball. And then came back?

Mr. Norman. Yes, sir.

Mr. Ball. After you had gone to the first floor?

Mr. Norman. Yes, sir.

Representative Ford. Did law enforcement officers make you go back or did you do it on your own initiative?

Mr. Norman. I remember, I don't know if this is the only time or not, but I remember the law enforcement saying not to let anybody leave from the building and I can't remember if that is the time we went back in the building or before or what.

Mr. Ball. Who did you go out with?

Mr. Norman. I know James Jarman and I went out. I can't remember.

Thus, Brennan was correct in his identification of Harold Norman as one of the two people from the fifth floor whom he saw on the front steps of the TSBD Building after the assassination. But what about James Jarman Jr.? Did he also leave the building after the assassination as Harold Norman claimed? And did Williams, who was in the window next to Norman, corroborate the testimony of Norman about hearing the bolt action of the rifle and the sound of the shells hitting the floor?

18

"AN ELEPHANT COULD WALK BY THERE AND YOU COULD NOT SEE HIM"

In some respects the plaza itself is queer. It rather resembles a crude baseball diamond built on a slope. The green is fan-shaped and flanked by curious little white concrete bleachers whose real function is obscure. They can only be meant to be ornamental. On most days the spectacle is quite boring—all you can see is the statuary, stagnant pools on either side, and three noisy streams of automobiles—and anyone anxious for a good view would ignore them and ascend to an upper floor of one of the adjacent buildings. The most prominent of these is the sore-eyed, tan brick structure at the corner of Houston and Elm which began as railroad offices, became a branch of the John Deere Plow Company, served later as the headquarters of a wholesaler for fancy groceries, and was converted, early in the 1960's, to a warehouse for the Texas School Book Depository. The interior is grimy, the two freight elevators are temperamental. But if you really want a proper perspective of the Dealey Memorial, the northeast window on the sixth floor of the warehouse is incomparable.

The only thing wrong with William Manchester's description in his book, *The Death of a President,* is that you cannot see Dealey Plaza from the *"northeast* window on the sixth floor of the warehouse" of the TSBD Building. But if you go to the *southeast* corner window of the sixth floor, the view "is incomparable" indeed.

On the morning of Nov. 22, 1963, the area around that window was shielded from the rest of the floor by cartons of books stacked in a semicircle in that corner. The shield had been constructed by employees who started to lay a new plywood floor moving from the west side of the building to the east. Bonnie Ray Williams was one of those employees.

Mr. Williams was 20 years old, married, and a high school graduate. He obtained a job at the TSBD around Sept. 8, 1963. Generally, his duties were to check, pack and fill orders. However, during November 1963, he and several other employees helped lay a new plywood floor over the old floor on the fifth floor. Several days before Nov. 22 these employees went to the sixth floor to lay a new plywood floor there.

Mr. Ball. Before you started to lay the floor, did you have to move any cartons?
Mr. Williams. Yes; we did.
Mr. Ball. From what part of the sixth floor did you move the cartons?
Mr. Williams. We moved cartons from, I believe, the west side of the sixth floor to the east side of the sixth floor, because I think there was a vacancy in there.

Commission Exhibit No. 723.
Shield of cartons of books around the sixth floor southeast corner window of TSBD Building. The shield had been constructed by employees who started to lay a new plywood floor, moving from the west side of the sixth floor to the east.

Williams said five employees were laying the floor on the sixth floor. At five or ten minutes before noon, they quit. Williams and another TSBD employee, Charles Givens, took the east freight elevator; the other employees took the west elevator and the two groups raced each other to the first floor.

Williams went to the first floor, washed, got his sack lunch in the Domino Room, purchased a soft drink from a vending machine, and then went back upstairs to the sixth floor to eat his lunch. He said that his lunch was in a small-sized paper bag and contained bread, some "chicken on the bone" and a bag of Fritos.

Mr. Ball. Why did you go to the sixth floor?

Mr. Williams. Well, at the time everybody was talking like they was going to watch from the sixth floor. I think Bill Lovelady said he wanted to watch from up there. And also my friend; this Spanish boy, by the name of Danny Arce, we had agreed at first to come back up to the sixth floor. So I thought everybody was going to be on the sixth floor.

Mr. Ball. Did anybody go back?

Mr. Williams. Nobody came back up. So I just left.

Mr. Ball. Where did you eat your lunch?

Mr. Williams. I ate my lunch—I am not sure about this, but the third or fourth set of windows, I believe . . . facing Elm Street on the sixth floor.

Mr. Dulles. And you were all alone?

Mr. Williams. Yes, sir.

Mr. Ball. What did you sit on while you ate your lunch?

Mr. Williams. First of all, I remember there was some boxes behind me. I just kind of leaned back on the boxes first. Then I began to get a little impatient, because there wasn't anyone coming up. So I decided to move to a two-wheeler.

Mr. Ball. A two-wheeler truck, you mean?

Mr. Williams. Yes, sir. I remember sitting on this two-wheeler.

By that time, I was through, and I got up and I just left then.

Mr. Dulles. How much of the room could you see as you finished your lunch there? Was your view obstructed by boxes of books, or could you see a good bit of the sixth floor?

Mr. Williams. Well, at the time I couldn't see too much of the sixth floor, because the books at the time were stacked so high. I could see only in the path that I was standing—as I remember, I could not possibly see anything to the east side of the building.

But just one aisle, the aisle I was standing in, I could see just about to the west side of the building. So far as seeing to the east and behind me, I could only see down the aisle behind me and the aisle to the west of me.

Williams said that he was eating his lunch at "about twelve" noon.

Mr. Ball. Did you see anyone else up there that day?

Mr. Williams. No, I did not.

Mr. Ball. How long did you stay there?

Mr. Williams. I was there from—five, ten, maybe twelve minutes.

Mr. Ball. Finish your lunch?

Mr. Williams. Yes, sir. No longer than it took me to finish the chicken sandwich.

Mr. Ball. Did you eat the chicken?

Mr. Williams. Yes, I did.

Mr. Ball. Where did you put the bones?

Mr. Williams. I don't remember exactly, but I think I put some of them back in the sack. Just as I was ready to go I threw the sack down.

Mr. Ball. What did you do with the sack?

Mr. Williams. I think I just dropped it there.

Mr. Ball. Anywhere near the two-wheeler?

Mr. Williams. I think it was.

Mr. Ball. What did you do with the Dr. Pepper bottle?

Mr. Williams. Just set it down on the floor.

Williams said that he had taken the east elevator from the first floor to the sixth floor. The west elevator can be worked by a pushbutton if all the gates are down, but the east elevator will not work unless someone on the elevator is operating it.

Mr. Ball. Where did you intend to go when you left the sixth floor?

Mr. Williams. I intended to stop on the fifth floor, and if there wasn't anyone there, I intended to get out of the building, to outside.

Mr. Ball. Why did you stop on the fifth floor?

Mr. Williams. To see if there was anyone there.

Mr. Ball. Did you know there was anyone there before you started down?

Mr. Williams. Well, I thought I heard somebody walking, the windows moving or something. I said maybe someone is down there, I said to myself. And I just went on down.

Mr. Ball. Did you find anybody there?

Mr. Williams. As I remember, when I was walking up, I think Harold Norman and James Jarman—as I remember, they was down facing the Elm Street on the fifth floor, as I remember.

There were two freight elevators in the north part of the building that were "back to back." Williams said he took the east elevator to the fifth floor and when he left the elevator both elevators were on the fifth floor, although he had no definite memory on this point.

He did not remember the exact time he left the sixth floor. Williams testified that after he went to the fifth floor, "I was there a while before it [the motorcade] came around."

Mr. Ball. You were at what window?

Mr. Williams. Well, I believe we was on the east side of the window, and I think Hank was—I think he was directly under the sixth floor window where Oswald was supposed to have shot the President from. And I think I was a window over. And I think James Jarman was two or three windows over.

He said that as the motorcade went by, he was by the window next to Harold Norman, in a squatting position.

Mr. Ball. Now tell us what happened after the President's car had passed your window.

Mr. Williams. After the President's car had passed my window, the last thing I remember seeing him do was, you know—it seemed to me he had a habit of pushing his hair back. The last thing I saw him do was he pushed his hand up like this. I assumed he was brushing his hair back. And then the thing that happened then was a loud shot—first I thought they were saluting the President, somebody—even maybe a motorcycle backfire. The first shot—there was two shots rather close together. The second and the third shot was closer together than the first shot and the second shot, as I remember.

Mr. Ball. Now, was your head out the window?

Mr. Williams. I could not say for sure. I do not remember.

Mr. Ball. Did you notice—where did you think the shots came from?

Mr. Williams. Well, the first shot—I really did not pay any attention to it, because I did not know what was happening. The second shot, it sounded like it was right in the building, the second and third shot. And it sounded—it even shook the building, the side we were on. Cement fell on my head.

Mr. Ball. You say cement fell on your head?

Mr. Williams. Cement, gravel, dirt, or something, from the old building, because it shook the windows and everything. Harold was sitting next to me, and he said it came right from over our head. If you want to know my exact words, I could tell you.

Mr. Ball. Tell us.

Mr. Williams. My exact words were, "No bull shit." And we jumped up.

Mr. Ball. Norman said what?

Mr. Williams. He said it came directly over our heads. "I can even hear the shell being ejected from the gun hitting the floor." But I did not hear the shell being ejected from the gun, probably because I wasn't paying attention.

Mr. Ball. Norman said he could hear it?

Mr. Williams. He said he could hear it. He was directly under the window that Oswald shot from.

Mr. Ball. After he made the statement that you mentioned, he thought it came from overhead, and you made some statement, did Jarman say anything?

Mr. Williams. I think Jarman, he—I think he moved before any of us. He moved towards us, and he said, "Man, somebody is shooting at the President." And I think I said again, "No bull shit." And then we all kind of got excited, you know, and, as I remember, I don't remember him saying that he thought the shots came from overhead. But we all decided we would run down to the west side of the building.

Mr. Ball. You ran down to the west side of the building?

Mr. Williams. Yes; we were on the fifth floor, the east side of the building. We saw the policemen and people running, scared, running—there are some tracks on the west side of the building, railroad tracks. They were running towards that way. And we thought maybe—well, to ourself, we know the shots practically came from over our head. But since everybody was running, you know, to the west side of the building, towards the railroad tracks, we assumed maybe somebody was down there. And so we all ran that way, the way that the people was running, and we was looking out the window.

Mr. Ball. When the cement fell on your head, did either one of the men notice it and say anything about it?

Mr. Williams. Yes, sir. I believe Harold was the first one.

Mr. Ball. That is Hank Norman?

Mr. Williams. I believe he was the first one. He said "Man, I know it came from there. It even shook the building." He said, "You got something on your head." And then James Jarman said, "Yes, man, don't you brush it out." By that time I just forgot about it. But after I got downstairs I think I brushed it out anyway.

Mr. Ball. Jarman is called Junior?

Mr. Williams. Yes, sir. . . .

Mr. Ball. Could you see light through the floor from the fifth to the sixth floor as you would look above your window?

Mr. Williams. Well, at the time, that day of Nov. 22, I did not notice that. But the other day when you were questioning me, even after the thick new floor that was put over the old floor on the sixth floor, well, you still could see light. And the new floor extended a little beyond the old floor. So therefore I would say that you could see light much more when the old floor was there.

Representative Ford asked the witness: "Why didn't you go up to the sixth floor?"

Mr. Williams gave a forthright reply: "I really don't know. We just never did think about it. And after we had made this last stop, James Jarman said, 'Maybe we better get the hell out of here.' And so we just ran down to the fourth floor, and came on down. We never did think about it, going up to the sixth floor. Maybe it was just because we were frightened."

Joe Ball asked Williams whether or not he heard anything at all upstairs. Williams replied, "No, sir; I didn't hear anything."

Mr. Ball. Any footsteps?

Mr. Williams. No, sir. Probably the reason we didn't hear anything is because, you know, after the shots we were running, too, and that was making a louder noise.

Mr. Dulles. Could I ask one question in connection with your last question?

Did you hear either of the elevators going up or down while you were eating your meal?

Mr. Williams. No, sir; I did not.

Mr. Dulles. If an elevator had come to that floor, would you have heard it then?

Mr. Williams. That all depends—

Mr. Dulles. Were they noisy elevators? The operation of the doors and so forth?

Mr. Williams. Yes, sir. The elevator that I came up on to the sixth floor, if you would listen—say you were listening for the boss, you could hear, because you would be paying attention. The elevator is worked by hand pedal. When you release the hand pedal, it makes a noise. It bangs—or maybe you can hear the old elevator when it is first coming up. But at that time I did not hear anything.

Now we come to one of the most crucial portions in the testimony of Williams. You have heard both Norman and Williams say that shortly after the shots were fired they ran from the southeast portion of the fifth floor to the *west* portion of the fifth floor because they saw all the people running toward the railroad tracks. There is a stairway in the northwest corner of the TSBD Building that runs from the seventh floor down to the first floor. To get downstairs from the top floor, someone either had to use the stairway or one of the two freight elevators. According to an FBI report signed by two FBI agents, on Nov. 23, Mr. Williams told them that while they were standing in the *southwest* portion of the fifth floor they would have seen anyone coming down from the sixth floor by way of the stairs.

Here is the testimony of Mr. Williams when he was interrogated about this FBI report:

Mr. Ball. They reported that you told them on the 23d of November that you and

Hank, that is Hank Norman, isn't it—

Mr. Williams. Yes, sir.

Mr. Ball. And Junior—that is Junior Jarman—were standing where they would have seen anyone coming down from the sixth floor by way of the stairs. Did you tell them that?

Mr. Williams. I could not possibly have told him that, because you cannot see anything coming down from that position.

Mr. Ball. And that you did not see anyone coming down.

Mr. Williams. No, sir. An elephant could walk by there and you could not see him.

In our visit in Dallas on Mar. 20, we had a photographer on the fifth floor take a picture from where Williams said he was standing with the camera pointing toward the stairway. It was impossible to see the stairway because there was a series of shelves extending from the floor almost to the ceiling and extending east from the west wall of the stairway, completely blocking the view of the stairway from the southwest corner of the fifth floor.

Mr. Ball. You saw these pictures taken?

Mr. Williams. Yes, sir.

Mr. Ball. Where was the camera?

Mr. Williams. The camera was located about the exact place I was standing looking out this window.

Mr. Dulles. How long has that shelving been there—for quite a long while? Or was it put there recently?

Mr. Williams. I think it was there from the time I started, as far as I can remember. . . .

Mr. Ball. Did you hear anyone going up or down the stairs?

Mr. Williams. No, I didn't.

Mr. Ball. Did you pay any attention to that?

Mr. Williams. No, sir.

Mr. Ball. As you were standing at the window, did you hear any footsteps?

Mr. Williams. No, sir.

Mr. Ball. Up above—hear any movement up above?

Mr. Williams. No, sir; I don't remember.

Mr. Ball. Were you paying any attention whether or not there was anyone up above?

Mr. Williams. No, sir; we wasn't paying any attention.

Mr. Ball. Now, in this FBI report that we have dated the 23d of November, 1963, the report that you said that someone might have been coming down on the elevator and you would not have noticed that. Did you say that?

Mr. Williams. I think I remember saying that.

Mr. Ball. After you stood at the west window for a while, what did you do?

Mr. Williams. After we stood at the west window for a while, we decided to go down. Then we left.

Mr. Ball. How did you go down?

Mr. Williams. By stairs.

Mr. Ball. Where did you go?

Mr. Williams. We went to the fourth floor first. Then we paused for a minute there, where we saw these women looking out of the window. Then we decided to go down to the first floor, and we ran on down.

Williams said that he did not recall how much time elapsed between his hearing the first shot and going to the first floor, although he thought it could be approximately 15 minutes. When he got to the first floor, "The first thing I noticed was that the policeman had rushed in."

Mr. McCloy. Do you know whether or not anybody got out of the building before the police could get there, did any of your friends or the people you were working with, did you hear whether any of them had left the building before the building was closed?

Mr. Williams. Yes, sir; I heard Mr. Truly—he said that—he mentioned that—he said, "Where is Lee?" That is what everybody called him. "Where is Lee?", he said, and therefore I assume he did not know where Lee was, that he was out of the building, because everybody else was there. And there was another colored fellow by the name of Charles Givens. He wasn't in the building at the time. He was downtown somewhere.

Mr. McCloy. Had he been at the building at the time of the shooting—Givens?

Mr. Williams. I don't believe he had.

Mr. Dulles. What did Mr. Truly say about Lee not being there?

Mr. Williams. The only thing I heard him say is—I think an officer asked him, "Is everyone here?" And he said, "Where is Lee?"—like that, you know.

Mr. Dulles: Mr. Truly said that?

Mr. Williams: Yes, sir.

19

"WE STARTED ASKING EACH OTHER, HAVE YOU SEEN LEE OSWALD"

"After the third shot was fired, I think I got up and I run over to Harold Norman and Bonnie Ray Williams, and told them, I said, I told them that it wasn't a backfire or anything, that somebody was shooting at the President."

Mr. Ball. And then did they say anything?

Mr. Jarman. Hank said, Harold Norman, rather, said that he thought the shots had come from above us, and I noticed that Bonnie Ray had a few debris in his head. It was sort of white stuff, or something, and I told him not to brush it out, but he did anyway.

Mr. Ball. He had some white what, like plaster?

Mr. Jarman. Like some come off a brick or plaster or something.

Mr. Ball. Did Norman say anything else that you remember?

Mr. Jarman. He said that he was sure that the shot came from inside the building because he had been used to guns and all that, and he said it didn't sound like it was too far off anyway. And so we ran down to the west side of the building.

The witness was James Jarman Jr., who had worked for the TSBD Company on a regular basis since 1961. Among fellow employees he was known as "Junior" (the only employee with that nickname).

He was 34 years old, married and had had a tenth-grade education.

According to Mr. Jarman, he had a conversation with Lee Harvey Oswald on the morning of Nov. 22 concerning the motorcade. Jarman stated that the conversation took place between 9:30 and 10:00 AM on the first floor of the TSBD Building.

Mr. Ball. And what was said by him and by you?

Mr. Jarman. Well, he was standing up in the window and I went to the window also, and he asked me what were the people gathering around on the corner for, and I told him that the President was supposed to pass that morning, and he asked me did I know which way he was coming, and I told him, yes; he probably come down Main and turn on Houston and then back again on Elm.

Then he said, "Oh, I see," and that was all.

Mr. Ball. Did you talk to him again?

Mr. Jarman. No, sir.

Mr. Jarman said that he quit for lunch about five minutes to twelve, went to the restroom and washed, "Got my sandwich" and went up to the second floor lounge to get a bottle of soda, and then went back down to the first floor where he ate his lunch.

Mr. Ball. Were you with anybody when you were walking around finishing your sandwich?

Mr. Jarman. No; I wasn't. I was trying to get through so I could get out on the street.

Mr. Ball. Did you see Lee Oswald?

Mr. Jarman. No; I didn't.

Mr. Ball. After his arrest, he stated to a police officer that he had had lunch with you. Did you have lunch with him?

Mr. Jarman. No, sir; I didn't.

Jarman said he then went out in front of the building and that he and Harold Norman went back up to the fifth floor at around 12:20 or 12:25 PM. They took the west elevator to the fifth floor and then went to the windows in the southeast corner where they watched the motorcade. Jarman said that he was on his knees at the time the motorcade was passing.

Mr. Ball. What did you hear him [Harold Norman] say?

Mr. Jarman. He said it was something sounded like cartridges hitting the floor, and he could hear the action of the rifle, I mean the bolt, as it were pulled back, or something like that.

Mr. Ball. Had you heard anything like that?

Mr. Jarman. No, sir; I hadn't.

Mr. Ball. Had you heard any person running upstairs?

Mr. Jarman. No, sir.

Mr. Ball. Or any steps upstairs?

Mr. Jarman. No, sir.

Mr. Ball. Any noise at all up there?

Mr. Jarman. None.

Mr. Jarman said that he did not remember any of the elevators coming up or down as he was standing at the west window.

Mr. Jarman verified the obstruction of the stairway by the bookshelves (as did Harold Norman).

Mr. Ball. What did you men do after you looked out the window toward the railroad tracks from the west window?

Mr. Jarman. Well, after Norman had made his statement that he had heard the cartridges hit the floor and his bolt action, I told him we'd better get the hell from up here.

Mr. Ball. Did anybody suggest you go up to the sixth floor?

Mr. Jarman. No, sir.

Jarman testified that after the assassination, he and Harold Norman went out the front door for a time and that he remembered seeing Brennan outside the building.

Mr. Ball. Where did you see him first?

Mr. Jarman. He was talking to a police officer.

Mr. Ball. How was he dressed?

Mr. Jarman. He was dressed in construction clothes.

Mr. Ball. Anything else, any other way to describe him?

Mr. Jarman. Well, he had on a silverlike helmet.

Mr. Ball. Hard-hat?

Mr. Jarman. Yes, sir.

Mr. Ball. Did you stay out there very long?

Mr. Jarman. Just a few minutes.

Mr. Ball. Then where did you go?

Mr. Jarman. We heard him talking to this officer about that he had heard these shots and he had seen the barrel of the gun sticking out the window, and he said that the shots came from inside the building, and I told the officer that I believed that they came from inside the building also, and then he rushed us back inside.

Mr. Ball. The officer did?

Mr. Jarman. Yes, sir.

Mr. Ball. How did you know this fellow was Brennan?

Mr. Jarman. Well, at that time I didn't know him at all.

Mr. Ball. Have you learned that since?

Mr. Jarman. Yes, sir.

Mr. Ball. Who told you that the man in the hard-hat was Brennan?

Mr. Jarman. Well, they have had him down there at the building a couple of times.

Mr. Ball. Were you taken to the police station?

Mr. Jarman. Yes, sir.

Mr. Ball. Did you make a statement?

Mr. Jarman. Yes, sir.

Mr. Ball. When?

Mr. Jarman. That Saturday morning.

Mr. Ball. The next day?

Mr. Jarman. Yes, sir.

Mr. Ball. How long did you stay in the building, the Texas School Book Depository Building that afternoon?

Mr. Jarman. I'd say it was somewhere between two and two-thirty when they turned us loose and told us to go home.

Mr. Ball. When you were there did you notice whether any of the employees were missing?

Mr. Jarman. Yes, sir.

Mr. Ball. When did you notice, and who was missing?

Mr. Jarman. When we started to line up to show our identification, quite a few of us asked where was Lee. That is what we called him, and he wasn't anywhere around. We started asking each other, have you seen Lee Oswald, and they said no.

Mr. Ball. Was there anybody else missing?

Mr. Jarman. Yes.

Mr. Ball. Who?

Mr. Jarman. Charles Douglas Givens, I believe.

When I took the testimony of Givens, he said that he went outside during the noon hour and watched the motorcade from the corner of Main and Record, two blocks from the TSBD Building. He heard three shots. With two friends, "We broke and ran down that way, and by the time we got to the corner down there of Houston and Elm, everybody was running, going toward the underpass over there by the railroad tracks.

And we asked—I asked someone—some white fellow there, "What happened?"

And he said, "Somebody shot the President." Like that. So I stood there for a while, and I went over to try to get to the building after they found out the shots came from there, and when I went over to try to get back in the officer at the door wouldn't let me in.

Mr. Belin. Did you tell him you worked there?

Mr. Givens. Yes; but he still wouldn't let me in. He told me he wouldn't let no one in.

Mr. Belin. This was the front of Elm Street?

Mr. Givens. Yes. So I goes back over to the parking lot and I wait until I seen Junior.

Mr. Belin. Is that Jarman?

Mr. Givens. Yes. They were on their way home, and they told me that they let them all go home for the evening, and I said, "I'd better go back and get my hat and coat."

So I started over there to pick up my hat and coat, and Officer Dawson saw me and he called me and asked me was my name Charles Givens, and I said, "yes."

And he said, "We want you to go downtown and make a statement."

And he puts me in the car and takes me down to the city hall and I made a statement to Will Fritz down there.

As for the other missing TSBD Building employee, Lee Harvey Oswald, he was also picked up by the Dallas police—but as you jurors know, under entirely different circumstances.

20

"HOWEVER, THE THOUGHT EVIDENTLY NEVER OCCURRED TO THEM"

Members of the jury, you will now hear the testimony of other witnesses at the scene of the assassination who said they saw a rifle. But before turning to these witnesses, you might be interested to see how the assassination sensationalists have treated the testimony of Brennan, Norman, Williams and Jarman. There are two basic techniques: distortion by omission and distortion by commission.

The first technique is illustrated in the Lane–de Antonio film: There is nothing in the film about Brennan, Norman, Williams or Jarman. The failure to include any of these key witnesses in such a film is a typical example of distortion by omission.

On the other hand, in his book, *Rush to Judgment,* Lane writes on page 90:

Later that day, however, when Brennan was confronted with Williams, Jarman and Norman in the hearing room and was asked to select the two whom he saw on November 22, whether at the window or coming out of the building, he was unable to make an identification. "I don't know which of those two," he said. "No; I won't say for sure. I can't tell which of those two it was . . . I saw two but I can't identify which one it was." The Commission found nonetheless that Brennan's statements constituted an identification: "When the three employees appeared before the Commission, Brennan identified the two whom he saw leave the building."

This is a typical example of distortion by commission. You have seen the actual testimony. You have seen that Brennan immediately identified Harold Norman. At first, he was not sure whether Bonnie Ray Williams or James Jarman Jr. was the other employee he saw. You have seen that I tried deliberately to trip up Brennan and asked him, "Could it have been neither one of these persons that you saw?" Brennan immediately replied: "I think it was one of them. I think it was this boy on the end," which was Norman, and he said that he believed the other person was Jarman. He asked whether he was right. Joe Ball immediately replied, "I don't know."

At that time, we did not know. But we found out subsequently when we interrogated all three employees that the two who left the building immediately afterward were Norman and Jarman, and that they remembered seeing Brennan talking to one of the officers in front of the building.

The assertion by Lane that Brennan ". . . was unable to make an identification" of any of the employees watching the motorcade from the fifth floor is another example of the distortions permeating the purported "brief for the defense" of Mr. Lane and the other post-assassination sensationalists' literature.

You members of the jury might pause and consider a matter that I am sure by now is readily apparent to you. Whereas it takes only a few sentences to assert a lie, it may take 10 or 20 pages to disclose all of the facts that disprove the lie.

This is the big advantage that an assassination sensationalist has in a film, a magazine interview, a television interview or a public debate. In 15 minutes of talk, he can make 15 false allegations, all of which may sound plausible to any person who does not have all the facts.

It may take 15 minutes to reply fully to just two or three of these false allegations. And generally the detailed assertion underlying the truth is not nearly as intriguing as the assertion of the falsity.

Just as we have seen the distortion and misrepresentation concerning Brennan's identification of the employees watching the motorcade from the fifth floor, just as we have seen the misrepresentation about the paraffin test, and just as we have determined the facts involving the cause of Lee Harvey Oswald's arrest, we can look at every other piece of sensationalist post-assassination literature and refute all of the attacks made upon the conclusions of our Warren Commission Report. The bedrock of this refutation lies in the Report and the 26 volumes of testimony and exhibits that form the foundation for our conclusions.

However, in this book I do not plan to take the several thousand pages necessary to give a detailed refutation of each of the misrepresentations of the assassination sensationalists. Rather, my primary goal is to give you jurors an inside view of the heart of the evidence through the testimony of key witnesses so that you can reach your own verdict. At the same time, I want you to understand from an inside view of the Warren Commission how we conducted our investigation and I want collaterally to expose the techniques that had been used to deceive, all too successfully, the jury of world opinion.

Here is another example in Lane's book (at page 105):

Norman, Jarman and Williams stated that they knew just after the last shot at the latest that it was an assassination attempt. If they believed that the shots came from overhead, they might have rushed upstairs to confront the assassin. Since he was presumably armed, they might not have wished to do so. However, the thought evidently never even occurred to them. Representative Gerald R. Ford asked Williams, "Why didn't you go up to the sixth floor?" Williams replied, "We just never did think about it."

One of the reasons I have included the entire testimony of these witnesses is to illustrate the technique of the sensationalists. Let us go back to the original testimony you have just read. You will remember that portion involving the question proposed by Representative Ford to Bonnie Ray Williams: "Why didn't you go up to the sixth floor?"

You will also remember Mr. Williams' forthright reply: "I really don't know. We just never did think about it. And after we had made this last stop, James Jarman said, 'Maybe we better get the hell out of here.' And so we just ran down to the fourth floor, and came on down. We never did think about it, going up to the sixth floor. Maybe it was just because we were frightened."

Thus, Lane uses only the sentence, "We never did think about it, going up to the sixth floor," and omits the next sentence, "Maybe it was just because we were frightened." The omission is all the more reprehensible because Lane has just stated: "Since he [the assassin] was presumably armed, they might not have wished to do so. However, the thought evidently never even occurred to them."

To all of this distortion, Lane adds his standard tactic of the "smear." Thus, on pages 104-105 of his book, Lane asserts with reference to the testimony of Harold Norman, Bonnie Ray Williams and James Jarman, Jr.:

Long before they appeared in front of the Commission, the official story had placed the source of the shots above the heads of these three men. They lived in the intolerant climate of Dallas; they were questioned by Commission counsel who addressed them as "boys." It is not unreasonable to conclude that many forces combined to impose on their testimony a uniform fidelity to the official view.

Having read this testimony yourself, I think that you would agree that the testimony shows fidelity to the truth rather than the imposition of any "official view." Such a false charge by Lane is typical of what virtually every assassination sensationalist does when he finds himself in a corner: He grasps for the "smear."

Our Warren Commission Report will stand the test of the final verdict of the jury of world opinion because it is basically accurate and because there are more than 6,500 footnotes in our 888-page Report, which are grounded in the 26 volumes of testimony and exhibits. When you examine every one of these footnotes you will find that there is none of the misrepresentation and distortion of the type Lane uses when he alleges that Brennan could not identify the two Negro men that he saw in the fifth floor window who came out of the building after the assassination. Nor will you find any distortion of the type used by Lane when he fragments the testimony and omits Williams' forthright statement about why he did not go to the sixth floor, "Maybe it was just because we were frightened."

In our final Report, we summarized Brennan's testimony in approximately three and a half pages. Although we included most of the salient facts, a summary of this nature does not give the reader an insight into the way the witness actually testified, as you jurors have just seen.

The ultimate decision we had to make was what to do with Brennan's eyewitness identification of Lee Harvey Oswald as the assassin. Brennan made this identification under oath. Nevertheless, because of an inherent skepticism that both Joe Ball and I had of the overall weight to be given to eyewitness identification, we did not rely on Brennan's identification of Oswald, even though Brennan could identify the two employees who ran out of the building from the fifth floor. Here is the crucial paragraph in the final Report:

Although the record indicates that Brennan was an accurate observer, he declined to make a positive identification of Oswald when he first saw him in the police lineup. The Commission, therefore, does not base its conclusion concerning the identity of the assassin on Brennan's subsequent certain identification of Lee Harvey Oswald as the man he saw fire the rifle. Immediately after the assassination, however, Brennan described to the police the man he saw in the window and then identified Oswald as the person who most nearly resembled the man he saw. The Commission is satisfied that, at the least, Brennan saw a man in the window who closely resembled Lee Harvey Oswald, and that Brennan believes the man he saw was in fact Lee Harvey Oswald.

Now that you have had an opportunity to read Brennan's testimony as well as the testimony of Harold Norman, Bonnie Ray Williams, and James Jarman Jr., how would you have written this paragraph?

21

"THERE IS THE GUN"

Picture a Presidential motorcade heading west on Main Street in downtown Dallas. At Houston Street, the lead car turns right and heads to the north. One block away is the front of the Texas School Book Depository Building at the northwest corner of the intersection of Houston and Elm Streets. At this intersection, the lead car makes a sharp reflex angle turn to the left and heads southwest on an entrance to the freeway. As the front cars of the motorcade make their turn and head to the southwest, the back cars of the motorcade are still going north on Houston Street.

Four members of the press were riding in one of the rear cars of the motorcade: Robert Jackson, Malcolm Couch, James Underwood and Thomas Dillard. At the time the shots were fired, the convertible car in which these four men were riding was heading north on Houston Street toward the front of the TSBD Building. It had not yet turned the corner.

Bob Jackson saw the rifle being withdrawn into the building from the assassination window. He yelled out, "There is the gun." The three others verified hearing this statement. One of them, Malcolm Couch, also looked up in time to see the rifle being withdrawn. Another, Dillard, took two photographs of the upper portion of the TSBD Building, one with a telephoto lens of the sixth floor southeast corner window. By the time the picture was taken, the assassin had disappeared from the window, although the three employees watching the motorcade from the southeast corner of the fifth floor were visible.

The fact that this picture was taken corroborates Jackson's testimony that he saw a rifle being withdrawn; otherwise, there would have been no occasion for a press photographer to make two pictures of the upper portion of the TSBD Building. You can see these pictures on pages 66 and 67 of the Warren Commission Report. They are vital evidence confirming the fact that the shots came from that window in the TSBD Building.

Here is the heart of the testimony of these four men: First, Robert H. Jackson, photographer for *The Dallas Times Herald*. Jackson was sitting in the back seat of a Chevrolet convertible with the top down. By prearrangement he was to toss a roll of film to another newspaper employee at the intersection of Main and Houston Streets.

Mr. Jackson. Well, on Main, as we neared Houston Street everyone was more or less in a relaxed state in our car, because we were near the end of the route, I guess, nothing unusual happened on Main Street.

The final block on Main, before we turned on Houston, I was in the process of unloading a camera and I was to toss it out of the car as we turned right on Houston Street to one of our reporters.

Mr. Specter. Had that been set up by prearrangement?

Mr. Jackson. Yes, sir. And that I did as we turned the corner, and when—it was in an interval and as I threw it out the wind blew it, caught it and blew it out into the street and our reporter chased it out into the street and the photographers in our car, one of the photographers, was a TV cameraman whom I do not recall his name, and he was joking about the film being thrown out and he was shooting my picture of throwing the film out.

. . . as our reporter chased the film out into the street, we all looked back at him and were laughing, and it was approximately that time that we heard the first shot, and we had already rounded the corner, of course, when we heard the first shot. We were approximately almost half a block on Houston Street.

Jackson marked on a Commission exhibit where he thought the automobile was at this point—on Houston Street about half-way between Main and Elm.

Mr. Jackson. Right here approximately. And as we heard the first shot, I believe it was Tom Dillard from Dallas News who made some remark as to that sounding like a firecracker, and it could have been somebody else who said that. But someone else did speak up and make that comment and before he actually finished the sentence we heard the other two shots. Then we realized or we thought that it was gunfire, and then we could not at that point see the President's car. We were still moving slowly, and after the third shot the second two shots seemed much closer together than the first shot, than they were to the first shot. Then after the last shot, I guess all of us were just looking all around and I just looked straight up ahead of me which would have been looking at the School Book Depository and I noticed two Negro men in a window straining to see directly above them, and my eyes followed right on up to the window above them and I saw the rifle or what looked like a rifle approximately half of the weapon, I guess I saw, and just as I looked at it, it was drawn fairly slowly back into the building, and I saw no one in the window with it.

I didn't even see a form in the window.

Mr. Specter. What did you do next?

Mr. Jackson. I said "There is the gun," or it came from that window. I tried to point it out. But by the time the other people looked up, of course, it was gone, and about that time we were beginning to turn the corner.

Mr. Specter. Which corner were you beginning to turn?

Mr. Jackson. Houston onto Elm.

Mr. Specter. I now show you a photograph marked as Commission Exhibit No. 348 and ask you if you can identify what that depicts?

Mr. Jackson. This is the School Book Depository. This is the window the two colored men were looking out of. This is the window where the rifle was.

The window where the rifle was, according to Jackson, was in the southeast sixth floor of the building—immediately above the window that "the two colored men" (Harold Norman and Bonnie Ray Williams) were looking out of.

James R. Underwood was the assistant news director and a photographer for television station KRLD in Dallas. He was riding in the front seat of the convertible.

Mr. Ball. From the time you turned, tell me what you observed after you made the turn at Main and Houston to drive north on Houston.

Mr. Underwood. After we turned onto Houston Street, the car I was in was about, as far as I can remember, about in the middle of the block or a little bit north of the center of the block, which is a short block, when I heard the first shot.

Mr. Ball. Between Main and Elm?

Mr. Underwood. Yes; between Main and Elm, closer to the Elm intersection, Elm and Houston intersection, when I heard the first shot fired. I thought it was an explosion. I have heard many rifles fired but it did not sound like a rifle to me. Evidently must have been a reverberation from the buildings or something. I believe I said to one of the other fellows it sounds like a giant firecracker and the car I was in was about in the intersection of Elm and Houston when I heard a second shot fired and moments later a third shot fired and I realized that they were by that time, the last two shots, I realized they were coming from overhead.

Mr. Ball. You realized they were coming from overhead and that would be from what source?

Mr. Underwood. That would be from the Texas School Book Depository Building.

Mr. Ball. It sounded like they were coming from that direction?

Mr. Underwood. Yes, sir; the last two. Now, the first was just a loud explosion but it sounded like a giant firecracker or something had gone off. By the time the third shot was fired, the car I was in stopped almost through the intersection in front of the Texas School Book Depository Building and I leaped out of the car before the car stopped. Bob Jackson from the Herald said he thought he saw a rifle in the window and I looked where he pointed and I saw nothing. Below the window he was pointing at, I saw two colored men leaning out there with their heads turned toward the top of the building, trying, I suppose, to determine where the shots were coming from.

Mr. Ball. What words did you hear Bob Jackson say?

Mr. Underwood. I don't know that I can remember exactly except I did hear him say words to the effect that "I saw a rifle" and I looked at that instant and I saw nothing myself. If he saw a rifle, I did not.

Mr. Ball. At that point when you looked, where was your car?

Mr. Underwood. Our car was in the intersection, in the intersection of Elm and Houston Street.

Mr. Ball. Had it made the turn yet?

Mr. Underwood. It had partially made the turn or had just begun to make the turn. Frankly, I was looking up and around and I saw at the same time people falling on the ground down the street toward the underpass and my first impression was some of these people falling to the ground had been shot.

Mr. Ball. Did your car stop?

Mr. Underwood. Our car stopped and the minute it stopped I leaped out of the car.

Tom Dillard, chief photographer of *The Dallas Morning News,* was also riding in the convertible in the right front seat.

Mr. Ball. Did you hear something unusual as you were driving north on Houston?

Mr. Dillard. Yes; I heard an explosion which I made the comment that I believe, in my memory, I believe I said, "My God, they've thrown a torpedo" and why I said "torpedo," I don't know. If you wish, I'll go ahead—

Mr. Ball. Go ahead with your story.

Mr. Dillard. Well, then I later estimated, immediately later, estimated, oh, 4, about 3 or 4 seconds, another explosion and my comment was, "No, it's heavy rifle fire," and I remember very distinctly I said, "It's very heavy rifle fire."

Mr. Ball. How many explosions did you hear?

Mr. Dillard. I heard three—the three approximately equally spaced.

Mr. Ball. What is the best estimate of the position of your car with reference to the turn at Main and Houston when you heard the first explosion?

Mr. Dillard. Perhaps, oh, just a few feet around the corner and it seems we had slowed a great deal. It seems that our car had slowed down so that we were moving rather slowly and perhaps just passed the turn when I heard the first explosion.

Mr. Ball. Did you hear anyone in your car say anything?

Mr. Dillard. Well, after the third shot I know my comment was, "They killed him." I don't know why I said that but Jackson—there was some running comment about what can we do or where is it coming from and we were all looking. We had an absolutely perfect view of the School Depository from our position in the open car, and Bob Jackson said, "There's a rifle barrel up there." I said, "Where?" I had my camera ready. He said, "It's in that open window." Of course, there were several open windows and I scanned the building.

Mr. Ball. Which building?

Mr. Dillard. The School Depository. And at the same time I brought my camera up and I was looking for the window. Now, this was after the third shot and Jackson said, "There's the rifle barrel up there," and then he said it was the second from the top in the right-hand side, and I swung to it and there was two figures below, and I just shot with one camera, 100-mm. lens on a 35-mm. camera which is approximately a two times daily photo twice normal lens and a wide angle on a 35-mm. which took in a considerable portion of the building and I shot those pictures in rapid sequence with the two cameras.

Mr. Ball. You shot how many pictures?

Mr. Dillard. Two pictures.

Mr. Ball. With one camera or two different cameras?

Mr. Dillard. Two different cameras—one daily photo, not extreme daily photo, but twice the normal lens.

Mr. Ball. You say your cameras were ready? How were they ready?

Mr. Dillard. Hung around my neck and held in my hand.

Malcolm Couch, television news cameraman with Station WFFA-TV, was sitting in the back seat of the convertible. He testified:

I remember I was talking and we were laughing and I was looking back to a fellow on my—that would be on my right—I don't know who it was—we were joking. We had just made the turn. And I heard the first shot.

Mr. Belin. What happened—or what did anyone say?

Mr. Couch. As I recall, nothing—there was no particular reaction; uh—nothing unusual. Maybe everybody sort of looked around a little, but didn't think much of it. And—uh—then, in a few seconds, I guess from 4-5 seconds later, or even less, we heard the second shot. And then we began to look—uh, not out of thinking necessarily it was a gunshot, but we began to look in front of us—in the motorcade in front of us. And, as I recall, I didn't have any particular fears or feelings at the second shot. By the third shot, I felt that it was a rifle. Almost sure it was. And, as I said, the shots or the noises were fairly close together, they were fairly even in sound—and—uh, by then one could recognize, or if he had heard a high-powered rifle, he would feel that it was a high-powered rifle. You would get that impression.

Mr. Belin. Do you remember where your vehicle was by the time you heard the third shot?

Mr. Couch. I'd say we were about 50 feet from making—or maybe 60 feet—from making the left-hand turn onto Elm.

Mr. Belin. Did you hear more than three shots?

Mr. Couch. No.

Mr. Belin. Had you heard any noises, what you'd describe like a motorcycle backfiring or firecrackers, prior to the time that you made your turn north onto Houston?

Mr. Couch. Well, way uptown on Main Street, a motorcycle did backfire right beside us—and we all jumped and had a good laugh over it. And the three shots sounded, at first—the first impression was that this was another motorcycle backfiring.

Mr. Belin. Now, between the first and the second shots, is there anything else you remember doing or you remember hearing or seeing that you haven't related here at this time?

Mr. Couch. Nothing unusual between the shots. Uh—as I say, the first shot, I had no particular impression; but the second shot, I remember turning—several of us turning—and looking ahead of us. It was unusual for a motorcycle to backfire that close together, it seemed like. And after the third shot, Bob Jackson, who was, as I recall, on my right, yelled something like, "Look up in the window! There's the rifle!"

And I remember glancing up to a window on the far right, which at the time impressed me as the sixth or seventh floor, and seeing about a foot of a rifle being—the barrel brought into the window.

I saw no one in that window—just a quick 1-second glance at the barrel.

Mr. Belin. In what building was that?

Mr. Couch. This was the Texas Book Depository Building.

Mr. Belin. At the corner of Houston and Elm in Dallas?

Mr. Couch. That's right.

Mr. Belin. You said it was the sixth or the seventh floor. Do you know how many floors there are in that building—or did you know at that time?

Mr. Couch. No; I didn't know at that time.

Mr. Belin. Did it look like to you he was on the top floor or next to the top floor or the second to the top floor—or—

Mr. Couch. It looked like it was the top. And when you first glance at the building, you're thrown off a little as to the floors because there's a ridge—uh, it almost looks like a structure added onto the top of the building, about one story above. So, you have to recount.

Of course, at the time, I wasn't counting, but—

Mr. Belin. You just remember, to the best of your recollection, that it was either the sixth or seventh floor?

Mr. Couch. That's right.

Mr. Belin. And when you say, "the far right"—

Mr. Couch. That would be the far east.

Mr. Belin. The far east of what side of the building?

Mr. Couch. The south side of the building.

Mr. Belin. Do you remember whether or not that window at which you saw the rifle, you say, being withdrawn—first of all, could you tell it was a rifle?

Mr. Couch. Yes, I'd say you could. Uh—if a person was just standing on the—as much as I saw, if the factors that did happen, did not happen, you might not say that it was a rifle. In other words, if you just saw an object being pulled back into a window, you wouldn't think anything of it. But with the excitement intense right after that third shot and what Bob yelled, my impression was that it was a rifle.

Mr. Belin. Did you see anything more than a steel barrel of a rifle?

Mr. Couch. No.

Mr. Belin. Could you tell whether or not the rifle had any telescopic sight on it?

Mr. Couch. No.

Mr. Belin. Did you see any of the stock of the rifle?

Mr. Couch. No.

Mr. Belin. Did you see any person pulling the rifle?

Mr. Couch. No.

Mr. Belin. Do you remember whether or not, if you can remember, the window was open or halfway open or what?

Mr. Couch. It was open. To say that it was half or three-quarters open, I wouldn't say. My impression was that it was all the way open—but that was an impression.

Mr. Belin. Did you see anything else in the window that you remember—any boxes or anything like that?

Mr. Couch. No; I didn't.

Our manner of interrogation of all these witnesses is typified by the following exchange in the concluding portion of my examination of Malcolm Couch:

Mr. Belin. Now, Mr. Couch, shortly before we commenced taking this deposition, you and I met for the first time. Is that correct?

Mr. Couch. That's correct.

Mr. Belin. And then we came to this room and we chatted for a few minutes before we started taking a formal deposition. Is that correct?

Mr. Couch. That's correct.

Mr. Belin. Now, is there anything that we talked about pertaining to the assassination that in any way differs or conflicts with the testimony that you have just given?

Mr. Couch. No; no.

Mr. Belin. What is the fact as to whether or not I questioned you in great detail about each question or whether or not I just asked you to relate the story to me?

Mr. Couch. You asked me to give general highlight impressions before we began.

Mr. Belin. And then, after you gave those to me, we started taking the deposition—is that correct?

Mr. Couch. That's correct.

Mr. Belin. And then you repeated on the deposition what we had talked about—is that right?

Mr. Couch. That's right—in more detail.

Mr. Belin. Is there anything else that you can think of at this time which, in any way, would affect the investigation of the assassination of President Kennedy?

Mr. Couch. No; I cannot think of anything.

Amos Lee Euins was a 15-year-old ninth-grade student at the time of the assassination. He was standing on the corner of Houston and Elm as the motorcade passed.

Mr. Specter. Tell us what you saw as the motorcade went by.

Mr. Euins. I was standing here on the corner. And then the President come around the corner right here. And I was standing here. And I was waving, because there wasn't hardly no one on the corner right there but me. I was waving. He looked that way and he waved back at me. And then I had seen a pipe, you know, up there in the window, I thought it was a pipe, some kind of pipe.

Mr. Specter. When had you first seen that thing you just described as a pipe?

Mr. Euins. Right as he turned the corner here.

Mr. Specter. Now, exactly where did you see that thing you have described as a pipe come from? And take a good look now before you tell us where it was.

Mr. Euins. Right here.

The witness placed on a picture of the TSBD Building an X on the southeast corner window on the sixth floor.

Mr. Specter. Proceed to tell us what happened, Amos.

Mr. Euins. Then I was standing here, and as the motorcade turned the corner, I was facing, looking dead at the building. And so I seen this pipe thing sticking out the window. I wasn't paying too much attention to it. Then when the first shot was fired, I started looking around, thinking it was a backfire. Everybody else started looking around. Then I looked up at the window, and he shot again. So—you know this fountain bench here, right around here. Well, anyway, there is a little fountain right here. I got behind this little fountain, and then he shot again.

So after he shot again, he just started looking down this, you know.

Mr. Specter. Who started looking down that way?

Mr. Euins. The man in the window. I could see his hand, and I could see his other hand on the trigger, and one hand was on the barrel thing.

Mr. Specter. Now, at the time the second shot was fired, where were you looking then?

Mr. Euins. I was still looking at the building, you know, behind this—I was looking at the building.

Mr. Specter. Looking at anything special in the building?

Mr. Euins. Yes, sir. I was looking where the barrel was sticking out.

Mr. Specter. How many shots did you hear altogether?

Mr. Euins. I believe there was four, to be exact.

Mr. Specter. Now, where were you looking at the time of the third shot, if you remember?

Mr. Euins. After he shot the first two times, I was just standing back here. And then after he shot again, he pulled the gun back in the window. And then all the police ran back over here in the track vicinity . . .

Mr. Specter. Now, when the third shot occurred, Amos, let me ask you again, where were you looking then?

Mr. Euins. I was still down here, looking up at the building.

Mr. Specter. What did you see in the building?

Mr. Euins. I seen a bald spot on this man's head, trying to look out the window. He had a bald spot on his head. I was looking at the bald spot. I could see his hand, you know, the rifle laying across in his hand. And I could see his hand sticking out on the trigger part. And after he got through, he just pulled it back in the window.

Mr. Specter. Did you see him pull it back in the window?

Mr. Euins. Yes, sir.

Euins said that he started walking toward the railroad tracks and he came to where a policeman was standing

. . . and told the policeman I had seen the shot, because they were looking at the railroad tracks. So he put me on the cycle and he went to here.

Mr. Specter. He put you on the cycle and took you where?

Mr. Euins. Up to the front of the building.

Mr. Specter. The Texas School Book Depository Building?

Mr. Euins. Yes, sir; and then he called some more cars. They got all around the building. And then the policemen came from the tracks, and they got around the building.

Mr. Specter. Did you see the policemen come from the tracks to go around the building?

Mr. Euins. Yes, sir.

Mr. Specter. Amos, would you tell us everything that you can remember about what you saw about the gun itself?

Mr. Euins. Well, when I first got here on the corner, the President was coming around the bend. That is when—I was looking at the building then.

Mr. Specter. What did you think it was when you first saw it?

Mr. Euins. I thought it was a piece of pipe or something sticking out the window.

Mr. Specter. Did it look like it was a piece of metal to you?

Mr. Euins. Yes, sir; just a little round piece of pipe.

Mr. Specter. About an inch in diameter, would you say?

Mr. Euins. Yes, sir.

Mr. Specter. And how long was the piece of pipe that you saw?

Mr. Euins. It was sticking out about that much.

Mr. Specter. About 14 or 15 inches?

Mr. Euins. Yes, sir. And then after I seen it sticking out, after awhile, that is when I heard the shot, and everybody started looking around.

Mr. Specter. At that time, Amos, did you see anything besides the end of the pipe?

Mr. Euins. No, sir.

Mr. Specter. For example, you didn't see anything about a stock or any other part of the rifle?

Mr. Euins. No, sir—not with the first shot. You see, the President was still right along down in here somewhere on the first shot.

Mr. Specter. Now, when you saw it on the first occasion, did you think it was a rifle then? Or did that thought enter your mind?

Mr. Euins. No, sir; I wasn't thinking about it then. But when I was looking at it, when he shot, it sounded like a high-powered rifle, after I listened to it awhile, because I had been in the NDCC for about a year.

Mr. Specter. What is NDCC?

Mr. Euins. We call it a military army for the boys, at our school.

Mr. Specter. Is that ROTC?

Mr. Euins. Yes, sir.

Mr. Specter. ROTC. And have you had any opportunity to fire a weapon in that ROTC class?

Mr. Euins. No, sir; not outside of just .22's. We fire them on the firing range.

Mr. Specter. Now, when you looked up at the rifle later, you described seeing some of the trigger part.

Mr. Euins. Yes, sir.

Mr. Specter. Now, describe as fully as you can for us what you saw then, Amos.

Mr. Euins. Well, when he stuck it out, you know—after the President had come on down the street further, you know he kind of stuck it out more, you know.

Mr. Specter. How far was it sticking out of the window would you say then, Amos?

Mr. Euins. I would say it was about something like that.

Mr. Specter. Indicating about 3 feet?

Mr. Euins. You know—the trigger housing and stock and receiver group out the window.

Mr. Specter. I can't understand you, Amos.

Mr. Euins. It was enough to get the stock and receiving house and the trigger housing to stick out the window.

Mr. Specter. Now, what direction was the rifle pointing?

Mr. Euins. Down—what did you say—Elm?

Mr. Specter. Elm Street?

Mr. Euins. Yes, sir; down Elm.

Mr. Specter. Was it pointing in the direction of the President?

Mr. Euins. Yes, sir.

Mr. Specter. Now, could you see anything else on the gun?

Mr. Euins. No, sir; I could not.

Mr. Specter. For example, could you see whether or not there was a telescopic lens on the gun?

Mr. Euins. No, sir.

Mr. Specter. Now, is there anything else about the gun that you can describe to us that you have not already told us about?

Mr. Euins. No, sir.

Mr. Specter. Now, what kind of a look, if any, did you have at the man who was there?

Mr. Euins. All I got to see was the man with a spot in his head, because he had his head something like this.

Mr. Specter. Indicating his face down, looking down the rifle?

Mr. Euins. Yes, sir; and I could see the spot on his head.

Mr. Specter. How would you describe that man for us?

Mr. Euins. I wouldn't know how to describe him, because all I could see was the spot and his hand.

Mr. Specter. Was he slender or was he fat?

Mr. Euins. I didn't get to see him.

Mr. Specter. Could you tell from where you looked whether he was tall or short?

Mr. Euins. No.

Mr. Specter. Of what race was he, Amos?

Mr. Euins. I couldn't tell, because these boxes were throwing a reflection, shaded.

Mr. Specter. Could you tell whether he was a Negro gentleman or a white man?

Mr. Euins. No, sir.

Mr. Specter. Couldn't even tell that? But you have described that he had a bald—

Mr. Euins. Spot in his head. Yes, sir; I could see the bald spot in his head.

Mr. Specter. Now, could you tell what color hair he had?

Mr. Euins. No, sir.

Mr. Specter. Could you tell whether his hair was dark or light?

Mr. Euins. No, sir.

Mr. Specter. How far back did the bald spot on his head go?

Mr. Euins. I would say about right along in here.

Mr. Specter. Indicating about 2 1/2 inches above where your hairline is. Is that about what you are saying?

Mr. Euins. Yes, sir; right along in here.

Mr. Specter. Now, did you get a very good look at that man, Amos?

Mr. Euins. No, sir; I did not.

Mr. Specter. Were you able to tell anything about the clothes he was wearing?

Mr. Euins. No, sir.

The Dallas Sheriff's Department had an affidavit signed by Euins in which Euins said that the man in the window had been a white man. However, when questioned about that, he testified that:

I told the man that I could see a white spot on his head, but I didn't actually say it was a white man. I said I couldn't tell. But I saw a white spot in his head.

Mr. Specter. Your best recollection at this moment is you still don't know whether he was a white man or a Negro? All you can say is that you saw a white spot on his head?

Mr. Euins. Yes, sir.

Mr. Specter. Then, did you tell the people at the police station that he was a white man, or did they make a mistake when they wrote that down here?

Mr. Euins. They must have made a mistake, because I told them I could see a white spot on his head.

On the other hand, Underwood, the TV director and cameraman, thought that he heard a "little colored boy whose last name I remember as 'Eunice'" talking with an officer on a motorcycle right after the assassination:

Mr. Ball. Euins?

Mr. Underwood. It may have been Euins. It was difficult to understand when he said his name. He was telling the motorcycle officer he had seen a colored man lean out of the window upstairs and he had a rifle. He was telling this to the officer and the officer took him over and put him in a squad car. By that time, motorcycle officers were arriving, homicide officers were arriving and I went over and asked this boy if he had seen someone with a rifle and he said "Yes, sir." I said, "Were they white or black?" He said, "It was a colored man." I said, "Are you sure it was a colored man?" He said, "Yes, sir" and I asked him his name and the only thing I could understand was what I thought his name was Eunice.

Mr. Ball. Was he about 15?

Mr. Underwood. I couldn't tell his age; looked to me to be younger. I would have expected him to be about 10 or 11 years old.

In stature, Euins was relatively small for his age. When I first saw him, I thought that he was younger than 15 or 16.

In all probability, Underwood did see Euins, but if this is true, we have a contradiction between Underwood's testimony and the testimony of Euins and Dallas Police Sergeant Harkness, whom you jurors will soon hear. Euins said he could not tell whether the man was white or black, and Sergeant

Harkness corroborates this testimony of Euins, but Underwood is sure that Euins said the man with the rifle was colored. Of course, Brennan said the man was a white man.

Sergeant Harkness testified that after the assassination he went into the crowd along Elm Street "and asked did anyone see any place where the shots came from, and there was an unidentified person pointed to him, said this boy here saw it, saw the shots, where the shots came from. . . ."

The boy was Amos Euins.

Mr. Belin. Then what did he say?

Mr. Harkness. He told me the shots came from the window under the ledge . . . of the School Book Depository.

The information Harkness called on the radio was that the witness said shots came from the "fifth floor, Texas Book Depository Store at Houston and Elm." I asked Sergeant Harkness: "What were the exact words of the witness?"

Mr. Harkness. The exact words of the witness, "It was under the ledge," which would put it on the sixth floor. It was my error in a hasty count of the floors.

When I specifically asked Sergeant Harkness, "Did your witness ever say whether the person he saw at the window was a white man or Negro?", Sergeant Harkness replied: "He just told me, he just said he couldn't identify him. That is what he told me."

There were two other witnesses who saw someone in the southeast corner window of the sixth floor of the TSBD Building seconds before the assassination: 25-year-old Ronald B. Fischer, an auditor for Dallas County, and his friend, Robert E. Edwards, who were standing on the corner of Houston and Elm as the motorcade approached. I asked Fischer to describe what he saw "as you were standing on the curb."

. . . about 10 or 15 seconds before the first car came around that corner, Bob punched me and said, "Look at that guy there in that window." And he made some remark—said, "He looks like he's uncomfortable"—or something.

And I looked up and I watched the man for, oh, I'd say, 10 or 15 seconds. It was until the first car came around the corner of Houston and Main. And, then, when that car did come around the corner, I took my attention off of the man in the window and started watching the parade. The man held my attention for 10 or 15 seconds, because he appeared uncomfortable for one, and secondly, he wasn't watching—uh—he didn't look like he was watching for the parade. He looked like he was looking down toward the Trinity River and the triple underpass down at the end—toward the end of Elm Street. And—uh—all the time I watched him, he never moved his head, he never—he never moved anything. Just was there transfixed.

Mr. Belin. In what window did you see the man?

Mr. Fischer. It was the corner window on Houston Street facing Elm, in the fifth or sixth floor. . . .

Mr. Belin. Do you remember anything about the man? Could you describe his appearance at all? First of all, how much of him could you see?

Mr. Fischer. I could see from about the middle of his chest past the top of his head . . . as you're looking toward that window, he was in the lower right portion of the window. He seemed to be sitting a little forward. . . . he had on an open-neck shirt, but it—uh—could have been a sport shirt or a T-shirt. It was light in color; probably white, I couldn't tell whether it had long sleeves or whether it was a short-sleeved shirt, but it was open-neck and light in color.

Uh—he had a slender face and neck—uh—and he had a light complexion—he was a white man. And he looked to be 22 or 24 years old.

Mr. Belin. Do you remember anything about the color of his hair?

Mr. Fischer. His hair seemed to be—uh—neither light nor dark; possibly a light—well, possibly a—well, it was a brown was what it was; but as to whether it was light or dark, I can't say.

Mr. Belin. Did he have a thick head of hair or did he have a receding hairline—or couldn't you tell?

Mr. Fischer. I couldn't tell. He couldn't have had very long hair, because his hair didn't seem to take up much space—of what I could see of his head. His hair must have been short and not long.

Mr. Belin. Well, did you see a full view of his face or more of a profile of it, or what was it?

Mr. Fischer. I saw it at an angle but, at the same time, I could see—I believe I could see the tip of his right cheek as he looked to my left.

Mr. Belin. Now, could you be anything more definite as to what direction he was looking at?

Mr. Fischer. He looked to me like he was looking straight at the triple underpass.

Mr. Belin. Down what street?

Mr. Fischer. Elm Street.

Mr. Belin. Down Elm?

Mr. Fischer. Toward the end of Elm Street.

Mr. Belin. As it angles there and goes under the triple underpass there?

Mr. Fischer. Yes, sir.

Mr. Belin. Could you see his hands?

Mr. Fischer. No.

Mr. Belin. Could you see whether or not he was holding anything?

Mr. Fischer. No; I couldn't see.

Mr. Belin. Could you see any other objects in the window?

Mr. Fischer. There were boxes and cases stacked all the way from the bottom to the top and from the left to the right behind him. It looked—uh—it's possible that there weren't cases directly behind him because I couldn't see because of him. But—uh—all the rest of the window—a portion behind the window—there were boxes. It looked like there was space for a man to walk through there between the window and the boxes. But there were boxes in the window, or close to the window there.

Mr. Belin. Could you see any other people in any other windows there that you remember?

Mr. Fischer. I couldn't see any other people in the windows. I don't remember seeing any others.

Mr. Belin. By this, do you mean that you are sure there were none, or that you just do not remember seeing any?

Mr. Fischer. I don't remember seeing any.

Mr. Belin. Now, after you saw the man, then the motorcade turned onto Houston from Main—is that correct?

Mr. Fischer. Yes.
Mr. Belin. Did you ever see the man again in the window?
Mr. Fischer. No.
Mr. Belin. Did you ever look back at the window?
Mr. Fischer. I never looked back at the window.

A week or so later, a policeman brought out a picture and asked Fischer to try and identify the man in the picture.

Mr. Belin. Whose picture did they say it was?
Mr. Fischer. Well, they actually showed me two pictures—one of Lee Harvey Oswald, and one of Jack Ruby.
Mr. Belin. All right. And what did you say?
Mr. Fischer. I told them that that could have been the man.
Mr. Belin. Now, which one did you say could have been the man?
Mr. Fischer. Lee Harvey Oswald. That could have been the man that I saw in the window of the School Book Depository Building, but that I was not sure. It's possible that a man fit the general description that I gave—but I can't say for sure.
Mr. Belin. Was there anything different—do you remember the picture?—between the picture you saw and the man you saw in the window?
Mr. Fischer. Yes; one thing—and that is in the picture he looked like he hadn't shaved in several days at least. And—uh—I don't know whether at that distance, looking at him from the street in the School Book Depository Building—if I could have been able to—if I could have seen that. I think, if he had been unshaven in the window, it would have made his complexion appear—well—rather dark; but I remember his complexion was light; that is, unless he had just a light beard.
Mr. Belin. Was the sun shining on his face when you saw him in the window or not—or don't you remember?
Mr. Fischer. No; uh—no, the sun wasn't shining on his face. He was back in the shadow of the window.
Mr. Belin. When did the policeman come out with this picture—on the same day or on the next day?
Mr. Fischer. No; it was—uh—no, it was several days after. I can't remember whether it was a week or 2 weeks or—it was at least a week. I don't remember exactly when it was but it was a week, at least.
Mr. Belin. Let me ask you this: Was there anything else different between the man you saw in the picture and the man you saw in the window?
Mr. Fischer. (Pausing before reply.) No.

I concluded my examination with my standard series of questions.

Mr. Belin. All right. Is there anything else you can think of that bears on the assassination, or anything you saw or did or heard that you haven't related here?
Mr. Fischer. (Pausing before reply.) No.
Mr. Belin. Did you say "No"?
Mr. Fischer. No—I can't think of anything.
Mr. Belin. Shortly before this interview began, you and I met for the first time—is that correct?
Mr. Fischer. Yes.
Mr. Belin. And we first chatted a few minutes about what you saw before we started taking your testimony on the record?

Mr. Fischer. Yes.

Mr. Belin. What is the fact as to whether or not I asked you to tell me your story or whether or not, instead, I asked you questions and tried to, in any way, lead you—or so forth?

Mr. Fischer. I answered the questions as I think that I saw the events happen—as I saw the events happen. I was not quizzed on what to say or anything of that nature. I've merely related what I think that I saw.

Mr. Belin. Is there anything that you told me of before we started taking the deposition that has not been included in this deposition—that you can think of?

Mr. Fischer. [Pausing before reply.] No; not that I can think of.

Robert E. Edwards was a college senior who was working at the Dallas County Court House at the time of the assassination.

He said that he looked at the south side of the TSBD Building shortly before the motorcade came by.

Mr. Belin. What did you see?

Mr. Edwards. Nothing of importance except maybe one individual who was up there in the corner room of the sixth floor which was crowded in among boxes.

Mr. Belin. You say on the sixth floor?

Mr. Edwards. Yes.

Mr. Belin. What portion of the sixth floor as you looked at the building, to your right or to your left?

Mr. Edwards. To my right.

Mr. Belin. How near the corner?

Mr. Edwards. The corner window.

Mr. Belin. The corner window there?

Mr. Edwards. Right.

Mr. Belin. Could you describe this individual at all? Was he a white man or a Negro?

Mr. Edwards. White man.

Mr. Belin. Tall or short, if you know?

Mr. Edwards. I couldn't say.

Mr. Belin. Did he have anything in his hand at all that you could see?

Mr. Edwards. No.

Mr. Belin. Could you see his hands?

Mr. Edwards. I don't remember.

Mr. Belin. What kind of clothes did he have on?

Mr. Edwards. Light colored shirt, short sleeve and open neck.

Mr. Belin. How much of him could you see? Shoulder up, waist up, knees up, or what?

Mr. Edwards. From the waist on. From the abdomen or stomach up.

Mr. Belin. Was the man fat, thin, or average in size?

Mr. Edwards. Oh, about average. Possibly thin.

Mr. Belin. Could you tell whether he was light skinned or medium skin or what, if you could tell?

Mr. Edwards. No.

Mr. Belin. Was the sun shining in or not, if you know?

Mr. Edwards. Don't know.

Mr. Belin. Was the sun out that day?

Mr. Edwards. Yes.

Mr. Belin. What color hair did the man have?

Mr. Edwards. Light brown.

Mr. Belin. Light brown hair?

Mr. Edwards. That is what I would say; yes, sir.

Mr. Belin. Did you see any other people on the sixth floor?

Mr. Edwards. No.

Mr. Belin. Did you notice whether or not there were any, or just did you look and see any?

Mr. Edwards. I noticed that there—I just didn't see any.

Mr. Belin. What about the next floor above? Did you see any people on the floor above?

Mr. Edwards. No.

Mr. Belin. What about on any floors below? See any people on the fifth floor?

Mr. Edwards. No.

Mr. Belin. Fourth floor?

Mr. Edwards. No.

Mr. Belin. Third floor?

Mr. Edwards. Possibly.

Mr. Belin. Second floor?

Mr. Edwards. I believe so.

Mr. Belin. First floor?

Mr. Edwards. I don't know.

I then asked Edwards if he remembered what he said to his friend, Ronald Fischer, as he saw the man in the sixth-floor window.

Mr. Edwards. I made a statement to Ronny that I wondered who he was hiding from since he was up there crowded in among the boxes, in a joking manner.

Mr. Belin. You mean you said it in a joking manner?

Mr. Edwards. Yes.

Mr. Belin. What did Fischer say to you?

Mr. Edwards. I don't recall what he said, but I know that we said a few things. It wasn't of any importance at the time. And we looked up at him, both of us.

Mr. Belin. How long did you look at him?

Mr. Edwards. Just a few seconds.

Mr. Belin. Then what took your attention away, if any, or did you just start looking somewhere else?

Mr. Edwards. Started looking somewhere else.

Mr. Belin. How long after that did the motorcade come by?

Mr. Edwards. Thirty seconds or a minute.

Mr. Belin. Anything else that you can remember that you or Ronald Fischer said?

Mr. Edwards. No.

Mr. Belin. Anything else you can think of that might be relevant at all?

Mr. Edwards. No.

Now, members of the jury, let us pause a moment. Howard Brennan said he saw a man fire a rifle from the southeast corner of the sixth floor of the TSBD Building. One of the witnesses in the fifth floor immediately below testified that he heard the cartridge cases hitting the floor. Amos Euins said he saw a rifle in the window. Robert Jackson testified he saw a rifle in the upper portion of the building. The fact that Dillard took two photographs of the building corroborated Jackson's testimony. Otherwise, there would have been no reason for Dillard to aim his camera and take a picture of the building and a telephoto-lens picture of the upper portion of the southeast corner of the building.

The testimony of Brennan is that the man in the window resembled Lee Harvey Oswald. The testimony of Edwards and Fischer is that the man had a general description that would be similar to that of Oswald.

However, I caution you to withhold reaching conclusions at this point. In the first place, you have not yet learned what evidence, if any, was found inside the upper floors of the TSBD Building. And in the second place, even if there was a rifleman in that place this doesn't preclude the possibility of there having been another rifleman somewhere else. And, even if you should find that all of the shots came from that portion of the TSBD Building, your ultimate verdict is not where the shots were fired from but who fired the shots.

One final note: You have heard the testimony of four witnesses, all of whom were riding in the same car at the same time. Because of their profession as news photographers, I think we could assume that all of them would have above-average ability to recall their observations. Yet, I am sure you will notice discrepancies in their testimony.

For instance, you will remember that Tom Dillard said that he heard the first explosion ". . . just a few feet around the corner and it seemed we had slowed a great deal." On the other hand, Robert Jackson said that when they heard the first shot, "We were approximately almost half a block on Houston Street." He also said the car was moving slowly.

Underwood said that he heard the first shot about half-way between Main and Elm on Houston. Malcolm Couch said that he heard the first shot about 15 or 20 feet from the turn.

In other words, of these four witnesses, two say they heard the first shot when their car was in the middle of the block and two say that they heard the first shot just after completing the turn from Main onto Houston.

This is a typical example of what I stated at the outset: Whenever there are two or more witnesses to a single event, you will always get at least two different versions of what happened.

However, there is one thing upon which each of the photographers agreed: His duty as a photographer for his employer was more important than his duty as a citizen to contact immediately the first police officer he saw and advise the officer of the source of the shots.

The Chevrolet convertible in which these four photographers were riding came to a stop just as it turned the intersection of Elm and Houston in front of the TSBD Building. Dallas policemen were stationed on the street in front of the TSBD Building, as they were stationed on the street throughout the motorcade route. Had any one of these four photographers contacted any of the nearby policemen, the TSBD Building could have been sealed off within a minute or two after the assassination. Had this been done, perhaps Dallas Police Officer J. D. Tippit would be alive today.

And the real irony is that one of these four cameramen—Robert Jackson—won a Pulitzer Prize because he wanted a picture of Lee Harvey Oswald as Oswald was being escorted through the basement of the Dallas Police Building and at the time Jackson took the picture, Jack Ruby darted forward and fired a shot into Oswald. For this, Jackson received one of the highest awards that can be bestowed on a member of the press.

But as citizens of the United States, Jackson should share with his three colleagues a last-place award in failing to do first whatever was possible to help catch a gunman firing at their President.

22

"THE WANTED PERSON IN THIS IS A SLENDER WHITE MALE, ABOUT 30"

I am sure that for you jurors the next step is obvious: We had better go inside the TSBD Building and search the sixth floor. Before conducting this search, let us see first if there are any witnesses who at the time of the assassination say they saw a rifle at any place other than the south side of the TSBD Building.

If there is any such witness in the world, please come forward! . . .

Members of the jury, there are none. Nonetheless, I caution you not to leap to the conclusion that no other rifle was fired. All we have at present is the fact that no one saw a rifle at the time of the assassination other than in the south side of the TSBD Building.

However, there were a number of people who, when they first heard the shots ring out, thought from the sound they heard that the shots came from the area of the "grassy knoll" or railroad tracks. This is readily apparent from transcriptions that we had prepared from the magnetic tape recordings of the Dallas Police Department radio calls on Nov. 22. These calls were broadcast on two channels, called Channel 1 and Channel 2. Periodically, the time would be interspersed in the radio broadcast.

The entire radio log transcription of the Dallas Police Department was independent documentary evidence of the fact that the chain of events after the first few minutes pointed toward the TSBD Building as the source of the shots. It is also independent evidence of the fact that—notwithstanding the claims of some of the assassination sensationalists—the Dallas police did not "want" Oswald within a few minutes after the assassination.

In Volume XXI of the supplementary volumes of hearings and exhibits that we published together with our Report, you can see the transcripts of the Dallas police radio broadcasts which were identified by Dallas Police Inspector J. H. Sawyer. You will see how first Chief Curry ordered men on top of the triple underpass and into the railroad yard—at 12:30 P.M.[1] If someone were trying to frame Oswald, he surely would not have first instructed that men go up to the top of the triple underpass. Then, at 12:34 P.M., you will see the reference to a passerby stating that the shots came

---

[1]The reverberations in the area led many witnesses to believe on the basis of their auditory senses that the shots came from the triple underpass. However, Dallas police officers and railroad employees standing by the railroad tracks over the triple underpass confirmed that no rifleman had fired any shots from that area. This will be discussed in more detail later.

from the TSBD Building. Officer No. 136 (B. W. Hargis) called in this information. At 12:35 P.M., that another police officer, No. 142 (C. A. Haygood), called in, "I talked to a guy at the scene who says the shots were fired from the Texas School Book Depository Building with the Hertz Rent-A-Sign on top."

And at 12:36 P.M., you will see that a third officer (B. V. Harkness) called in and said, "Witness says shots came from fifth floor Texas Book Depository Store at Houston and Elm. I have him with me now and we are sealing off the building." (Because the first floor of the building did not have windows at the front entrance, witnesses were often confused about the floor count.)

And at 12:37 P.M., Officer Haygood called in: "Get men to cover the building, Texas School Book Depository, believe the shots came from there, facing it on Elm Street. Looking at the building it will be the second window from the end in the upper righthand corner."

At 12:38 P.M., Officer E. D. Brewer called in: "A witness says he saw 'em pull the weapon from the window off the second floor on the southeast corner of the Depository Building." (What the witness probably said was the second floor from the top, the building being seven stories high. When I took Brewer's deposition he said he did not know if the witness said the second floor or the second floor from the top. However, the southeast corner window on the second floor was over the front stairway [which went from the second to the first floor] and could not have been used as a firing point.[2])

At 12:38 P.M., the transcript shows a call from the transmission center at police headquarters to Assistant Chief Batchelor. The radio-transmitting man states: "We have information the shots came from the fifth or fourth floor of the Book Depository store on the corner of Elm and Field. Officers are now surrounding and searching the building." Of course, this is an error—the Book Depository store is at the corner of Elm and Houston. And nowhere is there any information that they came from the fourth floor.

As a matter of fact, this points up the authenticity of the entire investigation of the Warren Commission. Wherever there are eyewitness reports and in turn reports of eyewitness reports, there are always inaccuracies. That there are such inaccuracies is indicative that these facts came through the natural flow of human events. There was no manufactured case; there was no prepared case. We just stated the facts as we found them.

Between the time indications of 12:32 P.M. and 12:45 P.M., Inspector J. H. Sawyer called in: "The wanted person in this is a slender white male about 30, 5 feet 10, 165, carrying what looked to be a 30-30 or some type of Winchester." The radio transmitter calls back, "It was a rifle?" And Inspector Sawyer replies, "Yes, a rifle."

---

[2]Also, the Dillard photograph showed that within seconds after the shooting, no windows were open on the southeast side of the Depository third floor, and only one window was open on the southeast side of the fourth floor. Victoria Adams, whose testimony will be discussed in Chapter 31, was watching the motorcade from that open fourth floor window.

This is the way it happened. There was no police report asking that Lee Harvey Oswald be apprehended for the assassination of President Kennedy.

What was the primary source of the description broadcast by Inspector Sawyer? Most probably it was Howard L. Brennan, but we cannot be sure because Inspector J. H. Sawyer—who called in the description on the Dallas police radio—did not remember the name of the person who gave him this description.

On Apr. 8, 1964, I took the testimony of Dallas Police Inspector J. Herbert Sawyer in Dallas. During the motorcade through Dallas he was in charge of controlling the crowds on Main Street at a point east of the TSBD Building. After the motorcade passed his area, he returned to his car, which faced west on Main Street.

The transcript shows that the first time the TSBD Building is mentioned on the Dallas police radio broadcast was at 12:34 P.M. when a call from an officer with call #136 states, "A passer-by states the shots came from Texas School Book Depository Building." Sawyer drove to the front of the building, parked his car, got out, went inside and took the passenger elevator in the front of the building as high as it would go (the fourth floor), looked around, then came back down and instructed that the building be sealed off. He does not believe that the building was sealed off before 12:37 P.M.

Inspector Sawyer's first call on the police radio was between 12:40 and 12:43 P.M. He used call #9. If you turn to Volume VI, page 321, of the 26 volumes of hearings and exhibits that we published with our Report, you will find the following testimony of Inspector Sawyer:

Mr. Belin. Would you read what it says that you said there? [Referring to the transcript of the Dallas police radio broadcast on Nov. 22.]

Mr. Sawyer. "We need more manpower down here at the Texas Book Depository; there should be a bunch on Main if somebody can pick them up and bring them down here."

Mr. Belin. Was that said before or after you came down from the elevator?

Mr. Sawyer. That was after.

Mr. Belin. Was that before or after you told the men there to guard the front door and not let anyone in or out?

Mr. Sawyer. That was after.

Mr. Belin. Now the next time that No. 9 appears is at what time?

Mr. Sawyer. Immediately after 12:43 and before 12:45.

Mr. Belin. What did you say then?

Mr. Sawyer. "The wanted person in this is a slender white male about 30, 5 feet 10, 165, carrying what looks to be a 30-30 or some type of Winchester."

Mr. Belin. Then the statement is made from the home office, "It was a rifle"?

Mr. Sawyer. I answered, "Yes, a rifle."

Mr. Belin. Then the reply to you, "Any clothing description?"

Mr. Sawyer. "Current witness can't remember that."

Mr. Belin. Then the statement is made sometime before 12:45 P.M., and after the 12:43 P.M. call, "Attention all squads, description was broadcast and no further information at this time."

Does that mean the description you made was rebroadcast?

Mr. Sawyer. I rebroadcast that description. That is what that means.

I asked Sawyer where he obtained the description of the gunman that he broadcast over the Dallas police radio. Inspector Sawyer replied:

That description came to me mainly from one witness who claimed to have been able to see the man up there.

Mr. Belin. Do you know this person's name?

Mr. Sawyer. I do not.

Mr. Belin. Do you know anything about him, what he was wearing?

Mr. Sawyer. Except that he was—I don't remember what he was wearing. I remember that he was a white man and that he wasn't young and he wasn't old. He was there. That is the only two things that I can remember about him. [Brennan was white. He was 45 years old. Had I been "preparing" a witness, I would have told Sawyer that Brennan was wearing a construction helmet.]

Mr. Belin. What age would you categorize as young?

Mr. Sawyer. Around 35 would be my best recollection of it, but it could be a few years either way.

Mr. Belin. Do you remember if he was tall or short, or can't you remember anything about him?

Mr. Sawyer. I can't remember that much about him. I was real hazy about that.

Mr. Belin. Do you remember where he said he was standing when he saw the person with the rifle?

Mr. Sawyer. I didn't go into detail with him except that from the best of my recollection, he was standing where he could have seen him. But there were too many people coming up with questions to go into detail. I got the description and sent him on over to the Sheriff's Office. [Brennan did go to the Sheriff's office.]

Mr. Belin. Inspector, do you remember anything else about this person who you say gave you the primary description?

Mr. Sawyer. No, I do not, except that I did send him with an escort to the Sheriff's Office to give fuller or more complete detail.

Mr. Belin. Do you know if he was taken there to see a lineup at the police station?

Mr. Sawyer. No.

Mr. Belin. Did you ever see him again?

Mr. Sawyer. Not to my knowledge.

Mr. Belin. Now, you talked to other people there that said they had some information with regard to where the shots may have come from?

Mr. Sawyer. Yes, through a number of people.

Mr. Belin. First, I am going to ask you if you talked to any other people who said they saw a rifle or part of a rifle?

Mr. Sawyer. Yes. There were a few who claimed that they had seen this.

Mr. Belin. Where did these people that claimed they saw a rifle or part of a rifle—

Mr. Sawyer. The ones that I talked to were pointing out one of the upper floors of the Texas School Book Depository, which at that time I thought was the fifth floor.

Mr. Belin. Do you know what portion, what side of the building it was?

Was it the northeast corner or west side of the building?

Mr. Sawyer. It was on the south side of the building, and in the southeast corner.

Mr. Belin. What about this person, who I will call the primary description witness, did he say what side of the building it was on?

Mr. Sawyer. He went and pointed out the window which I now note to be the sixth floor, but when I talked to him, I thought it was the fifth floor.

Mr. Belin. The fifth floor?

Mr. Sawyer. Yes.

Mr. Belin. What side of the building?

Mr. Sawyer. On the south side of the building, and the southeast corner.

Mr. Belin. Did you talk to any witness, or did any witness talk to you who claimed to see any rifle or portion of a rifle at any place other than a window in the Texas School Book Depository Building?

Mr. Sawyer. No, not to my knowledge.

When you compare this with the testimony of Howard Leslie Brennan, you will note an inconsistency between his identification and Inspector Sawyer's: Whereas Sawyer on the Dallas police radio stated that the current witness cannot remember any clothing description, Brennan testified that the man that he saw in the window was wearing light-colored clothing.

What about this inconsistency? Does this mean that we should throw out the testimony of either Brennan or Sawyer or both? We do know that when Brennan gave an affidavit to the Dallas Sheriff's office on the afternoon of the assassination, he stated that the gunman had light-colored clothing. I do not know whether this is something he recalled after his report to the Dallas police in front of the TSBD Building, or whether he told one of the Dallas police officers and in all of the activity shortly after the assassination the clothing description was lost. But regardless of that inconsistency between Brennan's testimony and the report of Inspector Sawyer, there can be no doubt that Brennan saw the gunman in the window, that Brennan told the Dallas police what he saw, and that the description broadcast by the Dallas police corresponded to that given by Brennan, except for the clothing.

Moreover, the only place that a rifle was seen at the time of the assassination was the southeast corner of the upper portion of the TSBD Building.

So, members of the jury, let us go inside the TSBD Building with the next witness, Luke Mooney, 40-year-old deputy sheriff in the civil law department of the Dallas County Sheriff's office.

23

"I SAW THE EXPENDED SHELLS"

The Dallas Sheriff's office is in a building at the intersection of Main and Houston—a block south of the TSBD Building. Luke Mooney, a deputy sheriff, was standing on Main Street in front of the sheriff's office and watched the motorcade pass.

"We heard this shot ring out. At that time, I didn't realize it was a shot. The wind was blowing pretty high, and, of course, it echoed." Mooney said he had turned his head to the right, looking west.

And there was a short lapse between these shots. I can still hear them distinctly—between the first and second shot. The second and third shot was pretty close together, but there was a short lapse there between the first and second shot. Why, I don't know. But when that began to take place—after the first shot we started moving out. And by the time I started running—all of us except Officer Ingram—he had a heart attack, and, of course, he wasn't qualified to do any running.

Mr. Ball. Which way?

Mr. Mooney. Due west, across Houston Street, went down across this lawn, across Elm Street there—I assume it is approximately the location the President was hit.

Of course, the motorcade was gone. There wasn't anything there except a bunch of people, a lot of them laying on the ground, taking on, various things. I was running at full speed.

Mr. Ball. When you ran across Elm, where did you go?

Mr. Mooney. Across Elm, up the embankment, which is a high terrace there, across—there is a kind of concrete building there, more or less of a little park.

Jumped over the fence and went into the railroad yards. And, of course, there was other officers over there. Who they were, I don't recall at this time. But Ralph Walters and I were running together. And we jumped into the railroad yards and began to look around there.

And, of course, we didn't see anything there. Of course the other officers had checked into the car there, and didn't find anything, I don't believe, but a Negro porter. Of course there were quite a few spectators milling around behind us. We were trying to clear the area out and get all the civilians out that wasn't officers.

Mr. Ball. Why did you go over to the railroad yard?

Mr. Mooney. Well, that was—from the echo of the shots, we thought they came from that direction.

Mr. Ball. That would be north and west from where you were standing?

Mr. Mooney. Yes, sir. To a certain extent—northwest. The way the echo sounded, the cracking of the shot. And we wasn't there many seconds—of course I never did look at my watch to see how many seconds it took us to run so many hundred yards there, and into the railroad yard. We were there only a few seconds until we had orders to cover the Texas Depository Building.

Mr. Ball. How did you get those orders?

Mr. Mooney. They were referred to us by the sheriff, Mr. Bill Decker.

Mr. Ball. Where was he when he gave you those orders?

Mr. Mooney. They were relayed on to us. I assume Mr. Decker was up near the intersection of Elm and Houston.

Mr. Ball. Did you hear it over a loudspeaker?

Mr. Mooney. No, sir. It come by word, by another officer.

Mr. Mooney took the west freight elevator to the sixth floor of the TSBD Building.

Mr. Ball. Was there any reason for you to go to the sixth floor?

Mr. Mooney. No, sir. That is what I say. I don't know why. I just stopped on that particular floor. I thought I was pretty close to the top.

Mr. Ball. Were there any other officers on the floor?

Mr. Mooney. I didn't see any at that time. I assume there had been other officers up there. But I didn't see them. And I begin criss-crossing it, round and round, through boxes, looking at open windows—some of them were open over on the south side.

And I believe they had started laying some flooring up there.

I was checking the fire escapes. And criss-crossing back and forth. And then I decided—I saw there was another floor. And I said I would go up. So I went up to the seventh floor. I approached Officers Webster and Vickery. They were up there—in this little old stairway there that leads up into the attic. So we climbed up in there and looked around right quick. We didn't climb all the way into the attic, almost into it. We said this is too dark, we have got to have floodlights, because we can't see. And so somebody made a statement that they believed floodlights was on the way. And I later found out that probably Officers Boone and Walters had gone after lights. I heard that.

And so we looked around up there for a short time. And then I says I am going back down on six.

At that time, some news reporter, or press, I don't know who he was—he was coming up with a camera. Of course he wasn't taking any pictures. He was just looking, too, I assume. So I went back down ahead of Officers Vickery and Webster. They come in behind me down to the sixth floor.

I went straight across to the southeast corner of the building, and I saw all these high boxes. Of course they were stacked all the way around over there. And I squeezed between two. And the minute I squeezed between these two stacks of boxes, I had to turn myself sideways to get in there—that is when I saw the expended shells and the boxes that were stacked up looked to be a rest for the weapon. And, also, there was a slight crease in the top box. Whether the recoil made the crease or it was placed there before the shots were fired, I don't know. But, anyway, there was a very slight crease in the box, where the rifle could have lain—at the same angle that the shots were fired from.

So, at that time, I didn't lay my hands on anything, because I wanted to save every evidence we could for fingerprints. So I leaned out the window, the same window from which the shots were fired, looked down, and I saw Sheriff Bill Decker and Captain Will Fritz standing right on the ground.

Well, so I hollered, or signaled—I hollered, I more or less hollered. I whistled a time or two before I got anybody to see me. And yet they was all looking that way, too—except the sheriff, they wasn't looking up.

And I told him to get the crime lab officers en route, that I had the location spotted.

So I stood guard to see that no one disturbed anything until Captain Will Fritz approached with his group of officers, city officers.

Mr. Mooney was then shown photographs taken by the crime lab officers of the Dallas Police Department after they arrived at the scene. One, marked Exhibit 510, showed three empty shells on the floor near the southeast corner window of the sixth floor of the TSBD Building.

Joe Ball handed Mr. Mooney the photograph, Exhibit 510.

Mr. Ball. Is that the empty shells you found?

Mr. Mooney. Yes, sir.

Mr. Ball. Are they shown there?

Mr. Mooney. Yes, sir. . . .

Mr. Ball. They were turned over to Captain Fritz?

Mr. Mooney. Yes, sir; he was the first officer that picked them up, as far as I know, because I stood there and watched him go over and pick them up and look at them. As far as I could tell, I couldn't even tell what caliber they were, because I didn't get down that close to them. They were brass cartridges, brass shells.

Mooney said that the window was open when he got there and that he had room enough to lean out this window, without disturbing the boxes.

Then, Joe Ball asked Luke Mooney how long he stayed on the sixth floor after he found the three cartridges.

Mr. Mooney. Well, I stayed up there not over 15 or 20 minutes longer—after Captain Will Fritz and his officers came over there, Captain Fritz picked up the cartridges, began to examine them, of course I left that particular area. By that time there was a number of officers up there. The floor was covered with officers. And we were searching, trying to find the weapon at that time.

Mr. Ball. Were you there when it was found?

Mr. Mooney. Yes, sir. I was searching under these books and between them and up on the ledges and the joists, we was just looking everywhere. And I was about 10 or 15 steps at the most from Officer Boone when he hollered, "Here is the gun."

Mr. Ball. Did you go over there?

Mr. Mooney. I stepped over there.

Mr. Ball. What did you see?

Mr. Mooney. I had to look twice before I actually saw the gun laying in there. I had to get around to the right angle before I could see it. And there the gun lay, stuck between these cartons in an upright position. The scope was up.

Whereas the cartridge cases had been found in the southeast corner of the sixth floor, Mr. Mooney said that the gun was found ". . . in the far northwest corner. Just right there at the staircase." We showed Luke Mooney two pictures of the rifle, which were later identified as having been taken before the rifle was moved from where it had been found. These pictures were marked Exhibits 514 and 515. Mooney said these pictures showed the gun in the position in which it had been found. "It was sitting in that position. The scope was up."

Eugene Boone, who found the rifle, was the next witness. He was 26 years old and, like Luke Mooney, was a high school graduate who worked for the Dallas County Sheriff's Department as a deputy sheriff. He was standing with Mr. Mooney on Main Street in front of the Sheriff's office when the motorcade passed them.

Mr. Ball. What happened there?

Mr. Boone. Well, it was approximately one o'clock when we heard the shots. The motorcade had already passed by us and turned back to the north on Houston Street. And we heard what we thought to be a shot. And there seemed to be a pause between the first shot and the second shot and third shots—a little longer pause. And we raced across the street there.

Mr. Ball. You raced across what street?

Mr. Boone. Houston Street.

Mr. Ball. You turned to your right and went west?

Mr. Boone. Well, there is a big cement works out there. We went on west across Houston Street, and then cut across the grass out there behind the large cement works there. Some of the bystanders over there seemed to think the shots came from up over the railroad in the freight yards, from over the triple underpass.

So there was some city officer, I don't know who he was, motorcycle officer had laid his motorcycle down and was running up the embankment to get over a little retaining wall that separates the freight yards there. He went over the wall first, and I was right behind him, going into the freight yards. We searched out the freight yards. We were unable to find anything.

Mr. Ball. A good many officers over there searching?

Mr. Boone. Yes; there were. Most all of the officers—well, all of the officers in front of the sheriff's office there. There were others that I don't recall. There were other officers in the area. Also, they all ran in that general direction, over around the depository and also down into the freight yards.

Mr. Ball. Any railroad employees around there?

Mr. Boone. There was one colored boy way on back down in the freight yards. He had been working on one of the pullmans down there.

Mr. Ball. And didn't you talk to somebody that was also in a tower?

Mr. Boone. Yes; I did.

Mr. Ball. A man named Bowers?

Mr. Boone. I don't know what his name was. He was up in the tower and I hollered up there to see if he had seen anybody running out there in the freight yards, or heard any shots. And he said he didn't hear any shots, and he hadn't seen anybody racing around out there in the yard.

Mr. Ball. That was a railroad tower?

Mr. Boone. Yes; it is situated between the tracks and the school book depository. Almost directly west of the building.

You jurors probably noticed the inaccuracy of Mr. Boone's statement that the shots took place at "approximately 1 o'clock." This is but one instance of the inaccuracies that inevitably arise from the testimony of different witnesses to an event.

Boone said he had learned that shells had been found on the sixth floor of the TSBD Building, so he went into the building and up to the sixth floor.

Mr. Ball. What did you do after you got up to the sixth floor?

Mr. Boone. Well, I proceeded to the east end of the building, I guess, and started working our way across the building to the west wall, looking in, under, and around all the boxes and pallets, and what-have-you that were on the floor. Looking for the weapon. And as I got to the west wall, there were a row of windows there, and a slight space between some boxes and the wall. I squeezed through them.

When I did—I had my light in my hand. I was slinging it around on the floor, and I caught a glimpse of the rifle, stuffed down between two rows of boxes with another box or so pulled over the top of it. And I hollered that the rifle was here.

Mr. Ball. What happened then?

Mr. Boone. Some of the other officers came over to look at it. I told them to stand back, not to get around close, they might want to take prints of some of the boxes, and not touch the rifle. And at that time Captain Fritz and an ID man came over. I believe the ID man's name was Lieutenant Day—I am not sure. They came over and the weapon was photographed as it lay. And at that time Captain Fritz picked it up by the strap, and it was removed from the place where it was.

Mr. Ball. You saw them take the photograph?

Mr. Boone. Yes.

Mr. Ball. Were you alone at that time?

Mr. Boone. There was an Officer Weitzman, I believe. He is a deputy constable.

Mr. Ball. Where was the rifle located on the floor, general location?

Mr. Boone. Well, it was almost—the stairwell is in the corner of the building, something like this, and there is a wall coming up here, making one side of the stairwell with the building acting as the other two sides. And from that, it was almost directly in front or about three feet south, I guess, it would be, from that partition wall that made up the stairwell.

Mr. Boone identified the same picture showing the rifle that Mr. Mooney identified.

Mr. Ball. This shows the rifle as you saw it, does it?

Mr. Boone. That is right. Then you could kneel down over here and see that it had a scope, a telescopic sight on it, by looking down underneath the boxes.

Then, Joe Ball asked the witness what time it was when he found the rifle.

Mr. Boone. 1:22 PM, in the afternoon.

Mr. Ball. 1:22?

Mr. Boone. Yes.

Mr. Ball. You looked at your watch?

Mr. Boone. That is correct.

Mr. Ball. And made a note of it?

Mr. Boone. Yes; I did.

Mr. Ball. I show you a rifle which is Commission Exhibit 139. Can you tell us whether or not that looks like the rifle you saw on the floor that day?

Mr. Boone. It looks like the same rifle. I have no way of being positive.

Mr. Ball. You never handled it?

Mr. Boone. I did not touch the weapon at all.

Boone testified that Captain Fritz of the Dallas Police Department "... was called to the location as soon as I found the rifle. He came over, and it was photographed then."

Mr. Ball. There is one question. Did you hear anybody refer to this rifle as a Mauser that day?

Mr. Boone. Yes, I did. And at first, not knowing what it was, I thought it was a 7.65 Mauser.

Mr. Ball. Who referred to it as a Mauser that day?

Mr. Boone. I believe Captain Fritz. He had knelt down there to look at it, and before he removed it, not knowing what it was, he said that is what it looks like. This is when Lieutenant Day, I believe his name is, the ID man, was getting ready to photograph it.

We were just discussing it back and forth. And he said it looks like a 7.65 Mauser.

The rifle was not a 7.65 Mauser. It was an Italian surplus Mannlicher-Carcano 6.5 mm. military rifle, Serial No. C-2766, as you jurors will learn from the next witness: Lt. J. C. Day of the Dallas Police Department. Lt. Day was the police officer who took over the crime-scene investigation and handled and examined the rifle.

24

"MAY HAVE BEEN USED
TO CARRY GUN"

Mr. Belin. I am going to hand you what has been marked Commission Exhibit 139 and ask you to state if you know what this is.

Mr. Day. This is the rifle found on the sixth floor of the Texas Book Store at 411 Elm Street, Nov. 23, 1963.

Mr. Belin. What date?

Mr. Day. Nov. 22, 1963.

Mr. Belin. Does it have any identification mark of yours on it?

Mr. Day. It has my name "J. C. Day" scratched on the stock.

Mr. Belin. And on the stock you are pointing to your name which is scratched as you would hold the rifle and rest it on the stock, approximately an inch or so from the bottom of the stock on the sling side of the stock, is that correct?

Mr. Day. Yes, sir.

Mr. Belin. Do you have any recollection as to what the serial number was of that?

Mr. Day. Yes sir; I recorded it at the time, C-2566.

Mr. Belin. Before you say that—

Mr. Day. C-2766, excuse me.

Mr. Belin. Do you have any record of that with you or not?

Mr. Day. Yes, sir; this is the record I made of the gun when I took it back to the office. Now, the gun did not leave my possession.

Mr. Belin. From the time it was found at the School Book Depository Building?

Mr. Day. Yes, sir; I took the gun myself and retained possession, took it to the office where I dictated—

Mr. Belin. Could you just read into the record what you dictated.

Mr. Day. To my secretary. She wrote on the typewriter: "4 x 18, coated, Ordinance Optics, Inc., Hollywood, California, 010 Japan. OSC inside a cloverleaf design."

Mr. Belin. What did that have reference to?

Mr. Day. That was stamped on the scopic sight on top of the gun. On the gun itself, "6.5 caliber C-2766, 1940 made in Italy." That was what was on the gun.

I dictated certain other stuff, other information, for her to type for me.

Mr. Belin. Well, you might just as well dictate the rest there.

Mr. Day. "When bolt opened one live round was in the barrel. No prints are on the live round. Captain Fritz and Lieutenant Day opened the barrel. Captain Fritz has the live round. Three spent hulls were found under the window. They were picked up by Detective Sims and witnessed by Lieutenant Day and Studebaker. The clip is stamped 'SMI, 9 x 2.'"

The witness was J. C. Day, 50-year-old Dallas Police Department lieutenant who was assigned to the Crime Scene Search Section of the identification bureau. He had been with the Dallas Police Department for 23 years and for the last seven years

I have had immediate supervision of the crime-scene search section. It is our responsibility to go to the scene of the crime, take photographs, check for fingerprints, collect any other evidence that might be available, and primarily we are to assist the investigators with certain technical parts of the investigation.

Mr. Belin. Do you carry any equipment of any kind with you when you go there?

Mr. Day. Yes, sir. We have a station wagon equipped with fingerprint equipment, cameras, containers, various other articles that might be needed at the scene of the crime.

Mr. Belin. Have you had any special education or training or background insofar as your crime-scene work is concerned?

Mr. Day. In the matter of fingerprints, I have been assigned to the identification bureau 15 years. During that time I have attended schools, the Texas Department of Public Safety, on fingerprinting; also an advanced latent-print school conducted in Dallas by the Federal Bureau of Investigation. I have also had other schooling with the Texas Department of Public Safety and in the local department on crime-scene search and general investigative work.

Mr. Belin. Were you on duty on Nov. 22, 1963?

Mr. Day. Yes, sir.

Mr. Belin. Could you describe your activities from about noon on of that day?

Mr. Day. I was in the identification bureau at the city hall. About a quarter of one I was in the basement of the city hall, which is three floors under me—actually I am on the fourth floor—and a rumor swept through there that the President had been shot.

I returned to my office to get on the radio and wait for the developments. Shortly before 1 o'clock I received a call from the police dispatcher to go to 411 Elm Street, Dallas.

Mr. Belin. Is there any particular building at that particular location?

Mr. Day. The Texas School Book Depository, I believe is the correct name on it.

Mr. Belin. Did you go there?

Mr. Day. Yes, sir; I went out of my office almost straight up 1 o'clock. I arrived at the location on Elm about 1:12.

Mr. Belin. What did you do when you got there?

Mr. Day. I was directed to the sixth floor by the police inspector who was at the front door when I arrived.

Mr. Belin. Do you know who that was?

Mr. Day. Inspector Sawyer.

Mr. Belin. What did you do when you got to the sixth floor?

Mr. Day. I had to go up the stairs. The elevator—we couldn't figure out how to run it. When I got to the head of the stairs, I believe it was the patrolman standing there, I am not sure, stated they had found some hulls over in the northeast corner of the building and I proceeded to that area—excuse me, southeast corner of the building.

I noted the witness was tense as he was giving his testimony. The Dallas Police Department had been the target of much criticism over its handling of the investigation, and Lt. Day was one of the chief officers at whom public scrutiny had been directed.

The first thing that Lt. Day did when he got to the southeast corner of the sixth floor was to supervise "photographs of the three hulls as they were found before they were moved." Detective Studebaker, who worked under his supervision, took the photographs. I had them marked as exhibits and introduced into evidence. On the pictures of several of the exhibits, I had Lt. Day circle the hulls.

Then I had him examine the picture taken by Dillard, the news photographer who was riding in the motorcade with Robert Jackson, which showed the east side of the TSBD Building. There were some boxes in the window. Lt. Day said that this was how it appeared when he arrived on the scene. The boxes may have been moved by Luke Mooney, the deputy sheriff who found the shells. Mr. Mooney said that he had leaned out of the window to call down and tell someone that he had found something.

After supervising photographs of the area, Lt. Day testified,

I processed these three hulls for fingerprints, using a powder. Mr. Sims picked them up by the ends and handed them to me. I processed each of the three: did not find fingerprints. As I had finished that, Captain Fritz sent word for me to come to the northwest part of the building, the rifle had been found, and he wanted photographs.

Mr. Belin. All right. You have mentioned these three hulls. Did you put any initials on those at all, any means of identification?

Mr. Day. At that time they were placed in an envelope and the envelope marked. The three hulls were not marked at that time. Mr. Sims took possession of them.

Mr. Belin. Well, did you at any time put any mark on the shells?

Mr. Day. Yes, sir.

Let me pause for a moment. You jurors now know how important cartridge cases can be in ballistic identification. Lt. Day knew this because of his seven years' experience in crime-scene search matters. Yet he was confused about when he marked the shells and their chain of possession from the time they were found in the TSBD Building until they were turned over to Special Agent Vincent Drain of the FBI. The confusion was not finally cleared up until late June, when Lt. Day executed an affidavit that concluded with the statement:

Both Detective R. L. Studebaker and Detective R. M. Sims, who were present at the window when the hulls were picked up, state I marked them as they were found under the window.

Signed this 23d day of June 1964.

Lt. Day tested the cartridge cases for fingerprints.

Mr. Day. I used fingerprint powder, dusted them with the powder, a dark powder. No legible prints were found.

Mr. Belin. After you did this, you dusted the prints and you put them in the envelope, 717, and then what did you do?

Mr. Day. I released them to Detective Sims or rather he took them.

Mr. Belin. And then what did you do?

Mr. Day. At that time I was summoned to the northwest corner of the building.

Mr. Belin. Then what did you do?

Mr. Day. I met Captain Fritz. He wanted photographs of the rifle before it was moved.

Mr. Belin. Do you remember if Captain Fritz told you that the rifle had not been moved?

Mr. Day. He told me he wanted photographs before it was moved, if I remember correctly. He definitely told me it had not been moved, and the reason for the photographs he wanted it photographed before it was moved.

I asked Lt. Day to identify the photographs made of the rifle in the location where it was found.

Mr. Belin. What else did you do in connection with the rifle at that particular time?

Mr. Day. Captain Fritz was present. After we got the photographs I asked him if he was ready for me to pick it up, and he said, yes. I picked the gun up by the wooden stock. I noted that the stock was too rough apparently to take fingerprints, so I picked it up, and Captain Fritz opened the bolt as I held the gun. A live round fell to the floor.

Mr. Belin. Did you initial that live round at all?

Mr. Day. Yes, sir; my name is on it.

Mr. Belin. When did you place your name on this live round, if you remember?

Mr. Day. How?

Mr. Belin. When?

Mr. Day. At the time, that was marked at the scene.

Mr. Belin. Handing you Commission Exhibit No. 141, I will ask you to state if you know what this is.

Mr. Day. It has "Day" on it where I scratched it on the small end where the slug goes into the shell.

Mr. Belin. What is this, what is Exhibit 141?

Mr. Day. That is the live round that fell from the rifle when Captain Fritz opened the bolt.

Mr. Belin. What did you do with this after you put your name on it?

Mr. Day. Captain Fritz took possession of it. I retained possession of the rifle.

Mr. Belin. Did you process this live round at all for prints?

Mr. Day. Yes, sir; I did. I did not find any prints.

The witness said that as he was processing the rifle for prints he was holding it in one hand and using a magnifying glass with the other.

After ejecting the live round, then I gave my attention to the rifle. I put fingerprint powder on the side of the rifle over the magazine housing. I noticed it was rather rough.

I also noticed there were traces of two prints visible. I told Captain Fritz it was too rough to do there, it should go to the office where I would have better facilities for trying to work with the fingerprints.

Mr. McCloy. But you could note with your naked eye or with a magnifying glass the remnants of fingerprints on the stock?

Mr. Day. Yes, sir; I could see traces of ridges, fingerprint ridges, on the side of the housing.

Lt. Day then identified the rifle and its serial number—C-2766. I then asked him to describe what other processing he did with the weapon.

Mr. Day. I took it to the office and tried to bring out the two prints I had seen on the side of the gun at the bookstore. They still were rather unclear. Due to the roughness of the metal, I photographed them rather than try to lift them.

I could also see a trace of a print on the side of the barrel that extended under the woodstock. I started to take the woodstock off and noted traces of a palmprint near the firing end of the barrel about 3 inches under the woodstock when I took the woodstock loose.

Mr. Belin. You mean 3 inches from the small end of the woodstock?

Mr. Day. Right—yes, sir.

Mr. McCloy. From the firing end of the barrel, you mean the muzzle?

Mr. Day. The muzzle; yes, sir.

Mr. Belin. Let me clarify the record. By that you mean you found it on the metal or you mean you found it on the wood?

Mr. Day. On the metal, after removing the wood.

Mr. Belin. The wood. You removed the wood, and then underneath the wood is where you found the print?

Mr. Day. On the bottom side of the barrel which was covered by the wood, I found traces of a palmprint. I dusted these and tried lifting them, the prints, with scotch tape in the usual manner. A faint palmprint came off.

I could still see traces of the print under the barrel and was going to try to use photography to bring off or bring out a better print. About this time I received instructions from the chief's office to go no further with the processing, it was to be released to the FBI for them to complete. I did not process the underside of the barrel under the scopic sight, did not get to this area of the gun.

Mr. Belin. Do you know what Commission Exhibit No. 637 is?

Mr. Day. This is the trace of palmprint I lifted off of the barrel of the gun after I had removed the wood.

Mr. Belin. Does it have your name on it or your handwriting?

Mr. Day. It has the name "J. C. Day," and also "11/22/63" written on it in my writing off the underside gun barrel near the end of foregrip, C-2766.

Mr. Belin. When you lift a print is it then harder to make a photograph of that print after it is lifted or doesn't it make any difference?

Mr. Day. It depends. If it is a fresh print, and by fresh I mean hadn't been there very long and dried, practically all the print will come off and there will be nothing left. If it is an old print, that is pretty well dried, many times you can still see it after the lift. In this case I could still see traces of print on that barrel.

Mr. Belin. Did you do anything with the other prints or partial prints that you said you thought you saw?

Mr. Day. I photographed them only. I did not try to lift them.

Mr. Belin. Do you have those photographs, sir? I will mark the two photographs which you have just produced Commission Exhibits 720 and 721. I will ask you to state what these are.

Mr. Day. These are prints or pictures, I should say, of the latent—of the traces of prints on the side of the magazine housing of the gun No. C-2766.

Mr. Belin. Were those prints in such condition as to be identifiable, if you know?

Mr. Day. No, sir; I could not make positive identification of these prints.

Mr. Belin. Did you have enough opportunity to work and get these pictures or not?

Mr. Day. I worked with them, yes. I could not exclude all possibility as to identification. I thought I knew which they were, but I could not positively identify them.

Mr. Belin. What was your opinion so far as it went as to whose they were?

Mr. Day. They appeared to be the right middle and right ring finger of Harvey Lee Oswald, Lee Harvey Oswald.

Mr. Belin. At the time you had this did you have any comparison fingerprints to make with the actual prints of Lee Harvey Oswald?

Mr. Day. Yes, sir; we had sets in Captain Fritz' office. Oswald was in his custody, we had made palmprints and fingerprints of him.

Mr. Belin. Is there any other processing that you did with the rifle?

Mr. Day. No, sir.

Mr. Belin. At what time, if you know, did you release the rifle to the FBI?

Mr. Day. 11:45 PM the rifle was released or picked up by them and taken from the office.

Mr. Belin. Was that on Nov. 22?

Mr. Day. Nov. 22, 1963.

However, Lt. Day did not release the "lift" of the palm print from the barrel of the gun until Nov. 26, when "we received instructions to send back to the FBI everything that we had."

John McCloy was following the interrogation closely:

Mr. McCloy. Am I to understand your testimony, Lieutenant, about the finger-prints to be you said you were positive—you couldn't make a positive identification, but it was your opinion that these were the fingerprints of Lee Oswald?

Mr. Day. Well, actually in fingerprinting it either is or is not the man. So I wouldn't say those were his prints. They appeared similar to these two, certainly bore further investigation to see if I could bring them out better. But from what I had I could not make a positive identification as being his prints.

Mr. McCloy. How about the palmprint?

Mr. Day. The palmprint again that I lifted appeared to be his right palm, but I didn't get to work enough on that to fully satisfy myself it was his palm. With a little more work I would have come up with the identification there.

Mr. Belin. Lieutenant Day, what is the fact as to whether or not palmprints are a sound means of identification of an individual?

Mr. Day. You have the same characteristics of the palms that you do the fingers, also on the soles of feet. They are just as good for identification purposes.

Mr. Belin. Is there anything else you did in connection with the rifle, the cartridges, the live cartridge, or the taking of prints from any of these metallic objects that you haven't talked about yet?

Mr. Day. No, sir; I believe that is the extent of the prints on any of those articles.

Mr. Belin. Did you make a positive identification of any palmprint or fingerprint?

Mr. Day. Not off the rifle or slug at that time.

Mr. Belin. At any other time did you off the rifle or the slugs?

Mr. Day. After I have been looking at that thing again here today, that is his right palm. But at that time I had not no—

Mr. Belin. When you are saying you looked at that thing today, to what are you referring?

Mr. Day. Your No. 637 is the right palm of Oswald.

Mr. Belin. Handing you what has been marked "Exhibit 629" I ask you to state if you know what this is.

Mr. Day. That is the right palm of Lee Harvey Oswald.

Mr. Belin. Do you know where this print was taken?

Mr. Day. Yes, sir; it was taken by Detective J. B. Hicks in Captain Fritz' office on Nov. 22, 1963.

Mr. Belin. Did you take more than one right palmprint on that day, if you know?

Mr. Day. Yes, sir; we took two, actually we took three. Two of them were taken in Captain Fritz' office, and one set which I witnessed taking myself in the identification bureau.

Mr. Belin. Any particular reason why you took more than one?

Mr. Day. In most cases, when making comparisons, we will take at least two to insure we have a good clear print of the entire palm.

Mr. Belin. Now, based—

Mr. Day. One might be smeared where the other would not.

Mr. Belin. Based on your experience, I will ask you now for a definitive statement as to whether or not you can positively identify the print shown on Commission Exhibit 637 as being from the right palm of Lee Harvey Oswald as shown on Commission Exhibit 629?

Mr. Day. Maybe I shouldn't absolutely make a positive statement without further checking that. I think it is his, but I would have to sit down and take two glasses to make an additional comparison before I would say absolutely, excluding all possibility, it is. I think it is, but I would have to do some more work on that. . . .

It was my understanding the prints had been identified by the FBI. I don't have official word on it. [Lt. Day was correct. Fingerprint experts Sebastian F. Latona of the FBI and Arthur Mandella, whom you jurors will hear in Chapter 30, unequivocally testified that the palmprint lifted from the underside of the gun barrel by Lt. Day was the right palmprint of Lee Harvey Oswald.]

Mr. Belin. Is there any other thing that you did with regard to the rifle that you haven't discussed this far that you can remember right now?

Mr. Day. No, sir; I released it to the FBI then, and they took possession of it.

Mr. Belin. Did you ever hear this rifle referred to as a 7.65 Mauser or as any type of a Mauser?

Mr. Day. Yes, sir; it wasn't referred to as that. Some of the newsmen, when I first carried the rifle out, asked me if it was a .30-06, and at another time they asked me if it was a Mauser. I did not give them an answer.

Mr. Belin. Were there newsmen on the sixth floor at the time the rifle was found, if you know?

Mr. Day. I think there was.

Mr. Belin. Did you ever describe the rifle as anything but a 6.5-caliber with regard to the rifle itself?

Mr. Day. I didn't describe the rifle to anyone other than police officers.

Mr. Belin. Is the description that you used with the police officers the same that you dictated here into the record from your notes?

Mr. Day. Yes, sir.

Mr. Belin. Anything else with regard to the rifle?

Mr. Day. I can't think of anything else that I did with it at the time.

I don't know whether you are interested in this or not, but about, it must have been about 8:30 I was processing the gun on the fourth floor—

Mr. Belin. Of the police department there?

Mr. Day. Of the police department where my office is. The identification bureau. And Captain Fritz came up and said he had Mrs. Oswald in his office on the third floor, but the place was so jammed with news cameramen and newsmen he did not want to bring her out into it.

Mr. Belin. Was this the wife or the mother of Lee Harvey Oswald?

Mr. Day. That was Marina. Oswald's wife. She had her baby with her, or babies, and there was an interpreter down there. He wanted her to look at the gun to see if she could identify it, didn't want to bring her in through the crowd, and wanted to know if we could carry it down. He said, "There is an awful mob down there."

I explained to him that I was still working with the prints, but I thought I could carry it down without disturbing the prints, which I did.

We waded through the mob with me holding the gun up high. No one touched it. Several of the newsmen asked me various questions about what the gun was at that time. I did not give them an answer.

When I went back to the office after Marina Oswald viewed the gun, they still were hounding me for it. I told them to check with the chief's office, he would have to give them the information, and as soon as I got back to my office I gave a complete description, and so forth, to Captain King on the gun.

Mr. Belin. Were you there when Marina Oswald was asked whether or not she could identify it?

Mr. Day. Yes, sir. But I didn't understand what she said. I was standing across the room from her where I couldn't understand. The interpreter said something to her and said something to Captain Fritz. I didn't catch what was said. I mentioned that because there was some talk about a Mauser and .30-06 at the time and various other things, that is the reason I mentioned it.

Mr. Belin. You just refused to answer all questions on that, is that correct?

Mr. Day. Yes, sir. It wasn't my place to give them that information. I didn't know whether they wanted it out yet or not.

Mr. McCloy. There was never any doubt in your mind what the rifle was from the minute you saw it?

Mr. Day. No, sir; it was stamped right on there, 6.5, and when en route to the office with Mr. Odum, the FBI agent who drove me in, he radioed it in, he radioed in what it was to the FBI over the air.

Mr. Belin. What else did you do, or what was the next thing you did after you completed photographing and inspecting the rifle on the sixth floor of the Texas School Book Depository Building for whatever prints you could find, what did you do next?

Mr. Day. I took the gun at the time to the office and locked it up in a box in my office at Captain Fritz' direction.

Another important piece of evidence was found in the southeast corner of the sixth floor, near where the cartridge cases were discovered. This was a large brown sack, which we had marked as Exhibit 142 and also as Exhibit 626. Lt. Day testified:

Mr. Day. This is the sack found on the sixth floor in the southeast corner of the building on Nov. 22, 1963.

Mr. Belin. Do you have any identification on that to so indicate?

Mr. Day. It has my name on it, and it also has other writing that I put on there for the information of the FBI.

Mr. Belin. Could you read what you wrote on there?

Mr. Day. "Found next to the sixth floor window gun fired from. May have been used to carry gun. Lieutenant J. C. Day."

Mr. Belin. When did you write that?

Mr. Day. I wrote that at the time the sack was found before it left our possession.

Mr. Belin. All right, anything else that you wrote on there?

Mr. Day. When the sack was released on Nov. 22 to the FBI about 11:45 PM, I put further information to the FBI reading as follows: "FBI: Has been dusted with metallic magnetic powder on outside only. Inside has not been processed. Lieut. J. C. Day."

Mr. Belin. Did you find anything, any print of any kind, in connection with the processing of this?

Mr. Day. No legible prints were found with the powder, no.

Mr. Belin. Do you know whether any legible prints were found by any other means or any other place?

Mr. Day. There is a legible print on it now. They were on there when it was returned to me from the FBI on Nov. 24.

Mr. Belin. Do you know by what means they found these?

Mr. Day. It is apparently silver nitrate. It could be another compound they have used. The sack had an orange color indicating it was silver nitrate.

Mr. Belin. You mean the sack when it came back from the FBI had a—

Mr. Day. Orange color. It is another method of processing paper for fingerprints.

Mr. Belin. Was there anything inside the bag, if you know, when you found it?

Mr. Day. I did not open the bag. I did not look inside of the bag at all.

Mr. Belin. What did you do with the bag after you found it and you put this writing on after you dusted it?

Mr. Day. I released it to the FBI agent.

As Lt. Day was leaving the building and was walking across the first floor,

. . . I noticed from their wrapping bench there was paper and tape of a similar—the tape was of the same width as this. I took the bag over and tried it, and I noticed that the tape was the same width as on the bag.

Mr. Belin. Did it appear to have the same color?

Mr. Day. Yes, sir.

Mr. Belin. All right. Then what did you do?

Mr. Day. I directed one of the officers standing by me, I don't know which, to get a piece of the tape and a piece of the paper from the wrapping bench.

Mr. Belin. Handing you what has been marked as Commission Exhibit 677, I will ask you to state if you know what this is.

Mr. Day. This is the tape and paper collected from the first floor in the shipping department of the Texas School Book Depository on Nov. 22, 1963.

Mr. Belin. Does this have any identification marks on it?

Mr. Day. It has my name, "J. C. Day, Dallas Police Department," and also in my writing, "Shipping Department."

Mr. Belin. Any other writing on there that you recognize?

Mr. Day. Yes, sir; Detective Studebaker, who was with me, and in his writing it says, "Paper sample from first floor, Texas School Book Depository, Studebaker, 11-22-63."

The tape also has Studebaker's writing on it, "Tape sample from first floor."

Lt. Day delivered the rifle to his office and then returned to the southeast corner of the sixth floor where

. . . we processed the boxes in that area, in the area of the window where the shooting apparently occurred, with powder. This particular box was processed and a palmprint, a legible palmprint, developed on the northwest corner of the box, on the top of the box as it was sitting on the floor.

Mr. Belin. Then what did you do when you developed this?

Mr. Day. I placed a piece of transparent tape, ordinary Scotch tape, which we use for fingerprint work, over the developed palmprint.

Mr. Belin. And then what did you do?

Mr. Day. I tore the cardboard from the box that contained the palmprint.

Mr. Belin. Then what did you do?

Mr. Day. The box was left in its position, but the palmprint was taken by me to the identification bureau.

Mr. Belin. Did you make any identification of it?

Mr. Day. Yes, sir. Later that night when I had a chance to get palmprints from Lee Harvey Oswald. I made a comparison with the palmprint off of the box, your 729, and determined that the palmprint on the box was made by the right palm of Lee Harvey Oswald.

Mr. Belin. Did you make any identification on Exhibit 649 which would indicate that this is the palmprint you took?

Mr. Day. It has in my writing. "From top of box Oswald apparently sat on to fire gun. Lieut. J. C. Day," and it is marked "right palm of Oswald. Lieut. J. C. Day."

There is also an arrow indicating north and where the palmprint was found. It further has Detective Studebaker's name on it, and he also wrote on there, "From top of box subject sat on."

Mr. Belin. Now, when was that placed on that exhibit, that writing of yours, when was it placed on there?

Mr. Day. It was placed on there Nov. 22, 1963.

There were boxes sitting in the windowsill with the words, "Ten Rolling Readers." Lt. Day dusted these boxes for prints and did not find any.

I then had the witness identify as Exhibit 627 a set of fingerprints taken of Lee Harvey Oswald on Nov. 22, 1963. I also introduced into evidence as Exhibits 735 and 736 a set of Oswald's palm prints.

As I came to the end of my interrogation, I asked my standard "any other evidence that you can think of?" The witness mentioned the paraffin test that was performed. Unfortunately, he did not mention the unreliability of the test.

Mr. Belin. Is there any other evidence pertaining to fingerprints or palmprints that you have not discussed?

Mr. Day. I can't think of any at the present time. I believe that pretty well covers my participation in this investigation.

Mr. Belin. Is there any other evidence that you can think of pertaining to the rifle that you have not discussed that you can think of at this time?

Mr. Day. Not that I can think of.

Mr. Belin. Is there any other thing that you did pertaining to the investigation of the assassination of the President that you can think of at this time?

Mr. Day. Under my direction they made paraffin casts of the hand of Lee Harvey Oswald in Captain Fritz' office.

Mr. Belin. This was done under your direction?

Mr. Day. I directed them to make it, and also paraffin casts or just of a piece of paraffin on the left side of the face to see if there were any nitrates there.

Mr. Belin. On the left side or right side of the face?

Mr. Day. Right side.

Mr. Belin. Do you know what the results of the paraffin tests were?

Mr. Day. The test on the face was negative.

Mr. Belin. Had you ever done a paraffin test on a face before?

Mr. Day. No; actually—had it not been for the particular type of case and this particular situation here—we would not have at this time. It was just something that was done to actually keep from someone saying later on, "Why didn't you do it?"

Actually, in my experience there, shooting a rifle with a telescopic sight there would be no chance for nitrates to get way back on the side of the face from a rifle.

Mr. Belin. Well, the chamber, the nature of the chamber of the rifle, would that have anything to do with that?

Mr. Day. Yes, sir.

Mr. Belin. In what way?

Mr. Day. A rifle such as that one we are talking about here from the sixth floor of the Texas School Book Depository, in my opinion, would not throw nitrates back to where a man's face was when he is looking through a telescopic sight.

Mr. Belin. Well, when you ran these tests you had understood that the man, Oswald, had fired a pistol, too, hadn't he?

Mr. Day. Yes, sir.

Mr. Belin. Would you expect to have any positive tests from a pistol on the cheek?

Mr. Day. I would expect more with a revolver with an open cylinder than I would from a rifle. Actually, for most practical purposes, I would not be surprised if there would be no nitrates from a man firing a rifle.

Mr. Belin. What about on the hands?

Mr. Day. Even on the hands. It is possible, but it is more likely with a revolver where you have a revolving cylinder and an opening between the cylinder and the actual barrel where the nitrates can come out.

Mr. McCloy. That was the type of pistol that was used to kill Tippit, wasn't it?

Mr. Day. Yes, sir.

Mr. McCloy. Did the paraffin show up nitrate?

Mr. Day. Yes, sir; nitrates were present on the cast made of Oswald's hands.

Mr. Belin. Is there anything else, are there any other comments you have with regard to the paraffin test, sir?

Mr. Day. No, sir.

25

"THIS BULLET FRAGMENT WAS FIRED IN THIS RIFLE, 139"

And I felt this windshield both inwardly and outwardly to determine first if there was something that was struck from the back of us or—and I was satisfied that it was.

Mr. Specter. When you say struck from in back of you, do you mean on the inside or outside of the windshield?

Mr. Kellerman. Inside, sir.

Mr. Specter. Inside of the car?

Mr. Kellerman. Right.

Mr. Specter. Did you have occasion to feel the outside of the windshield?

Mr. Kellerman. I did on that day; yes, sir.

Mr. Specter. What did you feel, if anything?

Mr. Kellerman. Not a thing; it was real smooth.

Mr. Specter. Did you have occasion to feel the inside of the windshield?

Mr. Kellerman. I did.

Mr. Specter. How did that feel to you?

Mr. Kellerman. My comparison was that the broken glass, broken windshield, there was enough little roughness in there from the cracks and split that I was positive, or it was my belief, that whatever hit it came into the inside of the car.

We not only had pictures of the windshield; we had the windshield itself, which we marked as Exhibit 251.

Mr. Specter. All right. Now, starting with the principal point of impact, where does that exist on this windshield?

Mr. Kellerman. The principal point of impact is located to the left of the mirror, to the right above the driver's head, and to the right of his, I am going to say, view line.

The witness was Secret Service Agent Roy H. Kellerman, who was sitting in the right-hand side of the front seat of the Presidential limousine. He had been with the Secret Service for 23 years and was the Assistant Special Agent in charge of the White House detail.

The windshield was examined by an FBI firearms expert, Robert A. Frazier, whom you jurors previously heard in connection with the ballistic identification testimony in the Tippit murder.

Mr. Specter. Did you have occasion then to examine the windshield of the Presidential limousine?

Mr. Frazier. Yes; I did.

Mr. Specter. What did that examination disclose?

Mr. Frazier. On the inside surface of the windshield there was a deposit of lead. This deposit was located when you look at the inside surface of the windshield, 13¹/₂ inches down from the top, 23 inches from the left-hand side or driver's side of the windshield, and was immediately in front of a small pattern of star-shaped cracks which appeared in the outer layer of the laminated windshield.

Mr. Dulles. What do you mean by the "outer layer of the laminated windshield"?

Mr. Frazier. The windshield is composed of two layers with a very thin layer of plastic in between which bonds them together in the form of safety glass. The inside layer of the glass was not broken, but the outside layer immediately on the outside of the lead residue had a very small pattern of cracks and there was a very minute particle of glass missing from the outside surface.

Mr. Dulles. And the outside surface was the surface away from where the occupants were sitting?

Mr. Frazier. That is correct; yes.

Mr. Dulles. And the inside surface was the surface nearest the occupants?

Mr. Frazier. Yes.

Mr. Specter. What do those characteristics indicate as to which side of the windshield was struck?

Mr. Frazier. It indicates that it could only have been struck on the inside surface. It could not have been struck on the outside surface because of the manner in which the glass broke and further because of the lead residue on the inside surface. The cracks appear in the outer layer of the glass because the glass is bent outward at the time of impact which stretches the outer layer of the glass to the point where these small radial or wagon spoke-wagon wheel spoke-type cracks appear on the outer surface.

Mr. Dulles. So the pressure must have come from the inside and not from the outside against the glass?

Mr. Frazier. Yes, sir; that is correct.

Mr. Dulles. As far as the car is concerned from the back to the front?

Mr. Frazier. Yes, sir.

Mr. Dulles. Not from outside against the glass—from the front against the glass.

Mr. Frazier. That is right.

Mr. Specter. Was a comparison made of the lead residues on the inside of the windshield with any of the bullet fragments recovered about which you have heretofore testified?

Mr. Frazier. Yes. They were compared with the bullet fragment found on the front seat, which in turn was compared with Commission 399. The lead was found to be similar in composition. However, that examination in detail was made by a spectrographer, Special Agent John F. Gallagher.

Mr. Specter. Was that examination made in the regular course of examining procedures by the FBI?

Mr. Frazier. Yes, sir.

Mr. Specter. And was that information made available to you through the normal conference procedures among FBI examiners?

Mr. Frazier. Yes, sir. He submitted his report to me and I prepared the formal report of the entire examination.

Mr. Specter. Are his report and your formal report a part of the permanent record of the FBI then?

Mr. Frazier. Yes, sir.

The windshield was demonstrative physical evidence that shots came from the rear. As to the bullet fragments and Exhibit 399 to which Frazier referred, the evidence was incontrovertible: Two bullet fragments of sufficient size to be ballistically identifiable were found in the front seat of the Presidential limousine when it was returned to Washington. One fragment found on the seat behind the driver consisted of the nose portion of a bullet and weighed 44.6 grains. The other fragment, found along the right side of the front seat, consisted of the base portion of a bullet and weighed 21.0 grains. Exhibit 399 was a nearly whole bullet that was found at Parkland Memorial Hospital. In the next chapter, you jurors will analyze the evidence concerning the question whether Exhibit 399 rolled off President Kennedy's stretcher or Governor Connally's stretcher.

As you jurors now know from the previous testimony of Robert Frazier, it is possible in examining an unmutilated bullet to determine whether that bullet came from a particular weapon to the exclusion of all other weapons in the world. What about substantial portions of bullets?

At this point I might add some background information. When we first came to Washington in January, 1964, we had before us the basic report of the FBI that included the ballistic identification of the cartridge cases found at the scene of the shooting of Officer Tippit, the cartridge cases found in the southeast corner window of the sixth floor of the TSBD Building, the large bullet fragments found in the front seat of the Presidential limousine, and the nearly whole bullet found at Parkland Memorial Hospital. Yet, we did not take any testimony in this area from expert witnesses until Mar. 31, when we called our first expert witness, Robert Frazier.

The reason we took so long to call any expert witnesses was simple: Before we discussed any matters with outside experts, we wanted to become wholly familiar with the field in which the expert testimony would be given. Among other things, this would enable us to determine the veracity of the witness and the significance of his testimony.

Moreover, if any of these expert witnesses were to try to mislead us, we would then be prepared to find the ultimate truth.

We studied the science of fiber analysis, photography, fingerprint and palm print identification and, most important of all, the science of firearms and firearms identification with particular reference to rifle bullets and cartridge cases.

We found that there is unanimous agreement among textbook writers as well as witnesses called from the FBI laboratory and independent experts retained by the Commission that when a shot is fired, the microscopic characteristics of the barrel of the weapon are engraved into the bullet (along with the rifling characteristics). At the same time, the microscopic characteristics of the firing pin and breach face are engraved into the base of the cartridge case.

The firearms identification expert will examine the suspect bullet or cartridge case under a comparison microscope, side by side with the test bullet or cartridge case that has been fired by the weapon. Under the microscope, the expert determines whether the pattern of the markings in the test and the suspect items are sufficiently similar to show that both were fired from the same weapon to the exclusion of all other weapons.

Obviously, this is a three-dimensional process. However, in preparing for our first meeting with the experts in the FBI laboratory, we had to rely on those texts on firearms identification that included pictures.

The day arrived for our appointment. Melvin Eisenberg and I sat before the comparison microscopes and familiarized ourselves with their operation and used comparisons of test cartridges. Then we examined test bullets.

After we had acclimated ourselves to the operation of the comparison microscope, in which one looks into an eyepiece to see portions of two different objects, we reviewed the background of firearms identification with FBI lab personnel. They were cooperative, and in our own cross-examination of them, using actual test cartridges and bullets, we found that they both knew their business and were 100% objective.

We placed the actual cartridge cases under the comparison microscope and compared these with the test cartridge cases fired from the rifle found on the sixth floor. That rifle had a great many individual characteristics on the firing pin and breach face. The similarity between the markings on the test cartridge cases and the cartridge case found by the window was remarkably clear.

We then looked at the whole bullet that had been found in Parkland Memorial Hospital and compared it with test bullets fired by the 6.5 mm. Mannlicher-Carcano rifle, C-2766, found on the sixth floor of the TSBD Building. You will hear more about this whole bullet in the next chapter.

And then we faced the task of examining under the comparison microscope the bullet fragments found in the front seat of the Presidential limousine that had come from the bullet that shattered as it tore off part of the President's skull. There were two fragments of fairly substantial size. One weighed 44.6 grains and had only one-fourth of its circumference available for identification. The other weighed 21.0 grains and had one-third of its circumference available. (A whole bullet of this type weighs approximately 161 grains, so both fragments could have come from the same bullet.) We knew beforehand that a minimum of one-fifth to one-sixth of the circumference was needed to make positive identification, so the minimum standards were met. Eisenberg and I examined these fragments separately and the identification could be seen clearly under the comparison microscope.

Only after we had completed our basic preparation did we take the testimony of the expert witness Frazier of the Federal Bureau of Investigation.

Frazier examined the first of the two bullet fragments found on the front seat of the Presidential limousine behind the driver. The FBI marking was Q-2; we marked it Exhibit 567.

Mr. Eisenberg. I now hand you a bullet fragment, what appears to be a bullet fragment, in a pill box which is labeled Jacket and Lead Q-2, and it has certain initials on it. For the record, this was found—this bullet fragment was found—in the front portion of the car in which the President was riding. I ask you whether you are familiar with this object.

Mr. Frazier. Yes; I am.

Mr. Eisenberg. Is your mark on it?

Mr. Frazier. Yes, sir.

Mr. Eisenberg. Did you examine this? Is this a bullet fragment, Mr. Frazier?

Mr. Frazier. Yes, sir. This consists of a piece of the jacket portion of a bullet from the nose area and a piece of the lead core from under the jacket.

Mr. Eisenberg. How were you able to conclude it is part of the nose area?

Mr. Frazier. Because of the rifling marks which extend part way up the side, and then have the characteristic leading edge impressions and no longer continue along the bullet, and by the fact that the bullet has a rounded contour to it which has not been mutilated.

Mr. Eisenberg. Did you examine this bullet to determine whether it had been fired from Exhibit 139 to the exclusion of all other weapons?

Mr. Frazier. Yes, sir.

Mr. Eisenberg. What was your conclusion?

Mr. Frazier. This bullet fragment was fired in this rifle, 139.

Mr. Eisenberg. Mr. Frazier, did you weigh this fragment?

Mr. Frazier. Yes; I did. It weighs 44.6 grains.

Frazier then reviewed magnified photographs of the bullet fragment, Exhibit 567, and compared this with a photograph of a test bullet fired from the rifle.

Mr. Eisenberg. What portion of the bullet fragment provided enough markings for purposes of identification, approximately?

Mr. Frazier. I would say that one-fourth, in this instance, one-fourth of 567's surface was available. One-fifth to one-sixth would have been sufficient for identification, based on the character of the marks present.

Mr. Eisenberg. Now this portion of the fragment was an even smaller portion of the bullet, the entire bullet, is that correct?

Mr. Frazier. Yes; it was.

Mr. Eisenberg. So when you say one-fifth and one-sixth, are you referring now to the proportion of marks on the fragment, as opposed to the proportion of marks you would want from an entire bullet?

Mr. Frazier. No; I am referring to the proportion of marks on the fragment which were used in the examination as compared to the total bullet circumference which would have existed on an unmutilated bullet.

Mr. Eisenberg. Mr. Frazier, do you feel that the amount of markings here were sufficient to make positive identification?

Mr. Frazier. Yes, sir.

Mr. Eisenberg. Have you made identifications in the past with as few or less markings as are present on this bullet fragment?

Mr. Frazier. Oh, yes; and on less, much less of an area. The character of the marks is more important than the number of the marks.

Mr. Eisenberg. Mr. Frazier, here you were of course unable to see all of the lines which were present on the bullet before mutilation. Have you ever had an occasion where you examined a bullet and saw one portion of it which was an apparent match and then found out that the balance of the bullet was not an apparent match?

Mr. Frazier. No, sir; and if I understand your words "apparent match," there is no such thing as an apparent match. It either is an identification or it isn't, and until you have made up your mind, you don't have an apparent match. We don't actually use that term in the FBI. Unless you have sufficient marks for an identification, you cannot say one way or the other as to whether or not two bullets were fired from a particular barrel.

In other words, you cannot nonidentify on the absence of similarities any more than you can identify when you have no similarities present.

Mr. Eisenberg. In other words, you won't make an identification unless you feel enough marks are present to constitute a basis for a positive identification?

Mr. Frazier. That is right, and I would not report any type of similarities unless they were sufficient for an identification, because unless you can say one bullet was fired from the same barrel as a second bullet, then there is room for error, and in this field of firearms identification, we try to avoid any possible chance of error creeping in.

Mr. Eisenberg. Do you avoid the category of "probable" identification?

Mr. Frazier. Oh, yes; we never use it, never.

Mr. Eisenberg. And why is that?

Mr. Frazier. There is no such thing as a probable identification. It either is or isn't as far as we are concerned.

Mr. Eisenberg. And in this case it is?

Mr. Frazier. It is, yes.

We then turned to the second major bullet fragment found in the front seat of the Presidential limousine, FBI identification Q-3, which we marked as Exhibit 569.

Mr. Eisenberg. Mr. Frazier, did you examine this bullet fragment with a view to determining whether it had been fired from the rifle, Exhibit 139?

Mr. Frazier. Yes, sir.

Mr. Eisenberg. What was your conclusion?

Mr. Frazier. This bullet fragment, Exhibit 569, was fired from this particular rifle, 139.

Mr. Eisenberg. Again to the exclusion of all other rifles?

Mr. Frazier. Yes, sir.

Mr. Eisenberg. Did you weigh this fragment, Mr. Frazier?

Mr. Frazier. Yes, I did. It weighs 21.0 grains.

Mr. Eisenberg. Can you describe the fragment?

Mr. Frazier. Yes. It consists of the base or most rearward portion of the jacket of a metal-jacketed bullet, from which the lead core is missing.

Mr. Eisenberg. How can you tell that it is the most rearward portion?

Mr. Frazier. It has the shape which bases of bullets have. It has the cannelure which is located at the rear, on the portion of bullets of this type.

Mr. Eisenberg. Can you determine whether this bullet fragment, 567, and 569 are portions of the originally same bullet?

Mr. Frazier. No, sir.

Mr. Eisenberg. You cannot?

Mr. Frazier. There is not enough of the two fragments in unmutilated condition to determine whether or not the fragments actually fit together.

However, it was determined that there is no area on one fragment, such as 567, which would overlap a corresponding area on the base section of 569, so that they could be parts of one bullet, and then, of course, be parts of separate bullets.

Frazier then illustrated his testimony with photographs of the bullet fragment, Exhibit 569, with photographs taken of a test bullet fired from the rifle.

Mr. Eisenberg. Mr. Frazier, what portion of the Exhibit 569 was unmutilated enough to allow you to make a comparison of its markings?

Mr. Frazier. Approximately one-third. Actually, the entire base section of the bullet was present, but approximately one-half of that base was mutilated. On the mutilated area, either marks were destroyed completely by striking some object, or being compressed or stretched, or they were thrown out of relationship with each other by stretching or compressing to the extent that they were of no value.

So I would estimate approximately one-third of the area was present.

Mr. Eisenberg. Now, when you say one-third, is this total area or circumference?

Mr. Frazier. Circumference—one third of the circumference.

The two test bullets that were fired by Frazier from the rifle, Exhibit 139, were then introduced into evidence.

The chain was almost complete: The two large bullet fragments found in the front seat of the Presidential limousine came from the rifle found on the sixth floor of the TSBD Building to the exclusion of all other weapons in the world.

Only two things remained: The cartridge cases found near the sixth floor window and the nearly whole bullet found at Parkland Memorial Hospital, Exhibit 399.

Frazier's testimony was concise.

Mr. Eisenberg. Mr. Frazier, returning to the cartridge cases which were marked earlier into evidence as Commission Exhibits 543, 544, and 545, and which, as I stated earlier for the record, had been found next to the window of the sixth floor of the Texas School Book Depository, can you tell us when you received those cartridge cases?

Mr. Frazier. Yes, sir; I received the first of the exhibits, 543 and 544, on Nov. 23, 1963. They were delivered to me by Special Agent Vincent Drain of the Dallas FBI Office.

And the other one I received on Nov. 27, 1963, which was delivered by Special Agents Vincent Drain and Warren De Brueys of the Dallas office.

Mr. Eisenberg. After receiving these cartridge cases, did you clean them up or in any way prepare them for examination?

Mr. Frazier. Yes. The bases were cleaned of a paint which was placed on them by the manufacturer. In spots this red lacquer on the base of the case was overlapping the head of the case where some of the microscopic marks were located, and some of that color was taken off.

Mr. Eisenberg. Why is that lacquer put on the cartridge cases?

Mr. Frazier. It seals the primer area against moisture.

Mr. Eisenberg. Were there any other changes made in the preparation of the cartridge cases?

Mr. Frazier. No, sir.

Mr. Eisenberg. You have examined the cartridge cases previously. Are they in the same condition now that they were when you received them in the laboratory except for the cleaning of the lacquer?

Mr. Frazier. Yes, sir; they are.

Mr. Eisenberg. After receiving the cartridge cases, did you examine them to determine whether they had been fired in Commission Exhibit 139?

Mr. Frazier. Yes, sir.

Mr. Eisenberg. When did you make the examinations?

Mr. Frazier. On the dates I mentioned, that is, Nov. 23, 1963, and Nov. 27, 1963.

Mr. Eisenberg. And what were your conclusions, Mr. Frazier?

Mr. Frazier. I found all three of the cartridge cases had been fired in this particular weapon.

Mr. Eisenberg. Can you describe the examination which you conducted to reach these conclusions?

Mr. Frazier. The first step was to fire test cartridge cases in this rifle to pick up the microscopic marks which are left on all cartridge cases fired in this weapon by the face of the bolt. Then those test cartridge cases were mounted on a comparison microscope, on the right-hand side, and on the left-hand side of the comparison microscope was mounted one of the three submitted cartridge cases, so that you could magnify the surfaces of the test and the evidence and compare the marks left on the cartridge cases by the bolt face and the firing pin of the rifle.

In an earlier chapter, you jurors heard Robert Frazier testify how one is able to conclude that a cartridge case was fired in a particular weapon to the exclusion of all other weapons in the world.

There could be no doubt: The rifle, Exhibit 139, was involved in the assassination of President Kennedy, since the two large bullet fragments found in the front seat of the Presidential limousine were fired from that rifle. So were the cartridge cases found on the sixth floor of the TSBD Building.

Let us now turn to the nearly whole bullet found at Parkland Memorial Hospital, Exhibit 399. From whose stretcher did it fall? And was it also fired by the Mannlicher-Carcano rifle, Exhibit 139?

26

"A SPENT CARTRIDGE
OR BULLET ROLLED OUT"

"He was moribund—he was lying across Mrs. Kennedy's knee and there seemed to be blood everywhere. When I went around to the other side of the car, I saw the condition of his head . . . it was very bad . . . I helped to lift his head and Mrs. Kennedy pushed me away and lifted his head herself" onto the stretcher cart. "We ran with it" to trauma (emergency) room No. 1.

The witness was Diana Bowron, a 22-year-old registered nurse from England, who had come to work at Parkland Memorial Hospital in Dallas on Aug. 4, 1963.

Diana Bowron testified that after President Kennedy was pronounced dead, his body was removed from the "stretcher," which was basically a metal cart on rubber wheels on which a rubber-covered mattress rested. With Margaret Henchliffe, the other emergency room nurse, Diana Bowron took all of the sheets off the stretcher and put them in the linen hamper.

Mr. Specter. Did you gather them up yourself?

Miss Bowron. Yes.

Mr. Specter. All of them?

Miss Bowron. Yes: with the help of Miss Henchliffe.

Mr. Specter. And did the two of you put them in the linen hamper?

Miss Bowron. Yes; I put them in the linen hamper myself.

Mr. Specter. What was done with the stretcher then?

Miss Bowron. The stretcher was then wheeled across into trauma room No. 2, which was empty.

Mr. Specter: Was there anything on the stretcher at all when it was wheeled into trauma room No. 2?

Miss Bowron. Not that we noticed, except the rubber mattress that was left on it.

Mr. Specter. Would you have noticed anything had anything been on that stretcher?

Miss Bowron. Yes; I think so.

Mr. Specter. And where was the stretcher when you last saw it?

Miss Bowron. Being wheeled across into trauma room 2.

Margaret Henchliffe verified that the sheets on President Kennedy's stretcher "were all rolled up and taken to the dirty linen hamper" and that the stretcher that President Kennedy had been on was rolled into emergency room No. 2 across the hall.

Mr. Specter. And, when it was rolled into emergency room 2, were the sheets still all on, or were they off at that time?

Miss Henchliffe. I believe they were off.

Mr. Specter. Is it possible that the stretcher that Mr. Kennedy was on was rolled with the sheets on it down into the area near the elevator?

Miss Henchliffe. No, sir.

Mr. Specter. Are you sure of that?

Miss Henchliffe. I am positive of that.

Meanwhile Governor Connally had been taken on the emergency elevator to the second floor operating room, where he was transferred from the stretcher to an operating table that was moved into the operating room. A hospital attendant wheeled the empty stretcher that Governor Connally had used into an elevator. Shortly afterward, Darrell C. Tomlinson, the hospital's senior engineer, removed the stretcher from the elevator and placed it in the corridor on the ground floor, alongside another stretcher unconnected with the care of Governor Connally. A few minutes later,

. . . I don't recall how long it had been exactly, but an intern or doctor, I didn't know which, came to use the men's room there in the elevator lobby . . . he pushed the stretcher out from the wall to get in and then when he came out he just walked off and didn't push the stretcher back up against the wall, so I pushed it out of the way where we would have clear area in front of the elevator.

Mr. Specter. And where did you push it to?

Mr. Tomlinson. I pushed it back up against the wall.

Mr. Specter. What if anything happened then?

Mr. Tomlinson. I bumped the wall and a spent cartridge or bullet rolled out that apparently had been lodged under the edge of the mat.

Tomlinson said that on the stretcher where the bullet rolled out, there were "one or two sheets rolled up . . . they were bloody . . . they were rolled up on the east end of it and there were a few surgical instruments on the opposite end and a sterile pack or so."

Tomlinson vacillated in his testimony about which stretcher the bullet came from. At first, he thought that it was not the stretcher that he took off the elevator. Later, he testified that he thought it was the stretcher that he took off the elevator. In the concluding portion of his testimony, Tomlinson said he was not certain, but that he believed the bullet had rolled off the stretcher that came off the elevator, which he marked on a diagram as Stretcher A.

Mr. Specter. When I first started to ask you about this, Mr. Tomlinson, you initially identified stretcher A as the one which came off of the elevator car?

Mr. Tomlinson. Yes; I think it's just like that.

Mr. Specter. And, then, when—

Mr. Tomlinson (interrupting). Here's the deal—I rolled that thing off, we got a call, and went to second floor, picked the man up and brought him down. He went on over across, to clear out of the emergency area, but across from it, and picked up two pints of, I believe it was, blood. He told me to hold for him, he had to get right back to the operating room, so I held, and the minute he hit there, we took off for the second floor and I came back to the ground. Now, I don't know how many people went through that—I don't know how many people hit them—I don't know anything about what could have happened to them in between the time I was gone, and I made several trips before I discovered the bullet on the end of it there.

Mr. Specter. You think, then, that this could have been either, you took out of the elevator as you sit here at the moment, or you just can't be sure?

Mr. Tomlinson. It could be, but I can't be positive or positively sure—I think it was A, but I'm not sure.

Mr. Specter. That you took off of the elevator?

Mr. Tomlinson. Yes.

It was a typical example of a witness's being confused, similar to Virginia Davis, who wavered about whether her sister-in-law called the police before or after they saw Oswald cutting across their front yard.

Obviously, the bullet could not have come from President Kennedy's stretcher because (1) it had been wheeled into Trauma Room 2, a separate room away from the elevator, and (2) the nurses had loaded up all of the linens and Miss Bowron said she took the dirty linens and "I put them in the linen hamper myself." Tomlinson said that on the stretcher where he found the bullet, there were "one or two sheets rolled up" which "were bloody" and "there were a few surgical instruments on the opposite end and a sterile pack or so."

By the process of elimination, the stretcher had to be the one on which Governor Connally had been placed.

This was confirmed by other hospital personnel as we followed Governor Connally's course after his arrival at the hospital.

Nurse Jane C. Webster, assistant supervisor in the operating room at Parkland Memorial Hospital, saw Governor Connally arrive in the operating room on a stretcher, helped in the transfer of Governor Connally from the stretcher onto an operating table, and then "took the stretcher and rolled it to the center area of the operating room suite—rolled the sheets up on the stretcher into a small bundle." At that point, R. J. Jimison, a hospital orderly, took the cart, according to Miss Webster, "and proceeded to the elevator with it and the last time I saw him he was standing at the elevator with the cart waiting . . . to be picked up."

According to R. J. Jimison, there were "a little flat mattress and two sheets as usual" on the cart. He did not notice anything else, although he said that there "could have been" empty packets of hypodermic needles or an alcohol sponge or other "small stuff." Jamison pushed the stretcher "onto the elevator myself and loaded it and pushed the door closed."

As you will soon learn in Chapter 37, there was a small wound to Governor Connally's thigh with very little soft tissue damage. No bullet was found by his physicians, undoubtedly because Exhibit 399 was dislodged while Governor Connally was being moved on the stretcher.

Thus we have the saga of how and where the nearly whole bullet was found. Although there was confusion in Tomlinson's mind about which stretcher the bullet was found on, there is one question of crucial importance about which there was no confusion: Whether that bullet was fired by the 6.5

mm. Mannlicher-Carcano rifle, our Exhibit 139. On this point there was no doubt whatsoever.

Mr. Eisenberg. Did you examine this exhibit to determine whether it had been fired in Exhibit 139?

Mr. Frazier. Yes, sir.

Mr. Eisenberg. And what was your conclusion?

Mr. Frazier. It was. Exhibit 399 was fired in the rifle 139.

Mr. Eisenberg. That is to the exclusion of all other rifles?

Mr. Frazier. Yes, sir.

The bullet itself was nearly whole.

Mr. Eisenberg. Mr. Frazier, did you determine the weight of the exhibit—that is, 399?

Mr. Frazier. Yes, sir. Exhibit 399 weighs 158.6 grains.

Mr. Eisenberg. How much weight loss does that show from the original bullet weight?

Mr. Frazier. We measured several standard bullets, and their weights varied, which is a normal situation, a portion of a grain, or two grains, from 161 grains—that is, they were all in the vicinity of 161 grains. One weighed—160.85, 161.5, 161.1 grains.

Mr. Eisenberg. In your opinion, was there any weight loss?

Mr. Frazier. There did not necessarily have to be any weight loss to the bullet. There may be a slight amount of lead missing from the base of the bullet, since it is exposed at the base, and the bullet is slightly flattened; there could be a slight weight loss from the end of the bullet, but it would not amount to more than 4 grains because 158.6 is only a grain and a half less than the normal weight, and at least a 2 grain variation would be allowed. So it would be approximately 3 or 4 grains.

Mr. Eisenberg. Were the markings on the bullet at all defaced?

Mr. Frazier. Yes; they were, in that the bullet is distorted by having been slightly flattened or twisted.

Mr. Eisenberg. How material would you call that defacement?

Mr. Frazier. It is hardly visible unless you look at the base of the bullet and notice it is not round.

Mr. Eisenberg. How far does it affect your examination for purposes of identification?

Mr. Frazier. It had no effect on it at all.

Mr. Eisenberg. Can you explain why?

Mr. Frazier. Because it did not mutilate or distort the original microscopic marks beyond the point where you could recognize the pattern and find the same pattern of marks on one bullet as were present on the other.

Frazier's testimony was concurred in by Joseph D. Nicol, who previously testified in connection with the bullets and cartridge cases involved in the Tippit murder.

Nicol first took a look at the nearly whole bullet and the two large bullet fragments, Exhibits 399, 567, and 569, and compared these with the test bullets, which we marked as Exhibit 572 and which were fired by the 6.5 mm. Mannlicher-Carcano rifle, our Exhibit 139.

Mr. Eisenberg. Now, Mr. Nicol, did you examine the three exhibits which were given to you as Q-1, Q-2, and Q-3, and which are now, I believe 567, 569, and 399?

Mr. Nicol. Yes, sir; I did.

Mr. Eisenberg. To determine whether or not they had come from the identical barrel as that in which the two—the bullets in Exhibit 572 had been fired?

Mr. Nicol. Yes, I did.

Mr. Eisenberg. Can you give us your conclusions?

Mr. Nicol. Yes. It is my opinion that the same weapon that fired Commission's Exhibit 572 also fired the projectiles in Commission's Exhibits 569, 567, and 399.

Mr. Eisenberg. That would be to the exclusion of all other weapons?

Mr. Nicol. Correct.

Nicol then testified concerning the three rifle cartridge cases found in the southeast corner of the sixth floor of the TSBD Building, our Exhibits 543, 544 and 545, and compared these with two test cartridge cases which we marked as Exhibit 557 and which were fired by the rifle.

Mr. Eisenberg. You are familiar with these shells?

Mr. Nicol. Yes, sir. And these were given to me by you on the same day I received the projectiles.

Mr. Eisenberg. I hand you Commission Exhibit 557, which also consists of—which consists of two expended shells, and I ask you whether you are familiar with them.

Mr. Nicol. Yes, sir. These are the specimens, the two shells which I used as standards or tests to compare against the other three fired cartridge cases.

Mr. Eisenberg. And you obtained these from what source?

Mr. Nicol. I obtained these from Mr. Eisenberg on the 24th of March here in this office.

Mr. Eisenberg. Again for the record. I obtained these shells from the FBI and turned them over directly to Mr. Nicol, and they have been identified earlier as having been fired by the FBI from Exhibit 139, the rifle found on the sixth floor of the TSBD building.

Now, Mr. Nicol, did you examine the shells in Exhibits 543, 544, and 545 to determine whether they had been fired from the same rifle as fired the shells in Exhibit 557?

Mr. Nicol. Yes, I did.

Mr. Eisenberg. And what was your conclusion?

Mr. Nicol. Based upon the similarity of the firing-pin impressions and the breech-block markings, as well as ejector and extractor marks, it is my opinion that all three of the exhibits, 545, 543, and 544, were fired in the same weapon as fired Exhibit 557.

Two other FBI experts also examined the three cartridge cases, the nearly whole bullet, Exhibit 399, and the two large bullet fragments. Each concurred in the conclusion of Robert Frazier that the bullet, the bullet fragments and the cartridge cases were all fired by the Mannlicher-Carcano rifle, serial No. C-2766, to the exclusion of all other weapons in the world.

Mr. Eisenberg. Mr. Frazier, did any other firearms experts in the FBI laboratory examine the three cartridge cases, the bullet, and the two bullet fragments which you have testified as to today?

Mr. Frazier. Yes, all of the actual firearms comparisons were also made by

Charles Killion and Cortlandt Cunningham. These examinations were made separately, that is, they made their examination individually and separately from mine, and there was no association between their examination and mine until both were finished.

Mr. Eisenberg. Did the three of you come to the conclusions which you have given us today as your own conclusions?

Mr. Frazier. Yes, sir.

Mr. Eisenberg. Did anyone in the FBI laboratory who examined the evidence come to a different conclusion as to any of the evidence you have discussed today?

Mr. Frazier. No, sir.

No other cartridge cases were found in the vicinity of the assassination. No other bullets or bullet fragments were found in the vicinity of the assassination, except for minute bullet fragments found in the Presidential limousine that were not of sufficient size to be ballistically identifiable.

The chain was complete: From the rifle to the victims.

The next question was obvious: Who fired the rifle? The first step to answer this question was to determine who owned the rifle.

27

"SHIPPED TO A MR. A.—LAST NAME— H-I-D-E-L-L, POST OFFICE BOX 2915, DALLAS, TEX."

The speed with which the FBI traced the ownership of the Italian-made rifle, Serial No. C-2766, was remarkable.

Within hours of the assassination, the FBI learned from retail outlets in Dallas that Crescent Firearms, Inc., of New York City was the distributor of surplus Italian 6.5 mm. military rifles. The FBI immediately contacted the president of Crescent Fire Arms, Louis Feldsott. During the evening of Nov. 22, he reviewed his company's records and found that the firm had shipped an Italian Mannlicher-Carcano, Serial C-2766, to Klein's Sporting Goods Co. in Chicago. We obtained an affidavit from Louis Feldsott.

I, Louis Feldsott, being duly sworn say:

1. I am the President of Crescent Firearms, Inc., 2 West 37th Street, New York 18, New York.

2. On Nov. 22, 1963, the FBI contacted me and asked if Crescent Firearms, Inc., had any records concerning the sale of an Italian made 6.5 m/m rifle with the serial number C 2766.

3. I was able to find a record of the sale of this rifle which indicated that the weapon had been sold to Klein's Sporting Goods, Inc., Chicago, Illinois on June 18, 1962. I conveyed this information to the FBI during the evening of Nov. 22, 1963.

4. Further records involving the purchase, sale, and transportation of the weapon have been turned over to the FBI.

That same night the officers of Klein's Sporting Goods searched their records. We took the testimony of William J. Waldman, vice president of Klein's Sporting Goods, at the company offices in Chicago. On Jan. 24, 1963, Klein's executed a purchase order to Crescent Firearms for 200 Carcano Italian rifles at a cost of $8.50 each. The rifles were received by Klein's on Sept. 21, 1963, in a series of cases, ten rifles to each case.

Mr. Belin. I'm going to hand you what has been marked as Waldman Deposition Exhibit No. 3 and ask you to state if you know what this is.

Mr. Waldman. Yes; these are memos prepared by Crescent Firearms showing serial numbers of rifles that were shipped to us and each of these represents those rifles that were contained in a case.

I asked the witness to examine the photostatic copy of the records from Crescent to see if the rifle, Serial No. C-2766, was included.

Mr. Belin. I notice that there are numbers on each of these papers with 10 serial numbers each. I see here No. 3672, 3504 on the first photostat of Waldman Deposition Exhibit No. 3. Do you see that?

Mr. Waldman. I do.

Mr. Belin. I'm going to ask you to search through these 10 photostats and see if you find any invoice number that has on it a serial number, C-2766.

Mr. Waldman. Crescent Firearms delivery memo No. 3620 covering carton or case No. 3376 does have a—indicate a rifle bearing serial No. 2766.

Mr. Belin. Well, is it 2766 or is there a prefix to it?

Mr. Waldman. There is a prefix, C-2766.

Waldman said that Klein's Sporting Goods assigned

to each rifle a control number which is a number used by us to record the history of the gun while it is in our possession and until it is sold, thus each rifle will be tagged with both this control number and with the serial number of the rifle which is stamped on the—imprinted on the gun by the manufacturer.

Mr. Belin. Do you have the same—does the same manufacturer give different serial numbers for each weapon that the manufacturer makes?

Mr. Waldman. The gun manufacturers imprint a different number on each gun. It's stamped into the frame of the gun and serves as a unique identification for each gun.

Mr. Belin. Well, I hand you what has been marked as Waldman Deposition Exhibit No. 4 and ask you to state if you know what this is.

Mr. Waldman. This is the record created by us showing the control number we have assigned to the gun together with the serial number that is imprinted in the frame of the gun.

Mr. Belin. Now, this is a photostat, I believe, of records you have in front of you on your desk right now?

Mr. Waldman. That's correct.

Mr. Belin. Do you find anywhere on Waldman Deposition No. 4 the serial number C-2766?

Mr. Waldman. Yes.

Mr. Belin. And what is your control number for that?

Mr. Waldman. Our control number for that is VC-836.

Having identified the receipt of the rifle into Chicago, the next question became where and to whom the rifle was shipped.

Mr. Belin. Mr. Waldman, were you ever contacted by any law enforcement agency about the disposition of this Mannlicher-Carcano rifle that had the serial number C-2766 on it?

Mr. Waldman. Yes; on the night of Nov. 22, 1963, the FBI contacted our company in an effort to determine whether the gun had been in our possession and if so, what disposition we had made of it.

Mr. Belin. Do you know how the FBI happened to contact you or your company?

Mr. Waldman. The FBI had a record of a gun of this type and with this serial number having been shipped to us by Crescent Firearms.

Mr. Belin. Do you mean that Crescent Firearms gave the FBI this information?

Mr. Waldman. Well, I—I must assume that's the case. I don't know it for a fact.

Mr. Belin. All right. What did you and your company do when you were contacted by the FBI?

Mr. Waldman. We met with the FBI in our offices.

Mr. Belin. Was this on Friday evening, Nov. 22?

Mr. Waldman. On Friday evening, Nov. 22.

Mr. Belin. Did the FBI indicate at what time, what period that they felt you might have received this rifle originally?

Mr. Waldman. We were able to determine from our purchase records the date in which the rifle had been received, and they also had a record of when it had been shipped, so we knew the approximate date of receipt by us, and from that we made—let's see, we examined our microfilm records which show orders from mail order customers and related papers, and from this determined to whom the gun had been shipped by us.

Mr. Belin. Are these microfilm records part of your customary recording of transactions of your company?

Mr. Waldman. Yes; they are.

Mr. Belin. I'm handing you what has been marked as an FBI Exhibit D-77 and ask you if you know what this is.

Mr. Waldman. This is a microfilm record that—of mail order transactions for a given period of time. It was turned over by us to the FBI.

Mr. Belin. Do you know when it was turned over to the FBI?

Mr. Waldman. It was turned over to them on Nov. 23, 1963.

Mr. Belin. Now, you are reading from the carton containing that microfilm. Do you know whose initials are on there?

Mr. Waldman. Yes; the initials on here are mine and they were put on the date on which this was turned over to the FBI concerned with the investigation.

Mr. Belin. You have on your premises a machine for looking at the microfilm prints?

Mr. Waldman. Yes.

Mr. Belin. And you can make copies of the microfilm prints?

Mr. Waldman. Yes.

Mr. Belin. I wonder if we can adjourn the deposition upstairs to take a look at these records in the microfilm and get copies of the appropriate records that you found on the evening of Nov. 22.

Mr. Waldman. Yes.

(Whereupon, the following proceedings were had at the microfilm machine.)

Mr. Belin. Mr. Waldman, you have just put the microfilm which we call D-77 into your viewer which is marked a Microfilm Reader-Printer, and you have identified this as No. 270502, according to your records. Is this just a record number of yours on this particular shipment?

Mr. Waldman. That's a number which we assign for identification purposes.

Mr. Belin. And on the microfilm record, would you please state who it shows this particular rifle was shipped to?

Mr. Waldman. Shipped to a Mr. A—last name—H-i-d-e-l-l, Post Office Box 2915, Dallas, Tex.

Mr. Belin. And does it show any serial number or control number?

Mr. Waldman. It shows shipment of a rifle bearing our control number VC-836 and serial number C-2766.

Mr. Belin. Is there a price shown for that?

Mr. Waldman. Price is $19.95, plus $1.50 postage and handling, or a total of $21.45.

Mr. Belin. Now, I see another number off to the left. What is this number?

Mr. Waldman. The number that you referred to, C20-T750 is a catalog number.

Mr. Belin. And after that, there appears some words of identification or description. Can you state what that is?

Mr. Waldman. The number designates an item which we sell, namely, an Italian carbine, 6.5 caliber rifle with the 4X scope.

Mr. Belin. Is there a date of shipment which appears on this microfilm record?

Mr. Waldman. Yes; the date of shipment was Mar. 20, 1963.

Mr. Belin. Does it show by what means it was shipped?

Mr. Waldman. It was shipped by parcel post as indicated by this circle around the letters "PP."

Mr. Belin. Does it show if any amount was enclosed with the order itself?

Mr. Waldman. Yes; the amount that was enclosed with the order was $21.45, as designated on the right-hand side of this order blank here.

Mr. Belin. Opposite the words "total amount enclosed"?

Mr. Waldman. Yes.

Mr. Belin. Is there anything which indicates in what form you received the money?

Mr. Waldman. Yes; below the amount is shown the letters "MO" designating money order.

Mr. Belin. Now, I see the extreme top of this microfilm, the date, Mar. 13, 1963; to what does that refer?

Mr. Waldman. This is an imprint made by our cash register indicating that the remittance received from the customer was passed through our register on that date.

Mr. Belin. And to the right of that, I see $21.45. Is that correct?

Mr. Waldman. That's correct.

Mr. Belin. Is there any other record that you have in connection with the shipment of this rifle other than the particular microfilm negative frame that we are looking at right now?

Mr. Waldman. We have a—this microfilm record of a coupon clipped from a portion of one of our advertisements, which indicates by writing of the customer on the coupon that he ordered our catalog No. C20-T750; and he has shown the price of the item, $19.95, and gives as his name A. Hidell, and his address as Post Office Box 2915, in Dallas, Tex.

Mr. Belin. Anything else on that negative microfilm frame?

Mr. Waldman. The coupon overlays the envelope in which the order was mailed and this shows in the upper left-hand corner the return address of A. Hidell, Post Office Box 2915, in Dallas, Tex.

There is a postmark of Dallas, Tex., and a postdate of Mar. 12, 1963, indicating that the order was mailed by airmail.

Mr. Belin. Can you see the actual cancelled stamp in the upper right-hand corner?

Mr. Waldman. Yes.

Mr. Belin. And the stamp itself says "United States Airmail"?

Mr. Waldman. That's correct.

Mr. Belin. And underneath that, someone has written "airmail"; is that correct?

Mr. Waldman. That's true.

Mr. Belin. And someone has written it addressed to you; is that correct?

Mr. Waldman. That's right.

I then made two prints from the microfilm records and introduced them into evidence as Waldman deposition Exhibits 7 and 8. The latter was the actual order coupon for the rifle. Then I turned to the actual money order that had been used to pay for the rifle.

Mr. Belin. Can you just give us one or more of the magazines in which this coupon might have been taken?

Mr. Waldman. Well, this coupon was specifically taken from American Rifleman Magazine, issue of Feb. 1963. It's identified by the department number which is shown as—now, if I can read this—shown as Department 358 on the coupon.

Mr. Belin. And that number also appears in the address on the envelope to you, is that correct, or to your company?

Mr. Waldman. That's correct.

Mr. Belin. Now, I believe that you said the total amount was $19.95, plus $1.50 for shipping charges, or $21.45; is that correct?

Mr. Waldman. The $1.50 is for both shipping charges and handling.

Mr. Belin. I hand you what has been marked as Commission Exhibit No. 788, which appears to be a U.S. postal money order payable to the order of Klein's Sporting Goods, and marked that it's from a purchaser named A. Hidell, and as the purchaser's street address is Post Office Box No. 2915, and the purchaser's city, Dallas, Tex.; Mar. 12, 1963; and underneath the amount of $21.45, the number 2,202,130,462. And on the reverse side there appears to be an endorsement of a bank.

I wonder if you would read that endorsement, if you would, and examine it, please.

Mr. Waldman. This is a stamped endorsement reading "Pay to the order of the First National Bank of Chicago," followed by our account No. 50 space 91144, and that, in turn, followed by "Klein's Sporting Goods, Inc."

Mr. Belin. Do you know whether or not that is your company's endorsement on that money order?

Mr. Waldman. It's identical to our endorsement.

Waldman said that the rifle could be bought either with or without a scope.

Mr. Belin. Now, when we examined Waldman Deposition Exhibit No. 1, you had a control number of which the last four numbers were T749, and when you shipped the rifle, you had the control number with the last four numbers as T750; otherwise the control number is the same. Could you tell us what accounts for the difference?

Mr. Waldman. Yes; these numbers that you referred to are not control numbers, as previously stated. These are known as catalog numbers. The number C20-T749 describes a rifle only, whereas the catalog No. C20-T750 describes the Italian carbine rifle with a four-power scope, which is sold as a package unit.

Mr. Belin. Do you remember what the rifle would have cost without the scope?

Mr. Waldman. As I recall, it was either $12.78 or $12.95.

Mr. Belin. Would the advertisement run in the Rifleman's Magazine of February 1963 have given the purchaser the option to buy with or without the scope, if you remember?

Mr. Waldman. Without specific reference to the ad, I would say that it did. Most usually we did.

Mr. Belin. And the purchaser would signify his preference in what manner?

Mr. Waldman. The customer designates whether he wants the rifle only or whether he wants the rifle with the scope by his selection of catalog numbers.

Mr. Belin. When this rifle came to your company, was the scope already mounted on it when you got it from Crescent?

Mr. Waldman. No.

Mr. Belin. Who put the scope on the rifle?

Mr. Waldman. The scope was mounted on the rifle in our gun shop, most probably by a gunsmith named William Sharp.

Mr. Belin. Would Mr. Sharp drill whatever holes were necessary for the mounting and do the actual mounting then himself?

Mr. Waldman. Yes.

Mr. Belin. Would Mr. Sharp or anyone else in your company in any way sight in the sight, whether it would be boresighting or actual firing with the sight?

Mr. Waldman. No; it's very unlikely in an inexpensive rifle of this sort that he would do anything other than roughly aline the scope with the rifle.

Mr. Belin. Do you have any records which show where you purchased the scope?

Mr. Waldman. It's reasonably certain the scope was purchased from Martin B. Retting, Inc., 1129 Washington Boulevard, Culver City, Calif.

Mr. Belin. Would it have any identification on the scope itself, if you know?

Mr. Waldman. It's most probable it carried the name "Ordnance Optics."

I then asked Waldman whether the rifle was shipped with the scope:

Mr. Waldman. Our catalog No. C20-T750, which was the number indicated on the coupon prepared by A. Hidell, designates a rifle with scope attached. And we would have so shipped it unless the customer specifically specified that he did not wish to have it attached. There is nothing in our records to indicate that there was any request made by the customer, and therefore we would have every reason to believe that it was shipped as a rifle with scope mounted.

Within 24 hours after the assassination, the FBI had traced the rifle to a post office box in Dallas.

The Post Office Department quickly found the postal money order sent to Klein's and determined who had rented Post Office Box 2915 in Dallas during the period when the rifle was shipped. Harry D. Holmes was a United States Post Office inspector in Dallas. He had joined the postal inspection service in 1942 and had been a postal inspector ever since, moving to Dallas in 1948. On Nov. 23,

I came into the lobby of the terminal annex, and the postal inspector that was on duty mentioned that the FBI agent had called to inquire as to how they could obtain an original post office money order.

He said he had told them that they would have to get it in Washington, but would have to know the number of the post office money order.

So he was worrying then as to how he could get that number.

So I knew about the post office money order. They said that Oswald—they said that also this FBI agent had passed on the information that, I don't know whether he told him or I called the FBI after—I went on up to my office, but somewhere I got the information that the FBI had knowledge that a gun of this particular Italian make and caliber had been purchased from Klein's Sporting Goods in Chicago, that it had been purchased, and the FBI furnished me the information that a money order of some description in the amount of $21.95 had been used as reimbursement for the gun that had been purchased from Klein's in Chicago, and that the purchase date was Mar. 20, 1963. I immediately had some men begin to search the Dallas money order records with the thought that they might have used a U.S. postal money order to buy this gun.

I didn't have any luck, so along about 11 o'clock in the morning, Saturday, I had my boys call the postal inspector. Oh, wait a minute, let's back up.

I had my secretary go out and purchase about half a dozen books on outdoor-type magazines such as Field and Stream, with the thought that I might locate this gun to identify it, and I did.

Mr. Belin. You have what magazine?

Mr. Holmes. Field and Stream of November 1963.

Mr. Belin. You found a Field and Stream magazine of just November 1963?

Mr. Holmes. It was the current magazine on the rack.

Mr. Belin. You got it to look for a gun and identified it in this magazine? Is this the page? I will call it Holmes Deposition Exhibit 2.

Mr. Holmes. Here, page 98.

Mr. Belin. Well, it is on the back of a page numbered 98, is that right?

Mr. Holmes. That's right.

Mr. Belin. On the front side. I am marking on the top of it, "Holmes Deposition Exhibit 2."

Was that the page you tore out?

Mr. Holmes. Yes, sir.

Mr. Belin. I see one circled in red, is that correct?

Mr. Holmes. That's correct.

Mr. Belin. Who circled that in red?

Mr. Holmes. I did.

Mr. Belin. Then I see that it is a picture with a gun with a scope on it and it says, "6.5 Italian carbine," in big black letters. And underneath it says, "Late military issue. Only 40 inches overall. Weighs 7 lbs. Shows only slight use, test-fired and head spaced, ready for shooting. Turned-down bolt. 6-shot, clip fed, rear sight." And it is marked "$12.78."

Mr. Holmes. With scope, it is $19.95.

Mr. Belin. There is a number. That $12.78 says "C20-1196." And underneath that is says, "C20-750, carbine with brand new 4x-$^{3}/_{4}$" diameter (illustrated) $19.95." Is that right?

Mr. Holmes. That's correct.

Mr. Belin. Then on the lower right-hand corner of the page there is a kind of place for clipping out of coupons. It is marked "Klein's Sporting Goods at 227 West Washington Street, Chicago 6, Illinois," then there is a place for a box to be checked. It says, "cash customers, send check or money order in full. Unless otherwise specified, send $1.00 postage and handling on any size order . . . $1.50 on shotgun and rifles."

Then there is a place at the bottom of the page. It is a place for putting the name and address and the city and state, is that correct?

Mr. Holmes. That's correct.

Mr. Belin. Now I notice on a piece of scrap paper you have taken the $19.95 which would be the exact amount for the rifle with the scope, and then added the $1.50 for the charge that the coupon says for postage and handling and you come up with a total of $21.45.

I thought you said the FBI said $21.95?

Mr. Holmes. He had, and that was the amount of money order I had been looking for. So I had my postal inspector in charge call our Chicago office and suggested that he get an inspector out to Klein's Sporting Goods and recheck it for accuracy, that if our looking at the right gun in the magazine, they were looking for the wrong money order.

Mr. Belin. So what happened?

Mr. Holmes. So in about an hour Postal Inspector McGee of Chicago called back then and said that the correct amount was $21.95—$21.45—excuse me, and that the shipping—they had received this money order on March the 13th, whereas I had been looking for Mar. 20.

So then I passed the information to the men who were looking for this money order stub to show which would designate, which would show the number of the money order, and that is the only way you could find one.

I relayed this information to them and told them to start on the 13th because he could have bought it that morning and that he could have gotten it by airmail that afternoon, so they began to search and within 10 minutes they called back and said they had a money order in that amount issued on, I don't know that I show, but it was that money order in an amount issued at the main post office, which is the same place as this post office box was at that time, box 2915, and the money order had been issued early on the morning of March the 12th, 1963.

Mr. Belin. To whom?

Mr. Holmes. They are issued in blank. He has to fill it in.

I then turned to the postal records concerning Box 2915 in Dallas.

Mr. Belin. I hand you what has been marked "Holmes Deposition Exhibit 3," and ask you to state what that is?

Mr. Holmes. That is a photostatic copy of the original box rental application covering the rental of box 2915, at the main post office in Dallas, Tex., which shows that it was completed on October the 9th, 1962. The applicant's name was Lee H. Oswald, home address, 3519 Fairmore Avenue, Dallas, Tex. Signed Lee H. Oswald. It shows that the box was closed on May 14, 1963.

Mr. Belin. Now, it is stamped date box opened, Oct. 9, 1962. And that is the same date that it appears to be written in handwriting at the bottom of it.

Mr. Holmes. That's correct.

Thus, the post office box had been in the name of Oswald during the period in which the rifle was shipped.

The money order number "was transmitted by phone to the Chief Inspector in Washington, who immediately got the money order center at Washington to begin a search, which they use IBM equipment to kick out this money order, and about 7 o'clock Saturday night they did kick out the original money order and sent it over by, so they said, by special conveyance to the Secret Service, chief of Secret Service at Washington now, and it turned out, so they said, to be the correct money order. I asked them by phone as to what it said on it, and it said it had been issued to A. J. Hidell, which to me then was the tip that I had the correct money order. Up to then I didn't know whether I had the correct money order or not."

Mr. Belin. How did you know about the use of the name A. J. Hidell?

Mr. Holmes. When the box was opened in the name of Lee H. Oswald. Because for two reasons. I—one is, when he rented the post office box in New Orleans, he used the name of A. J. Hidell as one of the persons entitled to receive mail in that box.

Mr. Belin. At that time did you know about that?

Mr. Holmes. Yes.

Mr. Belin. All right, what else?

Mr. Holmes. In his billfold the police had found a draft registration card in the name of A. J. Hidell on his person at the time of his arrest, and I had seen it.

After Post Office Box 2915 was closed on May 14, 1963, the application was thrown away in accordance with postal regulations. Even though the box was in the name of Lee Harvey Oswald and the rifle was addressed to A. Hidell, the usual postal procedure was to place a notice in the box when a package was received for a box, regardless whether the name on the package was listed on the application as a person entitled to receive mail through the box. The person having access to the box then takes the notice to the window and is given the package. Ordinarily, identification is not required because it is assumed that the person with the notice is entitled to the package.

In the case of Lee Harvey Oswald, it would have made no difference whether identification was requested, for when Oswald was arrested at the Texas Theatre he had purported identification cards in his wallet in the name of Hidell in addition to identification cards in his own name. These included a Selective Service notice of classification and a Marine certificate of service in the name of Alek James Hidell. On the Hidell Selective Service card there appeared a signature, "Alek J. Hidell," and the photograph of Lee Harvey Oswald. Experts on questioned documents from the Treasury Department and the FBI testified that the Hidell cards were counterfeit photographic reproductions made by photographing the Oswald cards, retouching the resulting negatives, and producing prints from the retouched negatives.

As you will soon learn, Oswald rented a room at 1026 North Beckley in the Oak Cliff section of Dallas. After his arrest, the room was searched.

In Oswald's personal effects found in his room at 1026 North Beckley Avenue in Dallas was a purported international certificate of vaccination signed by "Dr. A. J. Hideel," Post Office Box 30016, New Orleans. It certified that Lee Harvey Oswald had been vaccinated for smallpox on June 8, 1963. This, too, was a forgery. The signature of "A. J. Hideel" was in the handwriting of Lee Harvey Oswald. There is no "Dr. Hideel" licensed to practice medicine in Louisiana. There is no post office box 30016 in the New Orleans Post Office but Oswald [when he moved to New Orleans] had rented post office box 30061 in New Orleans on June 3, 1963, listing Marina Oswald and A. J. Hidell as additional persons entitled to receive mail in the box. The New Orleans postal authorities had not discarded the portion of the application listing the names of those, other than the owner of the box, entitled to receive mail through the box. [Warren Commission Report, pp. 121–122.]

The Commission lawyers working in Area III determined that Hidell was a fictitious name used by Oswald while he lived in New Orleans.

Marina Oswald testified that she first learned of Oswald's use of the fictitious name "Hidell" in connection with his pro-Castro activities in New Orleans. According to her testimony, he compelled her to write the name "Hidell" on membership cards in the space designated for the signature of the "Chapter President." The name "Hidell" was stamped on some of the "Chapter's" printed literature and on the membership application blanks. Marina Oswald testified, "I knew there was no such organization. And I know Hidell is merely an altered Fidel, and I laughed at such foolishness." Hidell was a fictitious president of an organization of which Oswald was the only member.

When seeking employment in New Orleans, Oswald listed a "Sgt. Robt. Hidell" as a reference on one job application and "George Hidell" as a reference on another. Both names were found to be fictitious. Moreover, the use of "Alek" as a first name for Hidell is a further link to Oswald because "Alek" was Oswald's nickname in Russia. Letters received by Marina Oswald from her husband signed "Alek" were given to the Commission. [Warren Commission Report, p. 122]

FBI experts examined all these documents and determined that the post office box application in Dallas, the post office box application in New Orleans, the Hidell signature on the forged notice of classification of Hidell, the coupon ordering rifle No. C-2766, the envelope in which the coupon was sent, the postal money order whereon there was printed opposite the words "Pay to the Order" the words "Klein's Sporting Goods" and opposite the printed word "From" the words, "A. Hidell, P. O. Box 2915, Dallas, Texas," were all in the handwriting or printing of Lee Harvey Oswald. Two experts, Alwyn Cole and James C. Cadigan, examined all these documents and concurred in these conclusions. We summarized the general principles involved in handwriting identification on pages 567-570 of our Report.

The area of questioned document examination encompasses many types of inquiries, the most familiar of which is the identification of handwriting. Handwriting identification is based upon the principle that every person's handwriting is distinctive. As Cole testified:

Q. Mr. Cole, could you explain the basis on which you were able to make an identification of a questioned writing as being authored by the person who wrote a standard writing?

Mr. Cole. This is based upon the principle that every handwriting is distinctive, that since the mental and physical equipment for producing handwriting is different in every individual, each person produces his own distinctive writing habits. Of course, everyone learns to write in the beginning by an endeavor to repeat ideal letter forms but practically no one is able to reproduce these forms exactly. Even though a person might have some initial success during the active period of instruction, he soon departs from these and develops his own habits. It may be said that habit in handwriting is that which makes handwriting possible. Habit is that which makes handwriting efficient. If it were not for the development of habit, one would be obliged to draw or sketch.

Some habit would be included even in those efforts. But the production of handwriting rapidly and fluently always involves a recording of personal writing habit. This has been confirmed by observation of a very large number of specimens over a long period of time, and it has further been demonstrated by, on my part, having a formal responsibility for rendering decisions about the identification of handwriting based upon an agreement of handwriting habit in situations where there would be a rigorous testing of the correctness of these decisions by field investigators, for example, of the law-enforcement agencies, and a demonstration that these results were confirmed by other evidence. This is the basis for identification of handwriting.

The same principles are generally applicable to hand printing, and in the balance of this section the term "handwriting" will be used to refer to both cursive or script writing and hand printing.

Not every letter in a questioned handwriting can be used as the basis of an identification. Most people learn to write letters in a standard or "copybook" form: a handwriting is distinctive only insofar as it departs significantly from such forms. Correspondingly, not every variation indicates nonidentification; no two acts are precisely alike and variations may be found within a single document. Like similarities, variations are significant only if they are distinctive. Moreover, since any single distinctive characteristic may not be unique to one person, in order to make an identification the expert must find a sufficient number of corresponding distinctive characteristics and a general absence of distinctive differences.

The possibility that one person could imitate the handwriting of another and successfully deceive an expert document examiner is very remote. A forger leaves two types of clue. First, he can seldom perfectly simulate the letter forms of the victim; concentrating on the reproduction of one detail, he is likely not to see others. Thus, the forger may successfully imitate the general form of a letter, but get proportions or letter connections wrong. In addition, the forger draws rather than writes. Forged writing is therefore distinguished by defects in the quality of its line, such as tremor, waver, patching, retouching, noncontinuous lines, and pen lifts in awkward and unusual places.

To make a handwriting identification, the handwriting in the document under examination (the questioned document) is compared against the handwriting in documents known to have been prepared by a suspect (the known or standard documents). This is exemplified by Cole's examination of Commission Exhibit No. 773, the photograph of the mail order for the rifle and the envelope in which it was sent:

Q. Now, Mr. Cole, returning to 773, the questioned document, can you tell the Commission how you formed the conclusion that it was prepared by the author of the standards, that is, what steps you followed in your examination and comparison, what things you considered, what instruments or equipment you used, and so forth?

Mr. Cole. I made first a careful study of the writing on Commission Exhibit 773 without reference to the standard writing, in an effort to determine whether or not this writing contained what I would regard as a basis for identification, contained a record of writing habit, and as that—as a result of that part of my examination, I concluded that this is a natural handwriting. By that I mean that it was made at a fair speed, that it doesn't show any evidence of an unnatural movement, poor line quality, tremor, waver, retouching, or the like. I regard it as being made in a fluent and fairly rapid manner which would record the normal writing habits of the person who made it.

I then made a separate examination of the standards, of all of the standard writings, to determine whether that record gave a record of writing habit which could be used for identification purposes, and I concluded that it, too, was a natural handwriting and gave a good record of writing habit.

I then brought the standard writings together with the questioned writing for a detailed and orderly comparison, considering details of letter forms, proportion, pen pressure, letter connections, and other details of handwriting habit.

The standards used by Cole and Cadigan consisted of a wide variety of documents known to be in the handwriting of Lee Harvey Oswald, including endorsements on his payroll checks, applications for employment, for a passport, for membership in the American Civil Liberties Union, and for a library card, and letters to the Immigration and Naturalization Service, the Marine Corps, the State Department, and the American Embassy in Russia.

The mail order and envelope for the C2766 rifle were photographed by Klein's on microfilm, and then destroyed. To identify the handwriting an enlarged photograph was made which showed the handwriting characteristics with sufficient clarity to form the basis of an identification. Based on a comparison with the standards, the handwriting on the purchase order and the envelope were identified as Lee Harvey Oswald's. The money order, which was retained by the post office after having been cashed by Klein's, was also identified as being in Oswald's handwriting. These identifications were made on the basis of numerous characteristics in which the writing in both the questioned and standard documents departed from conventional letter forms. For example, in the return address on the envelope, the left side of the "A" in "A. Hidell" was made by a downstroke followed by an upstroke which almost exactly traced the downstroke, the "i" showed an elongation of the approach stroke and an exaggerated slant to the right, and the second "l" was somewhat larger than the first; the "B" in "Box" had an upper lobe smaller than the lower lobe; the "D" in "Dallas" exhibited a distinctive construction of the looped form at the top of a letter, and the "s" was flattened and forced over on its side; and the "x" in "Texas" was made in the form of a "u" with a cross bar. These characteristics were also present in the standards. In addition, these items, as well as other questioned documents, resembled the standards in their use of certain erroneous combinations of capital and lowercase letters. For example, in the mail order, "Texas" was printed with a capital "T," "X," "A," and "S," but a lowercase "e"; a similar mixture of capital and lowercase letters in "Texas" was found in the standards.

The writing on the purchase order and envelope showed no significant evidence of disguise (subject to the qualification that the use of hand printing on the mail order, rather than handwriting, may have been used for that purpose). However, it is not unusual for a person using an alias not to disguise his writing. For example, Cole, who is document examiner for the Treasury Department, has frequently examined forgeries evidencing no attempt at disguise.

One other item was ordered in the name of A. J. Hidell and shipped to Post Office Box 2915 in Dallas during the time that Lee Harvey Oswald rented the box. This was the revolver used in the slaying of Officer Tippit, our Exhibit No. 143.

Just as it had done with the rifle, Serial No. C-2766, the FBI was able to trace quickly the source of the revolver used in the Tippit shooting. As our Report noted:

By checking certain importers and dealers after the assassination of President Kennedy and slaying of Officer Tippit, agents of the FBI determined that George Rose & Co. of Los Angeles was a major distributor of this type of revolver. Records of Seaport Traders, Inc., a mail-order division of George Rose & Co., disclosed that on Jan. 3, 1963, the company received from Empire Wholesale Sporting Goods, Ltd., Montreal, a shipment of 99 guns in one case. Among these guns was a .38 Special caliber Smith & Wesson revolver, serial No. V510210, the only revolver made by Smith & Wesson with this serial number. When first manufactured, it had a 5-inch barrel. George Rose & Co. had the barrel shortened by a gunsmith to 2¼ inches.

Sometime after Jan. 27, 1963, Seaport Traders, Inc., received through the mail a mail-order coupon for one ".38 St. W. 2" Bbl.," cost $29.95. Ten dollars in cash was enclosed. The order was signed in ink by "A. J. Hidell, aged 28." The date of the order was Jan. 27 (no year shown), and the return address was Post Office Box 2915, Dallas, Tex. Also on the order form was an order, written in ink, for one box of ammunition and one holster, but a line was drawn through these items. The mail-order form had a line for the name of a witness to attest that the person ordering the gun was a U.S. citizen and had not been convicted of a felony. The name written in this space was D. F. Drittal.

Heinz W. Michaelis, office manager of both George Rose & Co., Inc., and Seaport Traders, Inc., identified records of Seaport Traders, Inc., which showed that a ".38 S and W Special two-inch Commando, serial number V510210" was shipped on Mar. 20, 1963, to A. J. Hidell, Post Office Box 2915, Dallas, Tex. The invoice was prepared on Mar. 13, 1963; the revolver was actually shipped on Mar. 20 by Railway Express. The balance due on the purchase was $19.95. Michaelis furnished the shipping copy of the invoice, and the Railway Express Agency shipping documents, showing that $19.95, plus $1.27 shipping charge, had been collected from the consignee, Hidell.

Handwriting experts, Alwyn Cole of the Treasury Department and James C. Cadigan of the FBI, testified before the Commission that the writing on the coupon was Oswald's. The signature of the witness, D. F. Drittal, who attested that the fictitious Hidell was an American citizen and had not been convicted of a felony, was also in Oswald's handwriting.

Members of the jury, we have now identified Lee Harvey Oswald as the owner of the revolver used in the murder of Officer Tippit and as the owner of the rifle used in the assassination of President Kennedy. The next step for us is to examine his activities on that fateful Friday in Dallas.

28

"IT WAS RIGHT NEXT TO THE STAIRWAY—RIGHT IN THE CORNER"

I received a phone call from a lady in Irving who said her name was Mrs. Paine.

Mr. Belin. All right.

What did Mrs. Paine say, and what did you say?

Mr. Truly. She said, "Mr. Truly"—words to this effect—you understand—"Mr. Truly, you don't know who I am but I have a neighbor whose brother works for you. I don't know what his name is. But he tells his sister that you are very busy. And I am just wondering if you can use another man," or words to that effect.

And I told Mrs.—she said, "I have a fine young man living here with his wife and baby, and his wife is expecting a baby—another baby, in a few days, and he needs work desperately."

Now, this is not absolutely—this is as near as I can remember the conversation over the telephone.

And I told Mrs. Paine that—to send him down. and I would talk to him—that I didn't have anything in mind for him of a permanent nature, but if he was suited, we could possibly use him for a brief time.

Mr. Belin. Was there anything else from that conversation that you remember at all, or not?

Mr. Truly. No. I believe that was the first and the last time that I talked to Mrs. Paine.

In fact, I could not remember her name afterwards until I saw her name in print, and then it popped into my mind that this was the lady who called me.

Mr. Belin. All right.

Anything else on—what was this—Oct. 15th—about Lee Harvey Oswald?

Mr. Truly. Yes, sir; I am sure it was on Oct. 15th.

Mr. Belin. Anything else you can remember about Lee Harvey Oswald on that day?

Mr. Truly. She told me she would tell him to come down and see me.

So he came in, introduced himself to me, and I took him in my office and interviewed him. He seemed to be quiet and well mannered.

I gave him an application to fill out, which he did.

Roy S. Truly, 56-year-old superintendent of the TSBD Company, hired the "fine young man" that afternoon. The next morning he came to work as an order-filler.[1]

The Texas School Book Depository Company is a private corporation engaged in the business of selling school books.

[1]This was nearly a month before the final selection of the Trade Mart as the luncheon site and the determination of the motorcade route past the TSBD Building. See Chapter 15.

Mr. Belin. Well, perhaps you might explain to the Commission just what exactly the nature of your business is, and how an employee would go about filling orders.

Mr. Truly. We are agents for a number of publishers. We furnish offices for those who desire them in Texas. And our business is shipping, inventorying, collecting, doing all the bookkeeping work for the various publishers' books.

Now, we have—most of the publishers' stock is lined up alphabetically by titles or by stock numbers or code numbers, whichever determines that.

And the location of the books—each publisher's books are to themselves. They are not mixed in with several other publishers on the various floors.

On the first floor we have bin stock, shelf stock, we fill a lot of small orders from. And then in the basement the same. The fifth and the sixth floor, and part of the seventh floor is overflow stock. It is reserve stock. But the boys have to go to those floors all during the day to pick up stock and bring it to the first floor in order to process and complete the orders for the checker.

According to Truly, Oswald filled orders primarily for the publishing house of Scott, Foresman & Co., although "possibly he filled some of Gregg Publishing Co. and others."

Mr. Belin. Where, generally, are Scott, Foresman books kept?

Mr. Truly. On the first floor and the sixth floor. We have a large quantity of their books on the sixth floor.

Mr. Belin. And this is the area where Lee Harvey Oswald worked?

Mr. Truly. He had occasion to go to the sixth floor quite a number of times every day, each day, after books.

Mr. Belin. Now, when an order would come in, how would it get to the individual employee, so the employee would go out and pick out the books?

Mr. Truly. The orders came into our office and were processed by our girls, priced and billed by the bill clerks, and then were sent down a little chute to the first floor, a little dumbwaiter, regardless of publisher.

The boys would take them off of this dumbwaiter and carry them over on to a little table near the checker stand.

Various ones would sort out the publishers—sort out the orders by publishers. . .

Mr. Belin. Do they just pick up the piece of paper for the order and carry them around with them?

Mr. Truly. That is right. Most of them use a clipboard. They may have several orders at a time on the clipboard. That saves them going back to the table continually for one order. These orders amount from anything to $3 or $4 to $300 or $400, on up. . . .

Mr. Belin. Who else worked on Scott, Foresman other than Lee Harvey Oswald?

Mr. Truly. Well, I assume that all of our boys, all of our order fillers have worked at some time or other, because when the boys finish up the stocks they are working, the orders they are filling, if there is anything left, regardless of publisher, they go fill it.

But Scott, Foresman was one of our publishers that I would say would be easiest for a new man to learn how to fill. And we have a lot of those orders. . . .

Mr. Belin. When they fill the orders, they go and get the books, and bring them down to your wrapping and mailing section?

Mr. Truly. That is right. And they are checked to see that they are in correct quantities and titles and called for on the order, or the invoice.

Then they are weighed up on parcel post scales, if they go by parcel post, or they are processed over on the floor if they are big enough for freight. . . .

Mr. Belin. Anything else you can think of with regard to the particular nature of the type of work that Lee Harvey Oswald did when he was working for your company?

Mr. Truly. Nothing—except that we have occasionally—we would check the numbers of orders that each boy filled per day, to see if he is doing a day's work. And each invoice which is the billing of the order, has a little section for a checker's number. And the order filler's number. Our checker periodically would count at the end of the day the number of orders that each order filler filled that day. . . .

Mr. Belin. What did you find generally—would you classify Lee Harvey Oswald as an average employee—above average, or below average employee?

Mr. Truly. I would say for the nature of the work and the time he was there, the work that he did was a bit above average. I wasn't on that floor constantly. The boy, from all reports to me, and what I have seen kept working and talked little to anybody else. He just kept moving. And he did a good day's work.

Mr. Belin. What was his pay?

Mr. Truly. $1.25 an hour.

Prior to the assassination, the last known employee to see Oswald inside the building was Charles Givens, a 38-year-old Texas School Book Depository employee who had worked for the company for approximately six years. On the morning of Nov. 22, he was helping put down some new plywood on the west end of the sixth floor. Around 8:30 that morning, he had seen Oswald filling orders from some bins on the first floor.

Mr. Belin. All right. You saw him at 8:30 on the first floor?

Mr. Givens. Yes, sir.

Mr. Belin. Then what did you do?

Mr. Givens. Well, we went back upstairs and started to work.

Mr. Belin. You went back up to the sixth floor to continue laying the floor?

Mr. Givens. Yes, sir.

Mr. Belin. When did you see Lee Harvey Oswald next?

Mr. Givens. Next?

Mr. Belin. Yes.

Mr. Givens. Well, it was about a quarter till 12, we were on our way downstairs, and we passed him, and he was standing at the gate on the fifth floor.

I came downstairs, and I discovered I left my cigarettes in my jacket pocket upstairs, and I took the elevator back upstairs to get my jacket with my cigarettes in it. When I got back upstairs, he was on the sixth floor in that vicinity, coming from that way.

Mr. Belin. Coming from what way?

Mr. Givens. Toward the window up front where the shots were fired from.

According to Givens, when he last saw Oswald, he (Oswald) was walking toward the elevator from the southeast corner of the sixth floor with a clipboard in his hand.

Mr. Belin. Did you see all of his body or not?

Mr. Givens. Yes, sir: he had his clipboard in his hand.

Mr. Belin. He had his clipboard in his hand?

Mr. Givens. Yes, sir.

Mr. Belin. Was that kind of an aisleway over there right next to the east wall that he was walking along, or what?

Mr. Givens. Yes, sir; they have aisles.

Mr. Belin. Now, was there stock in back of him as well as in front of him? Were you where you had stacked it up, or not, or don't you remember?

Mr. Givens. Well, it was already some books stacked there.

Mr. Belin. Were there books stacked between where you saw him and the window itself?

Mr. Givens. Yes, sir.

Mr. Belin. All right, he was walking with his clipboard from that southeast corner?

Mr. Givens. Yes, sir.

Mr. Belin. Where did you see him walking? What direction did you see him walking in?

Mr. Givens. He was coming towards the elevators.

Mr. Belin. From the Elm Street side of the building?

Mr. Givens. Yes, sir.

Mr. Belin. So that would be walking in a northerly direction?

Mr. Givens. Yes, sir.

Mr. Belin. Now, you said that he had a clipboard in his hand?

Mr. Givens. Yes; he had his board with his orders on it.

Mr. Belin. Did you see the orders on the board?

Mr. Givens. Well, yes, sir; he had it in his hand.

Mr. Belin. Did he have any books in his hand that he was carrying?

Mr. Givens. No, sir.

Mr. Belin. Did you ever fill orders in November on the sixth floor?

Mr. Givens. Yes, sir.

Mr. Belin. Do you remember whether or not there were any books or book cartons over in that corner from which he might have been filling orders?

Mr. Givens. Well, yes, sir; it was possible.

Mr. Belin. Did you watch where he walked to?

Mr. Givens. Well, no, sir; I didn't pay much attention. I was getting ready to get on the elevator, and I say, "Boy, are you going downstairs?"

Mr. Belin. What did he say to you?

Mr. Givens. I say, "It's near lunch time."

He said, "No, sir. When you get downstairs, close the gate to the elevator."

That meant the elevator on the west side, you can pull both gates down and it will come up by itself.

Mr. Belin. What else did he say?

Mr. Givens. That is all.

Mr. Belin. What did you say to that? Did you say you would close the elevator gate, or not say anything?

Mr. Givens. I said, "Okay," and got on the elevator.

Mr. Belin. What elevator did you take down?

Mr. Givens. The east elevator.

Mr. Belin. Do you know whether or not when you got down to the first floor, the west elevator was there?

Mr. Givens. No, sir; it wasn't, because I looked over there to close the gate and it wasn't there.

Mr. Belin. Do you know where it was?

Mr. Givens. No, sir; I don't.

Mr. Belin. What time was this?

Mr. Givens. Well, I would say it was about 5 minutes to 12.

When Givens got to the first floor, he ate his lunch outside, standing in front of the building, and then walked one block east to the corner of Elm and Record Streets where he had a friend working at a parking lot.

Mr. Belin. Now you said you saw Lee Oswald on the sixth floor around 11:55?

Mr. Givens. Right.

Mr. Belin. Did you see Lee Oswald anywhere else in the building between 11:55 and the time you left the building?

Mr. Givens. No, sir.

Mr. Belin. On Nov. 22d?

Mr. Givens. No, sir.

Mr. Belin. Did you see him in the domino room at all around anywhere between 11:30 and 12 or 12:30?

Mr. Givens. No, sir . . .

Mr. Belin. Did you ever see Lee Oswald at any time after the time you saw him carrying the clipboard on the sixth floor?

Mr. Givens. No, sir. The next time I saw him was on television.

Mr. Belin. Is there anything else you can think of, whether I have asked it or not, that in any way is relevant to the assassination?

Mr. Givens. No, sir.

Mr. Belin. Anything else you can think of about Lee Oswald, whether I have asked it or not, that might in any way be helpful?

Mr. Givens. No, sir. Other than he is just a peculiar fellow. He is just a loner. Don't have much to say to anybody. Stayed by himself most of the time.

Mr. Belin. Did you ever notice any one person there he was more friendly with than the other?

Mr. Givens. Well, this boy he rode with.

Mr. Belin. Frazier?

Mr. Givens. Yes, sir. Every once in a while I would see him talking to him. Bonnie Ray told me—I never saw him, but Bonnie Ray told me he talked to he and Danny sometimes.

Mr. Belin. Anyone else?

Mr. Givens. Not that I know of; no, sir.

Mr. Belin. Anything else you can think of?

Mr. Givens. No, sir; that is about it.

Mr. Belin. Well, Mr. Givens, we surely appreciate your cooperation in coming down here.

Now you and I didn't talk about this at all until we started taking this deposition, did we?

Mr. Givens. No, sir.

Mr. Belin. You walked into the room and you raised your right hand and we started taking your testimony. Is that correct?

Mr. Givens. Yes, sir.

Mr. Belin. Have I ever met you before?

Mr. Givens. I don't believe so.

I don't believe I have.

No employee of the TSBD Company is known to have seen Oswald again until after the shooting.

The significance of Givens's testimony that Oswald was carrying his clipboard became apparent on Dec. 2, 1963.

You jurors will remember that the rifle was found in the northwest corner of the sixth floor near the stairway. About 10 days after the assassination, Frankie Kaiser, another Depository employee, was looking for a teacher's edition of Catholic Handbooks, copies of which were stored in the northwest corner of the sixth floor. While looking for these books, Kaiser found a clipboard hidden by book cartons in the northwest corner of the sixth floor at the west wall, a few feet from where the rifle had been found.

Mr. Ball. Where was it with reference to the stairway?
Mr. Kaiser. It was right next to the stairway—right in the corner.

When he found the clipboard,

I went downstairs and got my boss.
Mr. Ball. What is his name?
Mr. Kaiser. William H. Shelley.
Mr. Ball. And then what happened?
Mr. Kaiser. This FBI was standing there with me—he was standing there then and I told him I had a clipboard laying up there with the orders.

According to Kaiser, there were unfilled orders on the clipboard. He did not remember the date of the orders because he did not examine them. "I just went down and got my boss and then they took it down."

Mr. Ball. Now, Frankie, that clipboard you found, describe it—what was it?
Mr. Kaiser. It was made out of paper and tape and a little piece of pasteboard.
Mr. Ball. Who made it?
Mr. Kaiser. I did.
Mr. Ball. When?
Mr. Kaiser. Well, right after I started there—it had been a long time ago.
Mr. Ball. And how was it you weren't using it on this day?
Mr. Kaiser. You see, when he first started there—
Mr. Ball. Who is "he"?
Mr. Kaiser. Lee—when he first started to work there he got my clipboard and started using it.
Mr. Ball. Did you give it to him to use?
Mr. Kaiser. No, he just picked it up and started using it and I just went and made me another one.
Mr. Ball. You recognized that clipboard when you saw it?
Mr. Kaiser. Yes, because my name was all over it.
Mr. Ball. Your name was on it, too?
Mr. Kaiser. Yes, sir.
Mr. Ball. You put your name "Frankie Kaiser" on it?
Mr. Kaiser. You see, it don't do no good to get a clipboard around here—everybody is always running off with it.
Mr. Ball. That's the reason you put your name on it?
Mr. Kaiser. He come up and got it and started using it and I just let him keep it and made me another one.

William H. Shelley was the manager of the Miscellaneous Department of the TSBD. He was Lee Harvey Oswald's immediate supervisor. Shelley testified that Oswald had used a clipboard and that Frankie Kaiser had found Oswald's clipboard "on the sixth floor in the corner of the stairway." On the clipboard were unfilled orders for Scott, Foresman books. According to Shelley, Oswald "filled mostly Scott, Foresman orders."

Shelley said that at the time the clipboard was found, FBI Agent Nat Pinkston was in the TSBD Building, "and he and Frankie and I went up and got it."

Pinkston testified that on Dec. 2, 1963, he was at the TSBD Company when "Frankie Kaiser came down the stairs and said that he had found something on the sixth floor. I then accompanied him back to the sixth floor where he pointed out on the floor near the entrance to the stairwell, a clipboard with some orders on it."

The clipboard was found "in the northwest corner of the sixth floor" of the TSBD Building "on the floor behind the books against the wall of the stairwell." There were three unfilled orders on the clipboard, each of which was for Scott, Foresman books and each of which was dated Nov. 22, 1963. Pinkston copied all the information on each of the three order slips.

Mr. Ball. What did you do when you—with the orders after you made these notations?

Mr. Pinkston. I turned them over to Mr. Truly. He desired to fill the orders.

29

"AND IT HAD CURTAINS
AND VENETIAN BLINDS"

And so I wanted to make friends with everybody I could, because you know yourself friendship is something you can't buy with money and you always need friends, so I went up and introduced himself to myself, and he told me his name was Lee and I said, "We are glad to have you."

We got talking back and forth and he come to find out I knew his wife was staying down there at the time with this other woman and so I thought he would go out there and I said, "Are you going to be going home this afternoon?"

And he told me then, he told me that he didn't have a car, you know, and so I told him, I said, "Well, I live out there in Irving"—I found out he lived out there and so I said, "Any time you want to go just let me know."

So I thought he would go home every day like most men do but he told me no, that he wouldn't go home every day and then he asked me could he ride home say like Friday afternoon on weekends and come back on Monday morning and I told him that would be just fine with me.

I told him if he wanted a ride any other time just let me know before I go off and leave him because when it comes to quitting time some of these guys, you know, some of them mess around the bathroom and some of them quit early and some of them like that and some leave at different times than others.

But I said from talking to him then, I say, he just wanted to ride home on weekends with me and I said that was fine.

The witness was 19-year-old Buell Wesley Frazier, who came to work for the Texas School Book Depository Company in September, about four or five weeks before Lee Harvey Oswald began his employment there.

Frazier lived with his sister, Linnie Mae Randle, and her husband and their family in the Dallas suburb of Irving. In the immediate neighborhood lived Ruth Paine, who had offered a room in her home to Marina Oswald. Meanwhile, Lee Harvey Oswald stayed in a small bedroom in a rooming-house in the Oak Cliff section of Dallas.

Mr. Ball. Did he ride home with you in your car on weekends?
Mr. Frazier. Yes, sir; he did.
Mr. Ball. On Friday nights.
Mr. Frazier. Right.
Mr. Ball. From that time until Nov. 22, did he ride home with you every weekend?
Mr. Frazier. No, sir; he did every weekend but one.
Mr. Ball. Do you remember that date?
Mr. Frazier. No, sir; I don't.

Mr. Ball. In the statement you made I believe you said it was the 16th and 17th of November. I am just reminding you of that.

Does it refresh your memory any?

Mr. Frazier. I remember one weekend. I say, right now I can't recall because just to be frank with you I couldn't tell you roughly; I say I might have at that time but I say it slipped my mind but the thing is I do know he rode home with me every weekend up to that but one.

Mr. Ball. And why did—did he tell you why he wasn't going to ride home that weekend?

Mr. Frazier. Yes, he did. He said he was working on his driving license and he was going to go take a driving test.

Ball asked Frazier if Oswald had ever paid for any part of the trip. Frazier replied: "No, sir, he didn't."

I never did ask him. Because like I said I drove over there anyway and it doesn't take any more to drive one guy than it does to drive a carload.

Mr. Ball. Did he offer to pay any time?

Mr. Frazier. No, sir; he never did.

Mr. Ball. At any time coming back after a weekend did you ever stop at a restaurant for breakfast?

Mr. Frazier. No, sir; we never did.

Mr. Ball. Did you ever stop on the way home on Friday night and buy anything?

Mr. Frazier. No, sir; stopped one time and bought some gas, I remember.

Mr. Ball. Did he pay for it?

Mr. Frazier. No, sir; he didn't.

Mr. Ball. Did he offer to?

Mr. Frazier. No, sir; he didn't.

Mr. Ball. Did you ever see him have any money in his possession, bills, change?

Mr. Frazier. No, sir; I never did see him out playing around with any money.

Mr. Ball. On the way back and forth did you talk very much to each other?

Mr. Frazier. No, sir; not very much. He is, probably in your line of business you have probably seen a lot of guys who talk a lot and some don't and he was one of these types that just didn't talk. And I have seen, you know, I am not very old but I have seen a lot of guys in my time, just going to school, different boys and girls, some talk a lot and some don't, so I didn't think anything strange about that.

About the only time you could get anything out of the talking was about babies, you know, he had one and he was expecting another, that was one way he had him get that job because his wife was pregnant and I would always get something out of it when I asked him about the babies because it seemed he was very fond of children because when I asked him he chuckled and told me about what he was doing about the babies over the weekend and sometimes we would talk about the weather, and sometimes he would go to work and it would be cloudy in the morning and it would come out that afternoon after work, sometimes during the day and it would turn to be just one of the prettiest days you would want anywhere, and he would say some comment about that, but not very much.

He would say a few words and then he would cut off.

Ball then turned to the subject of lunches. The TSBD Company gave its employees 45 minutes for lunch. The lunch period was from 12 to 12:45 PM.

Mr. Ball. Did you pack your lunch from home?

Mr. Frazier. Yes, sir, I always took lunch.

Mr. Ball. Do you remember whether or not when Oswald came back with you on any Monday morning or any weekend did he pack his lunch?

Mr. Frazier. Yes, sir; he did.

Mr. Ball. He did?

Mr. Frazier. Yes, sir. When he rode with me, I say he always brought lunch except that one day on Nov. 22 he didn't bring his lunch that day.

Mr. Ball. But every other day he brought a lunch?

Mr. Frazier. Right, when he rode with me.

Mr. Ball. Would he bring it in a paper sack or what kind of a container?

Mr. Frazier. Yes, sir; like a little paper sack you get out of a grocery store, you have seen these little old sacks that you could buy, sandwich bag, sack.

Mr. Ball. Did you carry your lunch in a paper sack?

Mr. Frazier. Yes, sir; I did.

On one occasion Oswald rode home to Irving with Frazier on a Thursday night.

Now, there was the one date that Oswald came to you and asked you to drive him back to Irving, it was not a Friday, was it?

Mr. Frazier. No, sir; it wasn't.

Mr. Ball. It was on a Thursday.

Mr. Frazier. Right.

Mr. Ball. Was that the 21st of November?

Mr. Frazier. Yes, sir.

Mr. Ball. Well, tell us about that.

Mr. Frazier. Well, I say, we were standing like I said at the four-headed table about half as large as this, not quite half as large, but anyway I was standing there getting the orders in and he said, "Could I ride home with you this afternoon?"

And I said, "Sure. You know, like I told you, you can go home with me anytime you want to, like I say, anytime you want to go see your wife that is all right with me."

So automatically I knew it wasn't Friday, I come to think it wasn't Friday and I said, "Why are you going home today?"

And he says, "I am going home to get some curtain rods." He said, "You know, put in an apartment."

He wanted to hang up some curtains and I said, "Very well." And I never thought more about it and I had some invoices in my hands for some orders and I walked on off and started filling the orders.

That evening Frazier's sister, Linnie Mae Randle, asked Frazier why Oswald had come home on a Thursday night.

Mr. Ball. Did you tell her what he had told you?

Mr. Frazier. Yes, sir. I believe she said why did he come home now and I said, well, he says he was going to get some curtain rods.

The next morning Frazier arose about 6:30 AM and started eating breakfast about seven.

While Frazier was eating in the kitchen, he said, his mother "just happened to glance up and saw this man, you know, who was Lee looking in the window for me and she said, 'Who is that?'"

"And I said, 'That is Lee.' . . . He just looked through the kitchen window."

Mr. Ball. When your mother mentioned, "Who is that," you looked up and saw Lee Oswald in the kitchen window?

Mr. Frazier. I just saw him for a split second and when he saw I saw him, I guess he heard me say, "Well, it is time to go," and he walked down by the back door there.

Representative Ford. When he would go with you on Monday, on any Monday, was this the same procedure for getting to, getting in contact with you?

Mr. Frazier. You mean coming in there and looking through the window?

Representative Ford. Yes.

Mr. Frazier. No, sir; it wasn't. I say, that is the first time he had ever done that. I say, most times I would usually call him, you know, I was already out in the car fixing to go out the driveway there, and, you know, around to pick him up if he hadn't come down but most times, once in a while I picked him up at the house and another time he was already coming down the sidewalk to the house when I was fixing to pick him up and I usually picked him up around the corner there.

Frazier testified that both entered the car at about the same time.

Mr. Ball. When you got in the car did you say anything to him or did he say anything to you?

Mr. Frazier. Let's see, when I got in the car I have a kind of habit of glancing over my shoulder and so at that time I noticed there was a package laying on the back seat, I didn't pay too much attention and I said, "What's the package, Lee?"

And he said, "Curtain rods," and I said, "Oh, yes, you told me you was going to bring some today."

That is the reason, the main reason he was going over there that Thursday afternoon when he was to bring back some curtain rods, so I didn't think any more about it when he told me that.

Mr. Ball. What did the package look like?

Mr. Frazier. Well, I will be frank with you. I would just, it is right as you get out of the grocery store, just more or less out of a package, you have seen some of these brown paper sacks you can obtain from any, most of the stores, some varieties, but it was a package just roughly about two feet long.

Frazier said that the length of the package was "roughly . . . around two feet, give and take a few inches" and the package was "5, 6 inches or there" wide. The color of the package was like the "heavy duty bags you know like you obtain from the grocery store, something like that, about the same color of that paper sack you get there."

Mr. Ball. Was there anything more said about the paper sack on the way into town?

Mr. Frazier. No, sir; there wasn't.

The two men drove to Dallas. The route was approximately 15 miles. They parked in an employee parking lot two or three blocks from the building.

Mr. Ball. When you got to the parking lot who got out of the car first?

Mr. Frazier. He did.

Mr. Ball. You didn't get out immediately then?

Mr. Frazier. No, sir; I was sitting there, say, looked at my watch and somewhere around 7 or 8 minutes until I saw we had a few minutes and I sat there, and as I say you can see the Freeway, Stemmons Freeway, from the warehouse and also the trains coming back and forth and I was sitting there.

What I was doing—glanced up and watching cars for a minute but I was letting my engine run and getting to charge up my battery, because when you stop and start you have to charge up your battery.

Mr. Ball. Did you have your lunch beside you?

Mr. Frazier. Yes, sir; I did.

Mr. Ball. Did you notice whether or not Lee had a package that looked like a lunch package that morning?

Mr. Frazier. You know like I told you earlier, I say, he didn't take his lunch because I remember right when I got in the car I asked him where was his lunch and he said he was going to buy his lunch that day.

Mr. Ball. He told you that that day, did he?

Mr. Frazier. Right. That is right. So, I assumed he was going to buy it, you know, from that catering service man like a lot of the boys do. They don't bring their lunch but they go out and buy their lunch there.

Mr. Ball. What did he do about the package in the back seat when he got out of the car?

Mr. Frazier. Like I say, I was watching the gages and watched the car for a few minutes before I cut it off.

Mr. Ball. Yes.

Mr. Frazier. He got out of the car and he was wearing the jacket that has the big sleeves in them and he put the package that he had, you know, that he told me was curtain rods up under his arm, you know, and so he walked down behind the car and standing over there at the end of the cyclone fence waiting for me to get out of the car, and so quick as I cut the engine off and started out of the car, shut the door just as I was starting out just like getting out of the car, he started walking off and so I followed him in.

So, eventually there he kept getting a little further ahead of me and I noticed we had plenty of time to get there because it is not too far from the Depository and usually I walk around and watch them switching the trains because you have to watch where you are going if you have to cross the tracks.

One day you go across one track and maybe there would be some cars sitting there and there would be another diesel coming there, so you have to watch when you cross the tracks. I just walked along and I just like to watch them switch the cars, so eventually he kept getting a little further ahead of me and by that time we got down there pretty close to the Depository Building there, I say, he would be as much as, I would say, roughtly 50 feet in front of me but I didn't try to catch up with him because I knew I had plenty of time so I just took my time walking up there.

Mr. Ball. Did you usually walk up there together?

Mr. Frazier. Yes, sir; we did.

Mr. Ball. Is this the first time that he had ever walked ahead of you?

Mr. Frazier. Yes, sir; he did.

Mr. Ball. You say he had the package under his arm when you saw him?

Mr. Frazier. Yes, sir.

Mr. Ball. You mean one end of it under the armpit?

Mr. Frazier. Yes, sir; he had it up just like you stick it right under your arm like that.

Mr. Ball. And he had the lower part—

Mr. Frazier. The other part with his right hand.

Mr. Ball. Right hand?

Mr. Frazier. Right.

Mr. Ball. He carried it then parallel to his body?

Mr. Frazier. Right, straight up and down.

Representative Ford. Under his right arm?

Mr. Frazier. Yes, sir.

Ball then brought forward a paper sack made of paper similar to that used for wrapping books in the TSBD Building. Inside the sack was the rifle found in the building, Exhibit 139. The rifle had been disassembled.

Mr. Ball. When you saw him get out of the car, when you first saw him when he was out of the car before he started to walk, you noticed he had the package under the arm?

Mr. Frazier. Yes, sir.

Mr. Ball. One end of it was under the armpit and the other he had to hold it in his right hand. Did the package extend beyond the right hand?

Mr. Frazier. No, sir. Like I say if you put it under your armpits and put it down normal to the side.

Mr. Ball. But the right hand on, was it on the end or the side of the package?

Mr. Frazier. No; he had it cupped in his hand.

Mr. Ball. Cupped in his hand?

Mr. Frazier. Right.

Frazier was slightly over six feet tall. However, he could not carry the disassembled rifle with the bottom of the sack cupped in his hand and the top of the sack in his armpit. The rifle, even in a disassembled state, was several inches too long.

Frazier said, "Like I said, I remember I didn't look at the package very much, paying much attention, but when I did look at it he did have his hands on the package like that." And to demonstrate, he put his hands on the bottom of the package with the package cupped in his fingers.

Mr. Frazier. I didn't pay much attention, but when I did, I say, he had this part down here, like the bottom would be short he had cupped in his hand like that and, say, like walking from the back if you had a big arm jacket there you wouldn't tell much from a package back there, the physical features. If you could see it from the front like when you walk and meet somebody you could tell about the package, but walking from behind you couldn't tell much about the package whatsoever about the width. But he didn't carry it from the back. If this package were shorter he would have it cupped in his hands.

The Chairman. Could he have had the top of it behind his shoulder, or are you sure it was cupped under his shoulder there?

Mr. Frazier. Yes; because the way it looked, you know, like I say, he had it cupped in his hand.

The Chairman. I beg your pardon?

Mr. Frazier. I said from where I noticed he had it cupped in his hands. And I don't see how you could have it anywhere other than under your armpit because if you had it cupped in your hand it would stick over it.

Mr. Ball. Could he have carried it this way?

Mr. Frazier. No, sir. Never in front here. Like that. Now, that is what I was talking to you about. No, I say he couldn't because if he had you would have seen the package sticking up like that.

From what I seen walking behind he had it under his arm and you couldn't tell that he had a package from the back.

Mr. Ball. When you cupped the bottom of your package in the hands, will you stand up, again, please, and the upper part of the package is not under the armpit, the top of the package extends almost up to the level of your ear.

Mr. Frazier. Right.

Mr. Ball. Or your eye level, and when you put the package under your armpit, the upper part of the package, and take a hold of the side of it with your right hand, it extends on approximately about 8 inches, about the span of my hand, more than 8 inches, 8, 10 inches.

Mr. Frazier. If you were using a yardstick or one of these little—

Mr. Ball. I was using my hand.

Mr. Frazier. I know you were, but there are some different means to measure it. I will say it varies, if you use a yardstick. You can go and measure something with a tape measure, with a yardstick and come up with a different measurement altogether, maybe a quarter of an inch shorter or longer.

Although Frazier repeatedly stated that he "didn't pay much attention" to the package as Oswald was carrying it into the building, he nevertheless stated that the package was short enough so that it could be carried with the bottom cupped in a person's hands and the top tucked under the armpit. This would make the package approximately 28 inches long, at a maximum. The rifle, disassembled, had a minimum length of 34.8 inches.

If Frazier was accurate in his account of how the package was handled by Oswald, the package Oswald carried into the building that morning could not have contained the rifle, Exhibit 139.

Oswald walked into the building about 50 feet ahead of Frazier. By the time Frazier got to the door, Oswald could not be seen.

Frazier's sister, Linnie Mae Randle, also saw the package. Mrs. Randle had met Marina Oswald with Mrs. Paine at a neighbor's house in early October. Marina Oswald was pregnant with her second child.

Mr. Ball. Was there some conversation at that time about her husband Lee Oswald?

Mrs. Randle. Well, they had—it was just general knowledge in the neighborhood that he didn't have a job and she was expecting a baby. Of course, I didn't know where he was or anything. And of course you know just being neighborly and everything, we felt sorry for Marina because her baby was due right away as we understood it, and he didn't have any work, so they said, so it was just—

Mr. Ball. Mrs. Paine told you that Lee didn't have any work?

Mrs. Randle. Well, I suppose. It was just in conversation.

Mr. Ball. Marina didn't take part in the conversation?

Mrs. Randle. No. She couldn't. So far as I know, she couldn't speak.

Mr. Ball. You and Mrs. Roberts and Mrs. Paine talked about it?

Mrs. Randle. Yes.

Mr. Ball. Was there anything said then about the Texas School Book Depository as a place he might get a job?

Mrs. Randle. Well, we didn't say that he might get a job, because I didn't know there was a job open. The reason that we were being helpful, Wesley had just looked for a job, and I had helped him to try to find one. We listed several places that he might go to look for work. When you live in a place you know some places that someone with, you know, not very much of an education can find work.

So, it was among one of the places that we mentioned. We mentioned several others, and Mrs. Paine said that well, he couldn't apply for any of the jobs that would require driving because he couldn't drive, and it was just in conversation that you might talk just any day and not think a thing on earth about it.

Mrs. Randle recalled seeing Oswald get out of her brother's car on Thursday night, Nov. 21. She remembered that her brother had told her that Lee had ridden home to get some curtain rods.

The next morning she saw Oswald walking toward the house carrying a package.

Mr. Ball. What was he carrying?

Mrs. Randle. He was carrying a package in a sort of a heavy brown bag, heavier than a grocery bag it looked to me. It was about, if I might measure, about this long, I suppose, and he carried it in his right hand, had the top sort of folded down and had a grip like this, and the bottom, he carried it this way, you know, and it almost touched the ground as he carried it.

Mr. Ball. Let me see. He carried it in his right hand, did he?

Mrs. Randle. That is right.

Mr. Ball. And where was his hand gripping the middle of the package?

Mrs. Randle. No, sir; the top with just a little bit sticking up. You know just like you grab something like that.

Mr. Ball. And he was grabbing it with his right hand at the top of the package and the package almost touched the ground?

Mrs. Randle. Yes, sir.

Mr. Ball. He walked over to your house, did he?

Mrs. Randle. Well, I saw him as he started crossing the street. Where he come from then I couldn't say.

Mr. Ball. You don't know where he went from that?

Mrs. Randle. Where he went?

Mr. Ball. Did you see him go to the car?

Mrs. Randle. Yes.

Mr. Ball. What did he do?

Mrs. Randle. He opened the right back door and I just saw that he was laying the package down so I closed the door. I didn't recognize him as he walked across my carport and I at that moment, I wondered who was fixing to come to my back door so I opened the door slightly and saw that it—I assumed he was getting in the car but he didn't, so he come back and stood on the driveway.

Mr. Ball. He put the package in the car.

Mrs. Randle. Yes, sir; I don't know if he put it on the seat or on the floor but I just know he put it in the back.

Mrs. Randle thought the bag was about 27 inches long. It looked similar to the color of a bag made with wrapping paper used in the TSBD Building to wrap books.

Thus, both witnesses who saw Oswald carry the bag believed that it was six inches shorter than the minimum length that would have been required, had the bag contained the disassembled rifle.

Did the bag contain curtain rods?

No curtain rods were discovered in the TSBD Building after the assassination. No curtain rods were taken from the Paine home.

The next step is to examine the room that Oswald rented in the Oak Cliff section of Dallas. Did it need curtain rods?

For the answer, we can turn to Mrs. Arthur C. Johnson, a 63-year-old woman who with her husband operated a small restaurant in Dallas called Johnson's Cafe. For 21 years, she had lived at 1026 North Beckley Street, a large old frame house that contained about 22 rooms, most of which she rented to tenants.

Mr. Ball. Where was he when you first met him, at what place?

Mrs. Johnson. At my home—I was between serving hours and I come home for relaxation and to kind of help out. I cooperate in keeping the house and seeing after it, too, and I had returned home that afternoon and he seen the room for rent sign—the first time that he came by, I happened to have just rented the last room that one time. Occasionally, I will have them full and then they just go vacant; people just come in and out, stay a week and then are gone, anyway, at that time, I didn't have a room.

Mr. Ball. The first time he came to see you?

Mrs. Johnson. Yes; that's something about 3 weeks before he came back.

Mr. Ball. This was 1026 North Beckley?

Mrs. Johnson. Yes.

Mr. Ball. He talked to you?

Mrs. Johnson. Yes; the first time and the last time; the first time, he told me he wanted a room and I told him I was very sorry, I just rented the last room and he said he was very sorry, he wanted to get near his work and he didn't have a car and it being on the bus line, he was sorry he missed it. I said, "You noticed the sign." I hadn't had time to take the sign up and I told him, "I will take the sign up and if you notice the sign up again, you might stop by and I will have a room" and sure enough, he came by this second time and so this tiny, little room—it was at one time my library; that's what it was built for, and he came by and I said I only have this small room at the present time. I run an ad, it seems like, at that time, and I said I only have the small room and he looked at it and said, "I will take this room with the understanding I can have a larger room at the time you have one go vacant" and I said to him that's agreeable, so, at the time, I had other vacancies which in just 2 or 3 days I had two or three more accommodations go vacant, so I told him I had other accommodations that are larger and he said, "I find this room to be light and comfortable." It was four windows on the outside wall; it was all light. He said, "I find it to be light and comfortable and worth the money, if you don't mind, I will remain in this room," so he didn't even look at the other rooms. He just remained in that room, what I call my library. When I utilized it into a bedroom, my father-in-law lived with a family of people on a farm and they went to Arkansas to live and he was getting old and he didn't want to be that far away from his son, so he wanted to come and make his home with us and I fixed this little library room—it was off and private from the other roomers—for "Pappy" to sleep in and the living room for him to sit in and he was—that's about 9 years before he was deceased.

Mr. Ball. Do you remember the date Oswald rented the room?

Mrs. Johnson. Oct. 14.

Mr. Ball. What time of day did he come by?

Mrs. Johnson. It was between 4 and 5 o'clock, I do know that because I was home that day when he came back by and I said, when he came by, I said, "You did come back by."

Mr. Ball. Was your sign out at that time?

Mrs. Johnson. Yes; it was; he seen the sign.

Mr. Ball. How much did you charge him?

Mrs. Johnson. $8 a week, refrigerator and living room privileges.

Mr. Ball. The refrigerator was located where?

Mrs. Johnson. In my kitchen—he wanted to know if he could put milk and lunch meat in my refrigerator and I told him he could.

Mr. Ball. Did he tell you what his name was?

Mrs. Johnson. O. H. L-e-e [spelling].

Mr. Ball. Did he sign anything with that name?

Mrs. Johnson. Yes, sir; I have it in my purse.

Mr. Ball. May I see it?

Mrs. Johnson. I will be glad to—I don't want you to keep it. I want you to—I brought it for your information. I knew you was going to ask that.

Mr. Ball. Now, is this in his handwriting?

Mrs. Johnson. This "O. H. Lee" is in his handwriting and this other is in the housekeeper's handwriting—Mrs. Roberts. . . .

Mr. Ball. Did he sign that "O. H. Lee" in your presence?

Mrs. Johnson. Yes, sir.

Mr. Ball. On that day?

Mrs. Johnson. Yes, sir; the day he rented the room, they sign the register—they sign the register before I accept any money.

Mr. Ball. I'm talking about this "O. H. Lee" signature on this document; he signed that on that date?

Mrs. Johnson. Yes, sir.

Mr. Ball. Did he give you the money?

Mrs. Johnson. Yes.

Mr. Ball. $8?

Mrs. Johnson. Yes.

Mr. Ball. Did you ever know his true name was Lee Harvey Oswald?

Mrs. Johnson. No; not until we saw his picture flash on the television as the officers were out. Those particulars was found in his pocket after he killed Tippit, after his arrest. So I came from the restaurant, I guess 1 or 1:30, and these officers were there 1:30 or 2, something like that, anyway, it was after this assassination, and as I drove in, well, the officers were there and they told me that they was looking for this character and I told them I didn't think I had anyone by that name there for we went through the register carefully two or three times and there was no Oswald there and I had two new tenants, rather new tenants, so we had carried them around the house to show them and we was going to start in the new tenants' rooms and my husband was sitting in the living room and seen this picture flash on the television and he said, "Please go around that house and tell him it was this guy that lived in this room here"; and it was O. H. Lee.

Mr. Ball. That is the first time you learned his name was Oswald?

Mrs. Johnson. Yes.
Mr. Ball. You knew him as O. H. Lee?
Mrs. Johnson. Yes; I knew him as O. H. Lee. . . .

Ball then turned to the question of how the room was furnished at the time Oswald rented it.

Mr. Ball. How is this room furnished that Oswald rented?
Mrs. Johnson. A very small room; it had an old fashioned clothes closet that had a place to hang your clothes and drawer space for your underwear, your socks and everything, and then it also had a cabinet space anyone could have stored food or, well I mean bundles of things, you know, and then I had a dresser and a bed and a heater and a little refrigerated unit.
Mr. Ball. A refrigerating unit?
Mrs. Johnson. Yes, sir; a window unit.
Mr. Ball. You mean it cooled the room?
Mrs. Johnson. Yes, sir; and it had curtains and venetian blinds.
Mr. Ball. What kind of curtains did it have?
Mrs. Johnson. Well, it just had side drapes and panels.
Mr. Ball. Were the curtains on curtain rods?
Mrs. Johnson. Yes, sir.
Mr. Ball. They were in the room when he rented it?
Mrs. Johnson. Yes, sir.
Mr. Ball. Did Oswald ever talk to you about redecorating his room?
Mrs. Johnson. No, sir; never mentioned it.
Mr. Ball. Did he ever talk to you about putting up new curtains in his room?
Mrs. Johnson. No, sir.
Mr. Ball. Did he ever tell you he was going to get some curtain rods?
Mrs. Johnson. No; he didn't.
Mr. Ball. The room had curtain rods on the window when he came in there?
Mrs. Johnson. Yes, sir; sure did.
Mr. Ball. Also curtains?
Mrs. Johnson. Yes, sir.

Now, members of the jury, what do you think Oswald had in the brown package that he carried inside the building that morning?

You may want to withhold a decision until you hear what Oswald had to say about this during his interrogation. In the meantime, you should know that "the jacket that has the big sleeves" that Frazier said Oswald was wearing on the morning of Nov. 22 was found by Frankie Kaiser some days later "in the windowsill . . . in the domino room" on the first floor of the TSBD Building. "I just found the coat there. I didn't even know it was his until someone told me it was. I thought they were kidding."

You should also know that there is important additional evidence about the large bag found in the southeast corner of the sixth floor of the TSBD Building. For this we will turn to our next witness, Sebastian Latona of the FBI.

30

"THEY WERE IDENTIFIED AS A FINGERPRINT AND A PALM PRINT OF LEE HARVEY OSWALD"

Members of the jury, you may remember that Lt. J. C. Day found a brown paper bag on the floor near the southeast corner window of the sixth floor of the TSBD Building. You heard Lt. Day testify that he had treated the bag with black fingerprint dusting powder and had found no latent prints.

The bag was sent to Washington on Nov. 23, 1963, and received by Sebastian F. Latona, supervisor of the Latent Fingerprint Section of the Identification Division of the Federal Bureau of Investigation. Mr. Latona had been with the FBI for more than 32 years.

The principle of fingerprint identification is based on the fact primarily that the ridge formations that appear on the hands and on the soles of the feet actually are created approximately 2 to 3 months before birth, on the unborn child, and they remain constant in the same position in which they are formed until the person is dead and the body is consumed by decomposition.

Secondly, the fact that no two people, or no two fingers of the same person, have the same arrangement of these ridge formations, either on the fingers, the palms, or the soles and toes of the feet. Plus the fact that during the lifetime of a person this ridge formation does not change, it remains constant—from the time it is formed until actual destruction, either caused by voluntary or involuntary means, or upon the death of the body and decomposition.

Mr. Eisenberg. Mr. Latona, do you have any personal experience indicating the uniqueness of fingerprints?

Mr. Latona. Yes; I do. My experience is based primarily upon the work which I have actually done in connection with my work with the FBI. I have had the experience of working on one case in particular in which millions of comparisons were actually and literally made with a small portion of a fingerprint which was left on a piece of evidence in connection with this particular case, which was a kidnapping case.

This fragmentary latent print which we developed consisted of approximately seven to eight points. Most fingerprints will have in them an average roughly of from 85 to about 125.

This fragmentary latent print was compared with literally millions of single impressions for the purpose of trying to effect an identification. And we were unable, over a lengthy period while we were making these millions of comparisons, not able to identify these few fragmentary points.

The important thing is simply this; that on the basis of that fragmentary print, it was not possible to determine even the type of pattern that the impression was. Accordingly, we had to compare it with all types of fingerprint patterns, of which

245

there are really four basic types—the arch, tented arch, loop, and whorl. And we are still making comparisons in that case, and we have not been able to identify these few points.

Now, that means simply this—that the theory that we are going on an assumption that people do not have the same fingerprints—and we find it not necessary to compare, say for example, a loop pattern with a whorl pattern, and as there is a possibility that, it is contended by some of these so-called authorities, that maybe the points that you find in a loop may be found in the same arrangement in a whorl—is not true. I think that that case, a practical case we have actually worked on, disproves that theory so strongly in my mind that I am convinced that no two people can possibly have the same fingerprints.

Mr. Eisenberg. That is, you had a print with seven points, and these same seven points appeared in none of the millions—

Mr. Latona. Of the millions that we actually compared over a period—well, since 1937. You may recall the case. It was the Matson kidnapping case out in Tacoma, Wash. That is one of only three major kidnapping cases the FBI has not yet solved.

Mr. Eisenberg. Are palmprints as unique as fingerprints?

Mr. Latona. Yes; palmprints are. They are not as useful for purposes of setting up a file in order to conduct searches, for the simple reason that there are not as many variations of patterns occurring with any frequency in the palms as occur on the tips of the fingers. That is primarily why the fingertips are used—because you have 10 digits, and there is a possibility of finding variations of the four basic pattern types which can be additionally subdivided by utilizing certain focal points which occur in those particular patterns, which enable us to actually subdivide our files into millions of groups. Accordingly, when you make a search in the fingerprint file, it can be reduced actually to a matter of minutes, whereas to attempt to set up a palmprint file to the extent of the size of the fingerprint file we have in the FBI would be a practical impossibility, much less a waste of time.

Latona testified that "as far as I know" experts are unanimous in their opinion that identifications effected through the use of palmprints "are just as absolute as are those of fingerprints."

Eisenberg then handed Latona the large paper bag found in the southeast corner of the TSBD Building near the window where the cartridge cases had been discovered. Latona said that he received the bag on Nov. 23, 1963, and on that day examined it for latent prints.

Mr. Eisenberg. When you had received it, could you tell whether any previous examination had been conducted on it?

Mr. Latona. When I received this exhibit, 626, the brown wrapper, it had been treated with black dusting powder, black fingerprint powder. There was nothing visible in the way of any latent prints on there at that particular time.

Mr. Eisenberg. Were you informed whether any fingerprints had been developed by means of the fingerprint powder?

Mr. Latona. No; I determined that by simply examining the wrapper at that particular time.

Mr. Eisenberg. Could you briefly describe the powder process?

Mr. Latona. The powdering process is merely the utilizing of a fingerprint powder which is applied to any particular surface for purposes of developing any latent prints which may be on such a surface.

Now, we use powder in the FBI only on objects which have a hard, smooth, nonabsorbent finish, such as glass, tile, various types of highly polished metals, and the like.

In the FBI we do not use powder on paper, cardboard, unfinished wood, or various types of cloth. The reason is that the materials are absorbent. Accordingly, when any finger which has on it perspiration or sweat comes in contact with an absorbent material, the print starts to become absorbed into the surface. Accordingly, when an effort is made to develop latent prints by the use of a powder, if the surface is dry, the powder will not adhere.

On the other hand, where the surface is a hard and smooth object, with a nonabsorbent material, the perspiration or sweat which may have some oil in it at that time may remain there as moisture. Accordingly, when the dry powder is brushed across it, the moisture in the print will retain the powder giving an outline of the impression itself.

These powders come in various colors. We utilize a black and a gray. The black powder is used on objects which are white or light to give a resulting contrast of a black print on a white background. We use the gray powder on objects which are black or dark in order to give you a resulting contrast of a white print on a dark or black background.

Mr. Eisenberg. Now, Mr. Latona, how did you proceed to conduct your examination for fingerprints on this object?

Mr. Latona. Well, an effort was made to remove as much of the powder as possible. And then this was subjected to what is known as the iodine-fuming method, which simply means flowing iodine fumes, which are developed by what is known as an iodine-fuming gun—it is a very simple affair, in which there are a couple of tubes attached to each other, having in one of them iodine crystals. And by simply blowing through one end, you get iodine fumes.

The iodine fumes are brought in as close contact to the surface as possible. And if there are any prints which contain certain fatty material or protein material, the iodine fumes simply discolor it to a sort of brownish color. And of course such prints as are developed are photographed for record purposes.

That was done in this case here, but no latent prints were developed.

The next step then was to try an additional method, by chemicals. This was subsequently processed by a 3-percent solution of silver nitrate. The processing with silver nitrate resulted in developing two latent prints. One is what we call a latent palmprint, and the other is what we call a latent fingerprint.

Mr. Eisenberg. Can you briefly explain the action of the silver nitrate?

Mr. Latona. Silver nitrate solution in itself is colorless, and it reacts with the sodium chloride, which is ordinary salt which is found in the perspiration or sweat which is exuded by the sweat pores.

This material covers the fingers. When it touches a surface such as an absorbent material, like paper, it leaves an outline on the paper.

When this salt material, which is left by the fingers on the paper, is immersed in the silver nitrate solution, there is a combining, an immediate combining of—the elements themselves will break down, and they recombine into silver chloride and sodium nitrate. We know that silver is sensitive to light. So that material, after it has been treated with the silver nitrate solution, is placed under a strong light. We utilize a carbon arc lamp, which has considerable ultraviolet light in it. And it will immediately start to discolor the specimen. Wherever there is any salt material, it will discolor it, much more so than the rest of the object, and show exactly where the latent prints have been developed. It is simply a reaction of the silver nitrate with the sodium chloride.

That is all it is.

Mr. Eisenberg. Do you frequently find that the silver nitrate develops a print in a paper object which the iodine fuming cannot develop?

Mr. Latona. Yes; I would say that is true, considerably so. We have more success with silver nitrate than we do with the iodine fumes.

The reason we use both is because of the fact that this material which is exuded by the fingers may fall into one of two main types—protein material and salt material. The iodine fumes will develop protein material. Silver nitrate will develop the salt material.

The reason we use both is because we do not know what was in the subject's fingers or hands or feet. Accordingly, to insure complete coverage, we use both methods. And we use them in that sequence. The iodine first, then the silver nitrate. The iodine is used first because the iodine simply causes a temporary physical change. It will discolor, and then the fumes, upon being left in the open air, will disappear, and then the color will dissolve. Silver nitrate, on the other hand, causes a chemical change and it will permanently affect the change. So if we were to use the silver nitrate process first, then we could not use the iodine fumes. On occasion we have developed fingerprints and palmprints with iodine fumes which failed to develop with the silver nitrate and vice versa.

Mr. Eisenberg. Now, Mr. Latona, looking at that bag I see that almost all of it is an extremely dark brown color, except that there are patches of a lighter brown, a manila-paper brown. Could you explain why there are these two colors on the bag?

Mr. Latona. Yes. The dark portions of the paper bag are where the silver nitrate has taken effect. And the light portions of the bag are where we did not process the bag at that time, because additional examinations were to be made, and we did not wish the object to lose its identity as to what it may have been used for. Certain chemical tests were to be made after we finished with it. And we felt that the small section that was left in itself would not interfere with the general overall examination of the bag itself.

Mr. Eisenberg. That is, the small section of light brown corresponds to the color which the bag had when you received it?

Mr. Latona. That is the natural color of the wrapper at the time we received it.

Mr. Eisenberg. And the remaining color is caused by the silver nitrate process?

Mr. Latona. That is correct.

Mr. Eisenberg. Does paper normally turn this dark brown color when treated by silver nitrate?

Mr. Latona. Yes; it does. It will get darker, too, as time goes on and it is affected by light.

Mr. Eisenberg. Mr. Latona, does the silver nitrate process permanently fix the print into the paper?

Mr. Latona. Permanent in the sense that the print by itself will not disappear. Now, it can be removed, or the stains could be removed chemically, by the placing of the object into a 2 percent solution of mercuric nitrate, which will remove the stains and in addition will remove the prints. But the prints by themselves, if nothing is done to it, will simply continue to grow darker and eventually the whole specimen will lose its complete identity.

The Chairman. May I ask a question here?

So I understand from that that this particular document that you are looking at, or this bag, will continue to get darker as time goes on?

Mr. Latona. Yes; it will.

The Chairman. From this date?

Mr. Latona. That's right.

Mr. Eisenberg. Returning to the prints themselves, you stated, I believe, that you found a palmprint and a fingerprint on this paper bag?

Mr. Latona. That is correct.

Mr. Eisenberg. Did you find any other prints?

Mr. Latona. No; no other prints that we term of value in the sense that I felt that they could be identified or that a conclusion could be reached that they were not identical with the fingerprints or palmprints of some other person.

Mr. Eisenberg. Did you attempt to identify the palmprint and fingerprint?

Mr. Latona. The ones that I developed; yes.

Mr. Eisenberg. Were you able to identify these prints?

Mr. Latona. I—the ones I developed, I did identify.

Mr. Eisenberg. Whose prints did you find them to be?

Mr. Latona. They were identified as a fingerprint and a palmprint of Lee Harvey Oswald.

Mr. Eisenberg. Now, Mr. Latona, what known sample of Lee Harvey Oswald's prints, finger and palm, did you use in making this identification?

Mr. Latona. The known samples I used were the ones forwarded by our office at Dallas, the Dallas office.

Mr. Eisenberg. Do you have those with you?

Mr. Latona. I do.

In similar fashion, Latona testified that one of the cartons on the floor near the southeast corner window of the sixth floor of the TSBD Building contained a palmprint of Lee Harvey Oswald, and a Rolling Reader carton sitting near the windowsill of the southeast corner window contained the left palm print of Oswald as well as a fingerprint of Oswald's right index finger.

Latona's findings were concurred in by Arthur Mendella, a fingerprint instructor for the New York Police Department Bureau of Criminal Identification, who was retained as an independent expert by the Commission.

The fact that Oswald's palmprint was on the bottom of the paper bag indicated not only that he had handled the bag, but also that the bag contained a heavy or bulky object when he handled it, because a light object is usually held with the fingers. The palmprint found on the closed end of the bag was from Oswald's right hand—the hand in which he carried the long package as he walked from Frazier's car into the building.

The bag itself was home made. On the day of the assassination, the Dallas police obtained a sample of wrapping paper and tape from the shipping room of the Depository and forwarded it to the FBI Laboratory in Washington. James C. Cadigan, a questioned-documents expert with the bureau, compared the samples with the paper and tape in the actual bag.

Cadigan described how the bag had been put together. Paper had been torn off a large roll. Then, tape from a dispensing machine had been used to tape the bag together.

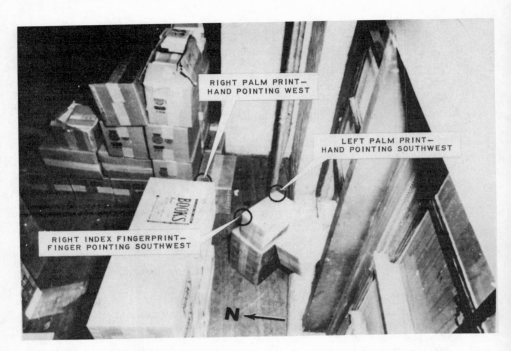

Commission Exhibit No. 1301
Southeast corner of sixth floor showing arrangement of cartons shortly after shots were fired.

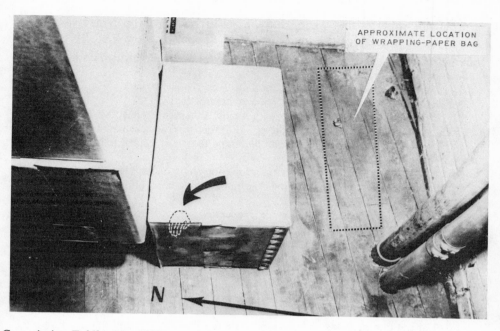

Commission Exhibit No. 1302
Approximate location of wrapping-paper bag and location of palm print on carton near window in southeast corner. (Hand position shown by dotted line on box)

Cadigan said he had examined the paper bag and the paper samples obtained on the day of the assassination, "comparing them visually

and under the microscope, I examined them under ultraviolet light. This is merely one additional step.

Here again I found that both of them fluoresced the same way.

Mr. Eisenberg. Could you explain the meaning of that?

Mr. Cadigan. Yes. Paper, along with many substances, has the property of absorbing or reflecting ultraviolet light rays differently. You can take two samples of paper and put them under an ultraviolet light, and they may appear to be the same or they may be markedly different.

Mr. Eisenberg. You mean even if they look the same under visual light?

Mr. Cadigan. Visually they may look the same and yet under ultraviolet light there may be very dramatic differences.

Mr. Eisenberg. What causes those differences?

Mr. Cadigan. Well, the chemicals that are in the paper itself; I think probably a very common example are the markings on shirts, so-called invisible dyes which, visually, you do not see, but you put them under ultraviolet light and the chemical is such that it glows brilliantly.

So, it is basically a chemical or chemicals in there, in this case, in the paper being examined under the ultraviolet, which gives a certain visual appearance, which you can say, it is the same or it is different.

In all of the observations and physical tests that I made, I found that for Exhibit 142, the bag, and the paper sample, Commission Exhibit 677, the results were the same.

Mr. Eisenberg. Can you just review those? That was the ultraviolet light—

Mr. Cadigan. Well, briefly, it would be the thickness of both the paper and the tape, the color under various lighting conditions of both the paper and the tape, the width of the tape, the knurled markings on the surface of the tape, the texture of the fiber, the felting pattern. I hadn't mentioned this before, but if you hold a piece of paper up to the light, you see light and dark areas caused by the way the fibers felt right at the beginning stages of paper manufacture.

There are light and dark areas, and these are called the felting pattern. This is something that will vary depending on how the paper is made, the thickness of the paper, the way that the fibers moved on the papermaking machine, and here again I found that they were the same for both the known sample, Commission Exhibit 677, and the paper bag, Commission Exhibit 142.

Mr. Eisenberg. In all these cases, did you make the examination both of the tape and the paper in each of the bag and the sample?

Mr. Cadigan. Oh, yes.

Mr. Eisenberg. And they were all identical?

Mr. Cadigan. Yes.

A number of days later, another paper sample was taken from the TSBD Building. Another sample bag was made.

Mr. Eisenberg. Have you any information as to whether the paper during the period between Nov. 22 and Dec. 1 used in the TSBD—whether it was the same or different rolls—would have come from the same ultimate manufacturer?

Mr. Cadigan. It is my understanding that they received a shipment of 58 rolls of paper that were shipped Mar. 19, 1963, from the St. Regis Paper Mill in Jacksonville,

Fla., and which lasted them until January of 1964. This would mean on an average, in a 9-month period, a little more than six rolls a month.

Mr. Eisenberg. The inference would therefore be that if the—although the papers in the replica bag obtained on December 1 and the paper in the sample obtained on Nov. 22 are distinguishable by you, they came from the same manufacturer, and—is that correct?

Mr. Cadigan. That is correct.

Mr. Eisenberg. And, therefore, that the state of your science is such that you can distinguish even rolls of paper made by the same manufacturer and assumedly made within a reasonably close time, is that correct also?

Mr. Cadigan. I don't know what period of time is involved here. But I can distinguish at least in this case between paper from the same shipment from the same mill.

Mr. Eisenberg. Could you proceed now to discuss the morphology of the fiber as you examined it under a microscope?

Mr. Cadigan. Well, I might state briefly what a fiber analysis is. We put samples of paper back into their, you might say, original state, in the form of fiber suspension.

You cook samples of paper for a couple of minutes in weak sodium hydroxide solution. Then you wash it, add water and shake it vigorously, and you get a suspension of fibers in the water. Samples of those fibers are put on glass slides and are stained by various reagents.

Then you examine them under a high-power comparison microscope or a binocular microscope under approximately 120 times magnification. In this particular case I used two different stains.

First a malachite green stain. This merely determines if there are any unbleached fibers, or if they are all bleached. I found that on both Commission Exhibit 677, the paper sample obtained on Nov. 22, and the paper sack, Commission Exhibit 142, that they are almost 100 percent unbleached fibers.

Then I stained other samples, with a stain known as Herzberg stain. It is an iodine-iodide stain, which will distinguish between rag fibers, chemical wood fibers, and ground wood fibers by different coloring. The chemical wood is stained blue, rag fibers are stained red, ground wood stained yellow.

I made and studied specimens or slides of fibers from Commission Exhibit 677, the known sample, and from Commission Exhibit 142, the paper sack, to see if the fiber composition is similar. What that means is, is this chemical wood, is it coniferous or deciduous, are there any rag fibers in there or are there any ground wood fibers in there, and I found here the fiber composition was similar and essentially it is a coniferous woodlike pine. There were a few stray rag fibers, which I think were probably accidental, and a few stray ground wood fragments in there.

Mr. Dulles. Let me get clearly what is similar, that is the paper bag, Exhibit—

Mr. Cadigan. 142; the paper comprising that sack and the paper comprising the known sample obtained Nov. 22, Exhibit 677.

Mr. Dulles. Right.

Mr. Cadigan. The papers I also found were similar in fiber composition, therefore, in addition to the visual characteristics, microscopic and UV characteristics.

Mr. Eisenberg. "UV" being ultraviolet?

Mr. Cadigan. Yes, sir. Then I had a spectrographic examination made of the paper from the sack, 142, and the known sample secured Nov. 22, Commission Exhibit 677.

Spectrographic tests involve, of course, burning the substance and capturing the light on a photographic plate to determine what metallic ions are present. This was done by our spectrographic section, and again the paper of Commission Exhibit 677, the paper sample, secured Nov. 22, was found to be similar spectrographically to the paper of the sack, Commission Exhibit 142.

Now, these were additional tests, the original examinations, under visual and ultraviolet light, were made by me on Nov. 23, 1963. Fiber analysis and the spectrographic examination was conducted on Mar. 25, 1964.

Mr. Eisenberg. Have you now reviewed all the points in which you compared the paper sack obtained from the TSBD, Exhibit 142, and the known sample obtained on Nov. 22, Exhibit 677?

Mr. Cadigan. Yes.

Mr. Eisenberg. Did you find any points of nonidentity?

Mr. Cadigan. No; I found none.

Mr. Eisenberg. They were identical on every point on which you measured them?

Mr. Cadigan. Yes.

The evidence was clear: The homemade paper bag found near the southeast corner window of the sixth floor of the TSBD Building had been made from paper available on the first floor of the building and used to wrap books. Lee Harvey Oswald had access to that paper. He also had access to the sixth floor, where the cartridge cases and rifle were found. Lee Harvey Oswald's prints were on the bag. Oswald owned the gun used in the assassination. The last time Oswald was seen by any employee prior to the assassination was by Charles Givens, approximately 35 minutes before the President's motorcade started down Elm Street toward the triple underpass. Oswald was then on the sixth floor—the place from which the shots were fired.

The next time that Oswald was seen by anyone inside the TSBD Building was on the second floor at approximately 12:32 PM. Let us find out what took place as we examine the other side of the FBI.

31

"IT WAS A LITTLE STRANGE THAT ONE OF THE WAREHOUSE BOYS WOULD BE UP IN THE OFFICE"

Millions of Americans have seen a weekly television series on the Federal Bureau of Investigation. Millions have seen movies concerning the work of the FBI. And in pre-television days millions of Americans regularly listened to a weekly radio program about the Bureau. Hundreds of thousands of visitors in Washington each year are conducted on tours of the FBI Headquarters.

The television programs, the movies, the radio programs, the tours, have all left their mark. Has there ever been a television show, a radio script, a movie or a tour that mentions mistakes as well as masterful exploits?

No one denies that the FBI is an outstanding organization. J. Edgar Hoover took it out of the political pork barrel and transformed it into a law enforcement agency with the highest professional standards in this country.

But there is another side to the FBI—a side that J. Edgar Hoover never discussed—a side that a vigilant society must constantly keep in mind. It is a side that has never before been documented by an independent investigation because prior to our work with the Warren Commission, no such independent appraisal had ever been made. To put it bluntly, the FBI at times is inaccurate in its reporting and at times is incomplete in its investigation. It does not happen often—but it happens.

The best-known instance of inaccurate reporting by the FBI in the course of the investigation of the assassination of President Kennedy is the Bureau's report of the autopsy of President Kennedy. On page 88 of our Report you will read this reference to the first bullet that struck the President near the base of the back of his neck:

Concluding that a bullet passed through the President's neck, the doctors at Bethesda Naval Hospital rejected a theory that the bullet lodged in the large muscles in the back of his neck and fell out through the point of entry when external heart massage was applied at Parkland Hospital. In the earlier stages of the autopsy, the surgeons were unable to find a path into any large muscle in the back of the neck. At that time they did not know that there had been a bullet hole in the front of the President's neck when he arrived at Parkland Hospital because the tracheotomy incision had completely eliminated that evidence. While the autopsy was being performed, surgeons learned that a whole bullet had been found at Parkland Hospital on a stretcher which, at that time, was thought to be the stretcher occupied by the President. This led to speculation that the bullet might have penetrated a short distance into the back of the neck and then dropped out onto the stretcher as a result of the external heart massage.

Further exploration during the autopsy disproved that theory. The surgeons determined that the bullet had passed between two large strap muscles and bruised them without leaving any channel, since the bullet merely passed between them. Commander Humes, who believed that a tracheotomy had been performed from his observations at the autopsy, talked by telephone with Dr. Perry early on the morning of Nov. 23, and learned that his assumption was correct and that Dr. Perry had used the missile wound in the neck as the point to make the incision. This confirmed the Bethesda surgeons' conclusion that the bullet had exited from the front part of the neck.

The conclusions of the autopsy physicians formed a part of the evidence that led to our conclusion that the same bullet that passed through President Kennedy's neck struck Governor Connally. Other evidence pertaining to this conclusion will be discussed in later chapters.

What we referred to in our Report as ". . . speculation that the bullet might have penetrated a short distance into the back of the neck and then dropped out onto the stretcher as a result of the external heart massage" was intensified by inaccurate reporting by FBI and Secret Service agents who were present at the autopsy. The reports of the FBI agents went only as far as the first preliminary thought that the bullet that struck the President near the base of his neck traveled only a short distance into his body and then dropped out during external heart massage. Ball and I read the secondary evidence of the FBI report of the autopsy before we read the report by the doctors themselves. We also read a supplemental summary report by the FBI on Jan. 13, which stated that "medical examination of the President's body had revealed that the bullet which entered his back had penetrated to a distance of less than a fingerlength." Perhaps that was accurate, but on the other hand Joe Ball and I were both surprised that a high-powered bullet that would enter the President's back would penetrate so short a distance.

It turned out that the FBI report was inaccurate. As you will find in a later chapter, wound ballistic tests performed on three different substances simulating the President's neck disclosed that the entrance velocity of the bullet as it entered the neck averaged 1,904 feet and the exit velocity averaged 1,772 to 1,798 feet per second, depending on the substance used.

Inaccurate reporting by the FBI thus became a tool that was used by the assassination sensationalists to sow their seeds of doubt.

Let me give you another example that involves both inaccurate FBI reporting and incomplete FBI investigation.

Ball and I were always looking for something that might shed new light on the assassination. Could it be that Oswald was not the assassin? Could it be that if Oswald was the assassin, one or more other people were involved? Could it be that Oswald merely aided the assassin, or that he unwittingly aided someone else?

As we pored over the thousands of pages of FBI and Secret Service reports and raised questions, it soon appeared that Oswald had to be involved in the assassination itself, if the testimony of witnesses and scientific experts confirmed our basic reports. To us, the most convincing evidence was the ballistic evidence which showed that cartridge cases found in the southeast corner window of the sixth floor of the School Book Depository Building, two large ballistically identifiable bullet fragments found in the front seat of the Presidential limousine, and one nearly whole bullet found at Parkland Memorial Hospital all came from a rifle found near the back stairway of the sixth floor of the TSBD Building, to the exclusion of all other weapons in the world. Four cartridge cases found near the scene of the Tippit shooting conclusively came from the revolver found in Oswald's possession at the time he was apprehended, to the exclusion of all other weapons in the world. Both the revolver and the rifle had been purchased by Lee Harvey Oswald.

But could it be that there was some other person involved with Oswald? Could Oswald have purchased the rifle and owned the rifle and killed Officer Tippit, and yet it was someone else who looked like Oswald whom Brennan saw in the sixth floor window? We analyzed the various ways that we might establish this and did everything within our power to check out the possibilities. One main way of establishing Oswald's innocence or the existence of co-conspirators was to prove that he could not have been on the sixth floor at the time of the assassination because he was seen on the second floor within such a short period thereafter. The possibilities of this were enhanced by three glaring omissions in all the investigative data that we had received before we went to Dallas:

1. Oswald was seen by Roy Truly, Superintendent of the TSBD Company, and Patrolman M. L. Baker of the Dallas Police Department in the second floor lunchroom of the TSBD Building shortly after the assassination. How soon after the shooting occurred we did not know, for nowhere in any investigative report had any officer or agent taken either Superintendent Truly or Patrolman M. L. Baker to the scene of the assassination and reconstructed a time sequence concerning the events of Nov. 22. This omission was all the more glaring because other time tests had been conducted, including tests involving the route taken by Oswald between the time of the assassination and the time of his apprehension in the Texas Theatre.

2. Oswald was also seen on the second floor of the TSBD Building by Mrs. Robert A. Reid. Again, no one had taken a time test to ascertain how soon after the assassination Oswald was seen by Mrs. Reid.

3. When Oswald was seen by Mrs. Reid, she was quoted as having said that he had a Coke in his hand. No one had verified from either Superintendent Truly or Patrolman Baker whether Oswald had a Coke in his hand when he was seen by them. Rather, it had been assumed that Oswald had had a Coke in his hand when he was first seen in the lunchroom by Patrolman Baker and Mr. Truly.

Finally, there was another major unanswered question: Oswald could get from the sixth floor to the second floor either by way of the freight elevators in the rear center portion of the building or by the stairway in the northwest corner of the building. There was fairly conclusive evidence that Oswald had not used the elevators because the elevators were not on the second floor when Patrolman Baker and Roy Truly arrived. Moreover, the method of operation of the elevators did not permit them to come down to the second floor and then be sent upstairs by someone who was not on the elevator itself.

By process of elimination, this left the stairway. However, according to a Nov. 23 FBI interview with Bonnie Ray Williams, the stairway was also eliminated. As you may remember, Williams and the two other men who were watching the motorcade from the southeast corner of the fifth floor of the TSBD Building shortly after the shots were fired ran to the southwest corner of the building to look out the window to see what was happening down Elm Street. In this FBI report, which Ball and I reviewed, Williams was quoted as saying that from his position in the southwest corner of the fifth floor he would have seen anyone coming down to the sixth floor via the stairway. Williams was further quoted as saying that he did not see anyone. Therefore, if Oswald did not use the elevator, and if he was not seen coming down the stairs and could have been seen coming down the stairs, he could not have been the assassin.

On Mar. 20, when Ball and I first met Bonnie Ray Williams and the other two employees who were watching the motorcade from the fifth floor, Mr. Williams denied ever having made such a statement to any law enforcement agency. We then had the three men reconstruct their actions as they went from the southeast corner of the sixth floor to the southwest corner. It was impossible to see the stairway from that point because there was a barrier of shelves that extended from the west wall approximately 15 feet and blocked off any possible view of the stairway. In Chapter 18 when you explored Williams' testimony in depth, you may recall what Williams said when we questioned him about this FBI report: "I could not possibly have told them that because you cannot see anything coming down there from that position . . . an elephant could walk by there, and you could not see him."

The only other question was whether these shelves, which were in place on Mar. 10, 1964, had also been in place on Nov. 22, 1963. We ascertained from Superintendent Roy Truly that the shelves or bins, which extended from the floor to the ceiling, had been in the TSBD Building "almost from the time we moved in" and were there on Nov. 22.

If Ball and I were to prove an alibi on the part of Oswald, we had to leave the testimony of Bonnie Ray Williams and turn rather to an analysis of the testimony of Patrolman Baker, Roy Truly and Mrs. Reid.

Oswald was first seen after the assassination by a Dallas patrolman, M. L. Baker. Patrolman Baker was riding a two-wheel motorcycle in the rear of the motorcade behind the last press car. He testified that the motorcade was traveling 5 to 10 miles an hour and that as he was turning right from Main to Houston the President's car had already turned left from Houston onto Elm heading toward the Expressway. As Baker turned the corner onto Houston he estimated his speed at 5 to perhaps 7 miles an hour. He said he had almost lost his balance on his motorcycle as a strong wind hit him and "as I got myself straightened up there, I guess it took me some 20, 30 feet, something like that, and it was about that time that I heard these shots come out . . . it seemed to me like they were high, and I just happened to look right straight up."

Baker testified that when he heard the first sound he thought it was a rifle shot "because I had just got back from deer hunting and I had heard them pop over there for about a week." It sounded like a high-powered rifle. He thought that "it sounded high and I immediately kind of looked up, and I had a feeling that it came from" either the TSBD Building, on the northwest corner, or the building across the street on the northeast corner. "As I was looking up, all these pigeons began to fly up to the top of the buildings here and I saw those come up and start flying around." He wasn't sure which building the pigeons came from "but I am pretty sure they came from the building right on the northwest corner."

He heard two more shots—the three shots together were spaced "pretty well even to me." After the third shot he revved up his motorcycle and parked it approximately ten feet from the signal light at the northwest corner of Elm and Houston.

I interviewed Patrolman Baker at the scene of the events on Friday, Mar. 20, 1964. In his testimony before the Commission Baker stated that at the Mar. 20 interview he walked with me to the point where he thought his motorcycle was located when he heard the first shot; this point was approximately 60 to 80 feet north of the north curbline of Main as it would be extended into the intersection of Main and Houston.

Baker also testified that on his Mar. 20 interview he paced off the distance from the position where he heard the first shot to the point at which he parked his motorcycle; this was approximately 180 to 200 feet. He observed as he was parking his motorcycle, people to the west were "falling and rolling around down there" and were rushing back, a lot of them grabbing their children, and he also observed a man run out into the crowd and back, and noticed a woman screaming, "Oh, they have shot that man, they have shot that man."

After surveying the situation, Baker said he "had it in mind that the shots came from the top of this building here," referring to the TSBD Building, and he ran to it.

He entered the lobby of the TSBD Building and there were people going in and he "spoke out and asked where the stairs or elevator was, and this man, Mr. Truly, spoke up and says, it seems to me like he says, I am a building manager. Follow me, Officer, and I will show you." He went through the second set of doors and ran into the swinging door—he bumped into the back of Mr. Truly—they backed up and got through the little swinging door and went at a "good trot" to the back of the building to the northwest corner.

Truly was trying to get the service elevator. He pushed the button to get it down. He hollered twice, "Bring that elevator down here." The elevator did not come, and Baker said to take the stairs, and he followed Truly up the stairway to the west of the elevator.

Mr. Belin. You went up the stairs then?

Mr. Baker. Yes, sir.

Mr. Belin. . . . when you started up the stairs, what was your intention at that time?

Mr. Baker. My intention was to go all the way to the top where I thought the shots had come from, to see if I could find something there, you know, to indicate that.

Mr. Belin. And did you go all the way to the top of the stairs right away?

Mr. Baker. No, sir, we didn't.

Mr. Belin. What happened?

Mr. Baker. As I came out to the second floor there, Mr. Truly was ahead of me, and as I came out I was kind of scanning, you know, the rooms, and I caught a glimpse of this man walking away from this—I happened to see him through this window in this door. I don't know how come I saw him, but I had a glimpse of him coming down there.

Mr. Dulles. Where was he coming from, do you know?

Mr. Baker. No, sir. All I seen of him was a glimpse of him go away from me.

Mr. Belin. What did you do then?

Mr. Baker. I ran on over there—

Representative Boggs. You mean where he was?

Mr. Baker. Yes, sir. There is a door there with a glass, it seemed to me like about a two by two, something like that, and then there is another door which was six foot on over there, and there is a hallway over there and a hallway entering into a lunchroom, and when I got to where I could see him he was walking away from me about 20 feet away from me in the lunchroom.

Mr. Belin. What did you do?

Mr. Baker. I hollered at him at that time and said, "Come here." He turned and walked right straight back at me.

Mr. Belin. Where were you at the time you hollered?

Mr. Baker. I was standing in the hallway between this door and the second door, right at the edge of the second door.

Mr. Belin. He walked back toward you then?

Mr. Baker. Yes, sir.

Baker said that when he first saw the man, the man "was walking east" and that the man was walking away from him. According to Baker, the man was evidently "hurrying" because when Baker first saw him he was 20 feet away and then when Baker ran over to the door to look into the lunchroom, notwithstanding the fact that Baker was running, the man was still "some 20 feet away from me." Baker said the man appeared to be calm and collected. "He never did say a word or nothing. In fact, he didn't change his expression one bit," and he did not flinch when Baker, who had his revolver out, thrust the weapon within three feet of the man's body.

Baker said that he did not say anything to the man for Mr. Truly had come up to his side "and I turned to Mr. Truly and I says, 'Do you know this man, does he work here?' And he (Truly) said yes, and I turned immediately and went on out up the stairs."

I asked Patrolman Baker: Was he carrying anything in his hands?

Mr. Baker. He had nothing at that time.

Later Officer Baker saw Lee Harvey Oswald in the homicide office and recognized him as the man he had seen on the second floor of the TSBD Building.

One of the most significant aspects of the testimony of Officer Baker is his statement that when Oswald was first seen he "was walking east" with his back toward Baker. Oswald was walking from the doorway of the lunchroom toward the Coke machine. Another significant aspect of the Baker testimony is that Oswald was not carrying anything in his hands when he was first seen by Baker. Much confusion has arisen about these facts because when Oswald was later seen by Mrs. Reid, she specifically noted that he had had a Coke in his hands. At the same time Oswald, in his interrogation, stated that he was holding a soft drink at the time of the lunchroom encounter with Patrolman Baker and Mr. Truly. However, in no prior interview with either Patrolman Baker or Mr. Truly was there any recording of the observations of either of these men concerning whether Oswald had a soft drink in his hand at the time of the lunchroom encounter.

For that matter, no law enforcement agency had a recorded affidavit or interview of Patrolman Baker concerning the details of the encounter in the lunchroom with Oswald in such areas as the various positions of Oswald when he was seen or the reason that Baker opened the first door into the lunchroom area rather than continuing up the stairs toward the roof. Nor had any law enforcement agency conducted any test with Patrolman Baker in an effort to determine the time between the firing of the shots and the lunchroom encounter.

On Mar. 20, 1964, I conducted two test runs with Officer Baker and Mr. Truly to reconstruct the events of Nov. 22. In making any factual determination as to whether Lee Harvey Oswald was the assassin beyond a reasonable doubt, the timing elements of the lunchroom encounter are obviously important. If the assassin could not have gotten down to the lunchroom from the southeast corner window on the sixth floor by the time Patrolman Baker saw Oswald, this would be an important consideration tending toward the conclusion either that Oswald was innocent or that, although Oswald might have been a part of a conspiracy to assassinate the President, someone else had pulled the trigger. Thus, when two test runs were made on Friday, Mar. 20, to reconstruct the events that took place on Nov. 22, the tests were run on a minimum-time basis.

In his testimony before the Commission, Baker was questioned about these test runs. He stated that on the first run one minute 30 seconds elapsed between the simulated first shot and the simulated lunchroom encounter, and that on the second test run there was a lapsed time of one minute 15 seconds. On the first run he walked from the motorcycle to the building and on the second run he ran. On both runs, once inside the building, he trotted. "We simulated the shots and by the time we got there we did everything that I had that day, and that would be the minimum, because I am sure that I, you know, it took me a little longer." There was no allowance for slowing down to push through the crowd of people who were on the front steps of the building on Nov. 22, nor was any allowance made for the amount of time it took Patrolman Baker to scan the scene outside the building.

There are several additional matters that indicate that the amount of time actually taken Nov. 22 was longer than the test runs. For instance, in the latter portion of his testimony before the Commission, Officer Baker stated that after he left the lunchroom he continued to the top of the TSBD Building and glanced over to the west side "because the last thing I heard on the radio was the Chief saying 'get some men up on that railroad.'" Baker said that he heard this message as he was getting off the motorcycle. In the test runs on Mar. 20 Baker was at the recessed door of the TSBD Building 15 seconds after the simulated first shot, and this included the time spent in parking the motorcycle and going the 45 feet from the motorcycle into the building.

Furthermore, when the TSBD foreman William Shelley was interviewed in Dallas immediately prior to the taking of his deposition, he testified that he was standing on the front steps of the TSBD Building, that he moved from there toward Elm Street after the shots were fired and that he saw Mr. Truly and Officer Baker running into the building—and he estimated this to be about a minute after the shots were fired. Because of the lack of precise judgment on time, he was not asked in his deposition to make such a specific time estimate. The conclusions that can be drawn are that in the excitement of the moment estimates of time can be either exaggerated or underestimated, and no matter how sincere the witness or how otherwise reliable his testimony, it is impossible to determine these matters with stop-watch accuracy.

Mr. Belin: You mentioned the relationship between what we did on Mar. 20 and what actually occurred on Nov. 22. Would you estimate that we, what we did on Mar. 20 was the maximum or the minimum as for the time we took?

Mr. Baker. I would say it would be the minimum.

Mr. Belin. For instance, on Mar. 20 did we do anything about trying to get through any people on the front steps of the building at all? Did we slow down at all for that?

Mr. Baker. No, sir.

Mr. Belin. Did we slow down at all on Mar. 20 for the time it took you to look over the scene as to what was happening in the area down Elm Street and the Parkway?

Mr. Baker. No, sir.

On Mar. 20, 1964, two additional test runs were made in the presence of Officer Baker from the southeast corner of the sixth floor to the lunchroom. The route taken was a simulated route of the assassin and commenced at the southeast corner of the sixth floor, from there along the east side of the building to the northeast corner and then along the north wall toward the west side of the building with the route going around the elevator and then to the northwest corner of the sixth floor where a Secret Service agent simulated the assassin placing a gun into the area where the rifle was found near the top of the stairway leading down to the fifth floor. The test run then continued down the stairway to the lunchroom. Baker testified that the first test run was done at a normal walking pace and took one minute 18 seconds and the second time the test run was made with a "fast walk" and took one minute 14 seconds.

The manner in which we made these test runs in effect shows that we were leaning over backward in seeking an alibi for Oswald. First we did the reconstruction to see how long it took Truly and Baker to get to the second floor. At that time we did not know how long it would have taken the gunman to get from the southeast corner of the sixth floor to the second floor. The shorter the time it took Baker and Truly to get to the second floor, the less likely it was that Oswald, if he were the gunman, could have gotten from the southeast corner of the sixth floor to the second floor. Therefore, when I ran through the reconstruction with Baker and Truly I made every effort to do this on a "minimum" time basis.

Since our reconstruction tests from the southeast corner of the sixth floor to the second floor lunchroom were made on the basis of the assassin's walking, I am sure that it is clear that if the assassin had moved at the pace of a trot or run, the elapsed time of the test would have been less. Thus, taking the minimum amount of time that it took for Patrolman Baker to reach the second floor lunchroom, it is obvious that in that amount of time the assassin could easily have come from the southeast corner of the sixth floor to that point.

Words are no substitute for an actual physical inspection of the scene. A picture does not even give full comprehension of the actual circumstances of the situation. In the TSBD Building the main stairway is in the northwest corner of the building and the stairs leading from one floor to the other are arranged in the shape of an "L," with both legs of the L approximately the same length. Going from the first to the second floor a person would head west on the first half of the stairway and south on the second half. The stairway itself is enclosed; as he came out of the stairway he would turn to his left and run to the north wall where he would find the stairs going from the second floor to the third floor, which would also be enclosed and also heading west as one went up the stairs. No person going up the stairs from the first to the second floor would be able to see anything in the hallway on the second floor until he got to the top of the stairs.

In the easterly part of this second floor hallway there is a door that leads into a vestibule going into the lunchroom. There is another doorway from the vestibule into the lunchroom and this doorway is generally open; the door from the hall into the vestibule, on the other hand, has a mechanism that keeps the door shut unless it is opened by hand or kept open with a prop. This door is solid except for a square piece of glass in the upper portion; it was through this glass section that Baker glanced as he came up the stairs from the first floor. See a diagram, opposite.

Mr. Belin. What did you see that caused you to turn away from going up to the third floor?

Mr. Baker. As I came out of that stairway running, Mr. Truly had already gone on around, see, and I don't know, as I came around—

Mr. Dulles. Gone on around and up?

Mr. Baker. He had already started around the bend to come to the next elevation going up, I was coming out this one on the second floor, and I don't know, I was kind of sweeping this area as I come up, I was looking from right to left and as I got to this door here I caught a glimpse of this man, just, you know, a sudden glimpse, that is all it was now, and it looked to me like he was going away from me.

Baker said he had stayed in the lunchroom with Oswald "just momentarily," and when Truly said, "'Yes, he works here,' I turned and walked up the stairs." He estimated that approximately 30 seconds elapsed between the time he first saw the movement through the doorway and the time he left to go back up the flight of stairs to the third floor.

One physical fact should be particularly noted; a person coming up the stairway from the first to the second floor and moving around from the head of the stairway toward the north wall where the stairway leading to the third floor begins, cannot look into the glass pane in the first door and see all the way into the lunchroom. This is because the first door is not parallel to the doorway leading from the vestibule into the lunchroom. Consequently, as one looks into the window of the first door he can see into the vestibule but he cannot readily see into the lunchroom itself. Thus, when Baker first saw the movement, Oswald must have just gotten through the door into the vestibule. Had Oswald been in the lunchroom itself no such movement could have been seen by Baker as he came from the top of the stairs leading up to the second floor.

Roy S. Truly, 56-year-old superintendent of the TSBD, was standing on Elm Street in front of the building when he heard an explosion, which he first thought was a firecracker; then he heard two more explosions, which he thought were some sort of rifle shots. People began screaming and the crowd pushed him back toward the first step of the entrance to the building.

I think there were a lot of people trying to get out of the way of something. The crowd in front of me kind of congealed around me and bore me back through weight of number, and I lost sight [of the President's car].

But as I came back here, and everybody was screaming and hollering, just moments later I saw a young motorcycle policeman run up to the building, up the steps to the entrance of our building. He ran right by me. And he was pushing people out of the way. He pushed a number of people out of the way before he got to me. I saw him coming through, I believe. As he ran . . . up the steps, I was almost to the steps, I ran up and caught up with him. I believe I caught up with him inside the lobby of the building, or possibly the front steps. I don't remember that close. But I remember it occurred to me that this man wants on top of the building. He doesn't

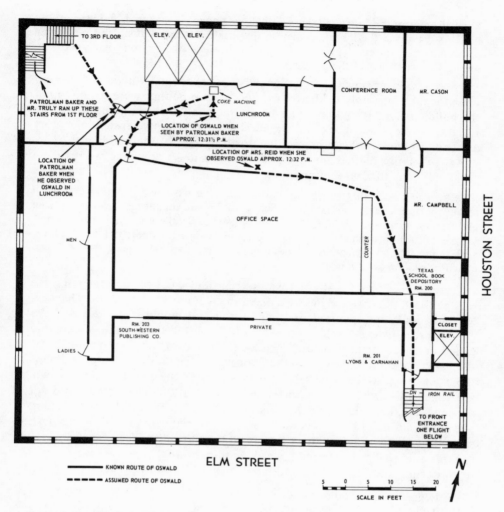

TO 3RD FLOOR

ELEV. ELEV.

CONFERENCE ROOM

MR. CASON

PATROLMAN BAKER AND
MR. TRULY RAN UP THESE
STAIRS FROM 1ST FLOOR

COKE MACHINE

LUNCHROOM

LOCATION OF OSWALD WHEN
SEEN BY PATROLMAN BAKER
APPROX. 12:31½ P.M.

LOCATION OF MRS. REID WHEN SHE
OBSERVED OSWALD APPROX. 12:32 P.M.

LOCATION OF
PATROLMAN
BAKER WHEN
HE OBSERVED
OSWALD IN
LUNCHROOM

OFFICE SPACE

MR. CAMPBELL

MEN

COUNTER

TEXAS
SCHOOL BOOK
DEPOSITORY
RM. 200

HOUSTON STREET

RM. 203
SOUTH-WESTERN
PUBLISHING CO.

PRIVATE

CLOSET

ELEV.

LADIES

RM. 201
LYONS & CARNAHAN

DN   IRON RAIL

TO FRONT
ENTRANCE
ONE FLIGHT
BELOW

ELM STREET

KNOWN ROUTE OF OSWALD
ASSUMED ROUTE OF OSWALD

5 0 5 10 15 20
SCALE IN FEET

N

Commission Exhibit No. 1118
Texas School Book Depository diagram of second floor showing route of Oswald.

know the plan of the floor. And that is—that just popped in my mind, and I ran in with him. As we got in the lobby, almost on the inside of the first floor, this policeman asked me where the stairway is. And I said, "This way." And I ran diagonally across to the northwest corner of the building.

There is a front stairway that runs only to the second floor and also a front elevator that runs only to the fourth floor. Since neither went to the top of the building, Truly took the policeman to the back of the building where the freight elevators and back stairway are situated. The two freight elevators are back to back in the center of the north portion of the building.

As Mr. Truly passed through the swinging glass doors he went to the "will-call" counter, where there is a

little swinging door that swings in and out that we have there. We never keep it locked. But on the bottom is a little bolt that you can lock it to keep people from pulling it out or pushing it in. And this bolt has slid out. It has done that on occasions. I started to run through this little opening, and I ran into the door, and the bolt hung against the side of the counter, and the policeman ran into my back. And so I just pulled it back and continued on through.

Truly then cut diagonally across the rear and went to the elevators. He thought both the east and the west elevators were on the fifth floor. The west elevator could be operated by push-button and would come down if the gates were down. He said there was a little button that he pressed and he called in a "real loud" voice, "Turn loose the elevator." That means that if the gates are up, the person on the floor where the elevator is stopped pulls the gates down so that when the button is pressed the elevator comes down. He yelled this twice after he first pushed the button. The elevator did not descend. He then started up the stairs with the officer a few feet behind him, and when he got to the second floor he ran "right on around to my left, started to continue on up the stairway to the third floor."

Truly said that as he started toward the third floor "I suppose I was up two or three steps before I realized the officer wasn't following me."

Mr. Belin. Then what did you do?

Mr. Truly. I came back to the second floor landing.

Mr. Belin. What did you see?

Mr. Truly. I heard some voices, or a voice, coming from the area of the lunchroom, on the inside vestibule. [He ran over and looked at the door and opened it. By that time Lee Harvey Oswald had turned and walked back to Baker.]

When I reached there the officer had his gun pointing at Oswald. The officer turned this way and said, "This man work here?" and I said, "Yes."

The officer's gun appeared to be almost touching the middle portion of Oswald's body.

Mr. Belin. Could you see Lee Harvey Oswald's hands?

Mr. Truly. Yes. [Truly said that he noticed nothing in either hand.]

Mr. Belin. Did you see both of his hands?

Mr. Truly. I am sure I did. I could be wrong, but I am almost sure I did.

Mr. Belin. About how long did Officer Baker stand there with Lee Harvey Oswald after you saw them?

Mr. Truly. He left immediately after I told him—after he asked me, does this man work here. I said yes. The officer left him immediately.

Mr. Belin. Did you hear Lee Harvey Oswald say anything?

Mr. Truly. Not a thing.

Truly was present at our reconstruction in Dallas on Mar. 20. He confirmed the facts of the reconstruction and said that when the incident was re-enacted "we trotted" and he got out of breath. He said that at the re-enactment he and Baker went at the speed that he felt he went on that day with Officer Baker. He said that he did not remember the time shown by the stop watch, but he thought it was between a minute and a half and two minutes. He further testified that on Nov. 22, "we had a few people we had to push our way through to start in the building the other time, and possibly didn't run quite so fast at first." According to Truly, the reconstruction was done in a "minimum amount of time."

On his testimony concerning the stop watch, Truly was slightly inaccurate. There was also an inaccuracy in his testimony concerning the amount of time it took to get from the southeast corner window on the sixth floor to the second floor lunchroom.

Mr. Belin. Mr. Truly, when we were there on Mar. 20th, did you take a walk down from the southeast corner window on the sixth floor with Officer Baker and a Secret Service Agent Howlett—we walked along from that window at the southeast corner of the sixth floor, walked along the east wall to the northeast corner of the building, and then across there around the elevators, and Secret Service Agent Howlett simulated putting a rifle at the spot where the rifle was found; and then we took the stairs down to the second floor lunchroom where Officer Baker encountered Lee Harvey Oswald? You remember us doing that?

Mr. Truly. Yes, sir.

Mr. Belin. How fast were we going—running, trotting, walking or what?

Mr. Truly. Walking at a brisk walk, and then a little bit faster, I would say.

(Here, Truly was inaccurate, as he was inaccurate in his recollection of what the stop watch showed on the reconstruction of the time to get up to the second floor. Whereas Truly testified the stop watch showed between a minute and a half and two minutes, the testimony of Officer Baker was correct: the first timing was one minute 30 seconds and the second timing was one minute 15 seconds. Similarly, the testimony of Officer Baker is correct that on the test runs from the southeast corner of the sixth floor to the lunchroom the first test run was at a normal walk and the second test run was at a brisk walk.)

Mr. Belin. You remember what time that was? How long did it take?

Mr. Truly. It seemed to me like it was a minute and 18 seconds, and a minute and 15 seconds. We tried it twice. I believe that is about as near as I remember.

Mr. Belin. If a person were in that southeast corner window, just knowing the way the books were laid up there, would that have been the most practicable route to use to get out of there, to get down the stairs?

Mr. Truly. I believe so. I believe it to be.

Even though the reconstruction tests with Truly and Baker showed that

Oswald could have gotten from the southeast corner of the sixth floor to the second floor within the time that Truly and Baker reached the second floor, we did not stop here. We also, on Mar. 20, subjected Mrs. R. A. Reid, clerical supervisor for the Texas School Book Depository, to a reconstruction test. Mrs. Reid said that at the time of the assassination she was standing in front of the main entrance of the TSBD and heard three shots after the motorcade passed by.

"And I turned to Mr. Campbell and I said, 'Oh, my goodness, I am afraid those came from our building,' because it seemed like they came just so directly over my head, and then I looked up in the windows, and saw three colored boys up there, I only recognized one because I didn't know the rest of them so well." She recognized James Jarman, according to her testimony. Campbell said to her: "Oh, Mrs. Reid, no, it came from the grassy area down this way," which was in the direction the parade was going.

She saw "a mass of confusion. I saw people beginning to fall, and the thoughts that went through my mind, my goodness I must get out of this line of shots, they may fire some more." She then went into the building and took the front stairs and went up the stairs into her office.

I went through a reconstruction with Mrs. Reid.

Mr. Belin. Do you remember how long by the stop watch it took you?

Mrs. Reid. Approximately 2 minutes. I kept walking and I looked up and Oswald was coming in the back door of the office. I met him by the time I passed my desk several feet and I told him, I said, "Oh, the President has been shot, but maybe they didn't hit him." He mumbled something to me, I kept walking, he did, too. I didn't pay any attention to what he said because I had no thoughts of anything of him having any connection with it at all because he was very calm. He had gotten a Coke and was holding it in his hand and I guess the reason it impressed me seeing him in there I thought it was a little strange that one of the warehouse boys would be up in the office at the time, not that he had done anything wrong. The only time I had seen him in the office was to come and get change and he already had his Coke in his hand so he didn't come for change and I dismissed him. I didn't think anything else.

Mrs. Reid said that the actual time on Nov. 22 "wasn't any less" than the two minutes it took in the reconstruction. As a matter of fact, she was rather out of breath by the time we were through on Mar. 20. In her words, "We did it three times and we ran."

Thus, our conclusions were that Oswald had used the stairs and that the fact that he was seen in the lunchroom after the assassination by Patrolman Baker and Superintendent Truly was not inconsistent with his having been on the sixth floor at the time of the assassination. This conclusion was still a tentative one because there was still another problem to be solved if the assassin had used the stairs. This concerned the testimony of Victoria Elizabeth Adams, a 23-year-old employee of Scott, Foresman Company's offices on the fourth floor of the TSBD Building. She was watching the motorcade from the fourth floor, looking out the west window of the third pair of windows, counting from the east side.

Miss Adams heard three shots and said that following the third shot "I went to the back of the building, down the back stairs, and encountered Bill Shelley and Billy Lovelady on the first floor" while she was on her way out to the Houston Street dock of the building. She said that she was running and that she encountered no one as she ran down the back stairs and saw no one when she got to the bottom of the stairs and no one by the elevator. The only persons she saw on the way out of the building, she said, were Bill Shelley and Billy Lovelady, at a point that "would be slightly east of the front of the east elevator, and about as far north as the length of the elevator, probably as far south as the length of the elevator." She did not see Oswald on the way down nor did she see any police officer or Roy Truly. When she got outside she went west toward the railroad tracks and then went back in front of the TSBD Building; she saw some employees there and heard a police radio report that the shots had been fired from the second floor of the TSBD Building and she went back inside. An officer allowed her to re-enter.

Miss Adams estimated from the time the shots were fired until she got back into the building five minutes elapsed.

She also said that from the time the shots were fired until she left the window to start toward the stairway 15 to 30 seconds elapsed, and she did not think it took her longer than a minute to get to the bottom of the stairs.

Miss Adams stated that she did not see any other person running down the stairs. She did not see Officer Baker or Mr. Truly running up the stairs. When she got to the bottom of the stairs she did not see them at the elevator shaft. If her testimony was correct that she started running down the stairs when she did and saw none of these persons, this conflicted with the other evidence that seemed to indicate that Oswald immediately came down the stairway from the southeast corner of the sixth floor to the second floor. It also conflicted with the promptness with which Officer Baker and Superintendent Truly said they had entered the building.

Since Miss Adams testified that the two people she saw when she got down to the first floor on her way out of the building were William Shelley and Billy Lovelady, these two men were asked in their depositions to describe their actions after the shots were fired.

Mr. Shelley said he was standing in front of the TSBD Building watching the motorcade. He heard something that sounded like a firecracker, a slight pause and then two more sounds a bit closer together that seemed to him to be coming from the west. A woman named Gloria Calvary ran up and said, "The President has been shot." Shelley and Billy Lovelady moved to the south—to the little "island," a portion of land between Elm as it turns down to the expressway and the extension of Elm Street as it runs immediately in front of the TSBD Building. They stopped there for a minute. An officer started running down the railroad yards. While they were at the island they saw Truly and the officer go into the building. (This would mean that Truly and Baker did not get into the building as fast as they thought they had.) Shelley and Lovelady then walked to the railroad yards to the first railroad track and watched officers searching cars in the parking lot. They then went back to the west side of the TSBD Building, walked to the rear of the building and entered the first floor from the rear entrance. Shelley does not remember whether he saw Victoria Adams at that time.

Billy Lovelady testified that he was on the steps of the TSBD Building when the motorcade went by. From his vantage point he was standing on the "right side" of the steps (as you face the street) and heard sounds he thought were firecrackers. Mr. Lovelady identified pictures of himself standing on the top step at the entrance to the building in Commission Exhibit 369, a photograph taken as the motorcade went by.[1] At the time the picture was taken, Lovelady was standing near Mr. Shelley on the top step at the entrance of the building. After the sounds were heard Gloria Calvary ran up and said the President had been shot—she worked at the Southwestern Publishing Company in the TSBD Building. Lovelady said that he left with Shelley and started toward the railroad tracks and that when he was 15 or 25 steps from the TSBD Building he looked back and saw Truly and the policeman running into the building. Shelley and Lovelady went on to the tracks, which Lovelady estimated as about 75 to 100 yards away, and then they moved to the rear of the TSBD Building, where they entered. Lovelady said that they went to the tracks at a medium trot or fast walk and that when he came back into the building from the west side through the raised doors he saw a girl on the first floor who he believes was "Vickie" (Victoria Adams).

Because Victoria Adams was sure that when she got to the bottom of the stairs from the fourth floor she saw Shelley and Lovelady before she left the building and because Shelley and Lovelady could not have gotten to the railroad tracks and returned within a minute after the shots were fired, we have two alternatives: Victoria Adams was inaccurate in her estimate of time, in which she states she left to go down the stairs 15 to 30 seconds after the shots were fired; or she is inaccurate about whom she saw when she got to the bottom of the stairs. It is obvious that the human mind is far more accurate on identification of known persons than it is on estimates of time. This is particularly true in this case because Miss Adams is so definite about whom she saw when she got to the first floor, and her observations are confirmed by the testimony of Billy Lovelady, who believed that he saw Miss Adams when they got back into the building.

Moreover, the testimony of Miss Adams is contradicted by the testimony of Officer Baker and Superintendent Truly, for Miss Adams saw neither of these persons as she was going down the stairs and did not see them at the

---

[1]This picture was the subject of much speculation because Lovelady resembled Oswald. There was speculation that the person in the photograph, Exhibit 369, might actually be Oswald. Lovelady, of course, put the matter to rest, although many sensationalists offered the picture as proof of Oswald's innocence. For instance, such misrepresentation is included in the Lane-de Antonio film.

elevator when she got down the stairs. The only possibility would be that Baker and Truly had already arrived at the second floor and were in the lunchroom, encountering Oswald when she came down the stairs—but she did not remember seeing anyone on the second floor either. The testimony of Victoria Adams, in summary, does not rebut the other facts, which indicate that the assassin, shortly after the time of the shooting, came down the stairway from the sixth floor. Rather, these facts seem to show that Victoria Adams was mistaken in her time estimate and that she did not get down to the first floor as soon as she thought she had, unless she ran down the stairs at the time of the lunchroom encounter when Oswald, Truly and Baker would not have been in view of anyone coming down the stairs.

On the basis of the overall testimony of these witnesses, Ball and I had come to another dead end in our efforts to establish the innocence of Oswald or the existence of a co-conspirator.

Just as the FBI was inaccurate in its report of what happened at the autopsy of President Kennedy, it was inaccurate in its report that Bonnie Ray Williams, from the southwest corner of the fifth floor, could see anyone coming down the stairway. And just as the FBI was incomplete in its investigation concerning the amount of time it took Patrolman Baker and Roy Truly to get to the second floor, the FBI was also incomplete in some other areas of its investigation.

The incompleteness of FBI investigations and the inaccuracies of some of the FBI reports have been exploited by assassination sensationalists. The technique is simple: When the FBI was right, as it generally was, sensationalists ignore the reports. When the FBI was wrong, the sensationalists say, "Look what the FBI said." Thus, they seek to have it both ways. A typical example concerns the first bullet that struck President Kennedy. According to the FBI investigation the fibers of the clothing on the back of President Kennedy pointed inward and the fibers on the front of President Kennedy's shirt pointed outward. This indicated a projectile entering from the rear and exiting from the front of the neck, which is at variance with the FBI report of the autopsy, which indicates the first bullet that struck President Kennedy went only a finger's length into his body. As you might expect, those who attack the Report of the Warren Commission ignore the FBI analysis of the President's clothing while relying heavily on the FBI report of what happened at the autopsy.

In contrast, Joe Ball and I did not limit ourselves to any single report, testimony, or item of physical evidence. Rather we conducted our investigation and reached our conclusions on the basis of the overall record.

By now, you have an insight into the method of our investigation. You also have an insight into the depth of the evidence that formed the foundation for our conclusions. You know that we did not blindly rely on the reports of any law enforcement agency and that even the best of these agencies can and does make mistakes.

Finally, you know that there is another, less-than-perfect side to the FBI.

32

"AND WE SAID, 'CAPTAIN, WE WILL SAVE YOU A TRIP ... BECAUSE THERE HE SITS'"

I was completing my questioning of Dallas Police Sergeant Gerald L. Hill, who had helped apprehend Lee Harvey Oswald in the Texas Theatre. Sergeant Hill rode in the police car with Oswald to police headquarters.

Mr. Belin. Now after, from the time you started in motion until the time you called in, do you remember anyone saying anything at all in the car?

Mr. Hill. The suspect was asked what his name was.

Mr. Belin. What did he say?

Mr. Hill. He never did answer. He just sat there.

Mr. Belin. Was he asked where he lived?

Mr. Hill. That was the second question that was asked the suspect, and he didn't answer it, either.

About the time I got through with the radio transmission, I asked Paul Bentley, "Why don't you see if he has any identification."

Paul was sitting sort of sideways in the seat, and with his right hand he reached down and felt of the suspect's left hip pocket and said, "Yes, he has a billfold," and took it out.

I never did have the billfold in my possession, but the name Lee Oswald was called out by Bentley from the back seat, and said this identification, I believe, was on the library card.

And he also made the statement that there was some more identification in this other name which I don't remember, but it was the same name that later came in the paper that he bought the gun under.

Mr. Belin. Would the name Hidell mean anything? Alek Hidell?

Mr. Hill. That would be similar. I couldn't say specifically that is what it was, because this was a conversation and I never did see it written down, but that sounds like the name that I heard.

Mr. Belin. Was this the first time you learned of the name?

Mr. Hill. Yes; it was.

Mr. Belin. All right; when did you learn of his address?

Mr. Hill. There were two different addresses on the identification.

One of them was in Oak Cliff. The other one was in Irving. But as near as I can recall of the conversation in the car, this was strictly conversation, because I didn't read any of the stuff. It didn't have an address on Beckley, that I recall hearing.

Mr. Belin. Let me ask you this. Now from the time you got in the car to the time you got to the station, I believe you said that at least the second question asked was where do you live, and the man didn't answer?

Mr. Hill. The man didn't answer.

Mr. Belin. Was he ever asked again where he lived, up to the time you got to the station?

Mr. Hill. No; I don't believe so, because when Bentley got the identification out, we had two different addresses. We had two different names, and the comment was made, "I guess we are going to have to wait until we get to the station to find out who he actually is."

After about the time Bentley reached in his pocket and got his billfold, the suspect made the statement, "I don't know why you are treating me like this. The only thing I have done is carry a pistol in a movie."

Then there was a remark made something to the effect, "Yes, sir; you have done a lot more. You have killed a policeman."

And then the suspect made a remark similar to "Well, you fry for that," or something to that effect.

Mr. Belin. Something to what effect?

Mr. Hill. Well, now, he either made the statement, "You only fry for that," or "You can fry for that," or a similar statement. Now the exact words of it, I don't recall.

Mr. Belin. All right; then what was said?

Mr. Hill. Some more questions were asked as to where he had been prior to going to the movie, which he did not answer. Some more questions were asked as to what was his true name, and in neither case did he ever answer them. He did make a comment, if I recall, about the handcuffs, about, "I don't see why you handcuffed me." And here again he repeated the statement, "The only crime I have committed was carrying a pistol in a movie."

We got the suspect to the city hall as rapidly as possible without using the siren and red light, but we took advantage of every open spot we had to make a little speed, and we explained to him this—I did, before we got into the basement, that there would probably be some reporters and photographers and cameramen waiting in the basement when we got to the station, and that if he so desired, we would hold him in a way that he could hide his face if he wanted to, and also told him he did not have to speak to the press if he didn't want to.

He didn't comment on this at this point, but as we pulled into the basement from the Main Street side, we were wanting to get out and get organized enough that we would set up our wedge again to get him in the station through the basement, and so we pulled over to what would have been the southeast side of the basement, got out of the car, and formed a wedge in the same position that we left the theatre, and told the suspect again he could hide his face if he wanted to.

And he said, "Why should I hide my face. I haven't done anything to be ashamed of."

And with that we started walking him up the aisle of the basement and walked him through the door into the basement of the city hall proper, put him on the elevator, stayed on the elevator with him, put him back behind the wall, and sort of formed a wall around him.

Some of the press pushed into the elevator with us.

Got him out on the third floor, walked him into the homicide and robbery office, placed him in the first interrogation room inside the homicide and robbery office, and left Officer Walker there with him.

At this point I stood in the door of the, or at the door of the room he was in.

Reporters wanted to see the pistol. I held it up to them but never relinquished control of it. I asked Baker at this time, who was Detective T. L. Baker, if he wanted the pistol, and he said, "No; hold on to it until later."

I explained to him that this was the suspect on Tippit and did he want us to make up the arrest sheet, or would they make them up.

We were trying to get together to decide who was going to make the offense report and get all the little technicalities out of the way when a detective named Richard Stovall and another one, G. F. Rose, came up, and the four of us were standing when Captain Fritz walked in.

He walked up to Rose and Stovall and made the statement to them, "Go get a search warrant and go out to some address on Fifth Street," and I don't recall the actual street number, in Irving, and "pick up a man named Lee Oswald."

And I asked the captain why he wanted him, and he said, "Well, he was employed down at the Book Depository and he had not been present for a roll call of the employees."

And we said, "Captain, we will save you a trip," or words to that effect, "Because there he sits."

And with that, we relinquished our prisoner to the homicide and robbery bureau, to Captain Fritz.

J. W. Fritz started as a patrolman with the Dallas Police Department in Jan. 1921. Since 1932 or 1933, he had been head of the homicide and robbery detail. On Nov. 22, he arrived at the TSBD Building at 12:58 PM.

Mr. Ball. What did you do when you got to this building?

Mr. Fritz. Some officer told us they thought he was in that building, so we had our guns—

Mr. McCloy. Thought who was in the building?

Mr. Fritz. The man who did the shooting was in the building. So, we, of course, took our shotguns and immediately entered the building and searched the building to see if we could find him.

Mr. Ball. Were there guards on the doors of the building at that time?

Mr. Fritz. I am not sure, but I don't—there has been some question about that, but the reason I don't think that—this may differ with someone else, but I am going to tell you what I know.

Mr. Ball. All right.

Mr. McCloy. By all means.

Mr. Fritz. After I arrived one of the officers asked me if I would like to have the building sealed and I told him I would.

Mr. Ball. What officer was that?

Mr. Fritz. That is a uniformed officer, but I don't know what his name was, he was outside, of course, I went upstairs and I don't know whether he did because I couldn't watch him.

Mr. Ball. Then what did you do?

Mr. Fritz. We began searching the floors, looking for anyone with a gun or looked suspicious, and we searched through hurriedly through most all the floors.

Mr. McCloy. Which floor did you start with?

Mr. Fritz. We started at the bottom; yes, sir. And, of course, and I think we went up probably to the top.

Different people would call me when they would find something that looked like something I should know about and I ran back and forth from floor to floor as we were searching, and it wasn't very long until someone called me and told me they wanted me to come to the front window, the corner window, they had found some empty cartridges.

Mr. Ball. That was on the sixth floor?

Mr. Fritz. That is right; the sixth floor, corner window.

Mr. Ball. What did you do?

Mr. Fritz. I told them not to move the cartridges, not to touch anything until we could get the crime lab to take pictures of them just as they were lying there and I left an officer assigned there to see that that was done, and the crime lab came almost immediately, and took pictures, and dusted the shelves for prints.

Mr. Ball. Which officers, which officer did you leave there?

Mr. Fritz. Carl Day was the man I talked to about taking pictures.

Mr. Ball. Day?

Mr. Fritz. Lieutenant Day; yes, sir.

Mr. Ball. Do you know whether he took the pictures or not?

Mr. Fritz. I feel like he did but I don't know because I didn't stay to see whether he could.

Mr. Ball. You didn't know whether he took the pictures?

Mr. Fritz. I went on searching the building. I just told them to preserve that evidence and I went right ahead.

Mr. Ball. What happened after that?

Mr. Fritz. A few minutes later some officer called me and said they had found the rifle over near the back stairway and I told them same thing, not to move it, not to touch it, not to move any of the boxes until we could get pictures, and as soon as Lieutenant Day could get over there he made pictures of that.

Mr. Ball. After the pictures had been taken of the rifle what happened then?

Mr. Fritz. After the pictures had been made then I ejected a live shell, a live cartridge from the rifle.

Mr. Ball. And who did you give that to?

Mr. Fritz. I believe that I kept that at that time myself. Later I gave it to the crime lab who, in turn, turned it over to the FBI.

While Captain Fritz was on the sixth floor of the TSBD Building, Superintendent Roy Truly—who had followed Patrolman Baker to the roof—returned to the first floor, then, according to Truly:

I noticed some of my boys were over in the west corner of the shipping department, and there were several officers over there taking their names and addresses and so forth.

There were other officers in other parts of the building taking other employees', like office people's names. I noticed that Lee Oswald was not among these boys. . . .

First I mentioned to Mr. Campbell—I asked Bill Shelley if he had seen him, he looked around and said no.

Mr. Belin. When you asked Bill Shelley if he had seen whom?

Mr. Truly. Lee Oswald. I said, "Have you seen him around lately," and he said no.

So Mr. Campbell is standing there, and I said, "I have a boy over here missing. I don't know whether to report it or not." Because I had another one or two out then. I didn't know whether they were all there or not. He said, "What do you think?" And

I got to thinking. He said, "Well, we better do it anyway." It was so quick after that.

So I picked the phone up then and called Mr. Aiken, at the warehouse, and got the boy's name and general description and telephone number and address at Irving.

Mr. Belin. Did you have any address for him in Dallas, or did you just have an address in Irving?

Mr. Truly. Just the address in Irving. I knew nothing of this Dallas address. I didn't know he was living away from his family.

Mr. Belin. Now, would that be the address and the description as shown on this application, Exhibit 496?

Mr. Truly. Yes, sir.

Mr. Belin. Did you ask for the name and addresses of any other employees who might have been missing?

Mr. Truly. No, sir.

Mr. Belin. Why didn't you ask for any other employees?

Mr. Truly. That is the only one that I could be certain right then was missing.

Mr. Belin. Then what did you do after you got that information?

Mr. Truly. Chief Lumpkin of the Dallas Police Department was standing a few feet from me. I told Chief Lumpkin that I had a boy missing over here—I don't know whether it amounts to anything or not. And I gave him his description. And he says, "Just a moment. We will go tell Captain Fritz."

Mr. Belin. All right. And then what happened?

Mr. Truly. So Chief Lumpkin had several officers there that he was talking to, and I assumed that he gave him some instructions of some nature—I didn't hear it. And then he turned to me and says, "Now we will go upstairs."

So we got on one of the elevators, I don't know which, and rode up to the sixth floor. I didn't know Captain Fritz was on the sixth floor. And he was over in the northwest corner of the building.

Mr. Belin. By the stairs there?

Mr. Truly. Yes; by the stairs.

Mr. Belin. All right.

Mr. Truly. And there were other officers with him. Chief Lumpkin stepped over and told Captain Fritz that I had something that I wanted to tell him.

Mr. Belin. All right. And then what happened?

Mr. Truly. So Captain Fritz left the men he was with and walked over about 8 or 10 feet and said, "What is it, Mr. Truly," or words to that effect.

And I told him about this boy missing and gave him his address and telephone number and general description. And he says, "Thank you, Mr. Truly. We will take care of it."

And I went back downstairs in a few minutes.

There was a reporter followed me away from that spot, and asked me who Oswald was. I told the reporter, "You must have ears like a bird, or something. I don't want to say anything about a boy I don't know anything about. This is a terrible thing." Or words to that effect.

Captain Fritz testified that after the rifle was found,

Mr. Truly came and told me that one of his employees had left the building, and I asked his name and he gave me his name, Lee Harvey Oswald, and I asked his address and he gave me the Irving address. . . .

Mr. Ball. How long did you stay at the Texas School Book Depository after you found the rifle?

Mr. Fritz. After he told me about this man almost, I left immediately after he told me that.

Mr. Ball. You left almost immediately after he told you that?

Mr. Fritz. Almost after he told me that man, I felt it important to hold that man.

Mr. Ball. Did you give descriptions to Sims and Boyd?

Mr. Fritz. Yes, sir; I told them to drive me to city hall and see if the man had a criminal record and we picked up two other officers and my intentions were to go to the house at Irving. When I got to the city hall, I asked, because, I will tell you why I asked because while we were in the building we heard that our officer had been killed, someone came in and told me. I asked when I got to my office who shot the officer, and they told me his name was Oswald, and I said, "His full name?" And they told me and I said, "That is the suspect we are looking for in the President's killing."

So, I then called some of my officers to go right quickly, and asked them about how much evidence we had on the officer's killing and they told me they had several eye witnesses, and they had some real good witnesses, and I instructed them to get those witnesses over for identification just as soon as they could, and for us to prepare a real good case on the officer's killing so we would have a case to hold him without bond while we investigated the President's killing where we didn't have so many witnesses.

Captain Fritz then directed some officers to go to the Irving address. While the officers were going to the residence in Irving, where Marina Oswald was staying, Captain Fritz started to interrogate Lee Harvey Oswald.

33

"THEY OPENED THE BLANKET BUT THERE WAS NO RIFLE THERE"

I went to the door. They announced themselves as from both the sheriff's office and the Dallas Police Office, showed me at least one package or two. I was very surprised.

Mr. Jenner. Did you say anything?

Mrs. Paine. I said nothing. I think I just dropped my jaw. And the man in front said by way of explanation, "We have Lee Oswald in custody. He is charged with shooting an officer." This is the first I had any idea that Lee might be in trouble with the police or in any way involved in the day's events. I asked them to come in. They said they wanted to search the house. I asked if they had a warrant. They said they didn't. They said they could get the sheriff out here right away with one if I insisted. And I said no, that was all right, they could be my guests.

They then did search the house. I directed them to the fact that most of the Oswalds' things were in storage in my garage and showed where the garage was, and to the room where Marina and the baby had stayed where they would find the other things which belonged to the Oswalds. Marina and I went with two or three of these police officers to the garage.

Mr. Jenner. How many police officers were there?

Mrs. Paine. There were six altogether, and they were busy in various parts of the house. The officer asked me in the garage did Lee Oswald have any weapons or guns. I said no, and translated the question to Marina, and she said yes; that she had seen a portion of it—had looked into—she indicated the blanket roll on the floor.

Mr. Jenner. Was the blanket roll on the floor at that time?

Mrs. Paine. She indicated the blanket roll on the floor very close to where I was standing. As she told me about it I stepped onto the blanket roll.

Mr. Jenner. This might be helpful. You had shaped that up yesterday and I will just put it on the floor.

Mrs. Paine. And she indicated to me that she had peered into this roll and saw a portion of what she took to be a gun she knew her husband to have, a rifle. And I then translated this to the officers that she knew that her husband had a gun that he had stored in here.

Mr. Jenner. Were you standing on the blanket when you advised—

Mrs. Paine. When I translated. I then stepped off of it and the officer picked it up in the middle and it bent so.

Mr. Jenner. It hung limp just as it now hangs limp in your hand?

Mrs. Paine. And at this moment I felt this man was in very deep trouble and may have done—

Mr. McCloy. Were the strings still on it?

Mrs. Paine. The strings were still on it. It looked exactly as it had at previous times

I had seen it. It was at this point I say I made the connection with the assassination, thinking that possibly, knowing already that the shot had been made from the School Book Depository, and that this was a rifle that was missing, I wondered if he would not also be charged before the day was out with the assassination.

The witness was Mrs. Ruth Paine, who had befriended Marina Oswald and in Sept., 1963, had invited Marina Oswald and her baby to live at her home in Irving. The officer in charge of the search of the Paine residence was Detective Guy F. Rose, who had seen Oswald earlier that afternoon at the Dallas police station.

Mr. Ball. What did you say to him [Oswald] or did he say to you?

Mr. Rose. Well, the first thing I asked him was what his name was and he told me it was Hidell. . . .

Mr. Ball. He didn't tell you it was Oswald?

Mr. Rose. No; he didn't, not right then—he did later. In a minute—I found two cards—I found a card that said "A. Hidell." And I found another card that said "Lee Oswald" on it, and I asked him which of the two was his correct name. He wouldn't tell me at the time, he just said, "You find out." And then in just a few minutes Captain Fritz came in and he told me to get two men and go to Irving and search his house.

Detective Rose went to the Irving residence with two other Dallas police officers and three detectives "from County CID."

Mr. Ball. You took part in the search, didn't you?

Mr. Rose. Yes; I did.

Mr. Ball. What part did you take?

Mr. Rose. Well, I was the senior detective that was there, and so I was sort of the spokesman for the group, I suppose, and Stovall went into the bedroom of Marina Oswald—Marina Oswald's bedroom, and I don't remember where Adamcik went first, but I talked with Ruth Paine a few minutes and she told me that Marina was there and that she was Lee Oswald's wife and that she was a citizen of Russia, and so I called Captain Fritz on the phone and told him what I had found out there and asked him if there was any special instructions, and he said, "Well, ask her about her husband, ask her if her husband has a rifle."

I turned and asked Marina, but she didn't seem to understand. She said she couldn't understand, so Ruth Paine spoke in Russian to her and Ruth Paine also interpreted for me, and she said that Marina said—first she said Marina said "No," and then in a minute Marina said, "Yes, he does have."

So, then I talked to Captain Fritz for a moment and hung up the phone and I asked Marina if she would show me where his rifle was and Ruth Paine interpreted and Marina pointed to the garage and she took me to the garage and she pointed to a blanket that was rolled up and laying on the floor near the wall of the garage and Ruth Paine said, "Says that that's where his rifle is."

Well, at the time I couldn't tell whether there was one in there or not. It appeared to be—it was in sort of an outline of a rifle.

Mr. Ball. You mean the blanket had the outline of a rifle?

Mr. Rose. Yes; it did.

Mr. Ball. Was it tied at one end?

Mr. Rose. Yes, sir; it was sort of rolled up, but it was flattened out from laying down and tied near the middle, I would say, with a cord and so I went on and picked the blanket up, but it was empty—it didn't have the rifle in it.

Mr. Ball. You brought that in?

Mr. Rose. Yes; I did.

Ten days later, on Dec. 2, 1963, Mrs. Paine turned over to the police some of the Oswalds' belongings, including a Russian volume entitled "Book of Useful Advice." In this book was an undated note written in Russian. In translation, the note read as follows:

1. This is the key to the mailbox which is located in the main post office in the city on Ervay Street. This is the same street where the drugstore, in which you always waited is located. You will find the mailbox in the post office which is located 4 blocks from the drugstore on that street. I paid for the box last month so don't worry about it.

2. Send the information as to what has happened to me to the Embassy and include newspaper clippings (should there be anything about me in the newspapers). I believe that the Embassy will come quickly to your assistance on learning everything.

3. I paid the house rent on the 2d so don't worry about it.

4. Recently I also paid for water and gas.

5. The money from work will possibly be coming. The money will be sent to our post office box. Go to the bank and cash the check.

6. You can either throw out or give my clothing, etc. away. Do not keep these. However, I prefer that you hold on to my personal papers (military, civil, etc.).

7. Certain of my documents are in the small blue valise.

8. The address book can be found on my table in the study should need same.

9. We have friends here. The Red Cross also will help you. (Red Cross in English). [sic]

10. I left you as much money as I could, $60 on the second of the month. You and the baby [apparently] can live for another 2 months using $10 per week.

11. If I am alive and taken prisoner, the city jail is located at the end of the bridge through which we always passed on going to the city (right in the beginning of the city after crossing the bridge).

James C. Cadigan, FBI handwriting expert, testified that this note was written by Lee Harvey Oswald.

The Commission used this note as the primary basis for its finding that Oswald was the person who on Apr. 10, 1963, fired a shot at Major General Edwin A. Walker, a controversial American political figure since his resignation from the Army in 1961. I did not believe we should have reached this conclusion. Even if there were sufficient overall evidence to prove Oswald tried to kill Walker, a major portion of such evidence was the testimony of Oswald's wife. Communications between a husband and wife are privileged under Texas law and would not have been admissible in a court had Oswald been tried for the crime.

General Walker was seated near his desk when a rifle bullet fired from outside his home passed near his head. The rifle bullet was found inside Walker's house. It was too mutilated to be ballistically identifiable.

Shortly before the Walker shooting, Oswald had been attending typing classes weeknights. But he quit these classes at least a week before the shooting, which occurred on a Wednesday night. That evening, Oswald went out; when he failed to return by 10 or 10:30 PM, according to his wife, she went to his room and discovered the note. She testified: "When he came back I asked him what had happened. He was very pale. I don't remember the exact time, but it was very late. And he told me not to ask him any questions. He only told me he had shot at General Walker." . . .

That evening he went out, I thought that he had gone to his classes or perhaps that he just walked out or went out on his own business. It got to be about 10 or 10:30, he wasn't home yet, and I began to be worried. Perhaps even later.

Then I went into his room. Somehow, I was drawn into it—you know—I was pacing around. Then I saw a note there.

Mr. Rankin. Did you look for the gun at that time?

Mrs. Oswald. No, I didn't understand anything. On the note it said, "If I am arrested" and there are certain other questions, such as, for example, the key to the mailbox is in such and such a place, and that he left me some money to last me for some time, and I couldn't understand at all what can he be arrested for. When he came back I asked him what had happened. He was very pale. I don't remember the exact time, but it was very late.

And he told me not to ask him any questions. He only told me that he had shot at General Walker.

Of course I didn't sleep all night. I thought that any minute now, the police will come. Of course I wanted to ask him a great deal. But in his state I decided I had best leave him alone—it would be purposeless to question him.

Mr. Rankin. Did he say any more than that about the shooting?

Mrs. Oswald. Of course in the morning I told him that I was worried, and that we can have a lot of trouble, and I asked him, "Where is the rifle? What did you do with it?"

He said that he had left it somewhere, that he had buried it, it seems to me, somewhere far from that place, because he said dogs could find it by smell.

I don't know—I am not a criminologist.

Mr. Rankin. Did he tell you why he had shot at General Walker?

Mrs. Oswald. I told him that he had no right to kill people in peacetime, he had no right to take their life because not everybody has the same ideas as he has. People cannot be all alike.

He said that this was a very bad man, that he was a fascist, that he was the leader of a fascist organization, and when I said that even though all of that might be true, just the same he had no right to take his life, he said if someone had killed Hitler in time it would have saved many lives. I told him that this is no method to prove your ideas, by means of a rifle.

Mr. Rankin. Did you ask him how long he had been planning to do this?

Mrs. Oswald. Yes. He said he had been planning for two months. Yes—perhaps he had planned to do so even earlier, but according to his conduct I could tell he was planning—he had been planning this for two months or perhaps a little even earlier.

According to Marina Oswald,

He said only that he had taken very good aim, that it was just chance that caused him to miss. He was very sorry that he had not hit him.

I asked him to give me his word that he would not repeat anything like that. I said that this chance shows that he must live and that he should not be shot at again. I told him that I would save the note and that if something like that should be repeated again, I would go to the police and I would have the proof in the form of that note.

He said he would not repeat anything like that again.

The Walker incident had a profound effect on Marina Oswald when she learned about the assassination of President Kennedy:

Mr. Rankin. How did you learn of the shooting of President Kennedy?

Mrs. Oswald. I was watching television, and Ruth by that time was already with me, and she said someone had shot at the President.

Mr. Rankin. What did you say?

Mrs. Oswald. It was hard for me to say anything. We both turned pale. I went to my room and cried.

Mr. Rankin. Did you think immediately that your husband might have been involved?

Mrs. Oswald. No.

Mr. Rankin. Did Mrs. Paine say anything about the possibility of your husband being involved?

Mrs. Oswald. No, but she only said that "By the way, they fired from the building in which Lee is working."

My heart dropped. I then went to the garage to see whether the rifle was there, and I saw that the blanket was still there, and I said, "Thank God." I thought, "Can there really be such a stupid man in the world that could do something like that?" But I was already rather upset at that time—I don't know why. Perhaps my intuition.

I didn't know what I was doing.

Mr. Rankin. Did you look in the blanket to see if the rifle was there?

Mrs. Oswald. I didn't unroll the blanket. It was in its usual position, and it appeared to have something inside.

Mr. Rankin. Did you at any time open the blanket to see if the rifle was there?

Mrs. Oswald. No, only once.

Mr. Rankin. You have told us about that.[1]

Mrs. Oswald. Yes.

Mr. Rankin. And what about Mrs. Paine? Did she look in the blanket to see if the rifle was there?

Mrs. Oswald. She didn't know about the rifle.

Perhaps she did know. But she never told me about it.

I don't know.

Mr. Rankin. When did you learn that the rifle was not in the blanket?

Mrs. Oswald. When the police arrived and asked whether my husband had a rifle, and I said "Yes."

Mr. Rankin. Then what happened?

Mrs. Oswald. They began to search the apartment. When they came to the garage and took the blanket, I thought, "Well, now, they will find it."

They opened the blanket but there was no rifle there.

Then, of course, I already knew that it was Lee.

[1]Marina moved from Dallas to New Orleans in May, 1963. Ruth Paine drove her and the baby back from New Orleans in late September. Marina said that she knew "that Lee loaded the rifle on" the Paine station wagon and that after she arrived at the Paine residence she tried to put "the child's crib together, the metallic parts, and I looked for a certain part, and I came upon something wrapped in a blanket. I thought that was part of the bed, but it turned out to be the rifle." The rifle wrapped in the blanket was "in the garage, where all the rest of the things were."

34

"... TO THE EXCLUSION OF ALL OTHER CAMERAS"

The most important evidence found in the search of Oswald's possessions were two photographs of him holding a rifle and wearing a pistol as well as a negative of one of these photographs and an Imperial Reflex camera.

You jurors will learn the import of the photographs in the next chapter when you will find that Oswald denied that these were photographs of him. Rather, he contended that the photograph was a composite, with his face placed on the picture of someone else with a rifle.

We found in our investigation that it is possible on the basis of a close microscopic examination of a negative known to have been made in a camera to determine whether another negative has been photographed by that camera to the exclusion of all other cameras in the world.

FBI expert Lyndal L. Shaneyfelt, a graduate of Southeastern University in Washington, had

been in photographic work since about 1937. I started working with the FBI in 1940. Three years prior to this I had worked as a newspaper photographer in Hastings, Nebr., and on entering the FBI I worked in the photographic section of the FBI for about 8 years before I became a special agent. I became an agent in 1951, spent a year in Detroit as a field investigator, and then was returned to the laboratory and assigned as a document examiner. I was also assigned cases involving photographic examinations, because of my extensive experience in photography.

He examined the two photographs of Oswald with the rifle and pistol, the camera and the negative that was found of one of the photographs.

As the film is placed across the aperture of the camera, and the shutter is opened, light comes through and exposes the film only in the opening within the edges. Where the film is out over the edges of the aperture it is not exposed, and your result is an exposed negative with a clear edge, and on the negative then, the edges of that exposure of the photograph are actually shadowgraphs of the edges of the aperture.

That would be true of every picture taken and is true of virtually every camera—every roll-film type camera. It would not be true of a press-type camera where the film is loaded into separate holders; then the holder becomes the thing that will leave identifying characteristics.

On any 35 mm. or Leica camera, roll-film camera, box cameras of all types, having an arrangement where the film goes across an opening leaving an exposed area at the aperture and unexposed area around the aperture, this would be true.

Mr. Eisenberg. When you say "virtually every camera" you are including every type of camera with this type of aperture?

Commission Exhibit No. 133A, 133B
Photographs of Oswald holding rifle.

Mr. Shaneyfelt. Yes; I would include every camera with this type of film arrangement and aperture.

Representative Ford. Is this a recognized technique or procedure used in or among experts such as yourself?

Mr. Shaneyfelt. Yes. We have used this technique of camera identification with film on several occasions. It doesn't arise too often. As it normally arises, the majority of examinations that I have made in this connection are the identification of a camera that has been stolen and the serial number removed so that it can't be identified, the owner cannot identify it. We then take the owner's film and the camera that has been recovered and make this examination and determine that this is in fact the camera that the owner's film was exposed in, thereby showing ownership.

So, it is a recognized technique, we do it regularly.

Mr. Eisenberg. And you have performed such examinations yourself, Mr. Shaneyfelt?

Mr. Shaneyfelt. Yes.

Mr. Eisenberg. Mr. Shaneyfelt, what is the basis of your statement, the theoretical basis of your statement, that every camera with this type of back aperture arrangement is unique in the characteristics of the shadowgraph it makes on the negative?

Mr. Shaneyfelt. It is because of the minute variations that even two cameras from the same mold will have. Additional handwork on cameras, or filing the edges where a little bit of plastic or a little bit of metal stays on, make individual characteristics apart from those that would be general characteristics on all of them from the same mold.

In addition, as the film moves across the camera and it is used for a considerable length of time, dirt and debris tend to accumulate a little—or if the aperture is painted, little lumps in the paint will make little bumps along that edge that would make that then individually different from every other camera.

Mr. Eisenberg. Is that similar then to toolmark identification?

Mr. Shaneyfelt. Very similar, yes.

Shaneyfelt then described his examination of the prints which we marked as Exhibits 133A and 133B and the test negative made from the camera as well as the negative found among Oswald's possessions.

Mr. Eisenberg. Now, Captain Fritz of the Dallas Police has stated that in his interrogations, Oswald—Lee Harvey Oswald—stated, in effect, that while the face in Exhibit 133A was his face, the rest of the picture was not of him—this is, that it was a composite of some type.

Have you examined 133A and 133B to determine whether either or both are composite pictures?

Mr. Shaneyfelt. Yes; I have.

Mr. Eisenberg. And have you—can you give us your conclusion on that question?

Mr. Shaneyfelt. Yes; it is my opinion that they are not composites. Again with very, very minor reservation, because I cannot entirely eliminate an extremely expert composite. I have examined many composite photographs, and there is always an inconsistency, either in lighting of the portion that is added, or the configuration indicating a different lens used for the part that was added to the original photograph, things many times that you can't point to and say this is a characteristic, or that is a characteristic, but they have definite variations that are not consistent throughout the picture.

I found no such characteristics in this picture.

In addition, with a composite it is always necessary to make a print that you then make a pasteup of. In this instance paste the face in, and rephotograph it, and then retouch out the area where the head was cut out, which would leave a characteristic that would be retouched out on the negative and then that would be printed.

Normally, this retouching can be seen under magnification in the resulting composite—points can be seen where the edge of the head had been added and it hadn't been entirely retouched out.

This can nearly always be detected under magnification. I found no such characteristics in these pictures.

Representative Ford. Did you use the technique of magnification in your analysis?

Mr. Shaneyfelt. Yes.

The negative of the picture of Oswald with the rifle was introduced into evidence as Exhibit 749. Oswald's camera—an "Imperial Reflex" simple box-type camera with a simple one-shutter speed and a fixed focus—was introduced as Exhibit 750. Then, the crucial questions:

Mr. Eisenberg. Mr. Shaneyfelt, did you compare the negative, Exhibit 749, with the camera, Exhibit 750, to determine whether the negative had been taken in that camera to the exclusion of all other cameras?

Mr. Shaneyfelt. Yes; I did.

Mr. Eisenberg. What conclusion did you come to?

Mr. Shaneyfelt. I reached the conclusion that the negative, which is Commission Exhibit 749, was exposed in the camera, Commission Exhibit 750, and no other camera.

We could not determine whether the other print of Oswald with the rifle, Exhibit 133A, had been taken by that camera because we did not have the negative from that picture and, according to Shaneyfelt,

you must have the negative or you must have a print of the negative that shows that shadowgraph area, and Commission Exhibit 133A does not show that shadowgraph area.

Therefore, no comparison could be made. It is not possible.

Mr. Eisenberg. Does the shadowgraph area show on 133B?

Mr. Shaneyfelt. No; it does not.

Mr. Eisenberg. Why does it not show on either 133 A or B?

Mr. Shaneyfelt. Because they are printed in a normal processing procedure, where this area is normally blocked out to give a nice white border and make the picture a little more artistic. In the printing process, masks are placed over the area, or the shadowgraph, in order to cover it up, and the resulting print is a photograph with a nice white border.

Mr. Eisenberg. So that you have to have the negative to make the kind of identification you have made for us earlier?

Mr. Shaneyfelt. That is correct.

Mr. Eisenberg. Looking at 133B, are the observable characteristics of the weapon pictured in this picture—shown in this picture—similar to the observable characteristics of Exhibit 139, the weapon used in the assassination?

Mr. Shaneyfelt. Yes; they are less apparent in this photograph—because it is a photograph of the bottom, or the base of the rifle, the bottom of the rifle along the trigger-guard area, but it does show this bottom of the rifle in that photograph.

However, the rifle sling shown in the photographs appears to be a homemade one that looks like a piece of rope; this was different from the sling that appeared on the weapon when it was found in the TSBD Building. We determined from the background in these pictures that they were taken between Mar. 2, 1963, and Apr. 24, 1963, when Lee Harvey Oswald and his wife lived on Neely Street in Dallas in a rented house with a small back yard. According to Marina Oswald, one Sunday Oswald asked her to take his picture as he was holding a rifle and wearing a holster with a pistol.

Mr. Rankin. Do you recall the day that you took the picture of him with the rifle and the pistol?

Mrs. Oswald. I think that that was towards the end of Feb., possibly the beginning of Mar. I can't say exactly. Because I didn't attach any significance to it at the time. That was the only time I took any pictures.

I don't know how to take pictures. He gave me a camera and asked me—if someone should ask me how to photograph, I don't know.

Mr. Rankin. Was it on a day off that you took the picture?

Mrs. Oswald. It was on a Sunday.

Mr. Rankin. How did it occur? Did he come to you and ask you to take the picture?

Mrs. Oswald. I was hanging up diapers, and he came up to me with the rifle and I was even a little scared, and he gave me the camera and asked me to press a certain button.

Mr. Rankin. And he was dressed up with a pistol at the same time, was he?

Mrs. Oswald. Yes.

Mr. Rankin. You have examined that picture since, and noticed that the telescopic lens was on at the time the picture was taken, have you not?

Mrs. Oswald. Now I paid attention to it. A specialist would see it immediately, of course. But at that time I did not pay any attention at all. I saw just Lee. These details are of great significance for everybody, but for me at that time it didn't mean anything. At the time that I was questioned, I had even forgotten that I had taken two photographs. I thought there was only one. I thought that there were two identical pictures, but they turned out to be two different poses.

Mr. Rankin. Did you have anything to do with the prints of the photograph after the prints were made? That is, did you put them in a photographic album yourself?

Mrs. Oswald. Lee gave me one photograph and asked me to keep it for June somewhere. Of course June doesn't need photographs like that. [June was Oswald's daughter.]

The picture with the rifle caused great confusion because *Life* Magazine produced the same picture on one of its covers. However, *Life* retouched the photograph, according to Shaneyfelt, "by placing a highlight along the stock almost up to the end of the bolt" which changed the contour of the rifle.

The purpose of the retouching in reproduction work is merely to enhance the detail so that it will not be lost in the engraving process.

Mr. Eisenberg. When you say "enhance the detail," why would a stock be retouched so as not only to enhance the detail, but actually to change the apparent configuration? Could you conceive of any reason for that?

Mr. Shaneyfelt. I think the reason that the stock was retouched straight in the photograph on Life magazine, and my interpretation would be that the individual retouching it does not have a familiarity with rifles and did not realize there was curvature there, and in doing it just made a straight-line highlight without even considering whether that curved or not. There was curvature in that area which is not readily apparent—it is quite indistinct—and I think it was just made without realizing that there was curvature there.

Now that you jurors have heard the testimony of Lyndal Shaneyfelt concerning these photographs, we can turn to the interrogation of Lee Harvey Oswald and learn what he had to say about the photographs, and about his activities on Nov. 22.

35

"HE SAID HE DIDN'T HAVE
ANY KNOWLEDGE OF THE
PICTURE AT ALL"

The flight and arrest of Lee Oswald must be seen in context, which is asking a lot. The mind instinctively rejects any connection between him and the nation's martyred Chief Executive. One feels that he slew in the criminal hope that reflected glory from the Kennedy nimbus might brighten his own anonymity—"Everybody will know who I am now," he told a police captain after he had been caught—and justice demands that while the deed cannot be undone the spoils should be destroyed. He shot the President of the United States in the back to attract attention. [William Manchester, *The Death of a President,* page 276.]

William Manchester constructs his theory of Oswald's motivation on the basis of what Oswald supposedly told a police captain.

But Manchester is inaccurate when he cites a captain in the Dallas Police Department as the source of his quotation. Actually, the source was Roger Craig—a deputy in the Dallas Sheriff's Office whose testimony you jurors will hear in a later chapter. Moreover, this testimony of Craig is contradicted by Captain Fritz of the Dallas police, who was in charge of the interrogation of Oswald.

Captain Fritz described the interrogation room on the third floor of police headquarters. It was a small room—"I believe it is 9½ feet by 14 feet, I have the exact measurements that I think are correct. Glass all around, and it has a door leading out into a hallway."

The first interrogation session with Oswald began about 2:15 PM on Nov. 22. In Captain Fritz's office with Oswald were several other police officers as well as FBI agents James P. Hosty, Jr. and James W. Bookhout.

Even though Oswald was already a suspect in the assassination of President Kennedy because of his flight from the building, Captain Fritz did not have a tape recorder in the room. He also failed to make notes during the interrogation; he put his notes together several days later.

Mr. Ball. Do you remember what you said to Oswald and what he said to you?

Mr. Fritz. I can remember the thing that I said to him and what he said to me, but I will have trouble telling you which period of questioning those questions were in because I kept no notes at the time, and these notes and things that I have made I would have to make several days later, and the questions may be in the wrong place.

Mr. Ball. What is your best memory of what you said to him when he first came in?

Mr. Fritz. I first asked him as I do of most people something about where he was from, and where he was raised and his education, and I asked him where he went to school and he told me he went to school in New York for a while, he had gone to school in Fort Worth some, that he didn't finish high school, that he went to the Marines, and the Marines, and finished high school training in the Marines.

And I don't remember just what else. I asked him just the general questions for getting acquainted with him, and so I would see about how to talk to him, and Mr. Hosty spoke up and asked him something about Russia, and asked him if he had been to Russia, and he asked him if he had been to Mexico City, and this irritated Oswald a great deal and he beat on the desk and went into a kind of a tantrum.

Mr. Ball. What did he say when he was asked if he had been to Mexico City?

Mr. Fritz. He said he had not been. He did say he had been to Russia, he was in Russia, I believe he said for some time.

Mr. Ball. He said he had not been in Mexico City?

Mr. Fritz. At that time he told me he had not been in Mexico City.

Mr. Ball. Who asked the question whether or not he had been to Mexico City?

Mr. Fritz. Mr. Hosty. I wouldn't have known anything about Mexico City.

The FBI had a background file on Oswald because during his trip to Russia, Oswald had tried to renounce his American citizenship. Except for standard government procedures that sought to discourage the renunciation of American citizenship, Oswald would have remained in Russia.

During the first interrogation session, the police learned of Oswald's room on Beckley Street. Captain Fritz sent some men to search the Beckley room.

Officer Potts called me back from out there and talked to me on the telephone and gave me a report from out there on the telephone, and I am sure that that is the time that he told me about the way he was registered, and I asked Oswald about why he was registered under this other name.

Mr. Ball. What other name?

Mr. Fritz. Of O. L. Lee.

Mr. Ball. O. H. Lee?

Mr. Fritz. O. H. Lee. He said, well, the lady didn't understand him, she put it down there and he just left it that way.

Captain Fritz said the first interrogation session had lasted about 30 or 40 minutes. Occasionally he left the room to speak to various police officers, giving them assignments and talking to them about witnesses.

I also asked Lt. Day to bring the rifle down after I sent after Mrs. Oswald, and had her to look at the rifle. She couldn't identify it positively but she said it looked like the rifle that he had, but she couldn't say for sure. She said she thought he brought it from New Orleans.

After Oswald arrived at the police station, he was searched and five .38 caliber cartridges were found in his pocket, as well as a transfer from the Dallas Transit Company.

Later that afternoon the Dallas police conducted their first showup.

Mr. Fritz. That first showup was for a lady who was an eye witness and we were trying to get that showup as soon as we could because she was beginning to faint and getting sick.

In fact, I had to leave the office and carry some ammonia across the hall, they were about to send her to the hospital or something and we needed that identification real quickly, and she got to feeling all right after using this ammonia.

Mr. Ball. Do you remember her name?

Mr. Fritz. I have her name here.

Mr. Ball. Was that Mrs. Markham?

Mr. Fritz. Yes, Helen Markham.

Mr. Ball. That was the first showup, was it?

Mr. Fritz. Yes, sir.

Mr. Ball. Were you there?

Mr. Fritz. Yes, sir.

Mr. Ball. With her?

Mr. Fritz. Yes, sir.

Mr. Ball. Will you tell me what happened there?

Mr. Fritz. She looked at these people very carefully, and she picked him out and made the positive identification.

Mr. Ball. What did she say?

Mr. Fritz. She said that is the man that I saw shoot the officer.

Mr. Ball. Who did she point out?

Mr. Fritz. She pointed out Oswald; yes, sir.

Mr. Ball. In your showup room you have the prisoners separated from the visitors?

Mr. Fritz. There is a screen. They are on a stage with numbers over their heads for identification, and measurements to show their height, and this is lighted back there so the people can see them plainly, and the people who are looking at them usually sit at desks out some distance, probably as far as here from that window, from the showup screen.

Mr. Ball. Near the window, you mean about 15, 20 feet.

Mr. Fritz. Yes; about that far.

Mr. Ball. And then, now in this showup there were two officers of the vice squad and an officer and a clerk from the jail that were in the showup with Oswald?

Mr. Fritz. That is true. I borrowed those officers. I was a little bit afraid some prisoner might hurt him, there was a lot of excitement and a lot of feeling right about that time so we didn't have an officer in my office the right size to show with him so I asked two of the special service officers if they would help me and they said they would be glad to, so they took off their coats and neckties and fixed themselves where they would look like prisoners and they were good enough to stand on each side of him in the showup and we used a man who works in the jail office, a civilian employee, as a third man.

Mr. Ball. Now, were they dressed a little better than Oswald, do you think, these three people?

Mr. Fritz. Well, I don't think there was a great deal of difference. They had on their regular working clothes and after they opened their shirts and took off their ties, why they looked very much like anyone else.

After the showup, Oswald was returned to Captain Fritz' office.

Mr. Ball. Did you ask him what happened that day; where he had been?

Mr. Fritz. Yes, sir.

Mr. Ball. What did he say?

Mr. Fritz. Well, he told me that he was eating lunch with some of the employees when this happened, and that he saw all the excitement and he didn't think—I also asked him why he left the building. He said there was so much excitement there then that "I didn't think there would be any work done that afternoon and we don't punch a clock and they don't keep very close time on our work and I just left."

Mr. Ball. At that time didn't you know that one of your officers, Baker, had seen Oswald on the second floor?

Mr. Fritz. They told me about that down at the bookstore; I believe Mr. Truly or someone told me about it, told me they had met him—I think he told me, person who told me about, I believe told me that they met him on the stairway, but our investigation shows that he actually saw him in a lunchroom, a little lunchroom where they were eating, and he held his gun on this man and Mr. Truly told him that he worked there, and the officer let him go.

Mr. Ball. Did you question Oswald about that?

Mr. Fritz. Yes, sir; I asked him about that and he knew that the officer stopped him all right.

Mr. Ball. Did you ask him what he was doing in the lunchroom?

Mr. Fritz. He said he was having his lunch. He had a cheese sandwich and a Coca-Cola.

Mr. Ball. Did he tell you he was up there to get a Coca-Cola?

Mr. Fritz. He said he had a Coca-Cola.

Mr. Ball. That same time you also asked him about the rifle.

Mr. Fritz. I am not sure that is the time I asked him about the rifle. I did ask him about the rifle sometime soon after that occurred, and after the showup; I am not sure which time I asked him about the rifle.

Mr. Ball. Did you bring the rifle down to your office?

Mr. Fritz. Not to him; not for him to see.

Mr. Ball. You never showed it to him?

Mr. Fritz. No, sir. I asked him if he owned a rifle and he said he did not. I asked him if he had ever owned a rifle. He said a good many years ago he owned a small rifle but he hadn't owned one for a long time. I asked him if he owned a rifle in Russia and he said, "You know you can't own a rifle in Russia." He said, "I had a shotgun over there. You can't own a rifle in Russia." And he denied owning a rifle of any kind.

Mr. Ball. Didn't he say that he had seen a rifle at the building?

Mr. Fritz. Yes, sir; he told me he had seen a rifle at the building 2 or 3 days before that Mr. Truly and some men were looking at.[1]

Mr. Ball. You asked him why he left the building, didn't you?

Mr. Fritz. Yes, sir.

Mr. Ball. He told you because he didn't think there would be any work?

Mr. Fritz. Yes, sir.

Mr. Ball. Did you ask him what he did after he left the building?

Mr. Fritz. Yes, sir.

Mr. Ball. What did he say?

Mr. Fritz. He told me he went over and caught a bus and rode the bus to North

---

[1]Oswald was referring to two rifles which had been purchased by Warren Caster, Manager of the Miscellaneous Department of the Texas School Book Depository on Nov. 20. During the noon hour on Nov. 20, he opened the gun cartons and showed them to Roy Truly and other employees. According to Truly, the rifles "were placed back in the carton and Mr. Caster carried them out of the door with him."

Beckley near where he lived and went by home and changed clothes and got his pistol and went to the show. I asked him why he took his pistol and he said, "Well, you know about a pistol; I just carried it." Let's see if I asked him anything else right that minute. That is just about it.

Mr. Ball. Did you ask him if he shot Tippit?

Mr. Fritz. Oh, yes.

Mr. Ball. What did he say?

Mr. Fritz. He denied it—that he did not. The only thing he said he had done wrong, "The only law I violated was in the show; I hit the officer in the show; he hit me in the eye and I guess I deserved it." He said, "That is the only law I violated." He said, "That is the only thing I have done wrong."

There was a showup around 6:30 that same evening at which Ted Callaway and Sam Guinyard, who had seen Oswald running with his pistol, identified him. At about 7:10 Oswald was arraigned for the murder of Tippit. Another showup was held about 7:50 PM for Barbara Jeanette Davis and Virginia Davis, who lived at the corner of Southeast Tenth and Patton and who had seen the gunman at the scene of the Tippit murder cut across their front yard and throw cartridge cases into the bushes. They also identified Oswald as the gunman.

Mr. Ball. Did you ever ask him if he had kept a rifle in the garage at Irving?

Mr. Fritz. Yes, sir; I did. I asked him and I asked him if he had brought one from New Orleans. He said he didn't.

Mr. Ball. He did not.

Mr. Fritz. That is right.

I told him the people at the Paine residence said he did have a rifle out there, and he kept it out there and he kept it wrapped in a blanket and he said that wasn't true.

Around 9 o'clock that night, a paraffin test was performed on Oswald and he was fingerprinted. Ball then turned to the curtain-rod story and Buell Frazier.

Mr. Ball. Did you ever talk to Oswald about that?

Mr. Fritz. Yes, sir; I did.

Mr. Ball. When?

Mr. Fritz. I talked to him about that on the last morning before his transfer.

Mr. Ball. That was on Sunday morning?

Mr. Fritz. Sunday morning, that would be the 24th, wouldn't it?

Mr. Ball. Yes.

Mr. Fritz. And I asked him about that and he denied having anything to do with any curtain rods. It is possible that I could have asked him that on one of those other times, too, but I know I asked him that question the last morning.

Mr. Ball. Well, you learned about it on Friday night according to your reports here when Mr. Frazier came in and you gave Frazier a polygraph test.

Mr. Fritz. I hesitated to ask him about those curtain rods and I will tell you why I hesitated, because I wanted to find out more about that package before I got started with the curtain rods because if there were curtain rods I didn't want to mention it to him but we couldn't find—I talked to his wife and asked her if they were going to use any curtain rods, while I was talking to her that afternoon and she didn't know anything about it.

No; I believe I talked to Mrs. Paine, one of them.

Mr. Ball. Do you think you talked to Oswald before Sunday morning about curtain rods?

Mr. Fritz. It is possible but I know I talked to him Sunday morning.

Mr. Ball. Now, did you tell him what Frazier had told you?

Mr. Fritz. I don't know that I told him what Frazier had told me but I told him someone had told me.

Mr. Ball. What did you tell him?

Mr. Fritz. I told him he had a package and put it in the back seat and it was a package about that long and it was curtain rods. He said he didn't have any kind of a package but his lunch. He said he had his lunch and that is all he had, and Mr. Frazier told me that he got out of the car with that package, he saw him go toward the building with this long package.

I asked him, I said, "Did you go toward the building carrying a long package?"

He said, "No. I didn't carry anything but my lunch."

Mr. Ball. Did Frazier ever tell you how long the package was?

Mr. Fritz. He just measured, told me about that long.

Mr. Ball. Approximately how long?

Mr. Fritz. I am guessing at this, the way he measured, probably 26 inches, 27 inches, something like that. Too short for the length of that rifle unless he took it down, I presume he took it down if it was in there, and I am sure it was.

Mr. Ball. Do you remember what time you—was it the way Frazier showed it to you—was it the size of a rifle that was broken down?

Mr. Fritz. Yes, sir; it would be just about right.

Around 1:30 AM on Nov. 23, Oswald was arraigned for the murder of President Kennedy.

Captain Fritz said that he had asked Oswald about identification cards found in Oswald's possession with the name "A. Hidell."

I believe he had three of those cards if I remember correctly, and he told me that was the name that he picked up in New Orleans that he had used sometimes. One of the cards looked like it might have been altered a little bit and one of them I believe was the Fair Play for Cuba and one looked like a Social Security card or something.

In an interrogation session on the morning of Nov. 23, Captain Fritz asked Oswald about the bus transfer that had been found in Oswald's shirt pocket.

He told me that was the transfer the busdriver had given him when he caught the bus to go home. But he had told me if you will remember in our previous conversation that he rode the bus or on North Beckley and had walked home but in the meantime, sometime had told me about him riding a cab.

So, when I asked him about a cab ride if he had ridden in a cab he said yes, he had, he told me wrong about the bus, he had rode a cab. He said the reason he changed, that he rode the bus for a short distance, and the crowd was so heavy and traffic was so bad that he got out and caught a cab, and I asked him some other questions about the cab and I asked him what happened there when he caught the cab and he said there was a lady trying to catch a cab and he told the busdriver, the busdriver told him to tell the lady to catch the cab behind him and he said he rode that cab over near his home, he rode home in a cab.

I asked him how much the cabfare was, he said 85 cents.

Mr. Ball. Did you ask him if he went directly to his home?

Mr. Fritz. Yes, sir; he said he went straight home.

Mr. Ball. Didn't you learn from the cabdriver that he hadn't taken him to 1026 North Beckley?

Mr. Fritz. I knew he had taken him near there but I am telling you what he told me, he told me he had taken him home.

Mr. Ball. Did you ask him whether he had gone directly home?

Mr. Fritz. No, sir; I don't think so.

Captain Fritz again asked Oswald "what he was doing at the time the President was shot."

Mr. Ball. What did he say?

Mr. Fritz. Well, he told me about the same story about this lunch.

Mr. Ball. He mentioned who he was having lunch with, did he not?

Mr. Fritz. Yes, sir; he told me he was having lunch when the President was shot.

Mr. Ball. With whom?

Mr. Fritz. With someone called Junior, someone he worked with down there, but he didn't remember the other boy's name.

According to Fritz's notes he talked to Oswald about the pistol "and asked him where he got it."

Mr. Ball. What did he say?

Mr. Fritz. He told me he had got it about 6 or 7 months before in Fort Worth but he wouldn't tell me where he got it. When I asked him a little further about that he told me he didn't want to talk any further about the pistol.

On the morning of the 23rd, Inspector Kelley of the Secret Service was present during the interrogation sessions. Oswald was asked "what he thought of President Kennedy or his family."

Mr. Ball. What did he say?

Mr. Fritz. What he thought about the family—he said he didn't have any particular comment to make about the President.

He said he had a nice family, that he admired his family, something to that effect. At one time, I don't have this in my report, but at one time I told him, I said, "You know you have killed the President, and this is a very serious charge."

He denied it and said he hadn't killed the President.

I said he had been killed. He said people will forget that within a few days and there would be another President.

Mr. Dulles. Did he say anything about Governor Connally?

Mr. Fritz. No, sir; I don't think I questioned him about the Governor at that time. I might have asked him at one time. I remember telling him at one time he shot the Governor.

Mr. Dulles. Will you give us that?

Mr. Fritz. He denied shooting any of them.

On Saturday afternoon, there was another interrogation session that started around 12:35 PM. In the meantime, officers searching the garage at Irving had found the pictures showing Oswald holding a rifle and wearing a pistol. The Dallas Police Department had had some enlargements made and Captain Fritz showed these to Oswald.

Mr. Ball. You had had your laboratory enlarge the picture that your men had brought back from Irving?

Mr. Fritz. Yes, sir; he said that wasn't his picture, he said, "I have been through that whole deal with all people in the cameras," he said. "One has taken my picture and that is my face and put a different body on it." He said, "I know all about photography, I worked with photography for a long time. That is a picture that someone else has made. I never saw that picture in my life."

I said, "Wait just a minute, and I will show you one you have seen probably," and I showed him the little one this one was made from and when I showed him the little one he said, "I never have seen that picture, either." He said, "That is a picture that has been reduced from the big one."

On Saturday evening, Nov. 23, around 6 PM there was another interrogation session that ended about 7:15 PM. The final interrogation was held Sunday morning starting around 9:30.

Mr. Ball. Did you ask him again about the rifle, did you ask him if that was the picture, that that rifle was his?

Mr. Fritz. Yes, sir; I am sure I did.

Mr. Ball. Look at your notes.

Mr. Fritz. All right, sir. Yes, sir; I did. I asked him again if that was his picture holding the rifle and he said it was not.

Mr. Ball. What did he say?

Mr. Fritz. He denied it. He said he didn't have any knowledge of the picture at all. He said someone else had made it, he didn't know a thing about it or the rifle.

Mr. Ball. Didn't you also that same morning again ask him if he brought a sack with him to work on the morning the President was killed?

Mr. Fritz. Well, I asked him. I believe that morning I might have asked him that. I believe I asked him about the sack.

Mr. Ball. Without looking at your notes there let me ask you this.

Mr. Fritz. All right.

Mr. Ball. When you did ask him about the sack, you did ask him about it, a sack at one time bringing a sack to work that morning?

Mr. Fritz. Yes; I did.

Mr. Ball. And you asked him the size and shape of the sack, didn't you?

Mr. Fritz. He never admitted bringing the sack. I showed him the size probably in asking him if he brought a sack that size and he denied it. He said he brought his lunch was all he brought.

Ball then asked Captain Fritz a series of questions, using a written summary of the interrogation that was prepared by Captain Fritz and included in our Warren Commission Report. The pages were numbered 136A, B, C and D, 137A, B, C and D, and 138A, B, C, D and E. The first series of questions related to the pistol Oswald had in his possession at the time of his arrest in the Texas Theatre.

Mr. Ball. You asked him when he got it and where he got it?

Mr. Fritz. He said he bought it in Fort Worth about 6 or 7 months ago.

Mr. Ball. How long ago?

Mr. Fritz. 6 or 7 months.

Mr. Ball. Did he tell you where in Fort Worth?

Mr. Fritz. No, sir; he wouldn't tell me.

Mr. Ball. Did you ask him?

Mr. Fritz. Yes, sir; I asked him.

Mr. Ball. What did he say?

Mr. Fritz. He just wouldn't tell me.

Ball then turned to the photograph of Oswald with his rifle and pistol that had been found in the garage in Irving, Texas.

Mr. Ball. What did he say?

Mr. Fritz. He said it was not his picture at all.

Mr. Ball. You did ask him if he had purchased a rifle from Klein's store in Chicago, Ill., didn't you?

Mr. Fritz. Yes; I did.

Mr. Ball. What did he say?

Mr. Fritz. He said he did not.

Mr. Ball. You did ask him how he explained the photograph, didn't you?

Mr. Fritz. How he explained the photograph?

Mr. Ball. Yes.

Mr. Fritz. I asked him about the photograph and he said someone else took it. It wasn't his picture at all. He said someone in the hall had taken his picture and made that photograph.

Mr. Ball. In other words, he said the face was his face but the picture was made by somebody superimposing his face?

Mr. Fritz. That is right; yes.

Mr. Ball. He denied ever having lived on Neely Street, did he?

Mr. Fritz. Yes, sir; he did.

Mr. Ball. And you asked him also if he had ever owned a rifle?

Mr. Fritz. Yes, sir.

Mr. Ball. What did he say?

Mr. Fritz. He said he had not. He said a long time ago he owned a small rifle.

Mr. Ball. What size did he say?

Mr. Fritz. He didn't say. He said small rifle.

Mr. Ball. Did you ask him if he kept a rifle in Mrs. Paine's garage at Irving, Tex.?

Mr. Fritz. Yes, sir; and I asked him if he brought it from New Orleans and he said no.

Mr. Ball. Did you ask him where he kept, if he did keep a rifle in a blanket?

Mr. Fritz. I asked him if he kept it in a blanket and he said no.

Mr. Ball. Didn't you tell him someone told you he had kept it there?

Mr. Fritz. Someone told me he had a rifle and wrapped in a blanket and kept it in the garage and he said he didn't. It wasn't true.

Mr. Ball. Did he at any time tell you when you asked him if he owned a rifle, did he say, "How could I afford to order a rifle on my salary of a dollar and a quarter an hour," something like that?

Mr. Fritz. I don't remember that.

Mr. Ball. You asked him whether or not he shot President Kennedy, didn't you?

Mr. Fritz. Yes, sir.

Mr. Ball. What did he say?

Mr. Fritz. He said he did not.

Mr. Ball. And you asked him if he shot Governor Connally?

Mr. Fritz. Yes, sir; he said he didn't do that, he said he didn't shoot Tippit.

Mr. Ball. With reference to where he was at the time the President was shot, did he tell you what floor of the building he was on?

Mr. Fritz. I feel sure that he told me he was on the second floor.

Mr. Ball. Look at 136B.

Mr. Fritz. All right, sir.

Mr. Ball. The second paragraph down, 136B.

Mr. Fritz. Yes, sir; second floor; yes, sir. He said he usually worked on the first floor. I asked him what part of the building at the time the President was shot. He said he was having lunch at about this time on the first floor.

Mr. Ball. In his first interview you say that Hosty asked him if he had been to Mexico.

Mr. Fritz. Yes; he did.

Mr. Ball. He denied it. Did he say he had been at Tijuana once?

Mr. Fritz. I don't remember him saying he had been at Tijuana.

Mr. Ball. What did you remember him saying?

Mr. Fritz. I remember him saying he had been to Russia, told me he had been to Russia, and was over there for some time, and he told Hosty that he had a record of that, knew he had been there, told him a number of things so far as that is concerned.

Mr. Ball. What did he say about Mexico?

Mr. Fritz. Mexico, I don't remember him admitting that he had been to any part of Mexico.

Mr. Ball. What do you remember him saying?

Mr. Fritz. I remember he said he did not go to Mexico City and I don't remember him saying he ever went to Tijuana.

Mr. Ball. In your report at 138E you have made a statement there of the conditions under which this interrogation proceeded, haven't you?

Mr. Fritz. Yes; I did.

Mr. Ball. Will you tell us about that. You can describe it either as you state it here or in your own words, but tell us what your difficulties were?

Mr. Fritz. I can tell you in just a minute. My office is small as you know, it is a small office, it doesn't have too much room to begin with.

With all the outer office full of officers who all wanted to help and we were glad to have their assistance and help, and we appreciate it, but in the hallway we had some 200 news reporters and cameramen with big cameras and little cameras and cables running on the floors to where we could hardly get in and out of the office.

In fact, we had to get two police officers assigned to the front door to keep them out of the office so we could work.

My office is badly arranged for a thing of this kind. We never had anything like this before, of course, I don't have a back door and I don't have a door to the jail elevator without having to go through that hall for 20 feet, and each time we went through that hallway to and from the jail we had to pull him through all those people, and they, of course, would holler at him and say things to him, and some of them were bad things that seemed to please him and some seemed to aggravate him, and I don't think that helped at all in questioning him. I think that all of that had a tendency to keep him upset.

Mr. Ball. What about the interview itself?

Mr. Fritz. Now the interview itself inside, of course, we did have a lot of people in the office there to be interviewing a man. It is much better, and you can keep a man's attention and his thoughts on what you are talking to him about better I think if there are not more than two or three people.

But in a case of this nature, as bad as this case was, we certainly couldn't tell the Secret Service and the FBI we didn't want them to work on it because they would have the same interest we would have, they would want to do anything they could do, so we, of course, invited them in too but it did make a pretty big crowd.

Mr. Ball. Did you have any tape recorder?

Mr. Fritz. No, sir; I don't have a tape recorder. We need one, if we had one at this time we could have handled these conversations far better.

Mr. Ball. The Dallas Police Department doesn't have one?

Mr. Fritz. No, sir; I have requested one several times but so far they haven't gotten me one.

Mr. Ball. And you had quite a few interruptions, too, during the questioning, didn't you?

Mr. Fritz. Yes, sir; we had quite a lot of interruptions. I wish we had had—under the circumstances, I don't think there is much that could have been done because I saw it as it was there and I don't think there was a lot that could have been done other than move that crowd out of there, but I think it would have been more apt to get a confession out of it or get more true facts from him if I could have got him to sit down and quietly talked with him.

Finally, Ball turned to the statement of Roger Craig that Oswald in his interrogation supposedly had said, "Everybody will know who I am now":

Mr. Ball. Did you ever know a man named Roger Craig, a deputy sheriff?

Mr. Fritz. Roger Craig, I might if I knew which one he was. Do we have it here?

Mr. Ball. He was a witness from whom you took a statement in your office or some of your men.

Mr. Fritz. Some of my officers.

Mr. Ball. He is a deputy sheriff.

Mr. Fritz. One deputy sheriff who started to talk to me but he was telling me some things that I knew wouldn't help us and I didn't talk to him but someone else took an affidavit from him. His story that he was telling didn't fit with what we knew to be true.

Mr. Ball. Roger Craig stated that about 15 minutes after the shooting he saw a man, a white man, leave the Texas State Book Depository Building, run across a lawn, and get into a white Rambler driven by a colored man.

Mr. Fritz. I don't think that is true.

Mr. Ball. I am stating this. You remember the witness now?

Mr. Fritz. I remember the witness; yes, sir.

Mr. Ball. Did that man ever come into your office and talk to you in the presence of Oswald?

Mr. Fritz. In the presence of Oswald?

Mr. Ball. Yes.

Mr. Fritz. No, sir; I am sure he did not. I believe that man did come to my office in that little hallway, you know outside my office, and I believe I stepped outside the door and talked to him for a minute and I let someone else take an affidavit from him. We should have that affidavit from him if it would help.

Mr. Ball. Now this man states that, has stated, that he came to your office and Oswald was in your office, and you asked him to look at Oswald and tell you whether or not this was the man he saw, and he says that in your presence he identified Oswald as the man that he had seen run across this lawn and get into the white Rambler sedan. Do you remember that?

Mr. Fritz. I think it was taken. I think it was one of my officers, and I think if he saw him he looked through that glass and saw him from the outside because I am sure of one thing that I didn't bring him in the office with Oswald.

Mr. Ball. You are sure you didn't?

Mr. Fritz. I am sure of that. I feel positive of that. I would remember that I am sure.

Mr. Ball. He also says that in that office—

Mr. Fritz. Yes, sir.

Mr. Ball. After he had said, "That is the man," that Oswald got up from his chair and slammed his hand on the table and said, "Now everybody will know who I am." Did that ever occur in your presence?

Mr. Fritz. If it did I never saw anything like that; no, sir.

Mr. Ball. That didn't occur?

Mr. Fritz. No, sir; it didn't. That man is not telling a true story if that is what he said.

You jurors will have an opportunity to hear Roger Craig's testimony in a later chapter when we discuss one of the aspects of possible conspiracy. You can then reach your own decision as to whether Roger Craig or Captain Fritz was accurately describing what transpired in the interrogation room.

In looking at the possibility of conspiracy, our starting point is "the single bullet theory"—a theory eventually adopted by the Warren Commission. In the next several chapters, you will learn how this theory was developed as you hear the testimony of Governor and Mrs. Connally, Governor Connally's attending physicians, the physicians who attended President Kennedy at Parkland Memorial Hospital, the physicians who performed the autopsy on President Kennedy and the experts who at our request conducted the wound ballistics experiments.

Before turning to the single bullet theory, you jurors may want to reflect on an overall pattern that appeared throughout Oswald's interrogation, a pattern confirmed by the written summaries of FBI agents and Secret Service personnel who were also present during the questioning of Oswald.

Oswald told Fritz that he bought his pistol in Fort Worth. This was false. He bought the pistol from a mail order house in Los Angeles in Mar., 1963. Why did he lie? Probably because the pistol was shipped to A. Hidell at Post Office Box 2915 in Dallas, and this was also the place to which the rifle was shipped.

Oswald denied owning a rifle. He said it was not true that the rifle had been wrapped in a blanket in the Paine garage. He said the photographs of him with the rifle were falsified photographs. Apart from the testimony of Marina Oswald, Lyndal Shaneyfelt's testimony led us to the conclusion that the photograph was taken with Oswald's camera to the exclusion of all other cameras in the world.

Oswald said that he was in the lunchroom having lunch with "Junior" at the time of the assassination. The only person who works for the TSBD Building named "Junior" was James Jarman Jr., who testified that he had had his lunch on the first floor around five minutes to twelve and that he did not see Oswald between that time and the assassination. Jarman was on the fifth floor with two other Depository employees, watching the motorcade, at the time of the assassination. Oswald denied shooting at President Kennedy and also denied killing Officer Tippit.

Oswald said the only sack he brought into the building on the morning of Nov. 22 was a lunch sack. He also denied mentioning anything to Buell Frazier about curtain rods.

All these lies involved major factors in our overall investigation of the two murders.

Oswald uttered another lie in the course of his interrogation: He said he had not gone to Mexico City. As I pondered about why he had lied about this trip, I went through all the other evidence and hit upon an idea: Could the bus transfer in Oswald's pocket at the time of his arrest have any possible significance with his destination at the time of the assassination, which might have been Mexico City?

You jurors will learn about this possibility in a later chapter when we look at my theory of Oswald's destination at the time he was stopped by Officer Tippit. But before getting into this area, let us first begin our exploration of "the single bullet theory"—a theory that has been the lightning rod for the greatest number of attacks on the conclusions of the Warren Commission Report.

36

"THE MINIMUM TIME FOR GETTING OFF TWO SUCCESSIVE WELL-AIMED SHOTS"

The "single bullet theory" is the conclusion in our Report that the first bullet that struck President Kennedy exited from the front of his neck and then struck Governor Connally. However, what is not generally known is that the beginning of the single bullet theory was an attempt on my part to prove that a second gunman was involved in the assassination.

You will recall that in the weeks following the assassination of President Kennedy, the majority of published reports said three shots were fired: the first hit President Kennedy, the second hit Governor Connally, and the third and fatal shot also hit President Kennedy. This was also the conclusion of the FBI and the Secret Service on the basis of their separate investigations of the assassination.

As many of you know, an amateur moving picture photographer took an 8 mm. color film of the assassination. The photographer, Abraham Zapruder, was standing on an abutment in the plaza southwest of the TSBD Building. Zapruder's testimony was eventually taken by Wesley J. Liebeler. As Zapruder, in his testimony, came to the point at which he saw the fatal shot hit the President and "saw his head opened up and the blood and everything came out," he broke into tears. Zapruder thought the shots had come from behind him, although he said there was too much reverberation to reach any definite opinion. When the films were developed, he sold the original print to *Life* Magazine for $25,000, donating the proceeds to the Firemen's and Policemen's Benevolence Association. At the same time, he gave Secret Service Agent Sorrels two copies of the film, one for the Secret Service and one for the FBI. Zapruder also let the FBI have his camera.

The FBI tested the speed of the Zapruder camera and also tested the minimum speed for firing successive shots in the bolt action rifle found on the sixth floor of the TSBD Building. According to FBI expert Lyndal L. Shaneyfelt, whose testimony on photographs and cameras you jurors heard in an earlier chapter: ". . . the Zapruder motion picture camera operates at an average speed of 18.3 frames per second . . ." Using the film camera speed as a guide and locating the position of the Presidential limousine at each frame of the movie film, the FBI was able to determine that the average speed of the Presidential limousine at the time of the assassination was 11.2 miles per hour.

Shaneyfelt also testified that FBI experiments were undertaken with the

302

rifle itself and "we have been advised that the minimum time for getting off two successive well-aimed shots on the rifle is approximately two and a quarter seconds."[1]

If I were to prove that there was another rifle involved, one means of proving this was to show that less than 2.25 seconds elapsed between the first and second shots or between the second and third shots.

We spent seven days with Shaneyfelt trying to analyze these films.

During our analysis, we had individual slides made from each frame of the Zapruder film to analyze the time sequence. We then numbered each of these slides. In frame number 313, we could clearly see the fatal shot hitting the President.

However, it was not possible to see precisely when the President was *first* struck, because the view from Mr. Zapruder's camera to the Presidential limousine was obstructed between frame 205 and 224 by a large freeway sign. As the Presidential car moved forward past the freeway sign from frame 225 onward, President Kennedy's hand is seen moving toward his throat and it is obvious that he has been struck. How long it took between the instant he was hit and the instant his hand moved toward his throat is, of course, impossible to determine. However, we know that prior to frame 210 foliage from a large oak tree obstructed the President from the gunman's view as seen through the telescopic lens of the rifle in the southeast corner of the sixth floor of the TSBD Building. This was ascertained in a reconstruction of the motorcade in which we used the slides from the Zapruder film and other photographs taken at the assassination. We pinpointed the location of the car on the street for each frame of the Zapruder film and correlated this with photographs through the telescopic sight of the rifle perched in the southeast corner window of the sixth floor of the TSBD Building. Except for a split instant at frame 186, the reconstruction revealed that the rifleman did not have a clear view from frame 166 to frame 210 and that at all times after frame 210 there was no obstruction from the sixth floor window.

We also found in the reconstruction that Governor Connally was in a position from frame 207 to frame 225 to receive a bullet that would have caused the wounds he suffered. Viewed through the telescopic sight of the C2766 Mannlicher-Carcano rifle from the sixth floor window during the test, marks that we placed on "stand-ins" for the President and the Governor simulating their wounds were in a straight line. In the words of Robert Frazier, "They both are in direct alignment with the telescopic sight at the window. The Governor is immediately behind the President in the field of view." You jurors can vividly see this in the reconstruction of frames 210 and 222, shown on page 305.

Since it was unlikely that the gunman would have shot at President

---

[1]The British Broadcasting Company, as a part of a four and one-half hour television program about the assassination of President Kennedy in 1967, had independent tests run with a similar rifle and found that it would be fired in less than two seconds between shots. However, there is a question as to whether or not those shots were "well aimed."

Kennedy with the view obstructed by the foliage of an oak tree when he was about to have a clear opportunity, we felt reasonably certain that President Kennedy was not hit before frame 210. Since the President shows signs of reacting to his first wound when his head comes into the view of the Zapruder camera at frame 225, we knew that the President was hit before frame 226. The next question was the point at which Governor Connally was struck.

Shaneyfelt examined the film, frame by frame with a microscope. He could not detect any facial expressions on Governor Connally that would give any precise instant of injury. Nor could he find any other significant action that would show precisely when Governor Connally had been hit.

We ran the film again and again. For several frames the police motorcycles are seen leading the motorcade. The cameraman then stopped taking pictures until the Presidential car rounded the corner and came into view. Zapruder started the camera again and kept it running throughout the route down Elm Street until the car went out of sight on his right. I would wake up in the middle of the night seeing the President waving to the crowds and then within a few seconds seeing the fatal shot and the head of the President jerk and then slump over.

Because the film that we were using was a copy of the original, which had been purchased by *Life* Magazine, I suggested that we ask *Life* for the temporary use of the original, because I was sure that it would be more definitive than the copy. I also suggested the possibility of making 35 mm. slides from each of the frames of the original.

Because of the value of the original film, *Life* Magazine was reluctant to release it to us. However, on Feb. 25, Herbert Orth, assistant chief of *Life*'s Photographic Laboratory, brought us the original, which had considerably more detail than any of the copies we had. In addition, Mr. Orth volunteered to prepare 35 mm. color slides, directly from the original movie, of all the pertinent frames of the assassination.

Meanwhile, long before we saw *Life*'s original Zapruder film, I had an idea to try to prove that the same rifle had not fired all of the shots. I wrote to the Dallas office of the Secret Service and asked them to contact the three physicians who had treated Governor Connally—one for a back wound, one for a hand wound, and one for a slight leg wound. I asked Secret Service to have these three doctors assemble and reconstruct the position of Governor Connally as it must have been to receive the wounds he received on Nov. 22. Secret Service did contact these physicians, and I received in the mail the reconstructed position of Governor Connally as it would be from *five* different viewpoints. The only difficulty was that in three of the poses the doctors showed that the bullet entered the back of Governor Connally's wrist and came out on the front side and in two poses it was shown vice versa.

I called this discrepancy to the attention of the Secret Service and asked that they in turn call this to the attention of Governor Connally's physicians.

PHOTOGRAPH THROUGH RIFLE SCOPE

PHOTOGRAPH FROM RE-ENACTMENT

DISTANCE TO STATION C .... 138.9 FT.

DISTANCE TO RIFLE IN WINDOW .... 176.9 FT.

ANGLE TO RIFLE IN WINDOW .... 21°34′

DISTANCE TO OVERPASS .... 348.0 FT.

ANGLE TO OVERPASS .... ⁺0°22′

FRAME 210

PHOTOGRAPH THROUGH RIFLE SCOPE

PHOTOGRAPH FROM RE-ENACTMENT

DISTANCE TO STATION C .... 151.4 FT.

DISTANCE TO RIFLE IN WINDOW .... 188.6 FT.

ANGLE TO RIFLE IN WINDOW .... 20°23′

DISTANCE TO OVERPASS .... 336.4 FT.

ANGLE TO OVERPASS .... ⁺0°24′

FRAME 222

Commission Exhibit 893.
Commission Exhibit 895.

I eventually received a revised set of drawings in which in all five poses the wrist wound was shown entering from the back or dorsal side of the wrist and exiting from the front.

Through a substantial portion of the Zapruder film, Governor Connally's right arm and wrist could be seen with relation to the rest of his body. I then asked the FBI experts to look at the drawings prepared by Governor Connally's physicians, compare them with the Zapruder film and tell us where Governor Connally could *not* have been hit on the film.

To have the full impact of what happened next, you should have this frame of reference: Almost everyone had assumed up to this point that the first shot struck President Kennedy, the second shot struck Governor Connally, the third shot struck President Kennedy, and all three shots had been fired from one weapon. The FBI had reached this conclusion, as had the Secret Service. No physical evidence had been found up to that point that would prove otherwise.

On the other hand, here was one independent person, a lawyer from Des Moines, Iowa, who was trying to prove—in the face of the FBI and the Secret Service—that this theory was wrong.

And I succeeded. According to the FBI photographic laboratory experts, Governor Connally was not in the position reconstructed by his doctors at any time after frame 240.

If Governor Connally could not have been hit after frame No. 240, and if President Kennedy was hit between frames 210 and 226, then there would be a maximum of 30 frames between the time President Kennedy was first hit and the time Governor Connally was hit. If the film speed was 18.3 frames per second, this meant that the elapsed time from President Kennedy's first wound to Governor Connally's wounds was less than two seconds. If the rifle could be operated no faster than 2.25 seconds, there were only two possibilities: (1) The first shot that struck President Kennedy also struck Governor Connally; (2) another rifle was involved in addition to the one that fired the bullet fragments found in the Presidential limousine. This, in turn, would mean a conspiracy involving at least two different riflemen.

These two possibilities were reinforced when we received from *Life* Magazine the 35 mm. slides. Governor Connally clearly shows signs of reacting before frame 250. The key question then became how long it took Governor Connally to react after he was struck. Our research disclosed that the reaction time could range from tenths of a second to several seconds or more.

We ultimately concluded that the same bullet that struck President Kennedy in the neck also struck Governor Connally. The evidence supporting this conclusion was overwhelming.

In the controversy that has followed the publication of the Warren Commission Report, most of the analysis pertaining to the single-bullet theory relates to the testimony of Governor Connally, Mrs. Connally, their physicians, and the physicians who performed the autopsy. Arlen Specter, who is now the District Attorney of Philadelphia, handled all of this interrogation. Specter had the rare combination of academic brilliance and down-to-earth common sense and judgment. A native of Kansas, he was a champion debater and a Phi Beta Kappa graduate of the University of Pennsylvania. At the Yale Law School he served as an editor of the Yale Law Journal. Methodically, he took all the witnesses through the salient facts.

Members of the jury, let us turn to the testimony of Governor Connally and his attending physicians.

37

"IT IS SOMETHING LESS
THAN THE WEIGHT
OF A POSTAGE STAMP"

It was a family argument. Governor and Mrs. Connally were so engrossed that they momentarily forgot those of us who were also present in the downstairs conference room in Washington as the film was being shown.

The film was horrible to watch—it was the footage, in color, that had been taken by Abraham Zapruder at the time of the assassination.

In the first portion of the film, you see the motorcade with a vibrant President and Mrs. Kennedy waving to the crowd. Then the President's head momentarily disappears behind a sign that is between the President's car and the photographer, Zapruder. When the President's head reappears, you see him clutching his throat. Within seconds, the fatal shot strikes the President in the head and you see a burst of orangish-red color as part of the President's head is torn away.

The film also shows Governor Connally starting to turn and then falling back into his wife's lap.

Prior to their testimony, Governor and Mrs. Connally saw the film and they gave an informal commentary as the film was shown and shown again in our conference room. According to Governor Connally, when he heard the first noise he took this to be a rifle shot and instinctively turned to his right because the sound appeared to have come over his right shoulder. He could not glimpse the President so he started to turn to the left when he felt he had been hit. He then started to turn right again, he said, doubled up and fell into Mrs. Connally's lap.

Mrs. Connally interrupted her husband: "No, John, you didn't fall into my lap; I pulled you over to my lap."

"No, Nellie, you didn't pull me over; I fell into your lap."

"No, John, you didn't fall—I pulled you."

"No, Nellie, you didn't pull me—" and Governor Connally stopped, realizing others were present in the room.

By the time the formal testimony of Governor and Mrs. Connally was taken, there was no disagreement between them on this point. First let us listen to the key testimony of Governor Connally. President and Mrs. Kennedy were sitting in the back seat of the Presidential limousine. Mrs. Kennedy was on the left and Mrs. Connally was on the jump seat immediately in front of her. Governor Connally was on the jump seat on the right, immediately in front of the President.

Mr. Specter. Describe in a general way the size and reaction of the crowd on the motorcade route, if you would, please, Governor?

Gov. Connally. When we got into Dallas there was quite a large crowd at the airport to greet their President. I would say several thousand people.

Part way downtown, in the thinly populated areas of Dallas, where we traveled, the crowds were not thick and were somewhat restrained in their reaction. By restrained, I mean they were not wildly enthusiastic, but they were grown people. There was a mature crowd as we went through some of the residential areas. They applauded and they were obviously very friendly in their conduct.

But as we, of course, approached downtown, the downtown area of Dallas, going down the main street, the crowds were tremendous. They were stacked from the curb and even outside the curb, back against the back walls. It was a huge crowd. I would estimate there were 250,000 people that had lined the streets that day as we went down.

The further you went the more enthusiastic the response was, and the reception. It was a tremendous reception, to the point where just as we turned on Houston Street off of Main, and turned on Houston, down by the courthouse, Mrs. Connally remarked to the President, "Well, Mr. President, you can't say there aren't some people in Dallas who love you." And the President replied, "That is very obvious" or words to that effect.

So I would say the reception that he got in Dallas was equal to, if not more, enthusiastic than those he had received in Fort Worth, San Antonio, and Houston.

Mr. Specter. Are there any other conversations which stand out in your mind on the portion of the motorcade trip through Dallas itself?

Gov. Connally. No; actually we had more or less desultory conversation as we rode along. The crowds were thick all the way down on both sides, and all of us were, particularly the President and Mrs. Kennedy were, acknowledging the crowds. They would turn frequently, smiling, waving to the people, and the opportunity for conversation was limited. So there was no particularly significant conversation or conversations which took place. It was, as I say, pretty desultory conversation.

Mr. Specter. Did the automobile stop at any point during this procession?

Gov. Connally. Yes; it did. There were at least two occasions on which the automobile stopped in Dallas and, perhaps, a third. There was one little girl, I believe it was, who was carrying a sign saying, "Mr. President, will you please stop and shake hands with me," or some—that was the import of the sign, and he just told the driver to stop, and he did stop and shook hands, and, of course, he was immediately mobbed by a bunch of youngsters, and the Secret Service men from the car following us had to immediately come up and wedge themselves in between the crowd and the car to keep them back away from the automobile, and it was a very short stop.

At another point along the route, a Sister, a Catholic nun, was there obviously from a Catholic school, with a bunch of little children, and he stopped and spoke to her and to the children; and I think there was one other stop on the way downtown, but I don't recall the precise occasion. But I know there were two, but I think there was still another one.

Mr. Specter. Are there any other events prior to the time of the shooting itself which stand out in your mind on the motorcade trip through Dallas?

Gov. Connally. No; not that have any particular significance.

Mr. Specter. As to the comment which Mrs. Connally had made to President Kennedy which you just described, where on the motor trip was that comment made, if you recall?

Gov. Connally. This was just before we turned on Elm Street, after we turned off of Main.

Mr. Specter. Onto Houston?

Gov. Connally. Onto Houston, right by the courthouse before we turned left onto Elm Street, almost at the end of the motorcade, and almost, I would say, perhaps a minute before the fatal shooting.

Mr. Specter. What was the condition of the crowd at that juncture of the motorcade, sir?

Gov. Connally. At that particular juncture, when she made this remark, the crowd was still very thick and very enthusiastic. It began to thin immediately after we turned onto Elm Street. We could look ahead and see that the crowd was beginning to thin along the banks, just east, I guess, of the overpass.

Mr. Specter. Was there any difficulty in hearing such a conversational comment?

Gov. Connally. No, no; we could talk without any, and hear very clearly, without any difficulty, without any particular strain. We didn't do it again because in trying to carry on a conversation it would be apparent to those who were the spectators on the sidewalk, and we didn't want to leave the impression we were not interested in them, and so we just didn't carry on a conversation, but we could do so without any trouble.

Mr. Specter. As the automobile turned left onto Elm from Houston, what did occur there, Governor?

Gov. Connally. We had—we had gone, I guess, 150 feet, maybe 200 feet, I don't recall how far it was, heading down to get on the freeway, the Stemmons Freeway, to go out to the hall where we were going to have lunch, and as I say, the crowds had begun to thin, and we could—I was anticipating that we were going to be at the hall in approximately 5 minutes from the time we turned on Elm Street.

We had just made the turn, well, when I heard what I thought was a shot. I heard this noise which I immediately took to be a rifle shot. I instinctively turned to my right because the sound appeared to come from over my right shoulder, so I turned to look back over my right shoulder, and I saw nothing unusual except just people in the crowd, but I did not catch the President in the corner of my eye, and I was interested, because once I heard the shot in my own mind I identified it as a rifle shot, and I immediately—the only thought that crossed my mind was that this is an assassination attempt.

So I looked, failing to see him, I was turning to look back over my left shoulder into the back seat, but I never got that far in my turn. I got about in the position I am in now facing you, looking a little bit to the left of center, and then I felt like someone had hit me in the back.

Mr. Specter. What is the best estimate that you have as to the time span between the sound of the first shot and the feeling of someone hitting you in the back which you just described?

Gov. Connally. A very, very brief span of time. Again my trend of thought just happened to be, I suppose along this line, I immediately thought that this—that I had been shot. I knew it when I just looked down and I was covered with blood, and the thought immediately passed through my mind that there were either two or three people involved or more in this or someone was shooting with an automatic rifle. These were just thoughts that went through my mind because of the rapidity of these two, of the first shot plus the blow that I took, and I knew I had been hit, and I immediately assumed, because of the amount of blood, and, in fact, that it had obviously passed through my chest, that I had probably been fatally hit.

So I merely doubled up, and then turned to my right again and began to—just sat there, and Mrs. Connally pulled me over to her lap. She was sitting, of course, on the jump seat, so I reclined with my head in her lap, conscious all the time, and with my eyes open; and then, of course, the third shot sounded, and I heard the shot very clearly. I heard it hit him. I heard the shot hit something, and I assumed again—it never entered my mind that it ever hit anybody but the President. I heard it hit. It was a very loud noise, just that audible, very clear.

Immediately I could see on my clothes, my clothing, I could see on the interior of the car which, as I recall, was a pale blue, brain tissue, which I immediately recognized, and I recall very well, on my trousers there was one chunk of brain tissue as big as almost my thumb, thumbnail, and again I did not see the President at any time either after the first, second, or third shots, but I assumed always that it was he who was hit and no one else.

I immediately, when I was hit, I said "Oh, no, no no." And then I said, "My God, they are going to kill us all." Nellie, when she pulled me over into her lap—

Mr. Specter. Nellie is Mrs. Connally?

Gov. Connally. Mrs. Connally. When she pulled me over into her lap, she could tell I was still breathing and moving, and she said, "Don't worry. Be quiet. You are going to be all right." She just kept telling me I was going to be all right.

After the third shot, and I heard Roy Kellerman tell the driver, "Bill, get out of line." And then I saw him move, and I assumed he was moving a button or something on the panel of the automobile, and he said, "Get us to a hospital quick." I assumed he was saying this to the patrolman, the motorcycle police who were leading us.

At about that time, we began to pull out of the cavalcade, out of the line, and I lost consciousness and didn't regain consciousness until we got to the hospital.

Arlen Specter then asked:

Governor, you have described hearing a first shot and a third shot. Did you hear a second shot?

Gov. Connally. No; I did not.

Mr. Specter. What is your best estimate as to the timespan between the first shot which you heard and the shot which you heretofore characterized as the third shot?

Gov. Connally. It was a very brief span of time; oh, I would have to say a matter of seconds. I don't know, 10, 12 seconds. It was extremely rapid, so much so that again I thought that whoever was firing must be firing with an automatic rifle because of the rapidity of the shots; a very short period of time.

Mr. Specter. What was your impression then as to the source of the shot?

Gov. Connally. From back over my right shoulder which, again, was where immediately when I heard the first shot I identified the sound as coming back over my right shoulder.

Mr. Specter. At an elevation?

Gov. Connally. At an elevation. I would have guessed at an elevation.

Mr. Specter. Did you have an impression as to the source of the third shot?

Gov. Connally. The same. I would say the same.

Mr. Specter. How fast was the President's automobile proceeding at that time?

Gov. Connally. I would guess between 20 and 22 miles an hour, and it is a guess because I didn't look at the speedometer, but I would say in that range.

Mr. Specter. Did President Kennedy make any statement during the time of the shooting or immediately prior thereto?

Gov. Connally. He never uttered a sound at all that I heard.

Mr. Specter. Did Mrs. Kennedy state anything at that time?

Gov. Connally. Yes; I have to—I would say it was after the third shot when she said, "They have killed my husband."

Mr. Specter. Did she say anything more?

Gov. Connally. Yes; she said, I heard her say one time, "I have got his brains in my hand."

Mr. Specter. Did that constitute everything that she said at that time?

Gov. Connally. That is all I heard her say.

Then Governor Connally was questioned about his wounds:

Mr. Specter. Did you experience any sensation of being struck any place other than that which you have described on your chest?

Gov. Connally. No.

Mr. Specter. What other wounds, if any, did you sustain?

Gov. Connally. A fractured wrist and a wound in the thigh, just above the knee.

Mr. Specter. What thigh?

Gov. Connally. Left thigh; just above the knee.

Mr. Specter. Where on the wrist were you injured, sir?

Gov. Connally. I don't know how you describe it.

Mr. Specter. About how many inches up from the wrist joint?

Gov. Connally. I would say an inch above the wrist bone, but on the inner bone of the wrist where the bullet went in here and came out almost in the center of the wrist on the underside.

Mr. Specter. About an inch from the base of the palm?

Gov. Connally. About an inch from the base of the palm, a little less than an inch, three-quarters of an inch.

Mr. Specter. Were you conscious of receiving that wound on the wrist at the time you sustained it?

Gov. Connally. No, sir; I was not.

Mr. Specter. When did you first know you were wounded in the right wrist?

Gov. Connally. When I came to in the hospital on Saturday, the next morning, and I looked up and my arm was tied up in a hospital bed, and I said, "What is wrong with my arm?" And they told me then that I had a shattered wrist, and that is when I also found out I had a wound in the thigh.

Mr. Specter. Can you describe the nature of the wound in the thigh?

Gov. Connally. Well, just a raw, open wound, looked like a fairly deep penetration.

Mr. Specter. Indicating about 2 inches?

Gov. Connally. No; I would say about an inch, an inch and a quarter long is all; fairly wide, I would say a quarter of an inch wide, maybe more, a third of an inch wide, and about an inch and a quarter, an inch and a half long.

Mr. Specter. Were you conscious that you had been wounded on the left thigh at the time it occurred?

Gov. Connally. No.

Mr. Specter. Did you first notice that in the hospital on the following day also?

Gov. Connally. Yes.

The next portion of Governor Connally's testimony is independent evidence of the fact that there was no effort on the part of the Commissioners or anyone else involved in the investigation of the assassination to "prepare" witnesses, for the testimony of Governor Connally basically disagreed with our ultimate conclusion that the first bullet that struck President Kennedy went through his neck and then struck Governor Connally:

Mr. Specter. In your view, which bullet caused the injury to your chest, Governor Connally?

Gov. Connally. The second one.

Mr. Specter. And what is your reason for that conclusion, sir?

Gov. Connally. Well, in my judgment, it just couldn't conceivably have been the first one because I heard the sound of the shot. In the first place, I don't know anything about the velocity of this particular bullet, but any rifle has a velocity that exceeds the speed of sound, and when I heard the sound of that first shot, that bullet had already reached where I was, or it had reached that far, and after I heard that shot, I had the time to turn to my right, and start to turn to my left before I felt anything.

It is not conceivable to me that I could have been hit by the first bullet, and then I felt the blow from something which was obviously a bullet, which I assumed was a bullet, and I never heard the second shot, didn't hear it. I didn't hear but two shots. I think I heard the first shot and the third shot.

Mr. Specter. Do you have any idea as to why you did not hear the second shot?

Gov. Connally. Well, first, again I assume the bullet was traveling faster than sound. I was hit by the bullet prior to the time the sound reached me, and I was in either a state of shock or the impact was such that the sound didn't even register on me, but I was never conscious of hearing the second shot at all.

Obviously, at least the major wound that I took in the shoulder through the chest couldn't have been anything but the second shot. Obviously, it couldn't have been the third, because when the third shot was fired I was in a reclining position, and heard it, saw it and the effects of it, rather—I didn't see it, I saw the effects of it—so it obviously could not have been the third, and couldn't have been the first, in my judgment.

Mr. Specter. What was the nature of the exit wound on the front side of your chest, Governor?

Gov. Connally. I would say, if the Committee would be interested, I would just as soon you look at it. Is there any objection to any of you looking at it?

The Chairman. No.

Gov. Connally. You can tell yourself.

I would say, to describe it for the record, however, that it, the bullet, went in my back just below the right shoulder blade, at just about the point that the right arm joins the shoulder, right in that groove, and exited about 2 inches toward the center of the body from the right nipple of my chest. I can identify these for you.

The bullet went in here—see if I properly describe that—about the juncture of the right arm and the shoulder.

Mr. Specter. Let the record show that the Governor has removed his shirt and we can view the wound on the back which he is pointing toward.

Governor Connally's physicians were present during his testimony and they commented on the wounds while the Governor had his shirt off. They had testified previously before the Commission. Medical testimony is often the most tedious part of any trial. If you members of the jury desire to skim the testimony of Governor Connally's physicians, you will find a summary of their key conclusions in the last five paragraphs of this chapter beginning on page 323.

Dr. Robert Shaw, a specialist in thoracic surgery, described the wound on the chest as being below the right nipple of the body and said it was an exit wound.

Mr. Specter. When did you first have an opportunity then to examine Governor Connally's wound on the posterior aspect of his chest?

Dr. Shaw. After the Governor had been anesthetized. As soon as he was asleep so we could manipulate him—before that time it was necessary for an endotracheal tube to be in place so his respirations could be controlled before we felt we could roll him over and accurately examine the wound entrance.

We knew this was the wound exit.

Mr. Specter. This [indicating an area below the right nipple on the body]?

Dr. Shaw. Yes.

Mr. Dulles. How did you know it was a wound exit?

Dr. Shaw. By the fact of its size, the ragged edges of the wound. This wound was covered by a dressing which could not be removed until the Governor was anesthetized.

Mr. Specter. Indicating this wound, the wound on the Governor's chest?

Dr. Shaw. Yes; the front part.

Mr. Specter. Will you describe in as much detail as you can the wound on the posterior side of the Governor's chest?

Dr. Shaw. This was a small wound approximately a centimeter and a half in its greatest diameter. It was roughly elliptical. It was just medial to the axillary fold or the crease of the armpit, but we could tell that this wound, the depth of the wound, had not penetrated the shoulder blade.

Mr. Specter. What were the characteristics, if any, which indicated to you that it was a wound of entrance then?

Dr. Shaw. Its small size, and the rather clean cut edges of the wound as compared to the usual more ragged wound of exit.

The bullet passed in an "angle of decline" from the entrance into Governor Connally's back near his armpit to the exit point below the right nipple on his chest. Dr. Shaw described his operative procedures and damage along the fifth rib at a point where the texture of the rib

is not of great density. The cortex of the rib in the lateral portions of our ribs is thin with the so-called cancellus portion of the rib being very spongy, offering very little resistance to pressure or to fracturing.

Mr. Specter. What effect, if any, would the striking of that rib have had to the trajectory of the bullet?

Dr. Shaw. It could have had a slight, caused a slight deflection of the rib, but probably not a great deflection of the rib, because of the angle at which it struck and also because of the texture of the rib at this time.

Mr. Specter. You say deflection of the rib or deflection of the bullet?

Dr. Shaw. Deflection of the bullet, I am sorry.

Mr. Specter. Was any metallic substance from the bullet left in the thoracic cage as a result of the passage of the bullet through the Governor's body?

Dr. Shaw. No. We saw no evidence of any metallic material in the x-ray that we had of the chest, and we found none during the operation.

Then we turned to the question of the bullet which caused the injury. Specter showed Dr. Shaw the bullet, Exhibit 399.

Mr. Specter. Is it possible that the bullet which went through the Governor's chest could have emerged being as fully intact as that bullet is?

Dr. Shaw. Yes; I believe it is possible because of the fact that the bullet struck the fifth rib at a very acute angle and struck a portion of the rib which would not offer a great amount of resistance. . . .

Mr. Specter. Now, as to the wound on the thigh, could that bullet have gone into the Governor's thigh without causing any more damage than appears on the face of that bullet?

Dr. Shaw. If it was a spent bullet; yes. As far as the bullet is concerned it could have caused the Governor's thigh wound as a spent missile. . . .

Mr. Specter. Dr. Shaw, assume if you will certain facts to be true in hypothetical form, that is, that the President was struck in the upper portion of the back or lower portion of the neck with a 6.5-mm. missile passing between the strap muscles of the President's neck, proceeding through a facia channel striking no bones, not violating the pleural cavity, and emerging through the anterior third of the neck, with the missile having been fired from a weapon having a muzzle velocity of approximately 2,000 feet per second, with the muzzle being approximately 160 to 250 feet from the President's body; that the missile was a copper jacketed bullet. Would it be possible for that bullet to have then proceeded approximately 4 or 5 feet and then would it be possible for it to have struck Governor Connally in the back and have inflicted the wound which you have described on the posterior aspect of his chest, and also on the anterior aspect of his chest?

Dr. Shaw. Yes.

Mr. Specter. And what would your reason be for giving an affirmative answer to that question, Dr. Shaw?

Dr. Shaw. Because I would feel that a missile with this velocity and weight striking no more than the soft tissues of the neck would have adequate velocity and mass to inflict the wound that we found on the Governor's chest.

Mr. Specter. Now, without respect to whether or not the bullet identified as Commission Exhibit 399 is or is not the one which inflicted the wound on the Governor, is it possible that a missile similar to the one which I have just described in the hypothetical question could have inflicted all of the Governor's wounds in accoradance with the theory which you have outlined on Commission Exhibit No. 689?

Dr. Shaw. . . . As far as the wounds of the chest are concerned, I feel that this bullet could have inflicted those wounds. But the examination of the wrist both by X-ray and at the time of surgery showed some fragments of metal that make it difficult to believe that the same missile could have caused these two wounds. There seems to be more than three grains of metal missing as far as the—I mean in the wrist.

Mr. Specter. Your answer there, though, depends upon the assumption that the bullet which we have identified as Exhibit 399 is the bullet which did the damage to the Governor. Aside from whether or not that is the bullet which inflicted the Governor's wounds.

Dr. Shaw. I see.

Mr. Specter. Could a bullet traveling in the path which I have described in the prior hypothetical question have inflicted all of the wounds on the Governor?

Dr. Shaw. Yes.

Mr. Specter. And so far as the velocity and the dimension of the bullet are concerned, is it possible that the same bullet could have gone through the President in the way that I have described and proceed through the Governor causing all of his wounds without regard to whether or not it was bullet 399?

Dr. Shaw. Yes.

Mr. Specter. When you started to comment about it not being possible, was that in reference to the exiting mass and shape of bullet 399?

Dr. Shaw. I thought you were referring directly to the bullet shown as Exhibit 399.

Mr. Specter. What is your opinion as to whether bullet 399 could have inflicted all of the wounds on the Governor, then, without respect at this point to the wound of the President's neck?

Dr. Shaw. I feel that there would be some difficulty in explaining all of the wounds as being inflicted by bullet Exhibit 399 without causing more in the way of loss of substance to the bullet or deformation of the bullet.

Before his testimony, Dr. Shaw had examined the pictures of the assassination taken by Zapruder and the slides we had made from the movies.

Mr. Specter. I have heretofore asked you questions about what possibly could have happened in terms of the various combinations of possibilities on missiles striking the Governor in relationship to striking the President as well. Do you have any opinion as to what, in fact, did happen?

Dr. Shaw. Yes. From the pictures, from the conversation with Governor Connally and Mrs. Connally, it seems that the first bullet hit the President in the shoulder and perforated the neck, but this was not the bullet that Governor Connally feels hit him; and in the sequence of films I think it is hard to say that the first bullet hit both of these men almost simultaneously.

Mr. Specter. Is that view based on the information which Governor Connally provided to you?

Dr. Shaw. Largely.

Mr. Specter. As opposed to any objectively determinable facts from the bullets, the situs of the wounds or your viewing of the pictures?

Dr. Shaw. Yes. I was influenced a great deal by what Governor Connally knew about his movements in the car at this particular time.

John McCloy then posed these questions:

Is it possible for a man to be hit some time before he realizes it?

Dr. Shaw. Yes. There can be a delay in the sensory reaction.

Mr. McCloy. Yes; so that a man can think as of a given instant he was not hit, and when actually he could have been hit.

Dr. Shaw. There can be an extending sensation and then just a gradual building up of a feeling of severe injury.

Mr. McCloy. But there could be a delay in any appreciable reaction between the time of the impact of the bullet and the occurrence?

Dr. Shaw. Yes; but in the case of a wound which strikes a bony substance such as a rib, usually the reaction is quite prompt.

Senator Cooper then asked:

I think, of course, it is evident from your testimony you have had wide experience in chest wounds and bullet wounds in the chest.

What experience have you had in, say, the field of ballistics? Would this experience—you have been dealing in chest wounds caused by bullets—have provided you knowledge also about the characteristics of missiles, particularly bullets of this type?

Dr. Shaw. No; Senator. I believe that my information about ballistics is just that of an average layman, no more. Perhaps a little more since I have seen deformed bullets from wounds, but I haven't gone into that aspect of wounds.

Sen. Cooper. In the answers to the hypothetical questions that were addressed to you, based upon the only actual knowledge which you could base that answer, was the fact that you had performed the operation on the wound caused in the chest, on the wound in the chest?

Dr. Shaw. That is true. I have seen many bullets that have passed through bodies or have penetrated bodies and have struck bone and I know manners from which they are deformed but I know very little about the caliber of bullets, the velocity of bullets, many things that other people have much more knowledge of than I have.

The physician who treated Governor Connally's wrist was Charles F. Gregory, who specialized in orthopedic surgery.

Mr. Specter. Now what did you observe with respect to the wound on the Governor's wrist?

Dr. Gregory. . . . The right wrist was the site of a perforating wound, which by assumption began on a dorsal lateral surface. In lay terms this is the back of the hand on the thumb side at a point approximately 5 centimeters above the wrist joint.

There is a second wound presumed to be the wound of exit which lay in the midline of the wrist on its palmar surface about 2 centimeters, something less than 1 inch above the wrist crease, the most distal wrist crease.

Mr. Specter. You say that the wound on the dorsal or back side of the wrist you assume to be the wound of entrance. What factors, if any, led you to that assumption?

Dr. Gregory. I assumed it to be a wound of entrance because of the general ragged appearance of the wound, but for other reasons which I can delineate in a lighter description which came to light during the operative procedure and which are also hallmarked to a certain extent by the X-rays.

Mr. Specter. Would you proceed to tell us, even though it is out of sequence, what those factors, later determined to be, were which led you to assume that it was the wound of entrance?

Dr. Gregory. Yes. Assuming that the wrist wound, which included a shattering fracture of the wrist bone, of the radial bone just above the wrist, was produced by a missile there were found in the vicinity of the wound two things which led me to believe that it passed from the dorsal or back side to the volar.

Mr. Specter. When you say volar what do you mean by that?

Dr. Gregory. The palm side.

Mr. Specter. Proceed.

Dr. Gregory. The first of these was evidence of clothing, bits of thread and cloth, apparently from a dark suit or something of that sort which had been carried into the wound, from the skin into the region of the bone.

The second of these were two or three small fragments of metal which presumably were shed by the missile after their encounter with the firm substance which is bone.

There was much comment after the assassination about whether the nearly whole bullet could have caused all the damage to Governor Connally, because X-rays showed metallic fragments in the wrist, whereas the bullet itself, Exhibit 399, weighed only one and one-half to three grains less than an ordinary bullet. Dr. Gregory put such speculation to rest with the following testimony:

Mr. Specter. Will you describe as specifically as you can what those metallic fragments are by way of size and shape, sir?

Dr. Gregory. I would identify these fragments as varying from five-tenths of a millimeter in diameter to approximately 2 millimeters in diameter, and each fragment is no more than a half millimeter in thickness. They would represent in lay terms flakes, flakes of metal.

Mr. Specter. What would your estimate be as to their weight in total?

Dr. Gregory. I would estimate that they would be weighed in micrograms which is very small amount of weight. I don't know how to reduce it to ordinary equivalents for you.

It is the kind of weighing that requires a microadjustable scale, which means that it is something less than the weight of a postage stamp.

Dr. Gregory was then asked about the bullet, Exhibit 399, which he had had an opportunity to examine:

Mr. Specter. What opinion, if any, do you have as to whether that bullet could have produced the wound on the Governor's right wrist and remained as intact as it is at the present time?

Dr. Gregory. In examining this bullet, I find a small flake has been either knocked off or removed from the rounded end of the missile.

I was told that this was removed for the purpose of analysis. The only other deformity which I find is at the base of the missile at the point where it joined the cartridge carrying the powder, I presume, and this is somewhat flattened and deflected, distorted. There is some irregularity of the darker metal within which I presume to represent lead.

The only way that this missile could have produced this wound, in my view, was to have entered the wrist backward. Now, this is not inconsistent with one of the characteristics known for missiles which is to tumble. All missiles in flight have two motions normally, a linear motion from the muzzle of the gun to the target, a second motion which is a spinning motion having to do with maintaining the integrity of the initial linear direction, but if they strike an object they may be caused to turn in their path and tumble end over, and if they do, they tend to produce a greater amount of destruction within the strike time or the target, and they could possibly, if tumbling in air upon emergence, tumble into another target backward. That is the only possible explanation I could offer to correlate this missile with this particular wound.

Mr. Specter. Is there sufficient metallic substance missing from the back or rear end of that bullet to account for the metallic substance which you have described in the Governor's wrist?

Dr. Gregory. It is possible but I don't know enough about the structure of bullets or this one in particular to know what is a normal complement of lead or for this particular missile. It is irregular, but how much it may have lost, I have no idea.

Mr. Dulles. Would the nature of the entry wound give you any indication as to whether it entered backward or whether it entered forward?

Dr. Gregory. My initial impression was that whatever produced the wound of the wrist was an irregular object, certainly not smooth nosed as the business end of this particular bullet is, because of two things. The size of the wound of entrance, and the fact that it is irregular surfaced permitted it to pick up organic debris, materials, threads and carry them into the wound with it.

Now, you will note that Dr. Shaw earlier in his testimony, and in all of my conversations with him, never did indicate that there was any such loss of material into the wrist, nor does the back of this coat which I have examined show that it lost significant amounts of cloth but I think the tear in this coat sleeve does imply that there were bits of fabric lost, and I think those were resident in the wrist. I think we recovered them.

Mr. Specter. Is the back of that bullet characteristic of an irregular missile so as to cause the wound in the wrist?

Dr. Gregory. I would say that the back of this being flat and having sharp edges is irregular, and would possibly tend to tear tissues more than does an inclined plane such as this.

Mr. Specter. Would the back of the missile be sufficiently irregular to have caused the wound of the right wrist, in your opinion?

Dr. Gregory. I think it could have; yes. It is possible.

Mr. Specter. Would it be consistent with your observations of the wrist for that missile to have penetrated and gone through the right wrist?

Dr. Gregory. It is possible; yes. It appears to me since the wound of exit was a small laceration, that much of the energy of the missile that struck the Governor's wrist was expended in breaking the bone reducing its velocity sufficient so that while it could make an emergence through the underlying soft tissues on his wrist, it did not do great damage to them.

Mr. Specter. Is there any indication from the extent of the damage to the wrist whether the bullet was pristine, that is: was the wrist struck first in flight or whether there had been some reduction in the velocity of the missile prior to striking the wrist?

Dr. Gregory. I would offer this opinion about a high velocity rifle bullet striking a forearm.

Mr. Specter. Permit me to inject factors which we have not put on the record although it has been brought to your attention previously: Assume this is a 6.5 millimeter missile which was shot from a rifle having a muzzle velocity of approximately 2,000 feet per second, with a distance of approximately 160 to 200 feet between the weapon and the victim; and answer the prior question, if you would, Dr. Gregory, with those factors in mind?

Dr. Gregory. I would fully expect the first object struck by that missile to be very badly damaged, and especially if it were a rigid bone such as the wrist bone is, to literally blow it apart. I have had some experience with rifle wound injuries of the forearm produced by this type of missile, and the last two which I attended myself have culminated in amputation of the limb because of the extensive damage produced by the missile as it passed through the arm.

Considerably more than was evidenced in the Governor's case either by examination of the limb itself or an examination of these X-rays.

Dr. Gregory brought with him some X-rays including X-rays of the thigh.

Careful examination of this set of X-rays illustrated or demonstrates, I should say, a number of artificial lines, this is one and there is one. These lines I think represent rather hurried development of these films for they were taken under emergency conditions. They were intended simply to let us know if there was another missile in the Governor's limb where it might be located.

The only missile turned up is the same one seen in the original film which lies directly opposite the area indicated as the site of the missile wound or the wound in the thigh, but a fragment of metal, again microscopic, measuring about five-tenths of a millimeter by 2 millimeters, lies just beneath the skin, about a half inch on the medial aspect of the thigh.

Mr. Specter. What is your best estimate of the weight of that metallic fragment?

Dr. Gregory. This again would be in micrograms, postage stamp weight thereabouts, not much more than that.

Mr. Specter. Could that fragment, in your opinion, have caused the wound which you observed in the Governor's left thigh?

Dr. Gregory. I do not believe it could have. The nature of the wound in the left thigh was such that so small a fragment as this would not have produced it and still have gone no further into the soft tissues than it did.

Mr. Specter. Would the wound that you observed in the soft tissue of the left thigh be consistent with having been made by a bullet such as that identified as Commission Exhibit 399?

Dr. Gregory. I think again that bullet, Exhibit 399, could very well have struck the thigh in a reverse fashion and have shed a bit of its lead core into the fascia immediately beneath the skin, yet never have penetrated the thigh sufficiently so that it eventually was dislodged and was found in the clothing.

I would like to add to that we were disconcerted by not finding a missile at all. Here was our patient with three discernible wounds, and no missile within him of sufficient magnitude to account for them, and we suggested that someone ought to search his belongings and other areas where he had been to see if it could be identified or found, rather.

Mr. Specter. Had the missile gone through his wrist in reverse, would it likely have continued in that same course until it reached his thigh in your opinion?

Dr. Gregory. The missile that struck his wrist had sufficient energy left after it passed through the radius to emerge from the soft tissues on the under surface of the skin. It could have had enough to partially enter his thigh, but not completely.

Mr. Specter. In the way which this thigh was wounded?

Dr. Gregory. I believe so; yes.

Both Dr. Shaw and Dr. Gregory believed that the wounds to Governor Connally came from a shot fired from the rear and above him. Both physicians also believed that a single bullet could have caused all three wounds to Governor Connally. However, they felt that the probability of a single bullet's doing this would be diminished if it had first passed through President Kennedy's neck:

Mr. Specter. Dr. Gregory, could all of the wounds which were inflicted on the Governor, that is, those described by Dr. Shaw, and those which you have described during your testimony, have been inflicted from one missile if that missile were a 6.5 millimeter bullet fired from a weapon having a muzzle velocity of approximately 2,000 feet per second at a distance of approximately 160 to 250 feet, if you assumed a trajectory with an angle of decline approximately 45 degrees?

Dr. Gregory. I believe that the three wounds could have accurred from a single missile under these specifications.

Mr. Specter. Assume, if you will another set of hypothetical circumstances: That the 6.5 millimeter bullet traveling at the same muzzle velocity, to wit, 2,000 feet per second, at approximately 165 feet between the weapon and the victim, struck the

President in the back of the neck passing through the large strap muscles, going through a fascia channel, missing the pleural cavity, striking no bones and emerging from the lower anterior third of the neck, after striking the trachea. Could such a projectile have then passed into the Governor's back and inflicted all three or all of the wounds which have been described here today?

Dr. Gregory. I believe one would have to concede the possibility, but I believe firmly that the probability is much diminished.

Mr. Specter. Why do you say that, sir?

Dr. Gregory. I think that to pass through the soft tissues of the President would certainly have decelerated the missile to some extent. Having then struck the Governor and shattered a rib, it is further decelerated, yet it has presumably retained sufficient energy to smash a radius.

Moreover, it escaped the forearm to penetrate at least the skin and fascia of the thigh, and I am not persuaded that this is very probable. I would have to yield to possibility. I am sure that those who deal with ballistics can do better for you than I can in this regard.

Mr. Specter. What would your assessment of the likelihood be for a bullet under those hypothetical circumstances to have passed through the neck of the President and to have passed through only the chest of the Governor without having gone through either the wrist or into the thigh?

Dr. Gregory. I think that is a much more plausible possibility or probability.

Mr. Specter. How about the likelihood of passing through the President and through the Governor's chest, but missing his wrist and passing into his thigh?

Dr. Gregory. That, too, is plausible, I believe.

Mr. Specter. Are there any other circumstances of this event which have been related to you, including the striking of the President's head by a third bullet, which would account in any way, under any possibility, in your view, for the fracture of the right wrist which was apparently caused by a missile?

Dr. Gregory. This morning I was shown two additional missiles or portions of missiles which are rather grossly distorted.

[These were the two large bullet fragments found in the front seat of the Presidential limousine.]

These are missiles having the characteristics which I mentioned earlier, which tend to carry organic debris into wounds and tend to create irregular wounds of entry. One of these, it seems to me, could conceivably have produced the injury which the Governor incurred in his wrist.

Mr. Dulles. And in his thigh?

Dr. Gregory. I don't know about that, sir. It is possible. But the rather remarkably round nature of the wound in the thigh leads me to believe that it was produced by something like the butt end of an intact missile.

Senator Cooper concluded the interrogation of the witness.

I would just ask this question. In your long experience of treating wounds, you said some 500 wounds caused by bullets, have you acquired, through that, knowledge of ballistics and characteristics of bullets?

Dr. Gregory. Within a very limited sphere.

Sen. Cooper. I know your testimony indicates that.

Dr. Gregory. I have been concerned with the behavior of missiles in contact with tissues, but I am not very knowledgeable about the design of a missile nor how many grains of powder there are behind it. My concern was with the dissipation of the energy which it carries and the havoc that it wreaks when it goes off.

Sen. Cooper. You derived that knowledge from your actual study of wounds and their treatment?

Dr. Gregory. Study of wounds together with what I have read from the Army proving grounds, various centers, for exploring this kind of thing. I don't own a gun myself.

Mr. McCloy. You are from Texas and you do not own a gun?

Dr. Gregory. Well, sir, I went from Indiana to Texas. My father gave me a .410 shotgun, but he took it away from me shortly after he gave it to me.

The physician who treated Governor Connally's leg wound was Dr. George T. Shires, professor of surgery and chairman of the department of surgery of the Southwestern Medical School in Dallas.

Mr. Specter. And what did you observe as to the wound on the thigh?

Dr. Shires. The wound on the thigh was a peculiar one. There was a 1 cm. punctate missile wound over the junction of the middle and lower third of the leg and the medial aspect of the thigh. The peculiarity came in that the X-rays of the left leg showed only a very small 1 mm. bullet fragment imbedded in the femur of the left leg. Upon exploration of this wound, the other peculiarity was that there was very little soft tissue damage, less than one would expect from an entrance wound of a centimeter in diameter, which was seen on the skin. So, it appeared, therefore, that the skin wound was either a tangential would or that a larger fragment had penetrated or stopped in the skin and had subsequently fallen out of the entrance wound.

Mr. Specter. What size fragment was there in the Governor's leg at that time?

Dr. Shires. We recovered none. The small one that was seen was on X-ray and it was still in the femur and being that small, with no tissue damage after the debridement, it was thought inadvisable to remove this small fragment.

Mr. Specter. Is that fragment in the bone itself at the present time?

Dr. Shires. Yes.

Mr. Specter. What would your best estimate be as to the size of that fragment?

Dr. Shires. One millimeter in diameter—one to two.

Mr. Specter. Would you have any estimate as to how much that might weigh in grains?

Dr. Shires. In grains—a fraction of a grain, maybe, a tenth of a grain—very small.

Mr. Specter. A tenth of one grain?

Dr. Shires. Yes.

Dr. Shires examined some diagrams, one of which was marked Diagram No. 5, which he said, "was the apparent position that he was in the car, which would explain one missile producing all three wounds."

Mr. Specter. Now, looking again at Diagram No. 5 what is your professional opinion, if you have one, as to whether Governor Connally's chest injury, wrist injury, and thigh injury were caused by the same bullet?

Dr. Shires. Well, we all thought, me included, that this was probably one missile, one bullet.

Mr. Specter. When you say "we all thought," whom do you mean by that?

Dr. Shires. Dr. Shaw, Dr. Gregory—as we were reconstructing the events in the operating room in an attempt to plot out trajectory as best we could, this appeared to be our opinion.

Mr. Specter. Did any of your assistants consult with you in those calculations?

Dr. Shires. I guess nearly all of them we have listed.

Mr. Specter. Dr. McClelland, Dr. Baxter and Dr. Patman?

Dr. Shires. Yes.

Mr. Specter. How about Dr. Osborne and Dr. Parker?

Dr. Shires. They were working with Dr. Gregory. If they discussed it, I'm sure they did—it was before I got there.

Mr. Specter. How about Dr. Boland and Dr. Duke who worked with Dr. Shaw?

Dr. Shires. Now again, I talked to them and they were discussing it as they did the chest procedure, and again thought the same thing. Everyone was under the impression this was one missile—through and through the chest, through and through the arm and the thigh.

Mr. Specter. Was there any one of the doctors on either of these three teams who had a different point of view?

Dr. Shires. Not that I remember.

Mr. Specter. Do you think it is possible that Governor Connally could have been struck by two bullets, one entering his back and emerging from his chest and the second going into his wrist?

Dr. Shires. I'm sure it is possible, because missile sites are so variable, depending upon the size of the bullet, the speed at which it travels, whether it was tumbling or not. We have seen all kinds of combinations of entrance and exit wounds and it's just impossible to state with any certainty, looking at a given wound, what the nature of the missile was, so I am sure it is possible.

Mr. Specter. Do you think it is possible that, assuming a missile being a bullet 6.5 mm. with a velocity of over 2,000 feet per second, and the distance between the weapon and the victim being approximately 160 to 250 feet, that the same bullet might have passed through President Kennedy, entering his back near the midline and emerging from his neck, and then entering Governor Connally in the back and emerging from his chest, into his wrist, through his wrist and into the thigh?

Dr. Shires. I assume that it would be possible. The main thing that would make me think that this was not the case is that he remembers so distinctly hearing a shot and having turned prior to the time he was hit, and in the position he must have been, particularly here in Figure 5, I think it's obvious that he did turn rather sharply to the right and this would make me think that it was a second shot, but this is purely conjecture, of course.

Mr. Specter. Well, is there anything, aside from what he told you, that is, anything in the characteristics of the wounds on President Kennedy and the wounds on Governor Connally which would lead you to conclude that it was not the same bullet?

Dr. Shires. No—there is nothing. It could have been—purely from the standpoint of the wounds, it is possible.

In the words of Dr. Shires, "we all thought" that Governor Connally's wounds were caused by one bullet. There was no doubt that the bullet that struck Governor Connally came from the rear and above him. Because of Governor Connally's opinion that he was struck by the second bullet, his physicians thought that the bullet that struck President Kennedy in the neck—i.e., the first bullet—did not cause the Governor's wounds. However, all the physicians agreed that it was possible for a single bullet to pass through the President's neck and cause the wounds to Governor Connally.

Most important of all, the testimony of Dr. Gregory and Dr. Shires was unequivocal on the amount of bullet fragments that remained in Governor Connally's wrist and in his thigh. The amount was infinitesimally small—a measurement in "micrograms," which are thousandths of a grain—there are 7,000 grains in an ounce. However, to a third party inspecting X-rays, such as Dr. Shaw, the opaque showing on the X-rays would give the impression of a substantially larger amount of fragments. This is of crucial importance in determining whether the nearly whole bullet found at Parkland Memorial Hospital caused all of the damage.

If Governor Connally's physicians had testified that the weight of the bullet fragments that remained in Governor Connally was four grains or more, it would have been physically impossible for the bullet found at Parkland to have caused all of the damage. In contrast, with the weight of the fragments measured in micrograms—thousandth parts of a grain and less than the weight of a postage stamp—it was obviously possible that all of the damage to Governor Connally could have come from the bullet, Exhibit 399.

Unfortunately, the physicians who conducted the autopsy of President Kennedy did not discuss Governor Connally's wounds with his attending physicians to determine the amount of the bullet fragments that remained in Governor Connally. Instead, the autopsy physicians relied on hearsay evidence—copies of Parkland Hospital records that did not specify the weight of the fragments involved.

Before turning to the autopsy as well as the physicians who attended President Kennedy at Parkland Hospital, let us hear the testimony of Mrs. Connally.

38

"I THOUGHT IT WAS
FROM BACK OF US"

Mr. Specter. Mrs. Connally, tell us what happened at the time of the assassination.

Mrs. Connally. We had just finished the motorcade through the downtown Dallas area, and it had been a wonderful motorcade. The people had been very responsive to the President and Mrs. Kennedy, and we were very pleased, I was very pleased.

As we got off Main Street—is that the main thoroughfare?

Mr. Specter. That is the street on which you were proceeding through the town, yes.

Mrs. Connally. In fact the receptions had been so good every place that I had showed much restraint by not mentioning something about it before.

I could resist no longer. When we got past this area I did turn to the President and said, "Mr. President, you can't say Dallas doesn't love you."

Then I don't know how soon, it seems to me it was very soon, that I heard a noise, and not being an expert rifleman, I was not aware that it was a rifle. It was just a frightening noise, and it came from the right.

I turned over my right shoulder and looked back, and saw the President as he had both hands at his neck.

Mr. Specter. And you are indicating with your own hands, two hands crossing over gripping your own neck?

Mrs. Connally. Yes; and it seemed to me there was—he made no utterance, no cry. I saw no blood, no anything. It was just sort of nothing, the expression on his face, and he just sort of slumped down.

Then very soon there was the second shot that hit John. As the first shot was hit, and I turned to look at the same time, I recall John saying, "Oh, no, no, no." Then there was a second shot, and it hit John, and as he recoiled to the right, just crumpled like a wounded animal to the right, he said, "My God, they are going to kill us all."

Now, jurors, we have a major difference in testimony: Governor Connally testified he said "Oh no, no, no" *after* he was hit. Mrs. Connally said this was *before the second shot.* So did Mrs. Kennedy.

I remember that he turned to the right and then just slumped down into the seat, so that I reached over to pull him toward me. I was trying to get him down and me down. The jump seats were not very roomy, so that there were reports that he slid into the seat of the car, which he did not; that he fell over into my lap, which he did not.

I just pulled him over into my arms because it would have been impossible to get us really both down with me sitting and me holding him. So that I looked out, I mean as he was in my arms, I put my head down over his head so that his head and my head were right together, and all I could see, too, were the people flashing by. I didn't look back any more.

The third shot that I heard I felt, it felt like spent buckshot falling all over us, and then, of course, I too could see that it was the matter, brain tissue, or whatever, just human matter, all over the car and both of us.

I thought John had been killed, and then there was some imperceptible movement, just some little something that let me know that there was still some life, and that is when I started saying to him, "It's all right. Be still."

Now, I did hear the Secret Service man say, "Pull out of the motorcade. Take us to the nearest hospital," and then we took out very rapidly to the hospital.

Just before we got to Parkland, we made a right-hand turn, he must have been going very fast, because as he turned the weight of my husband's body almost toppled us both.

Mr. Specter. How fast do you think he was going?

Mrs. Connally. I don't know; very rapidly. The people I could see going by were just rushing. We were just rushing by very fast.

We arrived at the hospital and sat there what seemed to me like an interminable time, and from what I know was just a few minutes, but the thoughts that went through my mind were how long must I sit here with this dying man in my arms while everybody is swarming over the President whom I felt very sure was dead, and just when I thought I could sit and wait no longer, John just sort of heaved himself up. He did not rise up in the car, he just sort of heaved himself up, and then collapsed down into the seat.

Mr. Specter. At that time you and Governor Connally were still on the jump seats of the car?

Mrs. Connally. Yes, and they had not—the President was still—and Mrs. Kennedy were still in the back. I still had not ever looked back at the back seat after the second shot. I could hear, you know, hear them talking about how sad, and lamenting the fact that the President was in such poor shape and, of course, they didn't know whether he was—I guess they didn't know whether he was alive or dead.

Mr. Specter. Did President Kennedy say anything at all after the shooting?

Mrs. Connally. He did not say anything. Mrs. Kennedy said, the first thing I recall her saying was, after the first shot, and I heard her say, "Jack, they have killed my husband" and then there was the second shot, and then after the third shot she said, "They have killed my husband. I have his brains in my hand," and she repeated that several times, and that was all the conversation.

Mr. Specter. From that point forward you say you had your eyes to the front so you did not have a chance—

Mrs. Connally. Yes, because I had him, and I really didn't think about looking back anyway, but I could just see the car rushing along, and people and things rushing past us. I remember thinking what a terrible sight this must be to those people, to see these two shot-up men, and it was a terribly horrifying thing, and I think that is about as I remember it.

Mr. Specter. What happened then after you got to the hospital?

Mrs. Connally. We got to the hospital and, like I said, John heaved himself over. They still could not seem to get Mrs. Kennedy or the President out of the back of the car, but someone scooped him up in their arms and put him on a stretcher. There were two stretchers there, and then they took him off immediately to the emergency room, and they ran down the hall with the stretcher, and I just ran along with them.

They took him into the emergency room, and right behind us came the President on a stretcher, and they took him and put him in a room to the right. There was much commotion and confusion. There were lots of what I assumed were Secret Service men rushing in with machine guns, I guess, or tommyguns. I am not real sure, they were big arms of some sort. There was no one—there were lots of people across the hall. There was no one with me and, of course, my thoughts then were, I guess like any other woman, I wondered if all the doctors were in the room on the left, and they were not taking too good care of my husband on the right. I shouldn't have worried about that, should I?

I knew no one in the hospital and I was alone. Twice I got up and opened the door into the emergency room, and I could hear John and I could see him moving, and I knew then that he was still alive.

Mrs. Connally waited at the hospital while the surgery was being performed.

As soon as Dr. Shaw found that he had some encouraging news, that the wounds were not as extensive as he had thought they could be or might be, he sent that word to me from the operating room, and that was good news.

I then asked if I couldn't go see Mrs. Kennedy, and they told me that she had left the hospital.

Mr. Specter. Mrs. Connally, what was your impression, if any, as to the source of the shots?

Mrs. Connally. Well, I had no thought of whether they were high or low or where. They just came from the right; sounded like they were to my right.

Mr. Specter. How many did you hear in all?

Mrs. Connally. I heard three.

Mr. Specter. What is your best estimate on the time that passed from the first to the last shot?

Mrs. Connally. Very short. It seemed to me that there was less time between the first and the second than between the second and the third.

Mr. Specter. About how fast do you think the car was going then?

Mrs. Connally. I don't really know. Not too fast. It was sort of a letdown time for us. We could relax for, we thought we could, for just a minute.

Mr. Specter. And you mean by that since the major part of the crowd had been passed?

Mrs. Connally. We had gone by them. The underpass was in sight, and I knew that as soon as we passed through the underpass that then we would be going straight to the Trade Mart for the luncheon, and I felt like we would then be moving fast and not have people on all sides of us.

Mr. Specter. Did you see the films this morning here in the Commission office?

Mrs. Connally. Yes, I did.

Mr. Specter. Did you have an opinion as to which frame it was that Governor Connally was shot?

Mrs. Connally. Yes. I was in agreement with the Governor. I am not sure I remember the numbers so correct me, but I thought at the time that it was that 229—it could have been through the next three or four frames.

Mr. Specter. Do you have anything—

Mrs. Connally. They were blurred.

Mr. Specter. With respect to the source, you say you thought it was to the right —did you have any reaction as to whether they were from the front, rear or side?

Mrs. Connally. I thought it was from back of us.

Mr. Specter. To the rear?
Mrs. Connally. To the right; that is right.
Mr. Specter. Did you have any reaction as to the question of elevation or level?
Mrs. Connally. No, I didn't.
Mr. Specter. Do you have anything else to add which you think would be helpful to the Commission in any way?
Mrs. Connally. I don't think so.

We knew Governor Connally could not have been hit after frame 236 to 240. We also knew that Governor Connally and President Kennedy between frames 210 and 225 were both "in direct alignment with the telescopic site at the window" of the TSBD Building. Governor and Mrs. Connally both thought he was hit around frames 229–233. If their impressions were only one-half of a second off, he would have been hit around frames 220–222 when he and the President were in the same trajectory line. In other words, if President Kennedy was hit at around frame 220, Governor Connally could also have been hit at frame 220 and, at 18.3 frames per second, if he had a delay of only one second in the reaction time, there would have been no visible indication that he was hit until the film reached frame 238. Actually, he is reacting before frame 250, and if the same shot that went through President Kennedy at around frame 220 also went through Governor Connally, this would mean a reaction time of a maximum of one and one-half seconds, which was well within the realm of possibility.

Although Governor Connally was sure that he was not hit at the time of the first shot, he also said that he had never felt that he was hit in the wrist or the leg. Because he was the Governor of Texas, the Commissioners were careful not to say that Governor Connally had erred in any portion of his testimony. However, I think that by now you have discerned that Governor Connally, who changed his story about falling into his wife's lap, is not infallible. He is no different from other eyewitnesses—human memories, especially under stress, are just not that precise.

In resolving conflicting evidence one cannot rely on the memory of one person. However, there is basis for giving weight to the collective memory of a large group of people. The overwhelming majority of those at the scene of the assassination believe three shots were fired, although some witnesses, like Howard Brennan, believe there were only two, and some thought there might have been four, five or six.

The large majority that believed three shots were fired could be divided into two groups: One felt that the shots were relatively evenly spaced. The other felt that the last two shots were closer together than the first two.

But if Governor Connally was not hit by the first shot, and yet was hit by frame 236 to frame 240, this would mean that a second shot was fired within one-quarter of a second to one second of the first shot and that more than four seconds elapsed between the shot that struck Governor Connally (assume at frame 230) and the fatal shot that struck the President at frame 313.

No witness thought that less than a second elapsed between the first and second shots or that more than four times as much time elapsed between the second and third shots.

Mrs. Connally realized the import of this problem. Consequently, with perhaps one or two other exceptions, she was the only witness who testified that more time elapsed between the second and third shots than between the first and the second shots.

Although auditory recollections surely are not entitled to be given as much weight as visual recollections, I felt that in looking at the overall problem of whether Governor Connally was struck by a second shot, we need to consider the collective auditory recollections of the spacing of the gunfire. If the second shot hit Governor Connally, then there would have been only one-quarter of a second to one second of elapsed time between the first two shots with the third shot more than four seconds after the second. Virtually no one at the scene of the assassination recalled that spacing of the shots. In addition, in another portion of his testimony Governor Connally undercut his conclusion that he was not struck by the first shot. Although he said he did not hear a middle shot, he said that he had heard the last shot, and that approximately 10 seconds elapsed between the first and the last shot. If Governor Connally was not struck by the first shot but was struck around frame 229–234, as he and his wife testified, this would mean a time sequence of less than a second between the first and second shot and nine seconds between the second and third shots. There is no testimony supporting such a time sequence. However, there could well have been a total of ten seconds between the first and last shot, assuming that the first shot struck President Kennedy in the back of the neck, that the second shot, approximately five to six seconds later, struck President Kennedy in the head, that the third shot missed, and that the time between the first and second shots and the second and third was approximately the same.

In any event, I felt that the eyewitness testimony of John Connally should not be given special treatment because he was the Governor of Texas. Like all eyewitness testimony, it was subject to the inherent inaccuracies in human recollection, especially under situations of stress.

Certainly, the evidence of the autopsy physicians of President Kennedy would be most important in resolving the question of the source of the shots and whether the first bullet exited from the front of the President's neck. Also, we would have to find out whether the fibers on the President's clothing gave any indication about the direction of the shots.

And most important of all were the practical physical aspects of the problem. If a bullet entered the front of President Kennedy's neck, where did that bullet go? Either there would be an exit wound or X-rays of the President would disclose a bullet still inside him. In the next two chapters, we will hear the heart of the testimony of the physicians who attended President Kennedy at Parkland Memorial Hospital and of the three physicians who conducted the autopsy examination.

By the same token, we had the other side of the practical physical facts: If a bullet *exited* from President Kennedy's neck at a relatively high velocity, where did it go? At such velocity at that point it would have had to cause extensive damage either to the car itself or to someone in the car. There was no such substantial damage to the car. And the only substantial injury to someone in the car was to Governor Connally, who was sitting in front of President Kennedy.

In an effort to resolve these physical facts, we reconstructed the entire motorcade, using 35 mm. slides made from each frame of the Zapruder movie film as a guide and putting the assassination weapon itself in the southeast corner window of the sixth floor of the TSBD Building. As you jurors know, we found that Governor Connally was riding in line with the telescopic sight of the rifle, No. C2766, at the approximate time that President Kennedy was hit. We also conducted wound ballistics tests and—as you will soon learn—found that the velocity of rifle bullets fired with that rifle at the approximate distance between the assassination window and the Presidential car was over 1,900 feet per second.

And finally, we found crucial evidence from the testimony of FBI expert Robert A. Frazier, who had examined President Kennedy's clothing:

Mr. Specter. In the course of your duties have you had an occasion to examine the clothing which was purportedly worn by President John Kennedy on Nov. 22, 1963?

Mr. Frazier. Yes, sir; I have.

Mr. Specter. And do you have that clothing with you at the present time, sir?

Mr. Frazier. I have certain parts of it. I have the coat, shirt, tie, and the bandages and support belt which he allegedly was wearing that day.

Mr. Specter. Would you refer at this time to the coat, if you please, which, may the record show, has heretofore been marked as Commission Exhibit 393.

And by referring to that coat will you describe what, if anything, you observed on the rear side of the coat?

Mr. Frazier. There was located on the rear of the coat 5-3/8 inches below the top of the collar, a hole, further located as 1-3/4 inches to the right of the midline or the seam down the center of the coat; all of these being as you look at the back of the coat.

Mr. Specter. What characteristics did you note, if any, on the nature of that hole?

Mr. Frazier. I noticed that the hole penetrated both the outer and lining areas of the coat, that it was roughly circular in shape. When I first examined it it was approximately one-fourth of an inch in diameter, and the cloth fibers around the margins of the hole were pushed inward at the time I first examined it in the laboratory.

Mr. Specter. Did any tests conducted on the coat disclose any metallic substance on that area of that hole?

Mr. Frazier. Yes, sir. I had a spectrographer run an analysis of a portion of the hole which accounts for its being slightly enlarged at the present time. He took a sample of cloth and made an analysis of it. I don't know actually whether I am expected to give the results of his analysis or not.

Mr. Specter. Yes; would you please, or let me ask you first of all, were those tests run by the Federal Bureau of Investigation in the regular course of its testing procedures?

Mr. Frazier. Yes, sir; they were.

Mr. Specter. And have those results been made available to you through the regular recordkeeping procedures of the FBI?

Mr. Frazier. Yes, sir.

Mr. Specter. Would you then please tell us what those tests disclose?

Mr. Frazier. Traces of copper were found around the margins of the hole in the back of the coat, and as a control, a very small section under the collar was taken, and no copper being found there, it was concluded that the copper was foreign to the coat itself.

Mr. Specter. Have you now described all of the characteristics of that hole, which you consider to be important for the Commission's consideration?

Mr. Frazier. Yes, sir.

Mr. Specter. Assuming that those clothes, that jacket, specifically, at this juncture, was worn by President Kennedy, and was in the same condition when that hole was made as it is now, and at the time when you made your examination, do you have a professional opinion as to what caused that hole in the back of the jacket?

Mr. Frazier. Yes, sir; I would say that it was an entrance hole for a bullet.

Mr. Specter. And what is the reason for that conclusion, please?

Mr. Frazier. It has all the physical appearance characteristics which are considered when examining holes, such as its shape, its size, and in particular the fact that the fibers around the margins of the hole were all pushed inward where the cloth was torn by the object which passed through, and the fibers were unraveled as they were pushed inward, which is characteristic of an entrance-type bullet hole.

Mr. Specter. Is the presence of the metallic substance relevant in your conclusion that it was a bullet hole?

Mr. Frazier. Not necessarily. It is a factor which corroborates that opinion but even without it, it would still have been my opinion that it was a bullet entrance hole.

Mr. Specter. Can you tell the size of the bullet from the hole in the jacket?

Mr. Frazier. The hole in the jacket is approximately a quarter of an inch in diameter.

Mr. Specter. Would that hole be consistent with a hole which would be caused by a 6.5 millimeter bullet?

Mr. Frazier. Yes, sir; the actual bullet which makes a hole cannot be determined because the cloth in one instance may stretch more than it does in another instance causing either a larger or smaller hole even for the same caliber, but it is consistent for a bullet of 6.5 millimeters in diameter to make a hole of approximately this size.

Mr. Specter. Were there any holes indicative of being bullet holes found on the front part of the President's jacket?

Mr. Frazier. No, sir.

Mr. Specter. Did you have further occasion to examine the President's shirt?

Mr. Frazier. I did.

Mr. Specter. May the record show that the shirt has heretofore been identified as Commission Exhibit 394?

The Chairman. Yes; it may be.

Mr. Specter. What, if anything, did you observe then on the back side of the shirt, Mr. Frazier?

Mr. Frazier. I found on the back of the shirt a hole, 5-3/4 inches below the top of the collar, and as you look at the back of the shirt 1-1/8 inch to the right of the midline of the shirt, which is this hole I am indicating.

Mr. Specter. May the record show the witness is examining the shirt, as he has the coat, to indicate the hole to the Commission.

The Chairman. The record may show that.

Mr. Frazier. In connection with this hole, I made the same examination as I did on the coat, Exhibit 393. I found the same situation to prevail, that is, the hole was approximately circular in shape, about one-fourth inch in diameter, and again the physical shape of it is characteristic of a bullet hole, that is, the edges are frayed, and there are slight radial tears in the cloth, which is characteristic of a bullet having passed through the cloth, and further, the fibers around the margin of the hole were—had been pressed inward, and assuming that when I first examined the shirt it was in the same condition as it was at the time the hole was made, it is my opinion that this hole, in addition, was caused by a bullet entering the shirt from the back at that point.

Mr. Specter. Is that hole consistent with having been caused by a 6.5 millimeter bullet?

Mr. Frazier. Yes; it is.

Mr. Specter. With respect to the front side of the shirt, what, if any, hole did you find there?

Mr. Frazier. Only one hole.

Mr. Dulles. May I ask one question there?

Mr. Frazier. Yes; certainly.

Mr. Dulles. Is the hole in the shirt and the hole in the coat you have just described in a position that indicates that the same instrument, whatever it was, or the same bullet, made the two?

Mr. Frazier. Yes; they are. They are both—the coat hole is 5-3/8 inches below the top of the collar. The shirt hole is 5-3/4 inches, which could be accounted for by a portion of the collar sticking up above the coat about a half inch.

Mr. Dulles. I see.

Mr. Frazier. And they are both located approximately the same distance to the right of the midline of both garments.

Now, on the front of the shirt, I found what amounts to one hole. Actually, it is a hole through both the button line of the shirt and the buttonhole line which overlap down the front of the shirt when it is buttoned.

Mr. Specter. Proceed.

Mr. Frazier. This hole is located immediately below the button being centered seven-eighths of an inch below the button on the shirt, and similarly seven-eighths of an inch below the buttonhole on the opposite side.

The Chairman. You are speaking of the collar button itself, aren't you?

Mr. Frazier. The collar button.

The Chairman. Yes.

Mr. Frazier. In each instance for these holes, the one through the button line and the one through the buttonhole line, the hole amounts to a ragged slit approximately one-half inch in height. It is oriented vertically, and the fibers of the cloth are protruding outward, that is, have been pushed from the inside out. I could not actually determine from the characteristics of the hole whether or not it was caused by a bullet. However, I can say that it was caused by a projectile of some type which exited from the shirt at that point and that is again assuming that when I first examined the shirt it was—it had not been altered from the condition it was in at the time the hole was made.

Mr. Specter. What characteristics differ between the hole in the rear of the shirt and the holes in the front of the shirt which lead you to conclude that the hole in the rear of the shirt was caused by a bullet but which are absent as to the holes in the front of the shirt?

Mr. Frazier. The hole in the front of the shirt does not have the round characteristic shape caused by a round bullet entering cloth. It is an irregular slit. It could have been caused by a round bullet, however, since the cloth could have torn in a long slitlike way as the bullet passed through it. But that is not specifically characteristic of a bullethole to the extent that you could say it was to the exclusion of being a piece of bone or some other type of projectile.

Mr. Specter. Have you now described all of the characteristics of the front of the shirt holes which you consider to be important?

Mr. Frazier. Yes sir.

Members of the jury, let us now undertake a brief subtotal of the evidence to this point. Governor Connally's physicians all agree that the wounds to Governor Connally were caused by one bullet. They also agree that the bullet came from above and to the rear of Governor Connally. Both Governor and Mrs. Connally thought that the shots came from behind. The clothing of President Kennedy shows that a shot entered through the back and also shows an exit from the front. The nearly whole bullet found at Parkland Memorial Hospital ballistically was fired by the rifle found in the TSBD Building to the exclusion of all other weapons in the world. The two large ballistically identifiable bullet fragments found in the front seat of the Presidential limousine were fired by that same rifle to the exclusion of all other weapons in the world.

Therefore, we are certain that the rifle found on the sixth floor of the TSBD Building was involved in the assassination. The next question we must answer is whether this was the only weapon involved in the assassination. To help us solve this question, let us first go to Parkland Memorial Hospital in Dallas on Nov. 22 as the President was carried into the emergency room known as Trauma (emergency) Room No. 1.

39

"A STRAIGHT AFFIRMATIVE WORD LIKE 'YES' IS NOT GOOD RELATIONS"

Mr. Specter. Now, what did you observe as to the condition of President Kennedy when you first saw him?

Dr. Carrico. He was on an ambulance cart, emergency cart, rather. His color was blue white, ashen. He had slow agonal respiration, spasmodic respirations without any coordination. He was making no voluntary movements. His eyes were open, pupils were seen to be dilated and later were seen not to react to light. This was the initial impression.

Mr. Specter. What was the status of his pulse at the time of arrival?

Dr. Carrico. He had no palpable pulse.

Mr. Specter. And was he making any movements at the time of arrival?

Dr. Carrico. No voluntary movements, only the spasmodic respirations.

Mr. Specter. Was any heartbeat noted at his arrival?

Dr. Carrico. After these initial observations we opened his shirt, coat, listened very briefly to his chest, heard a few sounds which we felt to be heartbeats and then proceeded with the remainder of the examination.

Mr. Specter. In your opinion was President Kennedy alive or dead on his arrival at Parkland?

Dr. Carrico. From a medical standpoint I suppose he was still alive in that he did still have a heartbeat.

The witness was 28-year-old Dr. Charles J. Carrico, who was serving as a resident in the surgery department at Parkland. Dr. Carrico was the first physician to see President Kennedy.

The President's clothes were removed by the nurses as Dr. Carrico proceeded with his examination.

Mr. Specter. What action did you take by way of treating President Kennedy on his arrival?

Dr. Carrico. After what we have described we completed an initial emergency examination, which consisted of, as we have already said, his color, his pulse, we felt his back, determined there were no large wounds which would be an immediate threat to life there. Looked very briefly at the head wound and then because of his inadequate respirations inserted an endotracheal tube to attempt to support these respirations.

Mr. Specter. Specifically what did you do with respect to the back, Dr. Carrico?

Dr. Carrico. This is a routine examination of critically ill patients where you haven't got time to examine him fully. I just placed my hands just above the belt, but in this case just above the brace, and ran my hands up his back.

Mr. Specter. To what point on his body?

Dr. Carrico. All the way up to his neck very briefly.

Mr. Specter. What did you feel by that?

Dr. Carrico. I felt nothing other than the blood and debris. There was no large wound there.

Mr. Specter. What source did you attribute the blood to at that time?

Dr. Carrico. As it could have come from the head wound, and it certainly could have been a back wound, but there was no way to tell whether this blood would have come from a back wound and not from his head.

Dr. Carrico then testified that he had inserted a plastic tube into President Kennedy's trachea (windpipe) to try to "allow an adequate airway" for breathing. Dr. Malcolm Perry then arrived in the emergency room and "took over supervision and treatment."

In the opinion of Dr. Carrico, the cause of the President's death was "the head wound," which he described as a large "defect in the posterior skull" with "shredded brain tissue present and initially considerable slow oozing. Then after we established some circulation there was more profuse bleeding from this wound." Dr. Carrico said that he observed "no other wound on the head."

Mr. Specter. Did you have any opportunity specifically to look for a small wound which was below the large opening of the skull on the right side of the head?

Dr. Carrico. No, sir; at least initially there was no time to examine the patient completely for all small wounds. As we said before, this was an acutely ill patient and all we had time to do was to determine what things were life-threatening right then and attempt to resuscitate him and after which a more complete examination would be carried out and we didn't have time to examine for other wounds.

Mr. Specter. Was such a more complete examination ever carried out by the doctors in Parkland?

Dr. Carrico. No, sir; not in my presence.

Mr. Specter. Why not?

Dr. Carrico. As we said initially this was an acute emergency situation and there was not time initially and when the cardiac massage was done this prevented any further examination during this time this was being done. After the President was pronounced dead his wife was there, he was the President, and we felt certainly that complete examination would be carried out and no one had the heart, I believe, to examine him then.

Dr. Carrico was then asked to describe the wound in the front of the President's neck. In the course of questioning, Allen Dulles referred to it as perhaps being an entrance wound. The response of Dr. Carrico was clear:

Mr. Specter. Will you describe, as specifically as you can then, the neck wounds which you heretofore mentioned briefly?

Dr. Carrico. There was a small wound, 5- to 8-mm. in size, located in the lower third of the neck, below the thyroid cartilage, the Adams apple.

Mr. Dulles. Will you show us about where it was?

Dr. Carrico. Just about where your tie would be.

Mr. Dulles. Where did it enter?

Dr. Carrico. It entered?

Mr. Dulles. Yes.

Dr. Carrico. At the time we did not know—

Mr. Dulles. I see.

Dr. Carrico. The entrance. All we knew this was a small wound here.

Mr. Dulles. I see, And you put your hand right above where your tie is?

Dr. Carrico. Yes, sir; just where the tie—

Mr. Dulles. A little bit to the left.

Dr. Carrico. To the right.

Mr. Dulles. Yes; to the right.

Dr. Carrico. Yes. And this wound was fairly round, had no jagged edges, no evidence of powder burns, and so forth.

Dr. Carrico thought that the wound in the neck was not a fatal wound and that if the President had not received the head wound it was "very likely" he would have survived the neck wound.

Mr. Specter. Based on your observations on the neck wound alone did you have a sufficient basis to form an opinion as to whether it was an entrance or an exit wound?

Dr. Carrico. No, sir; we did not. Not having completely evaluated all the wounds, traced out the course of the bullets, this wound would have been compatible with either entrance or exit wound depending upon the size, the velocity, the tissue structure and so forth.

Mr. Specter. Permit me to add some facts which I shall ask you to assume as being true for purposes of having you express an opinion.

First of all, assume that the President was struck by a 6.5 mm. copper-jacketed bullet from a rifle having a muzzle velocity of approximately 2,000 feet per second at a time when the President was approximately 160 to 250 feet from the weapon, with the President being struck from the rear at a downward angle of approximately 45 degrees, being struck on the upper right posterior thorax just above the upper border of the scapula 14 centimeters from the tip of the right acromion process and 14 centimeters below the tip of the right mastoid process.

Assume further that the missile passed through the body of the President striking no bones, traversing the neck and sliding between the large muscles in the posterior aspect of the President's body through a fascia channel without violating the pleural cavity, but bruising only the apex of the right pleural cavity and bruising the most apical portion of the right lung, then causing a hematoma to the right of the larynx which you have described, and creating a jagged wound in the trachea, then exiting precisely at the point where you observe the puncture wound to exist.

Now based on those facts was the appearance of the wound in your opinion consistent with being an exit wound?

Dr. Carrico. It certainly was. It could have been under the circumstances.

Mr. Specter. And assuming that all the facts which I have given you to be true, do you have an opinion with a reasonable degree of medical certainty as to whether, in fact, the wound was an entrance wound or an exit wound?

Dr. Carrico. With those facts and the fact as I understand it no other bullet was found this would be, this was, I believe, was an exit wound.

Mr. Specter. Were any bullets found in the President's body by the doctors at Parkland?

Dr. Carrico. No, sir.

Mr. Specter. Was the President's clothing ever examined by you, Dr. Carrico?

Dr. Carrico. No, sir; it was not.

Mr. Specter. What was the reason for no examination of the clothing?

Dr. Carrico. Again in the emergency situation the nurses removed the clothing after we had initially unbuttoned enough to get a look at him, at his chest, and as the routine is set up, the nurses remove the clothing and we just don't take time to look at it.

Mr. Specter. Was the President's body then ever turned over at any point by you or any of the other doctors at Parkland?

Dr. Carrico. No, sir.

Mr. Specter. Was President Kennedy lying on the emergency stretcher from the time he was brought into trauma room one until the treatment at Parkland Hospital was concluded?

Dr. Carrico. Yes; he was.

Mr. Specter. At what time was that treatment concluded, to the best of your recollection?

Dr. Carrico. At about 1 o'clock.

Mr. Specter. At approximately what time did you leave the trauma room where the President was brought?

Dr. Carrico. I left right at one when we decided that he was dead.

The autopsy of the President was conducted at Bethesda Naval Hospital near Washington, D.C. Less than a week after the death of the President, Dr. Carrico discussed these findings in Dallas with two representatives of the Secret Service.

Mr. Specter. And what questions were you asked specifically at that time, if any?

Dr. Carrico. I don't recall any specific questions I was asked. In general, I was asked some questions pertaining to his treatment, to the wounds, what I thought they were, and et cetera.

Mr. Specter. What opinions did you express at that time?

Dr. Carrico. Again, I said that on the basis of our initial examination, this wound in his neck could have been either an entrance or exit wound, which was what they were most concerned about, and assuming there was a wound in the back, somewhere similar to what you have described, that this certainly would be compatible with an exit wound.

Mr. Specter. Were your statements at that time different in any respect with the testimony which you have given here this morning?

Dr. Carrico. Not that I recall.

Mr. Specter. Were your views at that time consistent with the findings in the autopsy report, or did they vary in any way from the findings in that report?

Dr. Carrico. As I recall, the autopsy report is exactly as I remember it.

Mr. Specter. Were your opinions at that time consistent with the findings of the autopsy report?

Dr. Carrico. Yes.

Dr. Malcolm Perry entered the emergency room shortly after President Kennedy had arrived. Dr. Perry was a 34-year-old surgeon who was an assistant professor of surgery at Southwestern Medical School and who was an attending surgeon and vascular consultant for Parkland Hospital.

Dr. Perry said the President was lying on his back and "there was no evidence of voluntary motion. His eyes were open, deviated up and outward, and the pupils were dilated and fixed.

"I did not detect a heart beat and was told there was no blood pressure obtainable.

"He was, however, having ineffective spasmodic respiratory efforts," which Dr. Perry described as "short, rather jerky contractions of his chest and diaphragm, pulling for air."

After making a cursory observation of the wound on the President's head and noting the presence of lacerated brain tissue, Dr. Perry saw that "in the lower part of the neck below the Adams apple was a small, roughly circular wound of perhaps 5 mm. in diameter from which blood was exuding slowly. I did not see any other wounds."

He testified that he did

no further examination because it was obvious that if any treatment were to be carried out with any success a secure effective airway must be obtained immediately.

I asked Dr. Carrico if the wound on the neck was actually a wound or had he begun a tracheotomy and he replied in the negative, that it was a wound.

After calling in additional physicians because of the severe character of the head wound, Dr. Perry

then began the tracheotomy making a transverse incision right through the wound in the neck.

Mr. Specter. Why did you elect to make the tracheotomy incision through the wound in the neck, Dr. Perry?

Dr. Perry. The area of the wound, as pointed out to you, in the lower third of the neck anteriorly is customarily the spot one would electively perform the tracheotomy.

This is one of the safest and easiest spots to reach the trachea. In addition the presence of the wound indicated to me there was possibly an underlying wound to the neck muscles in the neck, the carotid artery or the jugular vein. If you are going to control these it is necessary that the incision be as low, that is, toward the heart or lungs, as the wound if you are going to obtain adequate control.

Therefore, for expediency's sake I went directly to that level to obtain control of the airway.

The purpose of the tracheotomy was to secure an adequate airway for the patient to maintain respiration.

The additional doctors, including Dr. William Kemp Clark of neurosurgery, arrived and Dr. Clark and Dr. Perry began external cardiac massage. This continued until Dr. Clark informed Dr. Perry that "there was no activity at all in the cardiotachyscope and that there had been no neurological or muscular response to our resuscitative effort at all and that the wound which the President sustained in his head was a mortal wound, and at that point we determined that he had expired and we abandoned efforts of resuscitation."

At approximately 1 PM, Dr. Clark "pronounced the President had died."

Mr. Specter. Will you now describe as specifically as you can, the injury which you noted in the President's head?

Dr. Perry. As I mentioned previously in the record, I made only a cursory examination of the President's head. I noted a large avulsive wound of the right parietal occipital area, in which both scalp and portions of skull were absent, and there was severe laceration of underlying brain tissue. My examination did not go any further than that.

Mr. Specter. Did you, to be specific, observe a smaller wound below the large avulsed area which you have described?

Dr. Perry. I did not.

Mr. Specter. Was there blood in that area of the President's head?

Dr. Perry. There was.

Mr. Specter. Which might have obscured such a wound?

Dr. Perry. There was a considerable amount of blood at the head of the cartilage.

Mr. Specter. Would you now describe as particularly as possible the neck wound you observed?

Dr. Perry. This was situated in the lower anterior one-third of the neck, approximately 5 mm. in diameter.

It was exuding blood slowly which partially obscured it. Its edges were neither ragged nor were they punched out, but rather clean.

Mr. Specter. Have you now described the neck wound as specifically as you can?

Dr. Perry. I have.

Now, members of the jury, we come to a portion of Dr. Perry's testimony that is most important in light of remarks attributed to him at a news conference held at Parkland Memorial Hospital shortly after the death of President Kennedy. This concerns whether the wound in President Kennedy's throat was an exit or an entrance wound. As you have already heard, neither Dr. Perry nor Dr. Carrico turned President Kennedy over to ascertain if there were any wounds in his back. Consequently, neither of these physicians knew of the wound on the back of President Kennedy's neck; the only neck wound that either of them had seen was the wound at the front of President Kennedy's neck, where the tracheotomy was performed.

First, let us hear Dr. Perry's testimony about the neck wound and then we can learn what he has to say about the press conference held at Parkland Memorial Hospital on Nov. 22.

Mr. Specter. Based on your observations of the neck wound alone, do you have a sufficient basis to form an opinion as to whether it was an entrance wound or an exit wound?

Dr. Perry. No, sir. I was unable to determine that since I did not ascertain the exact trajectory of the missile. The operative procedure which I performed was restricted to securing an adequate airway and insuring there was no injury to the carotid artery or jugular vein at that level and at that point I made the procedure.

Mr. Specter. Based on the appearance of the neck wound alone, could it have been either an entrance or an exit wound?

Dr. Perry. It could have been either.

Arlen Specter then turned to some hypothetical questions that had been developed on the basis of the autopsy of the President and wound ballistic tests:

Mr. Specter. Permit me to supply some additional facts, Dr. Perry, which I shall ask you to assume as being true for purposes of having you express an opinion.

Assume first of all that the President was struck by a 6.5-mm. copper-jacketed bullet fired from a gun having a muzzle velocity of approximately 2,000 feet per second, with the weapon being approximately 160 to 250 feet from the President, with the bullet striking him at an angle of declination of approximately 45 degrees, striking the President on the upper right posterior thorax just above the upper border of the scapula, being 14 cm. from the tip of the right acromion process and 14 cm. below the tip of the right mastoid process, passing through the President's body striking no bones, traversing the neck and sliding between the large muscles in the posterior portion of the President's body through a fascia channel without violating the pleural cavity but bruising the apex of the right lung, inflicting a hematoma to the right side of the larynx, which you have just described, and striking the trachea causing the injury which you described, and then exiting from the hole that you have described in the midline of the neck.

Now, assuming those facts to be true, would the hole which you observed in the neck of the President be consistent with an exit wound under those circumstances?

Dr. Perry. Certainly would be consistent with an exit wound.

Mr. Specter. Now, assuming one additional fact that there was no bullet found in the body of the President, and assuming the facts which I have just set forth to be true, do you have an opinion as to whether the wound which you observed in the President's neck was an entrance or an exit wound?

Dr. Perry. A full jacketed bullet without deformation passing through skin would leave a similar wound for an exit and entrance wound and with the facts which you have made available and with these assumptions, I believe that it was an exit wound.

Mr. Specter. Do you have sufficient facts available to you to render an opinion as to the cause of the injury which you observed in the President's head?

Dr. Perry. No, sir.

Mr. Specter. Have you had an opportunity to examine the autopsy report?

Dr. Perry. I have.

Mr. Specter. And are the facts set forth in the autopsy report consistent with your observations and views or are they inconsistent in any way with your findings and opinions?

Dr. Perry. They are quite consistent and I noted initially that they explained very nicely the circumstances as we observed them at the time.

Mr. Specter. Could you elaborate on that last answer, Dr. Perry?

Dr. Perry. Yes. There was some considerable speculation, as you will recall, as to whether there were one or two bullets and as to from whence they came. Dr. Clark and I were queried extensively in respect to this and in addition Dr. Carrico could not determine whether there were one or two bullets from our initial examination.

I say that because we did what was necessary in the emergency procedure, and abandoned any efforts of examination at the termination. I did not ascertain the trajectory of any of the missiles. As a result I did not know whether there was evidence for 1 or 2 or even 3 bullets entering and at the particular time it was of no importance.

Mr. Specter. But based on the additional factors provided in the autopsy report, do you have an opinion at this time as to the number of bullets there were?

Dr. Perry. The wounds as described from the autopsy report and coupled with the wounds I have observed it would appear there were two missiles that struck the President.

Mr. Specter. And based on the additional factors which I have provided to you by way of hypothetical assumption, and the factors present in the autopsy report, from your examination of that report, what does the source of the bullets seem to have been to you?

Dr. Perry. That I could not say. I can only determine their pathway, on the basis of these reports, within the President's body.

As to their ultimate source, not knowing any of the circumstances surrounding it, I would not have any speculation.

Mr. Specter. From what direction would the bullets have come based on all of those factors?

Dr. Perry. The bullets would have come from behind the President based on these factors.

Mr. Specter. And from the level, from below or above the President?

Dr. Perry. Not having examined any of the wounds with the exception of the anterior neck wounds, I could not say. This wound, as I noted, was about 5 mm., and roughly circular in shape. There is no way for me to determine.

Mr. Specter. Based upon a point of entrance in the body of the President which I described to you as being 14 cm. from the right acromion process and 14 cm. below the tip of the right mastoid process and coupling that with your observation of the neck wound, would that provide a sufficient basis for you to form an opinion as to the path of the bullet, as to whether it was level, up or down?

Dr. Perry. Yes, it would.

In view of the fact there was an injury to the right lateral portion of the trachea and a wound in the neck, if one were to extend a line roughly between these two, it would be going slightly superiorly, that is, cephalad toward the head, from anterior to posterior, which would indicate that the missile entered from slightly above and behind.

Arlen Specter then turned to the press conference held at Parkland Hospital after the death of the President. The conference was held in a classroom which "was packed with gentlemen and ladies of the press."

Mr. Specter. Would you state as specifically as you can the questions which were asked of you at that time and the answers which you gave?

Dr. Perry. Mr. Specter, I would preface this by saying that, as you know, I have been interviewed on numerous occasions subsequent to that time, and I cannot recall with accuracy the questions that were asked. They, in general, were similar to the questions that were asked here. The press were given essentially the same, but in no detail such as have been given here. I was asked, for example, what I felt caused the President's death, the nature of the wound, from whence they came, what measures were taken for resuscitation, who were the people in attendance, at what time was it determined that he was beyond our help.

Mr. Specter. What responses did you give to questions relating to the source of the bullets, if such questions were asked?

Dr. Perry. I could not. I pointed out that both Dr. Clark and I had no way of knowing from whence the bullets came.

Mr. Specter. Were you asked how many bullets there were?

Dr. Perry. We were, and our reply was it was impossible with the knowledge we had at hand to ascertain if there were 1 or 2 bullets, or more. We were given, similarly to the discussion here today, hypothetical situations. "Is it possible that such could have been the case, or such and such?" If it was possible that there was one bullet.

To this, I replied in the affirmative, it was possible and conceivable that it was only one bullet, but I did not know.

Mr. Specter. What would the trajectory, or conceivable course of one bullet have been, Dr. Perry, to account for the injuries which you observed in the President, as you stated it?

Dr. Perry. Since I observed only two wounds in my cursory examination it would have necessitated the missile striking probably a bony structure and being deviated in its course in order to account for these two wounds.

Mr. Specter. What bony structure was it conceivably?

Dr. Perry. It required striking the spine.

Mr. Specter. Did you express a professional opinion that it did, in fact, happen or it was a matter of speculation that it could have happened?

Dr. Perry. I expressed it as a matter of speculation that this was conceivable. But, again, Dr. Clark and I emphasized that we had no way of knowing.

Mr. Specter. Have you now recounted as specifically as you can recollect what occurred at that first press conference or is it practical for you to give any further detail to the contents of that press conference?

Dr. Perry. I do not recall any specific details any further than that.

Representative Ford. Mr. Specter—was there ever a recording kept of the questions and answers at that interview, Dr. Perry?

Dr. Perry. This was one of the things I was mad about, Mr. Ford. There were microphones, and cameras, and the whole bit, as you know, and during the course of it a lot of these hypothetical situations and questions that were asked to us would often be asked by someone on this side and recorded by someone on this, and I don't know who was recorded and whether they were broadcasting it directly. There were tape recorders there and there were television cameras with their microphones. I know there were recordings made but who made them I don't know and, of course, portions of it would be given to this group and questions answered here and, as a result, considerable questions were not answered in their entirety and even some of them that were asked, I am sure were misunderstood. It was bedlam.

Representative Ford, who, when present, always followed the testimony keenly, asked a cogent question:

You subsequently read or heard what was allegedly said by you and by Dr. Clark and Dr. Carrico. Were those reportings by the news media accurate or inaccurate as to what you and others said?

Dr. Perry. In general, they were inaccurate. There were some that were fairly close, but I, as you will probably surmise, was pretty full after both Friday and Sunday, and after the interviews again, following the operation of which I was a member on Sunday, I left town, and I did not read a lot of them, but of those which I saw I found none that portrayed it exactly as it happened. Nor did I find any that reported our statements exactly as they were given. They were frequently taken out of context. They were frequently mixed up as to who said what or identification as to which person was who.

Rep. Ford. This interview took place on Sunday, the 24th, did you say?

Dr. Perry. No, there were several interviews, Mr. Ford. We had one in the afternoon, Friday afternoon, and then I spent almost the entire day Saturday in the administrative suite at the hospital answering questions to people of the press, and some medical people of the American Medical Association. And then, of course,

Sunday, following the operation on Oswald, I again attended the press conference since I was the first in attendance with him. And, subsequently, there was another conference on Monday conducted by the American Medical Association, and a couple of more interviews with some people whom I don't even recall.

Rep. Ford. Would you say that these errors that were reported were because of a lack of technical knowledge as to what you as a physician were saying, or others were saying?

Dr. Perry. Certainly that could be it in part, but it was not all. Certainly a part of it was lack of attention. A question would be asked and you would incompletely answer it and another question would be asked and they had gotten what they wanted without really understanding, and they would go on and it would go out of context. For example, on the speculation on the ultimate source of bullets. I obviously knew less about it than most people because I was in the hospital at the time and didn't know the circumstances surrounding it until it was over. I was much too busy and yet I was quoted as saying that the bullet, there was probably one bullet, which struck and deviated upward which came from the front, and what I had replied was to a question, was it conceivable that this could have happened, and I said yes, it is conceivable.

I have subsequently learned that to use a straight affirmative word like "yes" is not good relations; that one should say it is conceivable and not give a straight yes or no answer.

"It is conceivable" was dropped and the "yes" was used, and this was happening over and over again. Of course, Dr. Shires, for example, who was the professor and chairman of the department, was identified in one press release as chief resident.

John McCloy then asked whether Dr. Perry discussed with any of the other doctors present

as to whether this was an exit wound or an entrance wound?

Dr. Perry. Yes, sir; we did at the time. But our discussion was necessarily limited by the fact that none of us knew, someone asked me now—you must remember that actually the only people who saw this wound for sure were Dr. Carrico and myself, and some of the other doctors were quoted as saying something about the wound which actually they never said at all because they never saw it, because on their arrival I had already made the incision through the wound, and despite what the press releases may have said neither Dr. Carrico nor myself could say whether it was an entrance or an exit wound from the nature of the wound itself and Dr. McClelland was quoted, for example, as saying he thought it was an exit wound, but that was not what he said at all because he didn't even see it.

Mr. McCloy. And it is a fact, is it not, that you did not see what we now are supposed to believe was the entrance wound?

Dr. Perry. No, sir; we did not examine him. At that time, we attended to the matters of expediency that were life-saving and the securing of an adequate airway and the stanching of massive hemorrhage are really the two medical emergencies; most everything else can wait, but those must be attended to in a matter of minutes and consequently to termination of treatment I had no morbid curiosity, my work was done, and actually I was rather anxious to leave.

Finally Specter questioned Dr. Perry about the nearly whole bullet that was found at Parkland Memorial Hospital.

Mr. Specter. Was any bullet found by you or by any other doctor at Parkland in the President's body?

Dr. Perry. I found none. To the best of my knowledge neither did anyone else.

Mr. Specter. Was the President ever turned over at any time?

Dr. Perry. Not by me nor did I see it done.

Thus, the attending physicians did not know of another wound to the President—in the back of his neck. This was discovered at the autopsy. Let us now hear from the three physicians who conducted the autopsy in Washington on the evening of Nov. 22.

40

"FROM A POINT ABOVE AND BEHIND HIM"

The President's body was received at 25 minutes before 8, and the autopsy began at approximately 8 PM on that evening. You must include the fact that certain X-rays and other examinations were made before the actual beginning of the routine type autopsy examination.

Mr. Specter. Precisely what X-rays or photographs were taken before the dissection started?

Dr. Humes. Some of these X-rays were taken before and some during the examination which also maintains for the photographs, which were made as the need became apparent to make such.

However, before the postmortem examination was begun, anterior, posterior and lateral X-rays of the head and of the torso were made, and identification type photographs, I recall having been made of the full face of the late President. A photograph showing the massive head wound with the large defect that was associated with it. To my recollection all of these were made before the proceedings began.

Several others, approximately 15 to 20 in number, were made in total before we finished the proceedings.

Mr. Specter. Now were those X-rays or photographs or both when you referred to the total number?

Dr. Humes. By the number I would say they are in number 15 to 20. There probably was 10 or 12 X-ray films exposed in addition.

Mr. Specter. What time did this autopsy end?

Dr. Humes. At approximately 11 PM.

Fifteen to twenty photographs and ten to twelve exposed X-ray films, and not one photograph or X-ray was introduced into evidence or seen by any lawyer or Commissioner. It was a disastrous decision. It was a decision with which Joe Ball and I, as well as Arlen Spector disagreed. It was a decision that gave rise to wild speculation and rumor. It was a decision that violated basic elementary rules of evidence familiar to every law student in America that when a person testifies he should have the "best evidence" available.

The Chief Justice knew better. For instance, when the FBI ballistic expert, Robert A. Frazier, testified in Washington on Mar. 31, 1964, you jurors may remember that part of the inquiry concerned the detailed description of the Mannlicher-Carcano Italian rifle found in the TSBD

Building. There were certain numbers and marks on that weapon. The record then shows:

Mr. Eisenberg. Has the Federal Bureau of Investigation been supplied with information concerning the meanings and significances of these various markings?

Mr. Frazier. Yes, sir; we have.

Mr. Eisenberg. Can you state the source of that information?

Mr. Frazier. This information came to us by mail as a result of an inquiry of the Italian Armed Forces Intelligence Service, abbreviated SIFAR, by letter dated Mar. 26, 1964, through the FBI representative in Rome, Italy.

This information is classified as secret by the Italian Government, who have advised that the material may be released to the Commission. However, they desire the retention of the information in a secret category.

The Chairman. Is this essential to the proof?

If it is not, I think we would rather not have it, because the fewer things we have to keep in secret, the better the situation is for us.

Yet, fifteen days earlier, on Mar. 16, the Chief Justice had made the determination that the autopsy photographs and X-rays would not be introduced into evidence.

The reason for this decision was that the Kennedy family, through Robert Kennedy, brother of the late President, did not want these pictures and X-rays to become a matter of public display. This was reinforced by the argument that such a decision would have no effect on the veracity of the testimony of the pathologists who performed the autopsy because these X-rays and photographs would eventually be released and the testimony could then be double-checked.

If this was the desire of the Kennedy family, perhaps a compromise could have been reached to keep the photographs out of the record and to introduce the X-rays. Even this, however, would have been a less-than-satisfactory solution.

My basic position as a citizen and as an independent attorney working with the Commission was that we were entitled to have all the evidence. The public had a right to know.[1] Although I could understand the desires of the Kennedy family, I nevertheless believed that their desire for privacy was outweighed by the need for public knowledge on what actually happened in Dallas on Nov. 22. Once a person runs for high national office, that person and his family have to expect a loss of privacy.

Moreover, even in the case of a private citizen, certain rights of privacy would yield to public policy in solving a murder. Thus, I argued that the widow of Officer J. D. Tippit could not have prevented any examination of her husband's body in connection with the investigation of a murder. Why should the widow or the family of President Kennedy be treated any differently?

This leads into an area that gave me the greatest cause for concern while I

[1] Secret records and proceedings always raise doubts, even if fairly conducted. This is one of the reasons our Constitution requires a public trial for accused persons.

served with the Warren Commission in Washington. There is a dangerous trend toward preferred treatment for high governmental officials, coupled with a dangerous trend in which high governmental officials tend to think of themselves as some sort of an élite, similar to the nobility of an eighteenth-century European monarchy.

This was evident in the relationship that developed between some of the Commissioners and the lawyers. For instance, even though the room where the Commissioners met was on the same floor of the small building where the Commission was headquartered, the Commissioners seldom took time to visit with the lawyers, working in their own offices, to find out how the investigation was developing. During the meetings of the Commissioners, the lawyers on the Commission staff were excluded, even though it was the lawyers who were undertaking the investigation.

The élite concept was also apparent from the fact that Robert Kennedy was able to prevail over the desires of counsel in Areas I and II by withholding the autopsy photographs and X-rays. When Governor Connally testified, even Senator Russell, otherwise seldom an active participant, was present—and surely Governor Connally was no more important a witness than Howard Brennan, who saw the assassin fire at the motorcade.

When the drafts of our final Report were presented for the Commissioners to review, their deference to Governor Connally was so great that they directed a revision in a major conclusion of the Commission that resulted in an outright misstatement of fact. This revision involved the single bullet theory; you will find it on page 19 of the Report, Conclusion No. 3:

Although it is not necessary to any essential findings of the Commission to determine just which shot hit Governor Connally, there is very persuasive evidence from the experts to indicate that the same bullet which pierced the President's throat also caused Governor Connally's wounds. However, Governor Connally's testimony and certain other factors have given rise to some difference of opinion as to this probability but there is no question in the mind of any member of the Commission that all the shots which caused the President's and Governor Connally's wounds were fired from the sixth floor window of the Texas School Book Depository.

The plain fact is that it is absolutely necessary to the findings of the Commission to determine whether the same bullet that pierced the President's throat also caused Governor Connally's wounds. Otherwise, where did that first bullet go? It was not in President Kennedy's body, and there was no extensive damage to the Presidential limousine of the nature that could be caused by a bullet traveling at the speed we determined under the wound ballistics tests, which you jurors will soon review.

Governor Connally was simply wrong in his testimony, just as President Johnson was wrong in some of his observations, and just as almost every witness to a sudden and startling event is incapable of being completely accurate.

In the case of President Johnson, he merely filed an affidavit. He did not undergo any interrogation by Commission counsel. Surely, if we could interrogate Mrs. Kennedy, whose husband had died before her eyes, there was no reason why President Johnson should not be examined in the same manner, as every other witness. Moreover, there was a special reason for not giving the President favored treatment: There was some speculation from abroad, however outlandish, that he might have had some indirect connection with the Dallas tragedy because it resulted in his elevation to the presidency.

One of the basic lessons of the Warren Commission investigation is the ramifications that arise when special treatment is given to a favored few. The reverberations from the decision to withhold publication of the autopsy photographs and X-rays will be felt for many decades as a part of the overall diminution of the confidence that the American people have in the integrity of their elected officials.

The three doctors who performed the autopsy were Commander James J. Humes, Director of Laboratories of the Naval Medical School at the Naval Medical Center at Bethesda, Commander J. Thornton Boswell, Chief of Pathology at the Navy Medical School, and Lieutenant-Colonel Pierre Finck, who was in the wound ballistics section of the Armed Forces Institute of Pathology.

Once again, the medical testimony will be highly technical. If you jurors desire to skim the testimony of Drs. Humes and Boswell, you will find their basic conclusions included in the testimony of Dr. Finck beginning on page 358.

In lieu of the photographs and X-rays, Commander Humes had had schematic drawings prepared. Even here, however, the artist did not have direct access to the photographs and X-rays. Rather,

he had to work under our description, verbal description, of what we had observed.

Mr. Specter. Would it be helpful to the artist, in redefining the drawings if that should become necessary, to have available to him the photographs or X-rays of the President?

Commander Humes. If it were necessary to have them absolutely true to scale. I think it would be virtually impossible for him to do this without the photographs.

Mr. Specter. And what is the reason for the necessity for having the photographs?

Commander Humes. I think that it is most difficult to transmit into physical measurements the—by word the—exact situation as it was seen to the naked eye. The photographs were—there is no problem of scale there because the wounds, if they are changed in size or changed in size and proportion to the structures of the body and so forth, when we attempt to give a description of these findings, it is the bony prominences, I cannot, which we used as points of references, I cannot transmit completely to the illustrator where they were situated.

Mr. Specter. Is the taking of photographs and X-rays routine or is this something out of the ordinary?

Commander Humes. No, sir; this is quite routine in cases of this sort of violent death in our training. In the field of forensic pathology we have found that the photographs and X-rays are of most value, the X-rays particularly in finding missiles which have a way of going in different directions sometimes, and particularly as documentary evidence these are considered invaluable in the field of forensic pathology.

Arlen Specter was furious. They did not even permit the artist preparing the schematic drawings to have access to the photographs and X-rays, even though photographs and X-rays were "quite routine" in cases of this sort. Specter wanted the record to include this testimony.

Initially, Commander Humes observed three wounds: (1) an "oval wound" in the back of the "low neck" which

was situated just above the upper border of the scapula, and measured 7 by 4 millimeters, with its long axis roughly parallel to the long axis of vertical column.

The second wound was found in the right posterior portion of the scalp. This wound was situated approximately 2.5 centimeters to the right, and slightly above the external occipital protuberance which is a bony prominence situated in the posterior portion of everyone's skull. This wound was then 2-1/2 centimeters to the right and slightly above that point.

The third obvious wound at the time of the examination was a huge defect over the right side of the skull. This defect involved both the scalp and the underlying skull, and from the brain substance was protruding.

This wound measured approximately 13 centimeters in greatest diameter. It was difficult to measure accurately because radiating at various points from the large defect were multiple crisscrossing fractures of the skull which extended in several directions.

I have noted in my report that a detailed description of the lines of these fractures and of the type of fragments that were thus made were very difficult of verbal description, and it was precisely for this reason that the photographs were made so one might appreciate more clearly how much damage had been done to the skull.

Commander Humes then turned to the wound at the top of the head, which he had referred to previously as the "second wound." The wound was approximately 15 x 6 mm. in size. Commander Humes explained that the skull is composed of two layers of bone and in between the two layers of skull bone is loose, somewhat irregular bone. The wound on the outer layer "had to us the characteristics of a wound of entrance for the following reasons: the defect in the outer table was oval in outline, quite similar to the defect in the skin . . ."

The wound on the inner table, however, was larger and had what in the field of wound ballistics is described as a shelving or a coning effect. To make an analogy to which the members of the Commission are probably most familiar, when a missile strikes a pane of glass, a typical example, a B-B fired by a child's air rifle, when this strikes a pane of glass there will be a small, usually round to oval defect on the side of the glass from whence the missile came and a belled-out or coned-out surface on the opposite side of the glass from whence the missile came.

Experience has shown and my associates and Colonel Finck, in particular, whose special field of interest is wound ballistics, can give additional testimony about this scientifically observed fact.

This wound then had the characteristics of wound of entrance from this direction through the two tables of the skull.

Mr. Specter. When you say "this direction," will you specify that direction in relationship to the skull?

Dr. Humes. At that point I mean only from without the skull to within.

Mr. Specter. Fine, proceed.

Dr. Humes. Having ascertained to our satisfaction, and incidentally photographs illustrating this phenomenon from both the external surface of the skull and from the internal surface were prepared, we concluded that the large defect to the upper right side of the skull, in fact, would represent a wound of exit.

A careful examination of the margins of the large bone defect at that point, however, failed to disclose a portion of the skull bearing again a wound of—a point of impact on the skull of this fragment of the missile, remembering, of course, that this area was devoid of any scalp or skull at this present time. We did not have the bone.

X-ray photographs showed tiny fragments extending from the wound to just above the right eye.

Commander Humes said that they then undertook an inspection of the defect of the scalp but could not find any of the minute particles or fragments.

I might say at this time that the X-ray pictures which were made would have a tendency to magnify these minute fragments somewhat in size and we were not too surprised in not being able to find the tiny fragments depicted in the X-ray.

Mr. Specter. Approximately how many fragments were observed, Dr. Humes, on the X-ray?

Dr. Humes. I would have to refer to them again, but I would say between 30 or 40 tiny dustlike particle fragments of radio opaque material, with the exception of this one I previously mentioned which was seen to be above and very slightly behind the right orbit . . .

To better examine the situation with regard to the skull, at this time, Dr. Boswell and I extended the lacerations of the scalp which were at the margins of this wound, down in the direction of both of the President's ears. At that point, we had even a better appreciation of the extensive damage which had been done to the skull by this injury.

We had to do virtually no work with a saw to remove these portions of the skull, they came apart in our hands very easily, and we attempted to further examine the brain, and seek specifically this fragment which was the one we felt to be of a size which would permit us to recover it.

Mr. Specter. When you refer to this fragment, and you are pointing there, are you referring to the fragment depicted right above the President's right eye?

Dr. Humes. Yes, sir; above and somewhat behind the President's eye.

Mr. Specter. Will you proceed, then, to tell us what you did then?

Dr. Humes. Yes, sir. We dissected carefully in this region and in fact located this small fragment, which was in a defect in the brain tissue in just precisely this location.

Mr. Specter. How large was that fragment, Dr. Humes?

Dr. Humes. I refer to my notes for the measurements of that fragment.

I find in going back to my report, sir, that we found, in fact, two small fragments in this approximate location. The larger of these measured 7 by 2 mm., the smaller 3 by 1 mm.

Sometime later that evening, agents of the FBI delivered three pieces of bone which had been recovered. The pathologists were able to put these fragments together to help reconstruct the skull.

To confirm that this was a missile wound, X-rays were made of that fragment of bone, which showed radio-opaque material consistent and similar in character to the particles seen within the skull to be deposited in the margins of this defect, in this portion of the bone.

Commander Humes used a drawing to show the point of entrance, which he labeled with the letter "A," and the point of exit, which he labeled "B." He testified that "a very significant portion, perhaps the largest portion" of the missile which struck the President's head exited at the point where the largest portion of the President's head had been torn off.

Asked about the kind of a bullet that caused the wound, Commander Humes said that from the characteristics of the head wound, "I believe that it must have had a very firm head rather than a soft head."

On the artist's drawings, Commander Humes drew an angle of declination.

Mr. Dulles. Is the angle of declination that you—one sees there from in and out approximately the angle you think at which the bullet was traveling at the time of impact and exit?

Dr. Humes. That is our impression, sir.

Mr. Dulles. So then the shot would have been fired from some point above the head of the person hit?

Dr. Humes. Yes, sir.

Mr. Specter. Dr. Humes, would you elaborate a bit on the differences in the paths, specifically why the bullet went in one direction in part and in part in the second direction, terminating with the fragment right over the right eye?

Dr. Humes. Yes, sir.

Why a fragment takes any particular direction like that is something which is difficult of scientific explanation. Those of us who have seen missiles strike bones, be it the skull or a bone in the extremity, have long since learned that portions of these missiles may go off in various directions and the precise physical laws governing them are not clearly understood.

Mr. Specter. Would the angle be accentuated in any way if you were to assume the President was in a moving automobile going in a slight downhill direction?

Dr. Humes. There are many variables under these circumstances. The most—the crucial point, I believe, to be the relative position of the President's head in relation to the flight of the missile.

Now, this would be influenced by how far his head was bent, by the situation with regard to the level of the seat in the vehicle, off of the horizontal, and so forth.

Mr. Specter. How about a decline in the path of the road itself?

Dr. Humes. I think that that would have a tendency to accentuate this angle, yes, sir. [John McCloy asked Commander Humes if there was] anything to indicate that this was, might have been a larger than a 6.5 or smaller than a 6.5?.

Dr. Humes. The size of the defect in the scalp caused by a projectile could vary from missile to missile because of elastic recoil and so forth of the tissues.

However, the size of the defect in the underlying bone is certainly not likely to get smaller than that of the missile which perforated it, and in this case, the smallest diameter of this was approximately 6 to 7 mm., so I would feel that that would be the absolute upper limit of the size of this missile, sir.

Mr. McCloy. Seven would be the absolute upper limit?

Dr. Humes. Yes, sir; and, of course, just a little tilt could make it a little larger, you see.

Then Mr. Dulles posed some questions, ending with the following:

Am I correct in assuming from what you have said that this wound is entirely inconsistent with a wound that might have been administered if the shot were fired from in front or the side of the President; it had to be fired from behind the President?

Dr. Humes. Scientifically, sir, it is impossible for it to have been fired from other than behind. Or to have exited from other than behind.

Mr. McCloy. This is so obvious that I rather hesitate to ask it. There is no question in your mind that it was a lethal bullet?

Dr. Humes. The President, sir, could not possibly have survived the effect of that injury no matter what would have been done for him.

The Chairman. Mr. Specter.

Mr. Specter. What conclusions did you reach then as to the trajectory or point of origin of the bullet, Dr. Humes, based on 388 [one of the schematic drawings]?

Dr. Humes. We reached the conclusion that this missile was fired toward the President from a point above and behind him, sir.

Thus, we have the head wounds of the President: A hard-jacketed missile fired toward the President from a point above and behind him had caused the wounds. We then turned to the wound in the back of the President's neck. According to Commander Humes, the doctors examined the bony structures of the body as well as X-rays

to see if there was any evidence of fracture or of deposition of metallic fragments in the depths of this wound, and we saw no such evidence, that is, no fracture of the bones of the shoulder girdle, or of the vertical column, and no metallic fragments were detectable by X-ray examination.

Attempts to probe in the vicinity of this wound were unsuccessful without fear of making a false passage.

Mr. Specter. What do you mean by that, Doctor?

Dr. Humes. Well, the defect in the fascia was quite similar, which is the first firm tissue over the muscle beneath the skin, was quite similar to this. We were unable, however, to take probes and have them satisfactorily fall through any definite path at this point.

Dr. Humes said that they noticed a "recent surgical defect in the low anterior neck" and he discussed this with Dr. Malcolm Perry of Parkland Hospital in Dallas on Saturday morning, Nov. 23:

I had the impression from seeing the wound that it represented a surgical tracheotomy wound, a wound frequently made by surgeons when people are in respiratory distress to give them a free airway.

To ascertain that point, I called on the telephone Dr. Malcolm Perry and discussed with him the situation of the President's neck when he first examined the President, and asked him had he in fact done a tracheotomy which was somewhat redundant because I was somewhat certain he had.

He said, yes; he had done a tracheotomy and that as the point to perform his tracheotomy he used a wound which he had interpreted as a missile wound in the low neck, as the point through which to make the tracheotomy incision.

Commander Humes then described the autopsy examination of the area of the neck and chest.

...we made the customary incision which we use in a routine postmortem examination which is a Y-shaped incision from the shoulders over the lower portion of the breastbone and over to the opposite shoulder and reflected the skin and tissues from the anterior portion of the chest.

We examined in the region of this incised surgical wound which was the tracheotomy wound and we saw that there was some bruising of the muscles of the neck in the depths of this wound as well as laceration or defect in the trachea. . . .

In attempting to relate findings within the President's body to this wound ' 'hich we had observed low in his neck, we then opened his chest cavity, and we very carefully examined the lining of his chest cavity and both of his lungs. We found that there was, in fact, no defect in the pleural lining of the President's chest.

It was completely intact. However . . . in the apex of the right pleural cavity there was a bruise or contusion or eemymosis of the parietal pleura as well as a bruise of the upper portion, the most apical portion of the right lung.

It, therefore, was our opinion that the missile while not penetrating physically the pleural cavity, as it passed that point bruised, either the missile itself, or the force of its passage through the tissues, bruised both the parietal and the visceral pleura.

The area of discoloration on the apical portion of the right upper lung measured five centimeters in greatest diameter, and was wedge shaped in configuration, with its base toward the top of the chest and its apex down towards the substance of the lung.

Commander Humes then said that Kodachrome photographs had been made of this area in the interior of the President's chest. Unfortunately, the Commission did not see the photographs. However, on a drawing that was marked Exhibit 385, Commander Humes marked point "C" as the wound on the back of the President's neck and point "D" as the wound in the front of the President's neck. He then came to the crucial question: Was the point of entry at the back of the neck (point"C") or at the front of the neck (point "D")?

Dr. Humes. We reached the conclusion that point "C" was a point of entry.

Mr. Specter. What characteristics of that wound led you to that conclusion?

Dr. Humes. The characteristics here were basically similar to the characteristics above, lacking one very valuable clue, or piece of evidence rather than clue, because it is more truly a piece of evidence in the skull. The skull as I mentioned before had the bone with the characteristic defect made as a missile traverses bone.

This missile, to the best of our ability to ascertain, struck no bone protuberances, no bony prominences, no bones as it traversed the President's body. But it was a sharply delineated wound. It was quite regular in its outline. It measured, as I mentioned, 7 by 4 mm. Its margins were similar in all respects when viewed with the naked eye to the wound in the skull, which we feel incontrovertibly was a wound of entrance.

The defect in the fascia which is that layer of connective tissue over the muscle just beneath the wound corresponded virtually exactly to the defect in the skin.

And for these reasons we felt that this was a wound of entrance.

Mr. Specter. Did you search the body to determine if there was any bullet inside the body?

Dr. Humes. Before the arrival of Colonel Finck we had made X-rays of the head, neck and torso of the President, and the upper portions of his major extremities, or both his upper and lower extremities. At Colonel Finck's suggestion, we then completed the X-ray examination by X-raying the President's body in toto, and those X-rays are available.

Mr. Specter. What did those X-rays disclose with respect to the possible presence of a missile in the President's body?

Dr. Humes. They showed no evidence of a missile in the President's body at any point. And these were examined by ourselves and by the radiologist, who assisted us in this endeavor.

Mr. Specter. What conclusion, if any, did you reach as to whether point "D" on 385 was the point of entrance or exit?

Dr. Humes. We concluded that this missile depicted in 385 "C" which entered the President's body traversed the President's body and made its exit through the wound observed by the physicians at Parkland Hospital and later extended as a tracheotomy wound . . . The angle which we observed in measuring, in comparing the point of entrance, our point of entrance labeled "C" on 385 and "D" point of exit is one that the point of exit is below the point of entrance compared with the vertical.

Commander Humes examined the clothing that President Kennedy had worn on Nov. 22. As you jurors remember from the testimony of Robert Frazier in an earlier chapter, there were holes and tears that showed that a missile entered the back of his clothing in the vicinity of his lower neck and exited through the front of his shirt.

Mr. Specter. Now, Doctor Humes, at one point in your examination of the President did you make an effort to probe the point of entry with your finger?

Dr. Humes. Yes, sir; I did.

Mr. Specter. And at or about that time when you were trying to ascertain, as you previously testified, whether there was any missile in the body of the President, did someone from the Secret Service call your attention to the fact that a bullet had been found on a stretcher at Parkland Hospital?

Dr. Humes. Yes, sir; they did.

Mr. Specter. And in that posture of your examination, having just learned of the presence of a bullet on a stretcher, did that call to your mind any tentative explanatory theory of the point of entry or exit of the bullet which you have described as entering at point "C" on Exhibit 385?

Dr. Humes. Yes, sir. We were able to ascertain with absolute certainty that the bullet had passed by the apical portion of the right lung producing the injury which we mentioned.

I did not at that point have the information from Doctor Perry about the wound in the anterior neck, and while that was a possible explanation for the point of exit, we also had to consider the possibility that the missile in some rather inexplicable fashion had been stopped in its path through the President's body and, in fact, then had fallen from the body onto the stretcher.

Mr. Specter. And what theory did you think possible, at that juncture, to explain the passing of the bullet back out the point of entry; or had you been provided with the fact that external heart massage had been performed on the President?

Dr. Humes. Yes, sir; we had, and we considered the possibility that some of the physical maneuvering performed by the doctors might have in some way caused this event to take place.

Mr. Specter. Now, have you since discounted that possibility, Doctor Humes?

Dr. Humes. Yes; in essence we have. When examining the wounds in the base of the President's neck anteriorly, the region of the tracheotomy performed at Parkland Hospital, we noted, and we noted in our record, some contusion and bruising of the muscles of the neck of the President. We noted that at the time of the postmortem examination.

Now, we also made note of the types of wounds which I mentioned to you before in this testimony on the chest which were going to be used by the doctors there to place chest tubes. They also made other wounds, one on the left arm, and a wound on the ankle of the President with the idea of administering intravenous blood and other fluids in hope of replacing the blood which the President had lost from his extensive wounds.

Those wounds showed no evidence of bruising or contusion or physical violence, which made us reach the conclusion that they were performed during the agonal moments of the late President, and when the circulation was, in essence, very seriously embarrassed, if not nonfunctional. So that these wounds, the wound of the chest and the wound of the arm and of the ankle were performed about the same time as the tracheotomy wound because only a very few moments of time elapsed when all this was going on.

So, therefore, we reached the conclusion that the damage to these muscles on the anterior neck just below this wound were received at approximately the same time that the wound here on the top of the pleural cavity was, while the President still lived and while his heart and lungs were operating in such a fashion to permit him to have a bruise in the vicinity, because that he did have in these strap muscles in the neck, but he didn't have in the areas of the other incisions that were made at Parkland Hospital. So we feel that, had this missile not made its path in that fashion, the wound made by Doctor Perry in the neck would not have been able to produce, wouldn't have been able to produce, these contusions of the musculature of the neck.

Thus, *the nature of these bruises where the President's heart and lungs were functioning when the bruises occurred* proved that the bullet entering the back of President Kennedy's neck passed through and exited at the front of the neck causing the bruises in the process. In contrast, where the incisions were made on the President's chest to insert tubes through the tracheotomy, *there was little bruising because this occurred after* the fatal bullet struck President Kennedy's head and there was *very little circulation.* This proof was independently corroborated by the wound ballistics tests that you will see in the next chapter.

In the conversation that Commander Humes had with Dr. Perry,

He told me that the President was on his back from the time he was brought into the hospital until the time he left it, and that at no time was he turned from his back by the doctors.

Mr. Specter. And at the time of your conversation with Doctor Perry did you tell Doctor Perry anything of your observations or conclusions?

Dr. Humes. No, sir; I did not.

Arlen Specter then returned to the autopsy photographs and X-rays, but he was interrupted by a very sensitive Chief Justice Warren.

Mr. Specter. Now that you have finished your major descriptions of the wounds, can you be any more specific in telling us in what way the availability of the X-rays would assist in further specifying the nature of the wounds?

Dr. Humes. I do not believe, sir, that the availability of the X-rays would materially assist the Commission.

Mr. Specter. How about the same question as to the pictures?

Dr. Humes. The pictures would show more accurately and in more detail the character of the wounds as depicted particularly in 385 and 386 and in 388-A. They would also perhaps give the Commissioners a better—better is not the best term, but a more graphic picture of the massive defect in 388.

Mr. Specter. Going back for a moment, Doctor Humes—

Chairman. Before we get off that, may I ask you this, Commander: If we had the pictures here and you could look them over again and restate your opinion, would it cause you to change any of the testimony you have given here?

Dr. Humes. To the best of my recollection, Mr. Chief Justice, it would not.

Then Commander Humes testified about an error of judgment on his part that further fanned the flames of speculation and rumor:

Mr. Specter. Are there any notes which you made at any time which are not included in this group of notes?

Dr. Humes. Yes, sir; there are.

Mr. Specter. And what do those consist of?

Dr. Humes. In privacy of my own home, early in the morning of Sunday, November 24th, I made a draft of this report which I later revised, and of which this represents the revision. That draft I personally burned in the fireplace of my recreation room.

There was no reason why the initial draft should have been burned by Commander Humes. My intuition told me that he had some mistakes in the original draft that may have been corrected by the telephone conversation to Dallas, when he learned about the tracheotomy. But regardless of the reason, once the Commission learned that the initial draft of the notes had been burned, I believe it was incumbent upon Chief Justice Warren to countermand the request of the Kennedy family and produce the autopsy photographs and X-rays.

After going through the notes and the drafts that the witness did have available, Specter asked the witness:

Will you first of all read into the record the final conclusion reflected in your final report.

Dr. Humes. I would rather read it from the final report. The final report reads:

"The projectiles were fired from a point behind and somewhat above the level of the deceased."

Mr. Specter. And what did the first draft of that sentence as shown on page 14 of your rough draft state?

Dr. Humes. It stated as follows:

"The projectiles were fired from a point behind and somewhat above a horizontal line to the vertical position of the body at the moment of impact."

Mr. Specter. Now would you state the reason for making that modification between draft and final report, please.

Dr. Humes. This examination, as I have indicated, was performed by myself with my two associates. The notes which we have just admitted as an exhibit are in my own hand and are my opinion, was my opinion at that time, as to the best way to present the facts which we had gleaned during this period.

Before submitting it to the typist, I went over this with great care with my two associates. One or the other of them raised the point that perhaps this sentence would state more than what was absolutely fact based upon our observations, pointing out that we did not know precisely at that time in what position the body of the President was when the missiles struck, and that therefore we should be somewhat less specific and somewhat more circumspect than the way we stated it. When I considered this suggestion, I agreed that it would be better to change it as noted, and accordingly, I did so.

Commander Humes did not think that the nearly whole bullet found at Parkland Memorial Hospital, Exhibit 399, had caused the wounds to the President's head. On the basis of the Parkland Hospital reports, he also did not believe that Exhibit 399 caused the wounds to Governor Connally's wrist because their reports referred to fragments in the wrist. Dr. Humes unfortunately failed to ascertain from Dr. Gergory that the weight of the fragments was only in micrograms—"less than the weight of a postage stamp." This exemplifies what can happen when a witness tries to testify from hearsay evidence, such as the hospital records of a patient treated by another doctor. Nevertheless, here is what Commander Humes said:

The X-rays of the wound in the head of the late President showed fragmentations of the missile. Some fragments we recovered and turned over, as has been previously noted. Also we have X-rays of the fragment of skull which was in the region of our opinion exit wound showing metallic fragments.

Also going to Exhibit 392, the report from Parkland Hospital, the following sentence referring to the examination of the wound of the wrist is found:

"Small bits of metal were encountered at various levels throughout the wound, and these were, wherever they were identified and could be picked up, picked up and submitted to the pathology department for identification and examination."

The reason I believe it most unlikely that this missile could have inflicted either of these wounds is that this missile is basically intact; its jacket appears to me to be intact, and I do not understand how it could possibly have left fragments in either of these locations.

We then asked the witness whether he felt the same bullet that caused the wound to President Kennedy's neck had also struck Governor Connally. As background, Dr. Humes examined a photograph, Exhibit 398, taken just after the President was struck by the first bullet.

Humes testified:

I would preface this statement by the following: As I testified earlier in the afternoon, as much as we could ascertain from our X-rays and physical examinations, this missile struck no bony structures in traversing the body of the late President. Therefore, I believe it was moving at its exit from the President's body at only very slightly less than that velocity, so it was still traveling at great speed.

I believe in looking at Exhibit 398, which purports to be at approximately the time the President was struck, I see that Governor Connally is sitting directly in front of the late President, and suggest the possibility that this missile, having traversed the low neck of the late President, in fact traversed the chest of Governor Connally.

Mr. Specter. How much of the velocity, if any, or would there be an appreciable diminution of the velocity of the projectile on passing through the portions of President Kennedy's body which you have described?

Dr. Humes. I would have to defer to my associate, Colonel Finck, for an opinion about this.

However, before Colonel Finck testified, the Commission heard briefly from Commander J. Thornton Boswell, who was also a certified pathologist. Dr. Boswell was chief of pathology at the National Naval Medical School and had been present during the interrogation of Dr. Humes.

Mr. Specter. Did you have occasion to participate in the autopsy of the late President Kennedy?

Dr. Boswell. I did.

Mr. Specter. And did you assist Doctor Humes at that time?

Dr. Boswell. Yes, sir.

Mr. Specter. Have you been present here today during the entire course of Doctor Humes' testimony?

Dr. Boswell. I have, sir; yes.

Mr. Specter. Do you have anything that you would like to add by way of elaboration or modification to that which Doctor Humes has testified?

Dr. Boswell. None, I believe. Doctor Humes has stated essentially what is the culmination of our examination and our subsequent conference, and everything is exactly as we had determined our conclusions.

Mr. Specter. And are you one of the three coauthors of the autopsy report which has been previously identified as a Commission Exhibit?

Dr. Boswell. Yes; I am.

Mr. Specter. All the facts set forth therein are correct in accordance with your analysis and evaluation of the situation?

Dr. Boswell. Yes,

Mr. Specter. And specifically, as to the points of entry and points of exit which have been testified to by Doctor Humes, do his views express yours as well?

Dr. Boswell. They do, yes.

Mr. Specter. Doctor Boswell, would you state for the record what your conclusion was as to the cause of death of President Kennedy?

Dr. Boswell. The brain injury was the cause of death.

Mr. Specter. And in the absence of brain injury, what, in your view, would have been the future status of President Kennedy's mortality, if he had only sustained the wound inflicted in 385?

Dr. Boswell. I believe it would have been essentially an uneventful recovery. It could have been easily repaired, and I think it would have been of little consequence.

Lt. Col. Pierre A. Finck was the third physician who participated in the autopsy. He was a certified pathologist who for three years had been Chief of the Wounds Ballistics Pathology Branch of the Armed Forces Institute of Pathology.

He concurred in the observations of Commander Humes.

Mr. Specter. Based on your observations and conclusions, was President Kennedy shot from the front, rear, side or what?

Dr. Finck. President Kennedy was, in my opinion, shot from the rear. The bullet entered in the back of the head and went out on the right side of his skull, producing a large wound, the greatest dimension of which was approximately 13 centimeters.

Mr. Specter. And as to angle, was he shot from below, from level, from above, or what, in your opinion?

Dr. Finck. In my opinion, the angle can be determined only approximately due to the fact that the wound of entrance is fairly small and could give enough precision in the determination of the path, but the dimension of the wound of exit, letter B of Exhibit 388, is so large that we can only give an approximate angle. In my opinion, the angle was within 45 degrees from the horizontal plane.

Mr. Specter. Is that to say that there was a 45-degree angle of declination from the point of origin to the point of impact, from the point of origin of the bullet where the bullet came from a gun until the point where it struck President Kennedy?

The Chairman. In other words, you mean was he shot from above or below.

Mr. Specter. Yes.

Dr. Finck. I think I can only state, sir, that he was shot from above and behind.

Colonel Finck was then questioned with regard to the President's neck wound. Point "C" on Exhibit 385 was on the back of the President's neck. Point "D" was on the front of the neck where the tracheotomy was performed.

Mr. Specter. As to Exhibit 385, Dr. Finck, was point C a point of entry or a point of exit, in your opinion?

Dr. Finck. In my opinion point C of Commission's Exhibit 385 is a wound of entrance.

Mr. Specter. And what is the basis for that conclusion?

Dr. Finck. The basis for that conclusion is that this wound was relatively small with clean edges. It was not a jagged wound, and that is what we see in wound of entrance at a long range.

Mr. Specter. Were you present here today and did you hear the entire testimony of Doctor Humes?

Dr. Finck. Yes; I did.

Mr. Specter. And do you concur in Dr. Humes' statements and opinions regarding the point of entry C, point of exit D, and general angle on the flight of the missile?

Dr. Finck. I certainly do.

Mr. Specter. Then from what direction was President Kennedy shot on entry point C?

Dr. Finck. From behind and above.

Finally, Colonel Finck was questioned about whether the bullet that passed through President Kennedy's neck had also struck Governor Connally.

Mr. Specter. With respect to the question of likelihood of Governor Connally having been wounded in the back and chest with the same bullet which passed through President Kennedy in 385, what reduction would there be, if any, in the velocity, considering the relative positions of the two men in the automobile as reflected in photograph, Exhibit 398?

Dr. Finck. Of course, to reach precise figures we would need experiments and similar circumstances with the same type ammunition at the same distance through two human cadavers, which I did not do.

On the basis that if we assume that this is one bullet going through President Kennedy's body and also through Governor Connally's body, the reduction of velocity would be of some extent after passing through President Kennedy's body, but not having hit bones, the reduction in velocity, after going through President Kennedy's body, would be minimal.

Mr. Specter. Would there be sufficient force then to inflict the wound which Dr. Humes described from the Parkland Hospital records having been inflicted on Governor Connally's back and chest?

Dr. Finck. There would be enough energy to go through the body of the Governor.

Mr. Specter. In expressing your opinion on that subject, Doctor Finck, have you taken into account the assumptions on distance, that we are dealing here with a weapon that has a muzzle velocity in the neighborhood of slightly in excess of 2,000, and that the vehicle carrying these two individuals was approximately 150, about 150 feet away from the site of origin of the missile?

Dr. Finck. At this range, a bullet of this velocity loses very little velocity, and keeps upon impact a large amount of kinetic energy.

Mr. Specter. You heard the whole of Doctor Humes' testimony, did you not?

Dr. Finck. Yes; I did.

Mr. Specter. Do you have anything that you would like to add to what he said?

Dr. Finck. No.

Mr. Specter. Or would you like to modify his testimony in any way?

Dr. Finck. No.

Mr. Specter. Do you subscribe to the observations and procedures which he outlined during the course of his testimony?

Dr. Finck. I do.

Mr. Specter. And do you share the opinions which he expressed in their entirety in the course of his testimony here today?

Dr. Finch. I do.

Colonel Finck was then asked to testify concerning the nearly whole bullet found in Parkland Memorial Hospital, Exhibit 399. Like Commander Humes, he was influenced considerably by the Parkland Hospital records showing fragments in Governor Connally's wrist.

Mr. Specter. Dr. Finck, have you had an opportunity to examine Commission's Exhibit 399?

Dr. Finck. For the first time this afternoon, sir.

Mr. Specter. And based upon your examination of that bullet, do you have an opinion as to whether in its current condition it could have passed through President Kennedy at point C-D in 385 and then inflicted the wound in the back and chest of Governor Connally?

Dr. Finck. Yes; I do. This is a bullet showing marks indicating the bullet was fired. The second point is that there was practically no loss of this bullet. It kept its original caliber and dimensions. There was no evidence that any major portion of the jacket was lost, and I consider this as one bullet which possibly could have gone through the wounds you described.

Mr. Specter. And could that bullet possibly have gone through President Kennedy in 388?

Dr. Finck. Through President Kennedy's head? 388?

Mr. Specter. And remained intact in the way you see it now?

Dr. Finck. Definitely not.

Mr. Specter. And could it have been the bullet which inflicted the wound on Governor Connally's right wrist?

Dr. Finck. No; for the reason that there are too many fragments described in that wrist.

Mr. Specter. And is the condition of Exhibit 399 consistent with the type of a wound which Doctor Humes described on Governor Connally's rib?

Dr. Finck. Yes.

Mr. McCloy. I have a question. . . . Are you familiar with the Mannlicher 6.5 rifle?

Dr. Finck. I am familiar with the caliber 6.5. I can draw the calibers for you on the blackboard.

Mr. McCloy. What is the initial velocity of a 6.5 mm. bullet of that character?

Dr. Finck. Of the order of 2,000 feet per second.

Mr. McCloy. And you say there would not be a substantial diminution of that velocity either at the point of impact or at the point of exit?

Dr. Finck. That is correct.

I was not present when Colonel Finck testified. However, when I read the transcript I was shocked to find that in a case involving the murder of the President of the United States, some of the supposedly leading doctors in the United States armed forces had failed to do their homework. They did not personally contact the physicians of Governor Connally and find from the primary source whether the weight of the fragments in Governor Connally's wrist precluded Exhibit 399 (the nearly whole bullet) from causing the Governor's wounds.

Had they done this, they would have learned from Dr. Gregory, who operated on Governor Connally's wrist, that the weight of the fragments that remained in Governor Connally's wrist was measured in micrograms and in no way precluded the possibility that all the Governor's wounds could have been caused by Exhibit 399.

If professional officers can jump to such false conclusions in a case involving the assassination of a President, is it unreasonable to assume that the military should expect objective questioning of their decisions by a free society? My inherent skepticism of governmental authority, be it civilian or military, was intensified as an outgrowth of my service with the Warren Commission. The autopsy physicians were very capable—but by no means perfect. The FBI and Secret Service were very capable— but by no means perfect. And although, by and large, Chief Justice Warren and his fellow Commissioners did a creditable job in conducting a fair and impartial investigation, surely errors were made, such as the failure to allow the attorneys conducting the work of the Commission to see the autopsy photographs and X-rays.

The position of the Kennedy family has not changed since the Warren

Commission investigation. On Jan. 5, 1972, I wrote a letter to Senator Edward Kennedy urging that he "undertake whatever steps are necessary to make available to the general public the autopsy photographs and X-rays which were taken following the assassination of President Kennedy." In the letter I said that although I understand the desire of the family "to avoid publication of matters of this kind" I nevertheless believed "that where the death of a President is involved the citizens of the country do have an overriding right to know all of the facts." Senator Kennedy did not reply to my letter, but turned it over to Burke Marshall, deputy dean of the Yale Law School. Marshall wrote me on Jan. 24, 1972, asserting "that the Kennedy family has some right of privacy" and that the Kennedy family, "particularly Robert F. Kennedy and the former Mrs. John Kennedy, could not accept the notion that the general public should have access to photographic materials of the nature that are created in an autopsy . . . Five distinguished totally independent experts have now examined the materials, as well as the three doctors who performed the autopsy. They have all stated publicly and in detail how the materials confirm the Warren Commission's other medical evidence, as you and I know . . . In any event, I intend to continue to protect the private feelings I have referred to, and which are also completely understandable, at least to me."

I replied on Feb. 2, restating my position that "the overwhelming right of the American public to have access to all of the facts involved in the murder of their President far outweighs the personal desires for privacy of the members of the victim's family . . . Where there is a judicial inquiry into any murder . . . any autopsy photographs and X-rays are a matter of public record."

I also repeated my concern "about the ever-increasing tendency of people in high government position or connected with other people in high government position who think of themselves as having special rules applicable to them which are not applicable to the public at large. It is as if we were starting to build up our own kind of 'nobility' in our country—a group of people who are above the normal standards of a democratic society.

"I would like to ask you why you feel the Kennedy family should be treated differently from the family of any other victim whose murder was being investigated in a judicial proceeding."

I concluded my letter with one question: ". . . if you and the Kennedy family do not wish to reconsider and release these key documents to the public, I would appreciate your advising me what in your opinion would be the proper forum in which to undertake a judicial determination of the right of the public to have full access to these documents." There was no reply by Marshall to my letter.

Now, members of the jury, let us go from the medical testimony and the testimony of the autopsy physicians to the final step in our exploration of the single bullet theory: the wound ballistics experiments.

41

"THAT SAME BULLET WAS CAPABLE"

Before turning to the wound ballistics tests, I will ask each juror a question: What was the distance from the assassination window to President Kennedy at the time he was struck by the first bullet? And what was the distance from the assassination window to President Kennedy's head when he was struck by the second bullet?

Using the Zapruder films, we determined that the President was shot through the neck at a point approximately 180 feet, or 60 yards, from the southeast corner window on the sixth floor of the TSBD Building. The rifle, C-2766, had a four-power scope, which would have reduced that range to approximately 15 yards in the gunman's eyes.

The distance from the window to the President's head at the time the fatal shot struck was 265.3 feet, or approximately 88 yards. With a four-power scope, this was reduced to 22 yards.

For a man such as Lee Harvey Oswald, who had been in the Marines and was a sharpshooter, this surely was not a difficult shot. And there was one other factor that made it an even easier shot. For this I would like you jurors to conduct another experiment.

Look out the window and hold your hands in front of you as if you were looking down a rifle barrel. Look at a car or someone walking across your line of vision from left to right or from right to left and try to follow the movement with your imaginary rifle. As you will note, you have to move the rifle materially as the person or object passes across your field of vision.

Now, pretend that instead of the person's walking across your field of vision from left to right or right to left, he is walking away from you, so that instead of having a "cross shot" you have a "line shot." You will notice that as a person walks away from you there is little need to change the position of the rifle.

As fate would have it, because of the reflex angle at which Elm Street turned into the freeway, the shot that the gunman had from the sixth floor window of the TSBD Building was an almost perfect "line shot." There was little need to move the rifle as it aimed toward the motorcade from the first shot that struck a victim, approximately 60 yards away, to the point of the next shot that hit, approximately 88 yards away. With this concept of a "line shot" as our frame of reference, let us explore the wound ballistics experiments that we requested in the course of our investigation. We had to determine whether the wounds to President Kennedy and Governor Connally could have been caused by the rifle found in the TSBD Building. We also had to determine what happened to rifle bullets similar to the ammunition used if they struck objects similar to the neck area where President Kennedy was first hit, his head, Governor Connally's back and chest and Governor Connally's wrist. Here is how we summarized the tests in our Warren Commission Report (pages 580–586):

WOUND BALLISTICS EXPERIMENTS

Purpose of the Test

During the course of the Commission's inquiry, questions arose as to whether the wounds inflicted on President Kennedy and Governor Connally could have been caused by the Mannlicher-Carcano rifle found on the sixth floor of the Texas School Book Depository Building and Western Cartridge Co. bullets and fragments of the type found on the Governor's stretcher and in the Presidential limousine. In analyzing the trajectory of the bullets after they struck their victims, further questions were posed on the bullet's velocity and penetration power after exiting from the person who was initially struck. To answer these and related questions, the Commission requested that a series of tests be conducted on substances resembling the wounded portions of the bodies of President Kennedy and Governor Connally under conditions which simulated the events of the assassination.

The Testers and Their Qualifications

In response to the Commission's request, an extensive series of tests were conducted by the Wound Ballistics Branch of the U. S. Army Chemical Research and Development Laboratories at Edgewood Arsenal, Md. Scientists working at that branch are engaged in full-time efforts to investigate the wound ballistics of missiles in order to test their effects on substances which simulate live human bodies. The tests for the Commission were performed by Dr. Alfred G. Olivier under the general supervision of Dr. Arthur J. Dziemian with consultation from Dr. Frederick W. Light, Jr. Dr. Olivier received his doctorate in veterinary medicine from the University of Pennsylvania in 1953. Since 1957 he has been engaged in research on wound ballistics at Edgewood Arsenal and is now chief of the Wound Ballistics Branch. His supervisor, Dr. Dziemian, who is chief of the Biophysics Division at Edgewood Arsenal, holds a PH.D. degree from Princeton in 1939, was a national research fellow in physiology at the University of Pennsylvania and was a fellow in anatomy at Johns Hopkins University Medical School. Since 1947, Dr. Dziemian has been continuously engaged in wound ballistics work at Edgewood Arsenal. In 1930, Dr. Light was awarded an M.D. degree from Johns Hopkins Medical School and in 1948 received his Ph.D. from the same institution. After serving a residency in pathology, he worked as a pathologist until 1940 when he returned to Johns Hopkins University to study mathematics. Since 1951, Dr. Light has been engaged in the study of the pathology of wounding at Edgewood Arsenal. All three of these distinguished scientists testified before the Commission.

General Testing Conditions

The Commission made available to the Edgewood Arsenal scientists all the relevant facts relating to the wounds which were inflicted on President Kennedy and Governor Connally including the autopsy report on the President, and the reports and X-rays from Parkland Hospital. In addition, Drs. Olivier and Light had an opportunity to discuss in detail the Governor's wounds with the Governor's surgeons, Drs. Robert R. Shaw and Charles F. Gregory. The Zapruder films of the assassination were viewed with Governor and Mrs. Connally to give the Edgewood scientists their version. The Commission also provided the Edgewood scientists with all known data on the source of the shots, the rifle and bullets used, and the distances involved. For purposes of the experiments, the Commission turned over to the Edgewood testers the Mannlicher-Carcano rifle found on the sixth floor of the Depository Building. From information provided by the Commission, the Edgewood scientists obtained Western bullets of the type used by the assassin.

Tests on Penetration Power and Bullet Stability

Comparisons were made of the penetrating power of Western bullets fired from the assassination rifle with other bullets. From the Mannlicher-Carcano rifle, the Western bullet was fired through two gelatin blocks totaling $72\frac{1}{2}$ centimeters in length. As evidenced by Commission Exhibit No. 844, which is a photograph from a high-speed motion picture, the Western bullets passed through $1\frac{1}{2}$ blocks in a straight line before their trajectory curved. After coming out of the second gelatin block, a number of the bullets buried themselves in a mound of earth.

Under similar circumstances, a bullet described as the NATO round M-80 was fired from a M-14 rifle. The penetrating power of the latter is depicted in Commission Exhibit No. 845 which shows that bullet possesses much less penetrating power with a quicker tumbling action. Those characteristics cause an early release of energy which brings the bullet to a stop at shorter distances. A further test was made with a 257 Winchester Roberts soft-nosed hunting bullet as depicted in Commission Exhibit No. 846. That bullet became deformed almost immediately upon entering the block of gelatin and released its energy very rapidly. From these tests, it was concluded that the Western bullet fired from the Mannlicher-Carcano had "terrific penetrating ability" and would retain substantial velocity after passing through objects such as the portions of the human body.

Tests Simulating President Kennedy's Neck Wound

After reviewing the autopsy report on President Kennedy, the Edgewood scientists simulated the portion of the President's neck through which the bullet passed. It was determined that the bullet traveled through $13\frac{1}{2}$ to $14\frac{1}{2}$ centimeters of tissue in the President's neck. That substance was simulated by constructing three blocks; one with a 20-percent gelatin composition, a second from one animal meat, and a third from another animal meat. Those substances duplicated as closely as possible the portion of the President's neck through which the bullet passed. At the time the tests were conducted, it was estimated that the President was struck at a range of approximately 180 feet, and the onsite tests which were conducted later at Dallas established that the President was shot through the neck at a range of 174.9 feet to

190.8 feet. At a range of 180 feet, the Western bullets were fired from the assassination weapon, which has a muzzle velocity of approximately 2,160 feet per second, through those substances which were placed beside a break-type screen for measuring velocity. The average entrance velocity at 180 feet was 1,904 feet per second.

To reconstruct the assassination situation as closely as possible both sides of the substances were covered with material and clipped animal skin to duplicate human skin. The average exit velocity was 1,779 feet from the gelatin, 1,798 feet from the first animal meat and 1,772 feet from the second animal meat. Commission Exhibit No. 847 depicts one of the animal meats compressed to $13^1/_2$ to $14^1/_2$ centimeters to approximate the President's neck and Commission Exhibit No. 848 shows the analogous arrangement for the gelatin. The photograph marked Commission Exhibit No. 849 shows the bullet passing through the gelatin in a straight line evidencing very stable characteristics.

Commission Exhibit No. 850 depicts the pieces of clipped animal skin placed on the points of entry and exit showing that the holes of entrance are round while the holes of exit are "a little more elongated." From these tests, it was concluded that the bullet lost little of its velocity in penetrating the President's neck so that there would have been substantial impact on the interior of the Presidential limousine or anyone else struck by the exiting bullet. In addition, these tests indicated that the bullet had retained most of its stability in penetrating the President's neck so that the exit hole would be only slightly different from the appearance of the entry hole.

Tests Simulating Governor Connally's Chest Wounds

To most closely approximate the Governor's chest injuries, the Edgewood scientists shot an animal with the assassination weapon using the Western bullets at a distance of 210 feet. The onsite tests later determined that the Governor was wounded at a distance of 176.9 feet to 190.8 feet from the sixth-floor window at the southeast corner of the Depository Building. The average striking velocity of 11 shots at 210 feet was 1,929 feet per second and the average exit velocity was 1,664 feet per second.

One of the shots produced an injury on the animal's rib very similar to that inflicted on Governor Connally. For purposes of comparison with the Governor's wound, the Edgewood scientists studied the Parkland Hospital report and X-rays, and they also discussed these wounds with Dr. Shaw, the Governor's chest surgeon. The similar animal injury passed along the animal's eighth left rib causing a fracture which removed a portion of the rib in a manner very similar to the wound sustained by the Governor. The X-ray of that wound on the animal is reproduced as Commission Exhibit No. 852. A comparison with the Governor's chest wound, shown in X-ray marked as Commission Exhibit No. 681, shows the remarkable similarity between those two wounds.

The bullet which produced the wound depicted in Commission Exhibits Nos. 851 and 852 was marked as Commission Exhibit No. 853 and possessed characteristics very similar to the bullet marked as Commission Exhibit No. 399 found on Governor Connally's stretcher and believed to have been the bullet which caused his chest wound. Those bullets, identified as Commission Exhibits Nos. 399 and 853, were flattened in similar fashion. In addition, the lead core was extruded from the rear in the same fashion on both bullets. One noticeable difference was that the bullet identified as Commission Exhibit No. 853, which penetrated the animal, was somewhat more flat than Commission Exhibit No. 399 which indicated that Commission Exhibit No. 853 was probably traveling at somewhat greater speed than the bullet which penetrated the Governor's chest. After the bullet passed through the animal, it left an imprint on the velocity screen immediately behind the animal which was almost the length of the bullet indicating that the bullet was traveling sideways or end over end. Taking into consideration the extra girth on the Governor, the reduction in the velocity of the bullet passing through his body was estimated at 400 feet. The conclusions from the animal shots are significant when taken in conjunction with the experiments performed simulating the injuries to the Governor's wrist.

Tests Simulating Governor Connally's Wrist Wounds

Following procedures identical to those employed in simulating the chest wound, the wound ballistics experts from Edgewood Arsenal reproduced, as closely as possible, the Governor's wrist wound. Again the scientists examined the reports and X-rays from Parkland Hospital and discussed the Governor's wrist wound with the attending orthopedic surgeon, Dr. Charles F. Gregory. Bone structures were then shot with Western bullets fired from the assassination weapon at a distance of 210 feet. The most similar bone-structure shot was analyzed in testimony before the Commission. An X-ray designated as Commission Exhibit No. 854 and a photograph of that X-ray which appears as Commission Exhibit No. 855 show a fracture at a location which is very similar to the Governor's wrist wound depicted in X-rays marked as Commission Exhibits Nos. 690 and 691.

The average striking velocity of the shots was 1,858 feet per second. The average exit velocity was 1,786 feet per second for the 7 out of 10 shots from bone structures which could be measured. These tests demonstrated that Governor Connally's wrist was not struck by a pristine bullet, which is a missile that strikes an object before hitting anything else. This conclusion was based on the following factors: (1) Greater damage was inflicted on the bone structure than that which was suffered by the Governor's wrist; and (2) the bone structure had a smaller entry wound and a larger exit wound which is characteristic of a pristine bullet as distinguished from the Governor's wrist which had a larger wound of entry indicating a bullet which was tumbling with substantial reduction in velocity. In addition, if the bullet found on the Governor's stretcher (Commission Exhibit No. 399) inflicted the wound on the Governor's wrist, then it could not have passed through the Governor's wrist had it been a pristine bullet, for the nose would have been considerably flattened, as was the bullet which struck the bone structure, identified as Commission Exhibit No. 856.

Conclusions From Simulating the Neck, Chest, and Wrist Wounds

Both Drs. Olivier and Dziemian expressed the opinion that one bullet caused all the wounds on Governor Connally. The wound to the Governor's wrist was explained by circumstances where the bullet passed through the Governor's chest, lost substantial velocity in doing so, tumbled through the wrist, and then slightly penetrated the

Governor's left thigh. Thus, the results of the wound ballistics tests support the conclusions of Governor Connally's doctors that all his wounds were caused by one bullet.

In addition, the wound ballistics tests indicated that it was most probable that the same bullet passed through the President's neck and then proceeded to inflict all the wounds on the Governor. That conclusion was reached by Drs. Olivier and Dziemian based on the medical evidence on the wounds of the President and the Governor and the tests they performed. It was their opinion that the wound on the Governor's wrist would have been more extensive had the bullet which inflicted that injury merely passed through the Governor's chest exiting at a velocity of approximately 1,500 feet per second. Thus, the Governor's wrist wound indicated that the bullet passed through the President's neck, began to yaw in the air between the President and the Governor, and then lost substantially more velocity than 400 feet per second in passing through the Governor's chest. A bullet which was yawing on entering into the Governor's back would lose substantially more velocity in passing through his body than a pristine bullet. In addition, the greater flattening of the bullet that struck the animal's rib (Commission Exhibit No. 853) than the bullet which presumably struck the Governor's rib (Commission Exhibit No. 399) indicates that the animal bullet was traveling at a greater velocity. That suggests that the bullet which entered the Governor's chest had already lost velocity by passing through the President's neck. Moreover, the large wound on the Governor's back would be explained by a bullet which was yawing although that type of wound might also be accounted for by a tangential striking.

Dr. Frederick W. Light, Jr., the third of the wound ballistics experts, testified that the anatomical findings alone were insufficient for him to formulate a firm opinion on whether the same bullet did or did not pass through the President's neck first before inflicting all the wounds on Governor Connally. Based on the other circumstances, such as the relative positions in the automobile of the President and the Governor, Dr. Light concluded that it was probable that the same bullet traversed the President's neck and inflicted all the wounds on Governor Connally.

Tests Simulating President Kennedy's Head Wounds

Additional tests were performed on inert skulls filled with a 20 percent gelatin substance and then coated with additional gelatin to approximate the soft tissues overlying the skull. The skull was then draped with simulated hair as depicted in Commission Exhibit No. 860. Using the Mannlicher-Carcano rifle and the Western bullets, 10 shots were fired at the reconstructed skulls from a distance of 270 feet which was the estimated distance at the time those tests were conducted. It was later determined through the onsite tests that President Kennedy was struck in the back of the head at a distance of 265.3 feet from the assassination weapon.

The general results of these tests were illustrated by the findings on one skull which was struck at a point most nearly approximating the wound of entry on President Kennedy's head. The whole skull, depicted in Commission Exhibit No. 860, was struck 2.9 centimeters to the right and almost horizontal to the occipital protuberance or slightly above it, which was virtually the precise point of entry on the President's head as described by the autopsy surgeons. That bullet blew out the right side of the reconstructed skull in a manner very similar to the head wounds of the President. The consequences on that skull are depicted in Commission Exhibits Nos. 861 and 862, which illustrate the testimony of Dr. Alfred G. Olivier, who supervised the experiments. Based on his review of the autopsy report, Dr. Olivier concluded that the damage to the reconstructed skull was very similar to the wound inflicted on the President.

Two fragments from the bullet which struck the test skull closely resembled the two fragments found in the front seat of the Presidential limousine. The fragment designated as Commission Exhibit No. 567 is a mutilated piece of copper recovered from the bullet which struck the skull depicted in Commission Exhibit No. 860. The other fragment, designated as Commission Exhibit No. 569 which was found in the front seat of the Presidential limousine, is the copper end of the bullet. Commission Exhibit No. 569 is very similar to a copper fragment of the end of the bullet which struck the test skull. The fragments from the test bullet are designated as Commission Exhibit No. 857 and are depicted in a photograph identified as Commission Exhibit 858. A group of small lead particles, recovered from the test bullet, are also very similar to the particles recovered under the left jump seat and in the President's head. The particles from the test bullet are a part of Commission Exhibit 857 and are depicted as Commission Exhibit No. 859. That skull was depicted as Commission Exhibit No. 862.

As a result of these tests, Dr. Olivier concluded that the Western bullet fired from the Mannlicher-Carcano rifle at a distance of 270 feet would make the same type of wound found on the President's head. Prior to the tests, Dr. Olivier had some doubt that such a stable bullet would cause a massive head wound like that inflicted on the President. He had thought it more likely that such a striking bullet would make small entrance and exit holes. The tests, however, showed that the bones of the skull were sufficient to deform the end of the bullet causing it to expend a great deal of energy and thereby blow out the side of the skull. These tests further confirmed the autopsy surgeons' opinions that the President's head wound was not caused by a dumdum bullet. Because of the test results, Dr. Olivier concluded that the fragments found on and under the front seat of the President's car most probably came from the bullet which struck the President's head. It was further concluded that the damage done to Governor Connally's wrist could not have resulted from a fragment from the bullet which struck President Kennedy's head.

The thoroughness of our inquiry is shown in the tests to simulate the tissue in the President's neck. When we were advised that there were three alternatives to simulate these neck tissues—a 20% gelatin composition, goat meat and horse meat—we directed that instead of using only one of these three alternatives, the wound ballistics experts would use all three so that we would have the most complete factual basis upon which to reach our conclusions.

Now that you have read the summary of these tests from our Warren Commission Report, let us turn to the testimony of the three experts who conducted the wound ballistics experiments.

If you desire to skim the testimony of the first witness, Dr. Olivier, you will find his basic conclusions included in the testimony of Dr. Dziemian beginning at page 374.

Dr. Alfred G. Olivier, Chief of the Wound Ballistics Branch at Edgewood

Arsenal, was certain that the wound to Governor Connally's wrist was not caused by a pristine bullet, i.e., a bullet that had not struck something else first. Test bullets were fired at bone structures similar to Governor Connally's wrist. The bullet that was the shot most similar to the point where Governor Connally's wrist was struck was introduced into the record and then compared with Exhibit 399, the nearly whole bullet found at Parkland Memorial Hospital.

Mr. Specter. Would you describe that bullet for the record, please?

Dr. Olivier: The nose of the bullet is quite flattened from striking the radius.

Mr. Specter. How does it compare, for example, with Commission Exhibit 399?

Dr. Olivier. It is not like it at all. I mean, Commission Exhibit 399 is not flattened on the end. This one is very severely flattened on the end.

Dr. Olivier then turned to the wounds on Governor Connally's wrist:

Mr. Specter. In your opinion, based on the tests which you have performed, was the damage inflicted on Governor Connally's wrist caused by a pristine bullet, a bullet fired from the Mannlicher-Carcano rifle 6.5 missile which did not hit anything before it struck the Governor's wrist?

Dr. Olivier. I don't believe so. I don't believe his wrist was struck by a pristine bullet.

Mr. Specter. What is the reason for your conclusion on that?

Dr. Olivier. In this case I go by the size of the entrance wound and exit wound on the Governor's wrist. The entrance wound was on the dorsal surface, it was described by the surgeon as being much larger than the exit wound. He said he almost overlooked that on the volar aspect of the wrist.

In every instance we had a larger exit wound than an entrance wound firing with a pristine bullet apparently at the same angle at which it entered and exited the Governor's wrist.

Also, and I don't believe they were mixed up on which was entrance and exit. For one thing the clothing, you know, the surgeon found pieces of clothing and the other thing, the human anatomy is such that I don't believe it would enter through the volar aspect and out the top.

So, I am pretty sure that the Governor's wrist was not hit by a pristine or a stable bullet.

Dr. Olivier testified that even if the velocity of the missile was decreased, the exit wound would still be larger than the entrance wound on the wrist "if the bullet is still stable."

. . . Now, on the other hand, to get a larger entrance wound and a smaller exit wound, this indicates the bullet probably hit with very much of a yaw. I mean, as this hole appeared in the velocity screen the bullet either tumbling or striking sideways, this would have made a larger entrance wound, lose considerable of its velocity in fracturing the bone, and coming out at a very low velocity, made a smaller hole.

Mr. Specter. So the crucial factor would be the analysis that the bullet was characterized with yaw at the time it struck?

Dr. Olivier. Yes.

Mr. Specter. Causing a larger wound of entry and a smaller wound of exit?

Dr. Olivier. Yes.

Mr. Specter. Now is there anything in the—

Dr. Olivier. Also at a reduced velocity because if it struck at considerable yaw at a high velocity as it could do if it hit something and deflected, it would have, it could make a larger wound of exit but it would have been even a more severe wound than we had here. It would have been very severe, could even amputate the wrist hitting at high velocity sideways. We have to say this bullet was characterized by an extreme amount of yaw and reduced velocity. How much reduced, I don't know, but considerably reduced.

Mr. Specter. So then the lesser damage on the Governor's wrist in and of itself indicates in your opinion—

Dr. Olivier. That it wasn't struck by a pristine bullet; yes.

Mr. Specter. Are there any other conclusions which flow from the experiments which you conducted on the wrist?

Dr. Olivier. We concluded that it wasn't struck by a pristine bullet. Also drew the conclusion that it was struck by an unstable bullet, a bullet at a much reduced velocity. The question that it brings up in my mind is if the same bullet that struck the wrist had passed through the Governor's chest, if the bullet that struck the Governor's chest had not hit anything else would it have been reduced low enough to do this, and I wonder, based on our work—it brings to mind the possibility the same bullet that struck the President striking the Governor would account for this more readily. I don't know, I don't think you can ever say this, but it is a very good possibility, I think more possible, more probable than not.

Chairman. What is more probable than not, Doctor?

Dr. Olivier. In my mind at least, and I don't know the angles at which the things went or anything, it seems to me more probable that the bullet that hit the Governor's chest had already been slowed down somewhat, in order to lose enough velocity to strike his wrist and do no more damage than it did. I don't know how you would ever determine it exactly. I think the best approach is to find out the angles of flight, whether it is possible. But I have a feeling that it might have been.

Chairman. The one that went through his chest went through his hand also?

Dr. Olivier. Yes; and also through the President.

Chairman. The first shot?

Dr. Olivier. Well, I don't know whether the first or second. The first one could have missed. It could have been the second that hit both.

Chairman. The one that went through his back and came out his trachea?

Dr. Olivier. It could have hit the Governor in the chest and went through because it had so little velocity after coming out of the wrist that it barely penetrated the thigh.

Chairman. May I ask one more question? Would you think that the same bullet could have done all three of those things?

Dr. Olivier. That same bullet was capable.

Chairman. Gone through the President's back as it did, gone through Governor Connally's chest as it did, and then through his hand as it did?

Dr. Olivier. It was certainly capable of doing all that.

Chairman. It was capable?

Dr. Olivier. Yes.

Chairman. The one shot?

Dr. Olivier. Yes.

Dr. Olivier then turned to the wound on Governor Connally's back. He testified that the relatively large size of the wound was indicative of the fact that either the bullet struck Governor Connally's back tangentially at a slight angle or that it was not perpendicular to the surface as it hit.

Then, Dr. Olivier returned to the wrist wound of Governor Connally and testified concerning conclusions that arose from the amount of the damage done to the wrist. It was his opinion that not only was it probable that the bullet went through Governor Connally's chest before striking Governor Connally's wrist, but also that it was more probable the bullet passed through President Kennedy's neck first before striking Governor Connally:

Mr. Specter. Would the damage done to the Governor's wrist indicate that a bullet which was fired approximately 160 to 250 feet away with the muzzle velocity of approximately 2,000 feet per second, would it indicate that the bullet was slowed up only by the passage through the Governor's body, in the way which you know, or would it indicate that there was some other factor which slowed up the bullet in addition?

Dr. Olivier. It would indicate there was some other factor that had slowed up the bullet in addition.

Mr. Specter. What is your reason for that conclusion, sir?

Dr. Olivier. The amount of damage alone; striking that end it would have caused more severe comminution as we found. You know—if it hadn't been slowed up in some other fashion. At that range it still had a striking velocity of 1,858 or in the vicinity of 1,800 feet per second, which is capable of doing more damage than was done to the Governor's wrist.

Mr. Specter. Had the same bullet which passed through the President, in the way heretofore described for the record, then struck the Governor as well, what effect would there have been in reducing its velocity as a result of that course?

Dr. Olivier. You say the bullet first struck the President. In coming out of the President's body it would have had a tendency to be slightly unstable. In striking the Governor it would have lost more velocity in his chest than if it had been a pristine bullet striking the Governor's chest, so it would have exited from the Governor's chest I would say at a considerably reduced velocity, probably with a good amount of yaw or tumbling, and this would account for the type of wound that the Governor did have in his wrist.

Mr. Specter. Had the bullet passed through only the Governor, losing velocity of 400 feet per second, would you have expected that the damage inflicted on the Governor's wrist would have been about the same as that inflicted on Governor Connally or greater?

Dr. Olivier. My feeling is it would have been greater.

Mr. Specter. Had the bullet passed through the President and then struck Governor Connally, would it have lost velocity of 400 feet per second in passing through Governor Connally or more?

Dr. Olivier. It would have lost more.

Mr. Specter. What is the reason for that?

Dr. Olivier. The bullet after passing through, say a dense medium, then through air and then through another dense medium tends to be more unstable, based on our past work. It appears to be that it would have tumbled more readily and lost energy more rapidly. How much velocity it would have lost, I couldn't say, but it would have lost more.

Mr. Specter. Are there any indications from the internal wounds on Governor

Connally as to whether or not the bullet which entered his body was an unstable bullet?

Dr. Olivier. The only thing that might give you an indication would be the skin wound of entrance, the type of rib fracture and all that I think could be accounted for by either type, because in our experiment we simulated, although not to as great a degree, the damage wasn't as severe, but I think it would be hard to say that.

One thing comes to my mind right now that might indicate it. There was a greater flattening of the bullet in our experiments than there was going through the Governor, which might indicate that it struck the rib which did the flattening at a lower velocity. This is only a thought.

Mr. Specter. It struck the rib of the Governor?

Dr. Olivier. It struck the rib of the Governor at a lower velocity because that bullet was less flattened than the bullet through the goat material.

Mr. Specter. Based on the nature of the wound inflicted on the Governor's wrist, and on the tests which you have conducted then, do you have an opinion as to which is more probable on whether the bullet passed through only the Governor's chest before striking his wrist, or passed through the President first and then the Governor's chest before striking the Governor's wrist?

Dr. Olivier. You couldn't say exactly at all. My feeling is that it would be more probable that it passed through the President first. At least I think it is important to establish line of flight to try to determine it.

Mr. Specter. Aside from the lines of flight, based on the factors which were known to you from the medical point of view and from the tests which you conducted, what would be the reason for the feeling which you just expressed?

Dr. Olivier. Because I believe you would need that, I mean to account for the damage to the wrist. I don't think you would have gotten a low enough velocity upon reaching the wrist unless you had gone through the President's body first.

Mr. Specter. The President's body as well as the Governor's body?

Dr. Olivier. As well as the Governor's.

Mr. Specter. Does the nature of the wound which was inflicted on Governor Connally's thigh shed any light on this subject?

Dr. Olivier. This, to my mind, at least, merely indicates the bullet at this time was about spent. In talking with Doctor, I believe it was Gregory, I don't think he did the operation on the thigh but at least he saw the wound, and he said it was about the size of an eraser on a lead pencil. This could be accounted for—and there was also this small fragment of bullet in this thigh wound—this, to me, indicates that this was a spent bullet that had gone through the wrist as the Governor was sitting there, went through the wrist into his thigh, just partly imbedded and then fell out and I believe this was the bullet that was found on the stretcher.

Dr. Olivier then turned to the experiments that were conducted to simulate the wounds to President Kennedy's head.

Mr. Specter. Dr. Olivier, in the regular course of your work for the U. S. Army, do you have occasion to perform tests on reconstructed human skulls to determine the effects of bullets on skulls?

Dr. Olivier. Yes; I do.

Mr. Specter. And did you have occasion to conduct such a test in connection with the series which you are now describing?

Dr. Olivier. Yes; I did.

Mr. Specter. And would you outline briefly the procedures for simulating the human skull?

Dr. Olivier. Human skulls, we take these human skulls and they are imbedded and filled with 20 percent gelatin. As I mentioned before, 20 percent gelatin is a pretty good simulant for body tissues.

They are in the moisture content. When I say 20 percent, it is 20 percent weight of the dry gelatin, 80 percent moisture.

The skull, the cranial cavity, is filled with this and the surface is coated with a gelatin and then it is trimmed down to approximate the thickness of the tissues overlying the skull, the soft tissues of the head.

Mr. Specter. And at what distance were these tests performed?

Dr. Olivier. These tests were performed at a distance of 90 yards.

Mr. Specter. And what gun was used?

Dr. Olivier. It was a 6.5 Mannlicher-Carcano that was marked Commission Exhibit 139.

Mr. Specter. What bullets were used?

Dr. Olivier. It was the 6.5 millimeter Mannlicher-Carcano Western ammunition lot 6,000.

Mr. Specter. What did that examination, or test rather, disclose?

Dr. Olivier. It disclosed that the type of head wounds that the President received could be done by this type of bullet. This surprised me very much, because this type of a stable bullet I didn't think would cause a massive head wound; I thought it would go through making a small entrance and exit, but the bones of the skull are enough to deform the end of this bullet causing it to expend a lot of energy and blowing out the side of the skull or blowing out fragments of the skull.

Mr. Specter. I now hand you a case containing bullet fragments marked Commission Exhibit 857 and ask if you have ever seen those fragments before.

Dr. Olivier. Yes, I have.

Mr. Specter. And under what circumstances have you viewed those before, please?

Dr. Olivier. There were, the two larger fragments were recovered outside of the skull in the cotton waste we were using to catch the fragments without deforming them. There are some smaller fragments in here that were obtained from the gelatin within the cranial cavity after the experiment. We melted the gelatin out and recovered the smallest fragments from within the cranial cavity.

Mr. Specter. Now, I show you two fragments designated as Commission Exhibits 567 and 579 heretofore identified as having been found on the front seat of the President's car on Nov. 22, 1963, and ask you if you have had an opportunity to examine those before.

Dr. Olivier. Yes, I have.

Mr. Specter. And have you had an opportunity to compare those to the two fragments identified as Commission Exhibit 857?

Dr. Olivier. Yes, I have.

Mr. Specter. And what did that comparison show?

Dr. Olivier. They are quite similar. These two fragments on, what is the number?

Mr. Specter. 857.

Dr. Olivier. On 857 there isn't as much of the front part in this one, but in other respects they are very similar.

Dr. Arthur J. Dziemian, Chief of the Biophysics Division at Edgewood

Arsenal, was present throughout the testimony of Dr. Olivier and concurred in Dr. Olivier's conclusions.

Now, based on the tests which have been performed and the other factors which I will ask you to assume, since you weren't present, for purposes of expressing an opinion, what is your opinion as to whether all of the wounds on Governor Connally were inflicted by one bullet?

Dr. Dziemian. My opinion is that it is most probably so, that one bullet produced all the wounds on Governor Connally.

Mr. Specter. And what is your opinion as to whether the wound through President Kennedy's neck and all of the wounds on Governor Connally were produced by one bullet?

Dr. Dziemian. I think the probability is very good that it is, that all the wounds were caused by one bullet.

Mr. Specter. When you say all the wounds, are you excluding from that the head wound on President Kennedy?

Dr. Dziemian. I am excluding the head wound, yes.

Mr. Specter. And what is the reasoning behind your conclusion that one bullet caused the neck wound on President Kennedy and all of the other wounds on Governor Connally?

Dr. Dziemian. I am saying that the probability is high that that was so.

Mr. Specter. What is the reason for your assessment of that high probability?

Dr. Dziemian. The same reasons that Dr. Olivier gave, based on the same information, that especially the wound to the wrist. That higher velocity strike on the wrist would be caused by the bullet slowing down by going through all this tissue would cause more damage to the wrist and also more damage to the thigh.

Mr. Specter. Had the bullet only gone through Governor Connally's chest then, what is your opinion as to whether or not there would have been greater damage to the Governor's wrist?

Dr. Dziemian. I think there would have been greater damage to the Governor's wrist, and also to the thigh from the information, from the experiments obtained by Dr. Olivier's group.

Mr. Dulles. Could I ask a question here? Does that take into account any evidence as to the angle of fire and the relative positions of the two men, or excluding that?

Dr. Dziemian. Excluding that. I do not know enough details about that to make an opinion on that. This is just on the basis of the velocities of the bullets.

Mr. Specter. Would the nature of the wounds on the Governor's wrist and thigh, then, be explained by the hypothesis that the bullet passed through the President first, then went through the Governor's chest before striking the wrist and in turn the thigh?

Dr. Dziemian. I think that could be a good explanation.

Mr. Specter. What is your opinion as to whether or not a fragment of a bullet striking the President's head could have caused the wound to Governor Connally's wrist?

Mr. Dziemian. I think it is unlikely.

Mr. Specter. What is your opinion as to whether or not Governor Connally's wrist wound could have been caused by a pristine bullet?

Dr. Dziemian. That is unlikely, too. Our results with pristine bullets were very different from the wound that the Governor had.

Mr. Specter. Based on the description provided to you of the nature of the wound in the Governor's back, what is your opinion as to whether, or not, that was a pristine bullet or had yaw in it, just on the basis of the nature of the wound on the Governor's back?

Dr. Dziemian. It could very well have yaw in it because of the rather large wound that was produced in the Governor's back. The wound from a nonyawing bullet could be considerably smaller.

Mr. Specter. For the record, would you define in lay terms what yaw means?

Dr. Dziemian. It is the procession of the bullet. The bullet is wobbling on its axis, so that as it wobbles, it presents different presented areas to the target or to the air, and this changes the drag coefficient of the bullet. It will slow down the bullet more both in the air and in tissues, in the yawing.

Mr. Specter. What is the course of a bullet, then, which is a pristine bullet or the nature of the bullet immediately after coming out of the muzzle of a rifle before it strikes anything?

Dr. Dziemian. A pristine bullet is normally stable. It does not wobble in the air. It presents the same presented area along most of its trajectory until it slows down, so that the drag coefficient in air or in the tissue of this type of bullet is less than the drag coefficient—

Mr. Specter. What do you mean by drag coefficient?

Dr. Dziemian. It is a measurement of the resistance of the target material or the air to the bullet. The greater the drag coefficient, the more the resistance to the bullet, the more the bullet slows down within a given time.

Mr. Specter. So would a bullet with yaw cause a greater or lesser hole on the surface which it strikes than a bullet without yaw?

Dr. Dziemian. It would normally cause a greater hole. It usually would have more presented area, that is, more of the surface of the bullet would hit the skin.

Mr. Specter. And would a bullet with yaw decrease in velocity to a greater, lesser, or the same extent as a bullet without yaw?

Dr. Dziemian. It would decrease in velocity to a greater extent.

Mr. Specter. Whether it passed through air or—

Dr. Dziemian. Or through tissue, and the important thing in tissue is that it transfers more energy to the target than would a nonyawing bullet.

Mr. Specter. Dr. Dziemian, Governor Connally testified that he experienced the sensation of a striking blow on his back which he described as being similar to a hard punch received from a doubled-up fist. Do you have an opinion as to whether that sensation would necessarily occur immediately upon impact of a wound such as that received by Governor Connally, or could there be a delayed reaction in sensing that feeling?

Dr. Dziemian. I don't have too much of an opinion on that. All I can say is that some people are struck by bullets and do not even know they are hit. This happens in wartime. But I don't know about that.

Mr. Specter. So that it is possible in some situations there is some delay in reaction?

Dr. Dziemian. I couldn't say.

Mr. Specter. Is it a highly individual matter as to the reaction of an individual on that subject?

Dr. Dziemian. I don't know.

Mr. Dulles. But take a wound like the wrist wound of Governor Connally. He couldn't get that without knowing it, could he?

Dr. Dziemian. I think he said that he didn't know he had a wrist wound until much later.

On the other hand, the testimony of Dr. Frederick W. Light Jr. was somewhat different.

Mr. Specter. Focusing on a few of the specific considerations, do you believe that there would have been the same amount of damage done to the Governor's wrist had the pristine bullet only passed through the Governor's body without striking the President first?

Dr. Light. I think that is possible; yes. It won't happen the same way twice in any case, so you have got a fairly wide range of things that can happen if a person is shot in more or less this way.

Mr. Specter. Do you think it is as likely that the damage would have been inflicted on the Governor's wrist as it was, with the bullet passing only through the Governor's chest as opposed to passing through the President's neck and the Governor's chest?

Dr. Light. I think the difference in likelihood is negligible on that basis alone.

Mr. Specter. So the damage on the Governor's wrist would be equally consistent—

Dr. Light. Equally consistent; yes.

Mr. Specter. With (A) passing only through the Governor's chest, or (B) passing through the President's neck and the Governor's chest?

Dr. Light. Yes.

Mr. Specter. Now, as to the damage on the thigh, would the nature of that wound again be equally consistent with either going through (A) the President's neck, the Governor's chest, the Governor's wrist, and then into the thigh, or (B) only through the Governor's chest, the Governor's wrist and into the thigh?

Dr. Light. I'd say equally consistent; yes.

Mr. Specter. And based on the descriptions which have been provided to you about the nature of the wound on the Governor's back, do you have an opinion as to whether the bullet was yawing or not at the time it struck the Governor's back?

Dr. Light. No; I don't. That is really one of the points—

Mr. Specter. It would be either way?

Dr. Light. Yes; I don't feel too certain that it was yawing. The measurements were not particularly precise as far as I could tell. You wouldn't expect them to be in an operating room. So I think it is difficult to be sure there that the missile wasn't presenting nose on. It undoubtedly struck not at normal instance, that is to say it was a certain obliquity, just in the nature of the way the shoulder is built.

Mr. Specter. Then do you think based on only the anatomical findings and the results of the tests which Dr. Olivier has performed that the scales are in equipoise as to whether the bullet passed through the President first and then through the Governor or passed only through the Governor?

Dr. Light. Yes; I would say I don't feel justified in drawing a conclusion one way or the other on that basis alone.

Mr. Specter. Do you have any preference of any sort?

Dr. Light. Yes; I do, for other reasons.

Mr. Specter. But only for the other reasons?

Dr. Light. As I mentioned, their positions in the automobile, the fact that if it wasn't the way—if one bullet didn't produce all of the wounds in both of the individuals, then that bullet ought to be somewhere, and hasn't been found. But those are not based on Dr. Olivier's tests nor are they based on the autopsy report or the surgeon's findings in my mind.

Dr. Light said that it was "barely conceivable" that the wounds on Governor Connally's wrist could have been caused by a fragment which first struck the President's head. ". . . it couldn't have produced that wound, in my mind, but it can't be ruled out with complete certainty."

The consistency in the testimony of all of the three physicians who treated Governor Connally and the three experts who conducted the wound ballistics experiments was that all of the wounds to Governor Connally were caused by one bullet.

If anyone is to argue that the nearly whole bullet found at Parkland Memorial Hospital, Exhibit 399, could not have caused the wounds to both President Kennedy's neck as well as to Governor Connally, he has to argue at the same time that Exhibit 399 could not have caused all of the wounds to Governor Connally, because the same arguments are equally applicable to both: the question of the amount of flattening of the bullet and the question of the amount of grains of fragments left in Governor Connally's wrist. Yet, we know that Governor Connally's wrist wound was not caused by a pristine bullet.

Could it have been caused by a bullet fragment from the bullet which struck the President's head? One witness, Dr. Light, thought that this was "barely conceivable but I do not believe that that is the case."

I did not believe that was the case because in addition to the testimony of Dr. Light, large bullet fragments were found imbedded in the front seat of the Presidential limousine, and they could not have gotten there after striking Governor Connally's wrist in the position of the wrist at the time the fatal shots were fired, frame 313. Governor Connally's wrist is below the top of the front seat of the Presidential limousine. Furthermore, threads of clothing were found in the wound, indicating the bullet passed through Governor Connally's chest and clothing before it hit his wrist.

Let us look at the alternate possibility that there was another bullet. In the first place, that bullet has never been found. In the second place, that bullet could not have struck Governor Connally's wrist without first striking something else. In the third place, what happened to the bullet that went through President Kennedy's neck if it did not hit Governor Connally, who was sitting directly in front of him? In the fourth place, if the bullet found at Parkland Memorial Hospital did not come from Governor Connally, how could it have been so flattened by striking President Kennedy when no bones were struck by the first shot? And finally, if the wound in the front of President Kennedy's neck was an entrance wound, instead of an exit wound, why were the fibers of his shirt pointed outward, instead of inward, and moreover, where is that bullet, since there was no exit point and the X-rays disclosed no bullets inside President Kennedy's body?

Anyone who seeks to challenge the single-bullet theory has to come up with a plausible alternative. And this plausible alternative must include the answer to all these questions.

The simple fact is that nowhere has there been any other theory advanced that is consistent with the physical evidence and that answers these questions.

The single-bullet theory—that the bullet that went through President Kennedy then struck Governor Connally—is the only possibility consistent with all the facts, including the ballistic examination of the bullet, Exhibit 399, the rifle found in the TSBD Building, the trajectory and the relative positions of President Kennedy and Governor Connally, the testimony of Governor Connally's physicians who unanimously agreed that Governor Connally was struck by a single bullet, the lack of substantial damage to the Presidential limousine from a bullet that might have exited from President Kennedy's neck, the wound ballistics experiments at Edgewood, the clothing worn by President Kennedy that showed on the back fibers pointed inward and on the front fibers pointed outward, the autopsy showing that he was struck from behind, the cartridge cases found on the sixth floor of the TSBD Building, and the fact that the only witnesses who saw a rifle at the time of the assassination saw this rifle in the upper portion of the southeast corner of the TSBD Building. There was simply no other way for it to have happened, based on the overwhelming weight of the evidence.

There is another matter that is relevant. It concerns the degree of difficulty of the shots and the marksmanship tests that were conducted by the Commission. Following our determination that the bullet that struck President Kennedy in the back of his neck exited through the front of his neck and then struck Governor Connally, we had to come to a determination as to which of the three shots had missed.

Just as there were contradictions between the testimony of witnesses concerning whether President Kennedy said anything after he was first shot, there were also contradictions concerning which of the three shots missed. We summarized the possibilities on pages 111-117 of our Report:

Some support for the contention that the first shot missed is found in the statement of Secret Service Agent Glen A. Bennett, stationed in the right rear seat of the President's followup car, who heard a sound like a firecracker as the motorcade proceeded down Elm Street. At that moment, Agent Bennett stated:

. . . I looked at the back of the President. I heard another firecracker noise and saw that shot hit the President about four inches down from the right shoulder. A second shot followed immediately and hit the right rear high of the President's head.

On the other hand, Secret Service agent Clinton J. Hill, who was on the left front running board of the President's follow-up car, immediately behind the Presidential limousine, thought that the first shot hit the President and a second shot hit the President's head. Here is how we summarized his testimony on pages 50-51 of our Report:

From the left front running board of the President's followup car, Special Agent Hill was scanning the few people standing on the south side of Elm Street after the motorcade had turned off Houston Street. He estimated that the motorcade had slowed down to approximately 9 or 10 miles per hour on the turn at the intersection of Houston and Elm Streets and then proceeded at a rate of 12 to 15 miles per hour with the followup car trailing the President's automobile by approximately 5 feet. Hill heard a noise, which seemed to be a firecracker, coming from his right rear. He immediately looked to his right, "and, in so doing, my eyes had to cross the Presidential limousine and I saw President Kennedy grab at himself and lurch forward and to the left." Hill jumped from the followup car and ran to the President's automobile. At about the time he reached the President's automobile, Hill heard a second shot, approximately 5 seconds after the first, which removed a portion of the President's head.

At the instant that Hill stepped onto the left rear step of the President's automobile and grasped the handhold, the car lurched forward, causing him to lose his footing. He ran three or four steps, regained his position and mounted the car. Between the time he originally seized the handhold and the time he mounted the car, Hill recalled that—

Mrs. Kennedy had jumped up from the seat and was, it appeared to me, reaching for something coming off the right rear bumper of the car, the right rear tail, when she noticed that I was trying to climb on the car. She turned toward me and I grabbed her and put her back in the back seat, crawled up on top of the back seat and lay there.

(There was much speculation as to whether Mrs. Kennedy was trying to get out of the seat that was the target of the rifle fire or whether she was trying to help Secret Service Agent Hill jump into the limousine. After examining the pictures and discussing the matter with Clint Hill, there was little doubt in my mind that Mrs. Kennedy was trying to get out of the limousine—a perfectly natural instinct under all the circumstances.)

My own analysis of all of the evidence led me to the conclusion that it was the last shot that missed. However, there were eyewitnesses near the scene who testified that it was the last shot that struck President Kennedy in the head. Here is how we summarized the evidence at pages 115-116 of our Report:

The last possibility, of course, is that it was the third shot which missed. This conclusion conforms most easily with the probability that the assassin would most likely have missed the farthest shot, particularly since there was an acceleration of the automobile after the shot which struck the President's head. The limousine also changed direction by following the curve to the right, whereas previously it had been proceeding in almost a straight line with a rifle protruding from the sixth-floor window of the Depository Building.

One must consider, however, the testimony of the witnesses who described the head shot as the concluding event in the assassination sequence. Illustrative is the testimony of Associated Press photographer Altgens, who had an excellent vantage point near the President's car. He recalled that the shot which hit the President's head "was the last shot—that much I will say with a great degree of certainty." On the other hand, Emmett J. Hudson, the grounds-keeper of Dealey Plaza, testified that from his position on Elm Street, midway between Houston Street and the Triple Underpass, he heard a third shot after the shot which hit the President in the head. In addition, Mrs. Kennedy's testimony indicated that neither the first nor the second shot missed. Immediately after the first noise she turned, because of the Governor's yell, and saw her husband raise his hand to his forehead. Then the second shot struck the President's head.

Some evidence suggested that a third shot may have entirely missed and hit the turf or street by the Triple Underpass. Royce G. Skelton, who watched the motorcade from the railroad bridge, testified that after two shots "the car came on down close to the Triple Underpass" and an additional shot "hit in the left front of the President's car on the cement." Skelton thought that there had been a total of four shots, either the third or fourth of which hit in the vicinity of the underpass. Dallas Patrolman J. W. Foster, who was also on the Triple Underpass, testified that a shot hit the turf near a manhole cover in the vicinity of the underpass. Examination of this area, however, disclosed no indication that a bullet struck at the locations indicated by Skelton or Foster.

The conflict between the testimony of Associated Press photographer Altgens, who testified that it was the last shot that hit the President's head, and that of Secret Service Agent Clint Hill, who testified that it was the second shot that hit the President's head, is typical of the conflicts in testimony that permeated our investigation.

Unfortunately, the marksmanship tests were conducted before we had developed the single-bullet theory. These tests were based on the assumption, supported by both the FBI and the Secret Service, that the first shot struck President Kennedy, the second shot hit Governor Connally, and the third shot struck President Kennedy and that the three were fired within approximately five and one-half seconds. But if the first shot struck President Kennedy's neck and then struck Governor Connally, and the second shot was at frame 313 and struck President Kennedy's head, this meant that approximately five seconds or more elapsed between the first and the second shots, and we never conducted any tests based on this theory. Moreover, although Oswald had been a marksman in the Marine Corps, the people that we used to conduct the test were far more proficient shooters, even though they had not had any previous experience with the weapon they fired.

As you can imagine, there was a great deal of argument about this matter among the lawyers on the staff. I wanted an actual test performed with moving vehicles and with people who were not outstanding marksmen. The argument against this was that we did not have to show that it was probable that these shots could have been made in the theoretical time span—all we had to show was that it was "possible," since if Oswald were to do it over again, perhaps he would have missed. This argument asserted that Oswald might have missed three of four times, but that nevertheless if it were possible for him to hit once in four times, this is all we had to show.

I agreed that perhaps all we had to show was that it was "possible," but I thought that we had an obligation to have the test performed in the manner most consistent with what we thought to be the facts. This would have required a moving target, riflemen perched at an elevation similar to the height of the southeast corner window of the sixth floor of the TSBD

Building, riflemen familiarizing themselves with the assassination weapon, and finally one test with five seconds of elapsed time between the first and the second shots, since that was a definite possibility.

That we did not do this I thought was a mistake, although not of crucial importance for four reasons: (1) We did demonstrate that it was "possible" to make this shot. According to FBI expert Frazier, Oswald's rifle was accurate. Without much practice, FBI experts were able to hit two out of three targets within a timespan of 4.6 to 8.0 seconds. (2) No one knows where Oswald was aiming when the shots were fired. The shot that struck the President in the lower portion of the neck might have been aimed at the President's head. Or, the shot that struck President Kennedy in the head could have been aimed at President Kennedy's back. (3) Oswald had undergone Marine Corps training and was a marksman. (4) The shot from the TSBD Building was a line shot with the rifle pointed in the same direction as Elm Street as it headed toward the triple underpass. As cars moved down Elm Street the angle of the rifle had to be moved only slightly from the place where the first shot struck the President to the place where the fatal shot struck the President.

Since my discharge from the United States Army in 1947, I had not fired a rifle. However, my conclusion as I sat in the southeast corner window of the sixth floor of the TSBD Building was that the shot was not a particularly difficult one under all the circumstances. You might disagree. Yet, I think that neither of us can disagree that even if the shot was difficult, it was still possible to make the shot. Regardless of the ease or difficulty of making such a shot, the physical facts were clear:

1. A rifle was found on the sixth floor of the TSBD Building near the stairway in the northwest corner.

2. Three cartridge cases were found on the floor near the southeast corner of the sixth floor of the TSBD Building. Ballistic evidence showed that these cartridge cases were fired by that rifle to the exclusion of all other weapons in the world.

3. Two large bullet fragments found in the front seat of the Presidential limousine were of sufficient size to be ballistically identifiable; those fragments came from the same rifle, to the exclusion of all other weapons in the world.

4. A nearly whole bullet rolled off a stretcher that had been used in Parkland Memorial Hospital to take Governor Connally to the operating room. That bullet was also fired from that same rifle to the exclusion of all other weapons in the world.

5. The only persons who saw a rifle at the time of the assassination saw that rifle in the southeast corner of the sixth floor of the TSBD Building. These witnesses include Howard Brennan, who saw the gunman aim and fire the last shot; Robert Jackson and Malcolm Couch, who were riding in the rear of the motorcade, and Amos Euins.

6. Harold Norman, who was watching the motorcade from the window

directly below the assassination window, heard cartridge cases hitting the floor and also heard the bolt action of the rifle. His testimony is confirmed by the testimony of two fellow employees who were watching the motorcade on the fifth floor in nearby windows: Bonnie Ray Williams and James Jarman Jr.

7. The clothing of President Kennedy showed that on the back of his jacket the fibers were pointed inward and on the front of his shirt the fibers were pointed outward.

8. The Presidential limousine showed no great damage that would come from a high-velocity bullet's hitting. Rather, a low-velocity bullet or fragment of bullet struck the windshield from the inside.

9. At the time the first shot struck President Kennedy, he and Governor Connally were virtually in the same line of fire, from the viewpoint of a gunman firing at the motorcade from the southeast corner window of the sixth floor of the TSBD Building.

10. Governor Connally's physicians agreed unanimously that he had been struck from behind, and they also believed that all his wounds were caused by one bullet.

11. The autopsy examination of President Kennedy showed no missiles inside him and that the wounds to his head had been inflicted from behind, and a path was traced from the back of his neck to the front of his neck following the flight of the first bullet which struck President Kennedy.

12. The wound ballistics examination proved that a 6.5 mm. bullet would pass through President Kennedy's neck and exit at a velocity of nearly 1,800 feet per second.

13. There was unanimous agreement between Dr. Gregory, who treated Governor Connally's wrist wound, and Edgewood Arsenal ballistics scientists that the wound to Governor Connally's wrist was not caused by a pristine bullet.

But what of the claims by the assassination sensationalists that there was another rifleman who supposedly fired a cross-shot over a high fence to the right of and in front of the Presidential limousine, a shot that struck the front of President Kennedy's neck? This leads us into the area of possible conspiracy, either another rifleman or someone assisting Lee Harvey Oswald in the assassination.

As we enter the area of possible conspiracy, let us first turn to the assassination sensationalists' alternate theory of the source of the shots and examine the evidence in the context of the entire record.

PART IV

The Possibility of Conspiracy

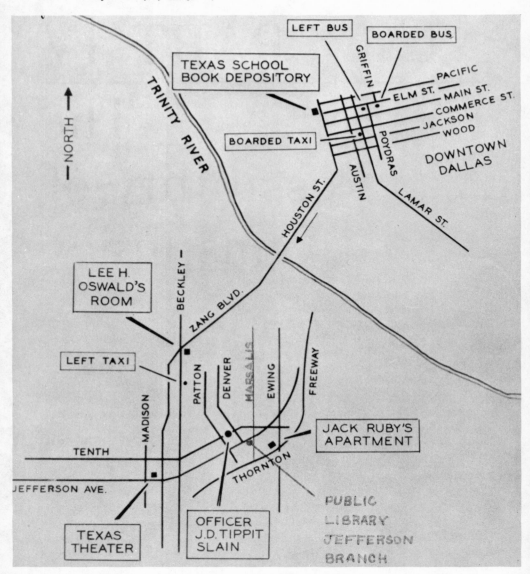

Whereabouts of Lee Harvey Oswald between 12:33 P.M. when he left the TSBD Building and 1:50 P.M. when he was apprehended at the Texas Theatre. (Map not drawn to scale.)

42
"A PUFF OF SMOKE"

I am signal supervisor for the Union Terminal and I was inspecting signal and switches and stopped to watch the parade. I was standing on top of the triple underpass and the President's car was coming down Elm Street and when they got just about to the arcade I heard what I thought for the moment was a firecracker and he slumped over and I looked over toward the arcade and trees and saw a puff of smoke come from the trees and I heard three more shots after the first shot but that was the only puff of smoke I saw. I immediately ran around to where I could see behind the arcade and did not see anyone running from there. But the puff of smoke I saw definitely came from behind the arcade through the trees. After the first shot the President slumped over and Mrs. Kennedy jumped up and tried to get over in the back seat to him and then the second shot rang out. After the first shot the secret service man raised up in the seat with a machine gun and then dropped back down in the seat. And they immediately sped off. Everything is spinning in my head and if I remember anything else later I will come back and tell Bill.

This affidavit by S. M. Holland is the fountainhead for speculation that there might have been another source of rifle shots. Holland, a signal supervisor for the Union Terminal Railroad, was standing with other railroad employees and Dallas policemen at the top of the triple underpass. We saw this affidavit early in our investigation, so we knew from the beginning that at least one witness thought he had seen a puff of smoke near a grassy knoll ahead of and to the right of the Presidential car.

Volume VI, pages 243-244, contains the testimony of Mr. Holland as he was being interrogated by Samuel A. Stern. Although Stern concentrated on Presidential protection in Area VI, he accompanied Joe Ball and me to Dallas one week to help us take depositions. After graduation from Harvard Law School, where he was Developments Editor of the Harvard Law Review, Sam served as a law clerk to Chief Justice Earl Warren and then became a member of a Washington, D.C., law firm. Mr. Holland testified that from where he was standing on the top of the triple underpass, looking to his left, he was sure that he had seen a puff of smoke:

There was a shot, a report, I don't know whether it was a shot. I can't say that. And a puff of smoke came out about 6 or 8 feet above the ground right out from under those trees. And at just about this location from where I was standing you could see that puff of smoke, like someone had thrown a firecracker, or something out, and that is just about the way it sounded. It wasn't as loud as the previous reports or shots.

Mr. Stern. What number would that have been in the—

Mr. Holland. Well, that would—they were so close together.

Mr. Stern. The second and third or the third and fourth?

Mr. Holland. The third and fourth. The third and the fourth.

Mr. Stern. So, that it might have been the third or the fourth?

Mr. Holland. It could have been the third or fourth, but there were definitely four reports.

Mr. Stern. You have no doubt about that?

Mr. Holland. I have no doubt about it. I have no doubt about seeing that puff of smoke come out from under those trees either.

The trees were more than 100 feet from Mr. Holland. Holland testified that he had seen Governor Connally knocked down in the seat of the limousine.

Mr. Stern. What did you then do?

Mr. Holland. Well, immediately after the shots was fired, I run around the end of this overpass, behind the fence to see if I could see anyone up there behind the fence.

Mr. Stern. That is the picket fence?

Mr. Holland. That is the picket fence.

Mr. Stern. On the north side of Elm Street?

Mr. Holland. Of course, this was this sea of cars in there and it was just a big—it wasn't an inch in there that wasn't automobiles and I couldn't see up in that corner. I ran on up to the corner of this fence behind the building. By the time I got there there were 12 or 15 policemen and plainclothesmen, and we looked for empty shells around there for quite a while, and I left because I had to get back to the office. I didn't give anyone my name. No one—didn't anyone ask for it, and it wasn't but an hour or so until the deputy sheriff came down to the office and took me back up to the courthouse.

We are going to return to the fact that no empty cartridge cases were found in the area, although many policemen searched for such evidence.

Other witnesses who stood on the triple underpass at the time of the assassination also testified before the Commission. For instance, I took the testimony of Austin L. Miller. He worked for the Texas-Louisiana Freight Bureau and said he was standing near some other people and police officers on the triple underpass.

Mr. Belin. Well, describe what happened. Did you see the motorcade come by?

Mr. Miller. Yes, sir; it came down Main Street and turned north on Houston Street and went over two blocks and turned left onto Elm Street.

Got about halfway down the hill going toward the underpass and that is when as far as I can recall the first shot was fired.

Mr. Belin. Did you know it was a shot when you heard it?

Mr. Miller. I didn't know it. I thought at first the motorcycle backfiring or somebody throwed some firecrackers out.

Mr. Belin. Then what did you hear or see?

Mr. Miller. After the first one, just a few seconds later, there was two more shots fired or, or sounded like a sound at the time. I didn't know for sure. And it was after that I saw some man in the car fall forward, and a woman next to him grab him and hollered, and just what, I don't know exactly what she said.

Mr. Belin. Then what did you see?

Mr. Miller. About that time I turned and looked toward the—there is a little plaza sitting on the hill. I looked over there to see if anything was there, who threw the firecracker or whatever it was, or see if anything was up there, and there wasn't nobody standing there, so I stepped back and looked on the tracks to see if anybody run across the railroad tracks, and there was nobody running across the railroad tracks.

So I turned right straight back just in time to see the convertible take off fast.

Mr. Belin. You mean the convertible in which the President was riding?

Mr. Miller. I wouldn't want to say it was the President. It was a convertible, but I saw a man fall over. I don't know whose convertible it was.

Mr. Belin. Where did the shots sound like they came from?

Mr. Miller. Well, the way it sounded like, it came from the, I would say from right there in the car. Would be to my left, the way I was looking at him over toward that incline.

Mr. Belin. Is there anything else that you can think of that you saw?

Mr. Miller. About the time I looked over to the side there, there was a police officer. No; a motorcycle running his motor under against the curb, and jumped off and come up to the hill toward the top and right behind him was some more officers and plainclothesmen, too.

Mr. Belin. Did you see anyone that might be, that gave any suspicious movements of any kind over there?

Mr. Miller. No, sir; I didn't.

Mr. Belin. Did you see anyone when you looked around on the railroad tracks, that you hadn't seen before?

Mr. Miller. No, sir; I didn't. We was all standing in one group right at the rail looking over, and the police officer, he was standing about 5 or 10 feet behind us.

The hill to which Mr. Miller referred is the so-called "grassy knoll," where assassination sensationalists have said a rifleman fired shots at President Kennedy and Governor Connally.

Mr. Belin. Did you ever see anyone else in that area at all or anything on the railroad tracks at any time?

Mr. Miller. No, sir; not until after the shots were fired and the police officers came up the hill and climbed over the fence and started searching.

Mr. Belin. That was the only other people that you saw?

Mr. Miller. That is all I recall seeing.

Mr. Belin. Anything else that you can add that might be of help in any way to the Commission, or to the investigation into the assassination?

Mr. Miller. Offhand, no, sir; I don't recall anything else. My statement at the time may have some more, but I don't recall exactly what all did happen for sure.

Mr. Belin. Well, you and I never met until just a few minutes ago, did we?

Mr. Miller. No, sir.

Mr. Belin. And as soon as you came in here, we started immediately taking your testimony under oath, is that correct?

Mr. Miller. Yes.

Mr. Belin. We never talked about the facts before then, did we?

Mr. Miller. No, sir.

Even though most of the witnesses we interviewed on the triple underpass did not see a puff of smoke, we nevertheless investigated every possibility to ascertain if the puff of smoke that Mr. Holland swore he saw rising six to eight feet above the ground was in any way connected with the assassination. We found that although there was general agreement that only three shots were fired, there was considerable disagreement among witnesses who heard the shots about the place from which they thought the shots emanated. A number of witnesses thought the shots had come from the TSBD Building.

For example, a photograph taken by the news photographer, Altgens, showed that Secret Service agents in the follow-up car, immediately after the shots were fired, were looking in the direction of the TSBD Building.

On the other hand, a substantial number of witnesses believed from what they heard that the shots came from either the triple underpass, the railroad tracks or the area ranging from the grassy knoll by the north side of the underpass to the trees beneath the arcade. Thus, immediately after the assassination a number of police officers, including motorcycle policemen, converged on the area. Holland testified that 12 to 15 policemen and plainclothesmen were there immediately, searching for cartridge cases.

Dallas Motorcycle Police Officer Clyde A. Haygood was riding on his motorcycle in the motorcade behind Officer M. L. Baker. He was on Houston Street when the shots were fired and, after hearing three shots, drove his motorcycle to where the Presidential limousine had been when the shots were fired "and I left my motor on the street and ran to the railroad yard."

Mr. Belin. What did you do when you got there?

Mr. Haygood. Well, there was nothing. There was quite a few people in the area, spectators, and at that time I went back to my motorcycle—it was on the street—to the radio.

Mr. Belin. Did you see any people running away from there?

Mr. Haygood. No. They was all going to it.

J. W. Foster, another Dallas police officer, was standing on the east side of the triple overpass with instructions "to keep all unauthorized personnel off that overpass."

Mr. Ball. Now, tell me what you saw happen after the President's car passed—turned onto Elm from Houston.

Mr. Foster. After he came onto Elm I was watching the men up on the track more than I was him. Then I heard a loud noise, sound like a large firecracker. Kind of dumbfounded at first, and then heard the second one. I moved to the banister of the overpass to see what was happening. Then the third explosion, and they were beginning to move around. I ran after I saw what was happening.

Mr. Ball. What did you see was happening?

Mr. Foster. Saw the President slump over in the car, and his head looked just like it blew up.

Mr. Ball. You saw that, did you?

Mr. Foster. Yes, sir.

Mr. Ball. And what did you do then?

Mr. Foster. Well, at that time I broke and ran around to my right—to the left—around to the bookstore.

Mr. Ball. Now, did you have any opinion at that time as to the source of the sounds, the direction of the sounds?

Mr. Foster. Yes, sir.

Mr. Ball. What?

Mr. Foster. It came from back in toward the corner of Elm and Houston Streets.

Mr. Ball. That was your impression at that time?

Mr. Foster. Yes, sir.

Mr. Ball. Was any shot fired from the overpass?

Mr. Foster. No, sir.

Mr. Ball. Did you see anyone with a weapon there?

Mr. Foster. No. Sir.

Mr. Ball. Or did you hear any sound that appeared to come from the overpass?

Mr. Foster. No, sir.

Mr. Ball Where did you go from there?

Mr. Foster. Went on around the back side of the bookstore.

Mr. Ball. Immediately?

Mr. Foster. Yes, sir.

Mr. Ball. Did you see anybody coming out of that side of the bookstore?

Mr. Foster. No, sir.

Mr. Ball. Back side? What do you mean by that?

Mr. Foster. Well, I guess you would say the northwest side of it.

Mr. Ball. Were there any people in the railroad yards around the bookstore at that time?

Mr. Foster. Yes, sir. There was a pretty good crowd beginning to gather back in that area.

Mr. Ball. At that time?

Mr. Foster. Yes, sir.

Mr. Ball. Had you seen anybody over at the railroad yard north and west of the bookstore before you heard the shots fired?

Mr. Foster. No; other than people that had come up there and I sent them back down the roadway.

Mr. Ball. I see. People had attempted to get on the overpass there?

Mr. Foster. Yes, sir.

Mr. Ball. And you had sent them away?

Mr. Foster. Yes, sir.

Not one bit of physical evidence was found to indicate that any rifle had been fired from any area near where Holland said he saw a puff of smoke (or from any other area, except the southeast corner of the sixth floor of the TSBD Building).

Moreover, from a personal inspection of this grassy knoll area, I determined that it would have been difficult for anyone there to hit an occupant in a moving car because (1) there was a lot of obstruction caused by trees and shrubbery, (2) there was a high wooden fence that would have almost necessitated that a gunman be standing on something, (3) the shot itself would have been a "cross shot" with the target moving from left to right across the field of vision of the gunman, and (4) a person seeking to fire a rifle from that point would have been exposed to the view of people to his north and northwest, including a railroad tower that was relatively nearby.

On page 73 or our Report you can see the view of this entire area from a camera location at this railroad tower.

There was a man in the railroad tower at the time of the assassination. He was Lee E. Bowers, Jr., and his tower was approximately 50 yards from the rear of the TSBD Building.

Although Bowers was viewing the overall area, he did not see any gunman.

You can find Lee Bower's testimony on pages 284-289 of Volume VI of our hearings, which we published together with our Report. He was observing the area from his position in the tower, approximately 14 feet above the ground. Between 12:00 and 12:30 PM on Nov. 22, he said, he noticed three cars enter the area in the vicinity of the tower. However, there is no "through street to anywhere" and the cars had to turn around and return the way they had come in. He saw these cars move away until his line of vision was obscured by the west wall of the TSBD Building.

The last of the three cars drove near the tower in attempting to get out, but it was forced to back out and head toward the extension of Elm Street in front of the TSBD Building. About eight minutes after this last car left, Bowers saw the Presidential motorcade as it headed down Elm toward the triple underpass.

Mr. Ball. Did you hear anything?

Mr. Bowers. I heard three shots. One, then a slight pause, then two very close together. Also reverberation from the shots.

Mr. Ball. And were you able to form an opinion as to the source of the sound or what direction it came from, I mean?

Mr. Bowers. The sounds came either from up against the School Depository Building or near the mouth of the triple underpass.

Mr. Ball. Were you able to tell which?

Mr. Bowers. No; I could not.

Mr. Ball. Well, now, had you had any experience before being in the tower as to sounds coming from those various places?

Mr. Bowers. Yes; I had worked this same tower for some 10 or 12 years, and was there during the time they were renovating the School Depository Building, and had noticed at that time the similarity of sounds occurring in either of those two locations.

Mr. Ball. Can you tell me now whether or not it came, the sounds you heard, the three shots came from the direction of the Depository Building or the triple underpass?

Mr. Bowers. No; I could not.

Mr. Ball. From your experience there, previous experience there in hearing sounds that originated at the Texas School Book Depository Building, did you notice that sometimes those sounds seem to come from the triple underpass? Is that what you told me a moment ago?

Mr. Bowers. There is a similarity of sound, because there is a reverberation which takes place from either location.

Mr. Ball. Had you heard sounds originating near the triple underpass before?

Mr. Bowers. Yes; quite often. Because trucks backfire and various occurrences.

Mr. Ball. And you had heard noises originating from the Texas School Depository when they were building there?

Mr. Bowers. They were renovating. I—did carpenter work as well as sandblasted the outside of the building.

Mr. Ball. Now, were there any people standing on the high side—high ground between your tower and where Elm Street goes down under the underpass toward the mouth of the underpass?

Mr. Bowers. Directly in line, towards the mouth of the underpass, there were two men. One man, middle-aged, or slightly older, fairly heavy-set, in a white shirt, fairly dark trousers. Another younger man, about midtwenties, in either a plaid shirt or plaid coat or jacket.

Mr. Ball. Were they standing together or standing separately?

Mr. Bowers. They were standing within 10 or 15 feet of each other, and gave no appearance of being together, as far as I knew.

Mr. Ball. In what direction were they facing?

Mr. Bowers. They were facing and looking up towards Main and Houston, and following the caravan as it came down.

Mr. Ball. Did you see anyone standing on the triple underpass?

Mr. Bowers. On the triple underpass, there were two policemen. One facing each direction, both east and west. There was one railroad employee, a signalman there with the Union Terminal Co., and two welders that worked for the Fort Worth Welding firm, and there was also a laborer's assistant furnished by the railroad to these welders.

Mr. Ball. You saw those before the President came by, you saw those people?

Mr. Bowers. Yes; they were there before and after.

Mr. Ball. And were they standing on the triple underpass?

Mr. Bowers. Yes; they were standing on top of it facing towards Houston Street, all except, of course, the one policeman on the west side.

Mr. Ball. Did you see any other people up on this high ground?

Mr. Bowers. There were one or two people in the area. Not in this same vicinity. One of them was a parking lot attendant that operates a parking lot there. One or two. Each had uniforms similar to those custodians at the courthouse. But they were some distance back, just a slight distance back.

Mr. Ball. When you heard the sound, which way were you looking?

Mr. Bowers. At the moment I heard the sound, I was looking directly towards the area —at the moment of the first shot, as close as my recollection serves, the car was out of sight behind this decorative masonry wall in the area.

Mr. Ball. And when you heard the second and third shot, could you see the car?

Mr. Bowers. No; at the moment of the shots, I could—I do not think that it was in sight. It came in sight immediately following the last shot.

Mr. Ball. Did you see any activity in this high ground above Elm after the shot?

Mr. Bowers. At the time of the shooting there seemed to be some commotion, and immediately following there was a motorcycle policeman who shot nearly all of the way to the top of the incline.

Mr. Ball. On his motorcycle?

Mr. Bowers. Yes.

Mr. Ball. Did he come by way of Elm Street?

Mr. Bowers. He was part of the motorcade and had left it for some reason, which I did not know.

Mr. Ball. He came up—

Mr. Bowers. He came almost to the top and I believe abandoned his motorcycle for a moment and then got on it and proceeded, I don't know.

Mr. Ball. How did he get up?

Mr. Bowers. He just shot up over the curb and up.

Mr. Ball. He didn't come then by way of Elm, which dead ends there?

Mr. Bowers. No; he left the motorcade and came up the incline on the motorcycle.

Mr. Ball. Was his motorcycle directed toward any particular people?

Mr. Bowers. He came up into this area where there are some trees, and where I had described the two men were in the general vicinity of this.

Mr. Ball. Were the two men there at the time?

Mr. Bowers. I—as far as I know, one of them was. The other I could not say. The darker dressed man was too hard to distinguish from the trees. The one in the white shirt, yes; I think he was.

Mr. Ball. When you said there was a commotion, what do you mean by that? What did it look like to you when you were looking at the commotion?

Mr. Bowers. I just am unable to describe rather than it was something out of the ordinary, a sort of milling around, but something occurred in this particular spot which was out of the ordinary, which attracted my eye for some reason, which I could not identify.

Mr. Ball. You couldn't describe it?

Mr. Bowers. Nothing that I could pinpoint as having happened that—

Mr. Ball. Afterwards did a good many people come up there on this high ground at the tower?

Mr. Bowers. A large number of people came, more than one direction. One group converged from the corner of Elm and Houston, and came down the extension of Elm and came into the high ground, and another line—another large group went across the triangular area between Houston and Elm and then across Elm and then up the incline. Some of them all the way up.

Many of them did, as well as, of course, between 50 and a hundred policemen within a maximum of 5 minutes.

Mr. Ball. In this area around your tower?

Mr. Bowers. That's right. Sealed off the area, and I held off the trains until they could be examined, and there was some transients taken on at least one train.

Mr. Ball. I believe you have talked this over with me before your deposition was taken, haven't we?

Mr. Bowers. Yes.

Mr. Ball. Is there anything that you told me that I haven't asked you about that you can think of?

Mr. Bowers. Nothing that I can recall.

Mr. Ball. You have told me all that you know about this, haven't you?

Mr. Bowers. Yes; I believe that I have related everything which I have told the city police, and also told to the FBI.

Mr. Ball. And everything you told me before we started taking the deposition?

Mr. Bowers. To my knowledge I can remember nothing else.

As I read Bowers' testimony, I wondered if the puff of smoke could have come from the motorcycle ridden by the policeman who Bowers said just turned up over the curb and came up the incline nearly to the top. This, of course, was conjecture, for Bowers did not see any puff of smoke.

A typical example of the misrepresentation of the assassination sensation-alists occurs with regard to Bowers's testimony. In the film produced by Messrs. Lane and de Antonio, the co-producers imply that Joe Ball was trying to cut Bowers off in the middle of a crucial statement and then never gave Bowers an opportunity to complete his statement. Thus, in the Lane–de Antonio movie Bowers says on film:

Immediately after the shots were fired there was of course mass confusion to put it mildly but the area was immediately sealed off by I would say at least fifty police within three to five minutes. The first . . . up here on the scene, other than those of course who were standing around including two on top of the triple underpass, was one who rode a motorcycle up the incline coming up from the lower portion of Elm Street and he rode perhaps two-thirds of the way up or more before he deserted his motorcycle. At the time of the shooting in the vicinity of where the two men I've described were, there was a flash of light and there was something which occurred which caught my eye in this immediate area on the embankment, and what this was I could not state at that time and at this time I could not identify it other than there was some unusual occurrence, a flash of light or smoke or something which caused me to feel like something out of the ordinary had occurred there.

Lane. In reading your testimony, Mr. Bowers, it appears that just as you were about to make that statement you were interrupted in the middle of a sentence by the Commission Counsel who then went into another area.

Bowers. Er, well, er, well that—that's correct. I was there only to tell them what they asked and so that when they seemed to want to cut off the conversation I felt like that was—as far as I was concerned that was the end of it.

In his book, at page 32, Lane refers to Joe Ball's question, "You couldn't describe it?" and Bowers' answer, "Nothing that I could pinpoint as having happened that—", and then Lane asserts: "Before Bowers could conclude this important sentence, the Commission lawyer interrupted with an unrelated question. A little later Bowers was excused as a witness, leaving unexplained what it was in the area behind the fence that caught his eyes at the moment the President was shot."

There are two things wrong with this statement:

In the first place, Lane ignores the immediately preceding question and answer in which Joe Ball asked: "When you said there was commotion, what do you mean by that? What did it look like to you when you were looking at the commotion?"

Mr. Bowers. I just am unable to describe rather than it was something out of the ordinary, a sort of milling around, but something occurred in this particular spot which was out of the ordinary, which attracted my eye for some reason, which I could not identify.

In other words, Bowers had already stated that he could not identify what it was that occurred.

In the second place, as you have now seen from reading Bowers testimony, Ball concluded his interrogation by asking?

Mr. Ball. Is there anything that you told me that I haven't asked you about that you can think of?

Mr. Bowers. Nothing that I can recall.

Mr. Ball. You have told me all that you know about this, haven't you?

Mr. Bowers. Yes; I believe that I have related everything which I have told the city police, and also told to the FBI.

Mr. Ball. And everything you told me before we started taking the deposition?

Mr. Bowers. To my knowledge I can remember nothing else.

When we boil down the case of the assassination sensationalists, we find the assumption that the Dallas police tried to frame Oswald coupled with the allegation that there were more than three shots, at least one of which came from the area behind the arcade, because (a) Holland said he had seen a puff of smoke six to eight feet above the ground; (b) a large number of people thought the shots came from either the triple underpass or the area extending northeast along the grassy knoll and behind the arcade; (c) although the overwhelming majority of witnesses say they heard three shots, some witnesses said they heard more than three—such as Mr. Holland, who said he heard four—and therefore there could have been an additional shot or shots from some area other than the TSBD Building.

But, this entire theory hangs on Holland's testimony that he saw a "puff of smoke" in the grassy knoll area behind the arcade, which the sensationalists assume must have come from a rifle.

Let us explore the possibility that a shot was fired from this area. We know that it did not hit Governor Connally, because he was struck from behind. We know that it did not strike President Kennedy's head, because the medical evidence was conclusive. The wound of entry was in the rear of the President's skull, and there was a large opening on the right side of his head which was the wound at exit.[1]

Thus, if a bullet was fired from the area of Holland's "puff of smoke" and struck President Kennedy, the only possible wound it could have inflicted was the wound in the front of President Kennedy's neck. The doctors who treated President Kennedy at Parkland Memorial Hospital never turned the President's body over; consequently they did not see the wound in the lower portion of the back of his neck. Moreover, the wound in the front of the neck was immediately obliterated by a tracheotomy, performed in an effort to save the President's life. There were discrepancies in immediate interviews with the doctors, who, not having seen the wound in the back of the President's neck, assumed that the wound in the front of the neck could have been an entrance wound.

The speculations and rumors that resulted from these early medical statements were fanned by the failure of the members of the Warren Commission and the lawyers conducting the investigation to have direct

---

[1]When the President was hit in the head his chin was down as a result of the first wound; thus, the path of the second missile through the head was at a different angle than it would have been had the President's head been erect at the time he was hit. The position of the President's head at the time of the second wound was confirmed by our examination of the slides made from the Zapruder film.

access to the photographs and X-rays taken at the autopsy of President Kennedy.

But let us first follow the thesis of the sensationalists.

If there was a shot that struck President Kennedy in the front of his neck, there are only two possibilities: Either the bullet exited at some other point or that bullet remained inside President Kennedy.

The deadend of the "puff of smoke" theory is that there is no other exit point for a bullet that entered the front of President Kennedy's neck. (In light of the absence of any large bony structure in the neck that would create a great deal of resistance to a bullet, it is unlikely that any bullet that entered the front of President Kennedy's neck would have met enough resistance to remain in the body.[2]) In the alternative, if the bullet did not exit, it assuredly would have shown on the X-rays taken of President Kennedy at the time of his autopsy.

We know conclusively that the only bullets and the only cartridge cases found came from the rifle, Serial No. C-2766, purchased by Lee Harvey Oswald and found in the northwest corner of the sixth floor of the TSBD Building. Since there was no exit for any bullet that might have entered the front of President Kennedy's neck, and since the autopsy disclosed the absence of any bullet having remained in the body of President Kennedy, the entire theory of the alleged second assassin falls flat. The theory of the second assassin also collapses because of the physical inconsistency between the contentions of such a theory and the physical facts of the President's clothing.

The theory of the sensationalists depends on a rifleman, whom no one sees, shooting a rifle that no one sees and that does not expel cartridge cases, shooting a cross-shot over the high fence and through the shrubbery with ammunition that leaves puffs of smoke but in some way enters the neck of the President and then vanishes, without an exit point, striking the front of President Kennedy's clothing, yet leaving the fibers pointing outward rather than inward.

When you jurors examine the *entire* record as a whole, I believe you will be compelled to reach the same conclusion that I reached: The "puff of smoke" theory of the assassination sensationalists that emanates from S. M. Holland (who said his head was "spinning" after the assassination) is overwhelmingly contradicted by the evidence pointing the other way: The testimony of Howard Brennan, who saw the gunman take aim and fire the last shot; the testimony of Robert Jackson and Robert Couch, who were riding in the press car in the motorcade and saw the rifle being withdrawn from the TSBD Building window, the actions of Tom Dillard, who was riding in Jackson's convertible and took two pictures of the upper portion of the TSBD Building; the testimony of the other witnesses who saw a rifle in

[2]The wound in the back of the neck could not be an exit point because it was higher than the wound in the front and because the fibers on the back of President Kennedy's coat and shirt were pointing inward.

the southeast corner window of the sixth floor of the TSBD Building; the absence of testimony from any other person who saw any rifle in any place other than the southeast corner of the TSBD Building; the testimony of Harold Norman, who was watching the motorcade from just below the assassination window; the testimony of the other two TSBD employees who were watching the motorcade next to Harold Norman; the presence of three cartridge cases by the southeast corner window of the sixth floor of the TSBD Building; the finding of Oswald's rifle in the northwest corner of the sixth floor by the back stairway; the ballistic evidence that proved that those three cartridge cases by the sixth floor window came from that rifle to the exclusion of all other weapons in the world; the ballistic evidence that the two large bullet fragments found in the front seat of the Presidential limousine came from that same rifle to the exclusion of all other weapons in the world; the ballistic evidence that the nearly whole bullet found at Parkland Memorial Hospital also came from that same rifle, Serial No. C-2766; the clothing of President Kennedy, which showed that on the back of his jacket and shirt the fibers were pointing inward and on the front of his shirt the fibers were pointed outward; the damage inflicted to the Presidential limousine, which showed that a low-velocity bullet or fragment of a bullet had struck the windshield from the inside; the wound ballistics experiments that proved that a bullet that went through President Kennedy's neck would exit at a velocity of nearly 1,800 feet per second; the medical testimony that Governor Connally was struck from behind and that all of Governor Connally's wounds were caused by one bullet; the medical evidence that the wounds to President Kennedy's head had been inflicted from behind; the lack of substantial damage to the Presidential limousine that would have been caused by a bullet exiting from the front of President Kennedy's neck if it did not hit Governor Connally; the testimony of the autopsy physicians that they traced a path through President Kennedy's neck of a bullet that first struck the President in the back of the neck; the unanimous agreement between Dr. Gregory, who treated Governor Connally's wrist wound, and the Edgewood Arsenal ballistic scientists that the wound to Governor Connally's wrist was not caused by a pristine bullet; and the relative positions of President Kennedy and Governor Connally, with the Governor sitting directly in front of President Kennedy and directly in line with the trajectory of a shot from the TSBD Building.

In the face of this overwhelming array of evidence, the invisible rifleman shooting the invisible rifle, leaving invisible cartridge cases and shooting an invisible bullet, goes up in a puff of smoke.

43

"SUCH EVIDENCE MAY BE SINCERE BUT IT IS UTTERLY RIDICULOUS"

In evaluating evidence, it is necessary not only to examine the record as a whole but also to recognize differences in the relative reliability of different categories of evidence, ranging from auditory recollections to scientific physical evidence.

If anyone expects the Report of the Warren Commission to set out a "perfect case," he is wrong. Had our investigation produced a perfect case, the only conclusion that could be reached is that the investigation was not complete. Wherever there are two witnesses to an event, there are often at least two different stories. You have already seen examples of this in comparing Secret Service Agent Kellerman's testimony that President Kennedy said, "My God, I am hit," with the testimony of Mrs. Kennedy, Mrs. Connally, Governor Connally and the driver of the Presidential limousine that the President never uttered a word.

You will also remember the James Jarman Jr., an employee of the TSBD Company who had daily contact with Lee Harvey Oswald, swore under oath that Oswald "never hardly worked in a shirt. He worked in a T-shirt." On the other hand, Troy Eugene West, also an employee of the TSBD Company and who also saw Lee Harvey Oswald every day, swore under oath: "I don't believe I ever seen him [Oswald] working in just a T-shirt. He worked in a shirt all right, but I never did see him work in a T-shirt."

In addition to conflicts between testimony of witnesses, you can also have conflicts in the testimony of the same witness. For instance, when we discussed the shooting of Officer J. D. Tippit, two sisters-in-law, Barbara Jeanette Davis and Virginia Davis, saw Oswald running across their front lawn at the corner of Patton and East Tenth Street emptying his gun. Each woman found one of the cartridge cases that Oswald tossed away as he was leaving the scene.

In her testimony Virginia Davis vacillated a number of times as to whether she and her sister-in-law called the police before or after they saw Oswald cut across their lawn. You will remember in her testimony that near the conclusion of my examination of her I asked her to pause several minutes and decide which way it had happened. After three minutes of silence, she testified that they called the police *before* they had seen Oswald cut across the lawn—and then changed her testimony to conclude that the police were called *after* they had seen Oswald cut across their front lawn and toss the cartridge cases into the bushes.

Because there are almost always differences in the observations of two or more witnesses to an event, it is relatively easy to select portions of the record and attack the conclusions of the Warren Commission Report. The fact that sensationalists such as de Antonio and Lane, like the others, go beyond selective distortion into affirmative misrepresentation is indicative of both the lack of substance to their allegations and the solidity of the foundation of the Report.

Furthermore, the major portion of the arguments of the fantasists, instead of being consistent with physical evidence, rests on the selected testimony of selected eyewitnesses and their selected recollection of what they say they saw or heard, including identifications of Oswald, Tippit, Ruby, etc., at a particular place or time.

Compared with other kinds of evidence, eyewitness observances have drawbacks. Before analyzing the relative quality of different categories of evidence, let us examine some of the limitations inherent in identification. Eyewitness identification should always be treated with great skepticism. For instance, one of the many memoranda circulated among the lawyers working with the Warren Commission was a memorandum on eyewitness identification prepared by Melvin Eisenberg. He included an excerpt from a recognized text in the area of identification, Wilder and Wentworth's *Personal Identification*.[1] After listing a number of cases of mistaken identity, the authors concluded:

Such cases might be indefinitely multiplied, each dealing with reliable witnesses, generally those who made their observations under favorable conditions, and resulting either in the punishment of the innocent, or the escape of the guilty. It must also be remembered that while these cases were selected because the truth eventually came out, there are countless others where it never does, and there are doubtless now behind the bars, deprived of their liberty and undergoing unmerited disgrace and punishment, many innocent men, convicted upon the uncertain testimony of sight recognition.

In view, then, of the facts presented in this chapter: first, the extraordinary resemblance possible between two individuals; second, the great amount of change in appearance of which a single individual is capable; third, the known unreliability of eyes, memory, and judgment under the influence of excitement, fear, or other mental emotion; and fourth, the numerous instances in which a sentence based upon sight recognition has proven erroneous and has worked the greatest injustice upon the innocent; is it not our duty to employ sight recognition as contributory evidence merely, and to seek for better and surer methods of effecting a true identification? The outcome of this inquiry is plainly and irrefutably this: Sight Recognition is not Identification.

This is one of the reasons that Ball and I treated with skepticism Howard Brennan's conclusive identification of Oswald.

In the case of the Tippit murder, however, we could not so readily discount eyewitness identification of Oswald because we had not one but six

[1] Copyright 1918 by Richard D. Badger (The Gorham Press, p. 40).

people who were able to identify the gunman: Scoggins, the taxi driver who saw Oswald from as close as 12 feet; Helen Markham, the waitress who was standing cater-cornered across the street; Barbara Jeanette Davis and Virginia Davis, who saw the gunman cut across their front lawn; and Ted Callaway and Sam Guinyard, who saw the gunman coming south on Patton with a revolver held high as they viewed the scene from across the street. This combination of six eyewitnesses must certainly be given a great deal of weight.

Moreover, there was even stronger evidence of Oswald's guilt: the cartridge cases at the scene of the Tippit shooting, which were shown scientifically to have come from the weapon that was ordered through the mail by Oswald—a weapon that Oswald pulled out in the Texas Theatre as he was approached by Patrolman McDonald.

This leads to another distinction that must be recognized: Some kinds of evidence are entitled to more weight than others. Physical evidence is obviously entitled to the greatest weight. The rifle, No. C-2766, found on the sixth floor of the TSBD Building is an example of physical evidence. The cartridge cases found at the southeast corner window of the sixth floor; the large bullet fragments found in the front seat of the Presidential limousine; the nearly whole bullet found at Parkland Memorial Hospital; the fibers of President Kennedy's clothing and the way they were pointing; the damage to the inside of the window of the Presidential limousine; the Zapruder film; the cartridge cases at the scene of the Tippit shooting; and the absence of any great damage to the Presidential limousine from a high-velocity bullet— these are typical examples of important physical evidence in this case.

One step below physical evidence is expert scientific testimony. For instance, we have the conclusive finding that the cartridge cases found at the scene of the Tippit shooting came from Oswald's revolver; the conclusive finding that the cartridge cases found near the southeast corner sixth-floor window of the TSBD Building came from Oswald's rifle found in that floor, Serial No. C-2766; the conclusive finding that the two large bullet fragments found in the front seat of the Presidential limousine as well as the nearly whole bullet found at Parkland Hospital came from Oswald's rifle, to the exclusion of all other weapons in the world; the conclusive finding that Governor Connally was struck from behind and that the wound to his wrist was not caused by a pristine bullet; and the conclusive finding that the handwriting on the order form for the assassination weapon as well as on the order form for Oswald's revolver was the handwriting of Lee Harvey Oswald.

On the other hand, there are points where experts disagree. For instance, although all three FBI ballistics experts thought that each of the four bullets removed from Tippit's body was too mutilated to be ballistically identifiable, Joseph Nicol believed that one of the four definitely came from Oswald's revolver. The physician who operated on Governor Connally's wrist, Dr. Gregory, thought the weight of the fragments remaining inside the wrist was consistent with the wound's having been caused by the nearly whole bullet found at Parkland Hospital; but the autopsy physicians at Washington, based on their reading of a portion of the Parkland Hospital reports, thought that the weight of the fragments remaining in the wrist was too great for the wound to have been caused by the nearly whole bullet. As you know, we resolved that conflict by relying more heavily on the testimony of the witness who saw the wound first-hand, coupled with the agreement by all the experts that the wrist wound to Governor Connally had not been caused by a pristine bullet and further coupled with our wound ballistic tests. The important point here is that you cannot take the testimony of one expert out of the context of the testimony of all of the experts on a given matter.

Eyewitness observation would fall within the next category of testimony, certainly on a level below physical evidence and the testimony of expert witnesses. You can expect to find many conflicts in the recollections of eyewitnesses, particularly where the observations are coupled with the excitement of an event that happens within a matter of seconds. Moreover, the first reports of what the eyewitnesses see are generally the most accurate. This is another of the reasons that we did not rely on Brennan's identification of Oswald. Notwithstanding his explanation that he feared a Communist conspiracy, the fact remains that when Brennan first saw Oswald in a police lineup, he did not make a positive identification. All he could say was that of the men he saw in the lineup, Oswald looked most like the man he had seen in the sixth-floor window firing the gun.

Even less accurate than human memory based on sight is human memory based on sound. For instance, although the great majority of witnesses at the scene of the assassination heard three shots, some, including Brennan, said they had heard only two and others said they heard four, five or six. Moreover, there is considerable disagreement among the witnesses concerning where they thought the shots had originated. Many witnesses who heard the shots thought they had come from the TSBD Building. On the other hand, many others thought that they had come from the direction of the triple underpass or the area near the railroad tracks or the grassy knoll behind the fence. Some even thought the shots came from the limousine itself.

Eisenberg researched this area and prepared a written memorandum that was circulated among us lawyers. Included in this memorandum is the following passage:

Among the most crucial questions to be considered in determining the identity of the President's assassin or assassins are the number of shots fired in the course of the assassination, the spacing between the shots, and the location of the site or sites from which the shots were fired. A great deal of evidence is relevant to these questions; for example, the number of wounds, the path of the missiles causing each wound, the position of the rifle believed to have fired the recovered bullet and bullet fragments, the position and number of the empty cartridge cases believed to have been fired in this rifle, the number of recovered bullets and bullet fragments, and visual observations of bystanders. In addition, a mass of evidence has been collected concerning the aural observation of bystanders. The purpose of this memorandum is to point out that very little weight can be assigned to this category of evidence.

A leading firearms textbook states flatly that "Little credence . . . should be put in what anyone says about a shot or even the number of shots." Hatcher, Jury, & Weller, *Firearms Investigation, Identification, and Evidence*, 420 (1957). This results from two interrelated factors: the difficulty of accurate perception of the sound of gunshots, and the acoustics of gunshots.

Perception. The sound of a shot comes upon a witness suddenly, and often unexpectedly. The witness is not "ready" to record his perception. The same is usually true of subsequent shots following hard on the heels of the first. For these reasons such sounds "are generally extremely inaccurately recorded in [one's] memory." *Ibid.* Hatcher cites an example in which a deer hunter was asked how many shots had been fired by another hunter who was less than one hundred yards away. The deer hunter said, "Five." Actually, only two shots had been fired.

The perception of distance is as unreliable as the perception of number:

"[T]he observation of a sound is often unclear and subjective. A loud noise may appear to have been produced nearby, while a weak sound may seem to have been transmitted from some distance. This difficulty of estimating the distance from the site at which the sound is produced to the place where it is heard is increased considerably if the sound is of a nature unknown to the listener." Soderman & O'Connell, *Modern Criminal Investigation*, 43 (5th ed. 1962).

Similarly, as to the characteristics of the sound:

"Another subject frequently discussed in criminal cases is the report made by various types of weapons. People will go into court and swear on occasion that a weapon fired was a certain type and even make and model. Unless a great many other factors are known, such evidence may be sincere but it is utterly ridiculous." Hatcher at 417.

Obviously, during the assassination the surprise, emotion, confusion, and noise were much greater than is even usually the case, and bystanders' aural perception of the gunshots is therefore to be accorded even less weight than is usually the case.

Acoustics. Apart from the difficulty of accurately recording aural perceptions of gunshots, the acoustics of gunshots are such that the witness' perceptions may lead him to draw inaccurate conclusions.

(a) *Number of shots.* The firing of a bullet causes *three* noises: (1) the muzzle blast, caused by the smashing of the hot gases which propel the bullet into the relatively stable air at the gun's muzzle; (2) the noise of the bullet, caused by the shock wave built up ahead of the bullet's nose as it travels through the air; (3) the noise caused by the impact of the bullet into its target. Each of these noises can be quite sharp and may be perceived as separate "shots" by an inexperienced or confused witness.

(b) *Direction.* If a bullet travels faster than the speed of sound the acoustics are such that an observer at right angles to the path of the bullet may perceive the shot to have been fired from a site somewhere *opposite to him.* "The reason for this is that since the bullet is traveling faster than the speed of sound, the noise caused by the bullet at the point it passes nearest the witness will reach him *before* the noise caused by the muzzle. Because the ear locates noises at right angles to the source of a sound wave, the witness first hearing the sound wave as the bullet passes closest to him will think that the bullet was fired from a point opposite him.

It must be emphasized that the above discussion is not merely theoretical, but is based on the analysis and observations of professional criminal investigators. Furthermore, this discussion is borne out by the fact that the testimony of the bystanders to the assassination varies enormously. (Similar variances occur in the testimony relating to the Tippit killing.)

It is significant that a major portion of the thesis of the assassination sensationalists that at least some of the shots came from the grassy knoll rests upon identification of sound direction by witnesses, for which there is no support through any physical evidence such as an empty cartridge case, a bullet from some other rifle, or clothing fibers on the front of the President's shirt pointing inward.

Even though little weight can be given to the auditory recollections of sound direction by witnesses, we investigated all areas from which people thought they heard shots in an effort to determine whether there was any physical or other evidence to support such conclusions. You have already seen that the overwhelming weight of the evidence shows that all of the shots came from the southeast corner window of the sixth floor of the TSBD Building. The important point is that unless you have an overall perspective and familiarity with all of the facts, it is easy to extract a few here and a few there and come up with something that at first blush seems plausible.

There were literally scores of witnesses at the scene of the assassination. By selecting several who on the basis of their auditory impressions were certain that the sound came from some place other than the TSBD Building, the sensationalists have given the impression that a large group was wantonly, purposely ignored by the Commission.

Nothing could be further from the truth. We took the testimony of many witnesses who, on the basis of what they had heard and the reverberations from the high buildings surrounding Dealey Plaza, thought the shots had come from the triple underpass, from the railroad tracks, from the grassy knoll, from the Presidential limousine itself. By the same token, we took the testimony of many witnesses who on the basis of what they heard thought the shots had come from the TSBD Building. Certainly, we did not question the honesty of any of these witnesses because their impressions might have differed from what we finally concluded. Rather, we tried to get a sampling of testimony of all witnesses to obtain every possible version about the source of the shots.

When we measured the great conflict of evidence based on auditory recollections with the overwhelming weight of the evidence about which there was no conflict, we could reach but one conclusion: All of the shots came from the southeast corner window of the sixth floor of the TSBD Building.

44

"I KEPT THINKING ABOUT THIS MAN THAT HAD RUN DOWN THE HILL"

ROGER CRAIG, 7711 Piedmont, Apartment B, phone EVergreen 1-4851, employed as a Deputy Sheriff, Dallas County Sheriff's Department, advised that he was standing in front of the Dallas Sheriff's Office, 505 Main Street, at the time the motorcade of President JOHN F. KENNEDY was approaching the triple underpass. He stated that he heard a shot and ran around the corner onto Houston Street and went through the parking area and briefly searched area on Elm Street. Shortly after this, approximately 3 or 4 minutes, came back across Elm Street and observed an individual run down the grass area from the direction of the Texas School Book Depository. He heard this individual whistle and a white Rambler station wagon, driven by a Negro male, pulled over to the curb and said individual got in and the car headed toward the Dallas-Fort Worth Turnpike.

CRAIG stated that at 5:18 PM, November 22, 1963, he was given an opportunity to observe LEE HARVEY OSWALD in the office of Captain J. W. FRITZ in the Homicide and Robbery Bureau, Dallas Police Department, and that he is positive that OSWALD is identical with the same individual he observed getting into the Rambler station wagon as mentioned above.

This was a report by FBI Special Agent James W. Bookhout. It was one of the thousands of such reports that came across our desks in Washington.

I took Roger Craig's testimony in Dallas on Apr. 1, 1964. Then 27 years old, he said he had been born in Wisconsin, raised in Minnesota, "and ran away from home when I was 12 and traveled all over the country." Although he did not go to school after running away from home, he joined the Army and said that when he was 19 he received a high school diploma by passing a "high school equivalent test" while in the service. Craig, married with two children and a stepson, had worked for the Dallas County Sheriff's office since Oct. 9, 1959. At the time of the assassination, Craig was in front of the Sheriff's office on the north curb of Main Street, one block south of the TSBD Building. He was watching the motorcade pass when he heard three shots.

Craig started running toward the railroad yards and then came back toward the TSBD Building, where he soon found

a young couple and the boy said he saw two men on the—uh—sixth floor of the Book Depository Building over there; one of them had a rifle with the telescopic sight on it—but he thought they were Secret Service agents on guard and didn't report it. This was about—uh—oh, he said, 15 minutes before the motorcade ever arrived.

Mr. Belin. Do you remember if that boy's name would have been Arnold Rowland—(spelling) R-o-w-l-a-n-d?

Mr. Craig. Yes.

Mr. Belin. Does that sound like it?

Mr. Craig. Yes; it sounds like the name—yes.

Mr. Belin. His wife might be Barbara Rowland?

Mr. Craig. Yes; I believe her name was Barbara.

Members of the jury, you will hear later the testimony of Arnold Rowland, and his wife, Barbara.

Craig said then he was searching the south curb of Elm Street near the TSBD Building about "fourteen or fifteen minutes" after he heard the first shot when he heard someone whistle, " . . . so I turned and—uh—saw a man start to run down the hill on the north side of Elm Street, running down toward Elm Street." According to Craig, the man started to run down the grassy portion of the park.

Mr. Belin. And then what did you see happen?

Mr. Craig. I saw a light-colored station wagon, driving real slow, coming west on Elm Street from Houston. Uh—actually, it was nearly in line with him. And the driver was leaning to his right looking up the hill at the man running down.

Mr. Belin. Uh-huh.

Mr. Craig. And the station wagon stopped almost directly across from me. And—uh—the man continued down the hill and got in the station wagon. And I attempted to cross the street. I wanted to talk to both of them. But the—uh—traffic was so heavy I couldn't get across the street. And—uh—they were gone before I could—

Mr. Belin. Where did the station wagon head?

Mr. Craig. West on Elm Street.

Mr. Belin. Under the triple underpass?

Mr. Craig. Yes.

Mr. Belin. Could you describe the man that you saw running down toward the station wagon?

Mr. Craig. Oh, he was a white male in his twenties, five nine, five eight, something like that; about 140 to 150; had kind of medium brown sandy hair—you know, it was like it'd been blown—you know, he'd been in the wind or something—it was all wild-looking; had on—uh—blue trousers—

Mr. Belin. What shade of blue? Dark blue, medium or light?

Mr. Craig. No; medium, probably; I'd say medium.

And, a—uh—light tan shirt, as I remember it.

Mr. Belin. Anything else about him?

Mr. Craig. No; nothing except that he looked like he was in an awful hurry.

Mr. Belin. What about the man who was driving the car?

Mr. Craig. Now, he struck me, at first, as being a colored male. He was very dark complected, had real dark short hair, and was wearing a thin white-looking jacket—uh, it looked like the short windbreaker type, you know, because it was real thin and had the collar that came out over the shoulder (indicating with hands) like that—just a short jacket.

Mr. Belin. You say that he first struck you that way. Do you now think that he was a Negro?

Mr. Craig. Well, I don't—I didn't get a real good look at him. But my first glance at him—I was more interested in the man coming down the hill—but my first glance at him, he struck me as a Negro.

Mr. Belin. Is that what your opinion is today?

Mr. Craig. Well, I—I couldn't say, because I didn't get a good enough look at him.

Mr. Craig testified that during the afternoon,

I kept thinking about this man that had run down the hill and got in this car, so—uh—it was about, oh, I don't recall exactly the time, nearly 5 or something like that, or after, when—uh—the city had apprehended a suspect in the city officer's shooting. And—uh—information was floating around that they were trying to connect him with the assassination of the President—as the assassin.

So—uh, in the meantime, I kept thinking about this subject that had run and got in the car. So, I called Captain Fritz' office and talked to one of his officers and—uh—told him what I had saw and give him a description of the man, asked him how it fit the man they had picked up as a suspect.

And—uh—it was then they asked me to come up and look at him at Captain Fritz' office.

Mr. Belin. All right.

Then what did you do?

Mr. Craig. I drove up to Fritz' office about, oh, after 5—about 5:30 or something like that—and—uh—talked to Captain Fritz and told him what I had saw. And he took me in his office—I believe it was his office—it was a little office, and had the suspect setting in a chair behind a desk—beside the desk. And another gentleman, I didn't know him, he was sitting in another chair to my left as I walked in the office.

And Captain Fritz asked me was this the man I saw—and I said, "Yes" it was.

Mr. Belin. All right.

Will you describe the man you saw in Captain Fritz' office?

Mr. Craig. Oh, he was sitting down but—uh—he had the same medium brown hair; it was still—well, it was kinda wild looking; he was slender, and—uh—what I could tell of him sitting there, he was—uh—short. By that, I mean not—myself, I'm five eleven—he was shorter than I was. And—uh—fairly light build.

Mr. Belin. Could you see his trousers?

Mr. Craig. No; I couldn't see his trousers at all.

Mr. Belin. What about his shirt?

Mr. Craig. I believe, as close as I can remember, a T-shirt—a whiteT-shirt.

Mr. Belin. All right.

But you didn't see him in a lineup? You just saw him sitting there?

Mr. Craig. No; he was sitting there by himself in a chair—off to one side.

Mr. Belin. All right.

Then, what did Captain Fritz say and what did you say and what did the suspect say?

Mr. Craig. Captain Fritz then asked him about the—uh—he said, "What about this station wagon?"

And the suspect interrupted him and said. "That station wagon belongs to Mrs. Paine"—I believe is what he said. "Don't try to tie her into this. She had nothing to do with it."

And—uh—Captain Fritz then told him, as close as I can remember, that, "All we're trying to do is find out what happened, and this man saw you leave from the scene."

And the suspect again interrupted Captain Fritz and said, "I told you people I did."

And—uh—yeah—then, he said—then he continued and he said, "Everybody will know who I am now."

And he was leaning over the desk. At this time, he had risen partially out of the chair and leaning over the desk, looking directly at Captain Fritz.

Mr. Belin. What was he wearing—or could you see the color of his trousers as he leaned over the desk?

Mr. Craig. No; because he never—he just leaned up, you know, sort of forward—not actually up, just out of his chair like that (indicating) forward.

Mr. Belin. Then, did you say anything more?

Mr. Craig. No; I then left.

Mr. Belin. Well, in other words, the only thing you ever said was, "This was the man"—or words to that effect?

Mr. Craig. Yes.

Mr. Belin. Did Captain Fritz say anything more?

Mr. Craig. No; I don't believe—not while I was there.

Mr. Belin. Did the suspect say anything more?

Mr. Craig. Not that I recall.

Mr. Belin. Did you say anything about that it was a Rambler station wagon there?

Mr. Craig. In the presence of the suspect?

Mr. Belin. Yes.

Mr. Craig. No.

Mr.Belin. You don't know whether Captain Fritz said anything to the suspect about this incident before you came, do you?

Mr. Craig. No; I don't.

Mr. Belin. Is there anything else that you can think of involving this interrogation at which you were present?

Mr. Craig. No. Nothing else was said after that point. I then left and give my name to the—uh—Secret Service agent and the FBI agent that was outside the office.

Mr. Belin. Anything else in connection with the assassination that you think might be important that we haven't discussed here?

Mr. Craig. No; except—uh—except for the fact that it came out later that Mrs. Paine does own a station wagon and—uh—it has a luggage rack on top. And this came out, of course, later, after I got back to the office. I didn't know about this. Buddy Walthers brought it up. I believe they went by the house and the car was parked in the driveway.

Mr. Belin. Anything else you can think of?

Mr. Craig. No. That's all. I forgot about it and went back to work.

Mr. Belin. Now, prior to the time we had your deposition taken, we chatted for a few minutes about some of these things—is that correct?

Mr. Craig. Yes.

Mr. Belin. For instance, we talked about your conversation with this young couple—this Arnold Rowland and his wife?

Mr. Craig. Yes.

Mr. Belin. Is there anything that we said before the deposition was taken that we haven't recorded here?

Mr. Craig. I don't believe so.

Mr. Belin. Is there anything that I said or you said in our conversation that is different from anything that was recorded here—to the best of your recollection?

Mr. Craig. No; except you asked me before, I believe, did I talk to any of the railroad employees.

Mr. Belin. That's right.

Mr. Craig. And I said, "No"—which I did not.

Mr. Belin. Anything else?

Mr. Craig. (Pausing before reply.) No—nothing that I recall.

Mr. Belin. In our conversation, did you just relate to me what your story was before we sat down to take the deposition?

Mr. Craig. Yes.

You jurors will remember that during Oswald's interrogation, he said that he boarded a bus after the assassination and later left the bus and took a taxi to his rooming house. You will also remember that when Oswald was apprehended, the Dallas police found a bus transfer in his pocket.

We know that Oswald was seen by Mrs. Reid in the TSBD Building, approximately two minutes after the assassination, on the second floor heading toward the stairs in the front of the building that go to the first floor entrance. We also know that at approximately 1:15 P.M., he was at the scene of the Tippit murder. The next question is whether Oswald was picked up by a station wagon approximately 15 minutes after the assassination in front of the building, as Roger Craig testified. If so, this would be strong evidence of conspiracy.

On the other hand, if Oswald left the building and boarded a bus and later a taxi, as he stated in his interrogation, this would rebut Craig's testimony. In either event, however, the actions of Oswald would be evidence of flight from the scene of the crime, particularly since Oswald was the only TSBD employee with access to the sixth floor who was inside the building at the time of the assassination and who left before the roll call of all warehouse employees.

Let us now determine if Oswald was picked up by a station wagon or if he boarded a bus.

"EVERY DRIVER HAS A
DIFFERENT PUNCH MARK"

Mr. Ball. Why did you tell him you wouldn't rent to him any more?
Mrs. Bledsoe. Because I didn't like him.
Mr. Ball. Why?
Mrs. Bledsoe. I didn't like his attitude. He was just kind of like this, you know, just big shot, you know, and I didn't have anything to say to him, and—but, I didn't like him. There was just something about him I didn't like or want him—just wasn't the kind of person I wanted. Just didn't want him around me.

Mary E. Bledsoe owned a house at 621 North Marsalis in the Oak Cliff section of Dallas in which she rented rooms. All her children were grown. "And I have four bedrooms, but I rent three."

Mrs. Bledsoe rented a room in her one-story house to Lee Harvey Oswald on Monday, Oct. 7, 1963. He moved into the room that same day, and stayed with Mrs. Bledsoe only one week.

Mrs. Bledsoe said she did not see Oswald again until the afternoon of Nov. 22. Mrs. Bledsoe had gone downtown to watch the motorcade and then caught a bus to go home. The bus was heading west on Elm Street.

Mr. Ball. All right, now, tell me what happened?
Mrs. Bledsoe. And, after we got past Akard, at Murphy—I figured it out. Let's see. I don't know for sure. Oswald got on. He looks like a maniac. His sleeve was out here [indicating]. His shirt was undone.
Mr. Ball. You are indicating a sleeve of a shirt?
Mrs. Bledsoe. Yes.
Mr. Ball. It was unraveled?
Mrs. Bledsoe. Was a hole in it, hole, and he was dirty, and I didn't look at him. I didn't want to know I even seen him, and just looked off, and then about that time the motorman said the President had been shot.

Mrs. Bledsoe said she was sitting on a side seat in the front of the bus facing the driver.

Mr. Ball. When Oswald got on, you then weren't facing him, were you?
Mrs. Bledsoe. No; but I saw that it was him.
Mr. Ball. How close did he pass to you as he boarded the bus?
Mrs. Bledsoe. Just in front of me. Just like this (indicating).
Mr. Ball. Just a matter of a foot or two?
Mrs. Bledsoe. Uh-huh.
Mr. Ball. When he got on the bus, did he say anything to the motorman?
Mrs. Bledsoe. Oh, the motorman? I think—I don't know. I don't know.

Mr. Ball. Where did he sit?

Mrs. Bledsoe. He sat about halfway back down.

Mr. Ball. On what side?

Mrs. Bledsoe. On the same side I was on.

Mr. Ball. Same side? Did you look at him?

Mrs. Bledsoe. No, sir.

Mr. Ball. Did he look at you as he went by? Did he look at you?

Mrs. Bledsoe. I don't know. I didn't look at him. That is—I was just—he looked so bad in his face, and his face was so distorted.

Mr. Ball. Did he have a hat on?

Mrs. Bledsoe. No.

Mr. Ball. Now, what color shirt did he have on?

Mrs. Bledsoe. He had a brown shirt.

Mr. Ball. And unraveled?

Mrs. Bledsoe. Hole in his sleeve right here [indicating].

Mr. Ball. Which is the elbow of the sleeve? That is, you pointed to the elbow?

Mrs. Bledsoe. Well, it is.

Mr. Ball. And that would be which elbow, right or left elbow?

Mrs. Bledsoe. Right.

Oswald did have a dark shirt with a hole in the elbow, so Mrs. Bledsoe's testimony was accurate in this respect. She testified that after Oswald had been on the bus for some time, the bus driver said,

"Well, the President has been shot, and I say—so, and the woman over— we all got to talking, about four of us sitting around talking, and Oswald was sitting back there, and one of them said, "Hope they don't shoot us," and I said, "I don't believe that—it is—I don't believe it. Somebody just said that."

And it was too crowded, you see, and Oswald had got off.

Mr. Ball. How far had he been on the bus before he got off? Until the time he got on until the time he got off?

Mrs. Bledsoe. About three or four blocks.

Mr. Ball. Did he say anything to the motorman when he got off?

Mrs. Bledsoe. They say he did, but I don't remember him saying anything.

Mr. Ball. Did you ever see the motorman give him a transfer?

Mrs. Bledsoe. No; I didn't pay any attention but I believe he did.

Mr. Ball. Well, what do you mean he—you believe he did? Did you remember seeing him get on or are you telling me something you read in the newspapers?

Mrs. Bledsoe. No; I don't remember. I don't remember.

Mr. Ball. Did you pay any attention at that time as to whether he did, or did not get a transfer?

Mrs. Bledsoe. I didn't pay any attention to him.

Mr. Ball. Well, did you look at him as he got off the bus?

Mrs. Bledsoe. No; I sure didn't. I didn't want to know him.

Mr. Ball. Well, you think you got enough of a glimpse of him to be able to recognize him?

Mrs. Bledsoe. Oh, yes.

Mr. Ball. You think you might be mistaken?

Mrs. Bledsoe. Oh, no.

Mr. Ball. You didn't look very carefully, did you?

Mrs. Bledsoe. No; I just glanced at him, and then looked the other way and I hoped he didn't see me.

The bus driver was Cecil J. McWatters, who was scheduled to leave the corner of St. Paul and Elm at 12:36 PM

Mr. Ball. And you think you left at the time you were supposed to leave?

Mr. McWatters. Well, I am almost positive I did, because, as I say, we generally come in on schedules on good time because from that street on is where we generally—for the next seven or eight blocks—is where we get all of our passengers going through the downtown area.

He headed west on Elm Street toward the TSBD Building with few passengers on the bus.

As I left Field Street, I pulled out into the, in other words, the first lane of traffic and traffic was beginning to back up then; in other words, it was blocked further down the street, and after I pulled out in it for a short distance there I come to a complete stop, and when I did, someone come up and beat on the door of the bus, and that is about even with Griffin Street . . .

Mr. Ball. And that is about seven or eight blocks from the Texas Book Depository Building, isn't it?

Mr. McWatters. Yes, sir. It would be seven, I would say that is seven, it would be about seven blocks.

Mr. Ball. What did the man look like who knocked on your door and got on your bus?

Mr. McWatters. Well, I didn't pay any particular attention to him. He was to me just dressed in what I would call work clothes, just some type of little old jacket on, and I didn't pay any particular attention to the man when he got on.

Mr. Ball. Paid his fare, did he?

Mr. McWatters. Yes, sir; he just paid his fare and sat down on the second cross seat on the right.

Mr. Ball. Do you remember whether or not you gave him a transfer?

Mr. McWatter. Not when he got on; no, sir.

Mr. Ball. You didn't. Did you ever give him a transfer?

Mr. McWatters. Yes, sir; I gave him one about two blocks from where he got on.

Mr. Ball. Did he ask you for a transfer?

Mr. McWatters. Yes, sir.

Mr. Ball. Do you remember what he said to you when he asked you for the transfer?

Mr. McWatters. Well, the reason I recall the incident, I had—there was a lady that when I stopped in this traffic, there was a lady who had a suitcase and she said, "I have got to make a 1 o'clock train at Union Station," and she said, "I don't believe—from the looks of this traffic you are going to be held up."

She said, "Would you give me a transfer and I am going to walk on down," which is about from where I was at that time about 7 or 8 blocks to Union Station and she asked me if I would give her a transfer in case I did get through the traffic if I would pick her up on the way.

So, I said, "I sure will." So I gave her a transfer and opened the door and as she was going out the gentleman I had picked up about 2 blocks asked for a transfer and got off at the same place in the middle of the block where the lady did.

Mr. Ball. Where was that near, what intersection?

Mr. McWatters. It was the intersection near Lamar Street, it was near Poydras and Lamar Street. It is a short block, but the main intersection there is Lamar Street.

Mr. Ball. He had been on the bus about 2 blocks?

Mr. McWatters. About 2 blocks; yes, sir.

Early that evening while McWatters was still on duty, he was contacted by the Dallas police.

Mr. McWatters. Well, they stopped me; it was, I would say around 6:15 or somewhere around 6:15 or 6:20 that afternoon.

Mr. Ball. You were still on duty, were you?

Mr. McWatters. Yes, sir.

Mr. Ball. Still on your bus?

Mr. McWatters. I was on duty but I was on a different line and a different bus.

Mr. Ball. What did they ask you when they came out?

Mr. McWatters. Well, they stopped me right by the city hall there when I come by there and they wanted me to come in, they wanted to ask me some questions. And I don't know what it was about or anything until I got in there and they told me what happened.

Mr. Ball. What did they tell you?

Mr. McWatters. Well, they told me that they had a transfer that I had issued that was cut for Lamar Street at 1 o'clock and they wanted to know if I knew anything about it. And I, after I looked at the transfer and my punch, I said yes, that is the transfer I issued because it had my punch mark on it.

Mr. Ball. Did your punch mark have a distinctive mark?

Mr. McWatters. It had a distinctive mark and it is registered, in other words, all the drivers, every driver has a different punch mark.

Mr. Ball. What makes it different?

Mr. McWatters. Well, it is, it would be, the symbol of it or angle, in other words, every one; it is different, in other words.

Mr. Ball. You have a punch there?

Mr. McWatters. Yes, sir; I have the punch right here.

Mr. Ball. Is that the punch that you used?

Mr. McWatters. That is the punch I used.

Mr. Ball. Will you punch a piece of paper and show us?

Mr. McWatters. In other words, that is the type of punch that this one makes right here, in other words.

Mr. Ball. On any bus in Dallas?

Mr. McWatters. In other words, the superintendent has a list, in other words, it would be just like this and every man has a punch and he has his name, and everything. In other words, if anyone calls in about a transfer or anything, I mean brings one in he can look right down the list by the punch mark and tell whose punch it is, and who it is registered to.

Mr. McWatters had been contacted by the police because in a search of Oswald at the Dallas police station following his arrest a bus transfer was found in Oswald's shirt pocket by Detective Richard M. Sims.

Mr. Ball. What did you find?

Mr. Sims. I found a bus transfer slip in his shirt pocket.

Mr. Ball. What did you do with the transfer?

Mr. Sims. I went back up to the office and I believe initialed it and placed it in an envelope for identification.

In Volume XVI of the Supplementary Volumes of testimony and exhibits published with our Report, you will see a picture of Commission Exhibit 381, which is the bus transfer. You will note the initials of Detective Sims on the back. You will also see on that same page Exhibit 381A, the envelope in which Detective Sims placed the transfer.

After the assassination, some sensationalists sought to say that the transfer was fabricated by the Dallas Police Department. However, Lee Harvey Oswald in his interrogation admitted he was on a bus, and the transfer had the distinctive punch mark of Cecil McWatters. Furthermore, in all our investigation of the Dallas Police Department, although we found many inadequacies, we found no fabrication of evidence.

The evidentiary import of the bus ride was that Oswald walked approximately seven blocks east from the TSBD Building to board a bus that he could have boarded in front of the TSBD Building. Moreover, instead of waiting for the Beckley Street bus, which would have taken Oswald directly to his rooming house, he took the first bus available, the Marsalis bus. At its closest point, the Marsalis bus route passed seven blocks away from Oswald's rooming house. This was indicative of flight from the scene of the assassination; furthermore, after traveling only two blocks Oswald left the bus when it became stalled in heavy traffic and, as you will soon learn, hailed a taxi.

The bus transfer was dated Friday, Nov. 22, 1963, was marked for the "Lakewood-Marsalis" route, and was punched in two places with the distinctive punchmark of the bus driver.

Although we were sure McWatters was accurate in his identification of his punch mark, we found him inaccurate in a number of other aspects of his testimony, including his identification of Oswald in a police lineup at around 6:30 PM on the day of the assassination. Therefore, in our final Report we wrote that "McWatters', recollection alone was too vague to be a basis for placing Oswald on the bus." However, the combination of Mrs. Mary Bledsoe plus the bus transfer, we felt, was evidence that Oswald had boarded the bus, and Oswald himself admitted in his interrogation that he had been on the bus.

In a reconstruction of this bus trip, agents of the Secret Service and the FBI walked the seven blocks from the front entrance of the Depository Building to Murphy and Elm three times, averaging 6-1/2 minutes for the three trips. A bus moving through heavy traffic on Elm from Murphy to Lamar was timed at 4 minutes. If Oswald left the Depository Building at 12:33 PM, walked seven blocks directly to Murphy and Elm, and boarded a bus almost immediately, he would have boarded the bus at approximately 12:40 PM, and left it at approximately 12:44 PM.

I double-checked the FBI time estimates on walking seven blocks east from the TSBD Building to the place where Oswald boarded the bus, and I also double-checked the time it took the bus to move through heavy traffic. The estimates were accurate.

After Oswald left the bus, he hailed a cab in front of the Greyhound Bus Depot. According to cab driver William Whaley, his trip sheet written records for Nov. 22 showed a trip from

Greyhound, 500 North Beckley, I think it is marked 12:30 to 12:45. Now that could have been 10 minutes off in each direction because I didn't use a watch, I just guess, in other words, all my trips are marked about 15 minutes each.

Mr. Ball. Tell me when you make the entries, you make the entries when?

Mr. Whaley. Sometimes I make them right after I make the trips, sir, and sometimes I make three or four trips before I make the entries.

Mr. Whaley had just pulled in front of the Greyhound Bus Depot, where he had dropped a passenger, when he noticed Oswald walking "south on Lamar from Commerce" on the west side of the street.

Mr. Whaley. He said, "May I have the cab?"

I said, "You sure can. Get in." And instead of opening the back door he opened the front door, which is allowable there, and got in.

Mr. Ball. Got in the front door?

Mr. Whaley. Yes, sir. The front seat. And about that tiime an old lady, I think she was an old lady, I don't remember nothing but her sticking her head down past him in the door and said, "Driver, will you call me a cab down here?"

She had seen him get this cab and she wanted one, too, and he opened the door a little bit like he was going to get out and he said, "I will let you have this one," and she says, "No, the driver can call me one."

So, I didn't call one because I knew before I could call one one would come around the block and keep it pretty well covered.

Mr. Ball. Is that what you said?

Mr. Whaley. No, sir; that is not what I said, but that is the reason I didn't call one at the time and I asked him where he wanted to go. And he said "500 North Beckley."

Well, I started up, I started to that address, and the police cars, the sirens was going, running crisscrossing everywhere, just a big uproar in that end of town and I said, "What the hell. I wonder what the hell is the uproar?"

And he never said anything. So I figured he was one of these people that don't like to talk so I never said any more to him.

But when I got pretty close to 500 block at Neches and North Beckley which is the 500 block, he said, "This will do fine," and I pulled over to the curb right there. He gave me a dollar bill, the trip was 95 cents. He gave me a dollar bill and didn't say anything, just got out and closed the door and walked around the front of the cab over to the other side of the street. Of course, traffic was moving through there and I put it in gear and moved on, that is the last I saw of him.

Whaley estimated the total trip was about two and one-half miles.

Mr. Ball. Can you give me any estimate of the time it took you to go that 2-1/2 miles?

Mr. Whaley. Not actually, sir. I run it again with the policeman because the policeman was worried, he run the same trip and he couldn't come out the same time I did. But he was turning off of Jackson and Lamar when the light was wrong, and he was hitting a red light at Wood—I mean at Austin and Jackson and he hit a red light at

Wood and Austin, then he hit a red light at Houston. Where I wait to make my turn until the light is right just after it has been green, almost ready for it to come red, turn right then, then the other lights turn green just as fast as you get to them, go on right through, you save about 2 minutes in traffic that way. That is where I got the 2 minutes on him he never could make up. So I had to go back with him to make that trip to show him I was right.

Mr. Ball. How much time, in that experiment, when you hit the lights right, how long did it take you?

Mr. Whaley. Nine minutes.

Representative Ford. Now on this particular trip with Oswald, do you recall the lights being with you?

Mr. Whaley. They were with me, sir; for I timed them that way before I took off. Because I made that so much that I know the light system and how they are going to turn.

Representative Ford. So this was a typical trip?

Mr. Whaley. Yes, sir.

The Chairman. The witness has been driving a taxicab in Dallas for 36 years.

Mr. Whaley. Thirty-seven, sir.

The Chairman. Thirty-seven.

Mr. Whaley. You name an intersection in the city of Dallas and I will tell you what is on all four corners.

Whaley was in error when he said he let the passenger off at "Neches and North Beckley."

We asked Whaley to mark on a map of Dallas with a large "X" what he thought was the intersection of Neches and Beckley. He said,

"Yes, sir; that is right, because that is the 500 block of North Beckley." However, Neches and Beckley do not intersect. Neches is within one-half block of the roominghouse at 1026 North Beckley where Oswald was living. The 500 block of North Beckley is five blocks south of the roominghouse.

Whaley's testimony was taken in Washington on Mar. 12. After examining the map that he marked and finding the error in his statement concerning where he dropped the passenger, Joe Ball and I decided to see Whaley during one of our trips to Dallas. I met with Whaley and we got into a car driven by a Secret Service agent. I asked Whaley to direct the driver along the same route that Whaley took on Nov. 22 while we timed the trip.

We left the Greyhound Bus Depot and Whaley told the driver the route to take. As we drove into the Oak Cliff section of Dallas, we turned onto Beckley Street and Whaley directed the driver to a point 20 feet north of the northwest corner of the intersection of Beckley and Neely, the point at which he said his passenger alighted. This was the 700 block of North Beckley. The elapsed time of the reconstructed run from the Greyhound Bus Depot to Neely and Beckley by stopwatch was 5 minutes 30 seconds.

I then timed the walk from Beckley and Neely to Oswald's rooming house at 1026 North Beckley. It took 5 minutes 45 seconds. I then interrogated Whaley in Dallas before a court reporter.

Mr. Belin. Mr. Whaley, today at noon there were six people including yourself that got in the car to travel that route that you drove a passenger on Nov. 22, is that correct?

Mr. Whaley. Yes, sir.

Mr. Belin. One of them is sitting here in this room, Dr. Goldberg, over there. Do you see him?

Mr. Whaley. Yes, sir.

Mr. Belin. Then you and I got in the car, and then Secret Service Agent John Joe Howlett. We drove in his car and he was the driver, wasn't he?

Mr. Whaley. Yes, sir.

Mr. Belin. Then there was Mr. Joe Ball, Joseph A. Ball, and then a Mr. Davis, this tall light-haired person?

Mr. Whaley. Yes, sir.

Mr. Belin. Mr. Davis is from the attorney general's office in Texas.

Now what is the fact as to whether or not we went to the Greyhound Bus Depot here in Dallas?

Mr. Whaley. Yes, sir.

Mr. Belin. Did you point out the place where you said you picked up this passenger?

Mr. Whaley. I did, sir.

Mr. Belin. We had a stopwatch, didn't we?

Mr. Whaley. Yes, sir.

Mr. Belin. Then you directed us to take a certain route, is that correct?

Mr. Whaley. That's correct.

Whaley then described the route from the Greyhound Bus Depot to Beckley Street.

Mr. Belin. Did we go about the speed you drove that day?

Mr. Whaley. Almost. Going across the viaduct is just about the speed, but he slowed down going up Zangs Boulevard. He slowed down a little slower than I was going.

My normal rate of speed, I don't remember the exact speed I was traveling, but I assume it was normal, because that is the way I travel all the time when traffic is clear enough.

Mr. Belin. Your normal rate of speed would be a little bit faster than the rate that he took?

Mr. Whaley. Yes, sir. In other words, not enough to make over half a minute difference in the timing.

Mr. Belin. Was traffic clearer on that particular day of Nov. 22?

Mr. Whaley. It was extra clear, for some reason. That street was clear except when I hit Beckley. When I hit Beckley, there was cars turning to the left, and I had to stop for the light.

Mr. Belin. When we got to Beckley at noon today, or shortly thereafter, the traffic light was green, but you told us you had stopped, so we waited through the red light, did we not?

Mr. Whaley. Yes, sir.

Mr. Belin. Then he turned on Beckley?

Mr. Whaley. Yes, sir.

Mr. Belin. Heading south?

Mr. Whaley. Yes, sir.

Mr. Belin. Now when this man that you picked up on Nov. 22 got into your cab, where did he say he wanted to go?

Mr. Whaley. To the 500 block of North Beckley.

Mr. Belin. I will take you back to Nov. 22.

You turned south on Beckley and then where did you go as you turned south on Beckley?

Mr. Whaley. I went right up on Beckley headed toward the 500 block.

Mr. Belin. Then what happened?

Mr. Whaley. When I got to Beckley almost to the intersection of Beckley and Neely, he said, "This will do right here," and I pulled up to the curb.

Mr. Belin. Was that the 500 block of North Beckley?

Mr. Whaley. No, sir; that was the 700 block.

Mr. Belin. You let him out not at the 500 block but the 700 block of North Beckley?

Mr. Whaley. Yes, sir.

Mr. Belin. Had you crossed Neely Street yet when you let him off?

Mr. Whaley. No, sir.

Mr. Belin. About how far north of Neely street did you let the man off?

Mr. Whaley. About 20 feet.

Whaley had testified in Washington that Oswald was wearing a jacket. He was in error, for Oswald had left his blue jacket in the domino room of the TSBD Building. Ball and I did not feel that Whaley was a particularly reliable witness. However, the question of whether Oswald rode in a taxi is resolved because Oswald said in his interrogation that he had taken a taxi-cab to the Oak Cliff section of Dallas. We wrote in our report:

The Greyhound Bus Station at Lamar and Jackson Streets, where Oswald entered Whaley's cab, is three to four short blocks south of Lamar and Elm. If Oswald left the bus at 12:44 PM and walked directly to the terminal, he would have entered the cab at 12:47 or 12:48 PM.

If he was discharged at Neely and Beckley and walked directly to his rooming-house, he would have arrived there about 12:59 to 1 PM. From the 500 block of North Beckley, the walk would be a few minutes longer, but in either event he would have been in the roominghouse at about 1 PM. This is the approximate time he entered the roominghouse, according to Earlene Roberts, the housekeeper there.

Mrs. Roberts knew Lee Harvey Oswald as "O. H. Lee":

He didn't spend Thursday night there and that was unusual, because he would always leave on Friday. That's the best I can do. He was just the type of person you just don't know—and I just thought he didn't like people and he would mix with nobody and he wouldn't say nothing. The only time he would ever say anything was when his rent was due and he was never behind.

On Nov. 22, Mrs. Roberts said that Oswald

came home that Friday in an unusual hurry.

Mr. Ball. And about what time was this?

Mrs. Roberts. Well, it was after President Kennedy had been shot and I had a friend that said, "Roberts, President Kennedy has been shot," and I said, "Oh, no." She said, "Turn on your television," and I said "What are you trying to do, pull my leg?" And she said, "Well, go turn it on." I went and turned it on and I was trying to clear it up—I could hear them talking but I couldn't get the picture and he come in and I just looked up and I said, "Oh, you are in a hurry." He never said a thing, not nothing. He went on to his room and stayed about 3 or 4 minutes.

Mr. Ball. As he came in, did you say anything else except, "You are in a hurry"?

Mrs. Roberts. No.

Mr. Ball. Did you say anything about the President being shot?

Mrs. Roberts. No.

Mr. Ball. You were working with the television?

Mrs. Roberts. I was trying to clear it up to see what was happening and try to find out about President Kennedy.

Mr. Ball. Why did you say to this man as he came in, "You are in a hurry"—why did you say that?

Mrs. Roberts. Well, he just never has come in and he was walking unusually fast and he just hadn't been that way and I just looked up and I said, "Oh, you are in a hurry."

Mr. Ball. You mean he was walking faster than he usually was?

Mrs. Roberts. Yes.

Mr. Ball. When he came in the door, what did he do?

Mrs. Roberts. He just walked in—he didn't look around at me—he didn't say nothing and went on to his room.

Mr. Ball. Did he run?

Mrs. Roberts. He wasn't running, but he was walking pretty fast—he was all but running.

Mr. Ball. Then, what happened after that?

Mrs. Roberts. He went to his room and he was in his shirt sleeves but I couldn't tell you whether it was a long-sleeved shirt or what color it was or nothing, and he got a jacket and put it on—it was kind of a zipper jacket. He was zipping it up as he went out the door.

I reconstructed the time it took to walk from the house at 1026 North Beckley to the scene of the Tippit murder. There were several possible routes. The most direct route required 12 minutes walking time. However, I also took a more indirect route, in light of the testimony of Helen Markham that she saw Oswald crossing Patton Street rather than walking in front of her along Patton (which would have been the most direct route) and this route at a normal walking pace could be readily done in 14 minutes. If Oswald arrived at his rooming house shortly before one o'clock and stayed three or four minutes, it was obvious that even at a normal walking pace he could be at the scene of the Tippit murder at the time it occurred—around 1:15 PM. See the map on page 386 showing Oswald's activities after he left the TSBD Building.

After the assassination, there was much comment about whether Oswald could have left the TSBD Building after the assassination, reached his rooming house and from there arrived at the scene of the Tippit murder. Apart from the fact that all of our time checks showed that this could be readily accomplished, the facts are that we know he was seen in the TSBD Building two or three minutes after the assassination, and we know he was the gunman who killed Officer Tippit.

Although Ball and I felt that Mrs. Roberts was a witness subject to the same kind of inaccuracies as the bus driver McWatters and the cab driver

Whaley, there is no reason not to believe Mrs. Roberts' testimony that she saw Oswald around one o'clock. Certainly, she knew Oswald, as did Mary Bledsoe.

Oswald had the bus transfer, which showed that he was on the bus. Insofar as the taxi ride is concerned, although we did not feel total reliance could be placed on Whaley's testimony because of its unreliability in several areas, Oswald himself admitted that he had taken a cab.

One aspect of Mrs. Roberts' testimony gave rise to great speculation and rumor. Mrs. Roberts testified, as summarized in our Report,

that at about 1 PM on Nov. 22, after Oswald had returned to the roominghouse, a Dallas police car drove slowly by the front of the 1026 North Beckley premises and stopped momentarily; she said she heard its horn several times. Mrs. Roberts stated that the occupants of the car were not known to her even though she had worked for some policemen who would occasionally come by.

She said the policeman she knew drove car No. 170 and that this was not the number on the police car that honked on Nov. 22. She testified that she first thought the car she saw was No. 106 and then said that it was No. 107. In an FBI interview she had stated that she looked out the front window and saw police car No. 207. Investigation has not produced any evidence that there was a police vehicle in the area of 1026 North Beckley at about 1 PM on Nov. 22. Squad car 207 was at the TSBD Building, as was car 106. Squad cars 170 and 107 were sold in Apr. 1963 and their numbers were not reassigned until Feb. 1964.

The testimony of Earlene Roberts, in light of the testimony of Roger Craig, is fertile breeding ground for the possibility that accomplices aided Oswald. From our observations as trial lawyers, Ball and I felt that neither Deputy Sheriff Roger Craig, landlady Mary Bledsoe, bus driver Cecil McWatters, cab driver William Whaley, nor housekeeper Earlene Roberts was a 100 per cent reliable witness and that the testimony of all of them should be viewed with some degree of skepticism.

However, there can be little doubt that Oswald was on a bus, in light of his own admissions during interrogation, the bus transfer in his pocket and the fact that Mary Bledsoe had a basis on which to recognize him; there was little doubt that Oswald, penurious though he was, took a taxicab, in light of his own admission during interrogation coupled with the testimony of Whaley; and there is little doubt that he went to his rooming house, in light of his own admission coupled with the testimony of Earlene Roberts.

The lawyers working in the areas of possible domestic conspiracy, possible foreign conspiracy and possible conspiracy involving Jack Ruby followed every possible lead to ascertain whether there was any reliable evidence showing that anyone other than Lee Harvey Oswald was involved in the assassination of President Kennedy or the murder of Officer J. D. Tippit. No such evidence was uncovered. However, there was one perplexing matter that troubled all of us; this concerned the possible destination of Lee Harvey Oswald when he was stopped by Officer Tippit in the Oak Cliff section of Dallas.

46
"THIS IS THE WAY
I WOULD GO ABOUT IT"

Having reached the conclusion that Lee Harvey Oswald was the assassin of President Kennedy, we had only one question remaining: Was anyone else involved in the assassination? Although in the course of our investigation Ball and I touched on this area, the basic responsibility for it fell on the six lawyers on the Warren Commission staff who were concentrating in Areas III, IV and V.

Albert E. Jenner, Jr., an outstanding Chicago trial attorney and past president of the American College of Trial Lawyers and a former professor of law at Northwestern University, and Wesley James Liebeler, a former managing editor of the University of Chicago Law Review, now a professor of law, worked in Area III, investigating Oswald's background in an effort to determine motive, assuming he was the assassin, and also investigating the possibility of domestic conspiracy (apart from Jack Ruby). These lawyers found no credible evidence that any group acted together to plan the assassination of President Kennedy on Nov. 22.

One of the depositions taken by Jim Liebeler provides a keen insight into the psychology of witnesses. The witness was Dr. Renatus Hartogs, who practiced psychiatry in New York. Since 1951, as part of his professional work, he had been the chief psychiatrist for the Youth House of New York City. In 1953, when Lee Harvey Oswald was living in New York, Dr. Hartogs examined Oswald, then 13½ years old.

Dr. Hartogs said he remembered the interview with Lee Harvey Oswald because he had used Oswald as a subject of discussion in a seminar. Recalling the seminar, Dr. Hartogs stated: "We gave a seminar on this boy in which we discussed him, because he came to us on a charge of truancy from school, and yet when I examined him, I found him to have definite traits of dangerousness. In other words, this child had a potential for explosive, aggressive, assaultive acting out which was rather unusual to find in a child who was sent to Youth House on such a mild charge as truancy from school."

Dr. Hartogs further testified that he recommended to the Court " . . . that this youngster should be committed to an institution."

You can find Dr. Hartogs' testimony in Volume VIII, beginning at page 214. After the deposition was completed, Jim Liebeler asked the court reporter to include Dr. Hartogs' 1953 report in it. This is shown in Volume VII, pages 223-224.

In the 1953 report Dr. Hartogs stated, " . . . strongly resistive and negativistic features were thus noted—but psychotic mental content was denied and no indication of psychotic mental changes was arrived at." Nowhere is there any mention of Lee Harvey Oswald having "definite traits of dangerousness" or "a potential for explosive, aggressive, assaultive acting out . . ." Nowhere is there any recommendation for committing Lee Harvey Oswald to an institution. Rather, the recommendation was that he be placed on probation on condition that he seek help from a child guidance clinic and that his mother be urged to seek psychotherapeutic guidance through contact with a family agency. In his deposition, Dr. Hartogs put himself out on a limb. With the original psychiatric report in hand, Jim Liebeler sawed off the limb.

The import of this is twofold: (1) The passage of time blurs the accuracy of human recollection, even of an expert witness such as a psychiatrist. (2) In trying to find all of the facts, Jim Liebeler had no inhibitions about destroying the testimony of a psychiatrist.[1]

Area IV was the foreign conspiracy area. Two lawyers, William T. Coleman Jr. and W. David Slawson, concentrated in Area IV. Bill Coleman was a magna cum laude graduate of the Harvard Law School and had served as an editor of the Harvard Law Review. After a clerkship with Justice Felix Frankfurter, he became associated with a Philadelphia law firm.

Dave Slawson, who is now a professor of law at the University of Southern California Law School, had graduated number one in his class at Amherst and had also been president of the student body. After graduate work under a science fellowship at Princeton University, he enrolled in the Harvard Law School, where he was graduated magna cum laude. He was a Note Editor of the Harvard Law Review.

In one sense, their work was the most frustrating of all because details of much of their investigation could not be disclosed for reasons of national security.

Some people have told me that they find the foreign conspiracy section in our Report the weakest because of its lack of detail. I agree with this criticism. The Commission was far too broad in its classification of "Top Secret," although I do admit that there was some specific detail which could not be included for reasons of national security—principally in the area of Presidential protection and certain sources of foreign information. We lawyers laughed about how *everything* was stamped "Top Secret," particularly since we were working with these papers for several months before security clearances were given to the entire staff.

---

[1]We all know that the passage of time dims the accuracy of our memories. It would not surprise me if in future years witnesses come forth with memories of conversations that on their face would indicate that others were implicated with Oswald. Although Lee Harvey Oswald at some time months ahead of the assassination might have told someone that he was going to kill the President, the faulty recollections of Dr. Hartogs are ample evidence of the skepticism with which we must treat all reports of conversations that allegedly took place years earlier.

Ultimately the reader was forced to rely on the professional integrity of the two lawyers who were concentrating in the foreign conspiracy area.

This was one of the great virtues of having an independent staff of lawyers selected from across the country that were not connected with any branch of government. The only exception was Howard P. Willens, who was Second Assistant in the Criminal Division of the U. S. Department of Justice and who acted both as an assistant counsel and as liaison between the Warren Commission and the Department of Justice. No government employee had more integrity or more devotion to his work than Howard Willens, a Phi Beta Kappa graduate of the University of Michigan, where he was president of the student government, and honor graduate of the Yale Law School, where he was an editor of the Yale Law Journal. Willens is now a partner in a Washington, D.C., law firm.

Although the foreign conspiracy area was frustrating to the extent that we were limited in what we could write in our Report, it was not the most frustrating. That dubious distinction belonged to Area V—the Jack Ruby area. Two fine lawyers worked for months, following every lead to determine whether Ruby was in any way connected with the assasination, other than as the killer of Lee Harvey Oswald. Ruby knew hundreds of people. He had a notebook with a large number of names, each of which had to be followed up. As you might expect, many people thought that they had seen Ruby and Oswald together on various occasions. Thousands of leads had to be followed up. Every one of them was a dead-end street.

The two lawyers who concentrated in this area were Leon D. Hubert, Jr., Phi Beta Kappa and Order of the Coif graduate of Tulane University and the Tulane Law School, experienced practitioner of law, and now professor of law at Tulane University, and Burt W. Griffin of Cleveland, graduate of Amherst College, Note and Comment Editor of the Yale Law Journal, and a former Assistant U. S. Attorney for the Northern District of Ohio. Just as I tried to find evidence contrary to the initial FBI and Secret Service determinations that Lee Harvey Oswald was the sole assassin of President Kennedy, Leon Hubert and Burt Griffin tried to find some evidence of conspiracy involving Jack Ruby. At the end of their investigation they were forced to concede that there were no grounds for believing that Ruby's killing of Oswald was part of a conspiracy.

I remember days when Leon would walk into my office and his eyes would light up as he would summarize his latest analysis of a possible link between Oswald and Ruby. Then, within a few days or a week or two, when I would ask him about what happened, he would say that there was just nothing to it.

As I talked with Leon and Burt about the course of our investigation, I would often go back to the one element that was to me most puzzling, and which, based on my conversations with people in Dallas, was also most puzzling to them: Where was Oswald heading at the time of his encounter with Dallas Police Officer J. D. Tippit? No one will ever know the answer. However, although it is pure conjecture, there was general agreement among us lawyers conducting the investigation that the most plausible theory was the one that I propounded, which had as its starting point the unused bus transfer found in Oswald's shirt pocket after his arrest in the Texas Theatre.

Because of the events of Nov. 24, when Ruby killed Oswald, there was wide speculation that there was some relationship between the two. The speculation was compounded because the apartment of Jack Ruby was approximately two-thirds of a mile from the scene of the shooting of Officer J. D. Tippit, and at the time of the shooting Oswald was headed in the general direction of that apartment.

We made every effort to uncover credible evidence of a possible link between Oswald and Ruby. No such evidence was discovered. Nor is there any definite evidence of any other specific destination of Oswald.

Perhaps Oswald was walking with no destination in mind. After the completion of the background study on Oswald's life, several Commission lawyers thought that this might be possible, either because he didn't ever expect to get out of the TSBD Building or because, psychologically, he almost wanted to be apprehended. And there was evidence pointing toward one or both of these possibilities. For instance, on the night before the assassination, for the first time Oswald left his wedding ring on the dresser in his wife's bedroom in Irving, Texas, where she was staying. He also left with her most of his money and, in contrast to past conduct, gave her permission to spend a portion of it for clothing.

On the other hand, these possibilities were never acceptable to many of us. I was certain that Oswald had a destination. After all, if he wanted to be captured, why had he rushed back to his room on Beckley Street to get his pistol?

If he had carried his pistol into the TSBD Building and if every employee had been searched after the assassination, the pistol would have been discovered and suspicion would have been immediately cast on Oswald. Besides, carrying a concealed weapon is against the law and this in itself would have meant immediate arrest. As a matter of fact, I believed that this was probably the basic reason that Oswald shot Tippit, because as Tippit got out of the car and headed toward Oswald, one of the first things he would have done would be to search Oswald. The search would have disclosed this pistol, and the pistol would have meant immediate arrest.

As the weeks went by, no one came up with any plausible theory.

June was approaching. We still had nothing. The Chief Justice and Congressman Ford were going to Dallas with Ball and Arlen Specter as their guides. Among other things, the final arrangements had been completed for our interview with Jack Ruby. An Army jet was to take them from Washington to Dallas and I was tempted to go along, primarily because I wanted to see Ruby and hear what he had to say about the shooting of Oswald. However, I had been working night and day to complete a first draft of the final report in our area, and I wanted to complete that draft before the birth of our fourth child, which we expected at the end of June.

On Memorial Day weekend the idea germinated. The bus transfer—why did Oswald ask for the bus transfer when he left the bus within a few blocks and hailed a cab? It could not be used any other day, for it was dated Nov. 22, 1963. It could not be used much later in the day because it was "cut" at the 1 PM mark to show when it might be used.

We had substantial evidence that Oswald was thrifty. We also knew he was very familiar with bus routes; he did not own a car. One possible answer was that he took a transfer because he expected to use a bus again and wanted to save a bus fare. Could it be that there was some nearby bus transfer point toward which Oswald was walking when he was stopped by Officer Tippit?

But if he were trying to get another Dallas bus, assuming that there was a nearby transfer point, where would that bus take him? Where would he be heading?

To me, the most obvious destination would have been Mexico and then Cuba. I knew that the men in Area IV had discovered that Oswald traveled to Mexico City on a bus on Sept. 26, 1963, and while there he tried to make some kind of arrangements to get to Cuba.[2]

My theory of his destination was Mexico and Cuba, but did we have any evidence in the record to back up this theory? When I asked Jim Liebeler, he called my attention to Nelson Delgado, a Marine buddy of Oswald's, who testified that Oswald once said that if he were every trying to escape law enforcement authorities in the United States, he would try to get to Mexico and from there go to Russia via Cuba. " 'This is the way I would go about it.' "

Moreover, Marina Oswald had testified that not only did Oswald desire to get to Cuba, but he had also talked about commandeering an airplane with a pistol and flying to Cuba.

The idea simmered. I asked Dave Slawson if they had ever checked bus schedules from Dallas to Mexico City. There was a report of an investigation by agents in the Secret Service office in Dallas. The report had maps attached and the Secret Service had marked the regular bus routes from Dallas on both the Greyhound and Trailways lines. I examined these routes—and my theory was shot full of holes. The Trailways bus routes went nowhere near the area and as for the Greyhound bus routes—Oswald had encountered Tippit somewhat *east* of Beckley Street, where his rooming house was, and the Greyhound routes out of Dallas went on Zangs Boulevard, slightly *west* of Beckley Street.

I was still troubled by the question of Oswald's possible destination. There must have been a reason for him to keep that bus transfer.

On June 13, I took a break from my other work and returned to the Secret Service file on the bus routes to Mexico. I looked again at the map prepared

[2]Oswald was a great admirer of Fidel Castro. I wondered if President Kennedy's handling of the Bay of Pigs incident could have had any influence on the actions of Oswald on Nov. 22.

by the Secret Service, which showed that the Greyhound busses followed
Highway 77 south, moving along Zangs Boulevard in Dallas, which was a
block or two *west* and parallel to Beckley Street.

What about the bus schedules—would these shed any more light? The
Secret Service report also included the official Greyhound schedules. There
were ten southbound busses out of Dallas. Two were expresses; and the
remaining eight made their first regular stop at a place called Waxahachie.

I studied the time it took for each of these eight busses to get from Dallas
to Waxahachie. Seven took either 42 or 43 minutes. The eighth took 47
minutes.

Could this eighth bus take longer because it went on a different route? I
analyzed the flag stops shown on the bus timetable. Of the eight busses, one
made no flag stops. But six of these seven others had flag stops at a place
called Pleasant Run; the seventh made no stop at Pleasant Run but rather
made a flag stop at places called Lisbon and Lancaster, where none of the
other busses made flag stops. It was the bus on the 47-minute run that made
these flag stops at Lisbon and Lancaster and none at Pleasant Run. If
Pleasant Run was important enough for the seven other busses, its absence
on the schedule of the eighth plus the longer time to Waxahachie indicated a
different route.

I went back to the Dallas map. There was an area of Dallas known as
Lisbon and also one known as Lancaster; both were in the *southeast* portion
of the city and would not be reached by the bus route on Zangs Boulevard
(Highway 77). However, another highway, 342, traveled along Lancaster
Road to Dallas. I checked a map of the Dallas city bus routes and found one
that went down Lancaster Road.

I quickly phoned Secret Service agent Sorrels at his home in Dallas. At the
time of the Tippit murder, Oswald was only three blocks away, heading
toward the intersection of Marsalis and Jefferson Streets in Dallas. The bus
transfer had been issued by a Marsalis bus. The transfer ticket was torn at
1:00 PM. I first wanted to know how long the transfer would be valid and
where the transfer could be used. I then wanted to know what bus routes
could be boarded at Marsalis and Jefferson.

Then I turned to the Greyhound bus schedule and asked Sorrels the route
of the Greyhound bus that stopped at the Lisbon flag stop. I also asked for
the precise location of the Lisbon flag stop. I also wanted to know if there
were any restaurants or theatres nearby where a person might wait for a bus,
rather than waiting on the street.

There was another reason for my interest: The first southbound bus out of
Dallas that Oswald could have taken after the assassination was the bus that
made the flag stop at Lisbon. It left downtown Dallas at 3:15 PM and went to
Laredo, Texas, at the Mexican border, where connections could be made
after a layover of 30 minutes for a bus to Mexico. By Monday, June 15, I had
the answers.

The original report on bus routes prepared by the Secret Service was accurate for only seven of the eight daily Greyhound southbound busses. I was correct in my hypothesis that the 3:15 PM Greyhound bus, which made the flag stop at Lisbon, did not follow the regular bus route on Highway 77 but rather a route along Lancaster on Highway 342 which first headed southeast and then, some miles after it left Dallas, returned to the southwest and eventually intersected Highway 77 midway between Dallas and Waxahachie. It made the bus route a little bit longer than the others and accounted for the extra few minutes on the bus timetables.

I was also correct in my hypothesis that a city transit company bus could be boarded at the intersection of Marsalis and Jefferson Streets near the scene of the Tippit murder, which went along Lancaster Road past the Lisbon flag stop. Finally, I was correct that the transfer would be valid for that bus. The rules of the bus line provided that the transfer was ordinarily valid for 15 minutes. However, the Lancaster Road bus route at that time had busses scheduled only every hour. If the bus for which the transfer was being used was scheduled an hour later, the transfer would be good for that bus, regardless of the time that had transpired after leaving the bus from which the transfer was obtained. In other words, the Marsalis bus line driver gave Oswald a transfer cut at 1:00 PM. However, the next bus at Lancaster Road would not have arrived at the transfer point until after 1:30. Accordingly, the transfer that Oswald had in his pocket was good for the Lancaster bus route.

There was one additional fact that supported my theory. The intersection at Jefferson and Marsalis Streets was the *only* transfer point in the Oak Cliff section of Dallas at which Oswald could have used his transfer. And there were restaurants and other businesses located in the vicinity of the Lisbon flag stop where Oswald could have readily awaited the arrival of the southbound Greyhound bus.

From the rooming house of Oswald at 1026 North Beckley, the nearest boarding point for the use of this transfer was at Jefferson and Marsalis, and he had almost arrived there at the time that he was stopped by Officer Tippit.

By now, most of my colleagues were aware of my original theory; I told them of the confirmation of my hypothesis. It seemed by far the best explanation of where Oswald was heading at the time of the Tippit shooting.

However, we had the basic question of whether to include this hypothesis in our published report. We even discussed the fact that at the transfer point of Jefferson and Marsalis Oswald could board a bus that might take him within walking distance of one of the two private airports in the southern part of Dallas. We recalled the discussion with Marina about commandeering an airplane and the pistol that Oswald had obtained at his rooming house.

We asked ourselves questions. If Oswald were going to Mexico, why had he left most of his money with his wife? One answer was that he had kept enough money to enable him to get to Mexico, and another was that even if he did not have enough money to get to Mexico, the pistol would have helped him obtain some.

I dictated a first draft of the summary of my theory and passed it to my colleagues for their comments. Then, on July 11, I dictated a final draft for possible inclusion in the Commission Report. The argument for inclusion: During the weeks that I spent in Dallas, the speculation that was the most prevalent (as a matter of fact, the only widespread speculation on this subject in Dallas) was that there must have been some connection between Oswald and Ruby because Oswald was heading toward Ruby's apartment, only two-thirds of a mile away. It was true that we had shown no connection between Oswald and Ruby. However, even though any theory on Oswald's destination was basically speculation, would it not be appropriate to show that there were possibilities of places that Oswald might have been heading other than Ruby's apartment? Then we could state that we had no evidence of any destination for Oswald and that there was not sufficient evidence upon which to conclude that he was heading for the bus transfer point at Marsalis and Jefferson, even though this might be a reasonable speculation.

Did we not have a duty to suggest the possibility of the bus transfer point in light of such wide speculation about Ruby? This was particularly true since we had a chapter entitled "Speculations and Rumors."

The two people who made most of the final decisions regarding what went into the final draft of the Report were Norman Redlich and Howard Willens. Norman acted as General Counsel Lee Rankin's executive assistant. Although I normally worked 60- to 70-hour weeks with the Commission, the standard for Norman Redlich was even higher. Magna cum laude graduate of Williams College, Executive Editor of the Yale Law Journal, Master of Law degree from New York University and professor at the New York University School of Law—he was an able lawyer.

Norman argued that because it was a theory and not a fact, no mention of it should be made in the final Report. Norman won the argument, even though we had a section in the Report entitled "Speculations and Rumors." This was just one of many differences I had concerning how the final Report should be prepared. For instance, I basically wanted a two-volume final Report, that would have included extensive portions of actual testimony, so that the reader would understand the ultimate foundation of many of the key summarizations of fact in our Report. I felt this would serve also as a better foundation upon which the Report could stand in the face of attacks that I knew would be coming, both at home and abroad. The rationale of the majority was that a two-volume Report would not be read by many people, and they wanted as wide dissemination of the Report as possible.

Be that as it may, you have already seen important portions of the actual testimony from witnesses, much of which I wanted included in the final Report. You have also seen my theory concerning Oswald's destination at the time of the Tippit shooting. As I said at the outset, it is pure speculation. Oswald might not have known about the route of the southbound Greyhound bus. He may have intended to use his pistol to commandeer an airplane. Or he may have had no specific destination in mind. No one will ever know the truth now that Oswald is dead.

47

"YOU KILLED MY
PRESIDENT, YOU RAT"

The time was July 18, 1964. The place was the Dallas County Jail. Against the advice of his chief attorney, Jack Ruby was scheduled to take a lie detector test arranged by the Warren Commission. Present with Ruby were his two attorneys, Clayton Fowler and Joe Tonahill. The man administering the test was one of the ablest in the field, FBI polygraph operator Bill P. Herndon. The representative from the Warren Commission was Arlen Specter.

At the last minute Clayton Fowler, then Ruby's chief counsel, tried to stop the test. He told Specter that Ruby had changed his mind. Specter was not to be denied. He immediately had the court reporter present in the room begin making a formal transcript of what was happening. The record is printed in Volume XIV, page 504, of the 26 volumes of testimony and exhibits that we published together with our Report.

Fowler said that he wanted to discuss it once again with his client. "And then Jack may say whether he wants to go ahead with this and how I have advised him, and that he has on numerous occasions requested it, and I will tell him that the Chief Justice promised to give it to him and they are hereby ready to do it, which I am going to tell him, and if he insists on it, I can't and won't try to hold him back. . . ."

Mr. Specter. Let the record show that Mr. Fowler left the room, and in approximately 5 minutes thereafter, returned to the room from his conference with Mr. Ruby.

Mr. Fowler. He says he's going to take this test regardless of his lawyers, and he says, "By God, I'm going to take the test."

Why did Jack Ruby determine that he was going to undergo a polygraph examination, regardless of the advice of his own chief counsel? Why did the Chief Justice of the United States finally agree to help arrange for such an exam, when the results of lie detector tests are inadmissible as evidence in a court of law? The answers to these questions have never before been told. We have to go back to late Jan., 1964, when I first discussed with Joe Ball the possibility of our asking for polygraph examinations of both Marina Oswald and Jack Ruby.

Joe Ball had 35 years of experience in trial work and had gained the reputation as being one of the outstanding defense lawyers on the West Coast. As a lecturer in criminal law at the University of Southern California

Law School and a member of the U. S. Judicial Conference Advisory Committee on the Federal Rules of Criminal Procedure, he was well aware of the limitations of the polygraph. It is not a *per se* determinant of whether a person has told the truth. In large part, the validity of the test depends upon the competency of the operator—the more experienced and the more able the operator, the more one can rely on the results of the test.

We knew that the FBI had capable polygraph operators. Even here, however, we did not want to rely blindly on the results of any test. However, we felt that it would be a valuable aid to our investigation, particularly in areas where we were limited in testing the credibility of statements by Marina Oswald.

Norman Redlich had submitted to the staff a long list of proposed questions for Marina Oswald, who was to testify the first week of February. To the list I had but one addition, which I submitted in a written memorandum on Jan. 29, 1964. I wanted to determine whether or not Marina Oswald would be willing to submit to a polygraph examination in addition to the regular interrogation.

In my written memorandum, I gave three basic reasons for my suggestion of a polygraph: "(1) A substantial portion of key testimony by Marina is not subject to ordinary tests of credibility; (2) insofar as the public is concerned, we believe that the submission to a polygraph examination by Marina Oswald would serve as a substantial addition upon final publication of the Report; (3) if under polygraph examination it were to be shown that Marina Oswald had not been truthful in her testimony, it could throw an entirely new light on aspects of the investigation." I suggested that in approaching Marina Oswald, it be stressed that this would enhance her future in America (she was a Soviet citizen) because it would show that she had done everything possible to tell the complete story truthfully.

There was an immediate battle among the members of the staff. One member undertook research to prove the limitations of the test and to prove also that one could not blindly rely upon the results of the test. In rebuttal, I stated that I concurred that a polygraph examination had limitations. However, I argued that a major portion of the limitations depended upon the qualifications and competency of the polygraph examiner. Moreover, my purpose in wanting the polygraph examination was not as an absolute determinant to find out whether or not the witness was telling the truth, but rather was for use as an investigative aid, which with an expert operator had a very high degree of accuracy.

To this there was the reply that polygraph examinations are not admissible into evidence in courts of law. My rejoinder was that this was not an adversary trial proceeding—this was merely an investigation, and all I wanted was to make use of what I thought to be an important investigative device.

The final decision was made by the Commission. On the basis of the fact that a polygraph examination is not admissible in a court of law, my request was denied.

Perhaps I should not have been so angry about this because there were few requests that I made that were not ultimately granted. But I was independent enough to want to be without any limitations at all and I felt that if the two lawyers in Area II wanted to have a request made that Marina Oswald submit herself to a polygraph examination, that request should have been honored.

After the decision had been made on the polygraph examination for Marina Oswald, I knew that it was hopeless to ask that the Commission request that Jack Ruby take a lie detector test, particularly when he was on trial for his life because of his murder of Lee Harvey Oswald. By the time the Ruby trial would be ultimately determined with all of the appellate procedures in Texas and to the United States Supreme Court, our investigation would have been long completed. Yet, though I was not working in the Ruby area, I was determined that somehow we had to find a way to encourage Jack Ruby to take a lie detector test.

In light of the position of the Commission on polygraph examinations, I decided to take matters into my own hands. I had one thing in my favor. During the summer of 1963 I had met (on a trip abroad) Rabbi Hillel E. Silverman, who was the spiritual leader for Congregation Shearith Israel in Dallas. After the assassination, Rabbi Silverman's name appeared in the media because Jack Ruby was a member of his congregation. Although Ruby seldom attended religious services, I found out that Rabbi Silverman was regularly visiting Ruby in the Dallas County Jail.

The plan I developed was basically a very simple one: Ruby proclaimed he was innocent of any conspiracy. Yet, the fact that he had killed Oswald gave rise to all sorts of speculations and rumors in the Dallas area. Rabbi Silverman knew this. Jack Ruby knew this.

One of the best means for Jack Ruby to gain public acceptance for his statements would be for him to submit to a polygraph examination. For the average layman the fact that Jack Ruby would submit to a lie detector test would give credence to Ruby's denial of involvement in any conspiracy. Moreover, if Ruby was telling the truth and this was substantiated by the polygraph examination, this would go a long way to overcome speculation and rumors concerning conspiracy.

I knew that the Commission would not ask that Ruby submit to a polygraph examination. However, I also knew that the Commission wanted the testimony of Ruby after the completion of his trial. Therefore, I thought I might—through Rabbi Silverman—encourage Ruby himself to ask the Commission for a polygraph examination. As a matter of fact, perhaps I could go one step further and have Ruby make it a condition precedent to any testimony before the Commission: He would not testify unless the Commission agreed to give him a polygraph examination.

Obviously there were many problems to overcome. First I had to have the cooperation of Rabbi Silverman. Second, Rabbi Silverman would have to convince Ruby that the plan would be followed even though Ruby's defense attorneys might try to block it.

The trial of Jack Ruby was not completed until the first part of Mar., 1964. We had decided not to undertake any field investigation in Dallas until the trial was over so that there would be no possibility of our prejudicing the Ruby trial. Finally, in the middle of March, Joe Ball and I flew to Dallas to conduct our initial field investigation at the scene of the assassination. The first evening there, I telephoned Rabbi Silverman and arranged to see him the following Friday night.

We had a cordial vist. Although during part of the conversation we naturally discussed the assassination, I did not broach the subject of a lie detector test. Rabbi Silverman said that based on his intimate conversations with Jack Ruby, he was sure that Ruby did not know Oswald prior to the assassination and that Ruby was not directly or indirectly involved in any conspiracy.

When I returned to Dallas in late March, one of the first things I did was to contact Rabbi Silverman again. We made arrangements to meet.

In that second meeting I did not wait long to bring my plan out into the open. First, I asked Rabbi Silverman if he was personally convinced that Ruby was not involved in any conspiracy. Without hesitation, he said that he was convinced that Ruby was innocent of any conspiracy. I replied that based on conversations I had already had with citizens both inside and outside of Dallas, I believed that Ruby would never convince the world in general—and Dallas in particular—of his innocence of any conspiracy unless he undertook a lie detector test. I then told Rabbi Silverman that I knew that the Warren Commission would never ask Ruby to submit to a lie detector test. "As a matter of fact, even if Jack Ruby requested that we give him a test, I do not know if we would even then submit to his request unless he made it a condition precedent to giving any testimony before the Commission."

By the end of our conversation, Rabbi Silverman was receptive to my suggestion. However, he said that there was a problem because Ruby had already requested that a lie detector test be given him and his attorneys had refused. After all, they were charged with the primary responsibility of defending Ruby against a charge of murder, for which he had already been convicted and sentenced to death in the Dallas criminal court.

I told Rabbi Silverman that I appreciated that Ruby's life was at stake and that as a lawyer I also appreciated the fact that when a client places himself in the hands of a competent attorney, he should normally follow that attorney's advice.

I admitted to Rabbi Silverman that I also knew there were inherent risks involved in the course of action I proposed. For instance, the defense of Ruby at the time of his trial was basically one of insanity. I knew that if a lie detector test were given to Ruby, it could show enough premeditation to completely destroy that defense. Yet Ruby had already been convicted and sentenced to death. Matters could not be much worse.

To be sure, there was a great potential conflict between the desire of

Ruby's attorneys to do everything possible to free their client and my desire to do everything possible to uncover the truth.

"But after all, Ruby, himself, had gotten into this predicament. It was he who had taken the law into his own hands. Did he now not have an obligation, even at the risk of imperiling his own life and liberty, to do everything possible to let the world know the whole truth?" This is the way I put it to Rabbi Silverman.

Finally, Rabbi Silverman reached a decision. He said he knew that Ruby was innocent of any conspiracy, and he felt that in the long run the most helpful thing for Jack Ruby would be to have this innocence of conspiracy accepted throughout the world. He agreed that there could be no better way for Jack Ruby to have this accepted than through a lie detector test.

I reiterated that the only way the test could be undertaken would be for Ruby to make this a condition precedent to giving any testimony before the Warren Commission. Jack Ruby would have to be determined to take this position because I was sure that his defense attorneys might do everything possible to interfere with the test, since it could disclose (as it ultimately did disclose) that the defense of insanity was not available.

During my next trip to Dallas Rabbi Silverman told me that he had discussed this matter with Ruby and that he was making much progress. And in the following week—when I talked to Rabbi Silverman—he said that Ruby had decided to demand that the Warren Commission give him a lie detector test.

Jack Ruby made his demand on June 7, 1964, in the interrogation room of the Dallas County Jail, where his testimony was taken before Chief Justice Earl Warren. With Ruby was one of his attorneys, Joe H. Tonahill. Here is how the testimony began:

Mr. Ruby. Without a lie detector test on my testimony, my verbal statements to you, how do you know if I am telling the truth?

Mr. Tonahill. Don't worry about that, Jack.

Mr. Ruby. Just a minute, gentlemen.

Chief Justice Warren. You wanted to ask something, did you, Mr. Ruby?

Mr. Ruby. I would like to be able to get a lie detector test or truth serum of what motivated me to do what I did at that particular time, and it seems as you get further into something, even though you know what you did, it operates against you somehow, brainwashes you, that you are weak in what you want to tell the truth about and what you want to say which is the truth.

Now, Mr. Warren, I don't know if you got any confidence in the lie detector test and the truth serum, and so on.

Chief Justice Warren. I can't tell you just how much confidence I have in it, because it depends so much on who is taking it, and so forth.

But I will say this to you, that if you and your counsel want any kind of test, I will arrange if for you. I would be glad to do that, if you want it.

I wouldn't suggest a lie detector test to testify the truth. We will treat you just the same as we do any other witness, but if you want such a test, I will arrange for it.

Mr. Ruby. I do want it. Will you agree to that, Joe?

Mr. Tonahill. I sure do, Jack.

Chief Justice Warren. Any kind of a test you want to verify what you say, we will be glad to do.

Mr. Ruby. I want it even if you put me into a sort of drowsiness so you can question me as to anything pertaining to my involvement in this particular act.

Mr. Tonahill. Jack, you have wanted to do that from the very beginning, haven't you?

Mr. Ruby. Yes; and the reason why I am asking for that is—are you limited for time?

Chief Justice Warren. No; we have all the time you want.

Mr. Ruby. As it started to trial—I don't know if you realize my reasoning how I happened to be involved—I was carried away tremendously emotionally, and all the time I tried to ask Mr. Belli,[1] I wanted to get up and say the truth regarding the steps that led me to do what I have got involved in, but since I have a spotty background in the night club business, I should have been the last person to ever want to do something that I had been involved in.

In other words, I was carried away tremendously.

You want to ask me questions?

Chief Justice Warren. You tell us what you want, and then we will ask you some questions.

Mr. Rankin. I think he ought to be sworn.

Mr. Ruby. Am I boring you?

Chief Justice Warren. Go ahead. All right, Mr. Ruby, tell us your story.

Mr. Ruby. That particular morning—where is Mr. Moore—I had to go down to the News Building, getting back to this—I don't want to interrupt.

Chief Justice Warren. What morning do you mean?

Mr. Ruby. Friday morning, the starting of the tragedy.

Mr. Belli evidently did not go into my case thoroughly, circumstantially. If he had gone into it, he wouldn't have tried to vindicate me on an insanity plea to relieve me of all responsibility, because circumstantially everything looks so bad for me.

It can happen—it happens to many people who happen to be at the wrong place at the right time.

Had Mr. Belli spent more time with me, he would have realized not to try to get me out completely free; at the time we are talking, technically, how attorneys operate.

Chief Justice Warren. I understand.

Mr. Ruby. Different things came up, flashed back into my mind, that it dirtied my background, that Mr. Belli and I decided—oh yes, when I went to say that I wanted to get on the stand and tell the truth what happened that morning, he said, "Jack, when they get you on the stand, you are actually speaking of a premeditated crime that you involved yourself in."

But I didn't care because I wanted to tell the truth.

Jack Ruby then told his entire story. His testimony is printed in full on pages 183-213 of Volume V of the 26 volumes of hearings that we published together with our Report. Ruby told how on the morning of Nov. 22 he learned about the assassination while he was in the advertising department of one of the Dallas newspapers composing an ad for his nightclubs. Ruby was with John Newnam, an advertising department employee. Ruby voiced

---

[1]Melvin Belli of San Francisco acted as Jack Ruby's chief attorney during the trial.

criticism of a black-bordered right-wing political advertisement sarcastically entitled "Welcome Mr. Kennedy" which appeared in the morning newspaper bearing the name of Bernard Weissman as the chairman of the committee sponsoring the advertisement.

After Ruby learned that President Kennedy had died, he placed a telephone call to his sister, Eva Grant. He told John Newnam, "John, I am not opening up tonight."

Ruby further testified: "And I don't know what else happened. I know people were just heartbroken. . . .

"I left the building and went down and got in my car and I couldn't stop crying. . . ."

Ruby then went to his nightclub, the Carousel Club, and instructed the bartender to notify employees that the club would be closed that night. Later that afternoon, he went to his sister's home and discussed with her whether the clubs should be closed for more than one day. Ruby testified that after placing a call from her home to Don Saffran, a columnist for the *Dallas Times Herald*:

I put the receiver down and talked to my sister, and I said, "Eva, what shall we do?"

And she said, "Jack, let's close for the 3 days." She said, "We don't have anything anyway, but we owe it to—" [Chokes up.]

So I called Don Saffran back immediately and I said, "Don, we decided to close for Friday, Saturday, and Sunday."

And he said, "Okay."

That night, Ruby went to Friday evening religious services at Congregation Shearith Israel. He testified that after attending services he stopped at a delicatessen and bought some sandwiches for some police officers who, he had heard on the radio, were working overtime and for some employees of radio station KLIF who had given him and his nightclub operations "free plugs" on some of their radio programs.

Later that night, around 11:30 PM he made his way up to the third floor of the Dallas Police Department where reporters were congregated near the homicide bureau. Ruby was present on the third floor when Dallas Police Chief Jesse Curry and District Attorney Henry Wade announced that Oswald would be shown to the newspapermen at a press conference in the basement.

Ruby was also present at the press conference where Lee Harvey Oswald was shown to newsmen, and he then left police headquarters, driving to radio station KLIF.

In meeting with Chief Justice Warren in Dallas, Ruby then told what happened on Sunday morning, Nov. 24, when he shot Lee Harvey Oswald. Ruby told of a letter that his sister, Eileen, wrote to Chief Justice Warren.

Mr. Ruby. Eileen wrote you a letter.

Chief Justice Warren. Wrote the letter to me and told us that you would like to testify, and that is one of the reasons that we came down here.

Mr. Ruby. But unfortunately, when did you get the letter, Chief Justice Warren?

Chief Justice Warren. It was a long time ago, I admit. I think it was, let's see, roughly between 2 and 3 months ago.

Mr. Ruby. Yes.

Chief Justice Warren. I think it was; yes.

Mr. Ruby. At that time when you first got the letter and I was begging Joe Tonahill and the other lawyers to know the truth about me, certain things that are happening now wouldn't be happening at this particular time.

Chief Justice Warren. Yes?

Mr. Ruby. Because then they would have known the truth about Jack Ruby and his emotional breakdown.

Chief Justice Warren. Yes?

Mr. Ruby. Of why that Sunday morning—that thought never entered my mind prior to that Sunday morning when I took it upon myself to try to be a martyr or some screwball, you might say.

But I felt very emotional and very carried away for Mrs. Kennedy, that with all the strife she had gone through—I had been following it pretty well—that someone owed it to our beloved President that she shouldn't be expected to come back to face trial of this heinous crime.

And I have never had the chance to tell that, to back it up, to prove it.

Consequently, right at this moment I am being victimized as a part of a plot in the world's worst tragedy and crime at this moment.

Months back had I been given a chance—I take that back. Sometime back a police officer of the Dallas Police Department wanted to know how I got into the building. And I don't know whether I requested a lie detector test or not, but my attorney wasn't available.

When you are a defendant in the case, you say "speak to your attorney," you know. But that was a different time. It was after the trial, whenever it happened.

At this moment, Lee Harvey Oswald isn't guilty of committing the crime of assassinating President Kennedy. Jack Ruby is.

How can I fight that, Chief Justice Warren?

Chief Justice Warren. Well now, I want to say, Mr. Ruby, that as far as this Commission is concerned, there is no implication of that in what we are doing.

Mr. Ruby. All right, there is a certain organization here—

Chief Justice Warren. That I can assure you.

Mr. Ruby. There is an organization here, Chief Justice Warren, if it takes my life at this moment to say it, and Bill Decker said be a man and say it, there is a John Birch Society right now in activity, and Edwin Walker is one of the top men of this organization—take it for what it is worth, Chief Justice Warren.

Unfortunately for me, for me giving the people the opportunity to get in power, because of the act I committed, has put a lot of people in jeopardy with their lives.

Don't register with you, does it?

Chief Justice Warren. No; I don't understand that.

Mr. Ruby. Would you rather I just delete what I said and just pretend that nothing is going on?

Chief Justice Warren. I would not indeed. I am only interested in what you want to tell this Commission. That is all I am interested in.

Mr. Ruby. Well, I said my life, I won't be living long now. I know that. My family's lives will be gone. When I left my apartment that morning—

Chief Justice Warren. What morning?

Mr. Ruby. Sunday morning.

Chief Justice Warren. Sunday morning.

Mr. Ruby. Let's go back. Saturday I watched Rabbi Seligman. Any of you watch it that Saturday morning?

Chief Justice Warren. No; I didn't happen to hear it.

Mr. Ruby. He went ahead and eulogized that here is a man that fought in every battle, went to every country, and had to come back to his own country to be shot in the back [starts crying].

I must be a great actor, I tell you that.

Chief Justice Warren. No.

Mr. Ruby. That created a tremendous emotional feeling for me, the way he said that. Prior to all the other times, I was carried away.

Then that Saturday night, I didn't do anything but visit a little club over here and had a Coca-Cola, because I was sort of depressed. A fellow that owns the Pago Club, Bob Norton, and he knew something was wrong with me in the certain mood I was in.

And I went home and that weekend, the Sunday morning, and saw a letter to Caroline, two columns about a 16-inch area. Someone had written a letter to Caroline. The most heartbreaking letter. I don't remember the contents. Do you remember that?

Mr. Moore. I think I saw it.

Mr. Ruby. Yes; and alongside that letter on the same sheet of paper was a small comment in the newspaper that, I don't know how it was stated, that Mrs. Kennedy may have to come back for the trial of Lee Harvey Oswald.

That caused me to go like I did; that caused me to go like I did.

I don't know, Chief Justice, but I got so carried away. And I remember prior to that thought, there has never been another thought in my mind; I was never malicious toward this person. No one else requested me to do anything.

I never spoke to anyone about attempting to do anything. No subversive organization gave me any idea. No underworld person made any effort to contact me. It all happened that Sunday morning.

The last thing I read was that Mrs. Kennedy may have to come back to Dallas for trial for Lee Harvey Oswald, and I don't know what bug got ahold of me. I don't know what it is, but I am going to tell the truth word for word.

I am taking a pill called Preludin. It is a harmless pill, and it is very easy to get in the drugstore. It isn't a highly prescribed pill. I use it for dieting.

I don't partake of that much food. I think that was a stimulus to give me an emotional feeling that suddenly I felt, which was so stupid, that I wanted to show my love for our faith, being of the Jewish faith, and I never used the term and I don't want to go into that—suddenly the feeling, the emotional feeling came within me that someone owed this debt to our beloved President to save her the ordeal of coming back. I don't know why that came through my mind.

And I drove past Main Street, past the County Building, and there was a crowd already gathered there. And I guess I thought I knew he was going to be moved at 10 o'clock, I don't know. I listened to the radio; and I passed a crowd and it looked—I am repeating myself—and I took it for granted he had already been moved.

And I parked my car in the lot across from the Western Union. Prior to that, I got a call from a little girl—she wanted some money—that worked for me, and I said, "Can't you wait till payday?" And she said, "Jack, you are going to be closed."

So my purpose was to go to the Western Union—my double purpose—but the thought of doing, committing the act wasn't until I left my apartment.

Sending the wire was when I had the phone call—or the money order.

I drove down Main Street—there was a little incident I left out, that I started to go down a driveway, but I wanted to go by the wreaths, and I saw them and started to cry again.

Then I drove, parked the car across from the Western Union, went into the Western Union, sent the money order, whatever it was, walked the distance from the Western Union to the ramp—I didn't sneak in. I didn't linger in there.

I didn't crouch or hide behind anyone, unless the television camera can make it seem that way.

There was an officer talking—I don't know what rank he had—talking to a Sam Pease in a car parked up on the curb.

I walked down those few steps, and there was the person that—I wouldn't say I saw red—it was a feeling I had for our beloved President and Mrs. Kennedy, that he was insignificant to what my purpose was.

And when I walked down the ramp—I would say there was an 8-foot clearance—not that I wanted to be a hero, or I didn't realize that even if the officer would have observed me, the klieg lights, but I can't take that.

I did not mingle with the crowd. There was no one near me when I walked down that ramp, because if you will time the time I sent the money order, I think it was 10:17 Sunday morning.

I think the actual act was committed—I take that back—was it 11 o'clock? You should know this.

Mr. Moore. 11:21.

Mr. Ruby. No, when Oswald was shot.

Mr. Moore. I understood it to be 11:22.

Mr. Ruby. The clock stopped and said 11:21. I was watching on that thing; yes. Then it must have been 11:17, closer to 18. That is the timing when I left the Western Union to the time of the bottom of the ramp.

You wouldn't have time enough to have any conspiracy, to be self-saving, to mingle with the crowd, as it was told about me.

I realize it is a terrible thing I have done, and it was a stupid thing, but I just was carried away emotionally. Do you follow that?

Chief Justice Warren. Yes; I do indeed, every word.

Mr. Ruby. I had the gun in my right hip pocket, and impulsively, if that is the correct word here, I saw him, and that is all I can say. I didn't care what happened to me.

I think I used the words, "You killed my President, you rat." The next thing, I was down on the floor.

I said, "I am Jack Ruby. You all know me."

I never used anything malicious, nothing like s.o.b. I never said that I wanted to get three more off, as they stated.

The only words, and I was highly emotional; to Ray Hall—he interrogated more than any other person down there—all I believe I said to him was, "I didn't want Mrs. Kennedy to come back to trial."

And I forget what else. And I used a little expression like being of the Jewish faith, I wanted to show that we love our President, even though we are not of the same faith.

And I have a friend of mine—do you mind if it is a slipshod story?

Chief Justice Warren. No; you tell us in your own way.

Mr. Ruby. A fellow whom I sort of idolized is of the Catholic faith, and a gambler. Naturally in my business you meet people of various backgrounds.

And the thought came, we were very close, and I always thought a lot of him, and I knew that Kennedy, being Catholic, I knew how heartbroken he was, and even his picture—of this Mr. McWillie—flashed across me, because I have a great fondness for him.

All that blended into the thing that, like a screwball, the way it turned out, that I thought that I would sacrifice myself for the few moments of saving Mrs. Kennedy the discomfiture of coming back to trial.

Chief Justice Warren asked Ruby, "Did you ever know Oswald?" Ruby replied, "No." Ruby said the first time he ever saw Oswald was on Friday evening, Nov. 22, when they brought him out in the assembly room of the Dallas Police Department.

General Counsel Lee Rankin, who was in Dallas with Chief Justice Warren, asked Ruby whether he knew Officer Tippit. Ruby replied, "I knew there was three Tippits on the force. The only one I knew used to work for the special services, and I am certain this wasn't the Tippit, this wasn't the man." Ruby maintained that "I am as innocent regarding any conspiracy as any of you gentlemen in the room, and I don't want anything to be run over lightly. I want you to dig into it with any biting, any question that might embarrass me, or anything that might bring up my background, which isn't so terribly spotted—I have never been a criminal—I have never been in jail . . ."

Ruby also testified concerning a conversation he had with Secret Service agent Sorrels, who interrogated him after the shooting of Oswald:

Mr. Rankin. There was a conversation with Mr. Sorrels in which you told him about the matter. Do you remember that?

Mr. Ruby. The only thing I ever recall I said to Mr. Ray Hall and Sorrels was, I said, "Being of Jewish faith, I wanted to show my love for my President and his lovely wife."

After I said whatever I said, then a statement came out that someone introduced Mr. Sorrels to me and I said, "What are you, a newsman?" Or something to that effect. Which is really—what I am trying to say is, the way it sounded is like I was looking for publicity and inquiring if you are a newsman, I wanted to see you.

But I am certain—I don't recall definitely, but I know in my right mind, because I know my motive for doing it, and certainly to gain publicity to take a chance of being mortally wounded, as I said before, and who else could have timed it so perfectly by seconds.

If it were timed that way, then someone in the police department is guilty of giving the information as to when Lee Harvey Oswald was coming down.

I never made a statement. I never inquired from the television man what time is Lee Harvey Oswald coming down. Because really, a man in his right mind would never ask that question. I never made the statement "I wanted to get three more off. Someone had to do it. You wouldn't do it." I never made those statements.

I never called the man by any obscene name, because as I stated earlier, there was no malice in me. He was insignificant, to my feelings for my love for Mrs. Kennedy and our beloved President. He was nothing comparable to them, so I can't explain it.

I never used any words—as a matter of fact, there were questions at the hearing with Roy Pryor and a few others—I may have used one word "a little weasel" or something, but I didn't use it, I don't remember, because Roy said it. If he said I did, I may have said it.

I never made the statement to anyone that I intended to get him. I never used the obscene words that were stated.

Anything I said was with emotional feeling of I didn't want Mrs. Kennedy to come back to trial.

Congressman Ford, who was also present at Ruby's interrogation in Dallas on June 7, reaffirmed the fact that Jack Ruby would be given the test:

Mr. Ford. In other words, the Chief Justice has agreed, and I on the Commission wholeheartedly concur, that you will be given a polygraph test as expeditiously as possible.

And I am sure you can rely on what has been stated here by the Chairman.

More than three hours after the testimony began, it concluded with the following exchange between Jack Ruby and Chief Justice Warren:

Mr. Ruby. All I want to do is tell the truth, and the only way you can do it is by the polygraph, as that is the only way you can know it.

Chief Justice Warren. That we will do for you.

The polygraph test itself was taken at the Dallas County Jail on July 18, 1964. One of the observers of the test was Dr. William Robert Beavers, a Dallas psychiatrist who was there as an expert observer to determine the competency of the witness during the course of the testimony. You can read the entire transcript of the lie detector test in Volume XIV, pages 504-570. The testimony of Dr. Beavers is in Volume XIV, pages 570-579, and the testimony of the person who administered the test, Bill P. Herndon, polygraph supervisor and polygraph examiner assigned to the FBI laboratory in Washington, is in Volume XIV, pages 579-598.

Included in the test were the following questions and answers, which Ruby answered truthfully, according to the test results:

Q. Did you know Oswald before Nov. 22, 1963?
A. No.
Q. Did you assist Oswald in the assassination?
A. No.
Q. Are you now a member of the Communist Party?
A. No.
Q. Have you ever been a member of the Communist Party?
A. No.
Q. Are you now a member of any group that advocates the violent overthrow of the United States Government?
A. No.
Q. Have you ever been a member of any group that advocates violent overthrow of the United States Government?
A. No.

Q. Between the assassination and the shooting, did anybody you know tell you they knew Oswald?

A. No.

Q. Aside from anything you said to George Senator on Sunday morning, did you ever tell anyone else that you intended to shoot Oswald?

A. No.[2]

Q. Did you shoot Oswald in order to silence him?

A. No.

Q. Did you first decide to shoot Oswald on Friday night?

A. No.

Q. Did you first decide to shoot Oswald on Saturday morning?

A. No.

Q. Did you first decide to shoot Oswald on Saturday night?

A. No.

Q. Did you first decide to shoot Oswald on Sunday Morning?

A. Yes.

Q. Were you on the sidewalk at the time Lieutenant Pierce's car stopped on the ramp exit?

A. Yes.

Q. Did you enter the jail by walking through an alleyway?

A. No.

Q. Did you walk past the guard at the time Lieutenant Pierce's car was parked on the ramp exit?

A. Yes.

Q. Did you talk with any Dallas police officers on Sunday, Nov. 24, prior to the shooting of Oswald?

A. No.

Q. Did you see the armored car before it entered the basement?

A. No.

Q. Did you enter the police department through a door at the rear of the east side of the jail?

A. No.

Q. After talking to Little Lynn did you hear any announcement that Oswald was about to be moved?[3]

A. No.

Q. Before you left your apartment Sunday morning, did anyone tell you the armored car was on the way to the police department?

A. No.

Q. Did you go to the synagogue that Friday night?

A. Yes.

Q. Did you see Oswald in the Dallas jail on Friday night?

A. Yes.

Q. Did you have a gun with you when you went to the Friday midnight press conference at the jail?

A. No.

[2]George Senator shared an apartment with Jack Ruby.

[3]"Little Lynn" was the stage name of Mrs. Karen Carlin, to whom Ruby wired $25 on Sunday morning at the Western Union office.

Q. Is everything you told the Warren Commission the entire truth?
A. Yes.
Q. Did any foreign influence cause you to shoot Oswald?
A. No.
Q. Did you shoot Oswald because of any influence of the underworld?
A. No.
Q. Did you shoot Oswald in order to save Mrs. Kennedy the ordeal of a trial?
A. Yes.
Q. Did you know the Tippit that was killed?
A. No.

Our summary of the interpretation of the test included the following:

A polygraph examination is designed to detect physiological responses to stimuli in a carefully controlled interrogation. Such responses may accompany and indicate deception. The polygraph instrument derives its name from the Greek derivative "poly" meaning many and the word "graph" meaning writings. The polygraph chart writings consist of three separate markings placed on a graph reflecting three separate physiological reactions. A rubber tube is placed around the subject's chest to record his breathing pattern on a pneumograph. That device records the respiratory ratio of inhalation and exhalation strokes. The second component is called a galvanic skin response which consists of electrodes placed on the examinee's fingers, through which a small amount of electrical current is passed to the skin. The galvanometer records the minute changes in electrical skin response. The third component consists of a cardiograph which is a tracing obtained by attaching a pneumatic cuff around the left arm in a manner very similar to an apparatus which takes blood pressure. When the cuff is inflated, that device records relative blood pressure or change in the heart rate.

From those testing devices, it is possible to measure psychological or emotional stress. This testing device is the product of observation by psychologists and physiologists who noted certain physiological responses when people lie. In about 1920 law enforcement officials with psychological and physiological training initiated the development of the instrument to serve as an investigative aid.

The polygraph may record responses indicative of deception, but it must be carefully interpreted. The relevant questions, as to which the interrogator is seeking to determine whether the subject is falsifying, are compared with control questions where the examiner obtains a known indication of deception or some expected emotional response. In evaluating the polygraph, due consideration must be given to the fact that a physiological response may be caused by factors other than deception, such as fear, anxiety, nervousness, dislike, and other emotions. There are no valid statistics as to the reliability of the polygraph. FBI Agent Herndon testified that, notwithstanding the absence of percentage indicators of reliability, an informed judgment may be obtained from a well-qualified examiner on the indications of deception in a normal person under appropriate standards of administration.

The results of the test are summarized in the last appendix to our Report at pages 807-816. Because of the question of Ruby's competency, we concluded this section of our Report with the statement that "the Commission did not rely on the results of this examination in reaching the conclusions stated in this Report."

However, the examination did show that Ruby was telling the truth when he denied ever knowing Oswald before Nov. 22, 1963, when he denied assisting Oswald in the assassination, when he denied shooting Oswald because of any foreign influence, when he said that he shot Oswald in order to save Mrs. Kennedy the ordeal of a trial, and when he said that everything he told the Warren Commission in his earlier testimony in June was the truth.

Now, the Warren Commission could very well afford to say that they did not rely on the lie detector test where the results of the test showed that Ruby was telling the truth on these important matters. *But suppose that the polygraph examination had showed that Ruby lied on any one of these matters. Do you think that the Warren Commission could have summarily dismissed the results of the test?*

Of course not. And this was one of the risks involved in giving the polygraph examination, for although a polygraph is often referred to as a "lie detector," in fact it is not such a device. Theoretically, Ruby might be telling the truth when he said he never knew Oswald before the assassination and yet the polygraph could perhaps show that he was not telling the truth. If this had happened, I will venture to say that no matter what we would have said in our Report, a large portion of the public would have pointed to the polygraph examination of Ruby and would have proclaimed, "He lied when he said he did not know Oswald."

In our Report we wrote at page 815: "Because Ruby not only volunteered but insisted upon taking a polygraph examination, the Commission agreed to the examination."

Thus, you have the story behind the lie detector test. I knew all along that there was always a tremendous risk in giving that test—the risk that even though Ruby might be innocent of any conspiracy, the fallibility of a polygraph examination could result in the test's reporting that Ruby lied when he asserted he was innocent of any conspiracy, even though in truth and in fact Ruby might have been innocent. The political ramifications of this possibility were world wide.

But so far as I was concerned, political considerations were totally irrelevant. My only concern was the truth. And to the best of my ability I left no stone unturned in an effort to arrive at the truth. It is here that I think the story behind the lie detector test has added significance. Even though the area in which I concentrated was not the Ruby area, I was concerned with that aspect of the investigation, just as all of the lawyers with the Commission were concerned with all areas of the investigation and not just the one in which they concentrated.

The story behind the polygraph examination of Jack Ruby is further evidence of the fact that we lawyers performed our work with a "total dedication to the determination of the truth."

This is what we wrote in the foreword to our Report. And this is what we did.

48

"THE FIRST TIME THAT THEY ASKED ME I SAID NO, I DIDN'T KNOW ANYTHING ABOUT IT"

The death of Oswald posed tremendous problems in investigating the possibility of a conspiracy. There is inherent difficulty in proving negatives to a certainty, and, therefore, we did not reject categorically the possibility of a conspiracy. Rather, we stated that despite the efforts of all of the investigative agencies and resources of the United States, no evidence of a conspiracy had come to our attention.

On June 11, 1964, Earl Warren wrote Robert Kennedy, who was then Attorney General of the United States:

The Commission is now in the process of completing its investigation. Prior to the publication of its report, the Commission would like to be advised whether you are aware of any additional information relating to the assassination of President John F. Kennedy which has not been sent to the Commission. In view of the widely circulated allegations on the subject, the Commission would like to be informed in particular whether you have any information suggesting that the assassination of President Kennedy was caused by a domestic or foreign conspiracy. Needless to say, if you have any suggestions to make regarding the investigation of these allegations or any other phase of the Commission's work, we stand ready to act upon them.

Robert F Kennedy replied on Aug. 4, 1964:

In response to your letter of June 11, 1964, I would like to assure you that all information relating in any way to the assassination of President John F. Kennedy in the possession of the Department of Justice has been referred to the President's Commission for appropriate review and investigation . . .

In response to your specific inquiry, I would like to state definitely that I know of no credible evidence to support the allegations that the assassination of President Kennedy was caused by a domestic or foreign conspiracy. I have no suggestions to make at this time regarding any additional investigation which should be undertaken by the Commission prior to the publication of its report. . . .

In our formal Report, we concluded that "the Commission has found no evidence that either Lee Harvey Oswald or Jack Ruby was part of any conspiracy, domestic or foreign, to assassinate President Kennedy" and we " . . . found no evidence of conspiracy, subversion, or disloyalty to the U. S. Government by any federal, state or local official." If any such credible evidence had been found, we lawyers would have pounced upon it. So would Robert Kennedy, who wanted to leave no stone unturned in investigating the death of his brother.

During the next hundred years it is reasonable to expect that some people may come forward and say that they heard someone confess to participating in such a conspiracy, or perhaps even themselves confess. Persons innocent of notorious crimes sometimes confess falsely for the sake of notoriety. So far as I am concerned, although I did not participate directly in Areas III, IV or V, I wholeheartedly concur in the conclusions summarized in our Report. I would state categorically that there was no conspiracy involving Ruby—a belief reinforced by a polygraph test taken by Ruby over the objections of his lawyers, as you have just learned. In addition, I would state categorically that there was no preconceived plan made weeks or months in advance concerning the assassination of President Kennedy in Dallas on Nov. 22.

However, because of the difficulty of proving negatives to a certainty, I could not state categorically that at some time prior to the assassination, Lee Harvey Oswald might not have talked to other parties about assassinating the President of the United States. In the first place, I have inherent skepticism that would almost block my categorically stating that Oswald never talked to anyone about murdering President Kennedy. Moreover, I never have been fully satisfied with the testimony of Marina Oswald. I urged that we request that she submit to a polygraph examination. One reason for my request emanated from a portion of the interrogation of Oswald with which I was especially concerned. This related to his denial that he had taken any trip to Mexico.

As you have learned in examining the various interrogation sessions with Oswald, he made other false statements; these included the denial of ownership of any rifle; the denial of the authenticity of the photograph of him holding a rifle, which we knew was taken by Oswald's camera, to the exclusion of all other cameras in the world; the denial of receiving a rifle through Post Office Box 2915; and the denial of what we called the "curtain rod story"—the excuse Oswald gave when he departed from custom on the Thursday night before the assassination and rode to Irving, Texas, where his wife was staying, and where his rifle was stored.

Oswald lied about other matters in his interrogation, and all were part of one consistent pattern: In almost every instance Oswald lied when it pertained to a matter of relative importance concerning the assassination of President Kennedy. Because Oswald lied about having taken a trip to Mexico, my question was whether there was any relationship between that trip and the assassination itself.

In our Report at page 413 we summarized Oswald's Mexican trip as follows:

Oswald left for Mexico City on Sept. 25, 1963, and arrived on Sept. 27, 1963. He went almost directly to the Cuban Embassy and applied for a visa to Cuba in transit to Russia. Representing himself as the head of the New Orleans branch of the "organization called 'Fair Play for Cuba,' he stated his desire that he should be accepted as a 'friend' of the Cuban Revolution." He apparently based his claim for a visa in transit to Russia on his previous residence, his work permit for that country, and several unidentified letters in the Russian language. The Cubans would not, however, give him a visa until he had received one from the Soviets, which involved a delay of several months. When faced with that situation Oswald became greatly agitated, and although he later unsuccessfully attempted to obtain a Soviet visa at the Soviet Embassy in Mexico City, he insisted that he was entitled to the Cuban visa because of his background, partisanship, and personal activities on behalf of the Cuban movement. He engaged in an angry argument with the consul who finally told him that "as far as he was concerned he would not give him a visa" and that "a person like him [Oswald] in place of aiding the Cuban Revolution, was doing it harm."

There is one other aspect of the Mexico City trip that was to me very disconcerting. Before we took the testimony of Marina Oswald, she underwent many interviews with the FBI. At all times she denied knowing that Oswald took a trip to Mexico City. Yet, when she testified under oath before us in Washington the first week of Feb., 1964, she changed her story. And she related conversations that she had with her husband when he returned from Mexico City. You can find her testimony in Volume I, page 27-28, of the supplementary hearings. Included in this testimony is the following:

Mr. Rankin. Did he tell you anything about his trip to Mexico City?

Mrs. Oswald. Yes, he told me that he had visited the two embassies, that he had received nothing, that the people who are there are too much—too bureaucratic. He said that he has spent the time pretty well. And I had told him that if he doesn't accomplish anything to at least take a good rest. I was hoping that the climate, if nothing else, would be beneficial to him.

Mr. Rankin. Did you ask him what he did the rest of the time?

Mrs. Oswald. Yes, I think he said that he visited a bull fight, that he spent most of his time in museums, and that he did some sightseeing in the city.

Mr. Rankin. Did he tell you about anyone that he met there?

Mrs. Oswald. No.

He said that he did not like the Mexican girls.

Mr. Rankin. Did he tell you anything about what happened at the Cuban Embassy, or consulate?

Mrs. Oswald. No. Only that he had talked to certain people there.

Mr. Rankin. Did he tell you what people he talked to?

Mrs. Oswald. He said that he first visited the Soviet Embassy in the hope that having been there first this would make it easier for him at the Cuban Embassy. But there they refused to have anything to do with him.

Mr. Rankin. And what did he say about the visit to the Cuban Embassy or consulate?

Mrs. Oswald. It was quite without results.

Mr. Rankin. Did he complain about the consular or any of the officials of the Cuban Embassy and the way they handled the matter?

Mrs. Oswald. Yes, he called them bureaucrats. He said that the Cubans seemed to have a system similar to the Russians—too much red tape before you get through there.

Mr. Rankin. Is there anything else that he told you about the Mexico City trip that you haven't related?

Mrs. Oswald. No, that is all that I can remember about it.

Mr. Rankin. Do you recall how long he was gone on his trip to Mexico City?

Mrs. Oswald. All of this took approximately 2 weeks, from the time that I left New Orleans, until the time that he returned.

Mr. Rankin. And from the time he left the United States to go to Mexico City to his return, was that about 7 days?

Mrs. Oswald. Yes. He said he was there for about a week.

Mr. Rankin. When you were asked before about the trip to Mexico, you did not say that you knew anything about it. Do you want to explain to the Commission how that happened?

Mrs. Oswald. Most of these questions were put to me by the FBI. I do not like them too much. I didn't want to be too sincere with them. Though I was quite sincere and answered most of their questions. They questioned me a great deal, and I was very tired of them, and I thought that, well, whether I knew about it or didn't know about it didn't change matters at all, it didn't help anything, because the fact that Lee had been there was already known, and whether or not I knew about it didn't make any difference.

Mr. Rankin. Was that the only reason that you did not tell about what you knew of the Mexico City trip before?

Mrs. Oswald. Yes, because the first time that they asked me I said no, I didn't know anything about it. And in all succeeding discussions I couldn't very well have said I did. There is nothing special in that. It wasn't because this was connected with some sort of secret.

Marina's change of heart may have been genuine. However, many of us, including Ball and me, did not have great confidence in the overall credibility of Marina Oswald as a witness. It was for this reason that I urged in a written memorandum prepared before she testified that we ask Marina Oswald to submit to a polygraph examination.

However, even though Marina Oswald did not tell the truth to the FBI when she was asked about her husband's trip to Mexico, and even though Marina Oswald did not undergo a polygraph examination, I do not want to leave you with the impression that my doubts about Marina Oswald's veracity affect my concurrence in the conclusions of our Report. I stand by what we wrote. We found no credible evidence that, in the frame of reference of the overall record, there was any conspiracy to assassinate President Kennedy in which someone participated with Lee Harvey Oswald. Moreover, we found many facts that pointed to no conspiracy. You will see some of these in the next chapter when we take a look at "what might have been."[1]

[1]The "Summary and Conclusions," Chapter 1 of the Warren Commission Report, forms the Appendix to this book. Included is a summary of the ultimate conclusions of the Commission on the question of motive and conspiracy as well as additional background information on Oswald's life.

49

"IT MUST BE A SECURITY MAN GUARDING THE MOTORCADE"

One of the most striking aspects of our investigation was the happenstance that changed the course of history. Much of this is included in Chapter VI of our Report where we summarize our investigation of possible conspiracy. Of itself, this happenstance was strong evidence tending to prove the absence of any conspiracy.

We can start with the selection of the motorcade route. As fate would have it, because of the angle at which Elm Street went to the southwest toward the freeway, the TSBD Building was perhaps the only place in Dallas where someone could have looked out of a high window and aimed a rifle at the motorcade with a direct-line shot. The motorcade route depended on the selection of the luncheon site. And it was not until Nov. 14 that Secret Service agent Lawson was notified that the Trade Mart had been selected as the luncheon site.

Pages 31-32 of our Report note that after the selection of the Trade Mart, Secret Service agent Lawson and Secret Service agent Sorrels met with Dallas police officials to discuss details of the motorcade and possible routes. It was not until Nov. 18 that representatives of the local host committee were advised of the actual route. And it was not until Nov. 19 that the route was published in the Dallas newspapers. This precluded the possibility that any conspiracy was planned weeks or months in advance to assassinate the President from the TSBD Building.

As a matter of fact, the presence of Oswald at the TSBD Building was really happenstance.

If you turn to page 246 of our Report you will find:

Oswald's presence as an employee in the Texas School Book Depository Building was the result of a series of happenings unrelated to the President's trip to Dallas. He obtained the Depository job after almost 2 weeks of job hunting which began immediately upon his arrival in Dallas from Mexico on Oct. 3, 1963. At that time he was in poor financial circumstances, having arrived from Mexico City with approximately $133 or less, and with his unemployment compensation benefits due to expire on Oct. 8. Oswald and his wife were expecting the birth of their second child, who was in fact born on Oct. 20. In attempting to procure work, Oswald utilized normal channels, including the Texas Employment Commission.

On Oct. 4, 1963, Oswald applied for a position with Padgett Printing Corp., which was located at 1313 Industrial Boulevard, several blocks from President Kennedy's parade route. Oswald favorably impressed the plant superintendent who checked his prior job references, one of which was Jaggars-Chiles-Stovall, the firm where Oswald had done photography work from Oct. 1962 to Apr. 1963. The following report was written by Padgett's plant superintendent on the reverse side of Oswald's job application:" Bob Stovall does not recommend this man. He was released because of his record as a troublemaker.—Has Communistic tendencies." Oswald received word that Padgett Printing had hired someone else.

If Bob Stovall had not vetoed the job application of Oswald on the basis of alleged "Communistic tendencies," then at the time of the motorcade Oswald, had he been hired by Padgett, would have been several blocks away from the motorcade route. In any event, he would not have had the unique position afforded by the southeast corner of the sixth floor of the TSBD Building.

How did Oswald ultimately get the job at the TSBD Building? You will find the answer at pages 246-247 of our Report:

Oswald's employment with the Texas School Book Depository came about through a chance conversation on Monday, Oct. 14, between Ruth Paine, with whom his family was staying while Oswald was living in a roominghouse in Dallas, and two of Mrs. Paine's neighbors. During a morning conversation over coffee, at which Marina Oswald was present, Oswald's search for employment was mentioned. The neighbors suggested several places where Oswald might apply for work. One of the neighbors present, Linnie Mae Randle, said that her brother had recently been hired as a schoolbook order filler at the Texas School Book Depository and she thought the Depository might need additional help. She testified, "and of course you know just being neighborly and everything, we felt sorry for Marina because her baby was due right away as we understood it, and he didn't have any work."

When Marina Oswald and Mrs. Paine returned home, Mrs. Paine promptly telephoned the Texas School Book Depository and spoke to Superintendent Roy Truly, whom she did not know. Truly agreed to interview Oswald, who at the time was in Dallas seeking employment. When Oswald called that evening, Mrs. Paine told him of her conversation with Truly. The next morning Oswald went to the Texas School Book Depository where he was interviewed and hired for the position of order filler.

When I took the testimony of Superintendent Roy Truly I asked him to relate the circumstances when he first heard the name Lee Harvey Oswald. You jurors remember from Chapter 28 that Truly testified, "I received a phone call from a lady in Irving who said her name was Mrs. Paine. . . . She said, 'I have a fine young man living here with his wife and baby, and his wife is expecting a baby—another baby, in a few days, and he needs work desperately. . . .' And I told Mrs. Paine that—to send him down, and I would talk to him—that I didn't have anything in mind for him of a permanent nature, but if he was suited, we could possibly use him for a brief time."

If Marina Oswald's neighbors had not been so friendly and concerned about her welfare, Oswald would never have obtained the job at the TSBD Building. As a matter of fact, if they had waited just one day, Oswald might have taken another job at pay $100 a month higher than that offered by the depository company. On Oct. 16, 1963, the Texas Employment Commission tried to advise Oswald of the availability of the other job. However, because Oswald had already been hired at the TSBD, the Texas Employment Commission referred the job to someone else.

Superintendent Truly's statement that "We could possibly use him for a brief time" is another happenstance that contributed to this tragic ending.

The Texas School Book Depository Company is a private corporation engaged in the sale of textbooks to schools. Naturally, there is a heavy volume of business in the period following the opening of schools in the early fall. Oswald was hired temporarily and ordinarily would have been laid off on Nov. 15. As a matter of fact, one other temporary employee who was hired that fall was let go on Nov. 15.

But Roy Truly decided that to keep the workforce busy he would have them lay a new plywood floor. In Volume III, page 237, you will find the following testimony by Roy Truly:

Actually, the end of our fall rush—if it hadn't existed a week or 2 weeks longer, or if we had not been using some of our regular boys putting down this plywood, we would not have had any need for Lee Oswald at the time, which is a tragic thing for me to think about.

This is another example of the strange tricks of fate—and another of the many facts that formed a part of our conclusion that there was no credible evidence of conspiracy.

The new plywood floor had another part to play in the assassination of President Kennedy. You may remember in the testimony of Bonnie Ray Williams that he and several other employees helped lay a new plywood floor over the old floor on the fifth floor and that several days before Nov. 22 these employees went to the sixth floor to lay a new floor there. Williams testified that he and the other employees moved cartons from the west side of the sixth floor to the east side.

You have seen on page 146 the picture showing the shield of cartons around the southeast corner sixth floor window, which made it a perfect spot, hidden from view from the rest of the floor. Paradoxically, the assassin did not even have to move most of these cartons—the "shield" had been placed there by the other employees laying the plywood floor. Williams' testimony was confirmed by Superintendent Truly.

The cartons at the window that appeared to be a gun rest included some small lightweight cartons marked "Rolling Readers," one of which contained a palmprint and a fingerprint that were identified by expert witness Latona as the left palmprint and right index fingerprint of Lee Harvey Oswald. The Rolling Reader cartons had been moved to the windowsill from some three aisles away. In addition, next to where the homemade paper bag was found with Oswald's palmprint and fingerprint, there was a large carton that had been moved near the southeast corner window, which appeared to be a place where someone could sit while looking out the window. On this carton was the right palmprint of Lee Harvey Oswald, in the same position it would be in if a person were sitting on the box looking out the window toward the freeway and placing his right hand along his right hip on top of the box. We determined that the prints had been placed on the box within three days of the time of the assassination. I did not place any more significance on these prints of Oswald because he handled cartons in the course of his duties as an employee. (see Pages 250–251.)

There were other tricks of fate that, had things been a little different, could have changed the course of history. For instance, Marina Oswald almost singlehandedly might have prevented the assassination. The relationship between Oswald and his wife, as we wrote on page 416 of our Report, was "stormy," to say the least. Certainly, a large part of the difficulty stemmed from the personality of Lee Harvey Oswald. But as in all interpersonal relationships, this was not a black-and-white situation. Marina Oswald, herself, contributed in large part. Thus, you will find at page 418 of our Report:

Although she denied it in some of her testimony before the Commission, it appears that Marina Oswald also complained that her husband was not able to provide more material things for her. On that issue George De Mohrenschildt, who was probably as close to the Oswalds as anyone else during their first stay in Dallas, said that:

"She was annoying him all the time—'Why don't you make some money?' Poor guy was going out of his mind.

"We told her she should not annoy him—poor guy, he is doing his best, 'Don't annoy him so much.'"

The De Mohrenschildts also testified that "right in front" of Oswald Marina Oswald complained about Oswald's inadequacy as a husband. Mrs. Oswald told another of her friends that Oswald was very cold to her, that they very seldom had sexual relations and that Oswald "was not a man." She also told Mrs. Paine that she was not satisfied with her sexual relations with Oswald.

Marina Oswald also ridiculed her husband's political views, thereby tearing down his view of his own importance. He was very much interested in autobiographical works of outstanding statesmen of the United States, to whom his wife thought he compared himself. She said he was different from other people in "At least his imagination, his fantasy, which was quite unfounded, as to the fact that he was an outstanding man." She said that she "always tried to point out to him that he was a man like any others who were around us. But he simply could not understand that." Jeanne De Mohrenschildt, however, thought that Marina Oswald "said things that will hurt men's pride." She said that if she ever spoke to her husband the way Marina Oswald spoke to her husband, "we would not last long." Mrs. De Mohrenschildt thought that Oswald, whom she compared to "a puppy dog that everybody kicked," had a lot of good qualities, in spite of the fact that "Nobody said anything good about him." She had "the impression that he was just pushed, pushed, pushed, and she [Marina Oswald] was probably nagging, nagging, nagging." She thought that he might not have become involved in the assassination if people had been kinder to him.

In the fall of 1963, Marina Oswald was staying with Mrs. Paine in the suburb of Irving. Generally, Oswald would visit his wife on weekends. However, on the weekend before the assassination his wife told him not to come because Mrs. Paine was planning a birthday party for one of her children.

On that Sunday night, Nov. 17, Ruth Paine and Marina Oswald decided to call Oswald at his roominghouse in Dallas. When they asked for him, they were told he did not live there. The reason was that, unknown to them, Oswald was living at the roominghouse under the name of O. H. Lee. When Oswald called his wife the next day, she became angry about the use of the alias, according to her testimony. His rationale was that he did not want the FBI to know where he lived "because their visits were not very pleasant for him and he thought that he loses jobs because the FBI visits the place of his employment."

She hung up on her husband. He called back several times on Monday (Nov. 18) but she refused to talk to him.

Then, Oswald arrived to visit his wife unexpectedly on Thursday, Nov. 21. Oswald's rifle was stored in the Paine garage. Undoubtedly, he was in the garage on the evening of Nov. 21; someone left the light on. But there was still time for Marina Oswald to change the course of history. Turn to page 420-421 of our Report:

"On Monday [Nov. 18, 1963] he called several times, but after I hung up on him and didn't want to talk to him he did not call again. He then arrived on Thursday [Nov. 21, 1963]."

The events of that evening can best be appreciated through Marina Oswald's testimony:

Q. Did your husband give any reason for coming home on Thursday?

A. He said that he was lonely because he hadn't come the preceding weekend, and he wanted to make his peace with me.

Q. Did you say anything to him then?

A. He tried to talk to me but I would not answer him, and he was very upset.

Q. Were you upset with him?

A. I was angry, of course. He was not angry—he was upset. I was angry. He tried very hard to please me. He spent quite a bit of time putting away diapers and played with the children on the street.

Q. How did you indicate to him that you were angry with him?

A. By not talking to him.

Q. And how did he show that he was upset?

A. He was upset over the fact that I would not answer him. He tried to start a conversation with me several times, but I would not answer. And he said that he didn't want me to be angry at him because this upsets him.

On that day, he suggested that we rent an apartment in Dallas. He said that he was tired of living alone and perhaps the reason for my being so angry was the fact that we were not living together. That if I want to he would rent an apartment in Dallas tomorrow—that he didn't want me to remain with Ruth any longer, but wanted me to live with him in Dallas.

He repeated this not once but several times, but I refused. And he said that once again I was preferring my friends to him, and that I didn't need him.

Q. What did you say to that?

A. I said it would be better if I remained with Ruth until the holidays, he would come, and we would all meet together. That this was better because while he was living alone and I stayed with Ruth, we were spending less money. And I told him to buy me a washing machine, because with two children it became too difficult to wash by hand.

Q. What did he say to that?

A. He said he would buy me a washing machine.

Q. What did you say to that?

A. Thank you. That it would be better if he bought something for himself—that I would manage.

That night Oswald went to bed before his wife retired. She did not speak to him when she joined him there, although she thought that he was still awake. The next morning he left for work before anyone else arose. For the first time he left his wedding ring in a cup on the dresser in his room. He also left $170 in a wallet in one of the dresser drawers. He took with him $13.87 and the long brown package that Frazier and Mrs. Randle saw him carry and which he was to take to the School Book Depository.

What would have happened had Marina offered to make up with Lee Harvey Oswald? What would have happened if Marina Oswald in reply to the plea of her husband had said, "Yes, let us rent an apartment in Dallas tomorrow—"?[1]

Of themselves, the events in Irving on the evening of Nov. 21, 1963, are important evidence showing there was no conspiracy. Moreover, the fact that Oswald did not get his rifle until the evening of Nov. 21 is also indicative of the fact that the assassination of President Kennedy was not part of any long-range preconceived plan.

Although Marina Oswald rebuffed the pleas of her husband, there was one other person who could have almost single-handedly prevented the assassination. His name was Arnold Rowland, an 18-year-old resident of Dallas, who was in the vicinity of the TSBD Building at least 15 minutes before the motorcade arrived. Rowland's testimony is an example of one of the most difficult problems in analyzing the testimony of a witness, when part of his testimony seems to check with other independent facts while other aspects are blatantly false.

[1]The tragedy of all of this is compounded when Marina Oswald later testified that her showing of anger was put on:

Rankin. Did the quarrel that you had at that time seem to cause him to be more disturbed than usual?

Oswald. No, not particularly. At least he didn't talk about that quarrel when he came. Usually he would remember about what happened. This time he didn't blame me for anything, didn't ask me any questions, just wanted to make up.

Rankin. I understood that when you didn't make up he was quite disturbed and you were still angry, is that right?

Oswald. I wasn't really very angry. I, of course, wanted to make up with him. But I gave the appearance of being very angry. I was smiling inside, but I had a serious expression on my face.

Rankin. And as a result of that, did he seem to be more disturbed than usual?

Oswald. As always, as usual. Perhaps a little more. At least when he went to bed he was very upset.

Sometime before the assassination, Rowland was standing near the TSBD Building with his young wife.

According to the testimony of both, they were discussing security precautions for the Presidential trip to Dallas. As they were talking, Rowland said that he had looked up at the TSBD Building and noticed a man back away from a window on the southwest corner of the sixth floor.

"He was standing and holding a rifle. This appeared to me to be a fairly high-powered rifle because of the scope and the relative proportion of the scope to the rifle, you can tell about what type of rifle it is. You can tell it isn't a 22, you know, and we thought momentarily that maybe we should tell someone but then the thought came to us that it is a security agent.

"We had seen in the movies before where they have security men up in windows and places like that with rifles to watch the crowds, and we brushed it aside as that, at that time, and thought nothing else about it until after the event happened."

Rowland said that the man was holding the rifle at a position similar to "port arms in military terms," and the rifle was held in that position during the entire time that he saw the man there. Rowland testified that the man was rather slender in proportion to his size, but he could give no estimate as to his height. He thought that the man was fair or light complected with dark hair, and was either a Caucasian or a light Latin.

"Right after I noticed the man, I brought him to my wife's attention, and she was looking at something else at that time, we looked at that, and when we both looked back she wanted to see also, and he was gone from our vision." Rowland said that he even pointed to the window with his wife, but that there was nothing there at that time. They talked about it for a few seconds, saying that it was most likely a security man, and thought no more about it. A policeman was about 12 feet away from them at the time.

This is one of the many ironic twists of fate that we discovered during our investigation.

The assassination of President Kennedy was a major event in American history. Future historians may even say that it changed the course of history. What would have happened had Arnold and Barbara Rowland called to that policeman 12 feet away and said, "What's that man doing with a rifle in that building?"

Senator Cooper asked Rowland that question in Washington, but rephrased it along the lines of "Why didn't you" tell anyone about this. This was not the first time that morning the question had been asked. Before Senator Cooper entered the hearing room, Rowland had answered this question once. When Senator Cooper asked it again, Rowland burst into tears, and the Chief Justice called for a recess.

Then Earl Warren walked to Rowland, put his arm over the young man's shoulder and sought to comfort him. It was an unforgettable experience to see the Chief Justice of the United States seeking to console an 18-year-old youth who had obviously confronted himself with the possibility that he might have prevented the assassination.

However, in other aspects of his testimony before the Commission Rowland was wholly inaccurate.

He testified that he had graduated from high school in June, 1963, had done post-graduate work while engaged in part-time employment and had been accepted at several colleges, including Rice, Southern Methodist University and Texas A & M. A supplementary investigation disclosed that this was untrue. As a matter of fact, he was dropped from high school on Dec. 8, 1962, for nonattendance.

Similarly, Rowland testified that in high school his grades were straight A's except for a couple of B's in his senior year, and that he had an IQ of 147. Independent investigation also showed that this was not true. Even his wife testified that Rowland was not a high school graduate and that his grades were A's and B's in some subjects and C's and D's in others. School district records showed that of twenty-seven final grades, Rowland received five A's and that the remaining 22 were B (good), C (fair), D (poor), E (poor, passing), and F (failure).

Rowland also said that on the morning of the assassination he was attending post-graduate high school classes until 11 o'clock and then went to pick up his wife, who was also attending school, to take her downtown to the motorcade. His wife said that they were not attending school and that both of them previously dropped out and that they had left from her mother's home, where both were living.

However, Barbara Rowland confirmed one aspect of her husband's testimony. She said that about 15 minutes before the motorcade came by "My husband I were talking about Mr. [Adlai E.] Stevenson's visit and the way the people had acted, and we were talking about security measures, and he said he saw a man on the sixth floor of the TSBD Building, and when I looked up there I didn't see the man, because I didn't know exactly what window he was talking about at first. And when I found out which window it was, the man had apparently stepped back, because I didn't see him."

As he faced the building it would be the window farthest west on the south side of the building. "He told me that he saw a man there who looked like he was holding a rifle, and that it must be a security man guarding the motorcade."

Mrs. Rowland said that she agreed that he must have been a security officer, although she did not see the man. She said that she thought her husband had said that the man was standing about 12 feet back from the window and that the man was a young man and either tall and well built or thin.

Mrs. Rowland said that she had seen other people, either earlier or later, looking out of the windows. She remembered some black men on a lower floor, at about the fourth floor nearer the center windows. She said that she and her husband had looked at the sixth floor for a few minutes but had not seen any other person on the sixth floor, which was about two or three minutes after the time her husband first saw the man. This would have been about 13 minutes before the motorcade came by. From then on she said she and her husband were just standing and talking "and looking" in the general area. He never told her that he was looking back at the building, and she never noticed his looking back at the building.

After the motorcade passed them she heard three shots—the second and the third were closer than the first and the second. People started running toward the railroad tracks, so she grabbed her husband's hand and "naturally followed." They stood around there and then her husband mentioned to a policeman the man he had seen in the TSBD Building, and the man took them to the Records Building, where her husband was questioned in her presence. Later, both Rowlands gave written statements, along with other witnesses. Her husband repeated the story that she had related.

Mr. Belin. Did your husband at that time say whether or not he had kept any watch on the window of the School Book Depository Building after he saw this man with the gun?

Mrs. Rowland. No.

Mrs. Rowland said that she knew there were no other people on the sixth floor looking out of windows that could be seen from the outside, because she was sure that she had glanced at the building more than once and had not seen them. All the people that she saw looking out of the building were on floors lower than the sixth.

Mrs. Rowland said that they had not been contacted by police officers again until Nov. 24, when her husband repeated the statement that he had made on the 22nd. The police officers showed him the written statement that he had signed and "asked him if that was in general what he had to say, and he said 'Yes.' " Her husband signed the statement—there might have been a change or two.

Mrs. Rowland testified that she was present with her husband on Sunday morning, Nov. 24, throughout the time that he was with police officers, and that at no time had he said in her presence that there was another man on the sixth floor other than the man with the rifle that he first saw about 15 minutes before the assassination. Her husband had never complained to her that any statement that he gave to any law enforcement agency was not recorded or that there had been anything inaccurate in any statements that he had given.

Mr. Belin. Now, has he ever told you that he had seen anyone else on the sixth floor other than this man with the gun that you described in the southwest corner window?

Mrs. Rowland. No, sir.

Mr. Belin. Has he ever told you that he told anyone else that he saw anyone else on the sixth floor?

Mrs. Rowland. No, sir.

Mrs. Rowland also said, with regard to her husband, "At times my husband is prone to exaggerate."

In his testimony before the Commission, Rowland described the man with the rifle as rather slender in proportion to his size, with dark hair. However, for the first time he went on to say that before he observed the man with the rifle in the southwest corner of the building, he noticed a Negro man "hanging out the window" on the southeast corner of the sixth floor.

Rowland testified: "My wife and I were both looking and making remarks that the people hanging out the windows, I think the majority of them were colored people, some of them were hanging out the windows to their waist, such as this, we made several remarks to this fact, and then she started watching the colored boy, and I continued to look, and then I saw the man with the rifle."

Rowland then circled, on a picture, the southeast corner window of the sixth floor of the TSBD Building and said that this was the window from which he had seen the person "hanging out" shortly before he saw the man with the rifle.

The person, Rowland said, "seemed to be an elderly Negro"; then he circled other windows where he thought he had seen people, including several on the second and third floors, but no one on the fourth.[2] Rowland said that he had looked back two or three times a minute from the time that he first saw the Negro man in the southeast corner window on the sixth floor, and that the man was there until five and a half or six minutes before the motorcade arrived but from that time on the man was not there.

Rowland heard three shots, and he and his wife went across the street, trying to see the President's car. They then went over to the railroad yards, he said, but they never looked back at the TSBD Building. Fifteen minutes after the shots were fired, he said, he went to a plainclothes officer and told him about the man in the building with the rifle, but he said nothing about seeing any other man on the sixth floor of the TSBD Building. An affidavit was prepared and signed by Rowland.

Even though some aspects of the testimony of Rowland were false and there was no other corroborating evidence about the elderly black man on the sixth floor of the TSBD Building, we made every effort to verify whether this part of Rowland's testimony was true. Among other things, we took the deposition of every employee in the building who might remotely resemble this description and we accounted for the whereabouts of these employees at the time of the assassination (as well as the whereabouts of all other employees in the TSBD Building). We also verified that there were no persons in the immediate area who were strangers to the building.

Whereas the statement of Rowland about the elderly balding black man that he claims he saw in the southeast corner of the TSBD Building from around 12:15 to 12:24 PM is uncorroborated and is contradicted by the testimony of his wife, his other testimony about the slender white man with dark hair holding a rifle is supported by his written affidavit and is further corroborated by his wife. On the basis of the overall record, our conclusion

[2]The Dillard photo showed no windows open on the southeast portion of the 3rd floor of the TSBD Building, and only one window open on the 4th floor. This was the window where Victoria Adams watched the motorcade.

was that he probably saw a man with a rifle appear briefly at the southwest corner of the sixth floor of the TSBD Building around 15 minutes before the assassination but that he did not see an elderly balding Negro man in the southeast corner of the sixth floor of the TSBD Building.

If only Arnold Rowland had told that police officer only 12 feet away . . .

As you might imagine, assassination sensationalists pounced on extracts from the testimony of Arnold Rowland. For corroboration, they relied on the testimony of Roger D. Craig, the deputy sheriff of Dallas County, who said that about 10 minutes after the assassination he talked to Mr. and Mrs. Rowland ". . . and the boy said he saw two men on the sixth floor of the Book Depository Building over there; one of them had a rifle with a telescopic sight on it—but he thought they were Secret Service agents or guards and didn't report it. This was about—oh, he said, 15 minutes before the motorcade ever arrived."

According to Craig, Rowland said that he looked back a few minutes later and "the other man was gone, and there was just one man—the man with the rifle." Craig further testified that Rowland told him that when he first saw the two men, they were walking back and forth in front of the window for several minutes. Both were white men and one had a rifle with a scope on it. This report by Craig is contradicted by the testimony of both the Rowlands, and by every recorded interview conducted with them by law enforcement agencies after the assassination.

When Mark Lane mentions in his book that Arnold Rowland's testimony was purportedly corroborated by Craig, he does not discuss Craig's assertion that he saw Oswald in Captain Fritz' office and that Oswald said, "Everybody will know who I am now." Nor is that statement by Craig mentioned by Edward J. Epstein in *Inquest,* which relies on Rowland and Craig to imply a second assassin. (Unfortunately, Epstein omits not only the fact that Craig's testimony is contradicted by Rowland and his wife, but he also omits reporting that the second person Rowland said he saw in another window was an elderly balding Negro, whereas, according to Craig, Rowland said he saw a second white man, in addition to the first white man with the rifle. Moreover, Epstein does not mention that Barbara Rowland contradicts her husband's contentions that he told FBI agents about seeing the elderly balding Negro man hanging out of the assassination window.)

Thus (at page 188 of Volume VI of the hearings), when questioning Mrs. Rowland I asked her about written statements that Rowland made to the FBI and the police in which he mentioned seeing the single man standing with a rifle in the southwest corner of the sixth floor 15 minutes before the assassination but failed to mention seeing any other man such as the elderly balding Negro.

Mr. Belin. Were you present at any of these times that your husband was contacted?

Mrs. Rowland. Yes.

Mr. Belin. Were you present, for instance, on the Sunday morning, Nov. 24th?

Mrs. Rowland. Yes.

Mr. Belin. Do you remember what your husband said at that time?

Mrs. Rowland. He repeated the statement he had made in the—well, the police officers brought a written statement and asked him if that was in general what he had to say, and he said, "Yes," and they asked him specific questions about it and he answered them.

Mr. Belin. Was there anything else that was said?

Mrs. Rowland. I don't believe so.

According to Mrs. Rowland, "He never said in my presence that there was another man other than the man with the rifle on the sixth floor."

I am sure that you would agree that when Arnold Rowland does not tell his wife that he saw an elderly balding Negro hanging out of the southeast corner window of the sixth floor approximately five minutes before the assassination and then makes this statement nearly four months later while testifying before us in Washington, we cannot give much weight to this late report—because there is no corroboration, because Rowland had signed an affidavit that mentions nothing about this, and because Rowland had deliberately misstated certain other matters in his testimony. On the other hand, we have to give some reliance to Rowland's statement that approximately 15 minutes before the assassination he saw a man on the sixth floor with a rifle, because he told it to his wife and to investigative officers immediately after the event, and also because this is included in his signed affidavit.

In future years I would predict any number of "Arnold Rowlands" or "Roger Craigs" or "Dr. Hartogs" will come forth with new revelations. No doubt these revelations will make the front pages of many newspapers. I am sure that you jurors now realize the skepticism with which such new stories must be treated.

There is yet another "what might have been" that we have previously examined. It involves the news photographer Robert H. Jackson, who was riding in the motorcade and saw a gun barrel in the assassination window. You may remember that the Chevrolet convertible in which Robert Jackson and the other photographers were riding came to a stop in front of the TSBD Building. Dallas policemen were stationed on the street in the immediate vicinity, just as they were stationed on the streets throughout the motorcade route.

Unfortunately, each of these four photographers thought his duty as a photographer was more important than his duty as a citizen to contact the first police officer he saw and report the source of the shots. Accordingly, each of these men continued at his work and none notified any policeman until after Oswald had had time to get out of the building.

If any one of these photographers had contacted any of the nearby policemen, the TSBD Building could have been sealed off within a minute or two after the assassination. And had the building been sealed off immediately, Police Officer J. D. Tippit would be alive.

There was also pure happenstance in the murder of Lee Harvey Oswald by Jack Ruby.

We can start with the murder of Oswald, which took place at 11:21 AM on Nov. 24.

At page 353 of our Report, you will find that we summarize a telephone conversation that Ruby had on Sunday morning, Nov. 24, with one of his entertainers, Mrs. Karen Carlin. She had called long distance from Fort Worth. The telephone company records showed that the call was placed at 10:19 AM. Mrs. Carlin asked that Jack Ruby send her $25 because her rent was delinquent and she needed groceries. According to Mrs. Carlin, Ruby, who seemed upset, mentioned that he was going downtown anyway and would send the money from the Western Union office.

The Western Union clerk who waited on Ruby was Doyle E. Lane. He identified the money order application and the duplicate receipt given to Jack Ruby. Photostatic copies of these documents appear in Volume XX, page 481, of the supplementary hearings which we published.

Doyle Lane identified his own handwriting on the application. And if you turn to Volume XIII, pages 223-224, you can find:

Mr. Hubert. I notice in the bottom right-hand corner of Exhibit 5118, the words and figures as follows: 1312½ Commerce. Whose handwriting is that?

Mr. Lane. It is mine.

Mr. Hubert. Where did you get the information?

Mr. Lane. From Mr. Ruby.

Mr. Hubert. You asked him?

Mr. Lane. I said, "Your address?" And he gave me his address.

Mr. Hubert. I notice that there apparently is a time stamp on the top of this document that says, "1963, November 24. AM 11:17." Would you explain what that is?

Mr. Lane. That is the time that money order was accepted for transmission at the counter.

Mr. Hubert. Now, explain when and how that stamp is placed—placed upon that document?

Mr. Lane. This stamp was placed here when I handed Mr. Ruby back his receipt for his money and his change, because in our language that is the—accepting a money order for transmission at that time.

Mr. Hubert. In other words, that was not stamped when Mr. Ruby first came to begin the transaction?

Mr. Lane. No; it was not.

Mr. Hubert. It was required that you do what you said you have done concerning the document, to make the correction about "Fort Worth," to do the rating?

Mr. Lane. Right.

Mr. Hubert. And did you write out the address at the bottom?

Mr. Lane. Yes.

Mr. Hubert. And to make the change and give it to him?

Mr. Lane. Yes.

Mr. Hubert. In other words, the 11:17, therefore, represents the moment when the transaction was over?

Mr. Lane. When it is completed.

Doyle Lane also testified that the customer who immediately preceded Jack Ruby turned around and left after the transaction and then "Ruby came up and was right there. He just handed me the money order, apparently he had come in while I was waiting on the other customer, because I believe there were only the two in the office."

It took only a minute and a half to get from the Western Union office to the basement of the Dallas Police Station where Ruby killed Oswald. The time of the murder of Oswald was 11:21 AM. Suppose there had been another customer or two waiting in line at the downtown Western Union office. This in itself could have caused sufficient delay so that Ruby could not have descended the ramp into the basement of the Dallas Police Station in time to kill Oswald.

Circumstances of this nature are strong proof of the fact there was no conspiracy. Moreover, if there had been some type of a conspiracy, it is doubtful that Ruby would have taken the time to stop first at the Western Union office to send the money order, for earlier press reports had said Oswald was to be moved sometime after 10 AM.

Here is another example of what might fall into the category of "what might have been." The original route for the transfer of Oswald was to move him down on a small jail elevator and then through the dimly lit corridor into the hallway that led to the ramp, where the transfer vehicle was waiting. On the other side of the ramp was an iron railing. Originally, all of the press people were to have been behind the railing. Had they been there, Ruby could not have darted forward and shot Oswald point-blank.

How could Ruby do this in the face of all of the police officers accompanying Oswald? I did not appreciate the answer until I walked the route Oswald took. If you can visualize walking through a relatively dimly lit corridor and then emerging into the open to face a mass of television lights and popping flashbulbs, I think you can understand how the security guards with Oswald were all but blinded as they came into the view of the more than 100 people present in the basement of police headquarters at the time of Oswald's transfer. Thus, the press itself, in failing to remain behind the iron railing and in thrusting upon the police accompanying Oswald the television lights and the flashbulbs, formed a part of the setting that contributed to the death of Oswald.

One of the most vivid descriptions of the actions of the press was given by Detective James R. Leavelle of the Dallas Police Department. If you will turn to Volume VII, pages 268-269, of our hearings, you will find the following from Detective Leavelle's deposition:

Mr. Ball. Did he have any marks on his face when you first saw him on Friday, the 22nd of November?

Mr. Leavelle. Well, no; not that I recall. He—I know he had a black eye. I remember seeing that some time along the way but I do not recall when I first noticed it.

Mr. Ball. Did you ever talk to Oswald about his black eye?

Mr. Leavelle. No.

Mr. Ball. Did you ever hear him say anything to anyone as to how he received the black eye?

Mr. Leavelle. Yes; I remember at one time when they were moving him. Of course, if you saw television that day, I am sure you saw what men we had in the hallway up there with the photographers and newsmen, all were sticking microphones out at arm's length and hollering questions at him, and at one time someone asked him how he got the black eye. He said "A cop hit me," but that was just a hollered response to some unknown question or unknown newsreporter asking him.

Mr. Ball. As you would move Oswald through the halls on the third floor from one room to another—.

Mr. Leavelle. Actually, it wasn't from one room to the other; it would be from our office to the elevator which is some 20 feet.

Mr. Ball. On those occasions would the hallway be crowded with reporters, newsmen, and television cameramen?

Mr. Leavelle. Yes; cameramen and television men all over the place; in fact, I was plumb up to my chin with those people.

Mr. Stern. How do you mean?

Mr. Leavelle. Well, I was disgusted with them.

Mr. Stern. Would they not cooperate with your request to stand in a particular place?

Mr. Leavelle. No; if you ever slopped hogs and throw down a pail of slop and saw them rush after it you would understand what that was like up there—about the same situation.

Mr. Ball. I'm through. Do you have some questions, Mr. Stern?

Mr. Stern. There was just no response. You asked them to cooperate with you?

Mr. Leavelle. Oh, yes; they would be asked to stand back and stay back but wouldn't do much good, and they would push forward and you had to hold them off physically. Of course, I realize I am not running the police department but if I had been running it wouldn't have been nobody up there; like I say, I was fed up. Fact of business, one time when I was trying to escort some witness out of there—I don't recall who it was at this time—but I was trying to get them through that crowd and taking them down the edge of the corridor and I stopped and I looked down and there was a joker had a camera stuck between my legs taking pictures so that's just some indication of how they acted.

This leads to another happenstance involving the murder of Oswald. If you turn to page 210 of our Report you will read:

Curry decided that Oswald would leave the building via the basement. He stated later that he reached this decision shortly after his arrival at the police building Sunday morning, when members of the press had already begun to gather in the basement. There is no evidence that anyone opposed this decision. Two members of the Dallas police did suggest to Captain Fritz that Oswald be taken from the building by another exit, leaving the press "waiting in the basement and on Commerce Street, and we could be to the county jail before anyone knew what was taking place." However, Fritz said that he did not think Curry would agree to such a plan because he had promised that Oswald would be transferred at a time when newsmen could take pictures. Forrest Sorrels also suggested to Fritz that Oswald be moved at an unannounced time when no one was around, but Fritz again responded that "Curry wanted to go along with the press and not try to put anything over on them."

You can read the testimony of Secret Service agent Sorrels in Volume XIII, page 63:

Mr. Hubert. Do you recall ever having spoken to either Curry or some other member of the police department about the possibility of moving Oswald in a way other than that which was planned?

Mr. Sorrels. When I heard that they were supposed to take him out at 10 o'clock—that was the announcement and so forth on the radio and in the papers—I remarked to Captain Fritz that if I were he, I would not remove Oswald from the city hall or city jail to the county jail at an announced time; that I would take him out at 3 or 4 o'clock in the morning when there was no one around.

Mr. Hubert. Do you know when you told that to Fritz?

Mr. Sorrels. That was on the Sunday morning, before he was removed.

Mr. Hubert. Did you tell that to any other person?

Mr. Sorrels. No.

Mr. Hubert. Was any other person present when you told that to Fritz?

Mr. Sorrels. No; not that I recall.

Mr. Hubert. What caused you to give that advice to Captain Fritz?

Mr. Sorrels. The importance of the prisoner, to my mind, was such that in order to remove the opportunity for some crackpot or anyone who might feel inclined to try to kill the prisoner, if the removal was made more or less unannounced or in secret, that those opportunities would have been at least lessened to a great degree.

Captain Fritz said that Chief Curry did not want to—let's reverse that just a bit—that Chief Curry wanted to go along with the press and not try to put anything over on them; or words to that effect.

Mr. Hubert. Did you gather from what Fritz told you that the reason why your suggestion was not acceptable was that Fritz at least thought that Captain—that Chief Curry did not want to break his word, as it were, to the press?

Mr. Sorrels. I didn't consider it so much as breaking his word as I would that he did not want to tell them one thing, or in other words, move him out without the press being aware of the fact—let's put it that way. That was my impression.

Mr. Hubert. What time was it, about, do you know, that you made that suggestion?

Mr. Sorrels. That was pretty close to 11:15 in the morning, just a short time before they got ready to move him.

Mr. Hubert. You do not know, do you, whether he conveyed your thought to Chief Curry?

Mr. Sorrels. No; I do not. I doubt that he did, because Chief Curry had left Fritz' office at that time, as I recall it.

Had Chief Curry not been concerned for the press, Oswald's transfer would have taken place at some unannounced time, and no one would have had an opportunity to kill him.

The time of the transfer, shortly after 11:15 AM, is a third example of happenstance. As recorded in Volume XV, pages 148-149, Captain Fritz testified that Chief Curry ". . . asked me about transferring him at 4 o'clock the day before, and I told him I didn't think we could be through with our questioning at that time.

"At that time he asked me about 10 o'clock the next morning, and I told him we thought we could be ready by 10 o'clock the next morning. We went,

I believe, an hour overtime with the interrogation, but we tried to finish up by 10 o'clock the next morning."

Had the "overtime" questioning lasted five minutes less, Oswald would have passed through the basement of the police station at 11:16 AM, while Ruby was still at the Western Union office.

Part of the reason for the "overtime" in the interrogation was that Postal Inspector Harry D. Holmes happened to participate in the interrogation on the morning of Nov. 24. When I took the testimony of Inspector Holmes, I asked him, "Just what was the occasion of your joining this interrogation? How did you happen to be there?"

At Volume VII, pages 296-297, you can see the answer of Inspector Holmes:

Mr. Holmes. I had been in and out of Captain Fritz' office on numerous occasions during this 2½-day period.

On this morning I had no appointment. I actually started to church with my wife. I got to church and I said," You get out, I am going down and see if I can do something for Captain Fritz. I imagine he is as sleepy as I am."

So I drove directly on down to the police station and walked in, and as I did, Captain Fritz motioned to me and said, "We are getting ready to have a last interrogation with Oswald before we transfer him to the county jail. Would you like to join us?"

I said, "I would."

We went into his private room and closed the door, and those present were Captain Will Fritz, of the Dallas Police Department, Forrest V. Sorrels, local agent in charge of Secret Service, and Thomas J. Kelley, inspector, Secret Service, from Washington, and also about three detectives who were not identified to me, but simply were guarding Oswald who was handcuffed and seated at Will Fritz' desk.

Holmes prepared a detailed memorandum of this interview, which you can find in our Report at pages 633-636. In his testimony, Inspector Holmes referred to several questions that he himself asked Oswald. For instance, at Volume VII, pages 298-299, there is Inspector Holmes's testimony that after Oswald said he did not own a rifle (Oswald's answer was "Absolutely not. How could I afford a rifle. I make $1.25 an hour. I can't hardly feed myself."), Oswald was asked about the name Alek Hidell. Inspector Holmes testified:

I brought it up first as to did he ever have a package sent to him from anywhere. I said, "Did you receive mail through this box 2915 under the name of any other name than Lee Oswald," and he said, "Absolutely not."

"What about a package to an A. J. Hidell?"

He said, "No."

"Well, did you order a gun in that name to come there?"

"No, absolutely not."

"Had one come under that name, could this fellow have gotten it?"

He said, "Nobody got mail out of that box but me; no, sir. Maybe my wife, but I couldn't say for sure whether my wife ever got mail, but it is possible she could have."

"Well, who is A. J. Hidell?" I asked him.

And he said, "I don't know any such person."

I showed him the box rental application for the post office box in New Orleans and I read from it. I said, "Here this shows as being able to receive, being entitled to receive mail is Marina Oswald." And he said, "Well, that is my wife, so what?"

And I said, "Also it says 'A. J. Hidell.' "

"Well, I don't know anything about that."

That is all he would say about it.

Then Captain Fritz interrupted and said, "Well, what about this card we got out of your billfold?" This draft registration card, he called it, where it showed A. J. Hidell.

Well, that is the only time that I recall he kind of flared up and he said, "Now, I have told you all I am going to tell you about that card in my billfold." He said, "You have the card yourself, and you know as much about it as I do." And he showed a little anger. Really the only time that he flared up.

Had Inspector Holmes continued on to church with his wife and not asked these questions, the length of interrogation would have been shortened and Jack Ruby would not have had the opportunity to kill Oswald.

50

THE VERDICT IS YOURS

The Rosetta Stone to the solution of President Kennedy's murder is the murder of Officer J. D. Tippit. To paraphrase Professor Hugh Trevor-Roper, once the "hypothesis is admitted" that Oswald killed Patrolman J. D. Tippit, there can be no doubt that the overall evidence shows that Lee Harvey Oswald was the assassin of John F. Kennedy.

The murder of J. D. Tippit is virtually an open-and-shut case because Oswald was apprehended with the murder weapon in hand. You jurors remember the testimony of Johnny Calvin Brewer, who saw Oswald duck into Brewer's storefront area as police sirens approached and then saw him leave and sneak into the Texas Theatre. Brewer followed Oswald into the theatre and had the cashier call the police. As a policeman approached, Oswald pulled out a revolver.

Carrying a concealed gun is a crime. The fact that Oswald had such a weapon in his possession and drew it in itself is highly suspicious. Irrefutable scientific evidence proved that this revolver to the exclusion of all other weapons in the world was the weapon that discharged the cartridge cases that witnesses saw the murderer of Officer Tippit toss away as he left the scene of the murder.

You jurors remember the testimony of taxicab driver W. W. Scoggins, who saw the murder and hid by the side of his cab as Oswald trotted by within 12 feet of Scoggins. You remember the testimony of Ted Callaway, who gave chase to Oswald, and the testimony of Sam Guinyard, who with Callaway and Scoggins identified Oswald as the gunman in a police lineup. Helen Markham, who witnessed the murder from across the street, and Barbara Jeanette Davis and Virginia Davis, who saw Oswald cut across their lawn and toss cartridge cases in the bushes, also identified Oswald as the gunman.

The combination of Oswald's actions at Brewer's shoe store and in the theatre and the scientific ballistics testimony linking this gun with the murder of Tippit would of itself would be sufficient. When you add to all this the positive identification by six independent eyewitnesses, there can be no doubt that Oswald killed Officer Tippit.

With the knowledge that Oswald had the capacity to kill, and with the additional knowledge that the pistol used in the Tippit murder was purchased by mail order under the same alias and sent to the same post office box in Dallas as the Kennedy assassination rifle, No. C-2766, the evidence in the murder of John F. Kennedy is placed in clear perspective.

The starting point is the testimony of Howard Brennan, who saw the gunman take aim and fire the last shot. Brennan's testimony is reinforced by the newsmen in the motorcade, including Robert Jackson and Malcolm Couch, who saw the rifle being withdrawn. It is also reinforced by Amos Euins, who saw the rifle, and by the testimony of the three employees watching the motorcade on the fifth floor, below the assassination window. Harold Norman heard the cartridge cases hit the floor above him and also heard the bolt action of the rifle. His testimony is reinforced by the testimony of Bonnie Ray Williams and James Jarman Jr.

As Brennan and Euins reported their observations to the police, the TSBD Building was searched. In the southeast corner of the sixth floor immediately above Harold Norman, three cartridge cases were found. In the northwest corner of the sixth floor near the stairway, a 6.5 mm. Mannlicher-Carcano rifle, Serial No. C-2766, was found stuffed between boxes. In the Presidential limousine, two bullet fragments of sufficient size to be ballistically identifiable were found. In Parkland Memorial Hospital, a nearly whole bullet rolled off a stretcher used to carry Governor Connally.

Scientific ballistic evidence proved that the cartridge cases found at the southeast corner of the sixth floor of the TSBD Building, the two ballistically identifiable bullet fragments in the front seat of the Presidential limousine, and the bullet found at Parkland Memorial Hospital all came from that rifle, No. C-2766, to the exclusion of all other weapons in the world.

Who was the owner of that weapon? Lee Harvey Oswald. Oswald had purchased the rifle through the mail from Klein's Sporting Goods in Chicago. He used the alias of A. J. Hidell, the same alias used to purchase the pistol. This same man, Oswald, closely met the physical description of Howard Brennan as Brennan saw the gunman fire the last shot. Oswald had ready access to the sixth floor of the TSBD Building, and he was the only employee who was inside the building at the time of the assassination who had access to the sixth floor and who left the building shortly after the assassination.

Where did Oswald go? He boarded a bus. But instead of waiting for a bus to pass in front of the TSBD Building, he walked seven blocks east to board one. The bus he boarded was not the one that went right by his rooming house. Rather, he took the first available bus, which came no closer than seven blocks from the house. And when that vehicle became stalled in traffic, he got out and hailed a taxicab that took him near his rooming house in the Oak Cliff section of Dallas, where he undoubtedly picked up his pistol and then left hastily toward an unknown destination.

The absence of Oswald from the TSBD Building was first noted by his fellow employees. They called this to the attention of the police officers searching the crime scene; the officers went to the police station, intending to send other officers to Oswald's residence to pick him up for questioning.

When the officers got to the police station, they found him already there; he had been apprehended in connection with the murder of Officer Tippit.

Oswald's rifle had been stored, wrapped in a blanket, in a garage of the Ruth Paine residence in the Dallas suburb of Irving. Oswald's wife and children were staying with Ruth Paine and ordinarily Oswald would visit them on weekends. However, on Thursday night, Nov. 21, Oswald varied his regular pattern and rode home with Buell Frazier. Oswald said he wanted to pick up some curtain rods for the room in which he stayed during the week. The next day Oswald carried a long package wrapped in brown paper into the TSBD Building—a package that Frazier thought contained curtain rods. However, the room where Oswald was staying already contained both curtains and curtain rods.

At the assassination window at the southeast corner of the sixth floor of the TSBD Building a large homemade paper bag was found. The paper was of the same type used to wrap books in the TSBD Building. It was of sufficient size to carry the disassembled rifle and it contained a fingerprint and palmprint of Lee Harvey Oswald.

A number of days after the assassination, the clipboard that Oswald used to fill orders of books was found with some unfilled book orders dated Nov. 22. The clipboard was found in the northwest corner near the back stairway—only a few feet from where the rifle, No. C-2766, had been discovered.

President Kennedy was struck twice—the first shot striking him in the back of his neck and exiting from his throat and the second striking him in the back of his head. The fibers on the back of President Kennedy's coat were pointed inward and the fibers on the front of his shirt were pointed outward. The autopsy physicians traced the path of the bullet through the President's neck and the autopsy X-rays disclosed that there was no missile inside the President's body. Wound ballistics tests showed that the bullet that struck President Kennedy's neck had entered at a velocity of approximately 1,900 feet per second and exited at a velocity of nearly 1,800 feet per second. Where did that bullet go?

It did not hit the Presidential limousine, because any missile of that velocity striking the limousine would have caused substantial damage. The only damage to the limousine was relatively minor and included damage to the inside of the front windshield, further evidence that the shots had come from behind.

At the time the first shot struck President Kennedy, the Presidential limousine was approximately 180 feet from the southeast corner window of the sixth floor of the TSBD Building. The four-power scope on the rifle made the actual distance appear to be only 45 feet—15 yards.

The autopsy showed that the second shot to hit President Kennedy came from the rear and above. At the time the fatal shot struck President Kennedy, the Presidential limousine was 265.3 feet away from the southeast corner window of the sixth floor of the TSBD Building, or approximately 88 yards. Through a four-power scope, this made him appear only 22 yards away. The trajectory was almost a perfect line shot as the limousine slowly headed down Elm Street toward the freeway at a speed of 11.2 miles per hour.

Sitting directly in front of President Kennedy was Governor Connally. At the time the shots were fired Governor Connally was in the same trajectory line as President Kennedy, with relation to the southeast corner window of the sixth floor of the TSBD Building. All of Governor Connally's physicians agreed that he was struck by one shot fired from above and behind. Governor Connally's physicians, as well as the wound ballistics experts at Edgewood Arsenal, agreed that Governor Connally's wrist had not been struck by a pristine bullet. The trajectory line of the shot, coupled with the medical testimony, the autopsy testimony and the wound ballistics experiments, and the fact that Governor Connally was sitting directly in front of President Kennedy led to the obvious conclusion: The bullet that exited from the front of President Kennedy's neck at a velocity of nearly 1,800 feet per second struck Governor Connally.

The bullet that hit Governor Connally was the nearly whole bullet found at Parkland Memorial Hospital. The total amount of materials from the bullet that remained in Governor Connally was measured in micrograms—less than one grain in total, according to the reports of physicians who operated on Governor Connally's wrist and thigh.

Some witnesses at the scene of the assassination thought they saw a puff of smoke near the grassy knoll. However, no one saw a rifle, except in the upper floor of the TSBD Building; no one found any cartridge cases, except on the sixth floor of the TSBD Building; and the only bullet or bullet fragments found came from that rifle, to the exclusion of all other weapons in the world.

When the Dallas police came to the Irving residence and asked about the location of a rifle, Marina Oswald pointed out a blanket roll in the garage. When the blanket was opened, the rifle was gone. Also found were two photographs and a negative of a picture taken of Oswald holding the rifle and having a pistol at his side. Scientific evidence showed that the picture negative was taken from Oswald's camera, to the exclusion of all other cameras in the world.

When Oswald was interrogated, he denied owning a rifle; he denied having purchased the rifle from Klein's Sporting Goods; he denied that the picture of him with the rifle and pistol was a true picture but rather said it was a composite; he denied having carried a long package into the TSBD Building on the morning of Nov. 22; and he said that at the time of the assassination he was having lunch with "Junior." The only employee known as "Junior" was James Jarman, Jr., who was watching the motorcade from the fifth floor.

Despite Oswald's denials that he shot Officer Tippit and President Kennedy, when you put all of these facts together and couple these facts with the evidence showing Oswald murdered J. D. Tippit, there can be no reasonable doubt that Lee Harvey Oswald murdered John F. Kennedy.

We found no evidence of any conspiracy involving any third party, particularly Jack Ruby. We found that Ruby was truthful in his testimony and in his polygraph examination when he said that he had shot Oswald to save Jacqueline Kennedy the hardship of going to Dallas and testifying at a trial of Oswald. We found innumerable instances of "happenstance," all of which reinforced our conclusion that there was no conspiracy.

But what about the assassination sensationalists who say there was a rifleman shooting a rifle that no one sees and that leaves no cartridge cases and leaves no bullets? This is the heart of the claims of assassination sensationalists typified by the film producers Lane and deAntonio. I was contacted by these producers in the summer of 1966:

JUDGMENT FILMS CORPORATION
BOX 1567
GRAND CENTRAL STATION
NEW YORK, N. Y. 10017

July 7, 1966 Mr. David W. Belin
HERRICK, LANGDON, SANDBLOM & BELIN
300 Home Federal Building
Des Moines, Iowa

Dear Mr. Belin,

We are completing a film on the assassination of President Kennedy, its aftermath, and "The President's Commission on the Assassination of President John F. Kennedy." The film, which is composed of interviews with witnesses in Dallas as well as stock footage, attacks both the methods and conclusions of the Commission.

We offer to screen a pre-release version of the film for you, and also offer you the opportunity to rebut the film on camera—with the understanding that anything you say on camera will be used intact without any cuts, additions or deletions on our part.

Sincerely,

/s/Mark Lane   /s/Emile deAntonio"

I knew Mark Lane through his testimony before the Warren Commission and through the public statements he had made starting months before we published our Report. Although not retained by Marina Oswald, Lane sought, with the support of Oswald's mother, to turn our fact-finding Commission into an adversary proceeding in which he would gain the limelight as "defense counsel" for Lee Harvey Oswald.

The Warren Commission was a fact-finding body—not a trial court. There were no prosecuting attorneys, and accordingly there were no defense attorneys. Our aim at all times was for an exhaustive impartial investigation—not a steam roller conviction of a dead man and not the carnival atmosphere of a mock trial that might enliven the front pages of newspapers throughout the world.

Thus, while the Commissioners did not accede to Mr. Lane's request to be considered as "defense counsel," they invited him to testify in the hope that he might have information that would shed additional light on the assassination and its aftermath. Mr. Lane's testimony before the Commission, like his subsequent lectures, debates, interviews, book, and film, was a concoction—a shrewd combination of specious arguments and selected extracts of newspaper articles.

Apparently, months before Mr. Lane saw our final Report, he realized the potentialities of sensationalizing the assassination. People were still buying books about Abraham Lincoln's assassination, which occurred more than 100 years ago. For someone who had a carefully cultivated mask of sincerity, coupled with sufficient shrewdness, cunning and lack of conscience, the assassination of President Kennedy could be almost a lifetime meal ticket.

Most recently [1973], Lane has co-authored a novel and a movie screenplay, both entitled Executive Action, and both based on the hokum that President Kennedy was killed as a part of a conspiracy by wealthy individuals, one of whom no doubt was "short, a little on the heavy side..."

Because all of us who served with the Warren Commission were familiar with Lane's methods, I felt that none of the seven Commissioners would answer the letter of Lane and deAntonio and that most if not all other lawyers who served with the Commission would throw the letter in the wastebasket.   We knew that Lane's claims were a sham. And although I did not agree with every decision made during our investigation, each of us felt that when we completed our investigation we had determined the truth: Lee Harvey Oswald was the assassin, and the sole assassin, of President John F. Kennedy, and Oswald was the killer of Officer J. D. Tippit.

Of course, not everyone in the court of world opinion agreed with these conclusions, and this was to be expected. In any democratic society it is important that we have doubters who are skeptical about every official report. Unfortunately, most doubters had not bothered to read the entire Report, and even those who studied the Report did not have the intimate knowledge of the evidence as did we lawyers.

The prevalence of relative ignorance of facts was a fertile breeding ground for the seeds of doubt cast by those critics who used sensationalism as their tool. There were speeches and newspaper articles, followed by magazine articles, followed by books. And at the top of the heap was the moving picture film that could reach an audience in the tens of millions. Most of the court of world opinion would not have to bother to read a book. They could get a spoon-fed version of the assassination of President Kennedy. In turn, this would create more doubts.

As I mused about Mark Lane's methods and his motive in extending to me the apparently fair-minded unconditional offer "to rebut the film on camera," I noticed the envelope in which the letter was sent. The letter was dated July 7, 1966, but the postmark on the envelope was August 5. Twenty-nine days is a long time to wait to mail a letter, particularly when the envelope is marked "Air Mail."

Why the delay? Could Lane and deAntonio have had some underlying motive? Could they have tendered such an offer to rebut their film to all of the members of the Warren Commission and its staff of lawyers with the expectation that it would be refused by all? If that were the case, they could then append to their film a statement proclaiming their unconditional offer and cast upon the universal rejection of the Commission and lawyers the damaging implication that the Warren Commission could not, dared not, defend itself against their accusations.

I was on vacation when the letter arrived at my law office. But on Aug. 15, as soon as I returned, I wrote the first of ten letters in which I sought to accept the offer. The first eight of these letters went unanswered, except for one postcard received on Sept. 12, 1966, from Emile deAntonio in response to my third letter. Mr. deAntonio wrote: "Please write to Mark Lane, 178 Spring St., N.Y., N.Y. I have sent him your letters. He is in Dallas and will return in 2 wks." On one occasion when I learned Mr. Lane was scheduled to speak in Des Moines, I arranged to have a sheriff serve the letters on Lane. Unfortunately, the speech was canceled.

Finally, after my ninth letter, Mark Lane replied on Dec. 19 and withdrew his offer, using the following as a rationale: "Since not a single member of the Commission has agreed to appear in the film and none of the senior counsel have agreed either we have decided not to settle for bit players."

In the original letter to me, there were no strings attached. The offer to rebut was unconditional. It was made to David Belin, and no one else. When I replied and accepted the offer, Lane tried to hide, hoping that perhaps I would go away. But I persistently pursued the offer. And whenever I wrote to Lane, I enclosed in each letter Xerox copies of all of my prior correspondence.

On Dec. 23, I replied to Mark Lane's withdrawal of the original unconditional offer to rebut, starting my letter with the simple factual statement: "Your bluff has been called . . ."

". . . True to form, you tried to hide from the person who could best demolish your fabricated case . . .

"You did not say that you had not received any of the prior correspondence, all of which was enclosed in my final letter. You did not say that my request for thirty minutes for rebuttal to your two-hour film was too long. You did not say that my request of fifteen days time to prepare my rebuttal was unreasonable.

Rather, your rationale for reneging on your original offer was your assertion that the lawyer who took the testimony of Howard Brennan, Roy Truly, Officer M. L. Baker,

Lieutenant Day, Domingo Benavides, William Scoggins, Johnny Calvin Brewer and William Waldman, the lawyer who was one of the two men concentrating in Area II, the lawyer who wrote the first draft of Chapter IV of the final Warren Commission Report, the lawyer who was one of the two persons with more first-hand knowledge of the key witnesses to the assassination of President Kennedy than any other individuals in the world, was not of sufficient stature to make a rebuttal. To quote your language, " . . . we have decided not to settle for bit players."

Although you are certainly entitled to your opinion that I was just a bit player, I would respectfully submit that I am fully qualified as an expert on the facts surrounding the assassination of President Kennedy and the murder of Officer J. D. Tippit.

Mr. Lane, you have welched on your offer of rebuttal. The reason is obvious: You are afraid . . . afraid of the truth.

Once again I challenge you, Mark Lane, to thirty minutes on film—that is all I need to demolish your manufactured case.

Although I won the battle of the letters, I unfortunately lost the war—for the film contains no rebuttal. Lane never replied to my final letter of Dec. 23, and wherever in the world the film is shown there will be no rebuttal.

However, there is no doubt in my mind that in the long run of history truth will prevail. It is for this reason that I have asked you to serve as a member of the jury of world opinion.

I have also wanted you to learn not only the heart of the evidence involved in these two murders but also the integrity with which we conducted our investigation.

Many times, members of the legal staff of the Warren Commission were referred to as "brilliant" lawyers. However, brilliance is only secondary. The primary considerations in an investigation of this kind are the same as in service of any governmental body: integrity and sound judgment. The tragedy of Watergate is a direct outgrowth of government servants ignoring these criteria and compounding this with placing as their highest priority loyalty to a person instead of loyalty to our constitutional republic.

There is a well-known axiom in the real estate business that the three most important criteria for success in a real estate venture are location, location and location. Similarly, the three most important criteria for governmental service of any kind must be intregrity and judgment, integrity and judgment and integrity and judgment.

I disagreed with a number of the decisions of my colleagues. I felt that some colleagues performed better than others. But there never was any question in my mind that the seven Commissioners, as well as all the lawyers working with the Commission, had absolute integrity in seeking the truth. There also is no doubt in my mind that the assassination sensationalists, in contrast, lack such integrity, as illustrated by the examples you have seen.

The last three sentences on the Lane–deAntonio film are ironic:

Having rushed to judgment, the Commission dissolved itself on Sept. 14, 1964, but that dissolution cannot bury the facts nor still the doubts. Our questions persist and we shall continue to go on asking them. And if today we cannot know the whole truth, at least we will know that truth which can be known and we shall continue to ask and ask and ask.

If you listen to such claims of people who attack fragments of the overall picture, you should not be content to merely let them ". . . continue to ask and ask and ask." Rather, you should demand that they produce some answers of their own.

Where are any eyewitnesses who saw a rifle at the time of the assassination, except in the TSBD Building? Where is any physical evidence of any other rifle being used—empty cartridge cases? Bullets that did not come from the assassination weapon, Serial No. C-2766?

How do they reconcile the fact that the fibers on President Kennedy's clothing and the autopsy of President Kennedy indicate that he was struck from behind? How do they reconcile the fact that all of the wounds to Governor Connally were caused by a single bullet fired from the rear and above and the fact that the wrist wound was not caused by a pristine bullet? If a bullet struck President Kennedy in the front of the neck, since there was no exit point for that bullet, where did it disappear? If the shots were not fired from the southeast corner window of the sixth floor of the TSBD Building, how do you reconcile the fact that the bullet fragments in the front seat of the Presidential limousine, the nearly whole bullet found at Parkland Memorial Hospital, the three cartridge cases found in the southeast corner window of the sixth floor of the TSBD Building, all came from Oswald's rifle, Serial No. C-2766, to the exclusion of all other weapons in the world? How do you reconcile the damage to the inside of the windshield of the Presidential limousine?

And you can ask additional questions. Why was Oswald the only employee who had regular access to the sixth floor of the TSBD Building who was inside the building at the time of the assassination and then left within a few minutes thereafter? Why did Oswald walk seven blocks east to get a bus when he could have boarded one in front of the TSBD Building? Why did Oswald board the first bus, that passed on Marsalis Street, instead of waiting for the Beckley bus which would have taken him to his rooming house? Why did Oswald leave the bus when it became stalled in a traffic jam as it approached the TSBD Building and take a taxicab?

Why did Oswald lie during his interrogation about owning a rifle? Why did Oswald lie when he was shown a picture of himself with a rifle and say that the picture was artificially manufactured to incriminate him when it was determined scientifically that the negative of that picture came from Oswald's reflex camera, to the exclusion of all other cameras in the world? Why did Oswald lie about having lunch with Junior Jarman at the time of the assassination? Why did Oswald lie about the "curtain rods"? Why, when Oswald ordered the rifle, did he use an alias, A. Hidell? Why, when Oswald ordered his revolver, did he use the alias A. Hidell? Why did Oswald lie about the place from which he purchased his revolver?

Why did Oswald duck into the lobby of Johnny Calvin Brewer's shoe store as police sirens approached? Why did Oswald, as he was approached by Patrolman McDonald in the Texas Theatre, strike Patrolman McDonald with one hand and pull out his revolver with the other? Most important of all, if Oswald was innocent of the assassination of President Kennedy, why did he kill Police Officer Tippit?

When someone charges that Jack Ruby was involved as a conspirator, you can ask additional questions, including such matters as the polygraph examination of Jack Ruby, the happenstance of Jack Ruby going to mail some money on that Sunday morning at around 11:15 AM, the happenstance of postal inspector Holmes who, on the spur of the moment, went to Captain Fritz' office and was responsible for the delay of Oswald's transfer, and all the other matters you may remember in your review of Jack Ruby's testimony.[1]

Finally, I hope that as you heard the evidence presented you will know that truth was my only goal and that our Warren Commission Report was prepared "in recognition of the right of people everywhere to full and truthful knowledge concerning" the events of the assassination of President Kennedy. As we wrote in the beginning:

This Report endeavors to fulfill that right and to appraise this tragedy by the light of reason and the standard of fairness. It has been prepared with a deep awareness of the Commission's responsibility to present to the American people an objective report of the facts relating to the assassination.

And now I will ask that you reach your verdict in the two cases before you:

1. Did Lee Harvey Oswald, beyond a reasonable doubt, murder Dallas Police Officer J. D. Tippit?

2. Did Lee Harvey Oswald, beyond a reasonable doubt, murder President John F. Kennedy?

The verdict is yours.

---

[1]Jack Ruby died while in prison.

APPENDIX

SUMMARY AND CONCLUSIONS
OF THE WARREN
COMMISSION REPORT

The assassination of John Fitzgerald Kennedy on November 22, 1963, was a cruel and shocking act of violence directed against a man, a family, a nation, and against all mankind. A young and vigorous leader whose years of public and private life stretched before him was the victim of the fourth Presidential assassination in the history of a country dedicated to the concepts of reasoned argument and peaceful political change. This Commission was created on November 29, 1963, in recognition of the right of people everywhere to full and truthful knowledge concerning these events. This report endeavors to fulfill that right to appraise this tragedy by the light of reason and the standard of fairness. It has been prepared with a deep awareness of the Commission's responsibility to present to the American people an objective report of the facts relating to the assassination.

NARRATIVE OF EVENTS

At 11:40 AM., c.s.t., on Friday, November 22, 1963, President John F. Kennedy, Mrs. Kennedy, and their party arrived at Love Field, Dallas, Tex. Behind them was the first day of a Texas trip planned 5 months before by the President, Vice President Lyndon B. Johnson, and John B. Connally, Jr., Governor of Texas. After leaving the White House on Thursday morning, the President had flown initially to San Antonio where Vice President Lyndon B. Johnson joined the party and the President dedicated new research facilities at the U. S. Air Force School of Aerospace Medicine. Following a testimonial dinner in Houston for U. S. Representative Albert Thomas, the President flew to Fort Worth where he spent the night and spoke at a large breakfast gathering on Friday.

Planned for later that day were a motorcade through downtown Dallas, a luncheon speech at the Trade Mart, and a flight to Austin where the President would attend a reception and speak at a Democratic fundraising dinner. From Austin he would proceed to the Texas ranch of the Vice President. Evident on this trip were the varied roles which an American President performs—Head of State, Chief Executive, party leader, and, in this instance, prospective candidate for reelection.

The Dallas motorcade, it was hoped, would evoke a demonstration of the President's personal popularity in a city which he had lost in the 1960 election. Once it had been decided that the trip to Texas would span 2 days, those responsible for planning, primarily Governor Connally and Kenneth O'Donnell, a special assistant to the President, agreed that a motorcade through Dallas would be desirable. The Secret Service was told on November 8 that 45 minutes had been allotted to a motorcade procession from Love Field to the site of a luncheon planned by Dallas business and civic leaders in honor of the President. After considering the facilities and security problems of several buildings, the Trade Mart was chosen as the luncheon site. Given this selection, and in accordance with the customary practice of affording the greatest number of people an opportunity to see the President, the motorcade route selected was a natural one. The route was approved by the local host committee and White House representatives on November 18 and publicized in the local papers starting on November 19. This advance publicity made it clear that the motorcade would leave Main Street and pass the intersection of Elm and Houston Streets as it proceeded to the Trade Mart by way of the Stemmons Freeway.

By midmorning of November 22, clearing skies in Dallas dispelled the threat of rain and the President greeted the crowds from his open limousine without the "bubbletop," which was at that time a plastic shield furnishing protection only against inclement weather. To the left of the President in the rear seat was Mrs. Kennedy. In the jump seats were Governor Connally, who was in front of the President, and Mrs. Connally at the Governor's left. Agent William R. Greer of the Secret Service was driving, and Agent Roy H. Kellerman was sitting to his right.

Directly behind the Presidential limousine was an open "followup" car with eight Secret Service agents, two in the front seat, two in the rear, and two on each running board. These agents, in accordance with normal Secret Service procedures, were instructed to scan the crowds, the roofs, and windows of buildings, overpasses, and crossings for signs of trouble. Behind the "followup" car was the Vice-Presidential car carrying the Vice President and Mrs. Johnson and Senator Ralph W. Yarborough. Next were a Vice-Presidential "followup" car and several cars and buses for additional dignitaries, press representatives, and others.

The motorcade left Love Field shortly after 11:50 AM, and proceeded through residential neighborhoods, stopping twice at the President's request to greet well-wishers among the friendly crowds. Each time the President's car halted, Secret Service agents from the "followup" car moved forward to assume a protective stance near the President and Mrs. Kennedy. As the motorcade reached Main Street, a principal east-west artery in downtown Dallas, the welcome became tumultuous. At the extreme west end of Main Street the motorcade turned right on Houston Street and proceeded north for one block in order to make a left turn on Elm Street, the most direct and convenient approach to the Stemmons Freeway and the Trade Mart. As the President's car approached the intersection of Houston and Elm Streets, there loomed directly ahead on the intersection's northwest corner a seven-story, orange brick warehouse and office building, the Texas School

Book Depository. Riding in the Vice President's car, Agent Rufus W. Youngblood of the Secret Service noticed that the clock atop the building indicated 12:30 PM, the scheduled arrival time at the Trade Mart.

The President's car, which had been going north, made a sharp turn toward the southwest onto Elm Street. At a speed of about 11 miles per hour, it started down the gradual descent toward a railroad overpass under which the motorcade would proceed before reaching the Stemmons Freeway. The front of the Texas School Book Depository was now on the President's right, and he waved to the crowd assembled there as he passed the building. Dealey Plaza—an open, landscaped area marking the western end of downtown Dallas—stretched out to the President's left. A Secret Service agent riding in the motorcade radioed the Trade Mart that the President would arrive in 5 minutes.

Seconds later shots resounded in rapid succession. The President's hands moved to his neck. He appeared to stiffen momentarily and lurch slightly forward in his seat. A bullet had entered the base of the back of his neck slightly to the right of the spine. It traveled downward and exited from the front of the neck, causing a nick in the left lower portion of the knot in the President's necktie. Before the shooting started, Governor Connally had been facing toward the crowd on the right. He started to turn toward the left and suddenly felt a blow on his back. The Governor had been hit by a bullet which entered at the extreme right side of his back at a point below his right armpit. The bullet traveled through his chest in a downward and forward direction, exited below his right nipple, passed through his right wrist which had been in his lap, and then caused a wound to his left thigh. The force of the bullet's impact appeared to spin the Governor to his right, and Mrs. Connally pulled him down into her lap. Another bullet then struck President Kennedy in the rear portion of his head, causing a massive and fatal wound. The President fell to the left into Mrs. Kennedy's lap.

Secret Service Agent Clinton J. Hill, riding on the left running board of the "followup" car, heard a noise which sounded like a firecracker and saw the President suddenly lean forward and to the left. Hill jumped off the car and raced toward the President's limousine. In the front seat of the Vice-Presidential car, Agent Youngblood heard an explosion and noticed unusual movements in the crowd. He vaulted into the rear seat and sat on the Vice President in order to protect him. At the same time Agent Kellerman in the front seat of the Presidential limousine turned to observe the President. Seeing that the President was struck, Kellerman instructed the driver, "Let's get out of here; we are hit." He radioed ahead to the lead car, "Get us to the hospital immediately." Agent Greer immediately accelerated the Presidential car. As it gained speed, Agent Hill managed to pull himself onto the back of the car where Mrs. Kennedy had climbed. Hill pushed her back into the rear seat and shielded the stricken President and Mrs. Kennedy as the President's car proceeded at high speed to Parkland Memorial Hospital, 4 miles away.

At Parkland, the President was immediately treated by a team of physicians who had been alerted for the President's arrival by the Dallas Police Department as the result of a radio message from the motorcade after the shooting. The doctors noted irregular breathing movements and a possible heartbeat, although they could not detect a pulsebeat. They observed the extensive wound in the President's head and a small wound approximately one-fourth inch in diameter in the lower third of his neck. In an effort to facilitate breathing, the physicians performed a tracheotomy by enlarging the throat wound and inserting a tube. Totally absorbed in the immediate task of trying to preserve the President's life, the attending doctors never turned the President over for an examination of his back. At 1 PM, after all heart activity ceased and the Last Rites were administered by a priest, President Kennedy was pronounced dead. Governor Connally underwent surgery and ultimately recovered from his serious wounds.

Upon learning of the President's death, Vice President Johnson left Parkland Hospital under close guard and proceeded to the Presidential plane at Love Field. Mrs. Kennedy, accompanying her husband's body, boarded the plane shortly thereafter. At 2:38 PM, in the central compartment of the plane, Lyndon B. Johnson was sworn in as the 36th President of the United States by Federal District Court Judge Sarah T. Hughes. The plane left immediately for Washington, D. C., arriving at Andrews AFB, Md., at 5:58 PM, e.s.t. The President's body was taken to the National Naval Medical Center, Bethesda, Md., where it was given a complete pathological examination. The autopsy disclosed the large head wound observed at Parkland and the wound in the front of the neck which had been enlarged by the Parkland doctors when they performed the tracheotomy. Both of these wounds were described in the autopsy report as being "presumably of exit." In addition the autopsy revealed a small wound of entry in the rear of the President's skull and another wound of entry near the base of the back of the neck. The autopsy report stated the cause of death as "Gunshot wound, head," and the bullets which struck the President were described as having been fired "from a point behind and somewhat above the level of the deceased."

At the scene of the shooting, there was evident confusion at the outset concerning the point of origin of the shots. Witnesses differed in their accounts of the direction from which the sound of the shots emanated. Within a few minutes, however, attention centered on the Texas School Book Depository Building as the source of the shots. The building was occupied by a private corporation, the Texas School Book Depository Co., which distributed school textbooks of several publishers and leased space to representatives of the publishers. Most of the employees in the building worked for these publishers. The balance, including a 15-man warehousing crew, were employees of the Texas School Book Depository Co. itself.

Several eyewitnesses in front of the building reported that they saw a rifle being fired from the southeast corner window on the sixth floor of the Texas School Book Depository. One eyewitness, Howard L. Brennan, had been watching the parade from a point on Elm Street directly opposite and facing the building. He promptly told a policeman that he had seen a slender man, about 5 feet 10 inches, in his early thirties, take deliberate aim from the sixth-floor corner window and fire a rifle in the direction of the President's car. Brennan thought he might be able to identify the man since he had noticed him in the window a few minutes before the motorcade made the turn onto Elm Street. At 12:34 PM, the Dallas police radio mentioned the Depository Building as a possible source of the shots, and at 12:45 PM, the police radio broadcast a description of the suspected assassin based primarily on Brennan's observations.

When the shots were fired, a Dallas motorcycle patrolman, Marrion L. Baker, was riding in the motorcade at a point several cars behind the President. He had turned right from Main Street onto Houston Street and was about 200 feet south of Elm Street when he heard a shot. Baker, having recently returned from a week of deer hunting, was certain the shot came from a high-powered rifle. He looked up and saw pigeons scattering in the air from their perches on the Texas School Book Depository Building. He raced his motorcycle to the building, dismounted, scanned the area to the west and pushed his way through the spectators toward the entrance. There he encountered Roy Truly, the building superintendent, who offered Baker his help. They entered the building, and ran toward the two elevators in the rear. Finding that both elevators were on an upper floor, they dashed up the stairs. Not more than 2 minutes had elapsed since the shooting.

When they reached the second-floor landing on their way up to the top of the building, Patrolman Baker thought he caught a glimpse of someone through the small glass window in the door separating the hall near the stairs from the small vestibule leading into the lunchroom. Gun in hand, he rushed to the door and saw a man about 20 feet away walking toward the other end of the lunchroom. The man was emptyhanded. At Baker's command, the man turned and approached him. Truly, who had started up the stairs to the third floor ahead of Baker, returned to see what had delayed the patrolman. Baker asked Truly whether he knew the man in the lunchroom. Truly replied that the man worked in the building, whereupon Baker turned from the man and proceeded, with Truly, up the stairs. The man they encountered had started working in the Texas School Book Depository Building on October 16, 1963. His fellow workers described him as very quiet—a "loner." His name was Lee Harvey Oswald.

Within about 1 minute after his encounter with Baker and Truly, Oswald was seen passing through the second-floor offices. In his hand was a full "Coke" bottle which he had purchased from a vending machine in the lunchroom. He was walking toward the front of the building where a passenger elevator and a short flight of stairs provided access to the main entrance of the building on the first floor. Approximately 7 minutes later, at about 12:40 PM, Oswald boarded a bus at a point on Elm Street seven short blocks east of the Depository Building. The bus was traveling west toward the very building from which Oswald had come. Its route lay through the

Oak Cliff section in southwest Dallas, where it would pass seven blocks east of the roominghouse in which Oswald was living, at 1026 North Beckley Street. On the bus was Mrs. Mary Bledsoe, one of Oswald's former landladies, who immediately recognized him. Oswald stayed on the bus approximately 3 or 4 minutes, during which time it proceeded only two blocks because of the traffic jam created by the motorcade and the assassination. Oswald then left the bus.

A few minutes later he entered a vacant taxi four blocks away and asked the driver to take him to a point on North Beckley Street several blocks beyond his roominghouse. The trip required 5 or 6 minutes. At about 1 PM Oswald arrived at the roominghouse. The housekeeper, Mrs. Earlene Roberts, was surprised to see Oswald at midday and remarked to him that he seemed to be in quite a hurry. He made no reply. A few minutes later Oswald emerged from his room zipping up his jacket and rushed out of the house.

Approximately 14 minutes later, and just 45 minutes after the assassination, another violent shooting occurred in Dallas, The victim was Patrolman J. D. Tippit of the Dallas police, an officer with a good record during his more than 11 years with the police force. He was shot near the intersection of 10th Street and Patton Street, about nine-tenths of a mile from Oswald's roominghouse. At the time of the assassination, Tippit was alone in his patrol car, the routine practice for most police patrol cars at this time of day. He had been ordered by radio at 12:45 PM to proceed to the central Oak Cliff area as part of a concentration of patrol car activity around the center of the city following the assassination. At 12:54 Tippit radioed that he had moved as directed and would be available for any emergency. By this time the police radio had broadcast several messages alerting the police to the suspect described by Brennan at the scene of the assassination—a slender white male, about 30 years old, 5 feet 10 inches and weighing about 165 pounds.

At approximately 1:15 PM, Tippit was driving slowly in an easterly direction on East 10th Street in Oak Cliff. About 100 feet past the intersection of 10th Street and Patton Avenue, Tippit pulled up alongside a man walking in the same direction. The man met the general description of the suspect wanted in connection with the assassination. He walked over to Tippit's car, rested his arms on the door on the right-hand side of the car, and apparently exchanged words with Tippit through the window. Tippit opened the door on the left side and started to walk around the front of his car. As he reached the front wheel on the driver's side, the man on the sidewalk drew a revolver and fired several shots in rapid succession, hitting Tippit four times and killing him instantly. An automobile repairman, Domingo Benavides, heard the shots and stopped his pickup truck on the opposite side of the street about 25 feet in front of Tippit's car. He observed the gunman start back toward Patton Avenue, removing the empty cartridge cases from the gun as he went. Benavides rushed to Tippit's side. The patrolman, apparently dead, was lying on his revolver, which was out of its holster. Benavides promptly reported the shooting to police headquarters over the radio in Tippit's car. The message was received shortly after 1:16 PM.

As the gunman left the scene, he walked hurriedly back toward Patton Avenue and turned left, heading south. Standing on the northwest corner of 10th Street and Patton Avenue was Helen Markham, who had been walking south on Patton Avenue and had seen both the killer and Tippit cross the intersection in front of her as she waited on the curb for traffic to pass. She witnessed the shooting and then saw the man with a gun in his hand walk back toward the corner and cut across the lawn of the corner house as he started south on Patton Avenue.

In the corner house itself, Mrs. Barbara Jeanette Davis and her sister-in-law, Mrs. Virginia Davis, heard the shots and rushed to the door in time to see the man walk rapidly across the lawn shaking a revolver as if he were emptying it of cartridge cases. Later that day each woman found a cartridge case near the house. As the gunman turned the corner he passed alongside a taxicab which was parked on Patton Avenue, a few feet from 10th Street. The driver, William W. Scoggins, had seen the slaying and was now crouched behind his cab on the street side. As the gunman cut through the shrubbery on the lawn, Scoggins looked up and saw the man approximately 12 feet away. In his hand was a pistol and he muttered words which sounded to Scoggins like "poor dumb cop" or "poor damn cop."

After passing Scoggins, the gunman crossed to the west side of Patton Avenue and ran south toward Jefferson Boulevard, a main Oak Cliff thoroughfare. On the east side of Patton, between 10th Street and Jefferson Boulevard, Ted Callaway, a used car salesman, heard the shots and ran to the sidewalk. As the man with the gun rushed past, Callaway shouted "What's going on?" The man merely shrugged, ran on to Jefferson Boulevard and turned right. On the next corner was a gas station with a parking lot in the rear. The assailant ran into the lot, discarded his jacket and then continued his flight west on Jefferson.

In a shoe store a few blocks farther west on Jefferson, the manager, Johnny Calvin Brewer, heard the siren of a police car moments after the radio in his store announced the shooting of the police officer in Oak Cliff. Brewer saw a man step quickly into the entranceway of the store and stand there with his back toward the street. When the police car made a U-turn and headed back in the direction of the Tippit shooting, the man left and Brewer followed him. He saw the man enter the Texas Theatre, a motion picture house about 60 feet away, without buying a ticket. Brewer pointed this out to the cashier, Mrs. Julia Postal, who called the police. The time was shortly after 1:40 PM.

At 1:29 PM, the police radio had noted the similarity in the descriptions of the suspects in the Tippit shooting and the assassination. At 1:45 PM, in response to Mrs. Postal's call, the police radio sounded the alarm: "Have information a suspect just went in the Texas Theatre on West Jefferson."

Within minutes the theater was surrounded. The house lights were then turned up. Patrolman M. N. McDonald and several other policemen approached the man, who had been pointed out to them by Brewer.

McDonald ordered the man to his feet and heard him say, "Well, it's all over now." The man drew a gun from his waist with one hand and struck the officer with the other. McDonald struck out with his right hand and grabbed the gun with his left hand. After a brief struggle McDonald and several other police officers disarmed and handcuffed the suspect and drove him to police headquarters, arriving at approximately 2 PM.

Following the assassination, police cars had rushed to the Texas School Book Depository in response to the many radio messages reporting that the shots had been fired from the Depository Building. Inspector J. Herbert Sawyer of the Dallas Police Department arrived at the scene shortly after hearing the first of these police radio messages at 12:34 PM. Some of the officers who had been assigned to the area of Elm and Houston Streets for the motorcade were talking to witnesses and watching the building when Sawyer arrived. Sawyer entered the building and rode a passenger elevator to the fourth floor, which was the top floor for this elevator. He conducted a quick search, returned to the main floor and, between approximately 12:37 and 12:40 PM, ordered that no one be permitted to leave the building.

Shortly before 1 PM Capt. J. Will Fritz, chief of the homicide and robbery bureau of the Dallas Police Department, arrived to take charge of the investigation. Searching the sixth floor, Deputy Sheriff Luke Mooney noticed a pile of cartons in the southeast corner. He squeezed through the boxes and realized immediately that he had discovered the point from which the shots had been fired. On the floor were three empty cartridge cases. A carton had apparently been placed on the floor at the side of the window so that a person sitting on the carton could look down Elm Street toward the overpass and scarcely be noticed from the outside. Between this carton and the half-open window were three additional cartons arranged at such an angle that a rifle resting on the top carton would be aimed directly at the motorcade as it moved away from the building. The high stack of boxes, which first attracted Mooney's attention, effectively screened a person at the window from the view of anyone else on the floor.

Mooney's discovery intensified the search for additional evidence on the sixth floor, and at 1:22 PM, approximately 10 minutes after the cartridge cases were found, Deputy Sheriff Eugene Boone turned his flashlight in the direction of two rows of boxes in the northwest corner near the staircase. Stuffed between the two rows was a bolt-action rifle with a telescopic sight. The rifle was not touched until it could be photographed. When Lt. J. C. Day of the police identification bureau decided that the wooden stock and the metal knob at the end of the bolt contained no prints, he held the rifle by the stock while Captain Fritz ejected a live shell by operating the bolt. Lieutenant Day promptly noted that stamped on the rifle itself was the serial number "C2766" as well as the markings "1940," "MADE ITALY" and

"CAL. 6.5." The rifle was about 40 inches long and when disassembled it could fit into a handmade paper sack which, after the assassination, was found in the southeast corner of the building within a few feet of the cartridge cases.

As Fritz and Day were completing their examination of this rifle on the sixth floor, Roy Truly, the building superintendent, approached with information which he felt should be brought to the attention of the police. Earlier, while the police were questioning the employees, Truly had observed that Lee Harvey Oswald, 1 of the 15 men who worked in the warehouse, was missing. After Truly provided Oswald's name, address, and general description, Fritz left for police headquarters. He arrived at headquarters shortly after 2 PM and asked two detectives to pick up the employee who was missing from the Texas School Book Depository. Standing nearby were the police officers who had just arrived with the man arrested in the Texas Theatre. When Fritz mentioned the name of the missing employee, he learned that the man was already in the interrogation room. The missing School Book Depository employee and the suspect who had been apprehended in the Texas Theatre were one and the same—Lee Harvey Oswald.

The suspect Fritz was about to question in connection with the assassination of the President and the murder of a policeman was born in New Orleans on October 18, 1939, 2 months after the death of his father. His mother, Marguerite Claverie Oswald, had two older children. One, John Pic, was a half-brother to Lee from an earlier marriage which had ended in divorce. The other was Robert Oswald, a full brother to Lee and 5 years older. When Lee Oswald was 3, Mrs. Oswald placed him in an orphanage where his brother and half-brother were already living, primarily because she had to work.

In January 1944, when Lee was 4, he was taken out of the orphanage, and shortly thereafter his mother moved with him to Dallas, Tex., where the older boys joined them at the end of the school year. In May of 1945 Marguerite Oswald married her third husband, Edwin A. Ekdahl. While the two older boys attended a military boarding school, Lee lived at home and developed a warm attachment to Ekdahl, occasionally accompanying his mother and stepfather on business trips around the country. Lee started school in Benbrook, Tex., but in the fall of 1946, after a separation from Ekdahl, Marguerite Oswald reentered Lee in the first grade in Covington, La. In January 1947, while Lee was still in the first grade, the family moved to Fort Worth, Tex., as the result of an attempted reconciliation between Ekdahl and Lee's mother. A year and half later, before Lee was 9, his mother was divorced from her third husband as the result of a divorce action instituted by Ekdahl. Lee's school record during the next 5-1/2 years in Fort Worth was average, although generally it grew poorer each year. The comments of teachers and others who knew him at that time do not reveal any unusual personality traits or characteristics.

Another change for Lee Oswald occurred in August 1952, a few months after he completed the sixth grade. Marguerite Oswald and her 12-year-old son moved to New York City where Marguerite's oldest son, John Pic, was stationed with the Coast Guard. The ensuing year and one-half in New York was marked by Lee's refusals to attend school and by emotional and psychological problems of a seemingly serious nature. Because he had become a chronic school truant, Lee underwent psychiatric study at Youth House, an institution in New York for juveniles who have had truancy problems or difficulties with the law, and who appear to require psychiatric observation, or other types of guidance. The social worker assigned to his case described him as "seriously detached" and "withdrawn" and noted "a rather pleasant, appealing quality about this emotionally starved, affectionless youngster." Lee expressed the feeling to the social worker that his mother did not care for him and regarded him as a burden. He experienced fantasies about being all powerful and hurting people, but during his stay at Youth House he was apparently not a behavior problem. He appeared withdrawn and evasive, a boy who preferred to spend his time alone, reading and watching television. His tests indicated that he was above average in intelligence for his age group. The chief psychiatrist of Youth House diagnosed Lee's problem as a "personality pattern disturbance with schizoid features and passive-aggressive tendencies." He concluded that the boy was "an emotionally quite disturbed youngster" and recommended psychiatric treatment.

In May 1953, after having been at Youth House for 3 weeks, Lee Oswald returned to school where his attendance and grades temporarily improved. By the following fall, however, the probation officer reported that virtually every teacher complained about the boy's behavior. His mother insisted that he did not need psychiatric assistance. Although there was apparently some improvement in Lee's behavior during the next few months, the court recommended further treatment. In January 1954, while Lee's case was still pending, Marguerite and Lee left for New Orleans, the city of Lee's birth.

Upon his return to New Orleans, Lee maintained mediocre grades but had no obvious behavior problems. Neighbors and others who knew him outside of school remembered him as a quiet, solitary and introverted boy who read a great deal and whose vocabulary made him quite articulate. About 1 month after he started the 10th grade and 11 days before his 16th birthday in October 1955, he brought to school a note purportedly written by his mother, stating that the family was moving to California. The note was written by Lee. A few days later he dropped out of school and almost immediately tried to join the Marine Corps. Because he was only 16, he was rejected.

After leaving school Lee worked for the next 10 months at several jobs in New Orleans as an office messenger or clerk. It was during this period that he started to read communist literature. Occasionally, in conversations with others, he praised communism and expressed to his fellow employees a desire to join the Communist Party. At about this time, when he was not yet 17, he wrote to the Socialist Party of America, professing his belief in Marxism.

Another move followed in July 1956 when Lee and his mother returned to Fort Worth. He reentered high school but again dropped out after a few weeks and enlisted in the Marine Corps on October 24, 1956, 6 days after his 17th birthday. On December 21, 1956, during boot camp in San Diego, Oswald fired a score of 212 for record with the M-1 rifle—2 points over the minimum for a rating of "sharpshooter" on a marksman/sharpshooter/expert scale. After his basic training, Oswald received training in aviation fundamentals and then in radar scanning.

Most people who knew Oswald in the Marines described him as a "loner" who resented the exercise of authority by others. He spent much of his free time reading. He was court-martialed once for possessing an unregistered privately owned weapon and, on another occasion, for using provocative language to a noncommissioned officer. He was, however, generally able to comply with Marine discipline, even though his experiences in the Marine Corps did not live up to his expectations.

Oswald served 15 months overseas until November 1958, most of it in Japan. During his final year in the Marine Corps he was stationed for the most part in Santa Ana, Calif., where he showed a marked interest in the Soviet Union and sometimes expressed politically radical views with dogmatic conviction. Oswald again fired the M-1 rifle for record on May 6, 1959, and this time he shot a score of 191 on a shorter course than before, only 1 point over the minimum required to be a "marksman." According to one of his fellow marines, Oswald was not particularly interested in his rifle performance, and his unit was not expected to exhibit the usual rifle proficiency. During this period he expressed strong admiration for Fidel Castro and an interest in joining the Cuban army. He tried to impress those around him as an intellectual, but his thinking appeared to some as shallow and rigid.

Oswald's Marine service terminated on September 11, 1959, when at his own request he was released from active service a few months ahead of his scheduled release. He offered as the reason for his release the ill health and economic plight of his mother. He returned to Fort Worth, remained with his mother only 3 days and left for New Orleans, telling his mother he planned to get work there in the shipping or import-export business. In New Orleans he booked passage on the freighter SS *Marion Lykes*, which sailed from New Orleans to Le Havre, France, on September 20, 1959.

Lee Harvey Oswald had presumably planned this step in his life for quite some time. In March of 1959 he had applied to the Albert Schweitzer College in Switzerland for admission to the spring 1960 term. His letter of application contained many blatant falsehoods concerning his qualifications and background. A few weeks before his discharge he had applied for and obtained a passport, listing the Soviet Union as one of the countries which he planned to visit. During his service in the Marines he had saved a comparatively large sum of money, possibly as much as $1,500, which would appear to have been accomplished by considerable frugality and apparently for a specific purpose.

The purpose of the accumulated fund soon became known. On October 16, 1959, Oswald arrived in Moscow by train after crossing the border from Finland, where he had secured a visa for a 6-day stay in the Soviet Union. He immediately applied for Soviet citizenship. On the afternoon of October 21, 1959, Oswald was ordered to leave the Soviet Union by 8 PM that evening. That same afternoon in his hotel room Oswald, in an apparent suicide attempt, slashed his left wrist. He was hospitalized immediately. On October 31, 3 days after his release from the hospital, Oswald appeared at the American Embassy, announced that he wished to renounce his U. S. citizenship and become a Russian citizen, and handed the Embassy officer a written statement he had prepared for the occasion. When asked his reasons, Oswald replied, "I am a Marxist." Oswald never formally complied with the legal steps necessary to renounce his American citizenship. The Soviet Government did not grant his request for citizenship, but in January 1960 he was given permission to remain in the Soviet Union on a year-to-year basis. At the same time Oswald was sent to Minsk where he worked in a radio factory as an unskilled laborer. In January 1961 his permission to remain in the Soviet Union was extended for another year. A few weeks later, in February 1961, he wrote to the American Embassy in Moscow expressing a desire to return to the United States.

The following month Oswald met a 19-year-old Russian girl, Marina Nikolaevna Prusakova, a pharmacist, who had been brought up in Leningrad but was then living with an aunt and uncle in Minsk. They were married on April 30, 1961. Throughout the following year he carried on a correspondence with American and Soviet authorities seeking approval for the departure of himself and his wife to the United States. In the course of his effort, Oswald and his wife visited the U. S. Embassy in Moscow in July of 1961. Primarily on the basis of an interview and questionnaire completed there, the Embassy concluded that Oswald had not lost his citizenship, a decision subsequently ratified by the Department of State in Washington, D. C. Upon their return to Minsk, Oswald and his wife filed with the Soviet authorities for permission to leave together. Their formal application was made in July 1961, and on December 25, 1961, Marina Oswald was advised it would be granted.

A daughter was born to the Oswalds in February 1962. In the months that followed they prepared for their return to the United States. On May 9, 1962, the U. S. Immigration and Naturalization Service, at the request of the Department of State, agreed to waive a restriction under the law which would have prevented the issuance of a United States visa to Oswald's Russian wife until she had left the Soviet Union. They finally left Moscow on June 1, 1962, and were assisted in meeting their travel expenses by a loan of $435.71 from the U. S. Department of State. Two weeks later they arrived in Fort Worth, Tex.

For a few weeks Oswald, his wife and child lived with Oswald's brother Robert. After a similar stay with Oswald's mother, they moved into their own apartment in early August. Oswald obtained a job on July 16 as a sheet metal worker. During this period in Fort Worth, Oswald was interviewed twice by agents of the FBI. The report of the first interview, which occurred on June 26, described him as arrogant and unwilling to discuss the reasons why he had gone to the Soviet Union. Oswald denied that he was involved in Soviet intelligence activities and promised to advise the FBI if Soviet representatives ever communicated with him. He was interviewed again on August 16, when he displayed a less belligerent attitude and once again agreed to inform the FBI of any attempt to enlist him in intelligence activities.

In early October 1962 Oswald quit his job at the sheet metal plant and moved to Dallas. While living in Fort Worth the Oswalds had been introduced to a group of Russian-speaking people in the Dallas-Fort Worth area. Many of them assisted the Oswalds by providing small amounts of food, clothing, and household items. Oswald himself was disliked by almost all of this group whose help to the family was prompted primarily by sympathy for Marina Oswald and the child. Despite the fact that he had left the Soviet Union, disillusioned with its Government, Oswald seemed more firmly committed than ever to his concepts of Marxism. He showed disdain for democracy, capitalism, and American society in general. He was highly critical of the Russian-speaking group because they seemed devoted to American concepts of democracy and capitalism and were ambitious to improve themselves economically.

In February 1963 the Oswalds met Ruth Paine at a social gathering. Ruth Paine was temporarily separated from her husband and living with her two children in their home in Irving, Tex., a suburb of Dallas. Because of an interest in the Russian language and sympathy for Marina Oswald, who spoke no English and had little funds, Ruth Paine befriended Marina and, during the next 2 months, visited her on several occasions.

On April 6, 1963, Oswald lost his job with a photography firm. A few days later, on April 10, he attempted to kill Maj. Gen. Edwin A. Walker (Resigned, U. S. Army), using a rifle which he had ordered by mail 1 month previously under an assumed name. Marina Oswald learned of her husband's act when she confronted him with a note which he had left, giving her instructions in the event he did not return. That incident and their general economic difficulties impelled Marina Oswald to suggest that her husband leave Dallas and go to New Orleans to look for work.

Oswald left for New Orleans on April 24, 1963. Ruth Paine, who knew nothing of the Walker shooting, invited Marina Oswald and the baby to stay with her in the Paines' modest home while Oswald sought work in New Orleans. Early in May, upon receiving word from Oswald that he had found a job, Ruth Paine drove Marina Oswald and the baby to New Orleans to rejoin Oswald.

During the stay in New Orleans, Oswald formed a fictitious New Orleans Chapter of the Fair Play for Cuba Committee. He posed as secretary of this organization and represented that the president was A. J. Hidell. In reality, Hidell was a completely fictitious person created by Oswald, the organization's only member. Oswald was arrested on August 9 in connection with a scuffle which occurred while he was distributing pro-Castro leaflets. The next day, while at the police station, he was interviewed by an FBI agent after Oswald requested the police to arrange such an interview. Oswald gave the agent false information about his own background and was evasive in his replies concerning Fair Play for Cuba activities. During the next 2 weeks Oswald appeared on radio programs twice, claiming to be the spokesman for the Fair Play for Cuba Committee in New Orleans.

On July 19, 1963, Oswald lost his job as a greaser of coffee processing machinery. In September, after an exchange of correspondence with Marina Oswald, Ruth Paine drove to New Orleans and on September 23, transported Marina, the child, and the family belongings to Irving, Tex. Ruth Paine suggested that Marina Oswald, who was expecting her second child in October, live at the Paine house until after the baby was born. Oswald remained behind, ostensibly to find work either in Houston or some other city. Instead, he departed by bus for Mexico, arriving in Mexico City on September 27, where he promptly visited the Cuban and Russian Embassies. His stated objective was to obtain official permission to visit Cuba, on his way to the Soviet Union. The Cuban Government would not grant his visa unless the Soviet Government would also issue a visa permitting his entry into Russia. Oswald's efforts to secure these visas failed, and he left for Dallas, where he arrived on October 3, 1963.

When he saw his wife the next day, it was decided that Oswald would rent a room in Dallas and visit his family on weekends. For 1 week he rented a room from Mrs. Bledsoe, the woman who later saw him on the bus shortly after the assassination. On October 14, 1963, he rented the Beckley Avenue room and listed his name as O. H. Lee. On the same day, at the suggestion of a neighbor, Mrs. Paine phoned the Texas School Book Depository and was told that there was a job opening. She informed Oswald who was interviewed the following day at the Depository and started to work there on October 16, 1963.

On October 20 the Oswalds' second daughter was born. During October and November Oswald established a general pattern of weekend visits to Irving, arriving on Friday afternoon and returning to Dallas Monday morning with a fellow employee, Buell Wesley Frazier, who lived near the Paines. On Friday, November 15, Oswald remained in Dallas at the suggestion of his wife who told him that the house would be crowded because of a birthday party for Ruth Paine's daughter. On Monday, November 18, Oswald and his wife quarreled bitterly during a telephone conversation, because she learned for the first time that he was living at the roominghouse under an assumed name. On Thursday, November 21, Oswald told Frazier that he would like to drive to Irving to pick up some curtain rods for an apartment in Dallas. His wife and Mrs. Paine were quite surprised to see him since it was a Thursday night. They thought he had returned to make up after Monday's quarrel. He was conciliatory, but Marina Oswald was still angry.

Later that evening, when Mrs. Paine had finished cleaning the kitchen, she went into the garage and noticed that the light was burning. She was certain that she had not left it on, although the incident appeared unimportant at the time. In the garage were most of the Oswalds' personal possessions. The following morning Oswald left while his wife was still in bed feeding the baby. She did not see him leave the house, nor did Ruth Paine. On the dresser in their room he left his wedding ring which he had never done before. His wallet containing $170 was left intact in a dresser-drawer.

Oswald walked to Frazier's house about half a block away and placed a long bulky package, made out of wrapping paper and tape, into the rear seat of the car. He told Frazier that the package contained curtain rods. When they reached the Depository parking lot, Oswald walked quickly ahead. Frazier followed and saw Oswald enter the Depository Building carrying the long bulky package with him.

During the morning of November 22, Marina Oswald followed President Kennedy's activities on television. She and Ruth Paine cried when they heard that the President had been shot. Ruth Paine translated the news of the shooting to Marina Oswald as it came over television, including the report that the shots were probably fired from the building where Oswald worked. When Marina Oswald heard this, she recalled the Walker episode and the fact that her husband still owned the rifle. She went quietly to the Paines' garage where the rifle had been concealed in a blanket among their other belongings. It appeared to her that the rifle was still there, although she did not actually open the blanket.

At about 3 PM the police arrived at the Paine house and asked Marina Oswald whether her husband owned a rifle. She said that he did and then led them into the garage and pointed to the rolled up blanket. As a police officer lifted it, the blanket hung limply over either side of his arm. The rifle was not there.

Meanwhile, at police headquarters, Captain Fritz had begun questioning Oswald. Soon after the start of the first interrogation, agents of the FBI and the U. S. Secret Service arrived and participated in the questioning. Oswald denied having anything to do with the assassination of President Kennedy or the murder of Patrolman Tippit. He claimed that he was eating lunch at the time of the assassination, and that he then spoke with his foreman for 5 to 10 minutes before going home. He denied that he owned a rifle and when confronted, in a subsequent interview, with a picture showing him holding a rifle and pistol, he claimed that his face had been superimposed on someone else's body. He refused to answer any questions about the presence in his wallet of a selective service card with his picture and the name "Alek J. Hidell."

During the questioning of Oswald on the third floor of the police department, more than 100 representatives of the press, radio, and television were crowded into the hallway through which Oswald had to pass when being taken from his cell to Captain Fritz' office for interrogation. Between Friday afternoon and Sunday morning he appeared in the hallway at least 16 times. The generally confused conditions outside and inside Captain Fritz' office increased the difficulty of police questioning. Advised by the police that he could communicate with an attorney, Oswald made several telephone calls on Saturday in an effort to procure representation of his own choice and discussed the matter with the president of the local bar association, who offered to obtain counsel. Oswald declined the offer saying that he would first try to obtain counsel by himself. By Sunday morning he had not yet engaged an attorney.

At 7:10 PM on November 22, 1963, Lee Harvey Oswald was formally advised that he had been charged with the murder of Patrolman J. D. Tippit. Several witnesses to the Tippit slaying and to the subsequent flight of the gunman had positively identified Oswald in police lineups. While positive firearm identification evidence was not available at the time, the revolver in Oswald's possession at the time of his arrest was of a type which could have fired the shots that killed Tippit.

The formal charge against Oswald for the assassination of President Kennedy was lodged shortly after 1:30 AM, on Saturday, November 23. By 10 PM of the day of the assassination, the FBI had traced the rifle found on the sixth floor of the Texas School Book Depository to a mailorder house in Chicago which had purchased it from a distributor in New York. Approximately 6 hours later the Chicago firm advised that this rifle had been ordered in March 1963 by an A. Hidell for shipment to post office box 2915, in Dallas, Tex., a box rented by Oswald. Payment for the rifle was remitted by a money order signed by A. Hidell. By 6:45 PM on November 23, the FBI was able to advise the Dallas police that, as a result of handwriting analysis of the documents used to purchase the rifle, it had concluded that the rifle had been ordered by Lee Harvey Oswald.

Throughout Friday and Saturday, the Dallas police released to the public many of the details concerning the alleged evidence against Oswald. Police officials discussed important aspects of the case, usually in the course of impromptu and confused press conferences in the third-floor corridor. Some of the information divulged was erroneous. Efforts by the news media representatives to reconstruct the crime and promptly report details frequently led to erroneous and often conflicting reports. At the urgings of the newsmen, Chief of Police Jesse E. Curry brought Oswald to a press conference in the police assembly room shortly after midnight of the day Oswald was arrested. The assembly room was crowded with newsmen who had come to Dallas from all over the country. They shouted questions at

Oswald and flashed cameras at him. Among this group was a 52-year-old Dallas nightclub operator—Jack Ruby.

On Sunday morning, November 24, arrangements were made for Oswald's transfer from the city jail to the Dallas County jail, about 1 mile away. The news media had been informed on Saturday night that the transfer of Oswald would not take place until after 10 AM on Sunday. Earlier on Sunday, between 2:30 and 3 AM, anonymous telephone calls threatening Oswald's life had been received by the Dallas office of the FBI and by the office of the county sheriff. Nevertheless, on Sunday morning, television, radio, and newspaper representatives crowded into the basement to record the transfer. As viewed through television cameras, Oswald would emerge from a door in front of the cameras and proceed to the transfer vehicle. To the right of the cameras was a "down" ramp from Main Street on the north. To the left was an "up" ramp leading to Commerce Street on the south.

The armored truck in which Oswald was to be transferred arrived shortly after 11 AM. Police officials then decided, however, that an unmarked police car would be preferable for the trip because of its greater speed and maneuverability. At approximately 11:20 AM Oswald emerged from the basement jail office flanked by detectives on either side and at his rear. He took a few steps toward the car and was in the glaring light of the television cameras when a man suddenly darted out from an area on the right of the cameras where newsmen had been assembled. The man was carrying a Colt .38 revolver in his right hand and, while millions watched on television, he moved quickly to within a few feet of Oswald and fired one shot into Oswald's abdomen. Oswald groaned with pain as he fell to the ground and quickly lost consciousness. Within 7 minutes Oswald was at Parkland Hospital where, without having regained consciousness, he was pronounced dead at 1:07 PM.

The man who killed Oswald was Jack Ruby. He was instantly arrested and, minutes later, confined in a cell on the fifth floor of the Dallas police jail. Under interrogation, he denied that the killing of Oswald was in any way connected with a conspiracy involving the assassination of President Kennedy. He maintained that he had killed Oswald in a temporary fit of depression and rage over the President's death. Ruby was transferred the following day to the county jail without notice to the press or to police officers not directly involved in the transfer. Indicted for the murder of Oswald by the State of Texas on November 26, 1963, Ruby was found guilty on March 14, 1964, and sentenced to death. As of September 1964, his case was pending on appeal.

CONCLUSIONS

This Commission was created to ascertain the facts relating to the preceding summary of events and to consider the important questions which they raised. The Commission has addressed itself to this task and has reached certain conclusions based on all the available evidence. No limitations have been placed on the Commission's inquiry; it has conducted its own investigation, and all Government agencies have fully discharged their responsibility to cooperate with the Commission in its investigation. These conclusions represent the reasoned judgment of all members of the Commission and are presented after an investigation which has satisfied the Commission that it has ascertained the truth concerning the assassination of President Kennedy to the extent that a prolonged and thorough search makes this possible.

1. The shots which killed President Kennedy and wounded Governor Connally were fired from the sixth floor window at the southeast corner of the Texas School Book Depository. This determination is based upon the following:

(a) Witnesses at the scene of the assassination saw a rifle being fired from the sixth floor window of the Depository Building, and some witnesses saw a rifle in the window immediately after the shots were fired.

(b) The nearly whole bullet found on Governor Connally's stretcher at Parkland Memorial Hospital and the two bullet fragments found in the front seat of the Presidential limousine were fired from the 6.5-millimeter Mannlicher-Carcano rifle found on the sixth floor of the Depository Building to the exclusion of all other weapons.

(c) The three used cartridge cases found near the window on the sixth floor at the southeast corner of the building were fired from the same rifle which fired the above-described bullet and fragments, to the exclusion of all other weapons.

(d) The windshield in the Presidential limousine was struck by a bullet fragment on the inside surface of the glass, but was not penetrated.

(e) The nature of the bullet wounds suffered by President Kennedy and Governor Connally and the location of the car at the time of the shots establish that the bullets were fired from above and behind the Presidential limousine, striking the President and the Governor as follows:

(1) President Kennedy was first struck by a bullet which entered at the back of his neck and exited through the lower front portion of his neck, causing a wound which would not necessarily have been lethal. The President was struck a second time by a bullet which entered the right-rear portion of his head, causing a massive and fatal wound.

(2) Governor Connally was struck by a bullet which entered on the right side of his back and traveled downward through the right side of his chest, exiting below his right nipple. This bullet then passed through his right wrist and entered his left thigh where it caused a superficial wound.

(f) There is no credible evidence that the shots were fired from the Triple Underpass, ahead of the motorcade, or from any other location.

2. The weight of the evidence indicates that there were three shots fired.

3. Although it is not necessary to any essential findings of the Commission to determine just which shot hit Governor Connally, there is very persuasive evidence from the experts to indicate that the same bullet which

pierced the President's throat also caused Governor Connally's wounds. However, Governor Connally's testimony and certain other factors have given rise to some difference of opinion as to this probability but there is no question in the mind of any member of the Commission that all the shots which caused the President's and Governor Connally's wounds were fired from the sixth floor window of the Texas School Book Depository.

4. The shots which killed President Kennedy and wounded Governor Connally were fired by Lee Harvey Oswald. This conclusion is based upon the following:

(a) The Mannlicher-Carcano 6.5-millimeter Italian rifle from which the shots were fired was owned by and in the possession of Oswald.

(b) Oswald carried this rifle into the Depository Building on the morning of November 22, 1963.

(c) Oswald, at the time of the assassination, was present at the window from which the shots were fired.

(d) Shortly after the assassination, the Mannlicher-Carcano rifle belonging to Oswald was found partially hidden between some cartons on the sixth floor and the improvised paper bag in which Oswald brought the rifle to the Depository was found close by the window from which the shots were fired.

(e) Based on testimony of the experts and their analysis of films of the assassination, the Commission has concluded that a rifleman of Lee Harvey Oswald's capabilities could have fired the shots from the rifle used in the assassination within the elapsed time of the shooting. The Commission has concluded further that Oswald possessed the capability with a rifle which enabled him to commit the assassination.

(f) Oswald lied to the police after his arrest concerning important substantive matters.

(g) Oswald had attempted to kill Maj. Gen. Edwin A. Walker (Resigned, U.S. Army) on April 10, 1963, thereby demonstrating his disposition to take human life.

5. Oswald killed Dallas Police Patrolman J. D. Tippit approximately 45 minutes after the assassination. This conclusion upholds the finding that Oswald fired the shots which killed President Kennedy and wounded Governor Connally and is supported by the following:

(a) Two eyewitnesses saw the Tippit shooting and seven eyewitnesses heard the shots and saw the gunman leave the scene with revolver in hand. These nine eyewitnesses positively identified Lee Harvey Oswald as the man they saw.

(b) The cartridge cases found at the scene of the shooting were fired from the revolver in the possession of Oswald at the time of his arrest to the exclusion of all other weapons.

(c) The revolver in Oswald's possession at the time of his arrest was purchased by and belonged to Oswald.

(d) Oswald's jacket was found along the path of flight taken by the gunman as he fled from the scene of the killing.

6. Within 80 minutes of the assassination and 35 minutes of the Tippit killing Oswald resisted arrest at the theatre by attempting to shoot another Dallas police officer.

7. The Commission has reached the following conclusions concerning Oswald's interrogation and detention by the Dallas police:

(a) Except for the force required to effect his arrest, Oswald was not subjected to any physical coercion by any law enforcement officials. He was advised that he could not be compelled to give any information and that any statements made by him might be used against him in court. He was advised of his right to counsel. He was given the opportunity to obtain counsel of his own choice and was offered legal assistance by the Dallas Bar Association, which he rejected at that time.

(b) Newspaper, radio, and television reporters were allowed uninhibited access to the area through which Oswald had to pass when he was moved from his cell to the interrogation room and other sections of the building, thereby subjecting Oswald to harassment and creating chaotic conditions which were not conducive to orderly interrogation or the protection of the rights of the prisoner.

(c) The numerous statements, sometimes erroneous, made to the press by various local law enforcement officials, during this period of confusion and disorder in the police station, would have presented serious obstacles to the obtaining of a fair trial for Oswald. To the extent that the information was erroneous or misleading, it helped to create doubts, speculations, and fears in the mind of the public which might otherwise not have arisen.

8. The Commission has reached the following conclusions concerning the killing of Oswald by Jack Ruby on November 24, 1963:

(a) Ruby entered the basement of the Dallas Police Department shortly after 11:17 AM and killed Lee Harvey Oswald at 11:21 AM

(b) Although the evidence on Ruby's means of entry is not conclusive, the weight of the evidence indicates that he walked down the ramp leading from Main Street to the basement of the police department.

(c) There is no evidence to support the rumor that Ruby may have been assisted by any members of the Dallas Police Department in the killing of Oswald.

(d) The Dallas Police Department's decision to transfer Oswald to the county jail in full public view was unsound. The arrangements made by the police department on Sunday morning, only a few hours before the attempted transfer, were inadequate. Of critical importance was the fact that news media representatives and others were not excluded from the basement even after the police were notified of threats to Oswald's life. These deficiencies contributed to the death of Lee Harvey Oswald.

9. The Commission has found no evidence that either Lee Harvey Oswald or Jack Ruby was part of any conspiracy, domestic or foreign, to assassinate President Kennedy. The reasons for this conclusion are:

(a) The Commission has found no evidence that anyone assisted

Oswald in planning or carrying out the assassination. In this connection it has thoroughly investigated, among other factors, the circumstances surrounding the planning of the motorcade route through Dallas, the hiring of Oswald by the Texas School Book Depository Co. on October 15, 1963, the method by which the rifle was brought into the building, the placing of cartons of books at the window, Oswald's escape from the building, and the testimony of eyewitnesses to the shooting.

(b) The Commission has found no evidence that Oswald was involved with any person or group in a conspiracy to assassinate the President, although it has thoroughly investigated, in addition to other possible leads, all facets of Oswald's associations, finances, and personal habits, particularly during the period following his return from the Soviet Union in June 1962.

(c) The Commission has found no evidence to show that Oswald was employed, persuaded, or encouraged by any foreign government to assassinate President Kennedy or that he was an agent of any foreign government, although the Commission has reviewed the circumstances surrounding Oswald's defection to the Soviet Union, his life there from October of 1959 to June of 1962 so far as it can be reconstructed, his known contacts with the Fair Play for Cuba Committee, and his visits to the Cuban and Soviet Embassies in Mexico City during his trip to Mexico from September 26 to October 3, 1963, and his known contacts with the Soviet Embassy in the United States.

(d) The Commission has explored all attempts of Oswald to identify himself with various political groups, including the Communist Party, U.S.A., the Fair Play for Cuba Committee, and the Socialist Workers Party, and has been unable to find any evidence that the contacts which he initiated were related to Oswald's subsequent assassination of the President.

(e) All of the evidence before the Commission established that there was nothing to support the speculation that Oswald was an agent, employee, or informant of the FBI, the CIA, or any other governmental agency. It has thoroughly investigated Oswald's relationships prior to the assassination with all agencies of the U.S. Government. All contacts with Oswald by any of these agencies were made in the regular exercise of their different responsibilities.

(f) No direct or indirect relationship between Lee Harvey Oswald and Jack Ruby has been discovered by the Commission, nor has it been able to find any credible evidence that either knew the other, although a thorough investigation was made of the many rumors and speculations of such a relationship.

(g) The Commission has found no evidence that Jack Ruby acted with any other person in the killing of Lee Harvey Oswald.

(h) After careful investigation the Commission has found no credible

---

[1]There were two Tippits on the Dallas Police Force—G. M. Tippit and J. D. Tippit. Ruby did know G. M. Tippit; he did not know J. D. Tippit.

evidence either that Ruby and Officer Tippit, who was killed by Oswald, knew each other or that Oswald and Tippit knew each other.[1]

Because of the difficulty of proving negatives to a certainty the possibility of others being involved with either Oswald or Ruby cannot be established categorically, but if there is any such evidence it has been beyond the reach of all the investigative agencies and resources of the United States and has not come to the attention of this Commission.

10. In its entire investigation the Commission has found no evidence of conspiracy, subversion, or disloyalty to the U.S. Government by any Federal, State, or local official.

11. On the basis of the evidence before the Commission it concludes that Oswald acted alone. Therefore, to determine the motives for the assassination of President Kennedy, one must look to the assassin himself. Clues to Oswald's motives can be found in his family history, his education or lack of it, his acts, his writings, and the recollections of those who had close contacts with him throughout his life. The Commission has presented with this report all of the background information bearing on motivation which it could discover. Thus, others may study Lee Oswald's life and arrive at their own conclusions as to his possible motives.

The Commission could not make any definitive determination of Oswald's motives. It has endeavored to isolate factors which contributed to his character and which might have influenced his decision to assassinate President Kennedy. These factors were:

(a) His deep-rooted resentment of all authority which was expressed in a hostility toward every society in which he lived;

(b) His inability to enter into meaningful relationships with people, and a continuous pattern of rejecting his environment in favor of new surroundings;

(c) His urge to try to find a place in history and despair at times over failures in his various undertakings;

(d) His capacity for violence as evidenced by his attempt to kill General Walker;

(e) His avowed commitment to Marxism and communism, as he understood the terms and developed his own interpretation of them; this was expressed by his antagonism toward the United States, by his defection to the Soviet Union, by his failure to be reconciled with life in the United States even after his disenchantment with the Soviet Union, and by his efforts, though frustrated, to go to Cuba.

Each of these contributed to his capacity to risk all in cruel and irresponsible actions.

12. The Commission recognizes that the varied responsibilities of the President require that he make frequent trips to all parts of the United States and abroad. Consistent with their high responsibilities Presidents can never be protected from every potential threat. The Secret Service's difficulty in meeting its protective responsibility varies with the activities and the nature

of the occupant of the Office of President and his willingness to conform to plans for his safety. In appraising the performance of the Secret Service it should be understood that it has to do its work within such limitations. Nevertheless, the Commission believes that recommendations for improvements in Presidential protection are compelled by the facts disclosed in this investigation.

(a) The complexities of the Presidency have increased so rapidly in recent years that the Secret Service has not been able to develop or to secure adequate resources of personnel and facilities to fulfill its important assignment. This situation should be promptly remedied.

(b) The Commission has concluded that the criteria and procedures of the Secret Service designed to identify and protect against persons considered threats to the President were not adequate prior to the assassination.

(1) The Protective Research Section of the Secret Service, which is responsible for its preventive work, lacked sufficient trained personnel and the mechanical and technical assistance needed to fulfill its responsibility.

(2) Prior to the assassination the Secret Service's criteria dealt with direct threats against the President. Although the Secret Service treated the direct threats against the President adequately, it failed to recognize the necessity of identifying other potential sources of danger to his security. The Secret Service did not develop adequate and specific criteria defining those persons or groups who might present a danger to the President. In effect, the Secret Service largely relied upon other Federal or State agencies to supply the information necessary for it to fulfill its preventive responsibilities, although it did ask for information about direct threats to the President.

(c) The Commission has concluded that there was insufficient liaison and coordination of information between the Secret Service and other Federal agencies necessarily concerned with Presidential protection. Although the FBI, in the normal exercise of its responsibility, had secured considerable information about Lee Harvey Oswald, it had no official responsibility, under the Secret Service criteria existing at the time of the President's trip to Dallas, to refer to the Secret Service the information it had about Oswald. The Commission has concluded, however, that the FBI took an unduly restrictive view of its role in preventive intelligence work prior to the assassination. A more carefully coordinated treatment of the Oswald case by the FBI might well have resulted in bringing Oswald's activities to the attention of the Secret Service.

(d) The Commission has concluded that some of the advance preparations in Dallas made by the Secret Service, such as the detailed security measures taken at Love Field and the Trade Mart, were thorough and well executed. In other respects, however, the Commission has concluded that the advance preparations for the President's trip were deficient.

(1) Although the Secret Service is compelled to rely to a great extent on local law enforcement officials, its procedures at the time of the Dallas trip did not call for well-defined instructions as to the respective responsibilities of the police officials and others assisting in the protection of the President.

(2) The procedures relied upon by the Secret Service for detecting the presence of an assassin located in a building along a motorcade route were inadequate. At the time of the trip to Dallas, the Secret Service as a matter of practice did not investigate, or cause to be checked, any building located along the motorcade route to be taken by the President. The responsibility for observing windows in these buildings during the motorcade was divided between local police personnel stationed on the streets to regulate crowds and Secret Service agents riding in the motorcade. Based on its investigation the Commission has concluded that these arrangements during the trip to Dallas were clearly not sufficient.

(e) The configuration of the Presidential car and the seating arrangements of the Secret Service agents in the car did not afford the Secret Service agents the opportunity they should have had to be of immediate assistance to the President at the first sign of danger.

(f) Within these limitations, however, the Commission finds that the agents most immediately responsible for the President's safety reacted promptly at the time the shots were fired from the Texas School Book Depository Building.

EPILOGUE

This book is too short, and yet it is too long.

There is so much more that I wanted to say, particularly in the areas of motive and possible conspiracy. The "Summary and Conclusions" chapter of the Warren Commission Report, therefore, has been added as an appendix. It includes a narration of events and some background on Oswald's life as well as the conclusions of the Commission on possible motive and conspiracy. Hopefully, some of you after reading the appendix will decide to read the entire report. Here you will find the bedrock supported by over 6,000 accurate footnotes keyed into the 26 volumes of testimony and exhibits. Collectively, these answer all of the claims and questions that are physically impossible to answer in one volume such as this, I have chosen the path of in-depth exploration of the key evidence.

In this book I have tried to combine three goals: (1) To bring the heart of the testimony of the primary witnesses before the jury of world opinion so that a true verdict can be reached concerning who killed President Kennedy and who killed Officer Tippit; (2) to give an inside view of the Warren Commission and to display the importance of independent citizen participation in governmental agencies and commissions of all kinds; (3) to expose the techniques of the assassination sensationalists—techniques of misrepresentation, fraudulent omission, and smear that have become all too common in public life and discussion of issues, both in this country and abroad.

We live in a great republic, a nation where it is possible for an independent citizen to become a part of a special commission investigating the assassination of a head of state, a country where a citizen can freely write a book criticizing the chief judicial officer, the highest law enforcement agency, and the head of state.

To maintain such freedom is not an easy task. It requires an informed citizenry, and the information upon which the people rely cannot merely be a mile wide and an inch deep. We must have depth of understanding.

If there is one thing that stands out in the minds of you jurors after reading this book, I hope it is the need for objective, in-depth exploration of all of the facts before deciding which or who is right or wrong. Mass-media techniques, spoon-fed sensationalism, and demagoguery are all the enemies of a free society.

These enemies cannot exist in an environment where the constant quest for accurate information on issues and answers is at least as important as the quest for personal luxury and entertainment. We must be aware of the facts, for our ultimate judgments will be no better than the accuracy of the information on which they are based.

One final comment. Just as Abraham Zapruder donated to a charity (the Fireman's and Policeman's Benevolence Fund) the proceeds of the sale of his film of the assassination, I have set aside for charitable purposes all royalties from the sale of this book.

INDEX

INDEX

Warren Commission report (*continued*)
on shot striking Kennedy, 380–381
Weapons. *See* Pistol; Rifle
Webster, Jane C., 184, 210
Weissman, Bernard, 435
Weitzman, 187
Weller, 403
Wentworth, 400
West, Troy Eugene, 4–5, 399
WFFA-TV, 164
Whaley, William, 415–418, 420
Wilder, 400
Willens, Howard P., 423, 428
Williams, Bonnie Ray, 132, 137–138,
139, 140, 141, 144, 145–152,
153, 157–160, 162, 258, 271,
383, 450, 467
Wound Ballistics Branch of the US
Army Chemical Research and
Development Laboratories, 364*ff*
Wounds. *See also* Shots; Single-bullet
theory; Wounds ballistic
experiments
of Connally, John, 210, 304, 306,
312
contradictory testimony on, 5–8
and grassy knoll as origin of shots,
396–397
of Kennedy, John F., 255–266, 334–
344, 468–469
Wounds ballistic experiments, 383,496

conclusions from simulating neck,
chest, and wrist wounds, 367–
368
general conditions for, 365
medical testimony on, 369–378
on penetration power and bullet
stability, 365
purpose of, 364
simulating Connally's chest wounds,
366
simulating Connally's head wounds,
368
simulating Kennedy's head wounds,
368
simulating Kennedy's back wound,
365–366

X-rays
of Connally's wounds, 318, 319–320
of Kennedy's body, 345–346, 348–
350, 353, 361–362, 397

Yablonski, Joseph, *xiii*
Yarborough, Ralph W., 480
Youngblood, Rufus W., 481
Youth House of New York, 421, 488

Zapruder, Abraham, 124*n*, 135, 302.
See also Zapruder film
Zapruder film, 302–307, 308, 316,
330, 363, 365, 401

ABOUT THE AUTHOR

DAVID W. BELIN is one of the Warren Commission lawyers who concentrated on the analysis of all evidence pertaining to the investigation to determine who killed President Kennedy and Officer Tippit. He has practiced law in Des Moines, Iowa, since graduating in 1954 from the University of Michigan, where in six years he earned undergraduate, Master of Business Administration, and Juris Doctor degrees—all with high distinction.

In college, he was a member of Phi Beta Kappa, Delta Sigma Rho, Beta Alpha Psi, Order of the Coif, and the Barristers Society, in addition to being Associate Editor of the *Michigan Law Review* and finalist in the Campbell Moot Court competition. His honors included 1950 Honors Orator, Michigamua (all-campus senior men's honorary society) and the 1954 Henry M. Bates Memorial Award made "to each of the two most outstanding seniors in the Law School."

As an attorney he has concentrated in the areas of corporation work and litigation, including constitutional issues. He was instrumental in the well-known Supreme Court decision upholding the constitutional rights of an indigent defendant to competent legal counsel on appeal, the *Entsminger* case; and the leading decision upholding the constitutional requirement of no more than one member in a state legislature district, the *Kruidenier* reapportionment case.

Belin studied to become a concert violinist, but after being admitted to the Juilliard School of Music enlisted in the U.S. Army. In the last four months of his service in Korea and Japan he was a concert violinist for Armed Forces Special Services.

He serves on the boards of directors of a number of corporations and has also lectured at numerous seminars and meetings across the country. Belin married Constance Newman, also a Phi Beta Kappa graduate of the University of Michigan. They reside in Des Moines with their five children.